The Abbasid Caliphate of Cairo, 1261–1517

Edinburgh Studies in Classical Islamic History and Culture
Series Editor: Carole Hillenbrand

Titles in the series include:

Arabian Drugs in Early Medieval Mediterranean Medicine
Zohar Amar and Efraim Lev

Towards a History of Libraries in Yemen
Hassan Ansari and Sabine Schmidtke

The Abbasid Caliphate of Cairo, 1261–1517: Out of the Shadows
Mustafa Banister

The Medieval Western Maghrib: Cities, Patronage and Power
Amira K. Bennison

Christian Monastic Life in Early Islam: Confessional Fluidity and Religious Ecumenism
Bradley Bowman

Keeping the Peace in Premodern Islam: Diplomacy under the Mamluk Sultanate, 1250–1517
Malika Dekkiche

Queens, Concubines and Eunuchs in Medieval Islam
Taef El-Azhari

Islamic Political Thought in the Mamluk Period
Mohamad El-Merheb

The Kharijites in Early Islamic Historical Tradition: Heroes and Villains
Hannah-Lena Hagemann

Medieval Damascus: Plurality and Diversity in an Arabic Library – The Ashrafiya Library Catalogue
Konrad Hirschler

A Monument to Medieval Syrian Book Culture: The Library of Ibn ʿAbd al-Hādī
Konrad Hirschler

The Popularisation of Sufism in Ayyubid and Mamluk Egypt: State and Society, 1173–1325
Nathan Hofer

Defining Anthropomorphism: The Challenge of Islamic Traditionalism
Livnat Holtzman

Making Mongol History: Rashid al-Din and the Jamiʿ al-Tawarikh
Stefan Kamola

Lyrics of Life: Saʿdi on Love, Cosmopolitanism and Care of the Self
Fatemeh Keshavarz

Art, Allegory and The Rise of Shiism In Iran, 1487–1565
Chad Kia

The Administration of Justice in Medieval Egypt: From the 7th to the 12th Century
Yaacov Lev

A History of the True Balsam of Matarea
Marcus Milwright

Ruling from a Red Canopy: Political Authority in the Medieval Islamic World, From Anatolia to South Asia
Colin P. Mitchell

Islam, Christianity and the Realms of the Miraculous: A Comparative Exploration
Ian Richard Netton

The Poetics of Spiritual Instruction: Farid al-Din ʿAttar and Persian Sufi Didacticism
Austin O'Malley

Sacred Place and Sacred Time in the Medieval Islamic Middle East: An Historical Perspective
Daniella Talmon-Heller

Conquered Populations in Early Islam: Non-Arabs, Slaves and the Sons of Slave Mothers
Elizabeth Urban

edinburghuniversitypress.com/series/escihc

The Abbasid Caliphate of Cairo, 1261–1517

Out of the Shadows

Mustafa Banister

EDINBURGH
University Press

For Shooshoo, Abdu, Joon, and Qas

Edinburgh University Press is one of the leading university presses in the UK. We publish academic books and journals in our selected subject areas across the humanities and social sciences, combining cutting-edge scholarship with high editorial and production values to produce academic works of lasting importance. For more information visit our website: edinburghuniversitypress.com

Edinburgh University Press Ltd
The Tun – Holyrood Road
12 (2f) Jackson's Entry
Edinburgh EH8 8PJ

First published in hardback by Edinburgh University Press 2021

Typeset in 11/15 Adobe Garamond by
Servis Filmsetting Ltd, Stockport, Cheshire

A CIP record for this book is available from the British Library

ISBN 978 1 4744 5336 3 (hardback)
ISBN 978 1 4744 5337 0 (paperback)
ISBN 978 1 4744 5339 4 (webready PDF)
ISBN 978 1 4744 5338 7 (epub)

Contents

List of Figures, Maps and Genealogical Tables vii
Acknowledgements viii

Introduction 1

PART ONE A History of the Abbasid Caliphate of Cairo

1 The Origins and Establishment of the Abbasid Caliphs in Cairo, 659–701/1261–1302 19

2 The Qalawunids and the Caliphate, 701–63/1302–63 60

3 Flirtations with Power and Political Intrigue, 763–815/1362–1412 91

4 Containing and Maintaining the Caliphate, 815–903/1412–97 141

5 The Last Abbasids of Cairo, 903–22/1497–1517 192

PART TWO The Legal, Historiographical and Chancery Dimensions of the Abbasid Caliphate of Cairo

6 Normative Perspectives on the Caliphate of Cairo: Jurisprudential, Advice and Courtly Literature 229

7 The Cairo Caliphate in Medieval Arabic Historiographical Literature 276

8 Caliphal Investiture Documents and the Ideality of a Cairo Caliphate 339

Figures, Maps and Genealogical Tables

Figures

1.1 Abbasid mausoleum, Cairo 47
2.1 Tombs inside the Abbasid mausoleum, Cairo 80
3.1 Royal decree of the caliph-sultan al-Mustaʿīn, Great Mosque of Gaza 120
3.2 Fifteenth-century silver and gold coins from the Syrian territories of the sultanate 125
5.1 Sketch of Yedikule hisarı fortress, Istanbul 217
7.1 Dedication page of al-Baghawī's *al-Maṣābīḥ* made for the caliph al-Mutawakkil in 778/1376–7 282

Maps

1.1 Mid-thirteenth-century Syro-Egypt and Mesopotamia 22
2.1 City of Cairo 65
3.1 Citadel of Cairo 102
4.1 Fifteenth-century west Asia 143

Tables

5.1 Disputed succession to al-Mustamsik, 1508 196
10.1 Descendants of al-Mustakfī I 441
10.2 Descendants of al-Mutawakkil I 442

Acknowledgements

As this book stems from my doctoral thesis, I must begin by thanking my *Doktormutter* Linda Northrup who set me on the path towards understanding the complex world of late medieval Cairo. Maria Subtelny, Victor Ostapchuk, Walid Saleh and Frédéric Bauden also carefully guided me towards a more complete reconstruction of the Abbasid Caliphate set up and supported by the sultans of Cairo. I would also recognise all of the former teachers and mentors in Michigan, Chicago and Toronto who helped to shape my outlook on medieval Islamic and world history, including Fred Donner, Cornell Fleischer, Lisa Golombek, Sebastian Günther, Todd Lawson, the late Chris Mayda, Rick Rogers, Michael Sells and, in particular, John Woods and Bruce Craig, who first introduced me to 'the Mamluks and their shadow caliph in Cairo' which piqued my interest so long ago.

A portion of this book was completed during my 2015–16 fellowship at the Annemarie Schimmel Kolleg 'History and Society during the Mamluk Era (1250–1517)' (University of Bonn), and I thank Stephan Conermann and Bethany Walker for their invitation and generous support. The book reached completion during my time as a postdoctoral researcher at Ghent University while engaged with the ERC-Consolidator Grant project, 'The Mamlukisation of the Mamluk Sultanate-II. Historiography, Political Order and State Formation in 15th-Century Egypt and Syria' (2018–21). I warmly thank Jo Van Steenbergen and Maya Termonia for providing sincere collegiality, stimulating discussions and a very fruitful work environment.

I am especially grateful to Reuven Amitai, Malika Dekkiche and Jo Van Steenbergen for kindly reading earlier drafts of the book and offering valuable feedback which helped to develop it further. Kenneth Goudie, Christian

Mauder and Gowaart Van Den Bossche also read sections of the book and shared helpful comments. I am also thankful to Mona Hassan, who allowed me to read an early version of her work on the Cairene Abbasids which was particularly eye-opening.

During my years in Canada, Germany and Belgium, the project has benefited greatly from conversations, emails and camaraderie shared with Noha Abou-Khatwa, Abdelkader Al Ghouz, Adam Ali, Ovamir Anjum, Nasrin Askari, Amar Baadj, Rihab Ben Othmen, Caterina Bori, Fien De Block, Kristof D'hulster, Mohammad Fadel, Nahyan Fancy, Kurt Franz, Yehoshua Frenkel, Noah Gardiner, Mohammad Gharaibeh, Usman Hamid, Hani Hamza, Stephen Humphreys, Matthew Ingalls, Lale Javanshir, Daniel Mahoney, Manhal Makhoul, Mohamed Maslouh, Haggai Mazuz, Richard McGregor, John Meloy, Zacharie Mochtari de Pierrepont, David Nicolle, Carl Petry, Nasser Rabbat, Fadi Ragheb, Tarek Sabraa, Marlis Saleh, Warren Schultz, Gül Şen, Bogdan Smarandache and Murat Yasar.

At Edinburgh University Press, I would like to thank series editor Carole Hillenbrand for her early enthusiasm for the project, as well as Nicola Ramsey, Kirsty Woods, Eddie Clark and freelance copy-editor Lyn Flight for their patience, help and direction throughout the publishing process. I also wish to thank the anonymous readers who provided helpful suggestions which improved the book. Ælfwine Mischler completed the index and Rebecca Mackenzie designed a beautiful cover. Naturally, I take responsibility for all remaining errors, oversights and omissions.

Finally, I must thank my family who humoured the colourful decade I spent on research for this project with patience and grace: my mother Noor (who always offered unwavering support) and my father Suhail Banister (who happily read early drafts and was always delighted to offer his 'two-cents'), my sister Aliyah and her husband Mustafa, and my cousin Jennifer Banister.

Last, but never least, I fail to find adequate words to thank my wife, best friend and life partner Shaima Yacoub who sacrificed in every way possible and frequently had to battle the Abbasid caliphs for my attention. She kept our life together in the meantime and always reminded me of the world outside the library. All the while, our three *luʾluʾs*, Abdallah, Ibrahim and Qasim, filled (and continue to fill) our home with sound, warmth and happiness. This book is for them.

'Know that faith and knowledge accompany the caliphate, wherever it may be.'

Jalāl al-Dīn al-Suyūṭī (d. 1505)

'The likes of me live by dying, and in passing on, attain their desires. For [the sultans of Cairo] is a succulent life, while I am left to merry speech. They are the possessors of outright kingship, while "for Sulaymān is the wind".'

Words attributed to the third Abbasid caliph of Cairo,
al-Mustakfī bi-llāh Sulaymān (d. 1340)

'There are no more virtuous people, *or even good people*, left to be sought after;
nor is there a generous person remaining to whom I can convey my melancholy.

People of no lineage have come to be the masters
and I am forlorn for having lived to see these days.'

Verses attributed to the last Abbasid caliph of Cairo,
al-Mutawakkil ʿalā Allāh III (d. 1539 or 1543)

Introduction

This book examines the final chapter of Abbasid history as it largely unfolded in Cairo over two and a half centuries (659–923/1261–1517), but more broadly took place within the interregional socio-political context of the late medieval Islamic polity commonly referred to as the 'Mamluk Sultanate' or the 'Mamluk Empire'. Here, however, I engage with this context as the Cairo Sultanate (or sultanate of Cairo).[1] The Abbasid Caliphate, arguably one of Islam's most enduring leadership institutions, remained an important fixture in the political culture of the time and was a recurring focal point for contemporary chroniclers and chancery scribes. Until recently, many conventional histories of Islam assumed that the declining Abbasid Caliphate received its *coup de grâce* with the Mongol capture of Baghdad in 656/1258 and the subsequent execution of the 'last caliph al-Mustaʿṣim', and largely ignored or passed over the line of Abbasids established in Cairo in 659/1261. We may put the earlier lack of interest in the Cairene Abbasid caliphs down to a wholesale dismissal of the dynasty's relevance from the thirteenth to the sixteenth centuries. Only in more recent decades has scholarly discussion moved beyond the installation of the first caliphs of Cairo by the sultan al-Ẓāhir Baybars (657–76/1260–77) and the political ramifications of that historical action.

When the orientalists of the late nineteenth and early twentieth centuries began studying the late medieval sultanate of Cairo, the restored Abbasid Caliphate simultaneously fell under their lens. This later incarnation, however, was typically dubbed a 'puppet' or 'shadow' caliphate, terms, it must be noted, with no Arabic analogues in the contemporary historiographical source material. This 'shadow caliphate' developed as convenient shorthand in modern studies to describe the powerless position of the Abbasid caliphs as well as the shadowy mystery hovering over their role within the social formations of late medieval Cairo. Thus, the institution itself, for the most part, likewise initially received the attention worthy of a shadow by mainstream Islamic historians. Extant presentations of the latter-day Abbasids, while offering an excellent starting point, have demonstrated the need for a comprehensive study of the Cairo caliphs to attain an even richer understanding of the caliphate in late medieval Egypt and Syria.

Among the specialists on Islam and the medieval Middle East that have studied the caliphate from the mid-thirteenth to early sixteenth centuries, several can be considered pioneers in explaining the political, social and cultural significance of the Abbasids of Cairo, including Gustav Weil,[2] William Muir,[3] Vasiliy V. Barthold,[4] Thomas Arnold,[5] Stanley Lane-Poole,[6] Maurice Gaudefroy-Demombynes[7] and Émile Tyan.[8]

Noting a growing interest in the subject in the decades since their works appeared, Jonathan Berkey in 2009 acknowledged the existence of 'a well-developed scholarly literature analysing the historical significance of the Abbasid caliphate of Cairo',[9] which highlighted the socio-political value of the caliphal family in Egypt. In 1942, Annemarie Schimmel examined the Cairene Abbasids in a substantial study focused on the uniquely Egyptian conditions of religious offices such as the caliphate and the chief judge-ships of late medieval Cairo. Schimmel outlined the powers of the caliphal office and offered general observations on the caliphs' investiture proceedings, succession and official duties.[10] Thirty years later Mounira Chapoutot-Remadi produced an important theme-oriented research article on the Abbasids of Cairo which made two notable contributions: the beginnings of a discussion on the living conditions of the caliphs as well as a section titled, 'Le chef des hommes de religion', in which the author observed that while the Abbasid caliph of Cairo carried greater political significance than religious importance for the sultans, his religious authority held deep ramifications for the scholarly class (*'ulamā'*) as well as for foreign policy.[11]

Although Schimmel cited several important anecdotes about the fifteenth-century Abbasid caliphs to illustrate broader points, it was not until 1967 that Jean-Claude Garcin, while examining the role of the caliphate in the historiography of the late fifteenth-century Egyptian religious scholar al-Suyūṭī, presented a detailed outline of the Cairene Abbasids. Using a variety of later Arabic sources, Garcin explored al-Suyūṭī's caliphate-centric worldview and described the political value of individual caliphs to the sultanate of Cairo.[12] Peter Holt's equally important 1984 article 'Some Observations on the 'Abbāsid Caliphate of Cairo', offers the author's remarks on key events involving the caliphate throughout the span of the late thirteenth to early sixteenth centuries. Holt focused heavily on the episode of the caliphate's restoration and its immediate relevance to sultanic legitimacy and foreign policy, though he also provided important research on the caliphate in late medieval Syro-Egyptian historiography.[13]

In 1950, the work of Richard Hartmann opened the question of elite attitudes towards the caliphate from 656–62/1258–61. Hartmann raised the issue of whether the Cairene political elite, like the rulers of Mecca, had recognised the Tunisian Hafsid caliphate in the years prior to the Abbasid installation at Cairo in 1261, and argued that the ruling sultans, having acknowledged the 'caliphate' of al-Mustanṣir (also the regnal title – *laqab* – of the Hafsid ruler of Tunis), later named their caliph with the same *laqab* to gloss over the earlier recognition.[14] David Ayalon, who recognised the re-establishment of the Abbasid Caliphate in Cairo as an 'event of major importance in Muslim history', put the matter to rest ten years later in an article that refuted Hartmann's thesis and concluded that the sultans ruling Egypt, Syria and (at times) parts of the Hijaz hastened to legitimate their status through the Abbasid family.[15]

The restoration of the post-Mongol Abbasid Caliphate, first in Aleppo and later in Cairo, did not receive a monograph of its own until 1994 with the appearance of a German study by Stefan Heidemann. Based on a comprehensive examination of literary sources and numismatic evidence, Heidemann detailed the re-establishment process of the caliphate in late thirteenth-century Egypt and Syria. While Heidemann carefully reconstructed the establishment of the Abbasids in Aleppo and later Cairo, the book is primarily a numismatic study that focuses only on the first decades of the dynasty's history in Egypt.

Longing for the Lost Caliphate: a Transregional History, the recent monograph by Mona Hassan, has demonstrated the enormous potential for examining the Abbasid Caliphate of Cairo as its own unique subject of inquiry. In a comparative study of the fall of the caliphate and its aftermath in both 1258 (to the invading Mongols) and 1924 (to the birth of the Turkish republic from the ashes of the Ottoman 'Caliphate'), Hassan conducted an extensive exploration of the enduring social and religious salience attached to the institution and made important contributions to our understanding of the unique place of the Abbasid Caliphate of Cairo in late medieval Arabic historiography and normative jurisprudential treatises. Significantly, Hassan's work links the symbol of the caliphate to the idea of a 'cultural grammar', which, in transcending the mere history of the institution, presents the resurrection of the Abbasid Caliphate in medieval Cairo in a way that demonstrates the very real meaning and significance it carried within the socio-political fabric of its time.[16] The book, which treats the Abbasid Caliphate for much of its incarnation in Cairo, is an excellent starting point for a study devoted exclusively to the Cairo Abbasids that goes further on the subject.

Thoughtful and dynamic reconsiderations of the caliphate's socio-religious and cultural significance beyond its potential for legitimating the reigning sultans of Cairo by, in particular, Schimmel, Garcin, Chapoutot-Remadi and Hassan, have thus helped to open the way for further discussion and exploration of the subtleties of the Cairo Caliphate in the present book.

The harsh reality of the curtailment of the caliphal office in late medieval Cairo has distracted from the fact that the figure of the caliph could remain an imposing, even potentially dangerous, presence, shrouded at court in mystique and enigma, in much the same way his forebears had been surrounded by courtiers and winding corridors at the height of the dynasty's power in Baghdad (132–656/750–1258). However, by the late fifteenth/early sixteenth centuries in Cairo, the status of the caliphate, whether attached to decline-oriented conceptions of 'demotion' or not, came to be accepted by all actors who engaged with it. Theoretically, as John Woods suggests, the Muslim community (*umma*) carried the responsibility for perpetuating and reproducing itself, and the caliphate served only as a function of the community, its common objectives and collective duties symbolically embodied in a single office holder.[17] Thus, the significance of the Abbasid Caliphate remained an undisputed constant in a social world of shifting political variables, particularly the making and unmaking of new political orders centred around elites based at the Citadel of Cairo.[18]

A Cairo Caliphate within a Cairo Sultanate

One aim of the current book is to contextualise the Abbasid Caliphate within the larger socio-cultural and political history of the interconnected Syro-Egyptian regions that made up the Cairo-based sultanate. The 'Mamluk Sultanate', which has developed as a common signifier over the course of nearly eighty years of modern scholarship, takes its name from the social status and servile origins of the ruling elites, particularly the social grouping of manumitted military slaves (*mamlūk*, pl. *mamālīk*) that dominated Egypt, Syria (Bilād al-Shām), and at times much of the Hijaz between the Mediterranean and Arabian seas for nearly two and a half centuries (typically, 648–923/1250–1517).[19] On their path to power in Cairo and beyond, many such *mamlūk*s had been Turkish slaves from the Qipchaq steppe who were later supplanted as the main source of manpower by Circassians from the Caucasus by the late fourteenth century. Trained and socialised in Cairo, the first group to obtain ruling power in the mid-thirteenth century were part of the military retinue of the last effectual sultan of the Ayyubid family, al-Ṣāliḥ Najm al-Dīn Ayyūb (637–47/1240–9).

Throughout the *longue durée* history of the sultanate these Turkish-speaking *mamlūk*s were not an isolated sector, but a socially integrated group comprising important actors.[20] Rather than a polity defined by military slavery throughout its existence, however, Jo Van Steenbergen has proposed engaging with the sultanate, particularly between 678 and 784/1279 and 1382, as part of the 'Military Patronage State' tradition characterised by 'military leadership, patronage ties, household bonds, and unstable devolved authorities', during a period in which power relations were dominated by a variety of ethnic groups, dynastic dispensations and political power networks.[21] The sultanate's tumultuous history between 1250 and 1517 was closely linked to the repeated disintegration and fragmentation of successful political orders around particular households and networks, as well as the sultans and their Cairo-based courts.[22]

Although the '*mamlūk*' element remained important throughout these two and a half centuries, it was not always crucial in defining how politics unfolded.[23] The *mamlūk*s themselves were nevertheless among the key manpower resources, which, along with financial and other resources, allowed political elites such as amirs and sultans like Baybars (r. 658–76/1260–77) or Qalāwūn (r. 678–89/1279–90) to create the political muscle they required, though in this they resembled earlier Muslim rulers like the Ghaznavids as well as other twelfth- or thirteenth-century rulers in pursuit of similar resources such as the sultans of Delhi.[24]

It is likewise important to acknowledge long periods in which dynastic rule reflected the general practices of social and political organisation rather than as a peculiar exception to a period of normative 'rule by slaves'. Dynastic and hereditary impulses appeared regularly and notably during much of the fourteenth century in which the Qalawunid dynasty (689–784/1290–1382) endured until it was supplanted by the sultan al-Ẓāhir Barqūq who sought to establish his own dynastic line at his death in 801/1399 with the succession of two of his sons. Indeed, hereditary impulses were widely exercised long into the fifteenth century, though seldom with successful results.[25]

Many later medieval Arabo-Muslim historians often understood the contemporary social and political order not as a 'Mamluk Sultanate' per se, but rather as part of an ongoing period of 'rule by the Turks' (*dawlat al-atrāk*, *dawlat al-turk* or *dawlat al-turkiyya*) and later that of the Circassians (*dawlat al-jarkas*). Within the overarching notion of a 'Dawlat al-Atrāk', however, could also be microcosmic '*dawlas*'– a complex and versatile term linked to notions of state, time and also the reign, dynasty or period of rule of a given sultan, such as the '*dawlat al-ẓāhiriyya*' of al-Ẓāhir Jaqmaq (r. 841–57/1438–53). Each new sultanic order thus established the authority of the ruler and his entourage through reproductive practices such as the 'recycling' or reintegration of elites from earlier orders representing a fresh state formation of its own.[26] What we perceive as the continuous sultanate is thus a series of social orders regularly produced by and around the sultans and their courts based in Cairo.

In addition to making room to focus on non-'*mamlūk*' actors such as the caliphs, the perspective of a 'Cairo Sultanate' provides an elastic way to identify the appearance of political order and to understand political power in late medieval Egypt and Syria as it was continuously and successfully projected outward from the Citadel of Cairo. Egypt, after all, represented the heartland of the sultanate and subsequent Cairo-based rulers often had to (re)consolidate Syria – which was occasionally treated as an eastern buffer zone – into their territory.[27]

How all of this was textually recreated and represented by contemporary authors, many of whom were linked directly or indirectly to military and political elites, is highly relevant to the current study of the Cairene Abbasid Caliphate. The normative act of creating structure and order was at the heart of much of the historiographical literature produced in the fourteenth and fifteenth centuries. Thus, texts which sought to invent textual realities of the state may have likewise lent a hand in creating factual reality through what they understood to be a fully realised expression and self-perception of reality.[28]

With power and authority frequently in tumult and flux, the sultans and their royal courts required a variety of ideological supports and vocabularies of legitimation to explicate and consolidate their rule. For its part, the Abbasid Caliphate offered a symbolic stability around which each new political order could establish itself. As a high-profile member of the sultanate's socio-political life, the name of the reining Abbasid caliph appeared frequently alongside the sultan and his 'Turkish' court atop political hierarchies of the region laid out in historiographical texts.[29]

This study engages with the latter-day Abbasid Caliphate and its relationship to sovereignty, authority and political agency through the historical lens of the late medieval Cairo Sultanate. The caliphs' participation in key social practices highlighted by Michael Chamberlain, Winslow Clifford and Jonathan Berkey, such as patronage, competition, intercession, and the construction of knowledge and institutions (from a historiographical perspective) are also of relevance to this study.[30] Rather than seeking answers to 'what went wrong' with the caliphate in this later period or understanding how the Cairo incarnation of the Abbasid Caliphate was unlike its Baghdadian predecessor, the book instead questions the ways in which the caliphate was made to appear as an ongoing reality – both as an unwavering institution and as a coherent practical idea when socio-political realities appeared to suggest the opposite.

The Caliphal Discourse of the Cairene Abbasids

Delegation of symbolic power from the Abbasid caliph to the sultan in Cairo after 659/1261, cast the polity in the form of the eleventh-century Seljuk-style government identified as a 'sultanate'.[31] The Cairo Sultanate's long-time patronage of the Abbasid Caliphate (no matter the realities of the latter's *actual* position) symbolised the upholding of religion which the religious elite (*ʿulamāʾ*) trumpeted as a demonstration of the sultan's regional dominance and ability to eclipse all other rival Muslim rulers.[32] The question of Abbasid legitimacy adds another wrinkle to the complexity and messiness of late medieval Syro-Egyptian politics in terms of a ruler's simultaneous need for caliphal legitimacy juxtaposed against the pressure to distance the caliphate from real power and authority. In studying the changes in the office of the Abbasid caliph during this period, lessons emerge about social organisation and the workings of governance. While the era has long been recognised as one of cooperation and symbiosis between political and religious elites, institutions like the caliphate were often used to mask very real tensions, power struggles and changing prerogatives of authority.[33] The caliphs were in many ways pawns to be removed or re-introduced into politics, and at times of uncertainty could find moments to seize new opportunities.

In some ways, the restoration of the caliphate in the context of the Cairo Sultanate resembled an important 'project', and contributed to a discourse that united the so-called 'men of the sword' and the 'men of the turban' even if they sometimes competed for influence.[34] Hassan's analysis of the caliphate as an ongoing interpretive framework or 'cultural grammar', has already linked it to a broader Islamic cultural discourse and structural language that creates meanings, textual realities and notions of unity across the Muslim world.[35]

'Discourse' is indeed a useful (though highly contextual and flexible) concept to apply as it allows us to transcend textual confines – moving beyond both text and conceptualisation, to a more complete and connected set of coherent ideas, practices, textual utterances, rituals and symbolic presentations.[36] These seemingly disparate elements represent different relationships and engagements with the discourse of the caliphate, signifying not just the ongoing discourse itself, but also medieval authors' attempts at making and remaking it anew, giving it form, and attempting to move it in a particular direction(s). The caliphate itself was functional as a part of the sultanate's ideological discourse on legitimacy – the discourse thereby functioning as a tool of power which also had an active hand in reproducing and reinforcing it.[37]

'Caliphate' itself is a highly contextual signifier that has taken on a variety of different meanings throughout its various appearances in space, time and text. As Hugh Kennedy points out, fundamental to all versions, however, is the idea of leadership concerned with ordering Muslim society in accordance with the will of God.[38] Caliphate, as an idea, is thus richly varied with no single defining template or legal framework.[39] It is important to emphasise that the Abbasid Caliphate as it existed in Cairo as an offshoot of Sunni juridical definitions of 'Caliphate', as religious and political successorship (*khilāfa*) of the Prophet, was but one strand of a broader discourse on caliphate and kingship in the Islamic world of the mid-thirteenth to early sixteenth centuries.[40] As recent studies by Christopher Markiewicz, Hüseyin Yılmaz and Evrim Binbaş have illustrated, in the centuries following the Mongol sack of Baghdad in 1258, there was no universally agreed-upon conception of rule among Islamicate polities. Indeed, the idea of the caliphate never again enjoyed the widespread acceptance it had held in earlier centuries. Nevertheless, in many regional contexts, Abbasid and/or Chinggisid lineage and legitimacy remained highly important until the rise of the Ottomans, Safavids and Mughals.[41] It is thus important for the reader to remember that, particularly during the fifteenth and sixteenth centuries, 'protection of the Abbasid Caliphate' was but one iteration among numerous competing claims to sovereignty.[42]

Reviving the Abbasid Caliphate in Cairo was not without tension between the local offices that contributed to the precariousness of power in the political order established around each new sultan and his entourage. In the tumultuous world of medieval Cairene politics, households of amirs constantly competed for influence and access to resources. The quest for Abbasid legitimacy (itself very much a resource) might thus be approached as a kind of 'arms race', and many incumbent sultans did their best to guard the caliph's sacred symbolic power from rivals.

Just as the Shiʿite Buyid amirs of tenth-century Iraq and Persia famously refused to restore a descendant of ʿAlī ibn Abī Ṭālib to the imamate for fear that they would lose their grip on rule, in late medieval Cairo some political elites were aware that a Sunni Abbasid caliph could be turned against them by sectors of their subject population.[43] Some of the sultans thus intended to control and exploit the discourse without getting destroyed by it, even as many, if not all, were at the same time awed by the caliph's gravitational pull on political rivals. The caliph, at various times in the long history of the Cairo Sultanate, was thus capable of expansion beyond his typical role of an on-demand performer of ceremonial legitimacy.[44]

It was incumbent upon the sultan of Cairo and his entourage to walk a complex and delicate line between appearing close to the caliph while also distancing the Abbasids from the limelight due to their mass appeal. After all, political and ecclesiastical currents periodically called for a 'return of the caliphate' in the Syro-Egyptian context. The caliph or sultan could often touch a 'third rail' and there were limitations that neither office could encroach upon easily. In other words, courtly and social expectations demanded there be boundaries which the sultan and caliph should not over-step. These lines, while never formally or explicitly defined, were largely subject to expediency as well as the tastes and socio-political expectations of elite social groupings.[45]

For specialists, this book provides the first comprehensive dynastic history of the Cairene Abbasids ever produced, as well as a study of the manifestations of 'Caliphate' in the Cairo Sultanate based on narrative, prescriptive and documentary sources. Some may wonder if yet another treatment of the Abbasids of Cairo is necessary, but the lacunae in the body of research has left us with several important and unanswered questions. What was the function of the caliph and his office amidst the breakdown and re-creation of each new social and political order? Did the blurring of social categories, particularly in the fifteenth century, afford the caliphs social or professional mobility? What was the nature of the many relationships and personal links established by members of the Abbasid family with individuals of similar and different social backgrounds? What part did the caliphate play in factional disputes? If the political elite wanted the Abbasid caliph to be nothing more than a compliant figurehead, why were they also willing to maintain the conceit that he was a reasonable candidate to hold power over affairs? How can the caliphal household be contextualised within the social practices and political processes of the sultanate? What kinds of symbolic, socio-political or cultural capital were available to non-Abbasid actors who associated with the caliphal family? Is the image of the caliphate that emerges from our late medieval sources best approached as an institution, an idea or a role? Residual traces of the caliphate's spiritual and religious authority prove central to the issues examined in *The Abbasid Caliphate of Cairo*.

The surviving image of the continuous Abbasid Caliphate was constructed across a very detailed body of Arabic historical writing from late medieval Egypt and Syria. Like all themes of the period traced through historiography, the discourse on the Abbasid Caliphate is shaped by the social context and dispositions of those who produced them.[46] The narrative history of the Abbasid caliphs in this book is constructed through a variety of stories and factoids preserved in late medieval Arabic sources. Each source presents only one reflection of the historical reality shaped by the socio-cultural context of its author. The five chapters of Part One draw heavily from the descriptions of accessions to the sultanate in which the Abbasid caliph typically appeared in the historical writing of the period, which is more thoroughly analysed in Chapter 7.

The Abbasid Caliphate of Cairo generated considerable archival materials, including works of Arabic historical literature, diplomatic protocol, numismatics, epigraphy and political theory.[47] By employing various strategies, including court ceremonial, marital alliances and diplomacy, members of late medieval Syro-Egyptian society sought to legitimate their own authority within a wider web of power relations. The history of the caliphate and its impact on late medieval Egyptian society in particular is thus addressed from different perspectives. Based on the dense and varied corpus of source material at my disposal, I have structured the book in two parts to elucidate the caliphal institution in the context of the Cairo Sultanate from several perspectives. Running through both parts of the book is the common notion that the caliphate itself was often more complex than its most basic representations, and that while it existed as a textual reality, it was also an open and ongoing social reality.

Part One of the book creates a sprawling historical narrative, which, over the course of Chapters 1–5, establishes a broad chronological framework that contextualises the rest of the work by presenting a detailed history of the Cairo Abbasids based on the reportage of contemporary and slightly later historians. The largely positive treatment of the rich narrative source material in these chapters results in an important work of reference on the Abbasid family during the late thirteenth to the early sixteenth centuries. A working periodisation inspired by Julien Loiseau and Jo Van Steenbergen has proven helpful. Thus, eras covered in Part One roughly correspond to a number of dynastic and pseudo-dynastic periods in which some sultans of Cairo and their supporters were successfully able to exert ruling coherence for different periods of time. The first part of the book can therefore be segmented into eras of rule by: the Salihids or Ṣāliḥiyya (1260–79) in Chapter 1; the Qalawunids (1279–1382) in Chapters 1, 2 and 3; the Barquqids or Barqūqiyya (1382–1412) in Chapter 3; the fifteenth-century sultanate of former '*mamlūks*' (1412–96) in Chapter 4; followed by Chapter 5 which covers the final twenty years before the Ottoman conquest and annexation of the Syro-Egyptian and Hijazi territories of the sultanate (1497–1517).

Part Two of the book, as a social and intellectual history, then broadens the focus of the study by analysing contemporary perceptions of the Abbasid Caliphate of Cairo. Chapter 6 surveys several specimens of so-called 'political literature' dealing with the normative or idealised theory of the imamate according to a sampling of jurists, religious scholars and courtiers from the thirteenth to the sixteenth centuries. The contemporary view of the Abbasid Caliphate is further enhanced by Chapter 7, which examines the attempt of medieval historians to transmit the Abbasid Caliphate of their own time to posterity. Chapters 8 and 9 analyse the functional aspects and formal expectations for the Cairene Abbasids based on existing investiture and succession documents to shed new light on the caliphal institution in the context of politics and religion in fourteenth- and fifteenth-century Syro-Egypt. In the aim of presenting a nuanced conceptualisation of the Cairo Caliphate, Chapter 10 synthesises the narrative, juridical and documentary images explored in the previous chapters in order to lead a discussion on how we may begin to see the Abbasid Caliphate of Cairo anew in the light of its social dimensions.

As a study of the uniquely medieval Egyptian conditions of a religious office such as the caliphate, this book thus seeks to engage with a re-thinking of the social dimensions of rulership. With its complex internal political landscape, frequently renegotiated networks and political formations, the caliphate offered a degree of uniformity essential to each new reorganisation of power in the sultanate.

In sum, this book is a contribution to Islamic social, cultural and political history by way of a thorough examination of its most outstanding leadership institution and organisational idea, the caliphate, as traced and presented through late medieval Syro-Egyptian literary and documentary evidence. While my intention is not to overstate the role of an often marginalised socio-political institution, I hope to add to the debate that the office itself occupied a role beyond the citadel that transcended mere concerns for political expediency.

Notes

1. The sultanate of Cairo (or Cairo Sultanate) is a more recent conceptualisation of the traditional 'Mamluk Sultanate', which takes the geographical nucleus of Cairo as its key defining feature rather than the servile military origins of some members of its ruling elite. See Van Steenbergen, 'Revisiting the Mamlūk Empire'; Van Steenbergen, 'Appearances of *dawla* and Political Order', 75–81; Van Steenbergen, 'Mamlukisation', 17–19.
2. Weil, *Geschichte des Abbasidenchalifats in Egypten.*
3. Muir, *Mameluke or Slave Dynasty of Egypt*, 16, 30, 64; Muir, *The Caliphate: Its Rise, Decline and Fall*, 599.
4. Barthold's original study on the caliphate appeared as: 'Khalif i Sultan', *Mir Islama* 1 (1912): 203–26, 345–400. Partial translations, notes and summaries of this study have been made available in other languages. See Becker, 'Barthold's Studien'; Barthold, 'Caliph and Sultan'.
5. Arnold, *Caliphate*, 89–106, 139–58.
6. Lane-Poole, *A History of Egypt in the Middle Ages*, 264.
7. Gaudefroy-Demombynes, *La Syrie à l'époque des mamelouks*, xix–xxix.
8. Tyan, *Institutions du droit public musulman*, 2:206–61.
9. Berkey, 'Mamluk Religious Policy', 11.
10. Schimmel, 'Kalif und Kadi', 5–27.
11. Chapoutot-Remadi, 'Une institution'. Chapoutot-Remadi's 1993 doctoral dissertation also includes a valuable treatment of the Cairene Abbasids. See Chapoutot-Remadi, 'Liens et relations', 23–62.
12. Garcin, 'Histoire', 53–65. See also Garcin's brief summary of the Abbasids reigning in late fourteenth- and fifteenth-century Cairo, 'The Regime of the Circassian Mamlūks', 303.

13. Holt, 'Some Observations'.
14. R. Hartmann, 'Zur Vorgeschichte des ʿabbāsidischen Schein-Chalifates von Cairo'.
15. Ayalon, 'Studies on the Transfer of the ʿAbbasid Caliphate from Baghdad to Cairo'.
16. Hassan, *Longing for the Lost Caliphate.*
17. Woods, *Aqquyunlu*, 4–6; Hodgson, *Venture of Islam*, 2:114–15; Gibb, 'Constitutional Organization', 3–4.
18. Van Steenbergen, 'Appearances of *dawla* and Political Order', 62, 76; Hassan, *Longing for the Lost Caliphate*, 29, 31.
19. For a reassessment of the 'Mamluk' signifier, see Van Steenbergen, 'Appearances of *dawla* and Political Order', 52–4; Van Steenbergen, 'Mamlukisation', 3–5.
20. Eychenne, *Liens personnels*, 19.
21. Van Steenbergen, 'The Mamluk Sultanate', 189–93; Van Steenbergen, Wing and D'hulster, 'Mamlukization Part I', 550–1; Loiseau, *Les Mamelouks*, 90.
22. The social primacy of the household was significant for its ability both to integrate elites as well as redistribute power and resources with the aim of reproducing itself. See Van Den Bossche, 'Past, Panegyric', 37–8; Onimus, *Les maîtres du jeu*, 15–17, 124; Van Steenbergen, 'Appearances of *dawla* and Political Order', 66–7; Eychenne, *Liens personnels*, 21; Chapoutot-Remadi, 'Liens et relations'.
23. For more recent 'Mamluk' readings of politics, see Fuess, 'Mamluk Politics'; Loiseau, *Les Mamelouks*.
24. Van Steenbergen, 'Mamlukisation', 18.
25. Van Steenbergen, 'The Mamluk Sultanate', 190–3; Van Steenbergen, 'Appearances of *dawla* and Political Order', 79.
26. Yosef, 'Dawlat al-Atrāk'; Van Steenbergen, *Caliphate and Kingship*, 16–17; Van Steenbergen, 'Appearances of *dawla* and Political Order', 54–5, 60; Yılmaz, *Caliphate Redefined*, 96–106; Van Den Bossche, 'Past, Panegyric', 28, 34–41.
27. Van Steenbergen, 'Appearances of *dawla* and Political Order', 76; Van Steenbergen, 'Mamlukisation', 18.
28. Van Den Bossche, 'Past, Panegyric', 41.
29. Van Steenbergen, 'Appearances of *dawla* and Political Order', 62; Van Steenbergen, 'Mamlukisation', 18; Van Steenbergen, 'ʿAṣabiyya, Messiness'.
30. Chamberlain, *Knowledge*, 8, 17, 37–8, 41–66; Clifford, 'Ubi Sumus?'; Berkey, *Transmission of Knowledge*.
31. Loiseau, *Les Mamelouks*, 106.

32. Hassan, *Longing for the Lost Caliphate*, 67, 75–9; Broadbridge, *Kingship and Ideology*, 14–16; Berkey, 'Mamluk Religious Policy', 7.
33. Hassan, *Longing for the Lost Caliphate*, 84; Lev, 'Symbiotic Relations'; Petry, 'Politics of Insult', 115; Berkey, 'Mamluks as Muslims', 166–7; Berkey, 'Mamluk Religious Policy', 7–8; Petry, 'Robing Ceremonials', 353; Lapidus, *Muslim Cities*, 134, 167; Petry, *Civilian Elite*, 320.
34. Hassan, *Longing for the Lost Caliphate*.
35. Hassan's work demonstrates that the notion of the 'Caliphate' was inherent in cultural discourses. See *Longing for the Lost Caliphate*, 5, 13, 19, 22–6, 30–3, 65, 85, 94, 108, 110–11, 120, 122, 127, 145, 259. See also Voll, 'Islam as a Community of Discourse'.
36. A discourse is most often understood as 'an extended stretch of connected speech or writing', or even a text itself. For Foucault, it was socially constructed knowledge of some aspect of reality. See Van Leeuwen, *Introducing Social Semiotics*, 94.
37. Van Steenbergen, *Caliphate and Kingship*, 101; Laoust, *Essai*, 46–9.
38. Kennedy, *Caliphate*, xiii.
39. Ibid., xvi.
40. On changing conceptions of caliphate over time, see Al-Azmeh, *Muslim Kingship*, 154–88.
41. Markiewicz, *Crisis of Kingship*, 7, 30, 155–6; Yılmaz, *Caliphate Redefined*, 1–4; Binbaş, *Intellectual Networks*, 20, 257–61; Moin, *Millennial Sovereign*, 1–14; Woods, *Aqquyunlu*, 9.
42. Markiewicz, *Crisis of Kingship*, 155–6; Moin, *Millennial Sovereign*, 6; Kennedy, *Caliphate*, 247–8; Woods, *Aqquyunlu*, 4–7.
43. Hassan, *Longing for the Lost Caliphate*, 92; Hanne, *Putting the Caliph in His Place*, 32; Ḍāḥī and Mizbān, *al-Raʾy al-ʿāmm*, 43–65.
44. Hassan, *Longing for the Lost Caliphate*, 92.
45. Hassan, *Longing for the Lost Caliphate*, 88–9, 92; Wiederhold, 'Legal-Religious Elite'.
46. Hassan, *Longing for the Lost Caliphate*, 13, 17, 19, 67–8, 85–6, 108–28; Van Steenbergen, Wing and D'hulster, 'Mamlukization Part I', 555.
47. Chapoutot-Remadi linked this abundance of material on the Cairo caliphs in fourteenth- and fifteenth-century Arabic sources to the past prestige of the family. See 'Liens et relations', 23.

PART ONE

A HISTORY OF THE ABBASID CALIPHATE OF CAIRO

1

The Origins and Establishment of the Abbasid Caliphs in Cairo, 659–701/1261–1302

Introduction

When assessing the caliphate in the minds of medieval Muslims, it is puzzling that the institution resonated in Islamic society as much as it did, considering the extent to which it lost much of its practical function long before the mid-thirteenth century. Nevertheless, as the work of Mona Hassan has demonstrated, for the interregional Muslim community it had been an utter catastrophe. In 656/1258, the Mongols destroyed Islam's imperial stronghold in Baghdad and executed the Abbasid caliph al-Mustaʿṣim (r. 640–56/1242–58), symbolic successor of the Prophet Muḥammad and *amīr al-muʾminīn* or 'Commander of the Faithful', a human representation of ecumenical Islamic leadership harking back to the earliest days of the faith. For most Sunni Muslims, by the mid-thirteenth century the caliph had come to represent a 'divinely ordained mediator for human action, who safeguarded the connection between his community, the Prophet's example, and divine Will'.[1] Recovering from the great ordeal of losing their caliph to infidel invaders proved to be a formidable setback with which the collective Muslim psyche grappled for more than three years (656–9/1258–61).[2]

After the caliph's execution in Baghdad, Abbasid claimants began surfacing west of the Euphrates in the hope of filling the vacant office. Individual attempts to realise wide-ranging acknowledgement often unfolded in similar circumstances: the aspiring Abbasid pretender, typically an individual fleeing Baghdad alone or with a small band of helpers, appeared and came under the protection of one of the Bedouin tribal configurations of northern

Mesopotamia and greater Syria (Bilād al-Shām).[3] Endeavours to find a patron more influential than the local tribal *shaykh* were frequently thwarted by the Mongols until the nearly subsequent (and successful) investitures of the caliphs al-Mustanṣir bi-llāh at Cairo in 659/1261 and that of al-Ḥākim bi-Amr Allāh in 661/1262.

Vagabond Caliph: Al-Ḥākim bi-Amr Allāh

Abū al-ʿAbbās Aḥmad ibn al-Ḥasan, ultimately invested as the Abbasid caliph al-Ḥākim bi-Amr Allāh (and eventual founding ancestor of the Abbasid line in Cairo), had a long and complicated journey to that office. After the siege of Baghdad, Aḥmad ibn al-Ḥasan went into hiding in early 657/1259. The young Abbasid spent time in the captivity of Mongol authorities who, as part of a policy of eliminating Abbasid family members, may have intended to immure him. The builder commissioned with the gruesome task took pity on the prince and instead abetted his escape with other sympathetic companions. The party fled westward in Jumādā II 657/May–June 1259 into the protective custody of the Khafāja Bedouin active on the lower Euphrates near al-Raḥba.[4]

The official claim of Aḥmad ibn al-Ḥasan as being a descendant of the Abbasid caliph al-Mustarshid (d. 529/1135) went unquestioned by his Bedouin hosts. The amir of the Khafāja forwarded al-Ḥākim and his companions to Syria. As he resumed his travels westward, al-Ḥākim visited important clan members of the Āl Faḍl Bedouin until he ultimately fell in with the prominent chieftain ʿĪsā ibn Muhannā (d. 683/1284), an influential leader in northern Syria and the Jazīra in the late thirteenth century.[5] ʿĪsā ibn Muhannā notified local authorities of his visitors from the east. As acting head of the unravelling Ayyubid family network of rulers, al-Nāṣir Yūsuf (648–58/1250–60) summoned the Abbasid prince to Damascus. Nevertheless, negotiations for al-Ḥākim's passage to Damascus crumbled with the first wave of Mongol attacks in northwestern Mesopotamia and Syria in 657/1259–60, forcing him to remain among the Āl Faḍl. The Mongols seized Damascus (around March 1260) and al-Nāṣir Yūsuf fled to Cairo.[6]

The upstart forces of the Ṣāliḥiyya *mamlūk* regiments (former slave-soldiers imported by the late Ayyubid sultan al-Ṣāliḥ Najm al-Dīn Ayyūb), led by al-Muẓaffar Quṭuz (657–8/1259–60) who had claimed the sultanate in Egypt, met the Mongols in Ramaḍān 658/September 1260 at the Battle of ʿAyn Jālūt in northern Palestine and ultimately crushed what remained of their Syrian forces, pushing the Mongols back behind the Euphrates. Victory at ʿAyn Jālūt furnished the *mamlūk* soldiers with prestige as valiant warriors, strengthening their hold in Egypt while aiding their consolidation of Syria. To better oversee the absorption and consolidation of the old Ayyubid domains in Syria after ʿAyn Jālūt, Quṭuz lingered in Damascus. There, ʿĪsā ibn Muhannā resumed the process of alerting the new political strongman of al-Ḥākim's eligibility for the vacant caliphate.

Quṭuz dispatched his amir Sayf al-Dīn Qilij al-Baghdādī to offer the oath of allegiance (*bayʿa*) to al-Ḥākim and ordered him to escort the caliph on a mission to reclaim Baghdad from the Mongols. Together, forces under their control overpowered several towns near the Euphrates such as ʿĀna, Ḥadītha, Hīt and al-Anbār. Al-Ḥākim's war party briefly clashed with Mongol forces at al-Fallūja (12 miles north of Baghdad) in late 658/1260. The tide turned when the Mongol commander Qarābughā advanced with a superior army and forced the caliph's men to retreat to Salāmiyya, the Syrian base of ʿĪsā ibn Muhannā.[7]

While we cannot know Quṭuz's long-term plans for the caliphate, some fourteenth-century sources report his order for ʿĪsā ibn Muhannā to send al-Ḥākim to Cairo for investiture at a later date. As a reward, the Bedouin amir received Salāmiyya as an *iqṭāʿ* land grant from the sultan, while wider recognition as caliph eluded al-Ḥākim once again. Two months after ʿAyn Jālūt a cadre of amirs (former *mamlūks*) assassinated Quṭuz. One of the co-conspirators, Baybars al-Bunduqdārī, ultimately rose to power as sultan of Egypt and continued the task of consolidating a political order that provided political, socio-economic and cultural stability for Egypt, Syria and the Hijaz.[8]

Al-Ḥākim and ʿĪsā ibn Muhannā secured no immediate advantages, though in the long run, as Hassan and Stefan Heidemann point out, even fleeting acknowledgement from the sultan in Cairo increased the prestige of the newly arrived caliph among the Bedouin, and the unstable situation in Syria encouraged other Abbasid claimants to make for Cairo, eager to fill the vacant position.[9]

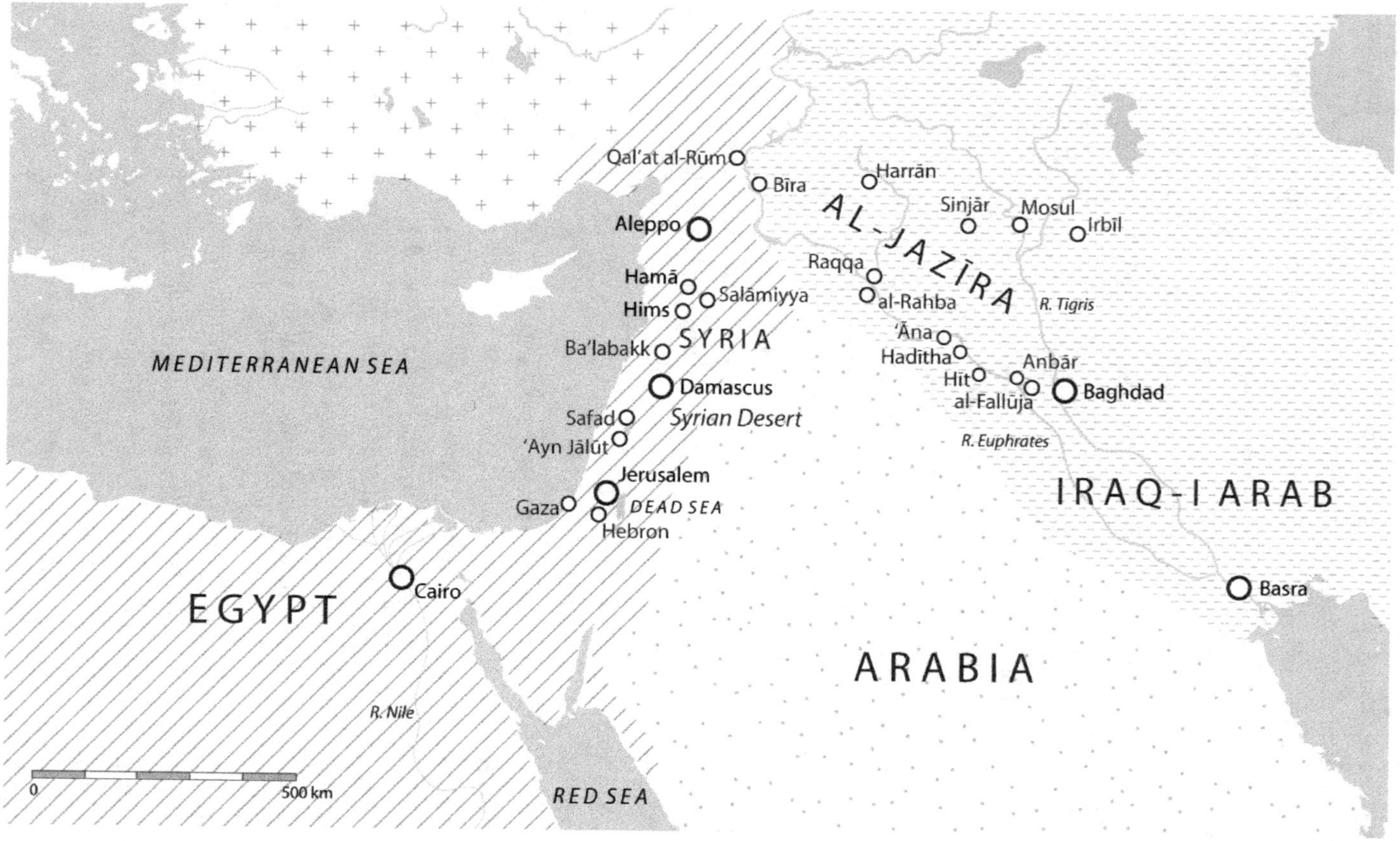

Map 1.1 Mid-thirteenth-century Syro-Egypt and Mesopotamia.

Al-Ḥākim's Search for Lasting Investiture

News of al-Ḥākim's activities did not escape the new political order established by Baybars. After several months in Salāmiyya, Ṭaybars al-Wazīrī, the sultan's governor of Damascus, summoned the caliph and his companions in Rajab 659/June 1261. Unbeknown to al-Ḥākim, several days earlier another Abbasid survivor, Aḥmad ibn al-Ẓāhir, the soon-to-be al-Mustanṣir bi-llāh of Cairo, had arrived in the city. Without informing al-Ḥākim, Ṭaybars al-Wazīrī sent the Abbasid survivor to the Egyptian capital along with his small band of Turkmen riders. At some point during the journey, al-Ḥākim learned that a caliph had already been invested by Baybars and that he himself was likely heading to incarceration or worse. Fearing uncertainty in Cairo, al-Ḥākim fled for the safety of the Syrian towns north of Salāmiyya.[10]

In the caliph's absence, ʿĪsā ibn Muhannā had fortified Salāmiyya against a siege by the local warlord Āqqūsh al-Barlī, a former *mamlūk* of the Ayyubid ruler of Aleppo, al-Malik al-ʿAzīz Muḥammad (613–34/1216–36). Coming to power on the strength of his own *mamlūk* factions, Āqqūsh became a major impediment to Baybars' consolidation of Syria. Āqqūsh sought recognition and leverage in his negotiations with Cairo, and successfully frustrated the forces of Baybars for several months by seizing Aleppo. As Bedouin control in Salāmiyya grew increasingly unstable, al-Ḥākim and his companions drifted towards Āqqūsh al-Barlī's camp. United by a common interest in wider acceptance for their respective ambitions, Āqqūsh helped al-Ḥākim acquire substantial acknowledgement as caliph of northern Syria and Mesopotamia. Nevertheless, Āqqūsh al-Barlī fled Aleppo when Baybars sent a force to take over, even though the latter only established short-term gains before Āqqūsh retook the city.[11]

After restoring influence in Aleppo for a second time in late Rajab 659/June 1261, Āqqūsh pledged allegiance (*bayʿa*) to al-Ḥākim, minted coins in his name and ordered mosque orators to mention the caliph's name in the Friday sermon (*khuṭba*). The pair had little choice but to flee Aleppo once again when Baybars renewed his efforts and Āqqūsh al-Barlī retreated to the former Mongol stronghold of Ḥarrān. Late thirteenth- and early fourteenth-century sources make little mention of al-Ḥākim after his flight from Aleppo, but modern scholarship suggests that knowledge of Baybars' investiture of al-Mustanṣir was widespread in Syria and the sultan of Cairo could only have interpreted the rival caliphate as a provocation. Bolstered by a resounding Abbasid endorsement, Āqqūsh emerged as a formidable regional threat to Baybars, and as Hassan and Heidemann confirm, his investiture of al-Ḥākim secured prestige and important oaths of loyalty from various elements in the towns and cities around Aleppo and Ḥarrān.[12]

After returning to recapture Aleppo from the amir Sanjar al-Ḥalabī in Ramaḍān 659/August 1261, Āqqūsh al-Barlī wrote to offer his obedience, but the sultan only agreed to accept it in person in Cairo. It was at this point that Āqqūsh and al-Ḥākim learned that Baybars had sent forces to Damascus with two objectives: half were to finally drive Āqqūsh from Aleppo, while a smaller portion led by al-Mustanṣir bi-llāh, the new caliph of Cairo, were to oust the Mongols from Baghdad.[13]

As if in competition, Āqqūsh equipped al-Ḥākim with about 1,000 Turkmen and other followers for their own adventure against the Mongols and sent the caliph to join the expedition of al-Mustanṣir. Āqqūsh then retreated back to Ḥarrān as Baybars' new governor took command in Aleppo. As al-Ḥākim and his forces travelled along the east bank of the Euphrates into Iraq, Āqqūsh and his army were drawn into conflict and devastated by the Mongols at Sinjār. Āqqūsh escaped and later went to submit to Baybars in Cairo in Dhū al-Ḥijja 660/October 1262.[14]

By acting as a pitchman for al-Ḥākim, ʿĪsā ibn Muhannā made the rounds with potential patrons on more than one occasion. In this, the Bedouin chief succeeded: Quṭuz rewarded him for looking after the caliph and allowed him to keep lands promised by the Ayyubids. Baybars likewise honoured him and made him *amīr al-ʿarab*. Previous studies of this period have shown that long before his investiture in Cairo, al-Ḥākim already enjoyed a political reputation and had amassed experience fighting the Mongols on several occasions. He had received a pledge of investiture from the proxy of the Cairo sultan and was treated with a modicum of respect as a brother-in-arms by powerful and influential commanders such as ʿĪsā ibn Muhannā and Āqqūsh al-Barlī.[15]

A Caliph for Cairo: the Investiture and Campaign of al-Mustanṣir bi-llāh, 659–60/1261

The first Abbasid claimant to arrive in Cairo was Abū al-Qāsim Aḥmad ibn al-Ẓāhir, an obscure figure prior to the Mongol invasion of Baghdad. Dark in complexion, he immediately claimed to be the son of the Baghdad caliph al-Ẓāhir (622–3/1225–6), brother of the caliph al-Mustanṣir bi-llāh (623–40/1226–42) and at the time of the Mongol invasion, a prisoner of his nephew, the reigning caliph al-Mustaʿṣim. After being freed by the Mongols, Aḥmad ibn al-Ẓāhir and a small escort of companions headed west to the Jazīra and found safety and honour among the Banū Khafāja, spending several months wandering rural areas with the tribesmen in search of support for his claims. In the company of a Bedouin escort, Aḥmad ibn al-Ẓāhir ultimately arrived at the Syrian oasis of al-Ghūṭa and two of Baybars' amirs stationed near Damascus, ʿAlāʾ al-Dīn al-Bunduqdār and Ṭaybars al-Wazīrī, alerted the ruler that a man from Iraq had arrived who might prove useful in the future. Baybars dispatched Qilij al-Baghdādī, who had earlier delivered a pledge of allegiance to al-Ḥākim on behalf of Quṭuz, to confirm the man's Abbasid identity. The chief commander instructed his Syrian officers to honour Aḥmad ibn al-Ẓāhir and guard him with chamberlains (*ḥujjāb*). Shortly thereafter, the Abbasid claimant arrived at the Cairo Citadel on 9 Rajab 659/9 June 1261 and met Baybars amidst throngs of onlookers on 'a very memorable day'. Even prominent Christians and Jews carrying their holy books came out to greet Aḥmad ibn al-Ẓāhir, who rode through the streets towards the Citadel on a horse decorated with Abbasid heraldry. Baybars arranged lodging for Aḥmad in the tower of the Citadel, while religious and political elites spent the next several days formalising plans for the debut of the Abbasid prince in their capital.[16]

On 13 Rajab 659/13 June 1261, Baybars, seating himself beside Aḥmad ibn al-Ẓāhir, assembled an audience of military officials, jurists, scholars, amirs, Sufis and merchants at the Columned or Pillar Hall (*Qāʿat al-ʿAwāmīd*) for a grand state ceremony. Contemporary chroniclers detailed the solemnity of the occasion; Baybars sat on the floor, on particularly good behaviour in the presence of the caliph, amid a noticeable absence of seats, a podium or any of the other trappings of a formal occasion. The ostensible purpose of the assembly was to hold a series of successive public confirmations of Aḥmad ibn al-Ẓāhir's Abbasid identity and to appoint him to the caliphate. First, his Bedouin travelling companions acknowledged that Aḥmad ibn al-Ẓāhir was indeed an '*imām*' of the Abbasid house and the uncle of the last caliph al-Mustaʿṣim. Next, the religious scholars presented a more formal testament naming Aḥmad as an authentic candidate whose noble pedigree satisfied the *ʿulamāʾ* enough for them to offer the *bayʿa* pledge on behalf of the religious leadership and the Muslim community (*umma*) at large. The chief Shāfiʿī magistrate, or qadi, Tāj al-Dīn ibn Bint al-Aʿazz, recorded the caliph's genealogy as sound before reading it to the gathering.[17]

The *bayʿa* itself was the most noteworthy aspect of the summit and introduced an important protocol for subsequent ceremonial practice involving the Abbasid Caliphate. Aḥmad ibn al-Ẓāhir received acknowledgement from the elites of Baybars' political order according to descending rank and included all classes of people without exception. The order in which participants pledged to the caliph sheds light on some tensions over which group had ownership over the caliphate project. Some sources claim Baybars himself was first to offer allegiance to Aḥmad ibn al-Ẓāhir as al-Mustanṣir, while alternative reports of the ceremony emphasise the participation and consent of high-level *ʿulamāʾ*. Many later accounts diverge from the 'official' version of Ibn ʿAbd al-Ẓāhir and assert that Ibn Bint al-Aʿazz first offered allegiance to al-Mustanṣir after having recorded the lineage of the caliph. Also of universal repute in the Syrian and Egyptian scholarly circles of the thirteenth-century sultanate was the independent scholar ʿIzz al-Dīn ʿAbd al-ʿAzīz ibn ʿAbd al-Salām (d. 660/1261), who lent crucial approval to the caliphal *bayʿa* ceremony.[18] As Hassan points out, Baybars had been obliged to learn how to perform the *bayʿa* ritual from an important Muslim scholar as a precaution to ensure that religious protocol was properly observed in restoring the caliphate. Islamic rulings on slave status had originally made Ibn ʿAbd al-Salām reluctant to lend support to Baybars, but in the end a pledge to a recognised Abbasid candidate secured critical support for the sultanate of Cairo from a noteworthy Islamic authority.[19]

Aḥmad ibn al-Ẓāhir received the regnal title (*laqab*) al-Mustanṣir bi-llāh, which, according to Heidemann, he may have already assumed among his Bedouin comrades, perhaps as homage to his deceased brother.[20] Immediately upon receiving *bayʿa* as caliph, al-Mustanṣir invested Baybars with the Islamic lands already in his possession as well as a pre-emptive authorisation to rule any future conquests made at the expense of non-Muslims. To underscore Baybars as the guarantor of the caliphate, al-Mustanṣir conferred the sobriquet 'Associate of the Commander of the Faithful' (*qasīm amīr al-muʾminīn*) on the sultan, which was subsequently struck on coins and included in inscriptions.[21]

After the ceremony, Baybars sent announcements to Syria and other regions under his control. The letters, often read publicly by a qadi, demanded *bayʿa* by proxy for the new caliph, and ordered coins be struck in the names of the sultan of Cairo and the Abbasid caliph, who must likewise be mentioned in all subsequent Friday sermons. Once Cairo formally became the new home of the Abbasid Caliphate, the *sharīf* ruler of Mecca, Abū Numayy Muḥammad (d. 701/1301), recognised Cairo's sovereignty and abandoned his acknowledgement of the Hafsid caliph of Tunis who also coincidentally made use of the title al-Mustanṣir.[22]

Clad in his family's traditional black ecclesiastical garb, al-Mustanṣir emerged some days later on 17 Rajab 659/17 June 1261 to deliver the Friday sermon before an elite crowd at the mosque of the Citadel. The caliph's emotional speech championed the Abbasid line and solicited God's assistance in *jihād* and blessings for the Prophet and his companions, as well as the sultan, before leading the congregational prayer with the mostly elite audience. Before adjourning, the sultan of Cairo, having been draped in a black Abbasid cloak by the caliph, showered the congregation with precious coins and later presented al-Mustanṣir with cash gifts.

News of the investiture reached Damascus several days after the ceremony and local officials read the announcement at the *madrasa* of the Ayyubid al-ʿĀdil. Syro-Egyptian sources describe jubilation among the masses who thanked God for the return of the Abbasid caliph after an absence of nearly four years. Mosques named al-Mustanṣir in the *khuṭba*, coins in Damascus bore his name, and a large street parade celebrated the news.[23] Meanwhile in Egypt, the historian al-Maqrīzī reports that the caliph and sultan briefly came down from the Citadel into Cairo to observe a demonstration of nautical war games including 'fire ships' (*ḥarāʾiq*) on the Nile, while locals came out to catch a glimpse.[24]

The caliph remained in Cairo for several weeks as the sultan's entourage plotted his triumphal return to Baghdad. On 4 Shaʿbān 659/4 July 1261, al-Mustanṣir was honoured at another ceremony unveiling Baybars' investiture diploma (*taqlīd*) combined with another round of robing for elites at the Bustān al-Kabīr pavilion erected outside Cairo. Baybars emerged from a private tent in full regalia, dressed in a black turban with gold embroidery, a violet robe, medallion and a sword hung at his side. Donning a yellow satin robe, Fakhr al-Dīn ibn Luqmān (d. 693/1294), the head of the chancery, ascended the *minbar* and read the investiture document that he had composed. Upon completion, Baybars paraded through the streets with the document displayed overhead while his men accompanied on foot.[25]

Securing the Caliphate in Egypt

Baybars, although a skilful commander and a master politician, began his career as a slave devoid of family connections or distinguished ancestors, a serious impediment in an Arabo-Muslim society connected viscerally to an Islamic past in which great stock was placed on lineage.[26] Therefore, it is no surprise that the Cairo sultan placed himself at the head of the project to restore the Abbasid Caliphate to make his own political order 'more palatable in the eyes of the *ʿulamāʾ* and pious public'.[27]

As several modern scholars have observed, Baybars' resurrection of the caliphate conforms to a conscious effort to follow earlier Seljuk, Zangid and Ayyubid models of political legitimisation in which caliphal suzerainty resided at the heart of the political system. Rulers had nominally acknowledged the reigning Abbasids in Baghdad as their overlords, sought letters of recognition and proclaimed their names on coins, inscriptions and in religious orations.[28] Baybars, as a short-term member of the inner circle of Quṭuz, was likely privy to the prior attempt to offer *bayʿa* to al-Ḥākim and was equally aware that Abbasid refugees had surfaced among the Bedouin tribes of greater Syria and Mesopotamia. While Baybars was essentially restoring the status quo, at the outset of his rule, he remained under pressure to distinguish his government or 'God-given turn in power' (*dawla*), silence competing claims, and destroy any grounds for accusation that he had come by his power unlawfully.[29]

Nevertheless, installing an Abbasid who could be persuaded to delegate all caliphal powers and prerogatives to a powerful sultan could not have stifled the criticisms of his detractors or quelled fears about his violent subduing of challengers in the region. In practical terms, Sherman Jackson is correct that *bayʿa* from the Abbasid caliph could only reinforce existing legitimacy that Baybars had already secured independently through military successes,[30] household expansion and ties of patronage.

Reclaiming Baghdad: a Deadly Mission?

Following the *bayʿa* ceremony and public appearances related to the arrival of al-Mustanṣir, Baybars began constructing a caliphal household by assigning servants and clients, and allocating wealth for Abbasid use in Shaʿbān 659/June 1261. The sultan and his amirs decided that al-Mustanṣir should be outfitted with a modest army to embark on an expedition to reclaim Baghdad. Baybars assigned numerous personnel to aid the caliph's mission, including chancery officials, religious functionaries and even doctors. Baybars appointed an *atābak* of 1,000 horsemen along with a eunuch over another 500 horsemen, an amir and treasurer charged with 200 horsemen, an *ustādār* over 500 horsemen, and a *dawādār* with 500 horsemen. Baybars also armed Bedouin fighters and distributed sizeable sums to cover several months' expenses. The sultan purchased and promoted 100 *mamlūk*s to guardsman (*jandār*) and arms' bearer (*silāḥdār*) positions, equipping each with three horses and camels all to carry the caliph's belongings and equipment.[31]

Together Baybars and al-Mustanṣir headed east towards Damascus on 19 Ramaḍān 659/17 August 1261 once the caliph's entourage and troops were flush with cash. After praying and celebrating the festival marking the end of Ramaḍān, al-Mustanṣir spent time in the sultan's tent. At an pre-agreed moment, the Abbasid caliph adorned the sultan in the garment of the *futuwwa* brotherhood (*libās al-futuwwa*) before a select group of unnamed dignitaries.[32]

The sons of the recently deceased ruler of Mosul, Badr al-Dīn al-Luʾluʾ (d. 657/1259) also accompanied the caliph's expedition. Finding life difficult as Mongol vassals, the two brothers Rukn al-Dīn Ismāʿīl of Mosul and Sayf al-Dīn Isḥāq of the Jazīra had fled west to petition the sultan of Egypt and Syria for aid. Baybars refused the request of the Luʾluʾid princes for an army of their own to reclaim their homelands from the Mongols, but allowed them to join al-Mustanṣir's expedition.[33]

On 6 Shawwāl 659/3 September 1261, the sultan and the caliph met the Syrian army after arriving at al-Kiswa. Damascene crowds, excited to welcome the pair, gathered to greet the Egyptian army when it arrived in the city on 10 Dhū al-Qaʿda 659/6 October 1261. The sultan lodged at the Damascus Citadel, while al-Mustanṣir camped near the *madrasa* and tomb complex of the Ayyubid sultan al-Nāṣir Yūsuf outside the city and later rejoined the sultan for public prayers at the Umayyad mosque. Before he sent the caliph to retake Baghdad, Baybars drastically scaled down the accompanying forces and left al-Mustanṣir with a paltry 300 men. Nevertheless, the sultan took the precaution of ordering the amirs Sayf al-Dīn al-Rashīdī, Shams al-Dīn Sunqur al-Rūmī and Aydakīn Bunduqdār to ride ahead to the Euphrates by way of Aleppo (with orders to seize the city from Āqqūsh al-Barlī). They were then to remain on standby with the vague order that they should await any request from al-Mustanṣir for assistance in Iraq if he required it.[34]

The caliph left for Iraq joined by Baybars' forces and the Luʾluʾid princes on 23 Dhū al-Qaʿda 659/19 October 1261 by way of al-Buriyya. The company landed near the town of al-Raḥba and camped for three days near the tomb of the fourth caliph ʿAlī ibn Abī Ṭālib. Changes to the expedition took place during the respite when al-Mustanṣir's forces encountered the Āl Faḍl Bedouin under the chieftain ʿAlī ibn Ḥadītha who appended 400 horsemen to the cause. Despite pleading from the caliph, the Luʾluʾids abandoned the mission to pursue their own interests in Iraq, taking roughly sixty *mamlūk*s and several camels with them. However, the amir ʿIzz al-Dīn Aydakīn from Ḥamā joined the caliph's expedition along with another thirty horsemen at roughly the same time.

After three days, al-Mustanṣir continued south towards the town of ʿĀna and encountered the aforementioned forces of the rival caliph al-Ḥākim, sent by Āqqūsh al-Barlī, advancing on the eastern bank of the Euphrates. The residents of ʿĀna, allegedly aware of al-Mustanṣir's investiture by Baybars in Egypt, denied al-Ḥākim allegiance and access to the town. The townspeople had vowed to open the gates *only* for al-Mustanṣir, 'the true caliph', arriving from the west. ʿĀna surrendered to al-Mustanṣir who presented it as an *iqṭāʿ* to the amir Nāṣir al-Dīn Aghlamish. The caliph rode on to al-Ḥadītha, whose inhabitants opened the gates and declared their willingness to submit to the Commander of the Faithful. Al-Mustanṣir took the town as his own property. When the two caliphal campaigns crossed paths, the majority of al-Ḥākim's nearly 700 Turkmen riders acknowledged al-Mustanṣir as the more powerful candidate, and abandoned the Aleppan caliph in favour of his Cairene rival. Al-Mustanṣir encouraged al-Ḥākim, who had little recourse but to set aside his claim, to unite (through *bayʿa* pledge) in the name of the Abbasid family (*Banī ʿAbbās*) and offered him shared space in his pavilion tent (*dihlīz*).[35]

Bolstered by the forces of al-Ḥākim, al-Mustanṣir wrote to Baybars of initial progress and the reclamation of the Iraqi towns ʿĀna and al-Ḥadītha. After departing the latter, al-Mustanṣir's forces alighted at a river bank before continuing on to Hīt. News of the caliph's arrival and modest triumphs quickly reached Qarābughā, the Mongol commander in Iraq (*muqaddam ʿaskar al-ṭaṭar bi-l-ʿIrāq*), who dispatched an army of his own to confront the caliph's forces. Qarābughā's army entered al-Anbār with 5,000 Mongols who plundered and massacred the population, while the military governor (*shiḥna*) of Baghdad ʿAlī Bahādur al-Khawarazmī brought up the remainder of the Mongol army from the rear. ʿAlī Bahādur ordered his son to continue on to Hīt to warn the Mongols of al-Mustanṣir's movements by setting the opposite river bank ablaze upon the caliph's approach.

As al-Mustanṣir advanced westward he encountered resistance when the inhabitants of Hīt closed the city gates in fear of impending violence. Laying siege to the town, the caliph's forces overwhelmed it on 29 Dhū al-Ḥijja 659/24 November 1261 and plundered the local non-Muslim population. Further south, the caliph camped at al-Dūr while a vanguard continued on in advance. Al-Mustanṣir spent the night of 3 Muḥarram 660/27 November 1261 encamped across the Euphrates from Qarābughā's Mongols in al-Anbār on the western bank of the river. At night, when Qarābughā noticed the caliph's vanguard he ordered his troops to cross the river and hostilities ensued the following morning. Before setting out, however, the Mongol commander purportedly ordered Muslim fighters in his ranks to hold back from the encounter, concerned that they would abandon the Mongols in favour of their Muslim caliph.[36]

Al-Mustanṣir or his amirs ordered the fighters into a classic battle formation with twelve squadrons of Bedouin on the right flank, Turkmen cavalry fighters on the left, and the caliph and his *mamlūk*s holding the centre.

Although present in the wings, the Bedouin and Turkmen deployments remained detached from the action. The 'Abbasid' army drove back ʿAlī Bahādur's forces, but the Mongols had launched a feigned retreat that drew the caliph's forces irresistibly into an ambush. The Bedouin and Turkmen flanks fled and left al-Mustanṣir's central fighters exposed to a subsequent encirclement and annihilation.[37]

The precise fate of al-Mustanṣir eluded contemporary writers and different speculative conclusions appear in the sources.[38] Al-Ḥākim, a shrewd politico not above suspicion for betraying his ally at a crucial moment, together with the Bedouin and Turkmen survived to fight another day and headed towards al-Raḥba and the protection of ʿĪsā ibn Muhannā, who contacted Baybars about the surviving Abbasid. Al-Ḥākim's party continued to the Damascus Citadel on 22 Ṣafar 660/16 January 1262 and reached the outskirts of Cairo by late Rabīʿ I 660/February 1262. Joined by a small band of survivors, al-Ḥākim journeyed towards safety and the newly vacant caliphate that awaited him in Cairo.[39]

Baybars had his own reading of what the caliphate should be and his intentions in arming the caliph are not entirely clear, suggesting that he did not see the caliphate as a wholly religious enterprise. In fact, he might even have interpreted the caliph as a junior sultan and his office thereby as an extension of the sultanate. This understanding would apparently evolve over time as the caliphate went on to play a lesser role.

The sultan's decision to dispatch the Abbasid caliph with limited resources puzzled medieval scholars and continues to confuse their modern counterparts. However, through the eyes of the political elite, the situation may have appeared ripe for expansion into an area of dubious Mongol control. For Baybars and his amirs to conclude that the time was right to reclaim Baghdad is thus not inconceivable in the years before Ilkhanid consolidation of Mesopotamia and Persia.[40]

Some historians believed Baybars deliberately intended to dispose of the Abbasid caliph over fears of his growing influence and popularity in the sultan's domains. Later fifteenth-century sources support this idea in their claims that a third party, perhaps one of the Luʾluʾid princes, poisoned Baybars against the caliph which culminated in the sultan sending al-Mustanṣir on a suicide mission. This assumption was absorbed by some modern scholars who believed Baybars wanted to clear the stage of a powerful political rival.[41] However, Reuven Amitai has summarised several flaws which demonstrate that this was not the case:

> First, it seems unlikely that Baybars would have contemplated at this early stage dispatching such a large force, which would have represented a sizeable chunk of the troops at his disposal, especially as he was still in the first stages of organizing his army. Second, it is difficult to see what exactly worried Baybars about al-Mustanṣir, who had given the Sultan complete power to rule in his name. Third, Baybars subsequently showed himself capable of keeping a Caliph (al-Ḥākim) in the background. Fourth, even taking Baybars' known cynicism and sense of *Realpolitik* into account, it is still hard to believe that he would deliberately send the Caliph on a suicide mission. Finally, one wonders how al-Mustanṣir would agree to embark on such an ill-fated campaign.[42]

Baybars' plans for Iraq after the expedition remain unclear. In the investiture document, the caliph legitimised any future holdings the sultan might secure from unbelievers, which surely included the re-conquest of Iraq.[43] Heidemann saw the expedition as more of an elongated raid, believing that Baybars was not interested in direct control of Baghdad otherwise he would have led the army himself. Holt acknowledges that the frontier zone separating the Mongols and the Syrian territories of the Cairo Sultanate after ʿAyn Jālūt was by no means stable and Baybars was in search of client rulers to place in power to his east such as al-Mustanṣir who already had inroads among the Bedouin. Amitai and Hassan, on the other hand, accept that the recovery of Baghdad and the subduing of contested areas was truly the aim of the conquest since that had been its stated purpose.[44]

The Mongol annihilation of the Baghdad caliphate in 656/1258 was not unexpected: the Mongols could hardly have tolerated a rival institution claiming universal sovereignty based on religion.[45] As some scholars have noted, Baybars' decision to send the caliph into Mongol territory reflected a desire to present a fully-developed religio-political alternative to Mongol or Chinggisid ideology.[46] For the Mongols, the resurrection of the Abbasid Caliphate was manifest proof that the sultans based in Cairo meant to stand as 'de facto leaders of the Muslim world',[47] including the part occupied by the invaders. Moreover, the restored Islamic caliphate may also have been a riposte to the sacred elements of Mongol ideology, thereby collectively casting Baybars and his entourage as the 'defenders of Islam, Muslims and the caliphate', and polar opposites to the Mongols of Hülegü's conquest.[48] Later claims emanating from Cairo that the caliph was still, in theory, the supreme authority in lands he no longer ruled directly no doubt offended Mongol ruling pretensions.[49]

It is noteworthy that Baybars set the caliph at the head of the army, in direct opposition to the Mongols' practice of having a Chinggisid lead their forces. There is also the similar notion of alleged Mongol reluctance to shed the 'royal' blood of the caliph in 656/1258, just as it was unacceptable to shed the blood of a Chinggisid. We might suggest that, at least in this micro instance, caliphal authority became the antithesis of Chinggisid charisma. Indeed, the Mongols would have interpreted the expedition of the Abbasid caliph as a potent provocation: he was a man of blood and power whom they had to respect, as well as a force applying a gravitational attraction upon the Muslims in their army.[50]

Al-Ḥākim bi-Amr Allāh in Cairo, 661–701/1262–1302

By the time Baybars welcomed him to Cairo in Rabīʿ II 660/March 1262, al-Ḥākim bi-Amr Allāh had already enjoyed a reputable political and military career. Late medieval Syro-Egyptian sources claim al-Ḥākim, his son and three travelling companions were greeted amid fanfare by Baybars, though in truth he arrived in Cairo as excitement for the recently martyred caliph al-Mustanṣir began to wane. Baybars was no longer preoccupied with caliphal investiture, and the name of al-Mustanṣir, whose caliphate had scarcely lasted six months, had already been removed from coinage. Upon arrival, the sultan assigned some expense money for al-Ḥākim and immediately sequestered him in the tower of the Citadel. Al-Ḥākim spent the majority of 660/1262 in limbo in the tower without receiving a formal pledge from Baybars.[51]

It was in dealing with the fallout from Mongol internecine struggles that the caliphate renewed its political importance for Baybars. Harmony among the descendants of Chinggis Khān disintegrated after the death of the Great Khān Möngke in 657/1259. Subsequent civil war between the brothers Ariq

Buqa and Qubilai ended in victory for the latter, who had been supported by Hülegü. Berke, the Khān of the Golden Horde since 655/1257, had supported the losing side and was left without allies in a bitter rivalry with his cousin Hülegü. Berke's isolation among the Mongols was compounded, moreover, by his early conversion to Islam in the 650s/1250s. This left him anxious to form an alliance with the sultan of Cairo.[52] Baybars reciprocated Berke's interest, due in part to his concerns about the unfriendly Mongol Ilkhanid power emerging in the east.

By reaching out to Berke in late 660/1262, Baybars stood to make strategic gains against their common Ilkhanid enemy as well as to secure a safe route to the Qipchāq steppe (northern Black Sea steppes), which served the Cairo Sultanate as a source of manpower and fell within Golden Horde territory. It was surely no accident that the eventual release and investiture of al-Ḥākim in Dhū al-Ḥijja 660/October 1262 coincided with the visit of Golden Horde ambassadors.[53] Baybars permitted the caliph to participate in the festivities celebrating the arrival of the embassy, which culminated in al-Ḥākim's *bayʿa* ceremony. On 2 Muḥarram 661/16 November 1262, Baybars prepared a gathering for his Citadel elite and the Golden Horde visitors to observe the allegiance ceremony for the new caliph. Al-Ḥākim solemnly rode into the Citadel, dismounted and sat beside Baybars as religious elites recited a genealogy linking the caliph to the Abbasid family. Baybars then pledged to the caliph before al-Ḥākim conferred authority on the sultan over the affairs of the lands and people before naming Baybars his associate (*qasīm*) in establishing justice. The notables and ambassadors then offered *bayʿa* to the new Abbasid caliph according to rank.[54]

Baybars was swift to emphasise the caliph's Islamic importance by making al-Ḥākim accessible to the Golden Horde ambassadors and presenting him as a central figure of religion protected by the sultan of Cairo. Shortly after the ceremony, Baybars brought the caliph to review the names of ambassadors selected for a return embassy to Berke Khān, which al-Ḥākim confirmed. The name of the caliph was subsequently mentioned on the *minbar*s of Egypt, followed soon after by Syrian mosques. Following the ceremony in Cairo, local elites and Golden Horde delegates attended al-Ḥākim's first Friday sermon and prayer. Emphasising the importance of the imamate and holy war, Baybars sent highlights of the *khuṭba* to Berke along with a copy of the genealogy linking the caliph to the Prophet. The embassy was dispatched north to Berke later in Muḥarram 661/November 1262.[55]

A Golden Horde embassy arrived in Cairo on 11 Rajab 661/21 May 1263, and the delegates presented Berke's formal request for support against Hülegü. The Mongol emissaries were treated to a special audience with the caliph as well as polo matches in his honour. To further strengthen Cairo's link with the Golden Horde, al-Ḥākim was ordered to name both Baybars and Berke in a *khuṭba* attended by Berke's ambassadors on 28 Shaʿbān 661/7 July 1263. After leading prayers in the Citadel, the caliph sat in with Baybars for a religious counselling session for the Golden Horde ambassadors.[56]

On 3 Ramaḍān 661/10 July 1263, during a late-night ceremony, the sultan capitalised on his previous initiation into the *futuwwa* brotherhood[57] by al-Mustanṣir. Baybars publicly inquired as to whether al-Ḥākim had ever been inducted into the *futuwwa* by his family members. After confirming the negative, the caliph, no doubt scripted by his handlers, expressed his wish to revive the *futuwwa* and donned its special garb. Shortly after doing so, the Abbasid caliph invested the Golden Horde visitors into the *futuwwa* and distributed the appropriate livery. Baybars carefully displayed his own ties to the brotherhood and recited the *silsila* which linked them all to the Abbasid caliph al-Nāṣir li-Dīn Allāh (575–622/1180–1225), and ultimately to prominent companions of the Prophet, including Salmān al-Fārisī and ʿAlī ibn Abī Ṭālib. *Futuwwa* initiation and the earlier *bayʿa* to the caliph of Cairo thus linked Berke's ambassadors to two Islamic institutions presented with keen importance. In both of his caliphal investitures, the idea of linking the Abbasid Caliphate to the *futuwwa* intrigued Baybars. The immediate successors of Baybars appeared to maintain the importance of investiture with *futuwwa* garments, issued documents associated with it, and inducted local amirs and foreign princes into it. The political elites' interest in the *futuwwa*s gradually waned in late medieval Egypt until its eventual disappearance by the fifteenth century.[58]

Heidemann speculates that the ambassadors were to return home, brief Berke on their collective experience in an authentic Islamic capital, and encourage their sovereign to cement ties with Baybars. In a parting address that underscored the necessity of *jihād* while commending Baybars for his service to Islam, the caliph called upon Berke to join the war effort and advised his ambassadors to praise Baybars to their master.[59] Once the alliance of Baybars and Berke had formalised, al-Ḥākim was gradually withdrawn from the political foreground. The caliph's name, which had been struck on coins, was soon removed. In Shawwāl 662/July–August 1264, Baybars also began to demonstrate interest in establishing his own dynasty by naming his son Berke Khān as heir apparent in a special ceremony that did not involve caliphal participation. The caliph likewise failed to serve in any ceremonial capacity at the prince's circumcision at the Citadel.[60]

In Dhū al-Qaʿda 662/August–September 1264, another Golden Horde embassy arrived in Cairo to deliver a letter thanking Baybars for his *second* restoration of the caliphate in as many years and agreeing to combine forces against Hülegü to achieve, among other things, the return of Baghdad to the abode of Islam.[61]

Early Years of Confinement

Shortly after his *bayʿa* ceremony, Baybars and his entourage permitted al-Ḥākim to receive visitors and travel among the civilian population on horseback. Wishing to separate the caliph from ambitious rival amirs, however, Baybars increased security around him. On 24 Dhū al-Ḥijja 663/7 October 1265, Baybars had the amir Sunqur al-Rūmī arrested on suspicions related to unauthorised meetings with al-Ḥākim. Henceforth, the sultan imposed a ban on military personnel visiting the Abbasid residence and restricted the caliph's movements, commencing a period of confinement that lasted nearly three decades.[62] In a time rife with failed coups and talk of overthrowing the sultan among his amirs, Baybars viewed the scholarly class as less of a liability and granted several of them access to al-Ḥākim.[63]

Although he was isolated for the majority of Baybars' reign, the sultan continued to make use of the caliph by widely publicising both of his investitures as noble deeds through inscriptions all over greater Syria. The caliphate, as presented in these inscriptions, was integral to the self-image Baybars, and his biographer Ibn ʿAbd al-Ẓāhir projected to Muslim audiences as a just and exemplary Islamic sovereign.[64]

Despite elaborate efforts at reinvigoration by Baybars the caliphate remained a fragile issue and could be questioned by rival claimants undeterred by widespread knowledge of Abbasid investitures in Cairo. The precise fate of several Abbasid claimants that emerged in interim years is unclear in the sources. Upon capture, Baybars would have guarded and isolated them in order to impede their ability to attract support among his enemies or otherwise disturb al-Ḥākim's reign in Cairo.[65]

The Sons of Baybars: Al-Malik al-Saʿīd Berke, 676–8/1277–9, and al-Malik al-ʿĀdil Salāmish, 678/1279

As Heidemann observed, conditions improved mildly for al-Ḥākim following the death of Baybars in 676/1277. After inheriting the sultanate from his father, al-Saʿīd Berke quickly became entangled in troubles of his own and offered the caliph a role in negotiations with rival amirs supporting the claim of his brother Salāmish. Al-Ḥākim and the four chief qadis were on hand in 678/1279–80 when Baybars' senior amirs revolted over Berke's preference for his own *mamlūk*s, demanding reappointment to their former positions. At the summons of the young sultan, the Abbasid caliph acted as a neutral mediator between the parties. When the caliph questioned the amirs concerning their demands, they responded that they sought the deposition of Berke. Ultimately, Berke's support base evaporated and his father's amirs laid siege to the Citadel until his surrender and abdication.[66]

The amirs exiled the son of Baybars to the desert fortress of al-Karak southeast of the Dead Sea and replaced him with his brother Salāmish, who ruled under the tutelage of his magnate the amir Qalāwūn. The caliph's name was removed from the coinage and replaced with Salāmish on one side and Qalāwūn on the other. In Rajab 678/November 1279, Qalāwūn seized the sultanate for himself with the throne title 'al-Manṣūr', an event which, in most fourteenth-century Syro-Egyptian historiographical sources, inaugurates a decade of near silence regarding the Abbasid Caliphate of Cairo.[67]

Al-Manṣūr Qalāwūn, 678–89/1279–90

Examination of the available sources for Qalāwūn's reign provides few reasons to believe that the Abbasid caliph played any active role in politics. In keeping with Baybars' practice, al-Ḥākim was excluded from many official ceremonies. This may have been due in part to an apparent shift in the sultan's understanding of his own office.[68] However, Qalāwūn still managed to benefit from the caliph's presence in the consolidation of his own political order.

While Qalāwūn's investiture document references the Abbasid Caliphate as a fount of authority, there is little evidence to suggest that al-Ḥākim was even present at the ceremony itself. Later historians claimed Qalāwūn did not bother to seek investiture from the caliph at all.[69]

Despite the caliph's marginal importance at the court of Qalāwūn, the sultan capitalised on his access to al-Ḥākim in both domestic and foreign disputes early in his reign. To maintain dominance among his peers, Qalāwūn had to behave as a first among equals and renegotiate his authority by expanding his military household with increased numbers of *mamlūk*s and amirs.[70]

As sultan, he left many of Baybars' religious policies in place and continued to support the four chief qadis and the caliphate, suppressing the latter while maintaining the title *qasīm amīr al-muʾminīn*. Although the sultan lacked serious rivals in Cairo at the time of his accession, a challenge soon appeared from the most senior amir Shams al-Dīn Sunqur al-Ashqar (d. 691/1292), who had been deputy or governor (*nāʾib al-salṭana*) in Damascus while Qalāwūn acted as ward to the sons of Baybars. From Syria, Sunqur al-Ashqar defied Qalāwūn, and by trying to establish a rival sultanate in Damascus emerged as a rallying point for unhappy elements seeking alternatives to the Manṣūrī *dawla* based in Cairo. On tenuous ideological footing in 679/1280, Sunqur al-Ashqar struck coins in the caliph's name and presented himself as '*al-sulṭān al-malik, qasīm amīr al-muʾminīn*', a direct challenge to Qalāwūn's authority. In reply, Qalāwūn wrote tersely to the amirs of Cairo that the caliph was under his 'protection', and not that of Sunqur al-Ashqar. This point was recapitulated in another letter from Qalāwūn to Sunqur preserved by the scribe and historian Shāfiʿ ibn ʿAlī.[71]

Qalāwūn likewise alluded to the caliph's presence in Cairo in his relations with his Mongol Muslim rivals. Hülegü's son Abaqa (663–81/1265–82) was succeeded by his brother, the convert to Islam, Tegüdar Aḥmad. The *ilkhan*'s change of faith might have brought a brief lull in the battle, but failed to end hostilities between the Cairo Sultanate and the Ilkhanids. It was widely held in Cairo that Tegüdar Aḥmad was not in search of 'right guidance'; rather, he was hoping to soften the resistance of Muslims who supported Qalāwūn against the infidel Mongols on chiefly religious and ideological grounds. In any case, the first of Aḥmad's two embassies to Qalāwūn in 681/1282 demanded that the sultan submit to the Ilkhanids on threat of war.[72]

Anne Broadbridge calls attention to the reply issued by Qalāwūn's chancery, which raises lasting implications for the sultan's view of the Abbasid Caliphate. In some versions of the letter preserved in fourteenth-century Egyptian chronicles, after praising God and the Prophet, Qalāwūn lauded al-Ḥākim, 'the master of rightly-guided (*mahdiyyūn*) caliphs, the cousin of the master of messengers and the caliph whom the people of religion cling to', implying that if Tegüdar Aḥmad was sincere in his wish to be a genuine Muslim, he too was obliged to acknowledge and obey the caliph who sanctified the authority of the sultanate of Cairo.[73]

It is a puzzling fact that with the exception of Bar Hebraeus (Ibn al-ʿIbrī) and Shāfiʿ ibn ʿAlī, most historians omit the references to al-Ḥākim, whereas Ilkhanid sources retained Qalāwūn's allusions to the Abbasid caliph. Perhaps learning from his earlier confrontation with Sunqur al-Ashqar, Qalāwūn recognised that the caliphate could be used against him if it figured too prominently in his correspondence. Broadbridge suggests that Qalāwūn, possibly uneasy about the role of al-Ḥākim in politics, wished to exploit the caliphate in his dealings abroad while hobbling it domestically.[74]

After the death of Berke Khān in 665/1267, Golden Horde leadership passed back to a non-Muslim branch of the family under Möngke Temür (665–79/1267–80), who found it politic to uphold the status quo with Cairo.[75] By 679/1280 leadership fell again into Muslim hands with Töde Möngke (679–87/1280–7), and the reinvigorated friendship between the two powers facilitated the flow of new slave recruits to help fill the manpower demands of the Cairo Sultanate. Qalāwūn's need to deal with friendly Muslim rulers demonstrated the enduring importance of the caliphate to the sultan of Cairo, even as he kept the caliph under close confinement. Controlling access to al-Ḥākim as a resource proved to be a powerful political asset for the sultan, and it is difficult to insist that the caliphate 'fell into disuse' during Qalāwūn's reign when evidence suggests that the symbolic and theoretical value continued as ever.[76]

Al-Ashraf Khalīl, 689–93/1290–3

The death of Qalāwūn inaugurates a nearly 100-year period of rule by his sons and grandsons as the Qalawunid dynasty. By way of an investiture deed, Qalāwūn had named his son al-Ṣāliḥ ʿAlī as his chosen replacement in 679/1280. However, al-Ṣāliḥ predeceased his father in 687/1288, and succession fell instead to another son, al-Ashraf Khalīl (689–93/1290–3).[77]

Early on critical disadvantages beset al-Ashraf Khalīl: his father had little confidence in him, and, worse still, Khalīl failed to win over the amirs who had earlier thrown in their lot with al-Ṣāliḥ ʿAlī. Because of this, modern researchers have suggested that a dire need for legitimacy drove Khalīl to reach for the Abbasid Caliphate.[78] Even so, as with his father, surviving records of Khalīl's investiture ceremony do not mention the presence or involvement of the caliph. Nevertheless, in Dhū al-Qaʿda 689/November 1290 Khalīl rode out donning a black caliphal robe.[79]

Several months into his reign, al-Ashraf Khalīl restored the caliphate to prominence in Cairo by renewing the *bayʿa* pledge to al-Ḥākim. After capturing the last Crusader stronghold at Acre in 690/1291, Khalīl returned to Cairo to provide special honours to al-Ḥākim at court on 25 Ramaḍān 690/21 September 1291. The caliph received gifts, clothing of distinction and a replica of Dhū al-Faqār, the famous two-pronged sword associated with the Prophet and ʿAlī ibn Abī Ṭālib.[80]

The Ilkhanids remained a substantial threat to the eastern Syrian territories of the sultanate, though they suffered a period of turbulence in the wake of the death of Arghūn in 690/1291, followed by the succession of his brother Gaikhatu (690–4/1291–5). Intelligence concerning the Mongol situation may have tempted Khalīl to consider making another attempt on Baghdad. Nevertheless, the sultan eventually decided against engaging the Ilkhanids directly and instead took aim at their Armenian allies.[81]

The caliph became a centrepiece in the sultan's war preparations. On 24 Shawwāl 690/10 October 1291 the Citadel mosque was decorated to receive the first public sermon delivered by al-Ḥākim in several decades. Abbasid emblems adorned the hall and Qurʾān reciters read verses and made prayers for the sultan. Al-Ashraf Khalīl ordered a company of amirs to wait on the caliph, and amirs vied to shake hands with al-Ḥākim and absorb the blessings of his presence. After meeting the sultan and basking in ornate praise, the caliph ascended the *minbar* and delivered a *khuṭba*.

The sultan ordered the jurist and scholar Badr al-Dīn ibn Jamāʿa, who, during the years of the caliph's seclusion, had been appointed chief Shāfiʿī qadi and orator of the Citadel mosque, to lead congregational prayers after the caliph's *khuṭba*. After the service, the caliph returned to his residence with a newly assigned retinue of caretakers and associates to enhance his household.

To commemorate the one-year anniversary of his father's death on the night of 4 Dhū al-Qaʿda 690/29 October 1291 al-Ashraf Khalīl ordered elite amirs and religious dignitaries to attend Qalāwūn's mausoleum complex for a Qurʾān-completion ceremony and religious retreat. Candle arrangements flooded the room with bright light as thick smoke from incense and ambergris wafted around the guests. Attendees spent the night reciting the Qurʾān and viewing the marvellous treasures on display. In the early morning, Khalīl, dressed in white, joined the caliph, clad in Abbasid black, and together they entered Qalāwūn's tomb to pay their respects. Poets sang and participants were honoured with robes. The caliph eloquently addressed the gathering to speak on the importance of *jihād* and the re-conquest of Iraq.

Before departing for the campaign, al-Ashraf Khalīl took the caliph to visit patients at Qalāwūn's hospital. For one observer, the mere sight of the pair was enough to raise the spirits and health of the inmates. From the hospital, the young sultan and elderly caliph embarked on another grand procession for inspections at the Citadel whilst alms were distributed to onlookers.[82]

Another Qurʾān-completion event occurred at the tomb of Qalāwūn several months later in Rabīʿ I 691/March 1292. At the end of the month al-Ḥākim delivered a final motivational sermon in the Citadel mosque before the sultan and his armies departed for Aleppo, the staging ground for their siege of the Armenian stronghold Qalʿat al-Rūm (Rumkale, Hromkla). The reign of al-Ashraf Khalīl, however, was not to last long; a group of conspirators, including the sultan's *nāʾib al-salṭana* Baydarā and Lājīn al-Manṣūrī, ambushed him on 8 Muḥarram 693/9 December 1293 during a hunting expedition.[83]

More than his father, Khalīl elevated the caliph, created a function for him in official ceremonies, spent sums on his household and was even seen accepting his counsel. 'Reviver of the Abbasid state' (*muḥyī al-dawla al-ʿabbāsiyya*) was an apt statement for the coins and inscriptions of al-Ashraf Khalīl, whereas his predecessors had contented themselves with '*qasīm amīr al-muʾminīn*'. To some extent this indicates Khalīl's interest in restoring a more universal Islamic empire comprising all the lands that the Abbasids ruled in their heyday.[84]

Modern scholars diverge on the relationship between al-Ashraf Khalīl and al-Ḥākim. On the one hand, the sultan needed to vindicate his sultanate before his father's sceptical amirs. Bringing the caliph into his father's tomb on several occasions represented an attempt to appeal to Qalāwūn's old supporters and rally them for the coming battle. On the other hand, these public appearances also struck a chord with a largely inchoate popular concept of the caliph as guide and protector of the Muslims in dangerous times.[85] Khalīl, by reputation, was a pious Muslim ruler, more so, it seems, than his father. It is hard to rule out the return of the caliph to prominence as an authentic act of the sultan's piety.[86] Nevertheless, Heidemann and Berkey argue that Khalīl's use of the caliph may have contributed to a 'political inertia' which mandated the caliph's appearance at all subsequent sultanic investiture ceremonies.[87]

Kitbughā and Lājīn

To give the appearance of stability and continuity after the assassination of Khalīl, the dominant faction of amirs loyal to the Qalawunid line nominally placed another son of Qalāwūn on the throne as al-Malik al-Nāṣir Muḥammad in 693/1293 before the eventual usurpation of the sultanate by the amir Kitbughā al-Manṣūrī (694–6/1295–7) in 694/1294.[88] Members of the political elite ordered al-Ḥākim and the chief judges to endorse the coup and furnish it with *sharī* approval. Under duress, the caliph denounced the youthfulness of al-Nāṣir Muḥammad as the formal reason for his inability to rule coherently.[89]

The former *mamlūk* of Qalāwūn, Lājīn al-Manṣūrī, a conspirator in the murder of al-Ashraf Khalīl who had escaped the wrath of that sultan's *mamlūk*s, emerged to be appointed *nāʾib al-salṭana* by Kitbughā. Lājīn grew ambitious in the months that followed and made an attempt on Kitbughā's life in 696/1296. The move ultimately forced the sultan into retirement in

Syria. After Kitbughā's flight from politics, the amirs agreed on the selection of Lājīn as sultan. On 10 Ṣafar 696/8 December 1296 al-Manṣūr Lājīn summoned al-Ḥākim to conclude a *mubāyaʿa* ceremony in which the pair mutually exchanged confirmation. When it was his turn, Lājīn received a black caliphal robe of honour (*al-khilʿa al-khalīfatiyya*) from the caliph who was also mentioned in his diploma of investiture. Some days later Lājīn appeared publicly to ride in an inaugural procession, dressed in caliphal honour garments with his investiture document paraded before him. To calm unrest regarding the turnover in leadership, the sultan sent a letter to Damascus announcing his attainment of approval from both the Cairo amirs and the Abbasid caliph.[90]

Lājīn continued to honour al-Ḥākim and maintained the caliph in the public eye. In addition to bankrolling the Abbasid household and bestowing gifts on the family, Lājīn offered the caliph opportunities to ride at his side during processions and to attend official functions as an esteemed guest. As Khalīl had done before him, Lājīn housed the Abbasids in a multi-storeyed, belvedered residential palace (*manāẓir*) in Cairo's al-Kabsh district near the Ibn Ṭūlūn mosque. The sultan likewise supplied the caliph with cash, provisions and pack animals to take on pilgrimage to the holy cities of the Hijaz in 697/1298 along with his children, various family members, and sons of Baybars and ʿĪsā ibn Muhannā.[91]

The sultans who reigned during al-Ḥākim's thirty-year caliphate had done little to extend or project his importance outside Cairo, and the caliph's pilgrimage was not without incident. In Mecca, a minor kerfuffle broke out when al-Ḥākim wished to have the *minbar*s of the holy city deliver orations and offer prayers in his name.[92] The local *sharīf* Abū Numayy felt threatened, suspicious or otherwise resentful towards the caliph's presence, and challenged al-Ḥākim over his Abbasid lineage in dialogue recreated by the Egyptian *amīr al-ḥajj* and reported by the fifteenth-century historian Badr al-Dīn al-ʿAynī: 'Who are you and what is said of you? Who was your father? You should be ashamed to mention your pedigree within earshot of my own!' The *sharīf* then began enumerating his noble ancestors as the elderly al-Ḥākim sat silent and failed to defend himself beyond a meek recitation of verses praising the *sharīf*'s lineage.[93] The *amīr al-ḥajj* stepped in to ease tensions and the caliph returned to Cairo with minor scuffs to his honour. The *sharīf* appears to have perceived the caliph as a threat and may also have felt able to attack him with impunity as the caravan was in a state of ritual purity (*iḥrām*) for the pilgrimage.

During his final years in Cairo, early fourteenth-century sources suggest the caliph and his family enjoyed autonomy in al-Kabsh, mixing freely among the common folk in public places, absorbing local culture, and appropriating the customs of townsfolk to the detriment of the last vestiges of their noble family reputation.[94]

The Second Reign of al-Nāṣir Muḥammad and the Death of the Caliph

When Lājīn's reign ended in assassination in 698/1299, the kingmakers recalled the Qalawunid prince al-Nāṣir Muḥammad from exile in al-Karak and restored him to the sultanate as they competed for real power behind the scenes. The two leading contenders had been active in Lājīn's circle, but helped to bring about their leader's demise. Sayf al-Dīn Salār, a Mongol by origin, led a faction of Turkish amirs, and Rukn al-Dīn Baybars al-Jāshinkīr had been the candidate favoured by the contingent of Circassian amirs imported by Qalāwūn. In al-Karak, al-Nāṣir Muḥammad received a letter confirming the unanimous consent of the important Cairene amirs, along with the blessing of the caliph. In Cairo, the chief amirs staged a show coronation for the young sultan attended by al-Ḥākim, the four chief and notable amirs in Jumādā I 698/February 1299. The Cairo chancery produced a new investiture diploma on behalf of the Abbasid caliph. Having aged several years, al-Ḥākim now welcomed the return of al-Nāṣir Muḥammad and delegated sultanic authority for a second time without incident. Several days later, the young sultan embarked on his inaugural procession cloaked in a black Abbasid robe and his investiture deed in full view.[95]

Meanwhile, the neighbouring eastern polity established by the Mongol Ilkhanids remained a serious threat for the sultanate at the end of the thirteenth century. Since 694/1295, governance had been in the hands of Ghāzān Khān who, shortly before his succession, converted to Islam on the advice of his general. Islam became the religion of Ghāzān's intimates and his army was compelled to embrace the faith. As in the past, the Ilkhanid ruler's adoption of Islam had little bearing on relations with Cairo. From the perspective of Muslim political ideology, not having a *bayʿa* to the recognised *imām* of the time (the sultan of Cairo and his symbolic liege lord, the Abbasid caliph), automatically removed enemies from the faith.[96]

In mid-Ṣafar 699/November 1299 al-Nāṣir Muḥammad, along with al-Ḥākim and his religious and military personnel, headed for Damascus to confront a Mongol advance towards Syria. After arriving the next month, the sultan's forces proceeded to Ḥims where they suffered an historic defeat near Wādī al-Khāzindār. Although mosques in Damascus delivered the *khuṭba* in the name of Ghāzān, the Mongols pulled out shortly after Jumādā I 699/ February 1300. A later Mongol invasion followed in 700/1300–1, which was confounded due to inclement weather though Ghāzān went on to launch a third and final attack in 702/1303.[97] That same year, the Cairene chancery sent a message to Ghāzān informing him that Baghdad must be restored to the Abbasid caliph. Although he favoured Chinggisid legitimacy and necessarily rejected Cairo's appeals to Abbasid authority, at least one of the reasons for Ghāzān's attacks on the eastern territories of the sultanate may have been a desire to bring the Abbasid Caliphate to Baghdad.[98]

Broadbridge characterised the unfavourable Mongol view of the Abbasid Caliphate under Ghāzān and his successor Öljeitü (703–15/1304–16) as being informed by a possible preference for Twelver Shiʿism. The Mongol rulers came to see all Sunni caliphal dynasties as illegitimate, which seems to have been exacerbated by the Cairo chancery's frequent diplomatic appeals to the Abbasid legitimacy of al-Ḥākim in communiqués written since the time of Qalāwūn. Any Ilkhanid interest in Shiʿism may thus be partially linked to a parallel Islamic legitimacy capable of challenging Cairo's claims of Abbasid supremacy.[99]

The Mongols traded diplomatic correspondence with the Cairo Citadel in these years reminiscent of the tone set by Qalāwūn and Aḥmad Tegüder thirty years earlier. Again, al-Ḥākim was referenced by al-Nāṣir Muḥammad's chancery in attempts to enlighten Ghāzān on obedience to the Abbasid caliph and the ruler who supported him. One letter warned the Ilkhanid *pādishāh-i Islām* that 'he who befriends (the caliph) is protected by God, and God takes him in hand, but God will humiliate the one who opposes (the caliph), or (opposes) the ruler who elevates him'.[100] This included the Syro-Egyptian territories of the sultanate, as hosts and protectors of the caliphate, within the sphere of divine protection.

Figure 1.1 Abbasid mausoleum, Cairo. Image courtesy of D. Fairchild Ruggles.

Upon returning to Cairo, al-Ḥākim lived out his final days at his estate in al-Kabsh where he succumbed to an unspecified disease on 18 Jumādā I 701/19 January 1302, aged between seventy and eighty years. Two days before his death the caliph called on judges and notaries to legally designate his son Sulaymān as heir to the caliphate. The political elite concealed the death of the caliph until the *nāʾib al-salṭana* Sayf al-Dīn Salār announced it before prayer and summoned all the amirs, dignitaries, Sufi *shaykh*s and religious personnel to attend. Overlap between Sufi holiness and the charisma of the Abbasid Caliphate occurred at times when the political elite invited Sufis to lend their sanctity to caliphal ceremonial. Karīm al-Dīn al-Āmulī, the *shaykh al-shuyūkh* of the Saʿīd al-Suʿadā *khānqāh* and the chief body-washer were ordered to perform the bathing ritual and other funerary rites for the caliph. Rank-and-file amirs came down to al-Kabsh to honour al-Ḥākim and participate in his funerary rituals. The amirs, chief judges and grandees solemnly marched from the caliph's neighbourhood to the nearby Ibn Ṭūlūn mosque. The *shaykh al-shuyūkh* then offered the farewell prayer for al-Ḥākim at the horse market below the Citadel after the afternoon prayer. The first Abbasid caliph to be buried in Egypt was then interred in the Qarāfa cemetery slightly south of Cairo near the shrine of Sayyida Nafīsa (d. 208/824), which became the traditional Abbasid burial ground in Cairo.[101]

The activities of Baybars and his power elite in the second half of the thirteenth century are often considered to be the foundation of the 'Mamluk' Sultanate and its long-term political system, but many of the important resources, institutions and value systems originated in the late twelfth century and lasted into the early sixteenth.[102] With power and authority often transitory and in a state of flux, would-be sultans and their entourages needed every kind of ideological support to bolster and consolidate their political orders. In addition to serving as a push-back against the Mongols, reinventing the Abbasid Caliphate in Cairo served as a transformative means through which military leaders could successfully attract and re-integrate Syro-Egyptian elites and scattered resources into the orbit of the Cairo Sultanate.[103] Abbasid ceremonial grew in importance after the reign of Qalāwūn, as the rituals each time helped to reproduce the new political order. In a response to the social climate, Baybars and his earliest political successors interacted with Abbasid ceremonial to publicly manipulate symbols granting access to social institutions, which in turn enabled them to exercise their sovereign agency.[104]

The following four chapters of Part One carry forth the theme of the establishment and perpetuation of a new Cairene incarnation of the Abbasid Caliphate introduced in this chapter. It is by turning to the later period of reigns by the descendants of al-Ḥākim that we begin to observe the development of the office and its interactions with the elite in subtle ways. By the start of the fourteenth century, uniquely Cairene traditions of the Abbasid Caliphate were beginning to unfold and take shape. Chapter 2 turns to the person of the caliph, who while undeniably suppressed, remained on hand to lend symbolic support to the established political orders of the Cairo sultans at important socio-political moments. Sequestration of the caliph often involved his betterment through religious and chancery training that continued through the fourteenth century and reach its peak in the fifteenth.

Notes

1. Van Steenbergen, *Caliphate and Kingship*, 16.
2. See, in particular, Hassan, *Longing for the Lost Caliphate*, 20–64; Heidemann, *Kalifat*, 67–9; Chapoutot-Remadi, 'Liens et relations', 29, 58.
3. Hassan, 'Loss of Caliphate', 119–42, 256–90; Heidemann, *Kalifat*, 78–107, 131–75. For closer analysis of these nomadic tribes, see Franz, 'The Castle and the Country', 368–76; Franz, 'Bedouin and States'; Amitai-Preiss, *Mongols and Mamluks*, 64–71.
4. Al-Yūnīnī, *Dhayl*, 1:483–4; Shāfiʿ ibn ʿAlī, *Ḥusn*, 54–5.
5. Al-Yūnīnī, *Dhayl*, 1:484–5; al-Maqrīzī, *Durar*, 2:208. See also Hassan, *Longing for the Lost Caliphate*, 69; Heidemann, *Kalifat*, 78–80; Franz, 'The Castle and the Country', 370–2; Franz, 'Bedouin and States', 49–51; Amitai-Preiss, *Mongols and Mamluks*, 62; Chapoutot-Remadi, 'Liens et relations', 34.
6. Al-Yūnīnī, *Dhayl*, 1:485; Abū al-Fidāʾ, *Mukhtaṣar*, 3:238–45; al-Nuwayrī, *Nihāya*, 30:40–2; Ibn al-Dawādārī, *Kanz*, 8:53, 87; al-Dhahabī, *Duwal*, 2:125–6; Mufaḍḍal, *Nahj*, 93; al-Ṣafadī, *Wāfī*, 6:317; al-Suyūṭī, *Taʾrīkh*, 382; Hassan, *Longing for the Lost Caliphate*, 69; Heidemann, *Kalifat*, 81–2; Humphreys, *From Saladin to the Mongols*, 323–4, 333–63.
7. Baybars al-Manṣūrī, *Zubdat al-fikra*, 50–2; al-Yūnīnī, *Dhayl*, 1:485–6; Ibn al-Dawādārī, *Kanz*, 8:87; Mufaḍḍal, *Nahj*, 93–4; al-Maqrīzī, *Durar*, 2:208; Ibn Ḥajar, *Durar*, 1:137–8; al-Suyūṭī, *Taʾrīkh*, 382; Hassan, *Longing for the Lost Caliphate*, 69–70; Franz, 'Bedouin and States', 50; Broadbridge, *Kingship and Ideology*, 14, 28–30; Amitai-Preiss, *Mongols and Mamluks*, 45–8, 62; Heidemann, *Kalifat*, 82–9; Chapoutot-Remadi, 'Liens et relations', 34; Holt, 'Some Observations', 501.
8. Ibn al-ʿIbrī, *Mukhtaṣar*, 282; Baybars al-Manṣūrī, *Zubdat al-fikra*, 53–5; al-Yūnīnī, *Dhayl*, 1:370–4; Abū al-Fidāʾ, *Mukhtaṣar*, 3:247; al-Nuwayrī, *Nihāya*, 30:13–16; Ibn al-Dawādārī, *Kanz*, 8:87; Mufaḍḍal, *Nahj*, 93–4; al-Ṣafadī, *Wāfī*, 6:318.
9. Hassan, *Longing for the Lost Caliphate*, 70; Heidemann, *Kalifat*, 87–8.
10. Al-Yūnīnī, *Dhayl*, 1:441, 2:94–5; Ibn al-Dawādārī, *Kanz*, 8:72; Hassan, *Longing for the Lost Caliphate*, 70; Franz, 'Bedouin and States', 53–4; Heidemann, *Kalifat*, 105–6; Chapoutot-Remadi, 'Liens et relations', 31–2.
11. Abū Shāma, *Tarājim*, 215–16; al-Yūnīnī, *Dhayl*, 1:486; Abū al-Fidāʾ, *Mukhtaṣar*, 3:250–1; al-Dhahabī, *Taʾrīkh*, 48:76, 81; al-Ṣafadī, *Wāfī*, 6:318; al-Maqrīzī, *Durar*, 2:208; Heidemann, *Kalifat*, 109–44; Hassan, *Longing for*

the Lost Caliphate, 76; Hassan, 'Loss of Caliphate', 126, 264–9; Amitai-Preiss, *Mongols and Mamluks*, 58, 60–1.

12. Abū Shāma, *Tarājim*, 215–16; al-Yūnīnī, *Dhayl*, 1:486, 2:105; al-Dhahabī, *ʿIbar*, 5:252; al-Dhahabī, *Taʾrīkh*, 48:75–6, 81, 49:5; al-Ṣafadī, *Wāfī*, 6:318; al-Ṣafadī, *Aʿyān al-ʿaṣr*, 1:209; Hassan, *Longing for the Lost Caliphate*, 76; Heidemann, *Kalifat*, 136–9, 144.
13. Al-Yūnīnī, *Dhayl*, 1:486; Hassan, *Longing for the Lost Caliphate*, 76; Hassan, 'Loss of Caliphate', 264–7; Heidemann, *Kalifat*, 139, 145.
14. Ibn Shaddād, *Aʿlāq*, 3:211; Baybars al-Manṣūrī, *Zubdat al-fikra*, 77; al-Yūnīnī, *Dhayl*, 1:486, 492–3; Shāfiʿ ibn ʿAlī, *Ḥusn*, 51; Ibn al-Dawādārī, *Kanz*, 8:88–9; al-Nuwayrī, *Nihāya*, 30:59–60; al-Dhahabī, *Taʾrīkh*, 48:76, 79, 81–3; al-Ṣafadī, *Wāfī*, 6:318; Hassan, *Longing for the Lost Caliphate*, 79; Heidemann, *Kalifat*, 159; Chapoutot-Remadi, 'Liens et relations', 35.
15. Hassan, *Longing for the Lost Caliphate*, 77–9; Heidemann, *Kalifat*, 80, 149. The real reason for maintaining good relations with ʿĪsā ibn Muhannā may have been more complicated, see Franz, 'The Castle and the Country', 350, 360–1, 370–6; Franz, 'Bedouin and States', 31–2.
16. Ibn ʿAbd al-Ẓāhir, *Rawḍ*, 99; Ibn Wāṣil, *Mufarrij*, 6:312; Baybars al-Manṣūrī, *Zubdat al-fikra*, 60–1; Ibn al-Ṣuqāʿī, *Tālī*, 2; al-Yūnīnī, *Dhayl*, 1:255, 441–2, 486, 2:95; Shāfiʿ ibn ʿAlī, *Ḥusn*, 37; Abū al-Fidāʾ, *Mukhtaṣar*, 3:253–4; al-Nuwayrī, *Nihāya*, 23:327, 30:29; Ibn al-Dawādārī, *Kanz*, 8:72–3; al-Dhahabī, *Siyar*, 23:168–9; al-Dhahabī, *Duwal*, 2:125; al-Dhahabī, *Taʾrīkh*, 48:407; Hassan, 'Loss of Caliphate', 267–70; Franz, 'Bedouin and States', 52–3; Aigle, *Mongol Empire*, 244–5; Heideman, *Kalifat*, 91–6; Chapoutot-Remadi, 'Liens et relations', 30–1.
17. Abū Shāma, *Tarājim*, 213; Ibn ʿAbd al-Ẓāhir, *Rawḍ*, 100; Ibn Wāṣil, *Mufarrij*, 6:312–13; Baybars al-Manṣūrī, *Zubdat al-fikra*, 60–1; al-Yūnīnī, *Dhayl*, 1:442, 2:96, 123, 163; Ibn al-Ṣuqāʿī, *Tālī*, 2; Shāfiʿ ibn ʿAlī, *Ḥusn*, 37; al-Nuwayrī, *Nihāya*, 23:327, 30:29; al-Dhahabī, *ʿIbar*, 5:252–3; al-Dhahabī, *Taʾrīkh*, 48:407; Hassan, *Longing for the Lost Caliphate*, 72; Heidemann, *Kalifat*, 95–6; Chapoutot-Remadi, 'Liens et relations', 32. See Aigle's discussion of the interrelationship between the oral and written components of the ceremony, *Mongol Empire*, 246–54. On the venue, see Behrens-Abouseif, 'Citadel of Cairo', 51–4; Rabbat, *Citadel of Cairo*, 93–4.
18. Ibn Wāṣil, *Mufarrij*, 6:312; al-Yūnīnī, *Dhayl*, 1:442, 2:96; Shāfiʿ ibn ʿAlī, *Ḥusn*, 37; Abū al-Fidāʾ, *Mukhtaṣar*, 2:121; Ibn al-Dawādārī, *Kanz*, 8:73; al-Qalqashandī, *Ṣubḥ*, 3:260; al-Qalqashandī, *Maʾāthir*, 2:112; Hassan,

Longing for the Lost Caliphate, 72; Heidemann, *Kalifat*, 96–8; Garcin, 'Histoire', 73–5.

19. On the relationship between Baybars and Ibn ʿAbd al-Salām, see Hassan, *Longing for the Lost Caliphate*, 67, 71–2, 84; Amitai, *Holy War*, 96–7; Knysh, *Ibn ʿArabi*, 62, 83. Al-Suyūṭī, who later clashed with the sultan Qāyitbāy in the late fifteenth century, harked back to Ibn ʿAbd al-Salām as a symbol of religious resistance against the political elite, see Garcin, 'Histoire', 73–4.
20. Heidemann, *Kalifat*, 75–7, 98.
21. Ibn ʿAbd al-Ẓāhir, *Rawḍ*, 100; Baybars al-Manṣūrī, *Zubdat al-fikra*, 61; al-Nuwayrī, *Nihāya*, 23:328, 30:29. I further discuss '*qasīm amīr al-muʾminīn*' in Chapter 8.
22. Ibn ʿAbd al-Ẓāhir, *Rawḍ*, 100–1; Baybars al-Manṣūrī, *Zubdat al-fikra*, 61; Shāfiʿ ibn ʿAlī, *Ḥusn*, 37; Abū al-Fidāʾ, *Mukhtaṣar*, 3:226–8; al-Nuwayrī, *Nihāya*, 23:328; Ibn al-Dawādārī, *Kanz*, 8:73; al-Dhahabī, *Siyār*, 23:170; Hassan, *Longing for the Lost Caliphate*, 73; Heidemann, *Kalifat*, 100; Little, 'History of Arabia', 17–23. The issue of whether or not the sultans of Cairo paid homage to the Hafsid caliphate was raised by R. Hartmann, 'Zur Vorgeschichte des ʿabbāsidischen Schein-Chalifates von Cairo', and debunked by Ayalon, 'Studies on the Transfer of the ʿAbbasid Caliphate from Baghdad to Cairo'. See also the various works of Chapoutot-Remadi on the subject: 'Liens et relations', 41–3; 'Les relations', 139–41; 'Une institution', 14–15.
23. Abū Shāma, *Tarājim*, 213; al-Yūnīnī, *Dhayl*, 1:451–2; al-Dhahabī, *Siyār*, 23:169–70; Ibn Taghrībirdī, *Manhal*, 2:73; Hassan, *Longing for the Lost Caliphate*, 73; Heidemann, *Kalifat*, 100.
24. Al-Maqrīzī, *Sulūk*, 1:451.
25. Ibn ʿAbd al-Ẓāhir, *Rawḍ*, 101; Ibn Wāṣil, *Mufarrij*, 6:313; Baybars al-Manṣūrī, *Zubdat al-fikra*, 61; al-Yūnīnī, *Dhayl*, 1:442–3, 2:97–8, 123–4; Shāfiʿ ibn ʿAlī, *Ḥusn*, 38, 44; Abū al-Fidāʾ, *Mukhtaṣar*, 3:253–4; al-Nuwayrī, *Nihāya*, 23:328, 30:29–30, 35; al-Dhahabī, *ʿIbar*, 5:258; al-Dhahabī, *Siyār*, 23:169–70; al-Dhahabī, *Taʾrīkh*, 48:407; Hassan, *Longing for the Lost Caliphate*, 74; Aigle, *Mongol Empire*, 251; Heidemann, *Kalifat*, 100–1. The text of the investiture document appears in Ibn ʿAbd al-Ẓāhir, *Rawḍ*, 102–10 and is discussed further in Chapters 8 and 9 below. On caliphal robing ritual in late medieval Cairo, see Yüksel Muslu, *Ottomans and Mamluks*, 41; Mājid, *Nuẓum*, 1:34.
26. Frenkel, 'Mamluks among the Nations', 74; Hassan, *Longing for the Lost Caliphate*, 26–9; Broadbridge, *Kingship and Ideology*, 12.

27. Berkey, 'Mamluk Religious Policy', 11. See also Hassan, *Longing for the Lost Caliphate*, 72; Aigle, *Mongol Empire*, 244–5.
28. Hassan, *Longing for the Lost Caliphate*, 110–11, 129, 130, 203; Lev, 'Symbiotic Relations', 13–14; Holt, 'Position and Power', 244–5; Holt, 'Structure of Government', 46.
29. Hassan, *Longing for the Lost Caliphate*, 77–9; Broadbridge, *Kingship and Ideology*, 30–1; Thorau, *Lion of Egypt*, 113; Holt, 'Virtuous Ruler', 31–3.
30. Jackson, 'Primacy of Domestic Politics', 58–9.
31. Thirteenth- and fourteenth-century Syro-Egyptian Arabic sources vary on the numbers of troops and names of specific officers involved. See Ibn ʿAbd al-Ẓāhir, *Rawḍ*, 110–11; Ibn Wāṣil, *Mufarrij*, 6:315–16; Baybars al-Manṣūrī, *Zubdat al-fikra*, 67; Ibn al-Ṣuqāʿī, *Tālī*, 2; al-Yūnīnī, *Dhayl*, 1:449, 2:104; Shāfiʿ ibn ʿAlī, *Ḥusn*, 44–5; Abū al-Fidāʾ, *Mukhtaṣar*, 3:253; al-Nuwayrī, *Nihāya*, 23:328–9, 30:36; Ibn al-Dawādārī, *Kanz*, 8:79–80; al-Dhahabī, *Taʾrīkh*, 48:408.
32. Ibn Shaddād, *Aʿlāq*, 3:208–9; Ibn ʿAbd al-Ẓāhir, *Rawḍ*, 111; Ibn Wāṣil, *Mufarrij*, 6:316; al-Yūnīnī, *Dhayl*, 1:450, 2:107; Shāfiʿ ibn ʿAlī, *Ḥusn*, 45; Hassan, *Longing for the Lost Caliphate*, 74–5; Heidemann, *Kalifat*, 104; Chapoutot-Remadi, 'Liens et relations', 32.
33. Ibn ʿAbd al-Ẓāhir, *Rawḍ*, 112; Ibn Wāṣil, *Mufarrij*, 6:317; Ibn Shaddād, *Aʿlāq*, 3:209; Baybars al-Manṣūrī, *Zubdat al-fikra*, 65–6; al-Yūnīnī, *Dhayl*, 1:452, 2:106, 124; al-Nuwayrī, *Nihāya*, 23:329–30; Ibn al-Dawādārī, *Kanz*, 8:81; al-Dhahabī, *Siyār*, 23:170; al-Dhahabī, *Taʾrīkh*, 48:408; Hassan, 'Loss of Caliphate', 277; Amitai-Preiss, *Mongols and Mamluks*, 57; Heidemann, *Kalifat*, 145; Chapoutot-Remadi, 'Liens et relations', 32.
34. Abū Shāma, *Tarājim*, 213–14; Ibn ʿAbd al-Ẓāhir, *Rawḍ*, 111–12; Ibn Wāṣil, *Mufarrij*, 6:316–17; Baybars al-Manṣūrī, *Zubdat al-fikra*, 66–7; al-Yūnīnī, *Dhayl*, 1:452; 2:106–7; Shāfiʿ ibn ʿAlī, *Ḥusn*, 45; Hassan, *Longing for the Lost Caliphate*, 75; Heidemann, *Kalifat*, 145–6.
35. Abū Shāma, *Tarājim*, 214–15; Ibn Shaddād, *Aʿlāq*, 3:208–9; Ibn al-Ṣuqāʿī, *Tālī*, 3; al-Yūnīnī, *Dhayl*, 1:452, 454–5, 2:108–10, 163; Ibn al-Dawādārī, *Kanz*, 8:82; al-Dhahabī, *Taʾrīkh*, 48:76, 408–9; al-Dhahabī, *Siyār*, 23:171; Hassan, *Longing for the Lost Caliphate*, 75; Hassan, 'Loss of Caliphate', 278–80; Franz, 'Bedouin and States', 54–5; Amitai-Preiss, *Mongols and Mamluks*, 57; Heidemann, *Kalifat*, 151–3; Chapoutot-Remadi, 'Liens et relations', 34; Holt, 'Some Observations', 502.
36. Jackson, *Mongols and the Islamic World*, 36, 264, 321, 324, 342.

37. Ibn ʿAbd al-Ẓāhir, *Rawḍ*, 112; Ibn Wāṣil, *Mufarrij*, 6:317–18; Abū Shāma, *Tarājim*, 215; Baybars al-Manṣūrī, *Zubdat al-fikra*, 68; Ibn al-Ṣuqāʿī, *Tālī*, 3; al-Yūnīnī, *Dhayl*, 1:455–6, 486, 500, 2:110–11; Shāfiʿ ibn ʿAlī, *Ḥusn*, 45–6; Abū al-Fidāʾ, *Mukhtaṣar*, 3:254; al-Nuwayrī, *Nihāya*, 23:330, 30:37; al-Kutubī, *ʿUyūn*, 20:255; Ibn al-Dawādārī, *Kanz*, 8:83; al-Dhahabī, *ʿIbar*, 5:253; al-Dhahabī, *Taʾrīkh*, 48:409; al-Dhahabī, *Siyār*, 23:171; Franz, 'Bedouin and States', 54–6; Hassan, 'Loss of Caliphate', 282–4; Amitai-Preiss, *Mongols and Mamluks*, 58; Heidemann, *Kalifat*, 88, 153–4; Chapoutot-Remadi, 'Liens et relations', 34.
38. Cf. Ibn al-Ṣuqāʿī, *Tālī*, 3; al-Yūnīnī, *Dhayl*, 1:457; al-Dhahabī, *Siyār*, 23:171; al-Maqrīzī, *Muqaffā*, 1:429; al-ʿAynī, *ʿIqd*, 1:328; Ibn Taghrībirdī, *Mawrid*, 1:239; al-Suyūṭī, *Ḥusn*, 2:58; al-Suyūṭī, *Taʾrīkh*, 382.
39. Abū Shāma, *Tarājim*, 216; al-Yūnīnī, *Dhayl*, 1:456, 483, 486, 2:111, 153; Ibn al-Dawādārī, *Kanz*, 8:83; al-Dhahabī, *Taʾrīkh*, 48:76; al-Dhahabī, *ʿIbar*, 5:253; al-Dhahabī, *Duwal*, 2:125; Mufaḍḍal, *Nahj*, 89, 105; al-Ṣafadī, *Wāfī*, 6:318; Hassan, *Longing for the Lost Caliphate*, 76, 79; Heidemann, *Kalifat*, 156.
40. Indeed, for several years immediately following the fall of Baghdad, the Mongols left Iraq thinly guarded. See Hassan, *Longing for the Lost Caliphate*, 70; Herzog, *Geschichte und Imaginaire*, 339–41; Holt, 'Some Observations', 502; Heidemann, *Kalifat*, 149–50; Amitai-Preiss, *Mongols and Mamluks*, 59–60; Amitai-Preiss, 'Fall and Rise', 491.
41. Al-Maqrīzī, *Sulūk*, 1:462; Aigle, *Mongol Empire*, 244; Khuwayṭir, *Baibars the First*, 34–6; Thorau, *Lion of Egypt*, 114–16; Irwin, *Middle East*, 43; Heidemann, *Kalifat*, 146–9; Amitai-Preiss, *Mongols and Mamluks*, 59; Holt, 'Some Observations', 501–2; Chapoutot-Remadi, 'Liens et relations', 33; Arnold, *Caliphate*, 94; Lane-Poole, *History of Egypt*, 265.
42. Amitai-Preiss, *Mongols and Mamluks*, 59.
43. Ibn ʿAbd al-Ẓāhir, *Rawḍ*, 104. See also Hassan, *Longing for the Lost Caliphate*, 74; Holt, 'Position and Power', 242; Arnold, *Caliphate*, 92–4.
44. Amitai-Preiss, 'Fall and Rise', 491; Hassan, *Longing for the Lost Caliphate*, 76; Heidemann, *Kalifat*, 148–50; Holt, 'Some Observations', 502.
45. Amitai-Preiss, 'Fall and Rise', 488; Jackson, *Mongols and the Islamic World*, 36.
46. In several places, Heidemann covers competing ideologies, notions of authority, and legitimate power between the Mongols and the sultans of Cairo: *Kalifat*, 36–8, 43–4, 55–61, 166, 195–7. See also Van Steenbergen, *Caliphate and Kingship*, 16, 18; Broadbridge, *Kingship and Ideology*, 6–26.

47. Amitai-Preiss, 'Mongol Imperial Ideology', 61–2.
48. De Rachewiltz, 'Some Remarks', 23–8; Broadbridge, 'Mamluk Legitimacy', 92, 95.
49. Amitai-Preiss, 'Fall and Rise', 488. See also Amitai's remarks in *Holy War*, 57, 98, 102–3.
50. Amitai-Preiss, 'Mongol Imperial Ideology', 61–2; Hassan, *Longing for the Lost Caliphate*, 117.
51. Abū Shāma, *Tarājim*, 221; Ibn Wāṣil, *Mufarrij*, 6:350; al-Yūnīnī, *Dhayl*, 1:483–4, 500, 530, 2:153; al-Nuwayrī, *Nihāya*, 23:331, 30:79; Ibn al-Dawādārī, *Kanz*, 8:86; al-Dhahabī, *Taʾrīkh*, 48:80; Hassan, 'Loss of Caliphate', 283–5; Heidemann, *Kalifat*, 156–7, 159, 177–9; Amitai-Preiss, *Mongols and Mamluks*, 61–3; Holt, 'Some Observations', 502–3.
52. Abū Shāma, *Tarājim*, 220; Baybars al-Manṣūrī, *Zubdat al-fikra*, 55–6, 82–4; al-Yūnīnī, *Dhayl*, 2:161–2; Jackson, *Mongols and the Islamic World*, 342; Favreau, 'Golden Horde and the Mamluks', 306–15; Hassan, *Longing for the Lost Caliphate*, 80; DeWeese, *Islamization and Native Religion*, 83–6; Holt, 'Some Observations', 503.
53. Aigle has argued that while the earlier investiture of al-Mustanṣir had been about domestic legitimacy for Baybars, the later ceremony for al-Ḥākim was geared instead towards external concerns, see *Mongol Empire*, 254. See also Hassan, *Longing for the Lost Caliphate*, 79–80; Heidemann, *Kalifat*, 167–75; Chapoutot-Remadi, 'Liens et relations', 36; Holt, 'Some Observations', 502–3.
54. Ibn ʿAbd al-Ẓāhir, *Rawḍ*, 141–2; Ibn Wāṣil, *Mufarrij*, 6:351; Baybars al-Manṣūrī, *Zubdat al-fikra*, 78; al-Yūnīnī, *Dhayl*, 1:530, 2:187; Shāfiʿ ibn ʿAlī, *Ḥusn*, 51–2; al-Dhahabī, *ʿIbar*, 5:263; al-Dhahabī, *Taʾrīkh*, 49:5–6; Hassan, *Longing for the Lost Caliphate*, 79–80; Heidemann, *Kalifat*, 163–4.
55. Ibn ʿAbd al-Ẓāhir, *Rawḍ*, 142, 145; Ibn Wāṣil, *Mufarrij*, 6:348, 351; Baybars al-Manṣūrī, *Zubdat al-fikra*, 78–80; al-Yūnīnī, *Dhayl*, 1:530, 2:187–90; Shāfiʿ ibn ʿAlī, *Ḥusn*, 51–2; al-Dhahabī, *Taʾrīkh*, 49:6; al-Maqrīzī, *Sulūk*, 1:477–80; Hassan, *Longing for the Lost Caliphate*, 80; Aigle, *Mongol Empire*, 248–51; Heidemann, *Kalifat*, 164–6. For a discussion of this *khuṭba*, see Chapter 8 below.
56. Ibn ʿAbd al-Ẓāhir, *Rawḍ*, 148, 171–2; Baybars al-Manṣūrī, *Zubdat al-fikra*, 81–4; al-Yūnīnī, *Dhayl*, 1:533–4, 2:191; al-Nuwayrī, *Nihāya*, 23:331, 30:82–4, 87; al-Suyūṭī, *Ḥusn*, 2:61; Hassan, 'Loss of Caliphate', 289–90; Heidemann, *Kalifat*, 168–9.

57. In the medieval Islamic world, *futuwwa*s, the urban networks with strong links to the Sufi *ṭarīqa*s, provided social services including welcoming travellers, and could also serve as ancillary militia forces. Between 950 and 1150 aid from the *futuwwa*s often proved decisive in political and military struggles. Baybars may have been interested in the activities of the existing orders in Cairo and Syria and wished to direct their activities through his association with the caliph. Others have suggested that he wanted to be seen as a simultaneous promoter of multiple classical Islamic institutions (caliphate and *futuwwa*). See Hanne, *Putting the Caliph in his Place*, 204; A. Hartmann, *An-Nāṣir li-Dīn Allāh*, 93–9, 111–18; Hassan, *Longing for the Lost Caliphate*, 74–5; Hodgson, *Venture of Islam*, 2:129; Holt, 'Virtuous Ruler'; Holt, 'Some Observations', 502–3. In the late thirteenth century, Cairene political elites integrated the initiation rituals of the *futuwwa* as a parallel structure that reinforced military culture and manliness (*muruwwa* or *javānmardi*). Its particular link to the caliphate in this period remains unclear.
58. Cairene amirs invested with the *futuwwa* displayed it in their coats of arms. Members of the *ʿulamāʾ* also composed documents opposing the *futuwwa*s. See Cahen, 'Futuwwa'; Irwin, 'Futuwwa', 162.
59. Ibn ʿAbd al-Ẓāhir, *Rawḍ*, 146–7, 173–4; Ibn Wāṣil, *Mufarrij*, 6:356–7; al-Yūnīnī, *Dhayl*, 1:537, 2:190–1; Shāfiʿ ibn ʿAlī, *Ḥusn*, 53–4; al-ʿAynī, *ʿIqd*, 1:353; Hassan, *Longing for the Lost Caliphate*, 74–5, 80; Amitai-Preiss, 'Fall and Rise', 492; Heidemann, *Kalifat*, 171; Irwin, 'Futuwwa', 162; Broadbridge, 'Mamluk Legitimacy', 99; Chapoutot-Remadi, 'Liens et relations', 47; Holt, 'Some Observations', 503. On the link between al-Nāṣir li-Dīn Allāh and the *futuwwa* in the late twelfth/early thirteenth century, see A. Hartmann, *An-Nāṣir li-Dīn Allāh*, 30–4, 92–108; Hanne, *Putting the Caliph in His Place*, 204; Hodgson, *Venture of Islam*, 2:129.
60. Ibn ʿAbd al-Ẓāhir, *Rawḍ*, 123, 203–4, 209, 218; Baybars al-Manṣūrī, *Zubdat al-fikra*, 89–90; al-Nuwayrī, *Nihāya*, 30:100–1; al-ʿAynī, *ʿIqd*, 1:377–8; Heidemann, *Kalifat*, 172–5; Holt, 'Some Observations', 503.
61. For details of the embassy's arrival, see Ibn ʿAbd al-Ẓāhir, *Rawḍ*, 214–18; al-Nuwayrī, *Nihāya*, 30:105; Heidemann, *Kalifat*, 172.
62. Shāfiʿ ibn ʿAlī, *Ḥusn*, 55; al-Nuwayrī, *Nihāya*, 23:331; al-Dhahabī, *ʿIbar*, 5:273; al-Dhahabī, *Taʾrīkh*, 49:22; Ibn al-Wardī, *Taʾrīkh*, 2:310; al-Qalqashandī, *Ṣubḥ*, 3:261, 275; al-Maqrīzī, *Sulūk*, 1:540; al-Suyūṭī, *Ḥusn*, 2:61; al-Suyūṭī, *Taʾrīkh*, 384; Clifford, *State Formation*, 97; Chapoutot-Remadi, 'Liens et relations', 37; Garcin, 'Histoire', 54.

63. On the religious learning of the Cairene Abbasid caliphs, see Banister, '*ʿĀlim*-Caliph'.
64. Hassan, *Longing for the Lost Caliphate*, 72; Aigle, *Mongol Empire*, 225–6; Aigle, 'Les inscriptions de Baybars', 63–6; Amitai, 'Some Remarks', 50–1; Holt, 'Virtuous Ruler', 27–8. For examples, see *RCEA* 12:4556, 4612 and 4690.
65. Mona Hassan has numbered at least three more erstwhile attempts (five in total) made by Abbasid claimants, see Hassan, *Longing for the Lost Caliphate*, 76–7, 80–3. Ibn ʿAbd al-Ẓāhir, *Rawḍ*, 248; al-Nuwayrī, *Nihāya*, 30:129; al-Maqrīzī, *Sulūk*, 1:554; al-ʿAynī, *ʿIqd*, 1:426; Broadbridge, 'Mamluk Legitimacy', 100; Heidemann, *Kalifat*, 179–80; Chapoutot-Remadi, 'Liens et relations', 38–9.
66. Shāfiʿ ibn ʿAlī, *Faḍl*, 37–51; Abū al-Fidāʾ, *Mukhtaṣar*, 4:19–20; al-Maqrīzī, *Sulūk*, 1:655; Clifford, *State Formation*, 114–25; Northrup, *From Slave to Sultan*, 86; Heidemann, *Kalifat*, 180; Chapoutot-Remadi, 'Liens et relations', 54.
67. Baybars al-Manṣūrī, *Zubdat al-fikra*, 162–4, 166–7, 169–74; Shāfiʿ ibn ʿAlī, *Faḍl*, 51–4; Abū al-Fidāʾ, *Mukhtaṣar*, 4:20; al-Birzālī, *Muqtafī*, 1:457–60; Ibn al-Dawādārī, *Kanz*, 8:229; al-Dhahabī, *Taʾrīkh*, 50:29–41; Ibn al-Wardī, *Taʾrīkh*, 2:324.
68. Northrup, *From Slave to Sultan*, 169–74.
69. Shāfiʿ ibn ʿAlī, *Faḍl*, 52; al-Dhahabī, *Taʾrīkh*, 51:56; al-Suyūṭī, *Taʾrīkh*, 385; Heidemann, *Kalifat*, 181.
70. Van Steenbergen, 'The Mamluk Sultanate', 198.
71. Shāfiʿ ibn ʿAlī, *Faḍl*, 62–3; Baybars al-Manṣūrī, *Zubdat al-fikra*, 178–9, 181–4; Abū al-Fidāʾ, *Mukhtaṣar*, 4:20–1; al-Nuwayrī, *Nihāya*, 31:14–17; al-Dhahabī, *Taʾrīkh*, 50:42–5; Heidemann, *Kalifat*, 181; Northrup, *From Slave to Sultan*, 90–7, 170, 174; Broadbridge, *Kingship and Ideology*, 42; Balog, 'A Dirhem of Al-Kāmil Shams Al-Dīn Sunqur', 296–9.
72. Baybars al-Manṣūrī, *Zubdat al-fikra*, 217–27; al-Nuwayrī, *Nihāya*, 31:90; Ibn al-Wardī, *Taʾrīkh*, 2:328; Jackson, *Mongols and the Islamic World*, 343, 366–7; Amitai, 'Conversion of Tegüder'; Holt, 'Chancery Clerk', 678; Holt, 'The Īlkhān Aḥmad's Embassies to Qalāwūn', 128–32; Allouche, 'Tegüder's Ultimatum'.
73. Shāfiʿ ibn ʿAlī, *Faḍl*, 102–3; Broadbridge, 'Mamluk Legitimacy', 115; Broadbridge, *Kingship and Ideology*, 42. See also Hassan, *Longing for the Lost Caliphate*, 117.
74. For a list of the sources which omit or include the reference to al-Ḥākim in the letter to Tegüdar Aḥmad, see Broadbridge, *Kingship and Ideology*, 42n.70. See

also Allouche, 'Tegüder's Ultimatum', 442; Northrup, *From Slave to Sultan*, 36.

75. Baybars al-Manṣūrī, *Zubdat al-fikra*, 108–9.
76. Hassan, *Longing for the Lost Caliphate*, 88–97; Heidemann, *Kalifat*, 182; Northrup, *From Slave to Sultan*, 174–6; Chapoutot-Remadi, 'Liens et relations', 49.
77. Ibn ʿAbd al-Ẓāhir, *Tashrīf*, 52–3; Baybars al-Manṣūrī, *Zubdat al-fikra*, 185, 263–4, 270–2; Abū al-Fidāʾ, *Mukhtaṣar*, 4:32–4; al-Nuwayrī, *Nihāya*, 31:68–9, 159–60, 177; al-Jazarī, *Ḥawādith*, 1:29; al-Dhahabī, *Taʾrīkh*, 50:51. See also Northrup, *From Slave to Sultan*, 243–9.
78. Heidemann, *Kalifat*, 187–8; Broadbridge, *Kingship and Ideology*, 45–8; Chapoutot-Remadi, 'Liens et relations', 49; Irwin, *Middle East*, 76–8; Haarmann, 'Khalīl'.
79. Abū al-Fidāʾ, *Mukhtaṣar*, 4:34; al-Nuwayrī, *Nihāya*, 31:177–8; Baktāsh al-Fākhirī, *Taʾrīkh*, 135; Ibn al-Wardī, *Taʾrīkh*, 2:336.
80. Ibn ʿAbd al-Ẓāhir, *Alṭāf*, 3, 6; al-Dhahabī, *Taʾrīkh*, 51:56; Ibn Ḥabīb, *Tadhkira*, 1:137–41; Ibn al-Furāt, *Taʾrīkh*, 8:128; al-Maqrīzī, *Sulūk*, 1:777; al-Maqrīzī, *Khiṭaṭ*, 3:784; al-ʿAynī, *ʿIqd*, 3:37. On the use of replicas of the sword in medieval Islamic ceremonial, see Alexander, 'Dhu'l-Faqār'.
81. Baybars al-Manṣūrī, *Zubdat al-fikra*, 238, 284–5; al-Birzālī, *Muqtafī*, 2:233–4. See also Broadbridge, *Kingship and Ideology*, 48–9; Boyle, 'Dynastic and Political History of the Il-Khāns', 372–3.
82. Ibn ʿAbd al-Ẓāhir, *Alṭāf*, 6–8, 11, 13, 17–19; al-Nuwayrī, *Nihāya*, 31:218–21; al-Jazarī, *Ḥawādith*, 1:56–7; al-Birzālī, *Muqtafī*, 2:257; al-Dhahabī, *Taʾrīkh*, 51:57, 52:10; Ibn al-Furāt, *Taʾrīkh*, 8:128–9; al-Qalqashandī, *Ṣubḥ*, 3:275; Broadbridge, *Kingship and Ideology*, 47.
83. Baybars al-Manṣūrī, *Zubdat al-fikra*, 288–9, 295–6; Abū al-Fidāʾ, *Mukhtaṣar*, 4:36–7, 40; al-Nuwayrī, *Nihāya*, 31:225–31, 259–62; al-Jazarī, *Ḥawādith*, 1:100–1, 190–3, 209–10; al-Birzālī, *Muqtafī*, 2:273, 346–7; al-Dhahabī, *Taʾrīkh*, 52:10, 13, 27; al-Dhahabī, *ʿIbar*, 5:377; Ibn al-Furāt, *Taʾrīkh*, 8:135; al-Maqrīzī, *Sulūk*, 1:777; Broadbridge, *Kingship and Ideology*, 48.
84. Heidemann, *Kalifat*, 188; Broadbridge, *Kingship and Ideology*, 45; Balog, *Coinage*, 120–4; *RCEA*, 13, No. 4959.
85. Hassan, *Longing for the Lost Caliphate*, 22, 37–8, 80, 101, 127.
86. Al-ʿAynī, *ʿIqd*, 3:87.
87. Heidemann, *Kalifat*, 187–9; Berkey, 'Mamluk Religious Policy', 9; Irwin, *Middle East*, 78.

88. Flinterman and Van Steenbergen, 'Al-Nasir Muhammad', 88.
89. Baybars al-Manṣūrī, *Zubdat al-fikra*, 298, 304–6; Abū al-Fidā', *Mukhtaṣar*, 4:41–2; al-Nuwayrī, *Nihāya*, 31:267, 282; al-Jazarī, *Ḥawādith*, 1:195–6, 248; al-Birzālī, *Muqtafī*, 2:347–8; al-Dhahabī, *Ta'rīkh*, 52:34, 44; al-Dhahabī, *Duwal*, 2:149 ; Chapoutot-Remadi, 'Liens et relations', 50.
90. Baybars al-Manṣūrī, *Zubdat al-fikra*, 310–14; Abū al-Fidā', *Mukhtaṣar*, 4:45–6; al-Nuwayrī, *Nihāya*, 31:313–14, 316, 319; al-Jazarī, *Ḥawādith*, 1:332–6; al-Birzālī, *Muqtafī*, 2:494–5; al-Dhahabī, *Ta'rīkh*, 52:49–52; Heidemann, *Kalifat*, 188–9. On the black caliphal robe as an emblem of specifically sultanic sovereignty, see Popper, *Systematic Notes*, 1:84.
91. Baybars al-Manṣūrī, *Zubdat al-fikra*, 315; Shāfi' ibn 'Alī, *Ḥusn*, 55; al-Nuwayrī, *Nihāya*, 23:331–2; Ibn Ḥabīb, *Tadhkira*, 1:195; Ibn al-Furāt, *Ta'rīkh*, 8:224, 230; al-Qalqashandī, *Ṣubḥ*, 3:261, 275; al-Maqrīzī, *Sulūk*, 1:828; al-Maqrīzī, *Khiṭaṭ*, 3:784; al-Maqrīzī, *Durar*, 2:209; al-Maqrīzī, *Muqaffā*, 1:472–3; al-'Aynī, *Iqd*, 3:359; al-Suyūṭī, *Ḥusn*, 2:62; Chapoutot-Remadi, 'Liens et relations', 37–8.
92. Van Steenbergen, *Caliphate and Kingship*, 301.
93. Ibid., 65, 96, 300–1; Heidemann, *Kalifat*, 190–1; Chapoutot-Remadi, 'Liens et relations', 61. According to al-'Aynī, the caliph went on pilgrimage in both 694/1295 and 697/1298, see *'Iqd*, 3:282, 413. See also Baybars al-Manṣūrī, *Zubdat al-fikra*, 315; al-Jazarī, *Ḥawādith*, 1:395; Ibn al-Dawādārī, *Kanz*, 8:371; al-Nuwayrī, *Nihāya*, 23:332.
94. Shāfi' ibn 'Alī, *Ḥusn*, 55.
95. Baybars al-Manṣūrī, *Zubdat al-fikra*, 323–6; Abū al-Fidā', *Mukhtaṣar*, 4:51–2; al-Jazarī, *Ḥawādith*, 1:428–34, 446; al-Nuwayrī, *Nihāya*, 31:357–63, 370–1; al-Dhahabī, *Ta'rīkh*, 52:63; al-Dhahabī, *Duwal*, 2:153; al-Dhahabī, *'Ibar*, 5:387; al-Kutubī, *'Uyūn*, 23:267–9; al-Qalqashandī, *Ṣubḥ*, 10:59–68; al-Maqrīzī, *Sulūk*, 1:872; Holt, 'Some Observations', 504.
96. Broadbridge, *Kingship and Ideology*, 42, 70, 84.
97. Baybars al-Manṣūrī, *Zubdat al-fikra*, 331–3; Abū al-Fidā', *Mukhtaṣar*, 4:55–8, 61; al-Jazarī, *Ḥawādith*, 1:461–3; al-Nuwayrī, *Nihāya*, 31:380, 384–5, 394–7; al-Dhahabī, *Ta'rīkh*, 52:69–81. Ibn Iyās reports that until his death, al-Ḥākim accompanied the sultan's forces in their attacks on the Mongols, see *Badā'i'*, 1:1:410. On Ghāzān's initial foray into Syrian territory, see Broadbridge, *Kingship and Ideology*, 73–80; Amitai, 'Whither the Ilkhanid Army'.
98. Jackson, *Mongols and the Islamic World*, 324, 342, 365; Amitai, *Holy War*, 72–3; Becker, 'Barthold's Studien', 369. See also Anne Broadbridge's review

of *al-Mughūl wa-al-mamālīk: al-siyāsa wa-al-sirāʿ* by ʿAbd al-Munʿim Ṣubḥī (*MSR* 11, No. 1 (2007): 221–2). Charles Melville points out that Ghāzān made use of black banners resembling those of the Abbasid Caliphate, see '*Pādishāh-i Islām*', 170–1.

99. Broadbridge, *Kingship and Ideology*, 67–70, 84, 94–6; Amitai-Preiss, 'Fall and Rise', 488.
100. Ibid.
101. Baybars al-Manṣūrī, *Zubdat al-fikra*, 362–3; al-Yūnīnī, *Dhayl Mirʾāt al-Zamān*, ed. and trans. Li Guo as *Early Mamluk Syrian Historiography*, 1:201–2 (English), 2:250–1 (Arabic) (cited hereafter as al-Yūnīnī/Guo, *Dhayl*); Abū al-Fidāʾ, *Mukhtaṣar*, 4:59; al-Nuwayrī, *Nihāya*, 23:332, 32:16; Ibn al-Dawādārī, *Kanz*, 9:78–9; al-Dhahabī, *Taʾrīkh*, 53:16; al-Dhahabī, *Duwal*, 2:157; Heidemann, *Kalifat*, 192–3; Tetsuya, 'Cairene Cemeteries', 101.
102. Van Steenbergen, Wing and D'hulster, 'Mamlukization Part II', 564.
103. Van Steenbergen, *Caliphate and Kingship*, 16; Hassan, *Longing for the Lost Caliphate*, 75–80.
104. Hassan, *Longing for the Lost Caliphate*, 88–97; Moin, *Millennial Sovereign*, 68.

2

The Qalawunids and the Caliphate, 701–63/1302–63

Introduction

The previous chapter engaged with the installation of a new Abbasid line in Cairo supported through the cooperation of the political and religious elite. By the end of his reign, Qalāwūn had helped to establish a social system in which his descendants generated a royal status due to the successful monopolisation of resources by members of his extended household that lasted for at least three generations. Flinterman and Van Steenbergen have argued that the social interactions of court elites from 689 to 709/1290 to 1309 were largely driven by an 'unsteady consensus over power and authority' which also involved a search for legitimacy in the face of rivals, the most powerful of which proved to be the representation of their master Qalāwūn's legacy through the enthronement of his sons. Although the hereditary legitimacy of the Qalawunid household remained supreme, some amirs in this period experimented with other forms of legitimacy including the Abbasid Caliphate.[1] This chapter focuses on the first Cairo-born Abbasid and his immediate successors as the caliphal office normalised and became an ongoing part of the socio-political vista of what can be understood as the Qalawunid period of the Cairo Sultanate.

Al-Nāṣir Muḥammad and the Caliphate of Sulaymān al-Mustakfī bi-llāh, 701–40/1302–40

Identified by fourteenth-century historians as the third Abbasid of Cairo and fortieth caliph of the dynasty overall, Abū Rabīʿa Sulaymān was born in early

684/1285 in the tower of the Citadel to a Turkish concubine. Sulaymān reached maturity during his father's isolation in the tower and later shared family accommodations at al-Kabsh. Reared in confinement, the Abbasid prince, described in early youth as brown-skinned with a wispy beard, befriended the young sultan al-Nāṣir Muḥammad, with whom he was close in age. The two princes bonded over polo matches, archery practice, hunting and promenading.[2]

During the seventeen years that followed the assassination of his brother al-Ashraf Khalīl (693–709/1293–1310), al-Nāṣir Muḥammad's reign was twice interrupted by usurpers. Although his father the caliph al-Ḥākim had been an active participant in the first ceremony, participating elites did not expect Sulaymān or the chief qadis to contribute much to the proceedings of the latter investiture, other than to attend as custom now required.[3] As with his first reign, al-Nāṣir Muḥammad resumed the part of figurehead sultan, diverting attention from the competition between rival amirs Salār and Baybars al-Jāshinkīr.

Sulaymān had not been his father's first choice for caliphal succession. Al-Ḥākim had originally planned to entrust an elder son, Muḥammad, with the family office, even concluding a covenant that named him al-Mustamsik bi-llāh. However, Muḥammad predeceased his father in late 695/October 1296. Al-Ḥākim next considered Ibrāhīm, a son of the late Muḥammad al-Mustamsik, but may have reconsidered after hearing rumours of his grandson's debauchery. Sulaymān, the next eldest surviving son thus emerged as a third candidate, though his father was reluctant due to his youthful inexperience. The young sultan al-Nāṣir Muḥammad was equally concerned about the adolescence of his friend and refused to pledge allegiance to Sulaymān as caliph until the chief Shāfiʿī qadi Taqī al-Dīn ibn Daqīq al-ʿĪd (d. 702/1302) attested to his suitability before a council of dignitaries.[4]

On his father's death, members of the political elite summoned Sulaymān, a young man largely uninstructed in formal Islamic training, to the Citadel to allow the amirs to testify that the new caliph had reaffirmed to al-Nāṣir Muḥammad all powers entrusted by his predecessor. Sulaymān confirmed the titles on the young sultan and draped him in black robes of honour. After the funerary prayers for al-Ḥākim, Sulaymān and his cousins who had led the funeral procession were sent back to the Kabsh palace under guard of five eunuchs who watched over them from the gate of the Abbasid residence. Some days later on 24 Jumādā I 701/25 January 1302, Sulaymān and the Abbasid delegation rejoined the amirs at the Citadel for a formal assumption of the caliphate. In the presence of important functionaries, al-Nāṣir Muḥammad officially granted Sulaymān the regnal title 'al-Mustakfī bi-llāh' along with the customary black robe and *ṭarḥa* headdress, while the caliph's cousins likewise received honour garments. The sultan and amirs completed a *bay'a* ceremony similar to that which had been performed with al-Ḥākim in years past. The sultan, followed by military and religious notables, swore allegiance to the new caliph before a grand feast and public reading of the investiture deed.[5] Shortly thereafter, al-Nāṣir Muḥammad set about making changes to the living conditions of the Abbasid family:

> The sultan then issued his orders to ask [the caliph] to stay in the Kabsh Palace and to give [the caliph and his brother] the stipend equal to their father's allowance during his last days in addition to some bonus (*ziyādāt*) by which he made them feel at ease and be optimistic. They stayed in the Kabsh Palace until Thursday, the beginning of Jumādā II (February 1, 1302), when the sultan sent a protocol officer (*mihmandār*) with a team of aides and a flock of camels to move the caliph, his brother, his nephews as well as their wives and all those under their shelter to the [Cairo] Jabal Citadel. They were given accommodations in two halls; one was called the Ṣāliḥīya Hall and the other the Ẓāhirīya Hall. They received their stipends as prescribed.[6]

The day after the *bay'a* ceremony, newly minted coinage bore the name of al-Mustakfī and Egyptian mosque orators named him in their *khuṭba*s. News of the accession arrived in Syria on 6 Jumādā II 701/6 February 1302 by postal courier and a copy of the investiture deed accompanied the announcement of the death and burial of al-Ḥākim which a Syrian qadi read before an assembled crowd. Three days later the congregation of the main mosque of Damascus heard the name of the new caliph and prayed for his late father.[7]

In 702/1302, the Ilkhanid ruler Ghāzān Khān renewed his efforts to intimidate Cairo by encroaching on land near Syria. In response, envoys of the sultan arrived at Hilla in Jumādā I 702/December 1302 to present Ghāzān with a letter restating Cairo's position that the sultan and his amirs were the true protectors of Islam against Ilkhan infidels. The letter demanded that in the interest of peace, Ghāzān must mint new coins: on one side, he could name himself alongside the caliph al-Mustakfī, while the lone name of al-Nāṣir Muḥammad should appear on the reverse.[8]

As al-Nāṣir Muḥammad departed Egypt with the battalions, word reached the Syrian amirs that the sultan would be arriving with the caliph, and reports of celebration and relief swept over the masses. In Ramaḍan 702/April 1303 Ghāzān ordered what was to be his final assault on Syria. The Mongols rode to Damascus and encountered Egyptian forces under Baybars al-Jāshinkīr, Salār and al-Nāṣir Muḥammad himself. The caliph journeyed with the sultan south of Damascus near Shaqḥab to serve as a living standard, safeguarding divine support and strengthening the resolve of the soldiers in battle. The caliph rode beside the sultan, mounted for all to see in a bulbous turban, black robe (*farjiyya*), and girded with an Arabian sword, while the amirs followed on foot. During the battle, al-Mustakfī recited from the Qurʾān and lectured portions of the army, reminding them that fighting for the sultan could not guarantee their place in heaven; instead, they must fight for their religion, their prophet and their families.[9] Although they absorbed heavy casualties, the sultan's forces successfully drove the Mongols from Syria, and as Donald Little suggests, 'won the battle, perhaps as a result, in part, of the caliph's inspiration'.[10] While the caliph's presence may not have played much of a practical role, it seems to have represented a larger attempt at morale-building. Al-Mustakfī was again at hand to lead al-Nāṣir Muḥammad's triumphal army into a jubilant Damascus.[11]

Although hostilities with the Ilkhanids ended after Ghāzān's death in 703/1304, a diplomatic row with Yemen in 706–7/1306–8 dragged the young caliph into foreign policy once again. Angered by the hubris of the Rasulid leader al-Malik al-Muʾayyad Ḥizabr al-Dīn Dāwūd (696–721/1296–1321), the Cairene ruling elite in 704/1304–5 had a letter drafted in the name of al-Mustakfī in the hope of reaffirming suzerainty over the Hijaz and Yemen. Annual Rasulid tribute for Cairo had diminished significantly by 705/1305–6 and the sultan's court expressed impatience to the Yemeni ruler who had ignored earlier reprimands. The outrage inspired an even more scathing letter from the Cairo chancery in 707/1307–8 issued in the name of al-Mustakfī. The message offered the possibility for a peaceful restoration of relations with

Yemen combined with the most likely hollow threat of invading armies and war-elephants.[12]

The second sultanate of al-Nāṣir Muḥammad came to an end in 708/1309 when the magnate amir Baybars al-Jāshinkīr, forced to the top by his Circassian following, came to prominence over the amir Salār. Lacking support to assert his claim, al-Nāṣir Muḥammad feigned a pilgrimage journey, abdicated and then fled to al-Karak, which became the base from which he secretly raised forces and invited sympathetic Syrian amirs to support his return to power.[13] Eventually, these counter-currents of intrigue would forever dissolve the old friendship between al-Nāṣir Muḥammad and his Abbasid caliph.

Alone in Cairo on 23 Shawwāl 708/5 April 1309, little recourse remained to al-Mustakfī who ultimately confirmed the sultanate of Baybars al-Jāshinkīr as al-Malik al-Muẓaffar, and dressed him in black Abbasid garb. Accompanied by great celebration in Cairo, the *ʿahd* document, encased in a black satin bag, was paraded over the head of Baybars al-Jāshinkīr in a great spectacle of caliphal favour.[14] Popular support for Baybars al-Jāshinkīr dwindled in subsequent months as plague and bad harvests undermined his reign. The position of the new sultan worsened when many troops defected in favour of al-Nāṣir Muḥammad. As news spread of the latter's impending return, Baybars summoned the caliph for a renewal of investiture. The resulting document refuted al-Nāṣir Muḥammad's kinship-based pretensions to the sultanate.[15] Notably, it took the position that 'kingship is childless' (*al-mulk ʿaqīm*).[16] It meant, in other words, that Baybars al-Jāshinkīr was no usurper against the House of Qalāwūn and, indeed, disobedience to a sultan sanctioned by the caliph was tantamount to disobeying the Prophet himself. Followed through to the end, the premise denies any right for the sultan to appoint his successors and leaves such power only to the caliph.

When mosque personnel read copies of the second investiture document of Baybars al-Jāshinkīr from the pulpits, many worshippers, after hearing mention of al-Nāṣir Muḥammad, proclaimed 'God grant him victory!' But after hearing Baybars al-Jāshinkīr named in the document, loudly voiced their rejection. In other mosques many common attendees (*ʿāmma*) dismissed the caliph's document and said 'We have no sultan except al-Malik

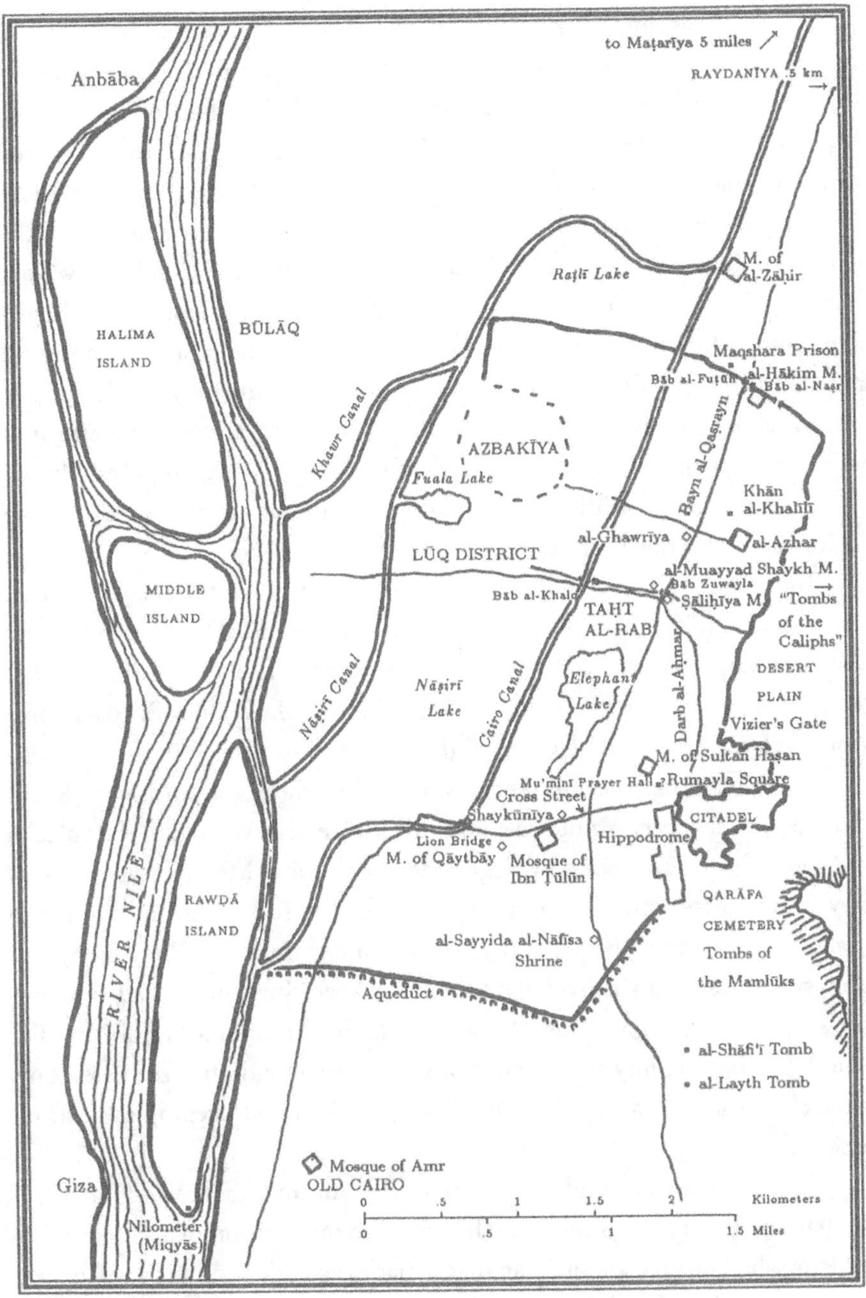

Map 2.1 City of Cairo. Image courtesy Carl Petry, *Twilight of Majesty: The Reigns of the Mamluk Sultans al-Ashraf Qāytbāy and Qānṣūh al-Ghawrī in Egypt*. London and Seattle: University of Washington Press, 1993.

al-Nāṣir'![17] Grasping at straws, Baybars al-Jāshinkīr sent a copy of the caliph's document to his own son-in-law, the amir Sayf al-Dīn Burulghay (or Burulghī) al-Ashrafī, whose troops had started to declare in favour of al-Nāṣir Muḥammad. Burulghay opened the document, noted the opening, 'Verily [this document is issued] from Sulaymān', then quoted the Qur'ān (34:12), ironically observing that '[To the prophet] Sulaymān [God has subjected] the wind!' To the messenger he said, 'Tell that fool [Baybars al-Jāshinkīr], by God, not a single person remains turned toward the caliph!'[18] Just like Kitbughā and Lājīn before him, Baybars failed to consolidate his position among his peers and thus the Qalawunid household remained 'the only viable alternative for elite consensus'.[19] Baybars fled Cairo mere days before the return of al-Nāṣir Muḥammad. Abandoned and vulnerable, al-Mustakfī found himself in the unattractive position of having ostentatiously denounced the ruling legitimacy of his boyhood friend.

The third and final enthronement of al-Nāṣir Muḥammad occurred on 2 Shawwāl 709/5 March 1310. Al-Mustakfī attended the ceremony and awkwardly approached to congratulate the sultan who spoke plainly to him; 'Are you here to greet a rebel (*khārijī*)? Was I a rebel? Does Baybars come from Abbasid stock (*sulālat Banī ʿAbbās*)?' Fearful, or wishing to keep his dignity, the crestfallen caliph kept silent.[20] Nevertheless, according to Shāfiʿ ibn ʿAlī, the chancery produced a new investiture deed written in the voice of al-Mustakfī, now *affirming* the legitimacy of al-Nāṣir Muḥammad's hereditary claim to the sultanate and emphasising that the caliph during a 'bad year' had recognised Baybars al-Jāshinkīr under duress.[21] The caliph, and even sworn testimony provided by the Shāfiʿī qadi Ibn Jamāʿa, failed to ease the sultan's misgivings. Thus, al-Nāṣir Muḥammad came to see al-Mustakfī as a dangerous liability for much of his third reign and after the ceremony, satisfied himself for a time by secluding the caliph and keeping tabs on his actions.[22]

Van Steenbergen underscores that the ultimate success of al-Nāṣir Muḥammad's long third reign can be linked to the creation of a varied political elite which he had subordinated and made dependent on his royal person by the end of his life. He managed his followers through purges and through a created 'language of power' as well as forms of elite identity[23] that developed independent of the Abbasid Caliphate.

Few details of al-Mustakfī's activities during al-Nāṣir Muḥammad's third reign have survived in fourteenth-century Arabic sources. While he was confined to the Citadel and brought out only to participate in official ceremonial, the caliph fathered several children. He prematurely selected his son Khiḍr as heir to the caliphal covenant (*walī al-ʿahd*), but the boy predeceased him in 710/1310 and was interred at the Abbasid mausoleum dedicated by Baybars. Another son, Baraka (d. 714/1315), also named presumptive heir as al-Mustawathiq (or possibly al-Muhtadī bi-llāh), failed to outlive his father.[24] Access to the caliph by the *ʿulamāʾ* remained unimpeded, and historians among them recorded details of his life in captivity. In their efforts to enshrine the caliph as a pious and versatile man wronged by the sultan, Syrian sources claim the caliph was a great aesthete with a keen interest in music and singing, and that he had nurtured a love for archery and polo throughout his life.[25] Although one source describes the caliph as indecisive in his personal affairs, he cultivated a rich social life and spoiled his intimates. When able, al-Mustakfī entertained prominent litterateurs such as Khalīl al-Ṣafadī (d. 763/1363), who visited the caliph numerous times and described him both as kingly and suited to the regency of his office. According to al-Dhahabī, the caliph, in true princely fashion, was particularly fond of treating select members of his entourage to private audiences with his singing slave girls.[26]

Despite his mistrust of the caliph, several instances indicate that al-Nāṣir Muḥammad continued to invoke the religious authority embodied by al-Mustakfī when need arose. In 713/1313, as a token of goodwill towards Toqtogha (or Toqta), the khān of the Golden Horde, al-Nāṣir Muḥammad sent several chests of fine fabric and a message stating that the two rulers would walk side-by-side to defeat their common enemies and after retaking Baghdad, 'return the caliph to the throne (*kursī*) of his caliphate'.[27]

The next year, to mark the completion of a new mosque adjoining the shrine of Sayyida Nafīsa, an important descendant of the Prophet buried in Cairo, al-Nāṣir Muḥammad invited al-Mustakfī in early 714/1314 to attend the first *khuṭba* delivered at the structure.[28] In 719/1320 the sultan, whose grip on power had grown secure enough that he could leave Cairo for pilgrimage on several occasions, brought the caliph and thirty amirs on *ḥajj* to the holy cities of the Hijaz.[29] Many years later, in 732/1331, the sultan ordered al-Mustakfī to provide formal recognition of his son Ānūk as heir before the qadis, but, fearing the probability that his offspring would develop into a rival during his lifetime, al-Nāṣir Muḥammad changed his mind.[30]

Yet the old rancour between caliph and sultan was never fully extinguished: events in 736/1335 culminated in the first banishment of an Abbasid from Cairo. While medieval Egyptian sources entertain colourful hearsay, the precise cause of the dispute is difficult to pinpoint, although it occurred against the backdrop of the notorious purges and paranoia associated with the otherwise highly successful third reign of al-Nāṣir Muḥammad. Some sources hint that security around the caliph was not as tight as the sultan wished. Al-Nāṣir Muḥammad was vexed by rumours that al-Mustakfī had created a network of amirs and scholars. Indeed, the caliph had several regular visitors, notably a *jandār* guardsman named Abū Shāma (d. 758/1357), a jurist associate and one of the sultan's *mamlūk*s. Together the trio called on the caliph at his family home in al-Kabsh.[31] The fisc supervisor of the sultan's private holdings (*nāẓir al-khāṣṣ*) Sharaf al-Dīn ʿAbd al-Wahhāb al-Nashw (d. 740/1339) also paid regular visits to the caliph's residence.[32] The sultan may have feared that al-Mustakfī was building a band of traitorous amirs and administrators to undermine his authority. When word reached the sultan that Abū Shāma was practically a fixture in the caliph's home, the *jandār* was accused of dereliction of duty, ordered a thrashing, and banished to Ṣafad in Syria for several months.[33]

Alternative evidence suggests that al-Mustakfī was seduced by the opportunity to increase his religious authority. A formal redress, evidently in the caliph's renowned handwriting, complained about the sultan's absence from sessions of holy law (*majlis al-sharīʿ al-sharīf*) and accused al-Nāṣir Muḥammad of negligence in religious matters, much to the sultan's irritation.[34]

Intrigue within the Abbasid house itself may have been the tipping point. Syrian chroniclers laid blame at the door of another ambitious son of al-Mustakfī, 'al-Qāʾim bi-Amr Allāh' Abū al-Faḍl Muḥammad (d. 738/1338).[35] According to al-Dhahabī, it was this Muḥammad (rather than al-Mustakfī himself) who had been a companion of Abū Shāma. Muḥammad also had two contacts amongst a nest of Ismāʿīlī assassins (*fidāʾīs* or *fidāwīs*) active in Cairo. The caliph wrote to his son warning him to curtail his clandestine activities, though the sultan's authorities ultimately caught up with the *fidāʾīs*, bisecting one and burning the other alive.[36]

Another son of the caliph, Ṣadaqa, brought disgrace on the Abbasid house both on account of his passion for a certain *mamlūk* and for coveting the lavish enjoyments at one of the family's Nile residences near Elephant Island (*Jazīrat al-Fīl*), which may have rekindled the sultan's resentment towards the caliph. Likewise, al-Mustakfī's nephew Ibrāhīm (later the caliph al-Wāthiq bi-llāh) allegedly went to the sultan to slander al-Mustakfī in the hope of obtaining the family office.[37]

In late 736/June 1336, the authorities again placed the caliph and his immediate family under close surveillance at their old Citadel quarters in the now colloquially-styled 'tower of the caliph', with a new *jandār* stationed at the door. The caliph's nephew Ibrāhīm was lodged in a nearby tower with his family and a sentry of their own. Both men were barred from leaving or accepting unauthorised visitors. The detention of al-Mustakfī lasted just over five months until 21 Rabīʿ I 737/28 October 1336, thanks in part to the intervention of the amir Qawṣūn (d. 742/1341) an influential intimate of al-Nāṣir Muḥammad who pleaded with the sultan to restore the caliph to his residence in al-Kabsh. Fourteenth- and fifteenth-century Arabic sources decried the decision to sequester the caliph as an unpopular move, which, according to al-Ṣafadī, 'most reasonable people found perplexing'.[38]

However, not all of the sultan's counsel concerning the caliph was favourable. At a private meeting with his advisers, the qadi Jalāl al-Dīn Muḥammad al-Qazwīnī urged al-Nāṣir Muḥammad to take drastic action lest the caliph take a public stand against him capable of producing dire political consequences.[39] Incensed, the sultan exiled al-Mustakfī and the roughly 100 members of the Abbasid household to the Upper Egyptian settlement of Qūṣ on 19 Dhū al-Ḥijja 737/19 July 1337. The new abode of the Abbasid family was a military outpost that served to maintain order among local tribes while also functioning as a containment area for 'potential troublemakers' from Cairo's perspective. Al-Nāṣir Muḥammad instructed the governor of Qūṣ to personally oversee the caliph and his family. The Abbasids remained in Qūṣ for several years, establishing local connections and attempting to draw attention to the disrespectful treatment suffered by the caliph and his kin. During these years, the caliph's yearly stipend gradually decreased from 5,000 dirhams to 1,000, forcing many women of the family to sell their clothes at nearby markets to produce income for the household.[40]

Nevertheless, the name of al-Mustakfī remained in the weekly *khuṭba*s of the Cairo Sultanate throughout Egypt and Syria. Contemporary observers suggest that the caliph's deportation unsettled the population, and inspired mass grief. Public opinion favoured the caliph, and dismay regarding the sultan's policy may have fomented an unspecified degree of civil unrest.[41]

Resigned to his fate, al-Mustakfī remained at Qūṣ for another four years. Several months before the caliph's death, Ṣadaqa, his latest presumptive heir passed away, hurling the caliph, we are told, into a deep depression until his own demise in Shaʿbān 740/February 1340, aged around fifty-six. Before his death, al-Mustakfī assembled forty witnesses and the governor (*ḥākim*) of Qūṣ and drew up a written statement (*mashrūḥ*) naming another son, Aḥmad, as heir to the caliphate. The governor of Qūṣ informed al-Nāṣir Muḥammad of the caliph's death and without the sultan's approval, the caliphate of Aḥmad al-Ḥākim was ratified in late Shawwāl 740/April 1340 and his name briefly mentioned from the *minbar*s of some mosques. The succession to al-Mustakfī proved to be anything but smooth, however, as al-Nāṣir Muḥammad, evidently seeking to thwart the caliph he despised even in death, scorned the testament and quickly suppressed al-Ḥākim II in favour of a rival Abbasid candidate of his own choosing.[42]

Memories of the caliph's tenure in Qūṣ survived into the seventeenth century. The Ottoman traveller Evliyā Çelebi (d. after 1096/1685) visited several sites in Qūṣ over the course of his travels in Egypt in the 1670s, including a large mosque built by the exiled Abbasid caliph near the main market.[43] Evliyā also described the *qubba* under which the caliph was likely buried. Nevertheless, Evliyā did not mention a reason for the caliph's exile and in claiming he had come from Baghdad and been invested by Baybars, apparently confused al-Mustakfī with al-Mustanṣir bi-llāh.[44]

Banished to Qūṣ for his intrusion into politics, the participation and authority of the caliph al-Mustakfī nevertheless proved to be crucial to sultans and amirs during moments of vulnerability. Moreover, the caliph enjoyed approval by the public at large, though we still know little about the nature of the support.[45] In the end, as Ḥayāt Nāṣir al-Ḥajjī points out, considering that al-Mustakfī had no military force of his own, it seems peculiar that al-Nāṣir Muḥammad could not content himself with simply isolating the caliph in the Citadel as his predecessors had done. The sultan's choice of exile to Qūṣ may have reflected a (perhaps reasonable) fear that the caliph could and would be used to support a new usurper of the sultanate or otherwise disrupt the sultan's own plans for succession. Exile to a remote outpost – though unpopular – was therefore more acceptable than a death sentence or even a beating. By allowing the caliph's name to remain in the *khuṭba*, al-Nāṣir Muḥammad also reminded subjects that the caliph was an ongoing part of the sultanate and had not been put to death.[46] Al-Mustakfī, despite banishment to a distant city, was still formally caliph until death. This allowed the sultan of Cairo to contain and ignore the Abbasid Caliphate, while keeping the caliph and his family beyond the reach of potential rivals.

The Brief Infamy of al-Wāthiq bi-llāh, 740–1/1340–1

Determined to settle the caliphate question himself, al-Nāṣir Muḥammad sent a postal courier (*barīdī*) carrying orders for the surviving Abbasids in Qūṣ to return to Cairo. Family representatives informed the sultan of the *ʿahd* document that named Aḥmad al-Ḥākim II to the caliphate in his father's name. Nevertheless, the sultan's estrangement from al-Mustakfī provoked his prompt dismissal of Aḥmad despite the powerful legal authority backing his designation in Upper Egypt. Amid confusion, Syro-Egyptian mosque orators went at least four months without naming a caliph on Fridays. Instead, the sultan ordered that the sermon be given in the name of Aḥmad's cousin Ibrāhīm, who had been canvassing for the office, even flaunting an *ʿahd* testament allegedly written by his grandfather al-Ḥākim I which named him successor. During a private meeting on 15 Shaʿbān 740/15 February 1340 al-Nāṣir Muḥammad concluded a secret *bayʿa* with Ibrāhīm, naming him al-Wāthiq bi-llāh before sending him home with a praetorian guard.[47]

Early the next month, al-Nāṣir Muḥammad summoned the political community (*ahl al-ḥall wa-l-ʿaqd*) to the Palace of Justice (*Dār al-ʿAdl*) for their monthly meeting and boldly commanded the participants to pledge allegiance to Ibrāhīm as caliph. No doubt bristling at the sultan's presumption, the qadis retorted that not only was the impious Ibrāhīm morally unfit for office, they had also accepted the legality of al-Mustakfī's designation of al-Ḥākim II which had been witnessed and ratified by religious authorities in Qūṣ. They emphasised to the sultan that 'none but [the late caliph al-Mustakfī] had the right to establish [a new caliph] and he had appointed his son Aḥmad'. After lukewarm assurances that Ibrāhīm would now 'walk a path of righteousness', the sultan informed the qadis that regardless of their consent or lack thereof, Ibrāhīm should henceforth be honoured as the caliph al-Wāthiq bi-llāh, a development reflected in Friday sermons beginning in Dhū al-Qaʿda 740/May 1340.[48]

The image of al-Wāthiq in some contemporary sources is far from positive. In an excerpt from the *Masālik al-absār* quoted by al-Suyūṭī, the Syrian official Ibn Faḍlallāh al-ʿUmarī paints a vivid picture of the antagonisms brought on by the caliphate of al-Wāthiq. For al-ʿUmarī, the caliph became an insufferable presence for both the *ʿulamāʾ* and other notables at court. Al-Nāṣir Muḥammad allegedly received numerous complaints about the caliph but entertained none of them. Al-ʿUmarī condemned the caliph as one who had been 'reared in dishonour and neglected piety', and at once described the caliph as pleasure-loving, extravagant and surrounded by base companionship.[49] The most objectionable points about the caliph were reports of his pigeon fancying, gambling on unlawful ram and cock fighting, and living beyond his means. According to al-ʿUmarī, al-Wāthiq constantly required funds to cover mounting debts which drew him into the seamy side of Cairene life through a vicious cycle of borrowing and extortion that scandalised religious and political elites alike. Common Cairenes were said to have mocked him, even before his investiture, as 'the beggar' (*al-Mustaʿṭī bi-llāh* – a taunt towards the sombre Abbasid regnal titles). The case of al-Wāthiq suggests that court expectations for the caliphate dictated what kind of man must occupy the office and surely not one whose follies 'inspired great pity in the hearts of the people'. More importantly, the sultan was accountable to ensure that the best candidate held the position. That the qadis and other courtiers felt they had the collective power to resist the sultan on this issue manifested itself as a hiatus on caliphal mention in the Friday sermons for a third of the year.[50]

Those offended by al-Wāthiq's notoriety found a champion in the grand qadi ʿIzz al-Dīn ibn Jamāʿa (d. 767/1366), who frequently pleaded with the sultan to remove the name of the unworthy caliph from the Friday sermon. Before al-Wāthiq's accession, Ibn Jamāʿa had gone to great lengths to expose his immorality, but al-Nāṣir Muḥammad stubbornly dismissed such concerns, arguing that 'he who has repented his sin is like one who has committed none. It was I who gave him the office, so observe the mandate.'[51]

Favoured by the religious community as the indisputable heir of al-Mustakfī, the counterclaim of al-Ḥākim II enjoyed support among those anxious to eject al-Wāthiq from office. Perhaps deliberately oblivious to the controversy, al-Nāṣir Muḥammad maintained al-Wāthiq's monthly stipend of 3,560 dirhams, nineteen units (*irdabb*, a weight measurement) of wheat, and ten *irdabb* of barley for his household and animals, which the caliph's enemies at court could not prevent.[52]

Later fourteenth-century Arabic sources, hardly uniform in emphasising the good character or deeds of al-Nāṣir Muḥammad, present an array of the sultan's alleged deathbed attitudes towards the caliphate. Some chroniclers, interested in placing the sultan on the right side of history and thereby preserving his legacy from the alleged infamy of al-Wāthiq, claim the sultan, having regretted his decision, acquiesced and heeded the complaints of Ibn Jamāʿa. Al-Wāthiq was removed and the sultan sanctioned the return to office of al-Ḥākim II on 1 Muḥarram 742/17 June 1341. Later Qalawunid-era chroniclers, including ʿUmar ibn al-Wardī (d. 749/1349) and Shams al-Dīn ibn al-Shujāʿī (d. after 756/1355), however, state that al-Nāṣir Muḥammad was content to leave al-Wāthiq in the caliphate until his death, while al-ʿUmarī claimed that personal piety finally forced the sultan to rescue the Muslims from an abhorrent and unscrupulous caliph.[53]

Little about the life of al-Wāthiq was recorded for subsequent years as most chroniclers of the era seemed happy to forget him. Nevertheless, he thrived in confinement until suffering partial paralysis and a likely plague-related death in Shaʿbān 748/November 1347.[54] Several children of al-Wāthiq were buried with their father in the Abbasid mausoleum along with his own father al-Mustamsik and several siblings. Al-Wāthiq, despite his brief tenure and allegations of depravity, appears to be one of only two Abbasid caliphs interred within the Abbasid mausoleum structure near the shrine of Sayyida Nafīsa in Cairo.[55]

Influenced by the scandalous reports of al-ʿUmarī and Ibn Jamāʿa, al-Suyūṭī later considered the line taken by al-Mustakfī as the only legitimate option and, according to Garcin, consistently denounced attempts by later sultans to impose caliphs from the 'rogue' line of al-Wāthiq, however briefly, as moves of an anti-caliphate. As the family continued to grow over the next century, the descendants of al-Wāthiq were often pitted as rivals against the descendants of al-Mustakfī.[56]

The Abbasid Caliphate and the Later Qalawunids: Al-Ḥākim bi-Amr Allāh II, 741–53/1341–52, and al-Muʿtaḍid bi-llāh, 753–63/1352–62

Modern historians have noted the complex politics of the amiral households that complicated the forty years of rule by the sons and grandsons of al-Nāṣir Muḥammad and the political elites who emerged from the ranks of his Qalawunid household.[57] Many amirs tended to lack widespread support and were instead compelled to rule (sometimes jointly) as regent *atābak*s of the reigning Qalawunid sultan, often a minor, though one capable of attracting support from the political elite and engaging in matters of rule.[58] By the mid-fourteenth century, the leading amirs were compelled to support those Qalawunid candidates who could best represent continuity as well as their interests. All the while, the sultan and his entourage continued to derive partial legitimacy from the Abbasid caliphs of the time.[59]

Nevertheless, perhaps to mask the ongoing rivalries among the amirs, settling the caliphate question became increasingly important in the wake of al-Nāṣir Muḥammad's death. The sultan had left behind a 'fully monopolised' political scene stocked by hand-picked amirs who had enjoyed close ties to him. Proof of this was the arrangement (and successful execution) of al-Nāṣir Muḥammad's chosen successor, his son Abū Bakr, to take the sultanate.[60] However, court protocol dictated that the next sultan should still have a caliph acceptable to the *ʿulamāʾ* and capable of underwriting the Islamic legitimacy of the political order. Members of the religious elite had expressed opposition to al-Wāthiq because his receipt of the office had been without true right. Nevertheless, formal recognition of Aḥmad as al-Ḥākim II was unlikely to have occurred before late 741/June 1341, when al-Manṣūr Abū Bakr came to the sultanate.

In the wake of al-Nāṣir Muḥammad's passing, the amir Qawṣūn (d. 742/1342) emerged as commander-in-chief of the armies (*atābak al-ʿasākir*) and began reorganising power structures in Cairo. Representatives of the elite called upon the rival Abbasid cousins to plead their respective cases before the court of the new sultan. Playing his part, Abū Bakr asked which cousin held legal right to the caliphate. Ibn Jamāʿa, again acting as interlocutor for the *ʿulamāʾ*, came forward to declare the legality of al-Ḥākim's designation, the confirmation of which had formally been received from the qadi of Qūṣ. He turned to al-Wāthiq, and informed him that the caliphate had been a temporary gift bestowed by al-Nāṣir Muḥammad, and that the late sultan's son al-Manṣūr Abū Bakr now requested its return. Indignant, al-Wāthiq claimed seniority and demanded to know why the new sultan wished to grant the caliphate to his younger cousin. Representatives of the religious establishment took the opportunity to set the record straight:

> It is our opinion that your caliphate has been disorderly. You have no possessions so we have stripped you of [office]. The caliphate (rightfully) belonged to Sulaymān [al-Mustakfī] and he delegated it to his son Aḥmad [al-Ḥākim II]. You may only seek mercy from the sultan that he continues to provide you with your salary (*maʿlūm*)![61]

Satisfied by the weightier claim of al-Ḥākim II which enjoyed the support of the Cairene *ʿulamāʾ*, sultan Abū Bakr and the amirs followed by the qadis and other grandees formally deposed al-Wāthiq and pledged allegiance to al-Mustakfī's 'true heir'. In contrast to some later Qalawunids, the sultanic investiture ceremony of Abū Bakr was a grand event covered in substantial detail.[62]

On 2 Muḥarram 742/18 June 1341, al-Ḥākim II attended the monthly session at the Palace of Justice (*Dār al-ʿAdl*) in the Citadel. Dressed in a green robe and a black turban with a gold-embroidered train, the caliph sat on the third step in front of the sultan's throne and stood up with other notables when the sultan entered. To display his own deference and respect for the Abbasid caliph, al-Manṣūr Abū Bakr symbolically sat one step below the Commander of the Faithful. Al-Ḥākim recited verses from the Qurʾān that referenced oath-taking (16:92 and 48:10) and delivered a sermon enjoining the young sultan to be kind to his subjects, to rule justly and to uphold Islam in his realm. The caliph then turned to Abū Bakr and announced: 'I have delegated to you jurisdiction over all the Muslims, and invested you with that which I have been invested in matters of the faith'.[63]

The caliph draped the sultan in a black robe and decorated him with an Arabian sword. Al-ʿUmarī, thrilled at last by al-Wāthiq's ouster, composed the text of the new caliphal diploma and read it aloud before presenting it to al-Ḥākim II, who signed it as 'Aḥmad the son of the Prophet's uncle'. It was notarised by the qadis who then offered their *bayʿa* to the caliph and sultan before all adjourned to attend a sumptuous banquet.[64] Indeed, such colourful descriptions of lavish ceremonial moments in our sources allow us to recover, as Hugh Kennedy points out, 'something of the delight and *joie de vivre* which attended the performance of the caliphate'.[65]

While al-Manṣūr Abū Bakr proved to be little more than a figurehead sultan, al-Suyūṭī later considered him 'a restorer of order' to the Abbasid family after the shame and scandal of al-Nāṣir Muḥammad's reign. The caliph's family returned to its respected position in Cairo, sequestered in a stately dwelling, while the name of the caliph, although without actual power, was briefly restored to the Friday sermons.[66]

The rivalry among al-Nāṣir Muḥammad's former amirs ensured Abū Bakr a brief time in power. Three weeks into his reign, the amir Qawṣūn overpowered his chief competitor Bashtāk and instead installed another son of al-Nāṣir Muḥammad, the child Kujuk, leaving Qawṣūn sultan in all but name. An older brother of Kujuk, Aḥmad, had grown to young adulthood in al-Karak thereby escaping the clutches of Qawṣūn and his entourage. Ultimately overthrown by factional strife in Cairo, Qawṣūn and Kujuk were swept away, and the remaining amirs, once in power, invited Aḥmad to the sultanate.[67]

On 10 Shawwāl 742/19 March 1342, the important amirs ascended the Citadel and prepared to install Aḥmad as sultan. Attendant officials dressed Aḥmad in the traditional black honorary robe of the caliph along with other finery. On horseback, amirs escorted the young sultan to the Columned Hall, in which he ascended his throne and awaited the caliph. Prominent Egyptian and Syrian qadis likewise showed their respect to Aḥmad before al-Ḥākim II entered, 'dressed in a black caliphal robe of honour and a black head shawl (*ṭarḥa*) as was the custom of the caliph. He climbed up and sat near the sultan on his throne. [After the entrance of the four chief qadis and several high-ranking amirs . . .] the caliph gave the sultan sovereignty (*al-mulk*) . . . and testified [to having completed the act]. Then the caliph and qadis descended.'[68]

Holt highlighted this episode as a noteworthy moment in Cairene Abbasid ritual, in that most chroniclers mention only that the caliph pledged *bayʿa* to the sultan without receiving *bayʿa* himself, which perhaps signifies an important break with tradition since the time of Baybars.[69] The amirs, through the accession of al-Nāṣir Aḥmad in 742/1342, had reconfigured caliphal ceremonial, turning the tables so that the Abbasid caliph, mirroring the *tafwīḍ* or delegation clause of many fourteenth- and fifteenth-century investiture deeds (as will be discussed further in Chapters 8 and 9), pledged his allegiance and authority to the sultan of Cairo.

After investing the new sultan, al-Ḥākim II briefly became entangled in political drama. Aḥmad failed to be the malleable candidate the amirs had expected; rather, he proved to be authoritative and curt, favouring the entourage he had brought from al-Karak at the expense of the amirs who had invited him. When tensions reached tipping point, Aḥmad fled Cairo, taking the Abbasid caliph and key members of the bureaucratic administration with him to re-establish his base in al-Karak. Egypt remained in the care of a deputy as Aḥmad prepared his comeback hoping to be free of interference from his father's amirs. To protect his fledgling political order, Aḥmad forwarded much of the treasury to al-Karak with a huge retinue. He likewise sent al-Ḥākim II to Palestine in Dhū al-Ḥijja 742/May 1342, presumably to station him at one of two holy cities, Jerusalem or Hebron, to better keep the caliph from the hands of his rivals. The amirs of Cairo retaliated by replacing him with his brother Ismāʿīl as al-Ṣāliḥ (without the presence of the caliph) followed by expeditions sent against al-Karak until Aḥmad was defeated. Early the next year in Ṣafar 743/July 1342, the caliph returned to Cairo, escorted through Gaza by several amirs.[70] Al-Ḥākim II later joined the four qadis to participate in the public deposition of Aḥmad in absentia.

Al-Ḥākim II enjoyed influence enough to develop and establish his own network of family members at court.[71] Advancing the interests and careers of his brothers and half-brothers in the government allowed the caliph to enhance Abbasid prestige and arrange possibilities for social reproduction that would enable future generations of the family to serve as courtiers or administrators. By virtue of their recognised lineage, the Abbasids already had social capital and may not have been in need of typical patronage practices as much as others. Nevertheless, salaried service at court was always an asset.[72]

Overall, political conditions inclined towards the betterment of the Abbasid family at large. In the atmosphere of uncertainty, the ruling amirs may well have considered it politic to shore up the interests of the Abbasid household, whose financial well-being had remained a concern. In Cairo the Abbasids had been permitted to collect income from a non-specific levy placed on goldsmiths, although the amount was precarious and often scarcely sufficient to feed the now sizeable household. In Qūṣ, the family's resources had been strained after increasingly severe cuts to the caliphal pension, though upon their return to Cairo, al-Nāṣir Muḥammad restored monthly payments for al-Wāthiq, which the former caliph had retained even after deposition. The administration of al-Manṣūr Abū Bakr likewise allotted amounts of cash and kind for the household of al-Ḥākim II.[73]

Important financial relief for the Abbasid family may have come as early as Shawwāl 742/April 1342 following the caliph's investiture of al-Nāṣir Aḥmad.[74] After several years of supervision by various notables, political authorities placed directorship (*naẓar*) of the shrine of Sayyida Nafīsa in the hands of al-Ḥākim II, a deed some sources attributed to the piety of sultan Aḥmad. For some decades the family had already exerted its influence in the area, as it was also the location of many Abbasid burials inside and outside the adjacent mausoleum set aside for their use. Pilgrims' donations, votive offerings (*nudhūr*) to the Nafīsī shrine, and revenue from the Abbasid family monopoly on the sale of donated candles and oil brought a significant source of income unencumbered by the sultans of Cairo. Each month the caliph or his delegate emptied donations from a large trunk at the head of the tomb. While there was no formal or regular contact between the caliphs and the masses, sporadic interaction took place at the shrine. Thus, through direct association with a well-attended religious landmark, the public profile of the Abbasid caliph enjoyed increased prominence, making the caliphs slightly more accessible to the masses after the earlier sultans had sought to isolate them. While sanctifying the place of pilgrimage with his own holy presence, we may speculate that the caliph also simultaneously tapped into the world of folk religion, popular culture and pietism in medieval Cairo that must have further endeared him to the *ʿāmma* and provided him entry into their social world. The Abbasids also received a residence near the Nafīsī shrine, an area thus deemed holy and suitable for caliphs.[75]

As had been the case with his recent ancestors, the caliph's scholarly credentials remained a concern among the political elite. Members of the

ʿulamāʾ and well-wishers visited al-Ḥākim II at his abode and received generous gifts from their host. The ability to reward his support-base and behave as a patron may be indicative of the caliph's increased access to property and financial resources.[76]

During the ten-year reign of al-Ḥākim II, the caliph invested no fewer than seven of al-Nāṣir Muḥammad's sons with the sultanate. Fourteenth-century sources regularly mention the caliph's involvement in sultanic investiture ceremonies for each new Qalawunid sultan.[77] The true holders of power – whether king-making amirs or indeed the sultans themselves – requested the caliph's presence for many investiture ceremonies and his official obligations included little else. The caliph witnessed many of their coronations: al-Manṣūr Abu Bakr (741–2/1341), al-Ashraf Kujuk (742/1341), al-Nāṣir Aḥmad (742/1342), al-Ṣāliḥ Ismāʿīl (743–6/1342–5), al-Kāmil Shaʿbān (746–7/1346–7), al-Muẓaffar Ḥājjī (747–8/1346–7), al-Nāṣir Ḥasan (748–52/1347–51) and al-Ṣāliḥ Ṣāliḥ (752–5/1351–4).[78]

Beyond participation in official functions narrative historical sources mention little about al-Ḥākim II.[79] The caliph remained, however, an attraction for important trading partners, notably India.[80] As it had during the Baghdad period of the Abbasid Caliphate, an investiture contracted through the caliph of Cairo secured local legitimacy for distant rulers and cemented goodwill with an important trading partner or strategic ally.

Some months prior to the toppling and murder of the young Qalawunid sultan Ḥājjī, a new generation of senior Qalawunid amirs came to power and approached al-Ḥākim II to offer him the sultanate in Dhū al-Ḥijja 747/March–April 1347. Fearing that he would fall victim and lose his life to politics, the caliph declined. The amirs ultimately installed another son of al-Nāṣir Muḥammad, al-Nāṣir Ḥasan (748–52/1347–51) in place of Ḥājjī.[81]

By mid-753/1352, al-Ḥākim II, who had played a part in public prayers against the Black Death (*ṭāʿūn*, or bubonic plague), joined the estimated one-third of the Egyptian masses who lost their lives to it. It remains unclear whether the caliph named his successor. The dominant amir of the era, Shaykhū al-ʿUmarī al-Nāṣirī, held a tribunal of the most powerful amirs, qadis and Abbasid representatives in the court of the Qalawunid sultan al-Ṣāliḥ Ṣāliḥ (752–5/1351–4) to select the next Abbasid to be raised to the caliphate.

Figure 2.1 Tombs inside the Abbasid mausoleum, Cairo. © Ashmolean Museum, University of Oxford. EA.CA.4423 by K. A. C. Creswell.

In due course, the triumvirate of Shaykhū, Ṭāz and Ṣarghitmish selected another son of al-Mustakfī, Abū Bakr Abū al-Fatḥ, and pledged loyalty to him as 'al-Muʿtaḍid bi-llāh' on 17 Shaʿbān 753/28 September 1352. The new caliph also received his brother's position as overseer of the tomb of Sayyida Nafīsa. After the ceremony a grand procession of qadis and other notables escorted the caliph from the Citadel to his residence. Perhaps confident in the brief stability they presided over, the ruling amirs permitted al-Muʿtaḍid, a man in his sixties, to perform the pilgrimage to the holy cities of the Hijaz at least twice, in 754/1353 and 760/1359, though few details of his escort are known.[82]

Contemporary Arabic sources mention little beyond the caliph's interaction with scholars and an apparent speech impediment.[83] Factional struggles plagued Cairene politics during much of al-Muʿtaḍid's caliphate, and the amirs frequently called upon him to engage in the ceremonial robing and *mubāyaʿa* for each new sultan. Like his predecessors, al-Muʿtaḍid attended the ceremonies to bestow sultans with 'the caliphal honour' (*al-tashrīf al-khalīfatī*) which frequently included black Abbasid robes.[84]

After a failed 752/1352 revolt in Syria by the deputy of Aleppo, Baybughā Rūs, who sought to name himself sultan in Damascus, the caliph al-Muʿtaḍid and the qadis arrived later in Shaʿbān 753/September 1352 to help to restore order.[85] At the Dammāghiyya *madrasa*, the caliph hobnobbed with local *ʿulamāʾ*, notably receiving, honouring and briefly reading Ḥanbalī ḥadīth literature with the Damascene scholar and Qurʾān exegete, Ismāʿīl ibn Kathīr. Ibn Kathīr wrote fondly of his encounter with al-Muʿtaḍid, blessing the caliph's ancestors after observing that 'he was a man [with a] handsome face, eloquent, humble and a quick learner who had a way with words'.[86] Having set affairs straight in Syria, the sultan's forces returned to Cairo amidst a massive celebration.

By Shawwāl 755/October 1354, the amirs ultimately forced al-Ṣāliḥ Ṣāliḥ into exile and returned al-Nāṣir Ḥasan to power for a second time (755–62/1354–6) after a ceremony involving al-Muʿtaḍid and the qadis. Al-Nāṣir Ḥasan ruled successfully in his own name until he in turn was deposed and executed in 762/1361–2. The first grandson of al-Nāṣir Muḥammad, al-Manṣūr Muḥammad was elevated in the absence of any surviving uncles, invested by the caliph and qadis, and dressed in a caliphal robe on 9 Jumādā I 762/17 March 1361. The next representative of the final generation of amirs to emerge among the extended Qalawunid military household was Yalbughā al-ʿUmarī al-Khāṣṣakī, a former *mamlūk* of the late sultan Ḥasan, who, in turn, enjoyed influence for eight years until his murder in 768/1366.[87]

In relative comparison with their father al-Mustakfī and grandfather al-Ḥākim, the Abbasid brothers al-Ḥākim II and al-Muʿtaḍid maintained a low profile and refrained from affairs of state while the Qalawunid amirs and their respective households competed for power. Both caliphs performed ceremonial duties, but avoided court intrigue, immersing themselves in religious studies and engagement with the scholarly class.[88] With the eclipse of the Mongols after the death of the last major Ilkhanid ruler Abū Saʿīd in 736/1335, the caliphate faded from foreign relations rhetoric, save for messages sent to Cairo from rulers abroad seeking caliphal sanction and investiture.

Al-Muʿtaḍid, shortly before his death in Jumādā I 763/March 1362, left the caliphate to his son Abū ʿAbd Allāh Muḥammad, who began his reign at the age of twenty-three as al-Mutawakkil ʿalā Allāh. Witnesses describe al-Muʿtaḍid's funeral as well-attended and memorable, the norm for an Abbasid caliph by the late fourteenth century.[89] Joining his cousin al-Wāthiq interred in the Abbasid mausoleum, al-Muʿtaḍid appears to be the only other Cairo caliph buried within the structure. The inscription on his tomb appears to be one of the more verbose epitaphs discovered in the mausoleum:

> Whosoever is upon [the earth] shall perish. Only God's face abides possessing majesty and glory. This is the grave of one who believes in His religion, seeking the grace of his Lord, Imām al-Muʿtaḍid bi-llāh Abū al-Fatḥ Abū Bakr, Commander of the Faithful.[90]

The endurance and longevity of Abbasid and Qalawunid symbolic dominance over much of the fourteenth century remains puzzling. The longer the Qalawunid sultans sat upon the throne, the more they became an abstraction of power. As their claims strengthened over time, the power and social order that flowed from their household in Syria and Egypt became increasingly difficult to imagine outside the existing socio-political context. This resulted in the presence of Qalawunid sultans (sanctioned by the caliph) on the throne that became part of the structural appearance of power which influenced subsequent representations and articulations of that power. To contest the structure brought about by such longevity, equally powerful symbolic or ideological tools would have been necessary to reshape imaginations of authority and sovereignty.[91]

Nevertheless, as Heidemann observed, in the decades following the exhilarating investitures of al-Mustanṣir and al-Ḥākim by Baybars discussed in Chapter 1, the caliphate was downgraded to a hereditary court office limited to a small variety of protocol functions. Political elites used Abbasid robing ceremonial and other rituals as a means to distract and gloss over rivalries, changing customs and uneasy alliances forged between the households of competing amirs, in the hope of making power struggles appear more subtle.[92] William Brinner described the caliphate and sultanate of Cairo, during much of the Qalawunid period, as being ceremonial offices outside the political system. Although recent research argues that many Qalawunid sultans were involved in politics,[93] Brinner may have been right in his assertion that no single office in the period could claim to represent a 'generally recognised supreme authority'.[94] As will be suggested later in Chapter 6, the two paradigms of sultanate and caliphate were not neatly separated by authors of the era, and the idea that the caliphate was more than the sum of its parts appears in various manifestations within the literature.[95]

As new caliphal protocols became routine in Cairo, interest in the office and the 'royal family' developed abroad. Among the rulers who began applying to Cairo for caliphal investiture deeds in the first half of the fourteenth century were the sultans of Delhi,[96] West Africa (Mali and Borno)[97] and the Muzaffarid dynasty of Fars.[98] Foreign embassies coming to Cairo in search of Abbasid delegation would continue into the early sixteenth century and enhanced the caliph's prestige. Interest from abroad also helped to create leverage for the position of the caliphal office.

The first Cairo-born caliph al-Mustakfī had taken office during an apparent dip in the caliphate's relevance at court. By the early fourteenth century, caliphal investiture was one of several viable sources of legitimacy on offer to the political elite: other powerful considerations such as Qalawunid dynastic legitimacy, consensus of the senior Cairo amirs, and designation by a previous sultan also retained influence.[99] The crowded field of legitimating modes led at least one modern scholar to suggest that Abbasid legitimacy could have quietly been omitted during the tumultuous forty-year period between the death of al-Nāṣir Muḥammad and the advent of the sultan Barqūq (741–84/1341–82). The reign of al-Ḥākim II is noteworthy as it marks one of the earliest attempts by the ruling amirs to hand power (temporarily) to a sitting caliph; a development that occurs with increased regularity beginning with the reign of al-Mutawakkil discussed in the next chapter. Although the Abbasid caliph appeared poised as an acceptable interim candidate for the sultanate, he remained in seclusion, expected to pledge allegiance to each new sultan. The socio-cultural context that developed around the court gave shape to politics,[100] and the social position of the caliph, like everything else, was largely driven by courtly expectations, which will be explored further in Chapter 9.

Notes

1. Flinterman and Van Steenbergen, 'Al-Nasir Muhammad', 89, 92; Van Steenbergen, 'The Mamluk Sultanate', 193, 197.
2. Al-Nuwayrī, *Nihāya*, 23:332–3; al-Yūnīnī/Guo, *Dhayl*, 1:203 (English), 2:252 (Arabic); al-Dhahabī, *Taʾrīkh*, 53:376; Mufaḍḍal, *Nahj*, 585–6; al-Shujāʿī, *Taʾrīkh*, 1:92; al-Ṣafadī, *Wāfī*, 15:349; Chapoutot-Remadi, 'Liens et relations', 52.
3. Holt, 'Some Observations', 504.
4. Baybars al-Manṣūrī, *Tuḥfa*, 162; Ibn al-Dawādārī, *Kanz*, 9:79; al-Birzālī, *Muqtafī*, 3:175; Mufaḍḍal, *Nahj*, 586; al-Suyūṭī, *Ḥusn*, 2:68; al-Suyūṭī, *Taʾrīkh*, 390.
5. Al-Yūnīnī/Guo, *Dhayl*, 1:202–3 (English), 2:251–2 (Arabic); al-Nuwayrī, *Nihāya*, 32:16; Ibn al-Dawādārī, *Kanz*, 9:79; al-Dhahabī, *Taʾrīkh*, 53:375; Chapoutot-Remadi, 'Liens et relations', 51–2.

6. English translation by L. Guo (*Early Mamluk Syrian Historiography*, 1:203); al-Nuwayrī, *Nihāya*, 23:333; al-Ṣafadī, *Wāfī*, 15:350.
7. Ibid. On the sultan's system of horseback mail delivery, see Franz, 'The Castle and the Country', 366–8.
8. Broadbridge, *Kingship and Ideology*, 87–8.
9. Baybars al-Manṣūrī, *Zubdat al-fikra*, 372; al-Nuwayrī, *Nihāya*, 23:332, 32:28; al-Dhahabī, *Ta'rīkh*, 53:375; al-Maqrīzī, *Sulūk*, 1:933; al-ʿAynī, *ʿIqd*, 4:233–4; Ibn Taghrībirdī, *Nujūm*, 8:160.
10. Little, 'Religion under the Mamluks', 173. On this phenomenon, see also Onimus, *Les maîtres du jeu*, 333–4.
11. Author Z, *Beiträge*, 113; al-Dhahabī, *Duwal*, 2:159. On the return celebration that greeted sultan and caliph in Cairo, see Shoshan, *Popular Culture*, 74–5.
12. Baybars al-Manṣūrī, *Zubdat al-fikra*, 395–9; al-Nuwayrī, *Nihāya*, 32:130–1; al-Maqrīzī, *Sulūk*, 2:7, 32–3. See also Vermeulen, 'Une lettre du Calife', 363–71; Behrens-Abouseif, *Practising Diplomacy*, 41; Van Steenbergen, *Caliphate and Kingship*, 99–100.
13. Abū al-Fidā', *Mukhtaṣar*, 4:68–70; al-Nuwayrī, *Nihāya*, 32:138–40; al-Maqrīzī, *Sulūk*, 2:43–7.
14. For the text of the document, see al-Nuwayrī, *Nihāya*, 8:128–35; al-Qalqashandī, *Ṣubḥ*, 10:68–75.
15. Baybars al-Manṣūrī, *Tuḥfa*, 191, 199–200; Baybars al-Manṣūrī, *Zubdat al-fikra*, 423; al-Nuwayrī, *Nihāya*, 32:144–6. See also Clifford, *State Formation*, 182–8; al-Ḥajjī, *Internal Affairs*, 21; Holt, 'Some Observations', 505–6; Shoshan, *Popular Culture*, 52–3.
16. Al-Maqrīzī, *Sulūk*, 2:65–7; Ibn Taghrībirdī, *Nujūm*, 8:263–4; al-Suyūṭī, *Ḥusn*, 2:113. On the implications of the statement, see Bauden, 'Sons of al-Nāṣir Muḥammad', 55–7; Loiseau, *Les Mamelouks*, 138–9; Van Steenbergen, 'Caught between Heredity and Merit', 430–4; al-Ḥajjī, *Internal Affairs*, 23–4.
17. Al-Nuwayrī, *Nihāya*, 32:146; al-Maqrīzī, *Sulūk*, 2:64.
18. Al-Maqrīzī, *Sulūk*, 2:64; Ibn Taghrībirdī, *Nujūm*, 8:262; al-Suyūṭī, *Ḥusn*, 2:112; Chapoutot-Remadi, 'Liens et relations', 54–7, 61–2; Holt, *Age of Crusades*, 112; Holt, 'Position and Power', 248; Holt, 'Some Observations', 506.
19. Van Steenbergen, 'The Mamluk Sultanate', 200.
20. Al-Nuwayrī, *Nihāya*, 32:155; al-Birzālī, *Muqtafī*, 3:442; Ibn Kathīr, *Bidāya*, 14:54; al-Maqrīzī, *Sulūk*, 2:73; Holt, *Age of Crusades*, 112.
21. Shāfiʿ ibn ʿAlī, [*Sīrat al-Malik al-Nāṣir*], fol. 94a–105b. See Van Den Bossche, 'Past, Panegyric', 181; al-Ḥajjī, *Internal Affairs*, 22–6.

22. Al-Shujāʿī, *Taʾrīkh*, 1:14, 70, 92–3; al-Maqrīzī, *Sulūk*, 2:416, 502–3; Ibn Ḥajar, *Durar*, 2:279; Ibn Kathīr, *Bidāya*, 14:187.
23. Van Steenbergen, 'Mamluk Elite', 196; Flinterman and Van Steenbergen, 'Al-Nasir Muhammad', 87, 96–9.
24. Al-Nuwayrī, *Nihāya*, 32:171; al-Dhahabī, *Taʾrīkh*, 53:344; al-Shujāʿī, *Taʾrīkh*, 1:92; al-Ṣafadī, *Aʿyān al-ʿaṣr*, 2:421; al-Qalqashandī, *Ṣubḥ*, 9:389; al-Qalqashandī, *Maʾāthir*, 2:337–9; Ibn Ḥajar, *Durar*, 2:204; al-Saḫmāwī, *Thaghr*, 2:578.
25. Indeed, the caliph was often spotted sporting a *jawkān* across his shoulder, a type of satchel associated with polo. See al-Dhahabī, *Taʾrīkh*, 53:376.
26. Al-Dhahabī, *Taʾrīkh*, 53:376; al-Shujāʿī, *Taʾrīkh*, 1:92; al-Yūsufī, *Nuzha*, 362; al-Ṣafadī, *Wāfī*, 15:349; al-Ṣafadī, *Aʿyān al-ʿaṣr*, 2:420; al-Qalqashandī, *Ṣubḥ*, 5:448; Ibn Taghrībirdī, *Manhal*, 6:21.
27. Ibn al-Dawādārī, *Kanz*, 9:281.
28. Mufaḍḍal, *Nahj*, 585n.1; al-Maqrīzī, *Khiṭaṭ*, 4:1:214; Ibn Taghrībirdī, *Nujūm*, 9:199. On the shrine of Sayyida Nafīsa, see Rāġib, 'Al-Sayyida Nafīsa'.
29. Abū al-Fidāʾ, *Mukhtaṣar*, 4:101–2; Ibn Iyās, *Badāʾiʿ*, 1:1:450. See Van Steenbergen, *Caliphate and Kingship*, 20–1; Flinterman and Van Steenbergen, 'Al-Nasir Muhammad', 95.
30. Al-Maqrīzī, *Sulūk*, 2:343; Ibn Ḥajar, *Durar*, 1:497–8; Ibn Taghrībirdī, *Nujūm*, 9:99.
31. Al-Maqrīzī, *Sulūk*, 2:416; al-Suyūṭī, *Taʾrīkh*, 387.
32. Ibn Taghrībirdī, *Manhal*, 6:20. On this intriguing and sometimes detested figure in fourteenth-century Egyptian historiography, see Holt, *Age of Crusades*, 118–19; Irwin, *Middle East*, 113–14; Levanoni, *Turning Point*, 73–80; Levanoni, 'The al-Nashw Episode'.
33. Al-Shujāʿī, *Taʾrīkh*, 1:14, 70; al-Yūsufī, *Nuzha*, 362; al-Maqrīzī, *Sulūk*, 2:416.
34. Ibn Ḥajar, *Durar*, 2:279; al-Suyūṭī, *Taʾrīkh*, 389; al-Ḥajjī, *Internal Affairs*, 27–8.
35. Al-Dhahabī, *Taʾrīkh*, 53:344; Ibn Ḥajar, *Durar*, 5:188. See also al-Ḥajjī, *Internal Affairs*, 27.
36. On the activities of the Ismāʿīlī *fidāʾī*s under the late thirteenth-/early fourteenth-century sultans of Cairo, see Melville, 'Sometimes by the Sword'; Thorau, *Lion of Egypt*, 147, 164, 169, 176, 194, 201–3, 208; Herzog, *Geschichte und Imaginaire*, 176–81.
37. Al-Ṣafadī, *Wāfī*, 15:350; al-Maqrīzī, *Sulūk*, 2:416; al-Suyūṭī, *Ḥusn*, 2:68; al-Suyūṭī, *Taʾrīkh*, 390; al-Ḥajjī, *Internal Affairs*, 27–8.

38. Al-Ṣafadī, *Wāfī*, 15:350; al-Ṣafadī, *Aʿyān al-ʿaṣr*, 2:420; al-Jazarī, *Ḥawādith*, 3:875, 929; Ibn Kathīr, *Bidāya*, 14:176–7; al-Maqrīzī, *Sulūk*, 2:403; Ibn Ḥajar, *Durar*, 2:281; al-ʿAynī, *ʿIqd*, 3:359.
39. On al-Qazwīnī's influence at court, see Eychenne, *Liens personnels*, 179, 211–13, 221–5.
40. Al-Dhahabī, *Taʾrīkh*, 53:376; al-Shujāʿī, *Taʾrīkh*, 1:14; Ibn al-Wardī, *Taʾrīkh*, 2:470; al-Yūsufī, *Nuzha*, 363; al-Ṣafadī, *Aʿyān al-ʿaṣr*, 2:420–1; al-Maqrīzī, *Sulūk*, 2:417; Ibn Ḥajar, *Durar*, 2:279–80; Ibn Taghrībirdī, *Mawrid*, 1:242–3; al-Suyūṭī, *Taʾrīkh*, 389; al-Suyūṭī, *Ḥusn*, 2:67. See also Garcin, *Qūṣ*, 200–1; Surūr, *Dawlat Banī Qalāwūn*, 80–1.
41. Ibn al-Wardī, *Taʾrīkh*, 2:469–70; al-Ṣafadī, *Aʿyān al-ʿaṣr*, 2:420–1; al-Maqrīzī, *Sulūk*, 2:403; al-Suyūṭī, *Ḥusn*, 2:67. On the motif of grief and loss surrounding al-Mustakfī's exile, see Hassan, *Longing for the Lost Caliphate*, 88–9.
42. Ibn al-Wardī, *Taʾrīkh*, 2:470; al-Dhahabī, *Taʾrīkh*, 53:376; al-Dhahabī, *Duwal*, 2:186; al-Shujāʿī, *Taʾrīkh*, 1:70, 92; Mufaḍḍal, *Chronik*, 88; al-Ṣafadī, *Aʿyān al-ʿaṣr*, 1:220–1, 2:421; al-Ṣafadī, *Wāfī*, 15:350, 30:103; Ibn Kathīr, *Bidāya*, 14:187, 191; Ibn Duqmāq, *Jawhar*, 189–90; al-Maqrīzī *Sulūk*, 2:502–3; al-Maqrīzī, *Muqaffā*, 1:177, 235; al-Ḥajjī, *Internal Affairs*, 33.
43. The mosque apparently stands today in the al-Baṭḥāʾ neighbourhood of Qūṣ, known as the Shaykh Sulaymān masjid.
44. Garcin, *Qūṣ*, 201n.4. Evliyā Çelebi also composed a brief dynastic sketch of the Abbasids of Cairo, see *Seyahatnâmesi*, 10:29–30, 426–7.
45. Al-Ṣafadī, *Aʿyān al-ʿaṣr*, 2:420–1.
46. Al-Ḥajjī, *Internal Affairs*, 27–30; al-Suyūṭī, *Ḥusn*, 2:67.
47. Al-Shujāʿī, *Taʾrīkh*, 1:70; al-Ṣafadī, *Aʿyān al-ʿaṣr*, 1:220, 2:421; Ibn Duqmāq, *Jawhar*, 189; al-Qalqashandī, *Ṣubḥ*, 3:261; al-Maqrīzī, *Sulūk*, 2:502–3; al-Maqrīzī, *Muqaffā*, 1:176, 235; al-Maqrīzī, *Durar*, 2:210; Ibn Taghrībirdī, *Mawrid*, 1:243; al-Suyūṭī, *Taʾrīkh*, 391; Chapoutot-Remadi, 'Liens et relations', 52–3.
48. Al-Shujāʿī, *Taʾrīkh*, 1:70; Mufaḍḍal, *Chronik*, 89; al-Maqrīzī, *Sulūk*, 2:502–3; al-Maqrīzī, *Khiṭaṭ*, 3:785; al-Maqrīzī, *Muqaffā*, 1:177; Ibn Ḥajar, *Durar*, 1:62. See also Hassan, *Longing for the Lost Caliphate*, 89; Surūr, *Dawlat Banī Qalāwūn*, 81; Levanoni, *Turning Point*, 29–30 and notes.
49. Al-ʿUmarī quoted in al-Suyūṭī, *Taʾrīkh*, 391–2; al-Suyūṭī, *Ḥusn*, 2:68; al-Maqrīzī, *Muqaffā*, 1:177.
50. Mufaḍḍal, *Chronik*, 89; al-Maqrīzī, *Sulūk*, 2:502–3; al-Maqrīzī, *Muqaffā*, 1:177; Ibn Ḥajar, *Durar*, 1:62; Hassan, *Longing for the Lost Caliphate*, 89;

Nielsen, *Secular Justice*, 117–18. It was perhaps jeering Cairene masses which encouraged the *ʿulamāʾ* to oppose the sultan's decision for fear that the caliphate was becoming a mockery, see Ḍāḥī and Mizbān, *al-Raʾy al-ʿāmm*, 59; Al-Azmeh, *Muslim Kingship*, 179; Chapoutot-Remadi, 'Liens et relations', 60–2.

51. Al-Maqrīzī, *Sulūk*, 2:503; al-Maqrīzī, *Muqaffā*, 1:177; Ibn Ḥajar, *Durar*, 1:62; Ibn Taghrībirdī, *Mawrid*, 1:243; al-Suyūṭī, *Ḥusn*, 2:68; al-Suyūṭī, *Taʾrīkh*, 391–2; Garcin, 'Histoire', 68–9. ʿIzz al-Dīn ibn Jamāʿa (d. 767/1366) was the son of the more famous qadi Badr al-Dīn ibn Jamāʿa.
52. Al-Shujāʿī, *Taʾrīkh*, 1:70, 126; al-Maqrīzī, *Sulūk*, 2:503.
53. Al-Dhahabī, *Duwal*, 2:188; al-Shujāʿī, *Taʾrīkh*, 1:70; Ibn al-Wardī, *Taʾrīkh*, 2:474; Ibn Ḥabīb, *Tadhkira*, 3:24; al-Suyūṭī, *Ḥusn*, 2:69; al-Suyūṭī, *Taʾrīkh*, 392.
54. Al-Qalqashandī, *Maʾāthir*, 2:148–9; al-Maqrīzī, *Muqaffā*, 1:177.
55. Tomb inscriptions name him 'Khiḍr' the son of al-Mustamsik, al-Wāthiq bi-llāh. A number of al-Wāthiq's children, including his daughter Zubayda (d. 712/1312) and son Abū ʿAbbās Aḥmad (d. 738/1338), are buried in the structure. For the partial inscription on the tomb of al-Wāthiq, see Rogers, 'Notice', 117–19, 122–3. For a listing of those interred in the tomb, Abbasids and otherwise, see Behrens-Abouseif, *Cairo of the Mamluks*, 126.
56. Garcin, 'Histoire', 57.
57. Van Steenbergen, *Order Out of Chaos*; Loiseau, *Les Mamelouks*, 118–24; Irwin, *Middle East*, 125; Holt, *Age of Crusades*, 121–9.
58. Van Steenbergen has argued that some of these sultans successfully accumulated power and generated support among high-ranking amirs, thereby becoming deeply involved in power politics. See Van Steenbergen, 'Is Anyone My Guardian', 56, 59.
59. For studies of the period, see Van Steenbergen, 'The Mamluk Sultanate'; Van Steenbergen, *Order Out of Chaos*; Brinner, 'Struggle for Power', 232–4; Broadbridge, *Kingship and Ideology*, 146–9, 167.
60. Van Steenbergen, 'Mamluk Elite', 196; Van Steenbergen, 'The Mamluk Sultanate', 201–2.
61. Al-Shujāʿī, *Taʾrīkh*, 1:126–7, 149–98; al-Ṣafadī, *Aʿyān al-ʿaṣr*, 1:220; al-Qalqashandī, *Ṣubḥ*, 3:276; al-Maqrīzī, *Sulūk*, 2:552; al-Maqrīzī, *Muqaffā*, 1:177; Ibn Qāḍī Shuhba, *Taʾrīkh*, 2:135–6; Ibn Ḥajar, *Durar*, 1:159.
62. Ibn Khaldūn, *Taʾrīkh*, 5:948, 973; al-Maqrīzī, *Sulūk*, 2:552, 558–9; al-Maqrīzī, *Muqaffā*, 1:177, 235; Ibn Ḥajar, *Durar*, 1:552–4.

63. Al-Dhahabī, *Duwal*, 2:188; Ibn al-Wardī, *Ta'rīkh*, 2:474; Ibn Ḥabīb, *Tadhkira*, 3:24; al-Maqrīzī, *Sulūk*, 2:558–9; al-Maqrīzī, *Muqaffā*, 1:235–6; Chapoutot-Remadi, 'Liens et relations', 44, 53–4, 61; Holt, 'Position and Power', 244.
64. Al-Shujā'ī, *Ta'rīkh*, 1:126, 130; Ibn Kathīr, *Bidāya*, 14:191; al-Qalqashandī, *Ṣubḥ*, 3:276–7; al-Maqrīzī, *Muqaffā*, 1:236; Ibn Qāḍī Shuhba, *Ta'rīkh*, 2:201; Ibn Taghrībirdī, *Nujūm*, 10:4–5; al-Suyūṭī, *Ḥusn*, 2:70, 80.
65. Kennedy, *Caliphate*, xv.
66. Al-Suyūṭī, *Ta'rīkh*, 392.
67. Ibn Taghrībirdī, *Nujūm*, 10:21–2, 42–59; Holt, *Age of Crusades*, 121–2.
68. Al-Shujā'ī, *Ta'rīkh*, 1:204–5; Ibn Kathīr, *Bidāya*, 14:200; al-Maqrīzī, *Sulūk*, 2:603; Ibn Taghrībirdī, *Nujūm*, 10:59–61. On the various items of the caliph's dress, see Fuess, 'Sultans with Horns', 75–6; Petry, 'Robing Ceremonials', 363; Chapoutot-Remadi, 'Liens et relations', 44; Mayer, *Mamluk Costume*, 13–14; Schimmel, 'Kalif und Kadi', 58.
69. Holt, 'Structure of Government', 45; Holt, 'Some Observations', 504.
70. Al-Shujā'ī, *Ta'rīkh*, 1:217, 224; al-Maqrīzī, *Sulūk*, 2:609–10, 620–1; Ibn Qāḍī Shuhba, *Ta'rīkh*, 2:246–51, 295, 299, 301; Ibn Taghrībirdī, *Nujūm*, 10:67–8, 70–2, 78–81.
71. Al-Suyūṭī, *Ta'rīkh*, 392.
72. Eychenne, *Liens personnels*, 300–1, 489–91.
73. Al-Shujā'ī, *Ta'rīkh*, 1:126; al-Maqrīzī, *Khiṭaṭ*, 3:785; Rāġib, 'Al-Sayyida Nafīsa', 41–2; Ṭarkhān, *Miṣr*, 54–5.
74. Ibn Ḥabīb, *Tadhkira*, 3:28; Ibn Iyās, *Badā'i'*, 1:1:495.
75. The shrine was assigned to the Abbasid family shortly after the death of al-Nāṣir Muḥammad. See al-Qalqashandī, *Ṣubḥ*, 3:275; al-Maqrīzī, *Sulūk*, 2:609, 3:76; al-Maqrīzī, *Khiṭaṭ*, 3:785; Ibn Taghrībirdī *Nujūm*, 10:66; al-Suyūṭī, *Ḥusn*, 2:81; Ibn Iyās, *Badā'i'*, 1:1:587–8, 5:192; Ṭarkhān, *Miṣr*, 60; Rāġib, 'Al-Sayyida Nafīsa', 41–2; Tetsuya, 'Cairene Cemeteries', 101–2; Garcin, 'Circassian Mamlūks', 303.
76. Al-Maqrīzī, *Muqaffā*, 1:236; Ibn Qāḍī Shuhba, *Ta'rīkh*, 3:38; Ibn Ḥajar, *Durar*, 1:159; al-Suyūṭī, *Ta'rīkh*, 392, 399; al-Malaṭī, *Nayl*, 1:234.
77. Holt, 'Some Observations', 504.
78. Al-Maqrīzī, *Sulūk*, 2:681, 714, 843; Ibn Ḥabīb, *Tadhkira*, 3:17, 26–7, 40, 80, 92, 102, 148; Ibn Taghrībirdī, *Nujūm*, 10:4–5, 16, 60, 66, 117, 149, 254.
79. Beyond sultanic investiture, the caliphal authority of al-Ḥākim II was also

invoked in the 740s/1340s to create other documents as well. Al-Maqrīzī reports that the sultan al-Ṣāliḥ Ismāʿīl commissioned the caliph to compose a caliphal deed honouring the *shaykh* of the Siryāqūs *khānqāh* in 744/1344 (*Muqaffā*, 1:236); and later, the chancery used the caliph's authority to address unlawful crossbow usage in Syria (see Chapter 8 below).

80. Al-Shujāʿī, *Taʾrīkh*, 1:257–8; al-Maqrīzī, *Sulūk*, 2:645; al-Maqrīzī, *Muqaffā*, 1:236; Ibn Qāḍī Shuhba, *Taʾrīkh*, 2:364. Relations between the Abbasids of Cairo and the rulers of medieval India have been well-covered, see Conermann and Kollatz, 'Some Remarks'; Auer, *Symbols of Authority*, 108–16; Hassan, *Longing for the Lost Caliphate*, 17, 95–7; al-Mashhadānī, *Al-ʿAlāqāt*, 46–56; Jackson, *Delhi Sultanate*, 296–8; Arnold, *Caliphate*, 105.
81. Tyan, *Institutions du droit public musulman*, 2:235–6; Van Steenbergen, 'The Mamluk Sultanate', 203, 205.
82. Al-Ṣafadī, *Wāfī*, 10:235, 30:148–9; al-Maqrīzī, *Sulūk*, 2:903, 3:77; al-Maqrīzī, *Khiṭaṭ*, 3:785; al-Maqrīzī, *Muqaffā*, 1:236; al-Maqrīzī, *Durar*, 2:210; Ibn Taghrībirdī, *Nujūm*, 10:204; Ibn Taghrībirdī, *Manhal*, 12:281–2.
83. Ibn Kathīr, *Bidāya*, 14:245; Ibn Duqmāq, *Jawhar*, 191–2; al-Maqrīzī, *Sulūk*, 3:77; Ibn Qāḍī Shuhba, *Taʾrīkh*, 3:517; Ibn Ḥajar, *Durar*, 1:529.
84. Ibn Taghrībirdī, *Nujūm*, 11:3; al-Sakhāwī, *Dhayl*, 1:139; Surūr, *Dawlat Banī Qalāwūn*, 85.
85. Van Steenbergen, 'The Mamluk Sultanate', 206. Contemporary sources are often vague regarding the identity of the caliph that accompanied al-Ṣāliḥ Ṣāliḥ in Shaʿbān 753/September 1352 when the latter rode out to Syria to deal with a group of recalcitrant amirs on the verge of revolt. Al-Sakhāwī attempts to have the last word by claiming that al-Muʿtaḍid had *twice* gone to Syria, once with Ṣāliḥ and again with al-Manṣūr Muḥammad, see *Dhayl*, 1:124–5, 188; al-Sakhāwī, *Wajīz*, 1:123.
86. Ibn Kathīr, *Bidāya*, 14:245.
87. Al-Ṣafadī, *Wāfī*, 30:149; al-Maqrīzī, *Sulūk*, 3:1, 62, 64–5; Ibn Taghrībirdī, *Nujūm*, 10:302, 11:3–5; Loiseau, *Les Mamelouks*, 122–3. After the elimination of Yalbughā's generation, the Qalawunid household seems to have been exhausted, see Van Steenbergen, 'The Mamluk Sultanate', 209; Loiseau, *Les Mamelouks*, 123.
88. Al-Malaṭī, *Nayl*, 1:340.
89. Ibn Kathīr, *Bidāya*, 14:293; Ibn Ḥabīb, *Tadhkira*, 3:248; Ibn Duqmāq, *Jawhar*, 191, 194; al-Qalqashandī, *Ṣubḥ*, 3:262; al-Maqrīzī, *Sulūk*, 3:76–7, 4:1:24; al-Maqrīzī, *Khiṭaṭ*, 3:785; al-Maqrīzī, *Durar*, 2:210, 3:292; Ibn Ḥajar,

Durar, 1:529; Ibn Ḥajar, *Inbāʾ al-ghumr*, 2:343; Ibn Taghrībirdī, *Manhal*, 12:282.

90. Rogers, 'Notice', 123–4; *RCEA*, 17, No. 763 002.
91. I thank Jo Van Steenbergen for sharing some of these observations.
92. Heidemann, *Kalifat*, 194. See also Petry, 'Robing Ceremonials', 353.
93. Van Steenbergen, 'Is Anyone My Guardian', 56–9.
94. Brinner, 'Struggle for Power', 233.
95. Ibn ʿAbd al-Ẓāhir, *Alṭāf*, 18; al-Qalqashandī, *Ṣubḥ*, 6:423, 9:373; al-Qalqashandī, *Maʾāthir*, 3:346.
96. See note 80, above.
97. Dewière, 'Diplomatic Practices', 674–9; Behrens-Abouseif, *Practising Diplomacy*, 57–8.
98. For an overview of Muzaffarid diplomacy involving al-Muʿtaḍid of Cairo, see Wing, 'Mozaffarids'.
99. Onimus, *Les maîtres du jeu*, 159; Levanoni, 'Mamluk Conception', 376, 379, 383; Heidemann, *Kalifat*, 182; Holt, 'Position and Power', 239; Gaudefroy-Demombynes, *La Syrie à l'époque des mamelouks*, xxi.
100. Flinterman and Van Steenbergen, 'Al-Nasir Muhammad', 87.

3

Flirtations with Power and Political Intrigue, 763–815/1362–1412

Introduction

The first century of the Abbasid Caliphate in Cairo, so far discussed, involved the establishment and consolidation of ceremonial traditions that the varied landscape of political and religious elites were comfortable with, while setting up the Abbasid family to be a financially self-sufficient source of ceremonial blessings (*baraka*) able to produce heirs for centuries to come. For the next 150 years, the Cairo Caliphate would retain importance as a valuable chip to be played by competing factions in medieval Syro-Egyptian politics. Caliphs would be at the centre of political revolts as individual officeholders struggled to stay in office while the family's income reached an all-time high. Nevertheless, as Garcin observed, in the fourteenth and early fifteenth centuries, it became routine for Cairene politics to disrupt the reign of a sitting Abbasid caliph.[1]

Continuing the discussion of the Qalawunid dynasty from the previous two chapters, we can identify the Abbasid Caliphate in this period alongside other languages of power used to generate and reproduce the normative dynastic order of the Qalawunids in the second half of the fourteenth century.[2] In this time, the sultanate of Cairo was essentially a delicate grouping of military households dominated by different Qalawunid leaders, none of whom were able to consolidate their positions at the expense of their peers. Thus, the Qalawunid household, buttressed to a lesser degree by caliphal delegation, remained the only option for elite consensus.[3]

Father of the Caliphs: The Long Reign of al-Mutawakkil ʿalā Allāh, 763–85/1362–83 and 791–808/1389–1406

Despite two intervals, the reign of al-Mutawakkil ʿalā Allāh, caliph for much of the period from 763/1362 to 808/1406, was the longest of the Cairene Abbasids. His tenure witnessed the fall of the Qalawunids, the emergence of al-Ẓāhir Barqūq and the so-called 'Circassian line' of sultans, as well as the horror of 'Mongol' revival that culminated in the invasion of Syria by the Central Asian warlord amīr Temür (Tamerlane, r. 771–807/1370–1405). Contemporary chroniclers were quick to acknowledge the legacy of al-Mutawakkil of Cairo. Among the one hundred children reportedly born to his wives and concubines, five sons and three grandsons reigned as caliphs until the end of the sultanate in Cairo – a development unique to both Abbasid and Islamic history. Indeed, by the late fifteenth century, every surviving member of the Abbasid clan allegedly drew descent from al-Mutawakkil after the extinction of all other lines.[4]

In addition to inaugurating the second century of the Abbasid restoration in Cairo, the reign of al-Mutawakkil was a time of financial prosperity for the family after accumulating a surplus of wealth and property from the Cairene political elite. The Abbasids had feathered their nest nicely thanks in large part to the lucrative administration of the shrine of Sayyida Nafīsa which al-Mutawakkil inherited along with the family office in 763/1362. However, the caliph was deprived of shrine revenues for a lengthy period beginning in 766/1364–5 when it was reassigned to the amir Jamāl al-Dīn ʿAbd Allāh ibn Baktimur until 789/1387.[5]

The early years of al-Mutawakkil's caliphate passed without incident, his duties involving little more than the expected investiture of Qalawunid princes. At the behest of the *atābak al-ʿasākir* Yalbughā al-Khāṣṣakī, the caliph confirmed the sultanate of al-Manṣūr Muḥammad ibn Ḥājjī (762–4/1361–3), though al-Mutawakkil was ultimately ordered to declare the latter deposed on the ground of mental inability and instead install al-Ashraf Shaʿbān as sultan in Shaʿbān 764/May 1363.[6]

The Cairo Caliphate entertained some interest from the east when in Jumādā I 767/1366 the Jalayrid governor of Baghdad, Khwāja Mirjān, rebelled against his overlord Shaykh Uvays (r. 757–76/1356–74) and replaced his name in the *khuṭba* and on coinage with that of the Qalawunid al-Ashraf Shaʿbān. Cairo, which had come to view Shaykh Uvays as hostile, welcomed the envoys of Khwāja Mirjān, who received a *taqlīd* of deputyship from Shaʿbān and the Abbasid caliph as well as caliphal standards to carry back to Baghdad.[7] A few years later in 770/1368, Shāh Shujāʿ (r. 765–86/1364–85), the Muzaffarid ruler of Fars, similarly requested and received an Abbasid investiture deed which was sent along with an Egyptian-made sword.[8]

In Rabīʿ II 768/December 1366, Yalbughā al-Khāṣṣakī, losing his grip on al-Ashraf Shaʿbān and hoping to regain control through a more malleable candidate, summoned al-Mutawakkil and Ānūk, another grandson of al-Nāṣir Muḥammad, and asked the caliph to delegate authority in place of his brother Shaʿbān. The caliph, however, refused and argued that Shaʿbān still had power (*shawka*). Unimpressed by the caliph's rebuff, Yalbughā ordered the sounding of drums and the display of sultanic symbols and, according to the historian al-Maqrīzī, remarked, 'I appoint and confirm [Ānūk], and who else holds power besides me?' After the murder of Yalbughā at court later that year, Shaʿbān succeeded in strengthening his power through the acquisition of many of the chief amir's former *mamlūk*s. Nevertheless, Shaʿbān's reign was hardly free of intrigue, and many of the amirs loyal to Yalbughā schemed to end his rule.[9]

After a quiet fifteen years, the caliph emerged from the side-lines in 778/1377 to join Shaʿbān for a lavish pilgrimage journey with other notables. Once the convoy crossed the Sinai Peninsula, however, the sultan's *mamlūk*s mutinied in ʿAqaba purportedly over diminished pay rations. Unable to calm the situation, Shaʿbān fled towards Cairo. Another report claimed the sultan had learned that his *mamlūk*s, in collusion with the amirs, sought to assassinate him on the pilgrimage. Unbeknown to the sultan, a separate coup by the Yalbughāwī amirs of Cairo had already removed him from power. Al-Mutawakkil, on the other hand, lingered in ʿAqaba. The rebellious *mamlūk*s led by the amir Ṭashtamur urged the caliph to take the sultanate and offered faithful assistance. After some hesitation, the caliph declined and offered instead to bestow authority on any other agreeable candidate. The caliph then proceeded to Cairo with the amirs and qadis.[10]

In Cairo, the amirs raised a son of Shaʿbān, al-Manṣūr ʿAlī (778–83/1377–82), to the sultanate without the presence of the caliph or chief magistrates who had yet to return from ʿAqaba.[11] Some amirs considered selecting a surrogate caliph until al-Mutawakkil arrived. Shortly after Shaʿbān emerged from hiding, a conspiracy of amirs (including the future sultan Barqūq) murdered him in late 778/1377. After al-Mutawakkil reached Cairo that same month, the caliph attended a ceremony at which the new political elite instructed him to read the appointment papers for the Qalawunid sultan al-Manṣūr ʿAlī before the religious elite. The caliph then offered *bayʿa* to the sultan and draped him in a black caliphal robe.[12]

Al-Mutawakkil made a powerful enemy of the ringleader of the Yalbughāwī amirs, Aynabak al-Badrī, who had risen against Shaʿbān and established himself in power in early 779/1377. At the outset, Aynabak demanded that al-Mutawakkil provide caliphal sanction for his stepson Aḥmad ibn Yalbughā al-Khāṣṣakī to take the sultanate along with a ruling that the murder of Shaʿbān had been lawful. Al-Mutawakkil refused to consent on the ground that Aḥmad was not from the House of Qalāwūn, allegedly stating that he would not depose the son of a king in favour of the son of an amir. Anticipating the charge, Aynabak argued that the mother of his stepson, a former wife of al-Nāṣir Ḥasan, had been impregnated by the late Qalawunid sultan before her marriages to Yalbughā and ultimately to Aynabak himself. Unconvinced and therefore unwilling, the caliph thus invited the wrath of Aynabak who accused him of neglecting the duties of his office in favour of worldly pleasure. Aynabak demanded that al-Mutawakkil be banished to Qūṣ and removed him from the caliphate to the dismay of many contemporary observers.[13] In need of a new Abbasid caliph to maintain legitimacy amidst his political rivals, Aynabak beckoned Abū Yaḥyā Najm al-Dīn Zakariyyāʾ, a son of al-Wāthiq, on 4 Rabīʿ I 779/11 July 1377 and robed him as al-Muʿtaṣim bi-llāh, albeit without obtaining a formal abdication from al-Mutawakkil or the consensus of the *ʿulamāʾ* or chief Cairene amirs.

Perhaps aware of Aynabak's fragile hold on power, al-Mutawakkil feigned preparation for the journey to Upper Egypt, even leaving his home for the day. Aynabak ultimately bowed to the pressure of the amirs and reinstated al-Mutawakkil some days later, al-Muʿtaṣim's fleeting caliphate having lasted scarcely more than a fortnight. The army ousted Aynabak shortly thereafter and imprisoned him in Alexandria until his death in 780/1378.[14]

Aynabak al-Badrī's interference with the caliphate would strengthen the precedent for later attempts to hand temporal power to al-Mutawakkil, or attempts to remove him from office. Brinner highlighted the incident as an instructive paradox demonstrating the simultaneous weakness and power of the caliph and his ability to influence sultanic succession.[15]

The Rise of al-Ẓāhir Barqūq, 784–801/1382–99

Ultimately it was Barqūq, a former *mamlūk* of Yalbughā al-Khāṣṣakī, who seized power as chief amir and army commander. After amassing support enough to dominate the networks and households that ran politics during 777–9/1376–8, the Circassian amir successfully ruled through the last two Qalawunid sultans, al-Manṣūr ʿAlī (778–83/1377–82) and his brother al-Ṣāliḥ Ḥājjī II (783–4/1382). All the while expanding his patronage, network and household to larger parts of the military elite, Barqūq successfully restored effective power and authority to the sultanate which he took for himself in 784/1382.[16] Although 'Turks' and 'Circassians' opposed each other, the conflict concerned more the competition for resources and factional solidarity than ethnicity. Nevertheless, solidarity and identity later formed around ethnic qualifiers as well.[17]

Amid the upheaval surrounding the succession various political actors (this time mostly Turks and Kurds) tried to deliver the sultanate to al-Mutawakkil as a stopgap ruler with limited power. The attempt resulted from competing power ideologies and brought the caliphate into conflict with the sultanate,[18] suggesting that some amirs preferred Abbasid legitimacy, which had been inseparable from the Qalawunids, over the pretensions of the nascent political order established by Barqūq, his clients and entourage.

Once entrenched as sultan, it was inevitable that Barqūq would brandish his access to the Abbasid caliph during his enthronement rites. The sultan's investiture proved to be a faithful rendition of routine ceremonial practices involving the caliph. After delivering an eloquent sermon, al-Mutawakkil delegated full powers to Barqūq as sultan, naming him al-Malik al-Ẓāhir, with the amirs, qadis and *shaykh al-islām* pledging support in turn. The sultan then donned the black Abbasid robe to demonstrate his righteous obligation to the caliphate. Five days later, on 24 Ramaḍān 784/1 December 1382, official representatives read Barqūq's diploma before the caliph and other robed religious and military officials.[19]

Intrigue and Revolt in the Name of the Caliph

Barqūq faced fierce pushback as he tried to reorient the socio-political order within the political contours of the sultanate. In the early months of his reign, the sultan appeased some opponents and crushed others in Egypt and Syria. He appointed his own *mamlūk*s to influential positions to safeguard their loyalty and the cohesion of his government.[20] In this erstwhile climate of purges and arrests, the Abbasid Caliphate can be linked to at least three attempts to unseat the sultan.

On 1 Rajab 785/30 August 1383, Barqūq granted audience to the amir Muḥammad ibn Tankiz who informed the sultan of an alleged plot in which the caliph al-Mutawakkil had colluded with two amirs, Quruṭ ibn ʿUmar al-Turkmānī and Ibrāhīm ibn Quṭluqtamur. According to Ibn Tankiz, the trio plotted to murder the sultan on the *maydān* below the Citadel and then place the caliph at the head of the government. Ibn Tankiz swore to the validity of his statement and encouraged Barqūq to investigate the allegations. Furious, Barqūq summoned the caliph and the offending amirs. The deputy of Egypt, Sūdūn al-Shaykhūnī, also present, scoffed at the notion that the caliph, 'an intelligent man incapable of such an act', might involve himself in open treason. At the hearing, al-Mutawakkil and Ibrāhīm ibn Quṭluqtamur promptly denied any wrongdoing, but in hoping to distance himself from the caliph – who unquestionably bore the brunt of the sultan's fury – Quruṭ hastily confessed:

> The caliph summoned me and said: 'These oppressors have seized kingship without my consent; I reluctantly invested Barqūq with the sultanate, and then he wrongfully took the wealth of the people'. [The caliph] asked that I stand with him and support the cause of righteousness; I agreed and promised to aid him by gathering 800 Kurds and Turkmen to his command.[21]

Cornered by Barqūq, the caliph clung to his vehement denial of Quruṭ's indictment, while Ibn Quṭluqtamur, equally anxious to get out of the hot seat, likewise inculpated the caliph by claiming ignorance of any negotiation between al-Mutawakkil and Quruṭ. Ibn Quṭluqtamur testified that al-Mutawakkil had in fact *invited* him to one of the caliphal residences on Elephant Island and urged him to join the cause against the sultan. Al-Mutawakkil maintained innocence even during a cross-examination by Ibn Quṭluqtamur, who grilled him on specific details that the caliph brushed off as baseless gossip. The hearing culminated with Barqūq unsheathing his sword and threatening to behead the caliph on the spot. Cooler heads prevailed, however, when Sūdūn and Aytamish al-Bujāsī attempted to intervene on behalf of the embattled trio. Nevertheless, Barqūq ordered crucifixion (*tasmīr*) for Ibn Quṭluqtamur and Quruṭ below the Citadel after a parade of shame through Cairo. Still unsatisfied, the sultan ordered the two offenders to be bisected, though court connections helped mitigate Ibn Quṭluqtamur's sentence to imprisonment at the Shamāʿil storehouse. As for the caliph, Barqūq convened a special tribunal of qadis in the hope of securing a death sentence. Reluctant to condemn the Commander of the Faithful to death, the qadis adjourned without providing Barqūq with religious sanction.[22]

Perplexed by having to deal with a dangerous enemy who could not be cleanly killed without deeply disturbing his religious elites, courtiers and the masses, Barqūq threw the caliph in irons in the tower of the Citadel. The Ḥanafī qadi Ṣadr al-Dīn al-Manṣūr produced and supported a fatwa dismissing al-Mutawakkil, perhaps to rescue the caliph from further abuse.[23] In order to select a new Abbasid caliph, the sultan called upon two sons of the former caliph al-Muʿtaṣim Zakariyyāʾ (r. 799/1377), Rukn al-Dīn ʿUmar and Muḥyī al-Dīn Zakariyyāʾ.[24] The sultan appointed ʿUmar as al-Wāthiq bi-llāh (II) for three years until that caliph's death on 19 Shawwāl 788/13 November 1386. Al-Mutawakkil spent the interim shackled in house arrest, stripped of his salary and properties, his future uncertain. In Ramaḍān 787/October 1385, the sultan also relieved the caliph of previous lands and gifts including financial control of the Abū Rajwān district in Giza. Public opinion appeared to remain firmly on the side of the ousted caliph, and by the end of Rajab 785/September 1383, several amirs passionately pleaded with Barqūq to restore al-Mutawakkil. When Barqūq reaffirmed his commitment to seeing the caliph executed as a traitor, they continued to cajole the sultan until at last he released al-Mutawakkil from tower imprisonment and allowed him to return to the Abbasid residence in the Citadel on the Muslim holy day of ʿArafa in late 785/February 1384.[25]

Barqūq was wise to exercise caution towards the inherent dangers of a popular Abbasid caliph. The unnamed amirs voicing concern and support for the caliph make for interesting actors in the narrative presented by our sources. Given the strength of al-Mutawakkil's dynastic claim, reinforced by the longevity of his career in office, it is not surprising that he developed networks of support and perhaps even patronage relationships in court circles, both as patron and client. In addition to commanding support from Turkish and Bedouin riders, al-Mutawakkil, from the time of his investiture nearly two decades earlier, had cultivated alliances among the amirs of Yalbughā al-Khāṣṣakī and various royal *mamlūks*. We must ask why contemporary historians wanted us to believe in the existence of this unknown mass of caliphal supporters. The caliph, of course, had previously represented the interests and legacy of the Qalawunid household against would-be usurpers and some, if they did not feel personally indebted to the caliph's favour, may have understood him as a symbolic check on the expanding power of Barqūq's household. Al-Wāthiq II, on the other hand, though described by historians as kind and good-natured, remained a non-entity. Contemporary fifteenth-century sources mention little concerning his three-year caliphate until his illness-related demise around aged seventy.[26]

Supporters of al-Mutawakkil continued to campaign for the caliph's reinstatement. Barqūq instead assigned the caliphate to the brother of al-Wāthiq II, Muḥyī al-Dīn Zakariyyā᾿ installed as al-Mustaʿṣim (d. 801/1399). The sultan arranged an impromptu *bayʿa* ceremony on 20 Shawwāl 788/14 November 1386 for qadis and notables to examine a testament produced by Zakariyyā᾿ naming him the legal successor to his uncle al-Muʿtaḍid. Barqūq robed his new caliph, assigned him a stipend, and a week later the amirs, qadis and *shaykh al-islām* returned for a formal *bayʿa* ceremony at the Citadel. After the new caliph entrusted Barqūq with authority over the Muslims, the participants were robed and authorities escorted al-Mustaʿṣim to his quarters. A final ceremony granted al-Mustaʿṣim (and the Abbasid family) a restoration of stewardship of the shrine of Sayyida Nafīsa in early Dhū al-Qaʿda 788/late November 1386, commemorated by another robing.[27]

The second attempt to restore power to the caliphate at the expense of

Barqūq involved disaffected *ʿulamāʾ* in Egypt and Syria rather than ambitious local amirs. The so-called *fitna Ẓāhiriyya* of 788/1386 in Damascus began as a revolt among several proponents attempting to revive the all-but-extinct Ẓāhirī school of Islam.[28] It is worth noting that some years earlier in 784/1382 Barqūq issued a decree ordering suspected Ẓāhirīs to be investigated and penalised. Significantly, the Ẓāhirī movement was a rebellion of religious scholars who did not agree with the caliphal institution that had evolved in the Islamic world over the preceding 400 years. Their goal was to depose Barqūq and restore political power to a new caliph descended from the Prophet's tribe of Quraysh. Interpreting al-Mutawakkil and his relatives as impotent figureheads compromised by their ties to elite circles, the Ẓāhirī scholars rejected the legitimacy of the Cairene Abbasids.[29] One important figure behind the revolt was the Egyptian scholar Abū Hishām Aḥmad ibn Muḥammad, known as Ibn al-Burhān (d. 808/1405), who was an admired acquaintance of al-Maqrīzī.[30]

Eventually, Barqūq had the conspirators arrested and sent to Cairo where he ordered them to be tortured until they revealed the names of amirs who had abetted them. The *fitna Ẓāhiriyya* also revealed powerful preachers capable of influencing the masses to agitate against the sultan's authority in the name of the caliph, whether he was an Abbasid or not.[31]

New challenges from abroad produced another moment of political importance for the Abbasid Caliphate. By the late 780s/1380s Barqūq struggled to balance both external and domestic threats. The career and conquests of Temür had started in earnest and the sultan and his entourage watched with fascination as the new enemy rapidly advanced westward.[32] As a non-Chinggisid, Temür's own claims to legitimacy involved a number of links to the legacy of Chinggis Khān; his status as royal 'son-in-law' by virtue of marriage ties to Chinggisid princesses, his claims to restore the Mongol Empire and uphold Mongol customary law, as well as his establishment and protection of Chinggisid puppet khāns.[33] The noteworthy fifteenth-century biographer of Temür, Aḥmad ibn ʿArabshāh (d. 854/1450) (who had been taken to Samarqand as a prisoner by the conqueror before returning to his native Syria in 824/1421–2), described the Chinggisids as the 'Quraysh of the Turks' and could not resist alluding to the similarity between puppet khāns and puppet caliphs:

> [Temür] set up [the Mongol puppet khān] Soyurghatmish to repel the calumnies of detractors and cut off the piercing point of every tongue . . . The khan was in his bondage, like a donkey in the mud, resembling the caliphs of this time in regard to the sultans.[34]

In Jumādā II 789/June 1387, Barqūq invited the caliph and other leading men of his administration to discuss Temür. To fund an expedition to stand against the latter in Syria and recoup his empty treasury, the sultan wanted to seize money from mosques and *waqf* endowments. After a lengthy debate in which the majority of the religious leadership opposed Barqūq, they reached an agreement to confiscate the wealth of the *waqfs* in the presence of the caliph.[35]

Despite relative calm during the reign of al-Mustaʿṣim, many of the amirs maintained an official position of antipathy attributed to the imprisonment of the caliph al-Mutawakkil, who persevered as an anti-Barquqid figurehead. Some of the Syrian amirs harnessed lingering resentment to stir up full-blown rebellion by Ṣafar 791/February 1389. At the centre was the governor of Aleppo, Yalbughā al-Nāṣirī, joined by Minṭāsh, a former *mamlūk* of Shaʿbān. Yalbughā al-Nāṣirī used the pretence of restoring a Qalawunid prince to power under the caliphal banner, to bolster his influence among the amirs of Syria, uniting them in opposition to Barqūq. Fearing that Yalbughā might capitalise on unresolved caliphate issues to undermine him, Barqūq returned al-Mutawakkil to tower confinement on 27 Ṣafar 791/25 February 1389 and banned all visits from the caliph's servants, family and entourage.[36]

Despite other precautions, an army that Barqūq sent to Damascus suffered defeat by Yalbughā al-Nāṣirī in mid-791/1389. The sultan sent peacemakers to Damascus thereafter, urging Yalbughā to fall into line with Barqūq, but the rebel amir declared his own status as a champion of al-Mutawakkil's right.

Evidently alive to the harm that mistreatment of the caliph had done to his image, Barqūq wasted no time in deposing al-Mustaʿṣim and publicly reattaching himself to al-Mutawakkil to strengthen his symbolic hold on power.[37] To this end the sultan invited the dishonoured caliph to the al-Rudaynī mosque in Rabīʿ I 791/March 1389, rising from his seat as al-Mutawakkil entered. The sultan begged the caliph to forgive the strained nature of their relationship and overlook the last six years of his incarceration. The two appeared to reconcile and mutually swore fidelity. Barqūq sent al-Mutawakkil home after lavishing him with gifts in excess of 10,000 dirhams; woollen garments, furs and Alexandrian silk.[38] The sultan also granted the caliph *iqṭāʿ* lands, reinstated his salary, as well as stewardship of the shrine of Sayyida Nafīsa which had been stripped from him along with its revenue streams some twenty-five years earlier.

Having united many of the Syrian amirs against the sultan, Yalbughā al-Nāṣirī himself raised the caliph's banners to destroy Barqūq, the 'usurper' of Qalawunids and Abbasids. As outposts such as Gaza and Ramla fell to the insurrection, the increasingly beleaguered sultan braced for a siege. Yalbughā's troops penetrated Egyptian territory and camped at Ṣāliḥiyya. Barqūq advanced to Maṭariyya, but fled back to Cairo after significant sectors of his forces deserted to the more powerful side.[39]

Desperation mounting, Barqūq announced the return of al-Mutawakkil to the caliphate and publicised his own position on 1 Jumādā I 791/28 April 1389 before a meeting of religious and military officials in the caliph's quarters of the Citadel. Again, Barqūq honoured the caliph and seated him, before the qadis administered a formal mutual pledge (*mubāyaʿa*) between caliph and sultan. The sultan gifted al-Mutawakkil with cash, fine goods and a gold-saddled grey mare from his own stock before allowing him to depart in great pomp. Barqūq staged another public reconciliation with the caliph some days later at the Nafīsī shrine in which the reinstatement of al-Mutawakkil was again acknowledged on 12 Jumādā I 791/9 May 1389, the caliph's name was officially restored to the Friday sermon, and his investiture diploma read aloud before the qadis and the viceroy (*nāʾib*) of Egypt. Attendees visited relics of the Prophet on display at the shrine, listened to readings from *Saḥīḥ Bukhārī*, and joined in prayers for Barqūq's victory in the impending showdown with the Syrian amirs. An entourage of scholars and qadis escorted al-Mutawakkil home from the ceremony. Some days before the caliph's name returned to the Friday sermon, Barqūq had sent al-Mutawakkil with a retinue of religious officials to ride through the streets of Cairo. In their company, a herald announced the rogue status of Yalbughā and Minṭāsh, the sultan's abolishment of non-canonical taxes and urged local denizens to fear God.[40]

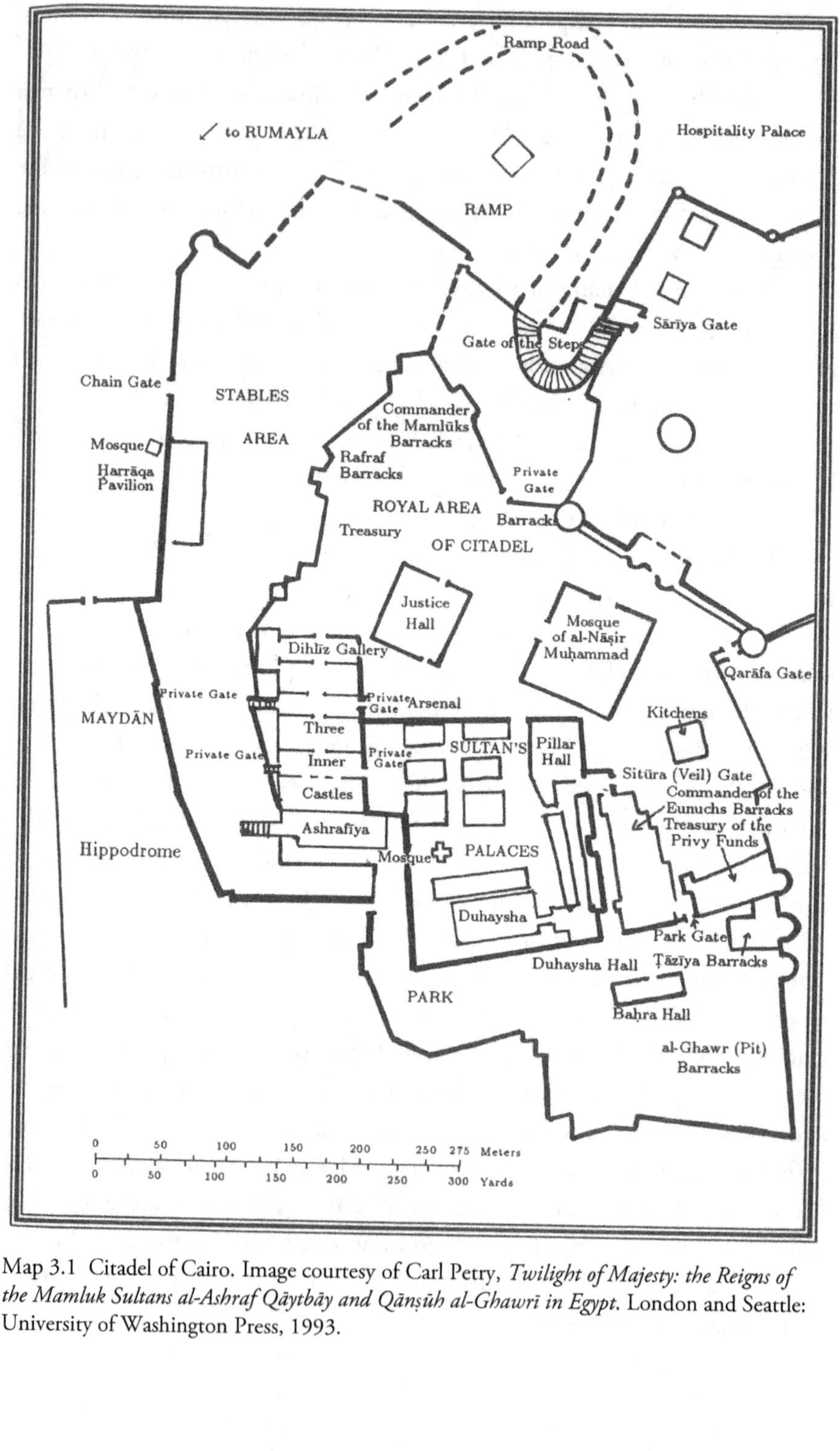

Map 3.1 Citadel of Cairo. Image courtesy of Carl Petry, *Twilight of Majesty: the Reigns of the Mamluk Sultans al-Ashraf Qāytbāy and Qānṣūh al-Ghawrī in Egypt*. London and Seattle: University of Washington Press, 1993.

Abundant, unconcealed pandering to al-Mutawakkil's position was Barqūq's attempt at retaining loyalty and popular support in the face of Yalbughā's power surge. This required, naturally, the denunciation of the caliphate of al-Mustaʿṣim whom the sultan arrested after formalising his deposition. Unsurprisingly, Barqūq's reinstatement of al-Mutawakkil failed to halt the rebel advance on Cairo. The sultan then hoped to settle matters with a confrontation beneath the city walls, though the battle fell short of a definitive outcome. Barqūq gradually lost the loyalty of his men as he continued attempts to raise morale. The caliph's endorsement was of minor consolation to the sultan who alternated fits of weeping with panicked disbursements to his *mamlūks*. At the same time, affairs improved for al-Mutawakkil, who received permission to come and go from his urban residence as he pleased.[41]

On 2 Jumādā II 791/29 May 1389, Barqūq and al-Mutawakkil made a final joint appearance to demonstrate mutual solidarity, this time mingling with the masses (*ʿāmma*) to whom they dispersed money behind the Palace of Hospitality (*Dār al-Ḍiyāfa*). Barqūq ultimately gained little from his eleventh-hour public relations campaign as it became evident that Cairo would soon be overwhelmed. As the forces of Yalbughā al-Nāṣirī closed in, Barqūq contemplated a formal surrender, but ultimately went into hiding, abandoning al-Mutawakkil at his unguarded dwelling after the final congregational prayer of the night.[42]

Upon entering Cairo, Yalbughā allowed his major collaborator Minṭāsh to seize the vacant Citadel on 5 Jumādā II 791/1 June 1389. While the victors busied themselves with plunder, al-Mutawakkil sauntered down from his quarters and introduced himself. Minṭāsh escorted the caliph to the Dome of Victory (*Qubbat al-Naṣr*) and entered the tent of Yalbughā, who respectfully engaged the Abbasid caliph in amiable conversation. The victorious amir reassured the caliph that all along, his sole intention had been to restore the caliph's rightful authority: 'O our master! Commander of the Faithful! My sword strikes not but to aid your cause!'[43]

The amirs included the caliph in advisory sessions at the Gate of the Chain (*Bāb al-Silsila*) to discuss the divisive issue of succession to Barqūq. Just as he had nipped in the bud any attempts to hand him the sultanate at ʿAqaba, al-Mutawakkil prudently recommended that the office be returned to a worthy Qalawunid, and thus al-Ṣāliḥ Ḥājjī was restored by way of caliphal *bayʿa* in Jumādā II 791/June 1389. Later that month, Ḥājjī conferred lofty honours (*tashrīf jalīl*) on al-Mutawakkil and other dignitaries as the investiture deed was read to observers. Compliant in signing all orders set before him, al-Mutawakkil sustained himself as an indispensable fount of legitimacy and later retired comfortably to his Citadel residence.[44]

Chaos crippled Cairo in the weeks that followed as victorious rebel forces pillaged the city and impoverished Cairenes helped themselves to the leftovers.[45] Yalbughā al-Nāṣirī stationed the caliph in a private tent secluded from the other qadis and notables who came to congratulate him. Despite enjoying majority support among the amirs, Yalbughā dared not risk alienating his powerful ally Minṭāsh. He made a show of refusing the sultanate when it was offered to him; instead, he produced an order co-signed by the caliph to free compatriots who Barqūq had imprisoned in Alexandria. With a manhunt for the fugitive sultan underway, Yalbughā began to make new appointments for every major position below the caliphate itself.

Rebel forces discovered Barqūq before long and exiled him to al-Karak, as escalating tensions between Yalbughā and Minṭāsh erupted in Shaʿbān 791/July–August 1389. Al-Mutawakkil, who had kept a low profile in the interim, found himself involved in politics once again. Minṭāsh had stealthily accumulated support and resources by winning Yalbughā's *mamlūk*s to his side. Yalbughā sent the caliph to parlay with his former rival, whereupon Minṭāsh feigned loyalty to Ḥājjī while vowing revenge against Yalbughā the 'usurper' who Minṭāsh claimed had deprived him of prime *iqṭāʿ*s and 500,000 dirhams. Disregarding the good offices of the Commander of the Faithful, Minṭāsh bellowed his grievances even as al-Mutawakkil turned his back and left.

After the caliph's debriefing, Yalbughā rallied his troops for a confrontation against Minṭāsh that resulted in stalemate. Eventually, Minṭāsh secured the upper hand over his former ally as news arrived that Barqūq had escaped from prison, rallied support at al-Karak and raised an army among the Bedouins. Against this new threat, Minṭāsh hoarded resources and attempted to attract the old stalwarts of Barqūq. He also took steps to strengthen his position by having Ḥājjī invest him in place of Yalbughā as *atābak al-ʿasākir* on 7 Shawwāl 791/29 September 1389. The same month, he also divorced his wife in order to marry a daughter of al-Mutawakkil.[46]

After a preliminary meeting to number the crimes of Barqūq, Minṭāsh summoned the caliph, qadis and *ʿulamāʾ* on 21 Dhū al-Qaʿda 791/11 November 1389 to finish drafting a fatwa on the legality of declaring war against the former sultan. Attending personnel drafted the document condemning Barqūq on the grounds that he had wrongfully deposed both Ḥājjī and al-Mutawakkil and fought Muslims with non-Muslim allies. Ten copies of the document were co-signed by qadis and notables. Four days later, Minṭāsh met with amirs and government officials, including al-Mutawakkil and the qadis, to confirm the maturity and competence of Ḥājjī. The first act of the sultan's majority was the declaration of war on Barqūq.[47]

Amid the upheaval unleashed on Cairo during the uprising against Barqūq, the Faraj Gate (*Bāb al-Faraj*) had sustained damage significant enough for authorities to order it sealed, effectively restricting access to the Aydugmish alleyway (*khūkha*) and disturbing daily life for a small sector of the populace. Although details remain sparse, unhappy residents managed to receive an audience with al-Mutawakkil, whom they prevailed upon to intercede with Minṭāsh, ultimately persuading him to clear the debris and re-open it.[48]

In exchange for a last-minute affirmation of al-Mutawakkil's support, Minṭāsh guaranteed that the caliph's cousin Zakariyyāʾ al-Mustaʿṣim would never again pose a threat to his caliphate. As a sign of good faith, Minṭāsh seized the former caliph from his home on 15 Dhū al-Ḥijja 791/5 December 1389, confiscated sensitive documents (including a diploma naming him *walī al-ʿahd* by his father), and imprisoned him in the Silver Hall (*Qāʿat al-Fiḍḍa*) of the Citadel.[49]

Minṭāsh ordered the qadis to join his camp on the outskirts of Cairo at Raydāniyya, and, on 22 Dhū al-Ḥijja 791/12 December 1389, led a vanguard of amirs as the remaining forces followed in the company of al-Mutawakkil and the qadis. After a pitched battle against the resurgent forces of Barqūq at Shaqḥab south of Damascus in early 792/1390, Minṭāsh fled, abandoning the sultan Ḥājjī, al-Mutawakkil and the chief qadis to Barqūq. After seizing the coffers of his foe and stripping the qadis of their possessions, the former sultan set minds at ease with gracious speech.[50]

Barqūq emerged victorious, and having captured Ḥājjī's royal banners, posed beneath them flanked by the vanquished sultan and the caliph, as soldiers from the defeated army steadily swelled his ranks.[51] At his camp in Shaqḥab, Barqūq assembled notables and amirs in the presence of al-Mutawakkil and the qadis. His first act was to depose Ḥājjī from the sultanate and renew his sovereignty through caliphal *bayʿa*. A new ceremony re-established Barqūq as sultan, after which he rode into a decorated Cairo on 14 Ṣafar 792/1 February 1390 with the caliph and qadis leading the way to calm tensions. Anxious to emphasise the validity of his return in Egypt, Barqūq wasted little time in staging a repeat of his installation ceremony with al-Mutawakkil, the qadis and the *shaykh al-islām*. Barqūq and the caliph exchanged black Abbasid robes, and on 23 Ṣafar 792/10 February 1390 a copy of the sultan's investiture deed was read at the Palace of Justice (*Dār al-ʿAdl*) after which al-Mutawakkil was robed in the company of other dignitaries.

Having repaired his troubled relationship with the caliph before his flight from Cairo, Barqūq made no attempt to penalise al-Mutawakkil for collaborating with Yalbughā and Minṭāsh. Late fourteenth-/early fifteenth-century historians such as Ibn Ṣaṣrā and Ibn Ḥajar claim the sultan was kind to the caliph for the remainder of his reign.[52] Al-Mutawakkil quietly resumed his reign during the second act of Barqūq's political career while the sultan focused his attention on Temür. However, neither Barqūq nor his chancery relied much on the sultan's proximity to the Abbasid Caliphate in official correspondence with Temür.[53]

Others in the region shared Cairo's disquiet over the ambitions of Temür. In late 796/1394, neighbouring rulers sent envoys to Egypt seeking anti-Temür alliances, including the Ottoman sultan Bāyezīd. In his communications with Bāyezīd, Temür had reminded the Ottoman sultan of Barqūq's slave status, as well as his audacious imprisonment of al-Mutawakkil and usurpation of the Qalawunid throne. In his correspondence with Temür, Barqūq, through his chancery, expressed incredulity that Temür should demand submission after the sultan of Cairo had already yielded to the authority of 'the commander of the faithful and caliph of the Prophet of God, lord of the worlds'.[54]

Despite growing Ottoman power fuelled by conquest and expansion, Bāyezīd encountered many rivals among the other march lords or beys of Anatolia, local dynastic rulers whose domains, the beyliks, the Ottomans ultimately absorbed. Bāyezīd requested an Abbasid investiture diploma recognising him as the heir of the Seljuks, and, according to some sources, Barqūq sent his governor of al-Karak to the Ottoman sultan with the requested document.[55] The blessing of the caliph, backed by the endorsement of Barqūq's strong political order carried clout in the region and may have supplemented other Ottoman legitimacy claims. In return, the sultan of Cairo wanted Bāyezīd to abandon his plans to attack other allies in the region. The Ottoman sultan obliged this request until Barqūq's death.[56]

Barqūq prepared to leave on expedition against Temür and dispersed dirhams to his subordinates, offering sums of 1,060 dirhams to every commander and 10,000 to the caliph. After borrowing thousands of dinars from local merchants, the sultan set out for Damascus with al-Mutawakkil and the other chief religious functionaries in 796/1394. After little more than a standoff interrupted by several skirmishes with Temür's forces near the Euphrates, the sultan returned to Cairo with the Egyptian army.[57]

Barring a number of public processions, Egyptian sources mention little concerning al-Mutawakkil during the final five years of Barqūq's rule.[58] Perhaps in the light of the sultan's troubled relationship with the caliphate, Clément Onimus also suggests that the role of the *shaykh al-islām* somewhat eclipsed that of the Abbasid caliph as spiritual guarantor of temporal authority during the second reign of Barqūq.[59]

Vassal polities subordinate to the Cairo Sultanate such as those of Mārdīn and Sīwās, minted coins and pronounced the *khuṭba* in Barqūq's name rather than that of al-Mutawakkil, which, according to Broadbridge, implies that they considered loyalty to the caliphate less a matter of Islamic unity and more a show of deference to Cairo's positioning atop the regional hierarchy.[60] At the dawn of the fifteenth century in Cairo, the caliph maintained his public persona and attended several funerary prayers as a high-profile guest of honour and occasional prayer leader for amirs, scholars, colleagues and family members.[61]

The sultan himself passed away after an illness on 15 Shawwāl 801/20 June 1399. The day before his death Barqūq, wishing to transmit the sultanate to his heirs the way that al-Nāṣir Muḥammad had done, summoned al-Mutawakkil, the qadis and prominent notables to discuss succession in his council chamber. Barqūq unwittingly set a precedent for the majority of his successors among the later Circassian sultans by having the caliph pledge to guarantee the succession of the sultan's son after the death of the father. The qadis, amirs and officials took the oath as well and swore to a succession list of Barqūq's eldest son Faraj followed by his brothers ʿAbd al-ʿAzīz and Ibrāhīm. Barqūq's testament included the stipulation that the executors of his final orders be formally subject to the sanction and supervision (*imḍāʾ*) of al-Mutawakkil. It was in this sense that the later sultans began to employ the caliph as guarantor of their dynastic aspirations, even though the caliph had no practical power to enforce any such requests.[62]

Al-Nāṣir Faraj, 801–15/1399–1412

After Barqūq died, his eldest son Faraj appeared before the amirs who summoned al-Mutawakkil and the religious dignitaries to the royal stables of the Citadel. The caliph delivered a sermon before pledging allegiance to the young Faraj as sultan with authority over the Muslims on 15 Shawwāl 801/20 June 1399. Donning Abbasid black, al-Malik al-Nāṣir Faraj ascended the Citadel on horseback with royal emblems and later draped al-Mutawakkil in a magnificent robe as his father's amirs prepared for the royal funeral. The next day the investiture deed for Faraj was read in the presence of the caliph, the chief secretary of the chancery (*kātib al-sirr*) Fatḥ al-Dīn Fatḥ Allāh (d. 816/1413), and other military and religious dignitaries.[63]

Controlled by his father's amirs from the outset and anxious to assert independence, Faraj spent several months prevailing upon Barqūq's executors to acknowledge his maturity. The amirs, deeply fragmented after the death of the sultan, were split over the decision. Faraj ultimately prevailed and al-Mutawakkil, the qadis and the *shaykh al-islām* appeared on 6 Rabīʿ I 802/6 November 1399 to officiate and receive commemorative robes.[64] A participant described the ceremony to the chancery scribe Aḥmad al-Qalqashandī:

> First, the caliph [al-Mutawakkil] and the *shaykh al-islām* Sirāj al-Dīn al-Bulqīnī presented themselves, [followed by] the four qadis, the scholars (*ahl al-ʿilm*), the notable amirs (*umarāʾ al-dawla*) at a location near the sultan's stables known as the Ḥarrāqa. The caliph sat in the centre of the congregation upon a seat which had been covered (*mafrūsh*) for him. Next entered the sultan, who at that time was very young (*hadathun*), and sat before [the caliph]. The *shaykh al-islām* asked if he had reached maturity,

> and the sultan confirmed that he had. The caliph delivered a *khuṭba*, and then informed the sultan that he had delegated authority to him according to the aforementioned ceremonial. A black garment was then brought to the caliph, an embroidered black turban, covered with a black embroidered *tarḥa*. The caliph returned to his seat, and a throne was erected next to the seat of the caliph for the sultan, who took his place. The qadis and amirs sat around him according to rank. For his investiture of the sultan, the caliph received a gift of one thousand dinars and fabric from Alexandria.[65]

Worried that the amirs of Syria would harbour initial misgivings about the succession of Barqūq's underage son, authorities in Cairo agreed on 16 Shawwāl 801/21 June 1399 to send al-Mutawakkil and a group of amirs with the courier rider (*ʿalā ʾl-barīd*) to reassure the deputies in Syria, secure their allegiance and return with testaments pledging their loyalty to Faraj.[66] Tensions between the amiral households created confusion during the early reign of Faraj, as some of his father's amirs attempted to wrest control from the young sultan. Ultimately, the political order established by the Barquqid sultanate of Cairo would crumble as it slid into a twelve-year civil war. Over the course of his troubled reign Faraj had to make at least seven expeditions to Syria to secure control there. To emphasise his moral superiority and divine favour, Faraj frequently travelled with the caliph and chief qadis.[67]

Meanwhile, Temür and his forces approached the frontier territory of the sultanate to exploit the chaos that had followed the death of the powerful Barqūq. Hitherto, the somewhat over-extended conqueror may have avoided a direct confrontation with Barqūq's polity due to the formidable military strength and the relative stability existing in the territories of the Cairo Sultanate by 801/1398–9.

To secure the loyalty of his officers in the face of Temür's renewed threat to the hinterland, Faraj maintained consistent payments to his supporters and soldiers. On 27 Muḥarram 803/17 September 1400, the sultan convened al-Mutawakkil, the qadis and his main administrators to obtain a fatwa permitting the extraction of money from merchants to cover the expenses of preparing to face Temür. The sultan's advisers cautioned him against acting in ways which contravened the *sharīʿa*, and other arrangements to obtain funds had to be made.[68]

The forces of Temür descended on the Syrian cities of Aleppo and Ḥamā in Rabīʿ I 803/October 1400, and after inflicting carnage on the inhabitants, headed towards Damascus. Faraj and the amirs mustered their forces to confront Temür early the next month with the caliph in tow, heading first towards Raydāniyya, then Gaza. Faraj and the caliph entered Damascus on 6 Jumādā I/23 December, and for several days awaited the arrival of Temür's forces. After minor scuffles between the opposing sides, the Egyptian amirs, plagued by internecine bickering, whisked Faraj back to Cairo. As Damascus fell to the same grisly plight as the other Syrian cities, Faraj returned to Cairo with al-Mutawakkil on 5 Jumādā II 803/21 January 1401.[69] Unsure of Temür's plans, the political elite struggled to gather funds to carry on a resistance and included the caliph, qadis and a group of *shaykh*s in preparations to return to Damascus.[70] As for Cairo, which had abandoned the Syrian territories to absorb the brunt of Temür's aggression, the conqueror demanded little from the vanquished beyond payment of tribute and the minting of coins in his name.[71]

Temür granted amnesty to Damascus a month later on 11 Rajab 803/25 February 1401. While encamped outside the city, he held a famous summit with Ibn Khaldūn. Among other things, the pair discussed assiduous support for Abbasid legitimacy within the territories of the Cairo Sultanate.[72]

In Ṣafar 804/September 1401, a group of leading Cairene amirs, including Nawrūz al-Ḥāfiẓī, Jakam, Sūdūn Ṭāz and others, increasingly frustrated both by their own internal struggles and by the unsatisfactory rule of Faraj, boycotted his court, sought to rebel against the sultan and fought each other for supremacy. Faraj sent the caliph and qadis to intercede with the disgruntled parties, but ultimately tried to appease them through coveted appointments and other gifts. When tensions flared up some months later, on 2 Shawwāl 804/5 May 1402, Faraj again called upon the chief religious functionaries and ordered them to descend into the city to visit the displeased amirs and persuade them to swear allegiance to the sultan. When the amirs planned to attack the Citadel, on 14 Shawwāl 804/17 May 1402, Faraj rode out with the caliph and brought the battle to Qarāfa. Those loyal to the sultan met their foes, whom they defeated and captured, while others like Nawrūz and Jakam fled. Faraj returned to the Citadel to celebrate his victory with the caliph and qadis.[73]

After the Battle of Ankara in 804/1402 Temür wrote to Cairo from Izmir to inform Faraj of the defeat of the Ottomans. In Jumādā I 805/November–December 1402, the sultan ordered the caliph, qadis and important amirs to be on hand to greet a pair of messengers sent by Temür who had arrived from Damietta the previous month. The meeting was to conclude the peace with Faraj and his amirs, and included the promise that Temür would not encroach on any territories of the sultanate of Cairo. Various amirs offered their counsel to the sultan, while al-Mutawakkil and the qadis also received a platform to sound out their opinions.[74] In the reply, the Egyptian chancery informed Temür that the sultan had met to confer with the caliph and other reputable men of his *dawla*, and that after careful consideration they had agreed to accept the peace. The language of the letter allowed the chancery to convey to Temür that Faraj (although officially a humbled vassal) had a choice in the matter and was able to consult the Abbasid caliph and other chief advisers.[75]

Sedition tended to escalate quickly in Syria, and amirs hostile to Faraj's rule ultimately bucked Cairo's authority in Damascus. Although the sultan's name was removed from the Friday sermon in many mosques of the city by Ramaḍān 807/March 1405, most continued to offer prayers in the name of al-Mutawakkil.[76]

By Dhū al-Ḥijja 807/June 1405, when a vanguard of rebel Syrian amirs approached Egypt, Faraj met them at Raydāniyya. The sultan lost the battle and hastily withdrew, leaving behind the Abbasid caliph, the qadis, 300 royal *mamlūk*s and much of his own baggage which briefly fell into enemy hands until the sultan's forces recovered them following a counterattack.[77]

Believing himself in a more secure position, Faraj pardoned the majority of vanquished amirs while imprisoning others in Alexandria to break their power. The sultan reorganised his realm and hoped to pacify Nawrūz by making him governor of Damascus at the expense of the amir Shaykh al-Maḥmūdī. Nevertheless, the Syrian amirs regrouped once more and forced the sultan into hiding in Cairo as unrest grew.

The rebels successfully occupied the Citadel on 25 Rabīʿ I 808/20 September 1405, but failed to agree on whom to name as sultan. After seizing al-Mutawakkil and the qadis, the amirs Yashbak and Baybars agreed on another Barquqid prince, ʿAbd al-ʿAzīz, who had already received the caliph's approval in accordance with Barqūq's final testament. The caliph, qadis and leading amirs administered the oath at the Citadel and dressed the third Barquqid sultan ʿAbd al-ʿAzīz in caliphal garb as al-Malik al-Manṣūr. Two months later Faraj emerged unexpectedly from hiding to recapture the Citadel with fresh forces on the morning of 5 Jumāda II 808/28 November 1405. He reaffirmed his pledge with al-Mutawakkil and the qadis, and announced the deposition of his younger brother in preparation for his return to the throne.[78]

Al-Mutawakkil's long reign ended a month later on 27 Rajab 808/ January 18 1406. He left the caliphate by testament to his son Aḥmad as al-Muʿtamid ʿalā Allāh, but removed him in favour of another son, Abū al-Faḍl al-ʿAbbās.[79] A grand state funeral demonstrated the esteem and adoration that al-Mutawakkil had enjoyed for decades among the populace. The caliph was then interred with his kinsmen near the Abbasid residence close to the shrine of Sayyida Nafīsa.[80]

The profile of the caliphal office rose domestically and externally during the reign of al-Mutawakkil. Competing factions even considered the caliph a viable candidate for the sultanate on at least three occasions, though he was frequently punished with deposition and imprisonment for crossing the line (voluntarily or not) into politics. Muḥammad Surūr suggests that Qalawunid charisma, even its vestiges, combined with the instability of the shorter Barquqid period, may have spurred al-Mutawakkil to turn away from opportunity and reject the sultanate. Even so, there is reason to believe that the caliph was not frightened by the possible consequences of reaching for the sultanate. There is room enough to imagine him biding his time, the better to revive the power and glory of the early caliphate once the Qalawunids had sufficiently faded.[81] The emergence of the Barquqid line, however, thwarted any such hopes. Even so, for many amirs the caliph remained a more palatable ruling symbol than a new patrimonial sultan. It is not without significance that Barqūq took great pains to demonstrate to his detractors that the caliph was pleased with him.[82]

With the reign of al-Mutawakkil, the position of the caliph began to receive opportunities to arbitrate between competing factions. Although the caliph tended to be the mouthpiece for the sultan or dominant amir, rival parties often had to accept that the caliph represented 'that which was most pleasing to God and the Prophet'. Yalbughā al-Nāṣirī and later Faraj could scarcely do better than to send al-Mutawakkil to negotiate with the very amirs who claimed to rebel in his name.

The Caliph-Sultan: Al-Mustaʿīn bi-llāh, 808–16/1406–14

Following the death of al-Mutawakkil, the caliphate passed to his son Abū al-Faḍl al-ʿAbbās. In an investiture ceremony on 1 Shaʿbān 808/22 January 1406, Faraj robed the new caliph as al-Mustaʿīn bi-llāh before dismissing him to return to the Abbasid residence.[83]

During his second reign, Faraj sought to concentrate power in the sultan's household and maintain the strength of his position. Although he was largely successful in Cairo, Syria, where he had sent many of the disgruntled actors from his Cairo conflicts, predictably became a hotbed of rebellion.[84] From 808 to 815/1405 to 1412, the rebel amirs Nawrūz and Shaykh pursued their attempts in Syria to establish authority independent of the sultan in Cairo. Faraj continued his expeditions to subdue them as the Syro-Egyptian territories of the sultanate further descended into a ruinous civil war. The new caliph al-Mustaʿīn and the chief qadis were regular participants in the sultan's ceremonial processions. On one official outing, after having arrived in Syria in Ṣafar 812/July 1409, the caliph and qadis read from long proclamations urging Damascenes to resist the amir Shaykh. Initially defeated by Faraj in Syria a month later, Shaykh was obliged to seek the sultan's forgiveness. A delegation consisting of al-Mustaʿīn, the amir Taghrībirdī and the *kātib al-sirr* Fatḥ Allāh greeted Shaykh near the moat (*al-khandaq*) at the gateway near the Citadel. As Taghrībirdī and Fatḥ Allāh scolded Shaykh for his rebellion against the sultan, the Abbasid caliph, charged with reporting the details of Shaykh's explanation to the sultan, observed the conversation. The presence of the caliph as a symbol of authority lent an official, albeit silent, theocratic approval to formal expressions of displeasure with Shaykh.[85]

Nevertheless, by 813/1410 Shaykh and Nawrūz resumed their defiance in Syria supported by some of Barqūq's former Ẓāhiriyya *mamlūk*s. Quelling the unrest occupied the final two years of Faraj's reign. The caliph and qadis attended another summer expedition to Damascus in Rabīʿ I 813/July 1410 in which the sultan intended to fight Shaykh once again.[86]

In late 814/March 1412, Faraj embarked on what was to be his last campaign against rebellious Syrian amirs. By the end of the year the sultan camped at Raydāniyya with al-Mustaʿīn and the four chief qadis near the shrine of Barqūq. During battle many of the sultan's troops deserted in favour of Shaykh and Nawrūz amid reports that Faraj was often too drunk to function. In Muḥarram 815/April 1412, victory appeared to be nigh for the rebel amirs, though without an agreeable candidate to replace Faraj.[87]

The Sultanate of the Caliph, 25 Muḥarram–1 Shaʿbān 815/ 7 May–6 November 1412

Poised to consolidate their victory over Faraj, the alliance between Shaykh, Nawrūz and another collaborator, Baktamur al-Ẓāhirī (known as Julaq), quickly unravelled as each sought to seize the sultanate. It became clear, however, that for the time being, an interim figurehead was required to prevent the exacerbation of the existing chaos. Opportunely, having been abandoned in al-Lajjūn by the fleeing sultan, the caliph al-Mustaʿīn and *kātib al-sirr* Fatḥ Allāh had fallen into the hands of the rebel amirs who wasted no time in summoning Fatḥ Allāh for his counsel on whom to appoint to the sultanate. Al-Mustaʿīn appeared to be a desirable contender, as his office had the potential to undermine critical support for Faraj, whose own popularity could not compete with the appeal of the black Abbasid standard.[88] Al-Mustaʿīn, himself the son of a popular caliph, was also more appealing than the infant son of Faraj. Acting on that advice, Shaykh called in al-Mustaʿīn before the amirs.

Fifteenth-century Egyptian sources emphasise that al-Mustaʿīn vehemently opposed the suggestion at once. Unwilling to accept refusal, the amirs embarked on a campaign of persuasion. They initially sent Fatḥ Allāh to the caliph, but al-Mustaʿīn could not be swayed due to his deep fear of deposition from the caliphate, or worse, death, and the lingering dread that Faraj would evade capture in Damascus, return to power and torture him. Fatḥ Allāh returned and advised the amirs that al-Mustaʿīn's unwillingness was such that they would have to pursue a different tack to finesse the compliance of the caliph.[89]

The amirs next approached the amir Nāṣir al-Dīn Muḥammad ibn Mubārakshāh al-Ṭāzī (d. 823/1420), a non-Abbasid half-brother of the caliph, to persuade al-Mustaʿīn to assume the sultanate. In exchange for his cooperation, Shaykh and Nawrūz offered Ibn Mubārakshāh a second-class amirate and the position of *dawādār* to the new sultan. Ibn Mubārakshāh set out to visit al-Mustaʿīn, while a herald rode before him to announce the deposition of Faraj by the caliph and to publicise bans against aiding the former sultan. The amirs sent an official document for al-Mustaʿīn to sign that inventoried the offences of Faraj and legitimised his deposition by the caliph. Such assurances did little to ease the caliph's anxiety over the possible return of Faraj, and al-Mustaʿīn chastised his half-brother for his dangerous meddling. Nevertheless, with Faraj weakened and besieged in Damascus, the caliph's fears gradually abated. After final negotiations with Fatḥ Allāh, al-Mustaʿīn agreed to assume the sultanate with some reservation. One of his reportedly numerous caveats, was that if he were ever to be removed from the sultanate al-Mustaʿīn must at least retain the caliphate, which all parties found agreeable. The qadis validated the unprecedented succession and al-Mustaʿīn assumed office as sultan on 25 Muḥarram 815/7 May 1412. A *bayʿa* ceremony for the first ever caliph-sultan followed so that the amirs could demonstrate fidelity and obedience. The attendees swore that the caliph would be free to act independently in matters of governance. The amirs arranged for the name of al-Mustaʿīn and news of his succession to the sultanate to be proclaimed in the streets of Damascus.[90]

As Hassan illustrates, the caliph's accession produced a new polarity in late medieval Syro-Egyptian politics, splitting the amirs and their households between those who accepted the sultanate of al-Mustaʿīn, in opposition to former supporters of Faraj. The issue received lively debate, with each side repudiating the other as rebels.[91]

With an improvised black 'caliphal robe' confiscated from the *khaṭīb* of the Karīm al-Dīn mosque, Shaykh's followers erected a makeshift throne for al-Mustaʿīn outside the building and stood before the caliph-sultan according to rank, with the exception of Nawrūz who was busy fighting forces loyal to Faraj. In line with the customs of a new sultan and breaking with caliphal protocol, the amirs all kissed the ground at al-Mustaʿīn's feet.[92] The caliph-sultan retained his Abbasid regnal name. While historiographical sources do not often provide any new honorific as sultan, other sources indicate that al-Mustaʿīn also reigned as 'al-Malik al-ʿĀdil', though some coins struck in the caliph's name fail to include his sultanic title.[93]

As sultan, al-Mustaʿīn followed the amirs on procession, while a herald warned supporters of Faraj to surrender within the week if they expected amnesty. Al-Mustaʿīn led the army further to al-Muṣallī before heading back to his previous position and ordered proclamations to be read in the eastern neighbourhoods of Damascus.[94]

The caliph's accession precipitated a minor spiritual crisis for Damascenes loyal to Faraj who deserted the beleaguered sultan, in fear 'of the results, in this world and the next, of disobedience to the Commander of the Faithful'.[95] We are told that al-Mustaʿīn then began to affix his mark or motto (*ʿalāma*) on the decrees (a task reserved to the sultan, which he was) and eased without reservation into certain sultanic prerogatives. Fifteenth-century Egyptian sources are unclear as to the nature of directives as well as the early power relationship between al-Mustaʿīn and Shaykh, though they suggest that the caliph-sultan initially received full executive control over appointments and removals combined with the issuing of proclamations in Syria. Al-Mustaʿīn wrote to the Egyptian amirs, demanded their submission as sultan, and announced his commitment to upholding religion by abolishing non-*sharīʿa* taxes (*maẓālim wa-mukūs*), a token gesture for any incoming sultan.[96]

The caliph-sultan invested a new grand qadi for the Shāfiʿī rite in Egypt, Shihāb al-Dīn Aḥmad al-Bāʿūnī, to replace the influential Jalāl al-Dīn al-Bulqīnī (d. 824/1421) who had remained in Damascus with Faraj as the latter desperately fought to maintain his position. Faraj and his supporters stepped up their efforts and even welcomed reinforcements among the amirs and fortress commanders sent by the head of the Aqquyunlu Turkmen configuration Qarā Yülük (805–39/1403–35). A proclamation advised the caliph-sultan's army to fight the Aqquyunlu reinforcements with the same fervour as if they had been dispatched by Temür himself.[97] In preparation, the amirs and *mamlūk*s reaffirmed their commitment to al-Mustaʿīn as caliph-sultan:

> [They] pledged to the Commander of the Faithful that they would maintain their obedience to him and obey his commands, that they were pleased that he was ruler over them, that he should have absolute control of affairs devoid of reference to anyone, and that they would not make anyone sultan so long as he lived. They then kissed the ground before him and all submitted to the Commander of the Faithful al-Mustaʿīn bi-llāh.[98]

Contemporary sources support the idea that the caliph's presence proved to be crucial for Shaykh and Nawrūz in their ongoing struggle against Faraj, who in addition to his sizeable Turkmen following, enjoyed popularity among the people.[99] Despite Shaykh's access to caliphal authority and his growing influence in Damascus, Nawrūz, busy on campaign, remained content for the time being as he tried to secure political advantage. Shaykh sent Fatḥ Allāh to Nawrūz to accept his pledge of loyalty to al-Mustaʿīn. Nawrūz kissed the ground for the caliph-sultan and expressed joy that al-Mustaʿīn had assumed 'unrestricted authority'. Delighted by anything that checked Shaykh's power, Nawrūz stressed that al-Mustaʿīn's authority must not be curtailed in any way and that the caliph-sultan should enjoy a free hand to take up governance.[100]

The amirs learned that supporters of Faraj planned to rescue him from Nawrūz's siege by setting Ḥajjāj castle ablaze thereby allowing the embattled sultan to reach Turkmen allies waiting on the other side. Shaykh rushed al-Mustaʿīn to the front to witness what appeared to be the last major battle against the soon-to-be deposed sultan. In the end, Faraj escaped again to the Damascus Citadel after several key amirs abandoned him in favour of rallying beneath the Abbasid banner.[101]

Encouraged by the unifying charisma of the caliph-sultan which held a magnetic draw over enemy forces, the amirs moved on to Damascus in pursuit of Faraj and lodged al-Mustaʿīn just outside the city. After a brief siege, Faraj sued for peace on 10 Ṣafar 815/22 May 1412. Ibn Mubārakshāh delivered an oath signed by the amirs to Faraj, who had no choice but submission. The amirs granted amnesty and forced him to concede that al-Mustaʿīn would remain sultan.[102]

A conference of amirs, scholars and jurists convened at al-Mustaʿīn's temporary residence in Damascus at the Palace of the Deputy (*Qaṣr al-Nāʾib*) to discuss the fate of Faraj. Amid intense deliberations, Shaykh, who had previously tasted the clemency of the deposed sultan, favoured deportation to Alexandria over execution. If Shaykh became sultan, allowing Faraj to survive would also prove to be useful in applying pressure on potential political rivals such as Nawrūz or even al-Mustaʿīn. Nawrūz, on the other hand, who had absorbed the brunt of the recent fighting against Faraj, lusted for blood and was likewise inclined towards any option that offered potential to thwart

Shaykh's interests. As for al-Mustaʿīn, his anxieties concerning Faraj were well-known and thus the caliph-sultan used his influence with the *ʿulamāʾ* to secure a death sentence for the ousted sultan. The Ḥanafī qadi Ibn al-ʿAdīm likewise advocated for execution and appealed to the weighted opinion of the caliph-sultan in arguments against jurists and amirs favouring exile. With support from al-Mustaʿīn, Nawrūz and Ibn al-ʿAdīm, the pro-execution party soon included Fatḥ Allāh. Ibn al-ʿAdīm testified to the legality of the decision and secured legal validation. Several days later Faraj was humiliated, tortured and made to suffer a gruesome death on 16 Ṣafar 815/28 May 1412.[103] The contentious execution became a sore point for many as Faraj had already surrendered on acceptable terms.

During the period of transition between Faraj and al-Mustaʿīn, in addition to living quarters the amirs established an interim court for the caliph-sultan at the Palace of the Deputy in Damascus which hosted weekly meetings for some time after the execution. While in session, Shaykh and Nawrūz flanked the caliph-sultan. Initially, the two amirs agreed to escort al-Mustaʿīn to Cairo with the understanding that they would wait on him: Shaykh as *amīr kabīr* and *atābak al-ʿasākir*; Nawrūz as *atābak* of the guard of the armies, and the pair divvied up *iqṭāʿ* land and finalised living arrangements. On 25 Ṣafar 815/6 June 1412, however, Shaykh managed to dupe Nawrūz into remaining in Syria. Al-Mustaʿīn named Nawrūz deputy of Syria after removing Baktamur Julaq, who was to return to Cairo. With Nawrūz invested over all of Syria, the domains of the sultanate were roughly partitioned in half.[104] Nawrūz received full rights over the cities of Syria with the power to assign land grants as he pleased, provided he informed al-Mustaʿīn of *de facto* appointments for purposes of issuing official diplomas. This granted Shaykh the free hand in Egypt he had desired all along.

Early during his time as sultan and apparently unaware of Shaykh's true ambitions, al-Mustaʿīn organised his government by selecting or deposing ministers and amirs. To all appearances, the caliph-sultan faced no restrictions in shoring up his administration as he saw fit. This freedom may have encouraged the impression that the caliph's sultanate was genuine and helped to ease some of his initial misgivings.[105] Confident in his control of affairs, the caliph-sultan expressed his orders to the Turkmen, Druze and Bedouin thus:

> From the servant of God and his *walī*, the *imām* al-Mustaʿīn bi-llāh, caliph of the Lord of the Worlds, cousin of the Master of the Prophets; the one to whom obedience is incumbent upon all creatures – God strengthen the faith through his preservation.[106]

The caliph-sultan sent his next communiqué to Cairene notables and the orators of the three important city mosques: Ibn Ṭūlūn, al-Ḥākim and al-Azhar. Mosque officials read the letters from the *minbars* and announced that Faraj had been defeated by the Abbasid caliph. According to some sources, the people rejoiced in the markets and called out for victory and aid to the Commander of the Faithful. A missive to Cairo dated 4 Rabīʿ I/14 June contained the earliest commands of al-Mustaʿīn, including an order for the release of amirs imprisoned at Alexandria and an order for the master of the armoury to prepare to surrender the Citadel.[107] Although the chronicles fail to explain the politics behind such moves, al-Mustaʿīn was likely preparing – or being directed to prepare – the ground for a smooth changeover from Faraj's deeply fractious political order to one more receptive to directives from Shaykh.[108]

Al-Mustaʿīn, Shaykh and Baktamur Julaq set out for Egypt on 8 Rabīʿ I 815/18 June 1412. Nawrūz lingered in Damascus for a week before moving on to Aleppo.[109] Further evidence of al-Mustaʿīn's alertness to the gravitas of his new position comes from an inscribed decree in Gaza concerning a tax repeal. Addressed to local residents, the caliph-sultan employed his own emblem and coat of arms in the middle of the inscription, intending to correct the injustices of his predecessor:

> In the name of God Most Merciful Most Beneficent. A decree of the venerable sublime *amīr al-muʾminīn*, the great *imām*, descendant of the Prophet, al-Mustaʿīnī, God increase and honour him: the repeal of earlier taxes from the days of sultan Faraj imposed on the inhabitants of Gaza on vineyards and orchards and agriculture and [let there be] no new introduction imposed upon them and no restoration of [illegal or non-canonical] tax collection upon them. 'Then whoever changes it after hearing it, the sin shall be upon those who make the change'. This being on the 18th of the month of Rabīʿ I the year 815 (28 June 1412).[110]

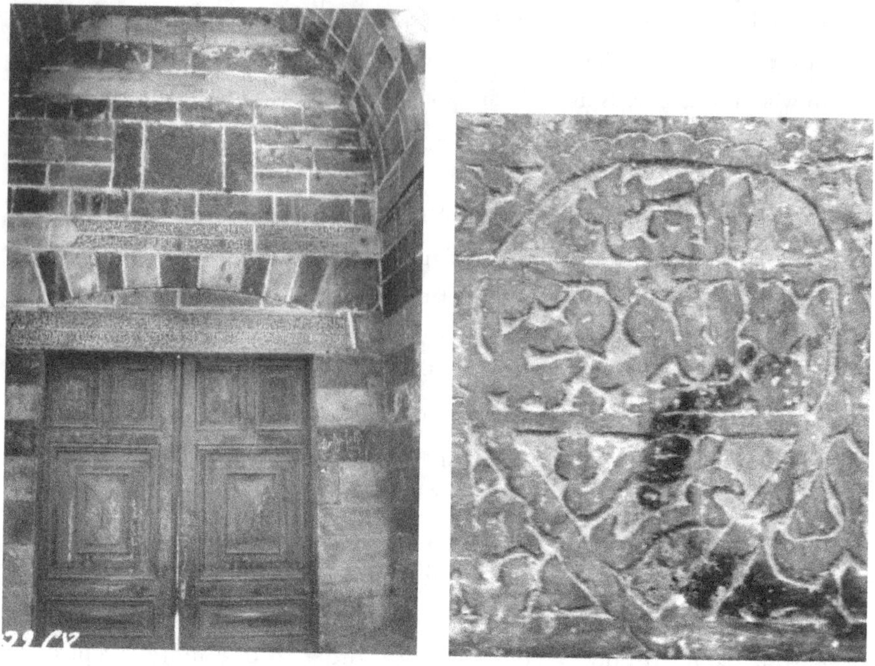

Figure 3.1 Royal decree of al-Mustaʿīn above northeast gate of the Great Mosque of Gaza (left); close-up of the caliph's sultanic medallion (right).
Image courtesy of Moshe Sharon, *Corpus Inscriptionum Arabicarum Palaestinae (CIAP), vol. 4: G–*, Leiden, Brill (Figs P13 and 46b).

Al-Mustaʿīn and Shaykh arrived in Cairo with the army some weeks later on 2 Rabīʿ II 815/12 July 1412, and ascended to the Citadel after passing through the decorated city and calling again for the removal of non-*sharīʿ* taxes. Ecstatic crowds of Egyptians flocked to welcome the caliph-sultan and the amirs of the city stood along his path adorned in their finest garments. People were eager to offer assistance, drawn by the prospect of aiding the curious new sultan. To the astonishment of Shaykh, the caliph-sultan moved into the sultan's palace in the Citadel, forcing him to settle in at the royal stables near the Gate of the Chain. That al-Mustaʿīn had not returned to his family home near the shrine of Sayyida Nafīsa alarmed Shaykh, who feared that Mustaʿīn truly 'intended to follow in the path of the sultan and depart from the path of the caliphs'.[111]

Joy in Cairo over the return of authority to the caliphate seemed genuine, as the masses celebrated. From his post as orator of al-Azhar mosque, Ibn

Ḥajar al-ʿAsqalānī composed and recited a lengthy *qaṣīda* praising Shaykh for having restored the 'stolen power' to the caliphate.[112] The caliph-sultan was not strictly involved in the business of running the government, however, and had time enough to participate in the wedding festivities of his sister-in-law, Bint al-Burhān al-Muhallī, with great pageantry.[113]

After his arrival in Cairo, the caliph-sultan's fortunes dwindled as Shaykh, rather than taper al-Mustaʿīn's power gradually, usurped it directly. Indeed, chroniclers were quick to acknowledge that the caliph was sultan in name only. Settled in the city, Shaykh set about the sabotage of al-Mustaʿīn in several ways: he cancelled the ceremonial procession traditionally held for new sultans and instead held a small service for the caliph-sultan at his own residence, citing journey fatigue as the reason most men would be unable to attend. Stifling al-Mustaʿīn's inaugural excitement was a great blow to the caliph-sultan's prestige and a calculated deflation of the public's unconcealed delight at his accession. In the resulting confusion, government officials in search of reassignment were redirected to Shaykh's door rather than the caliph-sultan. Al-Mustaʿīn received no new subordinates in Cairo other than the initial entourage he had taken to Syria with Faraj. He was also barred from looking over and selecting the best *mamlūk*s of his predecessor for his own household; a traditional perk reserved for new sultans.[114]

Shaykh cast pretences aside a week later, although he allowed ceremonies to commence in the caliph-sultan's castle on 8 Rabīʿ II 815/18 July 1412. Al-Mustaʿīn descended from his throne as the amirs entered and it quickly became apparent that the real focus of the ceremony was Shaykh. In the first major blow to his illusory hold on government, the caliph-sultan was forced to formally invest Shaykh both as *amīr kabīr* and *atābak al-ʿasākir* in Egypt, thereby making massive ceremonial concessions of sovereignty. At the meeting Shaykh received honorific *ṭirāẓ* garments along with the title 'organiser of the kingdom' (*niẓām al-mulk*). Although Shaykh actively worked to undermine al-Mustaʿīn's authority, he permitted the caliph-sultan to continue making appointments for a time, though always with the goal of rooting out unfriendly or uncooperative amirs from the previous administration. The limitations and restraints on his authority began to weigh heavily on al-Mustaʿīn who slowly became aware of his status as Shaykh's prisoner.[115] Al-Suyūṭī describes how the process may have unfolded:

> When the amirs were released from service at the palace [with the caliph-sultan], they returned to the service of Shaykh at the stables and paid their respects [before] carrying out administration in his presence. Then [Shaykh's] inkwell-bearer (*dawādār*) waited on al-Mustaʿīn whose signature was attached to royal mandates and letters. It became clear that the caliph was not empowered to attach the sign manual to a document until it had been shown to Shaykh. The caliph now felt trepidation: his heart strained and alarmed.[116]

Shaykh continued to assume sultanic prerogatives, and on 9 Rabīʿ II/19 July reviewed Faraj's *mamlūk*s and *iqṭā*ʿs and redistributed them among his own supporters. To further pin down al-Mustaʿīn, Shaykh assigned his inkwell-bearer (*dawādār*) Jaqmaq al-Arghūnshāwī to wait on the caliph-sultan, but in reality to spy on, isolate and frustrate him at every turn. Shaykh also instructed his agent to monitor the caliph-sultan's previous secretary and half-brother, Ibn Mubārakshāh. After only two and a half months as sultan, al-Mustaʿīn found himself sequestered once more with his family in their Citadel residence, barred from meeting anyone without Shaykh's approval and consumed by regret.[117]

The caliph was not alone in remorse. As news of Shaykh's activities and swelling influence in Egypt reached Nawrūz, he too began to lament his decision to remain in Syria, wrongly believing that Shaykh prized it above Egypt. The *coup de grâce* came on 16 Jumādā I 815/24 August 1412, when Shaykh commissioned an *ʿahd* diploma on behalf of al-Mustaʿīn that delegated 'everything beyond the throne (*sarīr*) of the caliphate' to Shaykh as he took a distinguished seat in the Ḥarrāqa pavilion of the royal stables before the qadis and heads of state. Al-Mustaʿīn remained caliph, but was barred from all meaningful political activity. Shaykh maintained his show of allegiance to the caliph and even ordered caliphal diplomas from al-Mustaʿīn on 24 Jumādā I/1 September to affirm Syrian viceroys appointed by Nawrūz.[118]

To be sure, Shaykh was sultan in all but name in Egypt, but still had to share Cairo with a powerful rival in the form of Baktamur Julaq, who posed a more immediate threat than Nawrūz in Syria. Fortune smiled on Shaykh when a scorpion bite claimed the life of Baktamur Julaq and left the way to ascendancy clear some weeks later on 8 Jumādā II/15 September. Predicting Shaykh's next move, Nawrūz convened his amirs and prepared to act.[119]

Unaware of the eclipse of the caliph-sultan's 'power' in Cairo, authorities in the Hijaz ordered prayers in honour of al-Mustaʿīn at the great mosque in Mecca on 23 Jumādā II/30 September and also over the holy well of Zamzam. The caliph-sultan's name was likewise mentioned at Friday prayers from the *minbar*s of Mecca and Medina. No previous Cairene Abbasid had received such distinction; in fact, the last Abbasid caliph to be prayed for publicly in the Hijaz had been al-Mustaʿṣim of Baghdad in the years prior to 656/1258.[120] In Dhū al-Qaʿda 815/February 1413 Shaykh ordered the halt of prayers for al-Mustaʿīn in Mecca and for prayers to be made in his name alone.[121] Whereas most contemporary chroniclers merely mentioned this fact, only al-Maqrīzī clarified that al-Mustaʿīn had been prayed for in Mecca solely on account of his brief status as sultan.[122]

Emboldened by the death of his nearest rival, Shaykh prepared to remove al-Mustaʿīn from the sultanate and put forth the idea to his amirs who vowed obedience but differed in their individual opinions. On 1 Shaʿbān/6 November, preparations for Shaykh's coronation began and Fatḥ Allāh was tapped to address a crowd at the royal stables, emphatically despairing of the practicality of 'caliphal' rule: 'Conditions are distressful; the name "caliph" is unknown to the people of the districts of Egypt; affairs will not proceed properly unless there is again a sultan according to custom.'[123]

The assembly testified both to their satisfaction with Shaykh as sultan and the deposition of the caliph. Shaykh, garbed in Abbasid black, was dubbed al-Malik al-Muʾayyad. As the new sultan ascended the palace, the caliph was escorted off the premises to a new residence outside the Sitāra Gate (*Bāb al-Sitāra*). The qadis had been present but the caliph did not attend. In need of caliphal sanction for the move, Shaykh ordered the qadis and *kātib al-sirr* to take the caliph's testimony at his house. Al-Mustaʿīn, now aware of the danger of total deposition, attempted to stall and secure assurances to safeguard his caliphate. He refused to testify that delegating the sultanate to Shaykh had been a free decision. Some sources depict the caliph as belligerent towards the qadis, requesting that he be allowed to return to his former home. In an attempt to bargain, al-Mustaʿīn tried to arrange for Shaykh to publicly swear loyalty to him as caliph, in exchange for firm support for the sultan's causes and aid against his foes. Largely unimpressed with the qadis' report and uninterested in negotiating with a caliph whose days were numbered, Shaykh ordered al-Mustaʿīn to remain under guard and return to his traditional role as caliph. Nevertheless, the sultan permitted the caliph to return to his apartments in the Citadel some days later in which he lived for a period with his family, barred from contact with the outside world.[124]

Nawrūz meanwhile attempted to capitalise on confusion in Cairo by throwing his support behind al-Mustaʿīn as legitimate sultan and carried out a rebellion in the name of 'justice for the caliph-sultan'. In 816/1413, Nawrūz ordered the caliph's name to be struck on coins, mentioned at Friday sermons in Syria, and frequently insulted Shaykh in their mutual correspondence by referring to him not as 'Sultan al-Malik al-Muʾayyad', but with appellations implying his subservience to 'Imām al-Mustaʿīn'.[125] From Damascus Nawrūz rallied forces to unseat Shaykh in the name of the caliph. Nawrūz gathered subordinate amirs from Aleppo and Tripoli and in their presence assembled local qadis to discuss the legality of Shaykh's imprisonment of al-Mustaʿīn and usurpation of the sultanate.[126] Near contemporary authors dispute the outcome of the hearing,[127] and Ḥayāt Nāṣir al-Ḥajjī has argued that the qadis may have deliberately adjourned without reaching a definitive answer for fear that issuing a fatwa labelling the deposition of the caliph from the sultanate as illegal carried the implication that *all* previous and subsequent sultans (weak or strong) had ruled unlawfully as usurpers. Many of the Syrian scholars may also have been weary of future retribution if Shaykh regained control there.[128]

Perhaps concerned that Nawrūz and al-Mustaʿīn might conspire against him, Shaykh began a purge of those he suspected of sympathy for Nawrūz, including Fatḥ Allāh whom he arrested. Shaykh then convened his own council and explained that the times required a powerful sultan and that the threat of *fitna* was sufficient to remove al-Mustaʿīn 'to preserve the blood of the Muslims and keep corruption from the flock'.[129] Taking on the issue directly, Shaykh invited the caliph's brother Dāwūd to the Citadel on 16 Dhū al-Ḥijja 816/9 March 1414 and cloaked him in black before the four qadis.[130] Dāwūd did not receive *bayʿa* at that time (nor was al-Mustaʿīn formally deposed), though he was named Abū al-Fatḥ al-Muʿtaḍid bi-llāh and recognised by Shaykh's court as acting caliph for the next three years.[131]

This new cleavage between caliphate and sultanate and the uncertainty over who, in fact, *was* caliph and sultan, created confusion for deliverers of the Friday *khuṭba*. The traditional formula had involved praying for the reigning sultan

Figure 3.2 Fifteenth-century silver and gold coins from the Syrian territories of the sultanate (dates unknown, c. 815/1412) recognising the name and titles of the caliph-sultan al-Mustaʿīn: (top) Damascus gold dinar recognising the caliph as *al-imām al-aʿẓam*, *amīr al-muʾminīn*, and (possibly also) *sulṭān*; (bottom) Aleppan silver dirham identifying the caliph al-Mustaʿīn as Abū al-Faḍl al-ʿAbbās. Images courtesy of Forschungsstelle für islamische Numismatik Tübingen: #1991-16-30 (dirham) and #2001-7-3 (dinar).

by reciting his agnomen or patronymic (*kunya*, i.e., Abū al-ʿAbbās) and his honorific title or regnal name (*laqab*, i.e., al-Mustaʿīn). The turmoil and turnover at the Citadel had rendered it unclear whether al-Mustaʿīn or his brother al-Muʿtaḍid II was the incumbent caliph. To add to the confusion in this period, al-Muʾayyad Shaykh's government officially barred preachers from praying for any caliph by name in what al-Maqrīzī denounced as an illegal 'vacancy' (*shughūr*) in the caliphate. Thus, some mosque orators changed the formula to 'O Lord, please maintain the righteousness of the caliph (*aṣlaḥ al-khalīfa*)', while others asked God to 'support the Abbasid Caliphate by strengthening our master the sultan'. It was evident that mosque orators, at least, were unhappy about the caliph's demotion from the sultanate and they remained sympathetic to the office itself, regardless of which brother held office.[132]

In Ramaḍān 815/November–December 1412, Shaykh moved the caliph and his family from the palace and settled them in one of the Citadel apartments, which would be their home for the next several years. In Ramaḍān 817/November–December 1414, while his brother Dāwūd joined Shaykh in a massive return parade from Syria, al-Mustaʿīn remained confined in the Citadel residence with his family and servants.[133] The dishonoured caliph was then moved to the tower in which Barqūq had imprisoned his father and lived in extremely tight confinement until he was sent off to Alexandria the next year. In Syria at the same time, Nawūz continued to strike his silver *Nawūzī* dirhams defiantly proclaiming al-Mustaʿīn as sultan.[134]

In Dhū al-Ḥijja 819/January 1417, the Cairene authorities despatched al-Mustaʿīn and his family to the Nile shore. Together with three surviving sons of Faraj, the caliph and others were exiled to the port of Alexandria under escort on the festival day of *ʿĪd al-Aḍḥā*, 10 Dhū al-Ḥijja/29 January.[135]

Al-Mustaʿīn remained in Alexandria for the duration of Shaykh's sultanate until 824/1421. The caliph spent time incarcerated in various locations around the port and may have initially gone without a stipend. The amir Ṭaṭar quickly deposed Shaykh's son and successor al-Muẓaffar Aḥmad, and as sultan, pardoned al-Mustaʿīn on 26 Dhū al-Qaʿda 824/22 November 1421 and offered him the option of returning to Cairo. Perhaps exhausted by his political follies, the caliph chose instead to live out the remainder of his life on the Mediterranean coast, enjoying a substantial salary drawn from levies on local merchants. Authorities in Alexandria granted al-Mustaʿīn permission to leave his residence frequently and the caliph occasionally rode down for Friday prayers on a gold-saddled stallion, a gift from al-Ẓāhir Ṭaṭar, along with embroidered clothes and fine fabrics.[136] Under the rule of al-Ashraf Barsbāy (825–41/1422–38), local authorities lodged al-Mustaʿīn in the hall of Alexandria's great fortress, where he remained until he went the way of all flesh afflicted by bubonic plague on 20 Jumādā II 833/16 March 1430 at about forty years of age.[137] Throughout his thirteen years of exile in Alexandria, al-Mustaʿīn considered himself to be caliph on the ground that he had never been legally deposed. He had even designated his son Yaḥyā (d. 847/1443) successor before leaving Cairo. When his uncle Dāwūd al-Muʿtaḍid II died in 845/1441, Yaḥyā, then a man of almost forty years, rode to Cairo in search of his birth right, but the *ʿahd* of his father failed to impress the court of the sultan Jaqmaq.[138]

At first glance, the career of al-Mustaʿīn appears (and was erroneously celebrated by some contemporaries) as a brief restoration of temporal power to the caliphate. It quickly became clear, however, that the caliph was merely a compromise candidate that fronted the rivalry underlying the uneasy duumvirate of Shaykh and Nawrūz. In the post-Qalawunid age and with no acceptable Barquqid heirs, al-Mustaʿīn served as an attractive figurehead capable of inspiring loyalty to Islam among all classes in the realm. Even though Shaykh emerged as the ultimate victor, the situation complicated his path to the sultanate.[139]

The fact remains that without an army of his own in the household and faction-dominated political world of the Cairo Sultanate, the caliph stood slim chance of securing long-term power. Nevertheless, Abbasid prestige had to be taken seriously: its formidable authority could still challenge a popular sultan, erode his support and sway public opinion against him. Some chroniclers assert that without the opposition fronted by al-Mustaʿīn, the desertion of Faraj by his adherents was unthinkable.[140]

Concerning authority, contemporary sources hint at a sense of independence for al-Mustaʿīn as he busied himself with appointments and depositions, none of which seemed to threaten the greater interests of Shaykh. If Shaykh and his entourage were not quietly organising their political order behind the scenes, al-Mustaʿīn's decisions were in large part guided by fear of Faraj and later his supporters. To those ends, al-Mustaʿīn shared the same vision as Shaykh, which involved clearing the political field of amirs and other personnel loyal to the Barquqid house.

Administrators and *ʿulamāʾ* directly involved in the affair of al-Mustaʿīn may have seen some of the writing on the wall. Fatḥ Allāh was eager to curry favour with Shaykh whom he identified as the driving force. Ibn Mubārakshāh likewise sought a better position, but perhaps succumbed to last-minute fraternal loyalty to the caliph especially after Shaykh made no secret of his eventual plans; but by that point, as the caliph's personal secretary (*dawādār*), Ibn Mubārakshāh's fate was already sealed to that of al-Mustaʿīn.

Decades later, narrative sources re-told the story of al-Mustaʿīn as a tragedy. Sympathetic historians presented him as an esteemed public figure and, after cataloguing his virtues – piety, modesty, generosity and humility – conclude that he was playing against a stacked deck, a victim of the same political situation that he had himself helped to bring about. Contemporary Egyptian historians al-Maqrīzī and Ibn Taghrībirdī shared the view that the caliph had been a tragic figure who stood little chance of survival, but that he somehow should have known better, as his father had.[141] In his contemporary obituary for al-Mustaʿīn, the historian al-ʿAynī astutely surmised the situation:

> [Shaykh and Nawrūz] contracted the sultanate [to al-Mustaʿīn] to give the outward appearance [of settling the issue] with respect to the sultanic title. [This was] because one of the commanding amirs had not yet been able to put himself forward or name another. Thus they contracted [the sultanate] to the caliph to prevent strife and repel malice from amongst themselves (*li-qaṭaʿ al-nizāʿ wa dafʿ al-sharr min baynihim*).[142]

Still it may be premature to dismiss the caliphate-sultanate as a doomed exercise from the outset. As it slowly gained momentum, it certainly had a great deal of potential considering the caliph's prestige, universal claim on loyalty, and ability to appoint whomever he wished to office. The real test would have been whether the caliph-sultan could succeed in building support while protecting and balancing the interests of multiple competing households and factions. Shaykh quickly exploited his power and used it to attract and integrate many key officials. If the caliph-sultan had better capitalised on the hearty welcome he received from Cairene amirs and attached various parties loyal to Faraj to his own charisma, could he have survived the schemes of Shaykh and captured control of the sultanate in a more tangible way?[143] This must remain in the realm of speculation, given al-Mustaʿīn's lack of practical access to the resources of real power.

For nearly fifty years, during the reigns of al-Mutawakkil and his son al-Mustaʿīn, the caliphate increased its political importance and emerged as an important symbol that could be used to run as a counter-current to the office of the sultanate. The caliph also served as an arbiter in this period, who acted as a high-profile messenger that represented royal authority and conveyed unspoken meanings to political actors.[144] The caliphate's quiet return to form as a courtly office during the fifteenth century (albeit with one exception) is the subject of the next chapter.

Notes

1. Garcin, 'Histoire', 58–62.
2. Van Steenbergen, 'Appearances of *dawla* and Political Order', 79; Flinterman and Van Steenbergen, 'Al-Nasir Muhammad', 89.

3. Loiseau, *Les Mamelouks*, 118; Van Steenbergen, 'The Mamluk Sultanate', 200, 212.
4. Ibn Taghrībirdī, *Mawrid*, 1:248; Ibn Taghrībirdī, *Ḥawādith*, 237; al-Sakhāwī, *Ḍaw'*, 7:168, 12:125; al-Suyūṭī, *Ḥusn*, 2:84; al-Suyūṭī, *Ta'rīkh*, 401.
5. Al-Qalqashandī, *Ṣubḥ*, 3:275; al-Maqrīzī, *Sulūk*, 3:76, 100; al-Maqrīzī, *Khiṭaṭ*, 3:786; al-Maqrīzī, *Durar*, 2:211; al-Malaṭī, *Nayl*, 3:132; al-Suyūṭī, *Ḥusn*, 2:84.
6. Al-Maqrīzī, *Sulūk*, 3:83; Ibn Taghrībirdī, *Nujūm*, 11:24.
7. Al-Maqrīzī, *Sulūk*, 3:112; al-Sakhāwī, *Dhayl*, 1:213; Broadbridge, *Kingship and Ideology*, 163–4. On the revolt of Khwāja Mirjān, see Wing, *Jalayrids*, 108–10; Gilli-Elewy 'Baghdad between Cairo and Tabriz', 351–8.
8. Alexander, 'Dhu'l-Faqār', 178.
9. Al-Maqrīzī, *Sulūk*, 3:133–4; Van Steenbergen, 'The Mamluk Sultanate', 209–10; Van Steenbergen, 'Is Anyone My Guardian', 61; Van Steenbergen, *Order Out of Chaos*, 117n.284; Van Steenbergen, 'On the Brink', 120.
10. Ibn Khaldūn, *Ta'rīkh*, 5:550–3; al-Maqrīzī, *Sulūk*, 3:269–76, 285; Ibn Qāḍī Shuhba, *Ta'rīkh*, 3:510; Ibn Ḥajar, *Inbā' al-ghumr*, 1:128, 132, 2:344.
11. Cairene amirs later restaged the investiture ceremony to include the caliph and qadis. See al-Maqrīzī, *Sulūk*, 3:290; Ibn Taghrībirdī, *Nujūm*, 11:148–9.
12. Ibn Khaldūn, *Ta'rīkh*, 5:553–4; al-Maqrīzī, *Sulūk*, 3:278, 284, 287; Ibn Ḥajar, *Inbā' al-ghumr*, 1:131–2.
13. Al-Qalqashandī, *Ṣubḥ*, 3:262; al-Qalqashandī, *Ma'āthir*, 2:167; Ibn Qāḍī Shuhba, *Ta'rīkh*, 3:543; al-Maqrīzī, *Sulūk*, 3:309, 4:24; Ibn Ḥajar, *Inbā' al-ghumr*, 1:151, 2:344; Ibn Taghrībirdī, *Manhal*, 9:232.
14. Al-Qalqashandī, *Ṣubḥ*, 3:262; al-Qalqashandī, *Ma'āthir*, 2:181; al-Maqrīzī, *Sulūk*, 3:309–10, 4:24; al-Maqrīzī, *Khiṭaṭ*, 3:786; Ibn Qāḍī Shuhba, *Ta'rīkh*, 3:543, 558; Ibn Ḥajar, *Inbā' al-ghumr*, 1:151–2, 170; Hassan, *Longing for the Lost Caliphate*, 90.
15. Brinner, 'Struggle for Power', 231–2.
16. Onimus, *Les maîtres du jeu*, 126–34, 147–50, 159–99; Loiseau, *Les Mamelouks*, 124; Ibn Qāḍī Shuhba, *Ta'rīkh*, 1:86–91; al-Maqrīzī, *Sulūk*, 3:439–40, 474–8; Ibn Taghrībirdī, *Manhal*, 3:287; al-Ṣayrafī, *Nuzhat*, 1:36–8.
17. Onimus, *Les maîtres du jeu*, 207–15; Loiseau, *Les Mamelouks*, 173–200.
18. Onimus, *Les maîtres du jeu*, 148.
19. Ibn Khaldūn, *Ta'rīkh*, 5:563–4; al-Maqrīzī, *Sulūk*, 3:477; Ibn Taghrībirdī, *Nujūm*, 11:221–2, 226, 228; al-Ṣayrafī, *Nuzhat*, 1:38, 46, 49.
20. Onimus, *Les maîtres du jeu*, 216–17.

21. Ibn Taghrībirdī, *Nujūm*, 11:234–5. See also Wiederhold, 'Legal-Religious Elite', 215.
22. Ibn Khaldūn, *Taʾrīkh*, 5:564–5; al-Maqrīzī, *Sulūk*, 3:494–5; al-Maqrīzī, *Durar*, 3:293; Ibn Ḥajar, *Inbāʾ al-ghumr*, 1:275; Ibn Qāḍī Shuhba, *Taʾrīkh*, 1:110, 124, 304; Ibn Taghrībirdī, *Nujūm*, 11:234–5; al-Ṣayrafī, *Nuzhat*, 1:71–2; Surūr, *Dawlat Banī Qalāwūn*, 88; Onimus, *Les maîtres du jeu*, 111, 147–8; Hassan, *Longing for the Lost Caliphate*, 90–1; Wiederhold, 'Legal-Religious Elite', 214.
23. Al-Qalqashandī, *Ṣubḥ*, 3:262; al-Maqrīzī, *Khiṭaṭ*, 3:786; al-Maqrīzī, *Durar*, 2:211, 3:293; Ibn Qāḍī Shuhba, *Taʾrīkh*, 1:110; Ibn Ḥajar, *Inbāʾ al-ghumr*, 1:275, 2:344; Ibn Taghrībirdī, *Nujūm*, 11:235; Hassan, *Longing for the Lost Caliphate*, 91; Wiederhold, 'Legal-Religious Elite', 214.
24. Al-Maqrīzī, *Sulūk*, 3:495; Ibn Qāḍī Shuhba, *Taʾrīkh*, 1:110; Ibn Taghrībirdī, *Nujūm*, 11:235, 13:8. The similarity of the regnal titles 'al-Muʿtaṣim' and 'al-Mustaʿṣim' confused many medieval observers' understanding of the succession. Most sources identify the pair as sons of al-Wāthiq bi-llāh instead of al-Muʿtaṣim. Several sources may have erroneously understood al-Muʿtaṣim (1377) to be the same as al-Mustaʿṣim (1386–9). Based on Ibn Qāḍī Shuhba and al-Maqrīzī, Wiederhold attempted to amend earlier Abbasid chronologies/genealogies by Bernard Lewis (in his *EI²* article, ''Abbāsids'), and C. E. Bosworth (*New Islamic Dynasties*, 7). According to the sources examined by Wiederhold 'caliphal succession proceeded as follows: "1377–83, al-Mutawakkil ʿala ʾl-lah Muhammad; 1383–86, al-Wathiq bi-ʾl-lah Rukn al-Din ʿUmar ibn Ibrahim – son of the Caliph al-Muʿtasim (r. 1377); 1386–89, al-Mustaʿsim bi-ʾl-lah Muhyi al-Din Zakariyya ibn al-Muʿtasim bi-ʾl-lah – brother of the Caliph al-Wathiq bi-ʾl-lah ʿUmar (not al-Muʿtasim!); 1389–1405, al-Mutawakkil ʿala ʾl-lah Muhammad', see 'Legal-Religious Elite', 231n.91. However, I must point out that even Ibn Qāḍī Shuhba elsewhere claims that al-Mustaʿṣim was the son of al-Wāthiq and was also the same Abbasid installed by Aynabak al-Badrī in 1377, thus further confounding efforts to understand caliphal succession in this period! See Ibn Qāḍī Shuhba, *Taʾrīkh*, 4:46.
25. Ibn Khaldūn, *Taʾrīkh*, 5:565; al-Maqrīzī, *Sulūk*, 3:496-6, 501, 504; al-Maqrīzī, *Khiṭaṭ*, 3:786; Ibn Ḥajar, *Inbāʾ al-ghumr*, 1:275, 2:344; Ibn Qāḍī Shuhba, *Taʾrīkh*, 1:113, 116; Ibn Taghrībirdī, *Nujūm*, 11:237; Ibn Taghrībirdī, *Manhal*, 8:261–2; al-Ṣayrafī, *Nuzhat*, 1:82, 121; al-Suyūṭī, *Ḥusn*, 2:84; Ibn Iyās, *Badāʾiʿ*, 1:2:333.
26. Al-Qalqashandī, *Ṣubḥ*, 3:262; Ibn Qāḍī Shuhba, *Taʾrīkh*, 1:201; Ibn Ḥajar, *Inbāʾ al-ghumr*, 1:315, 325–6, 2:344.

27. Al-Maqrīzī, *Sulūk*, 3:551–2, 975; Ibn Qāḍī Shuhba, *Taʾrīkh*, 1:110–11.
28. Ibn Qāḍī Shuhba, *Taʾrīkh*, 1:186–7. The Ẓāhirī school was obsolete by the fourteenth century, but I. Goldziher and Wiederhold have demonstrated that Ẓāhirī ideas remained important in Damascus. See Wiederhold, 'Legal-Religious Elite', 204–5, 214.
29. Wiederhold, 'Legal-Religious Elite', 208, 210–11, 214, 224; Hassan, *Longing for the Lost Caliphate*, 91; al-Maqrīzī, *Durar*, 1:298.
30. Al-Maqrīzī's biography of Ibn al-Burhān (*Durar*, 1:297–303) contains valuable details regarding the Ẓāhirī *fitna* and its motivations. Ibn al-Burhān's biography as well as his political 'manifesto', *Ṭarīq al-istiqāma li-maʿrifat al-imāma*, will provide interesting information for future studies.
31. Wiederhold, 'Legal-Religious Elite', 212–13, 224–6.
32. For the early career of Temür, see Subtelny, 'Tamerlane and his Descendants', 173–8, and for his three campaigns against the territories of the sultanate of Cairo, see Broadbridge, *Kingship and Ideology*, 171–97.
33. Markiewicz, *Crisis of Kingship*, 156–9; Broadbridge, *Kingship and Ideology*, 168–9.
34. Translation modified from Ibn ʿArabshāh (trans. Sanders), *Tamerlane*, 13.
35. Ibn Iyās, *Badāʾiʿ*, 1:2:386.
36. Ibn al-Furāt, *Taʾrīkh*, 9:56–7; al-Maqrīzī, *Durar*, 3:293; Ibn Ḥajar, *Inbāʾ al-ghumr*, 1:365; Ibn Taghrībirdī, *Manhal*, 3:92; Onimus, *Les maîtres du jeu*, 133, 305, 308; Hassan, *Longing for the Lost Caliphate*, 91.
37. Later sources offer little information concerning al-Mustaʿṣim, though after losing the caliphate he lived in solitary confinement until his death, see al-Sakhāwī, *Ḍawʾ*, 3:233; al-Sakhāwī, *Wajīz*, 1:340–1.
38. Ibn al-Furāt, *Taʾrīkh*, 9:57; al-Maqrīzī, *Sulūk*, 3:595, 605; Ibn Ḥajar, *Inbāʾ*, 1:366, 2:344; Ibn Qāḍī Shuhba, *Taʾrīkh*, 1:266, 4:46; Ibn Taghrībirdī, *Nujūm*, 11:261–2, 268; Ibn Taghrībirdī, *Manhal*, 3:299; al-Ṣayrafī, *Nuzhat*, 1:189. On fourteenth- and fifteenth-century Syro-Egyptian gifting practices, see Onimus, *Les maîtres du jeu*, 88–97; Eychenne, *Liens personnels*, 312–13; Behrens-Abouseif, *Practising Diplomacy*.
39. Ibn al-Furāt, *Taʾrīkh*, 9:56; al-Maqrīzī, *Sulūk*, 3:595; Ibn Ḥajar, *Inbāʾ al-ghumr*, 1:365, 2:344; Ibn Taghrībirdī, *Nujūm*, 11:262–3.
40. Ibn al-Furāt, *Taʾrīkh*, 9:69, 71–2; al-Maqrīzī, *Sulūk*, 3:602–3, 605; al-Maqrīzī, *Khiṭaṭ*, 3:786; al-Maqrīzī, *Durar*, 2:211, 3:294; Ibn Ḥajar, *Inbāʾ al-ghumr*, 1:367, 2:344; Ibn Ḥajar, *Dhayl*, 119; Ibn Qāḍī Shuhba, *Taʾrīkh*, 1:273–4; Ibn Taghrībirdī, *Nujūm*, 11:268-9, 272, 13:8; Ibn Taghrībirdī,

Mawrid, 1:254; al-Ṣayrafī, *Nuzhat*, 1:195–7, 199; Hassan, *Longing for the Lost Caliphate*, 92.

41. Ibn Ḥajar, *Dhayl*, 119; Ibn Taghrībirdī, *Nujūm*, 13:8; Ibn Taghrībirdī, *Mawrid*, 1:253; Wiet, 'Barḳūḳ'; Garcin, 'Histoire', 60.
42. Ibn al-Furāt, *Taʾrīkh*, 9:81–2, 87; al-Maqrīzī, *Sulūk*, 3:611–15; Ibn Ḥajar, *Dhayl*, 119; Ibn Taghrībirdī, *Nujūm*, 11:280, 285; Ibn Taghrībirdī, *Manhal*, 3:305; al-Ṣayrafī, *Nuzhat*, 1:206, 210.
43. Ibn al-Furāt, *Taʾrīkh*, 9:89; al-Maqrīzī, *Sulūk*, 3:620–1; al-Maqrīzī, *Durar*, 3:294; Ibn Ḥajar, *Inbāʾ al-ghumr*, 1:368, 2:344; Ibn Qāḍī Shuhba, *Taʾrīkh*, 1:277; Ibn Taghrībirdī, *Nujūm*, 11:286–7; al-Ṣayrafī, *Nuzhat*, 1:214; Hassan, *Longing for the Lost Caliphate*, 91.
44. Ibn al-Furāt, *Taʾrīkh*, 9:94, 105; al-Maqrīzī, *Sulūk*, 3:621–3, 630; Ibn Ḥajar, *Inbāʾ al-ghumr*, 1:368–9, 2:344; Ibn Taghrībirdī, *Nujūm*, 11:287, 319; al-Ṣayrafī, *Nuzhat*, 1:215; Garcin, 'Histoire', 60.
45. On the role of the *ʿāmma* and their support for Minṭāsh, see Perho, 'The Sultan and the Common People', 153–5.
46. Ibn al-Furāt, *Taʾrīkh*, 9:91, 120–1; al-Maqrīzī, *Sulūk*, 3:621, 644, 655–6; Ibn Ḥajar, *Inbāʾ al-ghumr*, 1:372–3; Ibn Taghrībirdī, *Nujūm*, 11:285–7, 332–7, 347–50; Ibn Taghrībirdī, *Manhal*, 3:312–13, 4:96–8; Ibn Taghrībirdī, *Mawrid*, 1:254; al-Ṣayrafī, *Nuzhat*, 1:237–9; Brinner, 'Struggle for Power', 232; ʿAbd ar-Rāziq, *La femme*, 172.
47. Ibn al-Furāt, *Taʾrīkh*, 9:155, 157; Ibn Ḥajar, *Inbāʾ al-ghumr*, 1:377; Ibn Qāḍī Shuhba, *Taʾrīkh*, 1:294–5, 299; al-Maqrīzī, *Sulūk*, 3:668–70, 673; Ibn Taghrībirdī, *Nujūm*, 11:357–61; al-Ṣayrafī, *Nuzhat*, 1:262–4, 266; Onimus, *Les maîtres du jeu*, 133–4, 305–6.
48. Al-Maqrīzī, *Sulūk*, 3:675; al-Maqrīzī, *Khiṭaṭ*, 2:280n. 2, 3:141–2; al-Ṣayrafī, *Nuzhat*, 1:267–8; Ibn al-Furāt, *Taʾrīkh*, 9:162; Ibn Iyās, *Badāʾiʿ*, 1:2:420–1.
49. Ibn al-Furāt, *Taʾrīkh*, 9:163, 166; Ibn Ḥajar, *Inbāʾ al-ghumr*, 1:377; Ibn Qāḍī Shuhba, *Taʾrīkh*, 1:302; al-Maqrīzī, *Sulūk*, 3:676, 678; Ibn Taghrībirdī, *Nujūm*, 11:362, 364; al-Ṣayrafī, *Nuzhat*, 1:269.
50. Ibn Ṣaṣrā/Brinner, *Durra*, 1:75–6 (English), 2:50–1 (Arabic); Ibn al-Furāt, *Taʾrīkh*, 9:167, 185–7; al-Maqrīzī, *Sulūk*, 3:680, 693–6; al-Maqrīzī, *Durar*, 3:294; Ibn Ḥajar, *Inbāʾ al-ghumr*, 1:391; Ibn Ḥajar, *Dhayl*, 119; Ibn Qāḍī Shuhba, *Taʾrīkh*, 1:303, 320; Ibn Taghrībirdī, *Nujūm*, 11:362–5; Ibn Taghrībirdī, *Manhal*, 3:314, 4:98; al-Ṣayrafī, *Nuzhat*, 1:282; De Mignanelli, *Ascensus Barcoch*, 23–4; Onimus, *Les maîtres du jeu*, 334.

51. On the symbolic importance of this strategy, see Onimus, *Les maîtres du jeu*, 333–6.
52. Ibn Ṣaṣrā/Brinner, *Durra*, 1:75–6 (English), 2:50–1 (Arabic); al-Maqrīzī, *Durar*, 3:294; Ibn Ḥajar, *Inbāʾ al-ghumr*, 2:345; Ibn Taghrībirdī, *Mawrid*, 1:254.
53. Broadbridge, *Kingship and Ideology*, 170–1, 183.
54. Ibid., 180, 183; Ibn Taghrībirdī, *Nujūm*, 12:58–9.
55. This may have occurred in Rabīʿ II 794/February 1392. See Ibn Qāḍī Shuhba, *Taʾrīkh*, 1:424. According to al-Suyūṭī, in 797/1395 Bāyezīd sent gifts to Cairo for al-Mutawakkil and a letter to Barqūq seeking a diploma that would recognise him as 'Sultan of Rūm', see *Ḥusn*, 2:85. Although contemporary sources mention few details about the request or exchange, Broadbridge believes it may have taken place when an Ottoman vizier made a brief sojourn in Damascus en route to pilgrimage in 798/1396, see *Kingship and Ideology*, 175n.40. On Bāyezīd's interest in the Abbasid Caliphate of Cairo, see Yüksel Muslu, *Ottomans and Mamluks*, 79; Har-El, *Struggle for Domination*, 66–7.
56. Ibn Taghrībirdī, *Nujūm*, 12:217, 269; al-Malaṭī, *Nayl*, 3:81; Broadbridge, *Kingship and Ideology*, 187.
57. Ibn Ṣaṣrā/Brinner, *Durra*, 1:194–5, 203–4 (English) 2:145–6, 150–1 (Arabic); Ibn Ḥajar, *Inbāʾ al-ghumr*, 1:470, 474; Onimus, *Les maîtres du jeu*, 138; Broadbridge, *Kingship and Ideology*, 185–6.
58. For some exceptions, see Ibn Taghrībirdī, *Nujūm*, 12:691–2; Ibn Iyās, *Badāʾiʿ*, 1:2:472.
59. Onimus, *Les maîtres du jeu*, 135.
60. Broadbridge, *Kingship and Ideology*, 150.
61. Al-Ṣayrafī, *Nuzhat*, 1:475, 2:27, 171; al-Sakhāwī, *Wajīz*, 1:373.
62. Al-Maqrīzī, *Sulūk*, 3:936; Ibn Taghrībirdī, *Nujūm*, 12:102, 104; al-Ṣayrafī, *Nuzhat*, 1:494–5, 2:6–7; al-Suyūṭī, *Ḥusn*, 2:120; Ibn Iyās, *Badāʾiʿ*, 1:2:524–5. On this peculiar practice see Banister, 'Naught Remains', 234; Onimus, *Les maîtres du jeu*, 139, 149, 224; Sievert, 'Family, Friend or Foe', 109–12, 116–17; Loiseau, *Les Mamelouks*, 131–2; Holt, 'Position and Power', 239–40.
63. Al-Qalqashandī, *Ṣubḥ*, 3:277; al-Maqrīzī, *Sulūk*, 3:959; Ibn Qāḍī Shuhba, *Taʾrīkh*, 4:19; Ibn Ḥajar, *Inbāʾ al-ghumr*, 2:50; Ibn Taghrībirdī, *Nujūm*, 12:169; al-Ṣayrafī, *Nuzhat*, 2:5–9, 18.
64. Ibn Qāḍī Shuhba, *Taʾrīkh*, 4:67–8; al-Maqrīzī, *Sulūk*, 3:985; Ibn Ḥajar, *Inbāʾ al-ghumr*, 2:94-5; Ibn Taghrībirdī, *Nujūm*, 12:182–3; al-Ṣayrafī, *Nuzhat*, 2:33–4 ; Onimus, *Les maîtres du jeu*, 229, 239–40.

65. Al-Qalqashandī, *Ṣubḥ*, 3:277.
66. Ibn Qāḍī Shuhba, *Taʾrīkh*, 4:73; Ibn Taghrībirdī, *Nujūm*, 12:172; al-Ṣayrafī, *Nuzhat*, 2:8–9.
67. Al-Maqrīzī, *Sulūk*, 3:1003; Ibn Ḥajar, *Inbāʾ al-ghumr*, 2:52, 99–102; Ibn Taghrībirdī, *Nujūm*, 12:200, 12:210–13; al-Ṣayrafī, *Nuzhat*, 2:47–8, 54–7.
68. Ibn Qāḍī Shuhba, *Taʾrīkh*, 4:145; al-Maqrīzī, *Sulūk*, 3:1028–9; Ibn Ḥajar, *Inbāʾ al-ghumr*, 2:134; Ibn Taghrībirdī, *Nujūm*, 12:218; al-Ṣayrafī, *Nuzhat*, 2:8.
69. Broadbridge, *Kingship and Ideology*, 191–2; Onimus, *Les maîtres du jeu*, 231–2; Massoud, *Chronicles*, 150. Temür's followers plundered Damascus and the other major Syrian towns before moving on in Rajab 803/March 1401. See Ibn Taghrībirdī, *Nujūm*, 12:245–6; al-Ṣayrafī, *Nuzhat*, 2:87–94. Faraj briefly sent the caliph and qadis to accompany an anti-Temür campaign to Ṣāliḥiyya leaving Cairo in Shaʿbān 803/April 1401.
70. Al-Maqrīzī, *Sulūk*, 3:1030–7, 1040–2, 1044; Ibn Qāḍī Shuhba, *Taʾrīkh*, 4:159–60, 170, 184; Ibn Ḥajar, *Inbāʾ al-ghumr*, 2:137; Ibn Taghrībirdī, *Nujūm*, 12:223–5, 229–30, 232–3, 236–7, 246; al-Ṣayrafī, *Nuzhat*, 2:74–7, 78–9, 82–7.
71. Broadbridge, *Kingship and Ideology*, 191.
72. Ibn Khaldūn, *Taʿrīf bi-Ibn Khaldūn*, 374–6; Ibn Qāḍī Shuhba, *Taʾrīkh*, 4:182. See Hassan, *Longing for the Lost Caliphate*, 125–6; Banister, 'Sword in the Caliph's Service', 10–11.
73. Al-Maqrīzī, *Sulūk*, 3:1083; Ibn Ḥajar, *Inbāʾ al-ghumr*, 2:203; Ibn Taghrībirdī, *Nujūm*, 12:281–7; al-Ṣayrafī, *Nuzhat*, 2:139–42; Massoud, *Chronicles*, 162–3, 369, 391–3, 398.
74. Ibn Qāḍī Shuhba, *Taʾrīkh*, 4:301.
75. Broadbridge, *Kingship and Ideology*, 193–4.
76. Ibn Taghrībirdī, *Nujūm*, 12:314; al-Malaṭī, *Nayl*, 3:116.
77. Ibn Qāḍī Shuhba includes more details surrounding the caliph's brief captivity, see *Taʾrīkh*, 4:421–3. See also Ibn Ḥijjī, *Taʾrīkh*, 2:680–4; al-Maqrīzī, *Sulūk*, 3:1163–4; Ibn Ḥajar, *Inbāʾ al-ghumr*, 2:296; Ibn Taghrībirdī, *Nujūm*, 12:319–20; al-Ṣayrafī, *Nuzhat*, 2:202–3; Onimus, *Les maîtres du jeu*, 334.
78. Al-Maqrīzī, *Sulūk*, 4:2, 7; Ibn Ḥajar, *Inbāʾ al-ghumr*, 2:319; Ibn Taghrībirdī, *Nujūm*, 12:331, 13:41–2, 48; al-Ṣayrafī, *Nuzhat*, 2:212–13.
79. According to al-Sakhāwī, al-Muʿtamid was returned to confinement by his father and remained incarcerated until death. See *Ḍawʾ*, 2:102–3. For the succession contract naming al-ʿAbbās the heir of al-Mutawakkil, see al-Qalqashandī, *Ṣubḥ*, 9:369–77.

80. Al-Qalqashandī, *Ṣubḥ*, 3:263; al-Qalqashandī, *Ma'āthir*, 2:203; al-Maqrīzī, *Sulūk*, 4:13, 23–4; al-Maqrīzī, *Khiṭaṭ*, 3:786; al-Maqrīzī, *Durar*, 2:211, 3:294–5; Ibn Ḥajar, *Inbā' al-ghumr*, 2:343–4; Ibn Ḥajar, *Dhayl*, 119; Ibn Taghrībirdī, *Nujūm*, 13:51, 155; Ibn Taghrībirdī, *Mawrid*, 1:254; al-Ṣayrafī, *Nuzhat*, 2:220.
81. Surūr, *Dawlat Banī Qalāwūn*, 86–7.
82. Hassan, *Longing for the Lost Caliphate*, 91–2.
83. Al-Maqrīzī, *Sulūk*, 4:14; Ibn Ḥajar, *Inbā' al-ghumr*, 2:343; Ibn Taghrībirdī, *Nujūm*, 13:51; al-Ṣayrafī, *Nuzhat*, 2:217.
84. Onimus, *Les maîtres du jeu*, 243–6.
85. Al-Maqrīzī, *Sulūk*, 4:93, 99, 104; al-Maqrīzī, *Durar*, 2:211; Ibn Ḥajar, *Inbā' al-ghumr*, 2:423; al-ʿAynī, *ʿIqd* (1985–9) 1:100–3; Ibn Taghrībirdī, *Nujūm*, 13:86. On conflict and conciliation between various political actors which could also involve the caliph as an intermediary, see Onimus, *Les maîtres du jeu*, 343–6.
86. Al-Ṣayrafī, *Nuzhat*, 2:263–7; Ibn Iyās, *Badā'iʿ*, 1:2:804.
87. Al-Maqrīzī, *Sulūk*, 4:174, 198; al-ʿAynī, *ʿIqd* (1985–9), 1:97; Ibn Taghrībirdī, *Nujūm*, 13:120, 189; Ibn Taghrībirdī, *Mawrid*, 1:255, 2:133; Ibn Taghrībirdī, *Manhal*, 6:283–4; al-Ṣayrafī, *Nuzhat*, 2:292–3, 305–8.
88. Al-Maqrīzī, *Sulūk*, 4:207–8, 214–15; al-Maqrīzī, *Durar*, 3:13; Ibn Ḥajar, *Inbā' al-ghumr*, 2:506–7; Ibn Taghrībirdī, *Nujūm*, 13:141, 145; Onimus, *Les maîtres du jeu*, 334–5; Hassan, *Longing for the Lost Caliphate*, 93–4; Holt, 'Al-Mustaʿīn (II) biʾllāh'. For a variety of examples describing public displays of the black Abbasid banners in the Cairo Sultanate, see Ibn Ḥijjī, *Ta'rīkh*, 1:455; Ibn Ṣaṣrā/Brinner, *Durra*, 1:179 (English), 2:134 (Arabic); Ibn Qāḍī Shuhba, *Ta'rīkh*, 2:129, 3:201; Ibn Iyās, *Badā'iʿ*, 5:36. The Abbasid standard retained its symbolic poignancy in some later literary specimens of the period, see Talib, 'Woven Together', 28–30.
89. Al-Maqrīzī, *Sulūk*, 4:214; al-Maqrīzī, *Durar*, 2:211, 3:13–14; Ibn Ḥajar, *Inbā' al-ghumr*, 2:507–8; Ibn Taghrībirdī, *Nujūm*, 13:147, 190; Ibn Taghrībirdī, *Manhal*, 761; Ibn Taghrībirdī, *Mawrid*, 1:256, 2:134; Onimus, *Les maîtres du jeu*, 287, 334–5, 396–7; Hassan, *Longing for the Lost Caliphate*, 93.
90. Al-Maqrīzī, *Sulūk*, 4:213–14, 216, 219, 543; al-Maqrīzī, *Khiṭaṭ*, 3:786; al-Maqrīzī, *Durar*, 2:212, 3:13–14; Ibn Ḥajar, *Inbā' al-ghumr*, 2:507–8; al-ʿAynī, *ʿIqd* (1985–9), 1:111; Ibn Taghrībirdī, *Nujūm*, 13:147, 190, 14:165; Ibn Taghrībirdī, *Manhal*, 6:284; Hassan, *Longing for the Lost Caliphate*, 93.
91. Hassan, *Longing for the Lost Caliphate*, 94; al-Maqrīzī, *Sulūk*, 4:216; al-Maqrīzī,

Durar, 2:212–13; al-ʿAynī, *ʿIqd* (1985–9), 1:113–15; Brinner, 'Struggle for Power', 233; Gaudefroy-Demombynes, *La Syrie à l'époque des mamelouks*, xxvi.

92. Ibn Ḥajar, *Inbāʾ al-ghumr*, 2:507–8; al-ʿAynī, *ʿIqd* (1985–9), 1:111; Ibn Taghrībirdī, *Nujūm*, 13:191; Hassan, *Longing for the Lost Caliphate*, 93–4.
93. On the caliph's use of the sultanic title al-ʿĀdil, see Irwin, 'Factions in Medieval Egypt', 231; Bosworth, *New Islamic Dynasties*, 77. While Balog and Schultz did not mention the 'al-ʿĀdil' title in their work on al-Mustaʿīn's coinage, the caliph-sultan was alternately identified as 'al-Sulṭān al-Malik al-ʿAbbās', see Schultz, 'Silver Coinage', 213–17. According to Balog, al-Mustaʿīn's coins, with the exception of his Cairo dirhams, styled the caliph-sultan as '*amīr al-muʾminīn*' or '*al-imām al-aʿẓam*'. Some coins may also have included the phrase *khallada Allāh mulkahu* as well as the caliph's apparent heraldry which resembles an upturned ribbon. See *Coinage*, 296–8. In addition to the gold and silver coins mentioned by Balog, Schultz mentions copper as well. The first silver reforms in the Cairo Sultanate occurred during the short reign of al-Mustaʿīn, and his silver coins are instantly recognisable because of their higher silver content and the thin flan design that later dominated fifteenth-century coinage, see Schultz, 'Silver Coinage', 212–13.
94. Al-Maqrīzī, *Sulūk*, 4:216; al-Maqrīzī, *Durar*, 2:212; al-ʿAynī, *ʿIqd* (1985–9), 1:111–12; Ibn Taghrībirdī, *Nujūm*, 13:191–2; Ibn Taghrībirdī, *Manhal*, 6:285.
95. Ibn Taghrībirdī, *Nujūm*, 13:192; Onimus, *Les maîtres du jeu*, 335–6; Hassan, *Longing for the Lost Caliphate*, 93–4.
96. Al-Qalqashandī, *Ṣubḥ*, 3:276; al-Maqrīzī, *Sulūk*, 4:209, 216–17; al-Maqrīzī, *Durar*, 2:212; Ibn Taghrībirdī, *Manhal*, 7:61.
97. Al-Maqrīzī, *Sulūk*, 4:217, 230; al-Maqrīzī, *Durar*, 2:212; Ibn Ḥajar, *Inbāʾ al-ghumr*, 2:508–9, 512; al-ʿAynī, *ʿIqd* (1985–9), 1:116, 126; Ibn Taghrībirdī, *Nujūm*, 13:193; Ibn Taghrībirdī, *Manhal*, 7:198–9.
98. Ibn Taghrībirdī, *Nujūm*, 13:193.
99. Hassan, *Longing for the Lost Caliphate*, 93–5.
100. Al-Maqrīzī, *Durar*, 2:213; Ibn Taghrībirdī, *Nujūm*, 13:193.
101. Al-Maqrīzī, *Sulūk*, 4:221; al-Maqrīzī, *Khiṭaṭ*, 3:786; al-Maqrīzī, *Durar*, 2:211; Ibn Taghrībirdī, *Nujūm*, 13:193–5; Ibn Taghrībirdī, *Manhal*, 6:285; Piloti, *Égypte*, 12–13.
102. Ibn Taghrībirdī, *Nujūm*, 13:197; Piloti, *Égypte*, 13; al-Ṣayrafī, *Nuzhat*, 2:308–9.
103. Al-Maqrīzī, *Sulūk*, 4:223–5; Ibn Ḥajar, *Inbāʾ al-ghumr*, 2:507, 510–1;

al-ʿAynī, *ʿIqd* (1985–9), 1:116–23; Ibn Taghrībirdī, *Nujūm*, 13:197–8; Ibn Taghrībirdī, *Manhal*, 6:285; Piloti, *Égypte*, 13; al-Ṣayrafī, *Nuzhat*, 2:309–10.

104. Al-Maqrīzī, *Khiṭaṭ*, 3:786; al-Maqrīzī, *Durar*, 2:213; Ibn Ḥajar, *Inbāʾ al-ghumr*, 2:508; al-ʿAynī, *ʿIqd* (1985–9), 1:124–5; Ibn Taghrībirdī, *Nujūm*, 13:199–200; Ibn Taghrībirdī, *Manhal*, 6:286; Ibn Taghrībirdī, *Mawrid*, 2:134; Hassan, *Longing for the Lost Caliphate*, 94.
105. Ibn Taghrībirdī, *Manhal*, 7:61; al-Malaṭī, *Nayl*, 3:234–5.
106. Al-ʿAynī, *ʿIqd* (1985–9), 1:123–4; Ibn Taghrībirdī, *Nujūm*, 13:201.
107. Al-Maqrīzī, *Sulūk*, 4:230–1; Ibn Ḥajar, *Inbāʾ al-ghumr*, 2:509; al-ʿAynī, *ʿIqd* (1985–9), 1:114–15; Ibn Taghrībirdī, *Nujūm*, 13:201–2.
108. Al-Qalqashandī, *Ṣubḥ*, 3:263; Ibn Ḥajar, *Inbāʾ al-ghumr*, 3:446.
109. Ibn Ḥajar, *Inbāʾ al-ghumr*, 2:512; al-Maqrīzī, *Sulūk*, 4:228, 231; al-Maqrīzī, *Durar*, 2:214; Ibn Ḥajar, *Inbāʾ al-ghumr*, 2:512–14; Ibn Taghrībirdī, *Nujūm*, 13:202; Ibn Taghrībirdī, *Mawrid*, 1:256.
110. Sharon, *Corpus Inscriptionum Arabicarum Palaestinae* (*CIAP*), 4:147–8; Sadek, *Architektur*, 98–9; Mayer, 'Decree of the Caliph', 27–9.
111. Al-Qalqashandī, *Maʾāthir*, 2:206; al-Maqrīzī, *Sulūk*, 4:229, 232–3; al-Maqrīzī, *Khiṭaṭ*, 3:786, 4:1:327; al-Maqrīzī, *Durar*, 2:214; Ibn Ḥajar, *Inbāʾ al-ghumr*, 2:512–13; al-ʿAynī, *ʿIqd* (1985–9), 1:131; al-Ṣayrafī, *Nuzhat*, 2:311; Ibn Taghrībirdī, *Nujūm*, 13:202; Ibn Taghrībirdī, *Manhal*, 6:286, 7:61; Ibn Taghrībirdī, *Mawrid*, 1:256, 2:134.
112. Hassan, 'Poetic Memories'.
113. Ibn Ḥajar, *Inbāʾ al-ghumr*, 2:513; al-ʿAynī, *ʿIqd* (1985–9), 1:130.
114. Al-Maqrīzī, *Sulūk*, 4:233; al-Maqrīzī, *Durar*, 2:214; Ibn Ḥajar, *Inbāʾ al-ghumr*, 3:446; Ibn Taghrībirdī, *Nujūm*, 13:202–4; Ibn Taghrībirdī, *Manhal*, 7:62; Ibn Taghrībirdī, *Mawrid*, 1:257; al-Suyūṭī, *Ḥusn*, 2:89; Ibn Iyās, *Badāʾiʿ*, 1:2:824, 827. See also Surūr, *Dawlat Banī Qalāwūn*, 95; Hassan, *Longing for the Lost Caliphate*, 95.
115. Al-Qalqashandī, *Ṣubḥ*, 3:263; al-Maqrīzī, *Sulūk*, 4:233–4; al-Maqrīzī, *Durar*, 2:214, 3:14; Ibn Ḥajar, *Inbāʾ al-ghumr*, 2:514; al-ʿAynī, *ʿIqd* (1985–9), 1:132; Ibn Taghrībirdī, *Nujūm*, 13:203–4; al-Ṣayrafī, *Nuzhat*, 2:313; al-Sakhāwī, *Dhayl*, 1:477; al-Suyūṭī, *Taʾrīkh*, 406; al-Suyūṭī, *Ḥusn*, 2:85–6, 89, 121. See also Surūr, *Dawlat Banī Qalāwūn*, 95; Holt, 'al-Mustaʿīn (II) biʾllāh'; Jaques, *Ibn Hajar*, 55, 58, 61.
116. Al-Suyūṭī, *Taʾrīkh*, 406. For more speculation on the emotional well-being of the caliph: Ibn Ḥajar, *Inbāʾ al-ghumr*, 3:446; Ibn Taghrībirdī, *Nujūm*, 13:203; al-Suyūṭī, *Ḥusn*, 2:89; Holt, *Age of the Crusades*, 182.

117. Al-Maqrīzī, *Sulūk*, 4:234, al-Maqrīzī, *Durar*, 2:214; al-ʿAynī, *ʿIqd* (1985–9), 1:134–6; Ibn Taghrībirdī, *Nujūm*, 13:203–4, 14:165; Ibn Taghrībirdī, *Mawrid*, 1:256; Ibn Ḥajar, *Inbāʾ al-ghumr*, 2:514; al-Ṣayrafī, *Nuzhat*, 2:314, 316; Ibn Iyās, *Badāʾiʿ*, 1:2:828. See also Surūr, *Dawlat Banī Qalāwūn*, 95; Holt, *Age of the Crusades*, 182.
118. Al-Maqrīzī, *Sulūk*, 4:234, 239; Ibn Ḥajar, *Inbāʾ al-ghumr*, 2:515; Ibn Taghrībirdī, *Nujūm*, 13:205–6; Ibn Taghrībirdī, *Mawrid*, 2:135; al-Qaramānī, *Akhbār*, 2:216. For the text of the *ʿahd* document, see al-Qalqashandī, *Ṣubḥ*, 10:120–8; al-Saḥmāwī, *Thaghr*, 2:594–604.
119. Al-Maqrīzī, *Sulūk*, 4:240; Ibn Taghrībirdī, *Nujūm*, 13:206–8; Ibn Iyās, *Badāʾiʿ*, 1:2:827; Hassan, *Longing for the Lost Caliphate*, 95.
120. Al-Maqrīzī, *Sulūk*, 4:240. The name of al-Mustaʿīn was mentioned in the prayers of the holy places of the Hijaz for about five months, until it was discontinued in Dhū al-Qaʿda 815/February 1413 and prayers instead made for Shaykh. See al-Ḥājjī, *Anmāṭ*, 24.
121. Ibn Ḥajar, *Inbāʾ al-ghumr*, 2:519. See also Ilisch, 'Inedita', 40.
122. Van Steenbergen, *Caliphate and Kingship*, 65–6, 77–8, 100.
123. Ibn Ḥajar, *Inbāʾ al-ghumr*, 2:516; al-Maqrīzī, *Sulūk*, 4:243–4; Ibn Taghrībirdī, *Nujūm*, 13:206; Ibn Taghrībirdī, *Manhal*, 6:287; al-Suyūṭī, *Taʾrīkh*, 406; Ibn Iyās, *Badāʾiʿ*, 1:2:828.
124. Al-Maqrīzī, *Sulūk*, 4:244; al-Maqrīzī, *Khiṭaṭ*, 3:204; al-Maqrīzī, *Durar*, 2:214, 3:14; Ibn Ḥajar, *Inbāʾ al-ghumr*, 2:516, 3:446; Ibn Taghrībirdī, *Nujūm*, 13:206–7, 14:1; Ibn Taghrībirdī, *Manhal*, 7:62; Ibn Taghrībirdī, *Mawrid*, 1:256, 2:134; al-Ṣayrafī, *Nuzhat*, 2:317; al-Sakhāwī, *Wajīz*, 2:421; al-Sakhwī, *Dhayl*, 1:478; al-Suyūṭī, *Ḥusn*, 2:89; al-Suyūṭī, *Taʾrīkh*, 406; Ibn Iyās, *Badāʾiʿ*, 1:2:827–8, 2:3–4; al-Qaramānī, *Akhbār*, 2:216; Piloti, *Egypte*, 13–14; Hassan, *Longing for the Lost Caliphate*, 95.
125. Al-Maqrīzī, *Sulūk*, 4:232, 255–6; Ibn Taghrībirdī, *Nujūm*, 14:7; Ibn Taghrībirdī, *Mawrid*, 2:137. Chroniclers refer to these coins as '*Nawrūzī dīnārs*', which imply that Nawrūz, rather than the caliph, ordered them to be minted. See Schultz, 'Silver Coinage', 211.
126. Al-Suyūṭī, *Ḥusn*, 2:89; Jaques, *Ibn Hajar*, 63–4; Hassan, *Longing for the Lost Caliphate*, 95.
127. Al-Qalqashandī, *Maʾāthir*, 2:206. Ibn Taghrībirdī claims the group adjourned without reaching a solid verdict (*Nujūm*, 14:5–6), while al-Suyūṭī suggests that the assembly condemned Shaykh's unlawful actions (*Taʾrīkh*, 406).
128. Al-Ḥajjī, *Anmāṭ*, 27–8.

129. Ibn Ḥajar, *Inbāʾ al-ghumr*, 2:518; Ibn Taghrībirdī, *Nujūm*, 15:5; al-Ṣayrafī, *Nuzhat*, 2:318–19; Ṭarkhān, *Miṣr*, 65.

130. Al-Maqrīzī, *Sulūk*, 4:273–4; Ibn Ḥajar, *Inbāʾ al-ghumr*, 3:15; al-ʿAynī, *ʿIqd* (1985–9), 1:181; Ibn Taghrībirdī, *Nujūm*, 13:207, 14:16; Ibn Taghrībirdī, *Manhal*, 6:295; Ibn Taghrībirdī, *Mawrid*, 1:257–8, 2:135; al-Ṣayrafī, *Nuzhat*, 2:334; al-Sakhāwī, *Wajīz*, 2:425; al-Sakhāwī, *Tibr*, 25; al-Suyūṭī, *Ḥusn*, 2:89–90.

131. Al-Maqrīzī, *Sulūk*, 4:273–4; Ibn Ḥajar, *Inbāʾ al-ghumr*, 3:15; Ibn Taghrībirdī, *Manhal*, 6:295, 7:63; Ibn Taghrībirdī, *Mawrid*, 2:135; al-Sakhāwī, *Dhayl*, 1:489; al-Sakhāwī, *Tibr*, 25; al-Qaramānī, *Akhbār*, 2:216. The precise arrangement of al-Mustaʿīn's caliphate remains curious. Some historians date the beginning of al-Muʿtaḍid II's caliphate to Dhū al-Ḥijja 816/February 1414, but al-Mustaʿīn was never formally deposed as he himself continued to claim from Alexandria. Sources agree that Shaykh exiled the former caliph-sultan from Cairo in 819/1417, but his official position, if he held one at all, is unclear and seemed to cause initial confusion on the *minbars*. Nevertheless, al-Maqrīzī begins the year 816/1413–14 by saying 'the caliph is al-Mustaʿīn bi-llāh who is forbidden from leaving', *Sulūk*, 4:255, while al-ʿAynī describes the caliph in the same year as 'restrained' (*muʿawwiq*) in the Citadel, *ʿIqd* (1985–9), 1:160. Al-Maqrīzī begins 817/1414–15 and 818/1415–16 by acknowledging al-Muʿtaḍid II as 'caliph of the time', *Sulūk*, 4:279, 298. According to the later historian al-Malaṭī, the name of al-Mustaʿīn remained in the caliphate from the day of his deposition as sultan, until Shaykh needed a caliph to bring to Syria and he selected Dāwūd al-Muʿtaḍid and named him caliph (*Nayl*, 3:261). It was indeed a bizarre moment (considering the explicit stance taken by Sunni political theory regarding multiple *imāms*) in which there were *two* Abbasid caliphs in Egypt. To explain Shaykh's appointment of a second caliph, Ḥayāt Nāṣir al-Ḥājjī suggested that the sultan may have wished to defy Nawrūz who continued to champion the cause of al-Mustaʿīn in Syria, and flaunt his unwillingness to recognise Shaykh's sultanate. Thus, the move provided a way for Shaykh to demonstrate his own power to suppress the office holder associated with the sultanate and caliphate and appoint two others (including himself) to take office instead, see al-Ḥajjī *Anmāṭ*, 25–6.

132. Al-Maqrīzī, *Sulūk*, 4:273–4; Ibn Ḥajar, *Inbāʾ al-ghumr*, 3:92–3; Ibn Taghrībirdī, *Manhal*, 7:63.

133. In Rajab 818/September 1415, Shaykh, joined by al-Muʿtaḍid II, returned to Syria to subdue rebels. See al-Maqrīzī, *Sulūk*, 4:327; Ibn Taghrībirdī, *Nujūm*, 14:34–6; al-Sakhāwī, *Wajīz*, 2:437; Ibn Iyās, *Badāʾiʿ*, 2:22–3.

134. Al-Maqrīzī, *Sulūk*, 4:282, 287–8, 373–4; Ibn Ḥajar, *Inbā' al-ghumr*, 2:519, 3:37; Ibn Taghrībirdī, *Mawrid*, 2:135; al-Sakhāwī, *Dhayl*, 1:482; al-Sakhāwī, *Wajīz*, 2:421; al-Malaṭī, *Rawḍ*, 1:236; Ibn Iyās, *Badā'i'*, 2:15. On the Nawrūzī coins, see Popper, *Systematic Notes*, 2:55–6; Ilisch, 'Inedita', 40.
135. Al-Maqrīzī, *Sulūk*, 4:373; al-Maqrīzī, *Khiṭaṭ*, 3:787; al-Maqrīzī, *Durar*, 2:215; Ibn Ḥajar, *Inbā' al-ghumr*, 3:85; al-'Aynī, *'Iqd* (1985–9), 2:385; Ibn Taghrībirdī, *Nujūm*, 13:207; Ibn Taghrībirdī, *Mawrid*, 1:257; al-Sakhāwī, *Ḍaw'*, 4:19–20; al-Sakhāwī, *Wajīz*, 2:425, 511; al-Suyūṭī, *Ḥusn*, 2:90.
136. Al-Maqrīzī, *Sulūk*, 4:587; Ibn Ḥajar, *Inbā' al-ghumr*, 3:446; Ibn Taghrībirdī, *Manhal*, 7:63; al-Sakhāwī, *Ḍaw'*, 4:20; al-Sakhāwī, *Wajīz*, 2:425; al-Suyūṭī, *Ta'rīkh*, 406.
137. Al-'Aynī, *'Iqd* (1985–9), 2:384. Several years earlier in 820/1417 Cairo received a report of the deaths of various exiled notables in Alexandria which erroneously numbered the caliph al-Musta'īn among the casualties. See Ibn Ḥajar, *Inbā' al-ghumr*, 3:139.
138. Al-Maqrīzī, *Sulūk*, 4:844; al-Maqrīzī, *Durar*, 2:215; Ibn Ḥajar, *Inbā' al-ghumr*, 3:273, 446; Ibn Taghrībirdī, *Nujūm*, 13:207–8, 15:163; Ibn Taghrībirdī, *Manhal*, 7:63, 12:78; Ibn Taghrībirdī, *Mawrid*, 1:257, 2:135; al-Malaṭī, *Nayl*, 4:274, 5:172; al-Malaṭī, *Rawḍ*, 1:237; al-Sakhāwī, *Ḍaw'*, 3:205, 4:20, 10:229; al-Sakhāwī, *Dhayl*, 1:567, 645; al-Sakhāwī, *Tibr*, 85; al-Sakhāwī, *Wajīz*, 2:511, 593; al-Suyūṭī, *Ḥusn*, 2:90; al-Suyūṭī, *Raf' al-bās*, 127; Ibn Iyās, *Badā'i'*, 2:12, 237–8; al-Qaramānī, *Akhbār*, 2:217. Although he spent most of his life in Alexandria, Yaḥyā later settled in Cairo. His caliphal claim no doubt queering relations with the Abbasid family already in Cairo, Yaḥyā lived in isolation near Yellow Lane (*al-Darb al-Aṣfar*), a small alley adjoining the Baybarsiyya *madrasa* and *khānqāh* complex to the central thoroughfare Bayn al-Qaṣrayn. Several sources mention him honourably among the notables who died in Muḥarram 847/May 1443.
139. Hassan, *Longing for the Lost Caliphate*, 93–4.
140. Ibn Taghrībirdī, *Nujūm*, 13:193; Hassan, *Longing for the Lost Caliphate*, 93; Garcin, 'Histoire', 62.
141. Al-Maqrīzī, *Sulūk*, 4:844; Ibn Taghrībirdī, *Manhal*, 7:63–4; al-Sakhāwī, *Ḍaw'*, 4:20.
142. Al-'Aynī, *'Iqd* (1985–9), 2:384.
143. Surūr, *Dawlat Banī Qalāwūn*, 96.
144. Garcin, 'Histoire', 61–2.

4

Containing and Maintaining the Caliphate, 815–903/1412–97

Introduction

The fifteenth-century sultanate of Cairo can be approached as the end-product of a long history, and a break from the earlier (longer dynastic) patterns of the late thirteenth and fourteenth centuries.[1] To contextualise the changes in the Abbasid Caliphate taking place during this transformative period, it is first necessary to comment on the evolving nature of the socio-political order in the sultanate. The reigns of al-Mutawakkil and al-Mustaʿīn discussed in Chapter 3, unfolded during the last successful 'dynastic experiment' of the sultanate in the form of the short-lived 'Barquqid' dynasty (784–815/1382–1412) comprising of al-Ẓāhir Barqūq and his son al-Nāṣir Faraj. The disastrous reign of the latter – plagued by internecine strife compounded by plague outbreaks as well as the destruction of Syrian cities by Temür – led to the execution of the sultan, the complete breakdown of the social order, and the loss of Egyptian control of Syria during the first decades of the fifteenth century. Amid a peculiar moment of transition and fragmented authority, the caliph al-Mustaʿīn was briefly named sultan until a new group, led by al-Muʾayyad Shaykh, established a new social and political order.[2]

The period between 815 and 872/1412 and 1468 in particular witnessed at least five sultans (all genuine former '*mamlūk*' military slaves from the household of Barqūq) who came to power as the 'state' was made and re-made around them and their courts. Although appearing as a constant centre of legitimacy, the court of each new sultan was largely unrelated to the one that preceded it.[3] There was also a common Circassian ethnic origin and social identity among many of the political elite which had begun in the late fourteenth century.[4]

In this context, the symbolic authority of the Abbasid Caliphate was sustained as a dependable mode of legitimacy in perpetually shifting Cairene politics. As each new sultan came to power, the political elites underwent processes of fragmentation, integration and, in some cases, a 'recycling' as they struggled to re-emerge in new political orders restored via the renegotiation of networks and the redistribution of power and resources.[5] As Chapter 3 demonstrates, politics frequently forced the caliphs of the late fourteenth/early fifteenth centuries to participate against their will. With only one later exception, this was not the case for much of the fifteenth century. The Abbasid caliphs of this period tried to maintain the living standard and properties held by their household, actively pursued scholarship, and in most cases distanced themselves from non-ceremonial affairs of state. The Abbasids appear in our sources as a family that had learned from recent mistakes and wanted to keep a low profile after al-Mutawakkil and al-Mustaʿīn. The caliphs of the fifteenth century resembled earlier predecessors such as al-Ḥākim II and al-Muʿtaḍid I, quiet 'men of good works' and religion who cultivated academic profiles and participated in the social networks of the scholarly class. In the meantime, they enjoyed modest scholarly careers as the religious dimensions of the office continued to develop along with the privileges and assets of their household.

An Ideal Caliph: the Reign of al-Muʿtaḍid bi-llāh II, 816–45/1414–41

With his brother the former caliph-sultan al-Mustaʿīn in confinement until exile in 819/1417, al-Muʿtaḍid II served as acting Abbasid caliph and joined the sultan al-Muʾayyad Shaykh on an offensive against Nawrūz in Syria in early 817/1414. Nevertheless, the memory of al-Mustaʿīn continued to haunt Shaykh's sultanate as *Nawrūzī* dinars naming the former caliph-sultan continued to appear in Syrian cities. A final showdown with Nawrūz ended the threat in Syria that year as Shaykh's sultanate began to stabilise. To symbolically protect his own position as sultan, Shaykh brought al-Muʿtaḍid II along for the journey, putting him beyond the reach of competitors. The sultan continued to use the Abbasid Caliphate and the chief qadis as sources of legitimacy in his domestic policy when in Rajab 818/September 1415 he

Map 4.1 Fifteenth-century west Asia.

headed to Syria to fight the former *nāʾib* Qānībāy and others who challenged his appointment of the amir Ṭaṭar as governor.[6]

To construct a new political elite and restore the regional dominance and symbolic authority of the sultanate of Cairo, Shaykh and his entourage integrated diverse elites in Syria and Anatolia.[7] Adriaenssens and Van Steenbergen have described a 'complex Anatolian arena' that included the northern frontier zone buffering the Syro-Egyptian territories of the Cairo Sultanate:

> There was an external complexity of constantly shifting and crisscrossing allegiances and authorities of local, regional and transregional rulers in many parts of Anatolia. This coalesced into the competition of many Turkmen leaders for access to land and resources and simultaneously of the rulers of Cairo, Bursa and Herat for geopolitical hegemony and for local military and economic control.[8]

By acting in southern and eastern Anatolia, Shaykh sought to counter the regional threat posed by Temür's successor Shāh Rukh (807–50/1405–47) and the Turkmen polities empowered by his father following the defeat of the Ottomans at Ankara in 804/1402. Chief among them was the growing power of the Qaraquyunlu under Qarā Yūsuf (792–823/1390–1420) in Baghdad. In the north, several independent Turkmen principalities were clients of Cairo such as the Ramadanids who dominated Cilicia from Adana, while their eastern neighbours, the Dulqadirids of Elbistan, held influence in Marʿash and Malaṭya. Stronger powers existed in the west, the Qaramanids of Konya, as well as the Turkmen configurations of the Aqquyunlu and Qaraquyunlu further east.[9] The Qaramanid Nāṣir al-Dīn Muḥammad Beg seized Ṭarsūs from the Cairo-allied Ramadanids which Shaykh later recovered. Each grouping or tribal formation competed for influence and resources in a highly fluid social space 'by challenging their integration into the sultan's orbit or by bringing their claims to court in Cairo'.[10] The sultan grew increasingly troubled by the Qaramanids and the Qaraquyunlu. Perhaps worried that competition between the two would spill into Aleppo, Shaykh made the city his base of operations for staging expeditions into Anatolia. As the Timurids and Ottomans recovered from regional struggles, the sultan headed to Damascus with al-Muʿtaḍid II and the qadis,[11] and, over the course of

820–2/1417–19, restored Cairo's authority deep into Anatolia via military engagement.[12]

The Qaraquyunlu remained a threat for Shaykh, particularly in the Aleppan theatre. In Shaʿbān 821/September 1418, the sultan summoned the caliph and the *ʿulamāʾ* to publicly declare Qarā Yūsuf an infidel for his transgressions against the faith. The *shaykh al-islām* Jalāl al-Dīn al-Bulqīnī composed a document enumerating the Qaraquyunlu chief's infractions against *sharīʿa* and the qadis wrote an approval for his death that al-Muʿtaḍid and others signed. It was thus that the caliph and other *ʿulamāʾ* facilitated the excommunication and killing of the sultan's enemies. When tensions began to escalate, Qarā Yūsuf ultimately withdrew, claiming that revenge against the Aqquyunlu leader Qarā Yülük, who dominated the Erzincan and Diyar Bakr regions with his family, had been his true interest in the region.[13]

Qarā Yülük sent word to Cairo on 27 Rajab 823/7 August 1420 that he had captured and beheaded Pīr ʿUmar, Qarā Yūsuf's proxy in Erzincan. Shortly before his own death Shaykh prepared an expedition against Qarā Yūsuf and on 4 Shaʿbān 823/14 August 1420 proclaimed the lawfulness of fighting Qarā Yūsuf, and in the caliph's presence called on men to take up arms against him.[14]

Al-Muʿtaḍid II also joined other members of the religious establishment in attempts to curb plague outbreaks that menaced Shaykh's time in power. By spring 822/1419, the epidemic had again grown widespread in Cairo, claiming nearly half the fellahin population. The sultan took the threat seriously and saw faith as an effective way to combat it. To this end Shaykh ordered three days of public fasting which culminated in a ceremony on the desert plain on 15 Rabīʿ II/11 May. Shaykh himself beseeched God to end the plague and encouraged the caliph, positioned at his right side, as well as other scholars, jurists and Sufis on his left, to lend their efforts. Pious people including al-Muʿtaḍid, dressed in white cloaks, held caliphal standards overhead. Likewise clad in white, Shaykh led a sombre ceremony at Barqūq's tomb bereft of the usual sultanic pomp and focused on Quranic recitations in modest surroundings. On foot, Shaykh led Friday prayers flanked by the caliph and other men of religion. Egyptian sources declared the event a success when the severity of the plague was said to have diminished shortly thereafter.[15]

Al-Muʿtaḍid II and al-Ẓāhir Ṭaṭar

As Shaykh neared the end of his life, on 20 Shawwāl 823/28 October 1420 he invited the caliph and other religious dignitaries to name his infant son Aḥmad to the sultanate after him. In a matter of months, Shaykh's former deputy, the amir Ṭaṭar, emerged as the most powerful strongman and before long, aided by his comrades, triumphed over the younger supporters of the sultan. Ṭaṭar became regent to Shaykh's son after the father's death on 9 Muḥarram 824/14 January 1421. The amirs again summoned al-Muʿtaḍid II to establish the child as sultan. Aḥmad received *bayʿa* as al-Malik al-Muẓaffar in the presence of the caliph and the qadis, after which the caliph led funerary prayers for Shaykh.[16]

Shaykh's successors continued the various processes of restoration and reformation he had begun, although through the use of their own subordinates and followers rather than his.[17] Faced with the mounting tensions stirred by malcontent Syrian amirs, Ṭaṭar was anxious to receive formal authority as *amīr kabīr*. He ordered al-Muʿtaḍid to attend the Ashrafiyya barracks of the Citadel on 10 Ṣafar 824/14 February 1421 to testify before a gathering of notables that he had entrusted Ṭaṭar with the affairs of the subjects and granted him power to depose and appoint at will, although al-Muẓaffar Aḥmad would retain the title of sultan. The qadis then validated and ratified the caliph's testament.[18]

On 14 Rabīʿ II 824/18 April 1421, Ṭaṭar advanced on Syria to confront the opposition. He camped at Raydāniyya, joined by al-Muʿtaḍid II, the sultan, amirs and important government officials before heading to Damascus a week later. After he secured Syria, Ṭaṭar moved to depose Aḥmad and establish his own sultanate while in Damascus on 29 Shaʿbān 824/29 August 1421. The caliph and qadis swore allegiance to Ṭaṭar followed by the amirs and *mamlūk*s.[19] During the ceremony al-Muʿtaḍid questioned the attendees on Ṭaṭar's installation, whereupon the assembly unanimously confirmed the *amīr kabīr* as sultan. Ṭaṭar donned the traditional black caliphal cloak and was prayed for from the pulpits of Damascus that same day.

Ṭaṭar's initiative to free the former caliph al-Mustaʿīn from Alexandria on 26 Dhū al-Qaʿda 824/22 November 1421 was received favourably by elites.[20] The new sultan's pardon of the exiled caliph represented benevolence towards the Abbasid family and was a reversal of Shaykh's unfavourable policy. With al-Muʿtaḍid firmly established in the caliphate, Ṭaṭar had little to lose by freeing al-Mustaʿīn as a public act of goodwill.

Although illness shortened the sultanate of Ṭaṭar to just three months, before his death he ordered al-Muʿtaḍid II, the qadis and important notables to attend him in the Citadel to receive his final instructions. Just as Barqūq and Shaykh had hoped to secure their dynasties, on 2 Dhū al-Ḥijja 824/28 November 1421 Ṭaṭar requested that al-Muʿtaḍid II oversee the investiture of his own son Muḥammad as successor. The boy was called to the sultan's palace and seated by the caliph who swore allegiance to him as sultan al-Malik al-Ṣāliḥ. Draped in black caliphal robes and adorned with royal symbols (*shiʿār*), al-Ṣāliḥ Muḥammad led a procession on horseback. The masquerade lasted four months until Ṭaṭar's amirs reached the outcome of a new succession struggle. The amirs Barsbāy and Jānibak al-Ṣūfī emerged as the two leading contenders, the former ultimately taking power as regent to the young sultan as the latter went on to wage various resistance campaigns across the southern and eastern frontier zone of Anatolia.[21]

Al-Muʿtaḍid II and Al-Ashraf Barsbāy

On 16 Dhū al-Ḥijja 824/12 December 1421, al-Muʿtaḍid II invested Barsbāy as *niẓām al-mulk* with administrative control over government affairs, acting as regent for al-Sālih Muḥammad until he reached puberty. In accordance with sultanic custom, al-Muʿtaḍid featured prominently in the enthronement ceremony on 8 Rabīʿ II 825/1 April 1422, after Barsbāy seized the sultanate for himself. At the event, the amirs kissed the ground before Barsbāy and the caliph invested him with a customary caliphal robe.[22] Historiographical sources mention little regarding al-Muʿtaḍid's involvement at the court of Barsbāy, reinforcing the idea that the caliph's political role was negligible and that he remained a primarily religious figure with minimal responsibility.

Benefiting from Shaykh's earlier model of state formation and political reformation, Barsbāy continued previous policies of active representation, diplomacy and campaigning in Anatolia, while also expanding the influence of his political order into neighbouring areas such as the Hijaz and Cyprus which he subdued as a vassal. As sultan, he topped a new regional political order which emanated from his court in Cairo.[23] The Timurid ruler Shāh

Rukh, who had risen in the east, was said to have pointedly abandoned the Mongol customs of his father, moving instead towards embracing and applying the Islamic *sharīʿa*. Shāh Rukh, in competition with rival members of his family, presented himself, at least for a time, as a 'caliph' from approximately 807 to 821/1405 to 1418 and on numismatic evidence from 819 to 825/1416 to 1422. After his early western campaigns, which would have also made him aware of the 150-year-old Cairene Abbasid Caliphate, the Timurid ruler abandoned or lost interest in the title.[24]

Although the sultans of Cairo had enjoyed greater regional dominance since the reign of Barqūq, at various times Barsbāy found himself in ideological contests with Sunni rivals including Shāh Rukh and the Aqquyunlu Turkmen.[25] Upon asserting hegemony over the Hijaz and the lucrative Red Sea trade, Barsbāy revived the notion, dating from the Ayyubids, that authority over the two holy cities and the Muslim *ḥajj* was the right of the sovereign of Cairo. This he emphasised symbolically by exercising the exclusive prerogative of sending the *kiswa* cloth covering for the Kaʿba at each major pilgrimage.[26]

Anxious to affirm his own counterclaim to Islam's holiest of holies, Shāh Rukh regularly offered to send inner *kiswa* drapes for the Kaʿba. Barsbāy, in addition to his desire to maintain prestige, however, was worried that Shāh Rukh might disturb his own commercial interests by gaining a foothold in the Hijaz. The Timurid ruler renewed his *kiswa* campaign in 838/1434–5, but Barsbāy and the *ʿulamāʾ* found a religious loophole by which to deny him.[27] Thus, protection of the Hijaz, rather than support for the caliph gained strength within the legitimating arsenal of the fifteenth-century Cairo Sultanate.[28]

In another apparent Timurid 'break' with Mongol tradition, Temür's grandson Pīr Muḥammad ibn ʿUmar Shaykh (d. 812/1409) may have tried to reach for new kinds of legitimating principles. Relying on the narratives of fifteenth-century Timurid chroniclers such as Ḥāfiẓ-i Abrū and ʿAbd al-Razzāq Samarqandī, modern historians have argued that while trying to assert his authority as governor in southern Iran after Temür's death, some advisers briefly recommended that the Timurid prince request an investiture deed from the Abbasid caliph in Cairo.[29]

Cairene political elites of the time, perhaps wishing to project the superiority of their court across Muslim west Asia, sent robes of honour in the name of the caliph to the Qaraquyunlu ruler of Iraq and Azerbaijan, Jahānshāh (837–53/1434–49), as well as years later to the conqueror of Constantinople, the Ottoman sultan Meḥmed II (855–86/1451–81). Emissaries sent on behalf of the caliph of Cairo met with hostility at both courts. Jahānshāh warned the emissary that if it were not for his status as a visiting messenger, he would have lost his tongue. The Qaraquyunlu ruler then ordered the emissary to don the caliphal robe himself and gifted him 300 dinars to make the journey. Meḥmed II ordered his robe be shredded and informed the emissary that he himself was the caliph of the world.[30]

Barsbāy's Āmid Campaign

The growing influence of Shāh Rukh in the east complicated Barsbāy's relationship with the Aqquyunlu Turkmen. As Patrick Wing observed, the protection and status Qarā Yülük enjoyed as a client of Barsbāy suddenly became secondary to Shāh Rukh's ability to deal with his Turkmen rivals. Seizing on a moment of Qaraquyunlu weakness, Qarā Yülük expanded his influence into Anatolian towns on the Euphrates that were loyal to Barsbāy, thus making them rivals.[31] To preserve his patrimony and humble the Aqquyunlu, the sultan headed towards Syria with his entire court on 19 Rajab 836/11 March 1433, joined by the four chief qadis and al-Muʿtaḍid II donning a turban worn in the so-called Baghdādī-style of the earlier Abbasid caliphs.[32]

As part of the campaign preparations the sultan disbursed 500 dinars to the caliph and provided him with a special escort. Nevertheless, the pair rode east together from Raydāniyya.[33] The caliph was an important focal point in Barsbāy's procession, the qadis walked before him with the caliphal standard paraded over their heads. After several weeks of travel through Syria, Barsbāy left the qadis in Aleppo but continued on with al-Muʿtaḍid II; the caliph personally accompanied by the second-class amir Qarāsunqur.[34] The company entered al-Ruhā (Edessa) after crossing the Euphrates and found it levelled by forces loyal to Barsbāy who had also brutalised the local population. The sultan withdrew and camped near the Turkmen capital of Āmid on 8 Shawwāl 836/28 May 1433. Al-Muʿtaḍid II rode alongside the sultan before lines of troops surrounded by unarmed government administrators. Wishing to demonstrate an air of religious supremacy, Barsbāy ordered his officials to dress in the cloaks of jurists and marched them before the soldiers.

When the sultan's forces reached the city, Qarā Yülük unleashed the dammed waters of the Tigris and trapped them in an ambush. At best, Barsbāy's campaign amounted to a draw, and although they forced Qarā Yülük to yield some Egyptian sources called the campaign a failure. Nevertheless, with the caliph and qadis preceding him on the way back, Barsbāy returned to Cairo in early 837/1433 and received a hero's welcome, with the city decorated in his honour.[35]

Five years later in 841/1438, the dying sultan summoned al-Muʿtaḍid II, the qadis and amirs to perform the familiar deathbed ceremony witnessing the delegation of his son Jamāl al-Dīn Yūsuf as successor. In his final hours, Barsbāy sat in a serene pavilion, encircled by the caliph and members of his entourage. When prompted, al-Muʿtaḍid, who formally received supervision (*imḍāʾ*) over the affair, approved the decision and praised Barsbāy's selection. The qadi and deputy secretary testified to the selection of Yūsuf and the caliph validated the statement. Following the increasingly typical pattern, the amir Jaqmaq, as Yūsuf's regent, prepared to seize the government in his own name. The caliph duly robed Jaqmaq in Dhū al-Qaʿda 841/April–May 1438 as *atābak* and recognised his authority as *niẓām al-mulk* over matters of governance. Al-Muʿtaḍid later met with Jaqmaq and other elites to invest Yūsuf as sultan al-Malik al-ʿAzīz. Although many courtiers had hoped the caliph would lead the funeral prayers for Barsbāy, the honour ultimately fell to the grand qadi Ibn Ḥajar al-ʿAsqalānī when pious participants observed that the double-satin robe, deemed unacceptable by the *sharīʿa* and bestowed on the caliph by Yūsuf, had negated al-Muʿtaḍid's permissibility to perform prayers.[36]

The caliph invested and robed Yūsuf in black as sultan on 13 Dhū al-Ḥijja 841/7 June 1438. The next day at a ceremony in the castle, al-Muʿtaḍid received the gift of Ṣābūnī Island in addition to other landholdings possessed by the Abbasid household and a few other *iqṭāʿ* disbursements. Tensions mounted as the army split between supporters of Jaqmaq as *amīr kabīr* and the Ashrafī *mamlūk*s of Barsbāy cloistered in the Citadel, who, while less-experienced, had the advantage of access to important resources including the treasury, the armoury and the Abbasid caliph. Although he had failed to protect the sons of Shaykh and Ṭaṭar from being swept away by ambitious amirs, al-Muʿtaḍid, perhaps to safeguard his recent acquisition of Ṣābūnī Island, expressed his intention to uphold the oath sworn to Barsbāy and supported the young sultan against Jaqmaq as the latter prepared to seize power.[37]

Al-Muʿtaḍid II and al-Ẓāhir Jaqmaq

On 17 Rabīʿ I 842/7 September 1438, the amir Qurqumās al-Shaʿbānī called the attention of al-Muʿtaḍid II and the qadis to the sultan's youth and argued that Jaqmaq was better suited to safeguard the welfare of the Muslims. After the assembly attested to a transfer of power to Jaqmaq, it fell to the Abbasid caliph (evidently swayed in favour of Jaqmaq) who, after public prayers for the government, initiated the *bay*ʿa followed by the qadis and amirs. Al-Muʿtaḍid II arrived at the Ḥarrāqa pavilion near the royal stables according to custom.[38] Egyptian sources do not indicate whether Jaqmaq begrudged the caliph's earlier loyalty to al-ʿAzīz Yūsuf. To demonstrate his error and subsequent acknowledgement of the unsuitability of al-ʿAzīz Yūsuf, al-Muʿtaḍid proclaimed before the amirs, 'I am aware of this, and I testify to you that I have removed al-Malik al-ʿAzīz from the sultanate and have rendered the *amīr kabīr* Jaqmaq sultan [in his place].' In turn, Jaqmaq invested al-Muʿtaḍid with a robe and gave him a lavishly decorated horse. Inaugural festivities concluded with a public reading of Jaqmaq's diploma in the Citadel on 9 Rabīʿ II 842/29 September 1438 in the presence of al-Muʿtaḍid, the qadis and the *kātib al-sirr*. Before the congregation dispersed, Jaqmaq again presented the caliph and others with robes and horses.[39]

Cihan Yüksel Muslu points out that shortly after his investiture as sultan, Jaqmaq emphasised the deciding role that al-Muʿtaḍid II had played in 'electing' him alongside other members of the religio-political elite in correspondence sent to the Ottoman sultan Murād II to inform him about changes in the Syro-Egyptian political order. The myth of election or consultation involving the caliph was occasionally exploited by the Cairo sultans to strengthen their claims to sovereignty.[40]

From the start of his reign, Jaqmaq had to subdue a number of the former Ashrafī amirs of Barsbāy, including Qurqumās al-Shaʿbānī, who revolted and sought to restore the rights of al-ʿAzīz Yūsuf or otherwise create their own rival political orders in Damascus and Aleppo. After Jaqmaq and his agents defeated the opposition, the period of his sultanate (842–57/1438–53) began in earnest.

Some months later, in Rabīʿ I 843/August 1439, the amir and Bedouin leader Baybars ibn Baqar[41] (d. 866/1461), who had fallen afoul of the sultan and temporarily escaped his wrath earlier in his career, threw himself on the mercy and good graces of al-Muʿtaḍid II whom he begged to mediate on his behalf. The caliph spoke kindly of the disgraced amir, and Jaqmaq, after accepting the caliphal intercession, granted Baybars ibn Baqar safe passage to leave his presence unharmed. Some years after the death of al-Muʿtaḍid II, however, the anger of the sultan caught up with Baybars on 25 Jumādā II 849/28 September 1445, and he was imprisoned in the tower of the Citadel. Presented with a list of his crimes, the sultan cancelled the previous caliphal pardon and demanded that Baybars answer for past offences.[42]

Man of Knowledge, Man of Religion

For nearly thirty years al-Muʿtaḍid II participated in solemn pageantry at the behest of new Cairo sultans, investing no fewer than seven. His mundane caliphate is attributable to his isolation from politics. The caliph focused on a quiet life of religion and did no more than the ceremonial requirements expected of him. More importantly, no opportunities emerged which might have thrust him into the complex web of power politics.[43] Thus, the caliph remained a religious and political cipher available to lend authority to public programmes such as prayer against the plague or to officially castigate the enemies of the sultan as infidels.

Biographical dictionaries and caliphal histories stress the generosity and piety of the caliph and list his intellectual pursuits, including private studies and public engagement in scholarly salons. In spite of his own modest status as a scholar, al-Muʿtaḍid II, a skilled orator, was happy to address and advise students of religion and enjoyed explaining challenging concepts to other courtiers.[44] The caliph actively patronised and sought the company of men of letters. He enjoyed a patronage relationship with the famous Ibn Ḥajar to whom he gave numerous gifts before departing for Āmid with Barsbāy, and to whom Ibn Ḥajar dedicated florid verses of thanks and praise.[45] The fifteenth-century scribe al-Qalqashandī and the jurist al-Shīrāzī dedicated extensive works on the caliphate and advice literature to him,[46] while Ibn Taghrībirdī frequented the caliph's household and closely studied his behaviour as a youth. Ibn Taghrībirdī knew the caliph personally and wrote that in all the time he had spent with al-Muʿtaḍid II, the caliph had always been an exemplary pillar of manners and good etiquette. Additionally, Ibn Taghrībirdī describes the caliph as a man committed to reciting daily devotions and verses from the Qurʾān at specific times (*lahu awrād fī kulli yawm*).[47] The historian and physician ʿAbd al-Bāsiṭ al-Malaṭī (d. 920/1515) mentions that the caliph enjoyed a close personal relationship with his father, the courtier and administrator Khalīl ibn Shāhīn al-Ẓāhirī (d. 872/1468). In addition to sharing frequent written correspondence with the caliph, Khalīl al-Ẓāhirī also took on a concubine from the household of al-Muʿtaḍid II.[48] In the caliph, biographers recalled a man who strove to emulate the standards of the Rāshidūn caliphs and other notable rulers that preceded him. The political elites of the early fifteenth century likewise made some unconventional use of the caliph's religious authority in both a welcoming ritual for Christian ambassadors and in negotiations to relieve diplomatic pressure placed on the sultan by the Catalans.[49]

Like his father al-Mutawakkil, al-Muʿtaḍid II participated in the funerary prayers of the elite, including amirs such as Yashbak al-Sāqī al-Aʿraj, the *atābak* of Egypt in 831/1427–8, as well as members of the *ʿulamāʾ*, including the qadi and chancery chief Nāṣir al-Dīn Muḥammad ibn al-Bārizī (d. 823/1420). The caliph likewise led funeral prayers for Barsbāy's *kātib al-sirr* Burhān al-Dīn Aḥmad al-Ḥalabī in 835/1431.[50]

The Cairo chancery of the time relied on the name of al-Muʿtaḍid II in which it issued many surviving investiture documents and other deeds of appointment. Like his brother al-Mustaʿīn, al-Muʿtaḍid lent himself to the duty of sanctifying investiture deeds requested by medieval Indian rulers such as the sultan of Bengal, Jalāl al-Dīn Muḥammad Shāh (d. 836/1433), which in turn encouraged diplomatic ties and good relations between the sultanates of India and Cairo.[51]

Unlike his father, however, and in spite of his connections and close association with the courts of several sultans, al-Muʿtaḍid II struggled with a difficult financial situation compounded by the strains of supporting a sizeable household. The demands of his family, entourage and servants, combined with his philanthropic activities could not be maintained by his primary source of income – an *iqṭāʿ* which yielded little more than 4,000 dinars per year. Even revenues from the Nafīsī shrine and al-Ṣābūnī Island seemed to be of little help, forcing the caliph and his family, for at least part of his reign, into a sparse lifestyle.[52]

The investiture of Jaqmaq proved to be the final major public act of al-Muʿtaḍid II. The caliph's choice for succession was unknown during his caliphate, although he had frequently left his only son Ibrāhīm (d. 837/1433), an accomplished Shāfiʿī Qurʾān scholar, as his deputy in Cairo whenever he travelled with Barsbāy. Nevertheless, Ibrāhīm, who did not live past thirty, died of tuberculosis, predeceasing his father.[53] As the caliph himself reached the end of a long sickness in his late sixties,[54] he arranged to pass the family office to his full brother Sulaymān, whom he praised as one who had 'never committed a major sin in youth or in adulthood'. Al-Muʿtaḍid II died on 4 Rabīʿ I 845/23 July 1441 and after a lavish funeral at the Muʾminī Muṣallā of sultan Ḥasan below the Citadel, which even included the pious prayers of Jaqmaq, the caliph was interred in the family fashion near the Nafīsī shrine.[55]

A Life beyond Reproach: al-Mustakfī bi-llāh II, r. 845–55/1441–51

In the summer of 845/1441 at roughly fifty years of age, Sulaymān ibn al-Mutawakkil assumed the caliphate as al-Mustakfī bi-llāh II shortly after the death of his elder brother. A magnificent procession followed his *bayʿa* ceremony and the new caliph paraded home on a stately horse trailing qadis and notables. For the ten years of his caliphate, al-Mustakfī II, a skilled novice in the Shāfiʿī rite, remained aloof from the intrigues and politics of the sultan's court. As a result little has been preserved about him in the annals and most information comes from biographical dictionaries, which above all seek to enumerate his pious and praiseworthy qualities.[56]

A respected courtier with ties to the *ʿulamāʾ*, al-Mustakfī had been a notable participant in the funeral for Ibn Ḥajar in 852/1448.[57] The caliph also secured an illustrious position for the father of Jalāl al-Dīn al-Suyūṭī, the Shāfiʿī scholar Abū Bakr Kamāl al-Dīn (d. 885/1480) as an *imām* and distinguished himself as a great benefactor of the Suyūṭī family.[58] Thus, al-Suyūṭī's warm remembrance of growing up in the caliph's service and praise for his piety come as little surprise:

> [Al-Mustakfī II] was among the most virtuous and devoted of the caliphs; pious, religious, and engaged in worship. He occupied himself with many

> acts of devotion, prayer and reading the Qurʾān. He held his tongue from idle talk and led an irreproachable life.[59]

The caliphate of al-Mustakfī II unfolded entirely within the reign of Jaqmaq's sultanate. Egyptian sources claim the sultan was particularly fond of the caliph with whom he had completed a mutual investiture.[60] As an important symbol of the socio-political order the caliph featured in Jaqmaq's public acts of piety.

When drought dangerously diminished the Nile in Rajab 854/August 1450, Jaqmaq ordered al-Mustakfī II and other notables to visit local holy sites in Cairo. Encouraged by a slight increase in the water level, the sultan sent alms to al-Mustakfī II on 9 Rajab/18 August and ordered the caliph to distribute them at the Ribāṭ al-Āthār shrine (*maḥall al-āthār al-nabawiyya*) and, in the presence of relics associated with the Prophet, pray for God to send more water as his ancestor al-ʿAbbās had done.[61] The sultan then sent notables to prepare and distribute food at the Nilometer (*miqyās*). Al-Mustakfī had again received instructions to pray with the people at the Rawḍa Mosque wherein he stood to lead the congregation in supplications for rain, which other mosques repeated. Some days later on 15 Rajab/24 August Jaqmaq ordered the people to fast and pray for water in the desert. A massive assembly including the caliph, chief qadis, amirs, Sufis and other religious notables travelled to the tomb of Barqūq to pray for rain. The ceremony included an eloquent *khuṭba* by the Shāfiʿī qadi, who, flanked by al-Mustakfī and the three other chief qadis, delivered an impassioned plea for God to send rain.[62]

On 2 Muḥarram 855/4 February 1451 after a brief illness the ascetic caliph reportedly died in his sixties at the Abbasid residence near the shrine of Sayyida Nafīsa. Biographers stress the caliph's piety and position at court, although Ibn Taghrībirdī characterises the caliph as a recluse who seldom interacted with people and remained scrupulously focused on the religious duties and dimensions of his office. Revered for his exceptional sagacity, al-Mustakfī II was said to be silent for lengthy periods, seldom speaking unless he had something profound or valuable to say, or to share an unwavering judgement. In this, he chose not to follow his opinionated brother al-Muʿtaḍid II who frequently interacted with members of court, engaging with *ʿulamāʾ* of various rank. Instead, al-Mustakfī found pleasure in seclusion during his caliphate. Political elites, who seemed highly appreciative of a caliph who bolstered his authority by rare and thus heavily weighted speech, admired the caliph. Indeed, Jaqmaq reportedly put great stock in the wisdom of al-Mustakfī, and was said to be aware of his intellectual assets. Eulogies for the caliph likewise demonstrate that contemporaries regarded him as a near perfect archetype for his office: frequently silent, pious, prudent, reserved, thoughtful, inclined towards great acts of charity and actively engaged in the spiritual protection of the state.[63]

Both al-Muʿtaḍid II and al-Mustakfī II stayed away from political affairs after the disastrous forays of their elder brother and father into amiral politics. As caliphs in the first half of the fifteenth century, they focused on strengthening the religious authority of the sultans who invested them and busied themselves in pious and academic pursuits.[64] While al-Muʿtaḍid actively engaged in courtly life and knew how to navigate its contours, al-Mustakfī tended to remain aloof from things beyond the scope of religion.

The body of the caliph lay in state at the Muʾminī Muṣallā, and his funeral proved to be a well-attended affair with the air of tragedy and loss for a beloved public figure. After the funerary prayer Jaqmaq personally served as a pallbearer for the caliph's coffin during the journey to its final resting place near the tomb of Sayyida Nafīsa.[65]

Al-Qāʾim bi-Amr Allāh, 855–9/1451–5: a Last Grasp for Power

Consumed by illness at the end of his life, al-Mustakfī II failed to provide the elites of the sultan's court with a complete testament for the caliphate. Succession thus became a government issue and fell to Jaqmaq who summoned the surviving sons of al-Mutawakkil I. A fourth son, Abū al-Baqāʾ (or al-Faḍl) Ḥamza, had grown up during the reigns of his father and elder brothers, his qualifications seem merely to have been that he was the eldest living brother of al-Mustakfī II. The political community thus invested Ḥamza as al-Qāʾim bi-Amr Allāh on 5 Muḥarram 855/7 February 1451. After he had received *bayʿa* from the notables, a member of the judiciary interviewed the new caliph to obtain his consent to confirm Jaqmaq as sultan over the Muslims. Upon answering all questions in the affirmative, the caliph dressed Jaqmaq in the caliphal robe (*al-tashrīf al-khalīfatī*), sat, and recited the opening chapter of the Qurʾān before respectfully conveying formal greetings to the sultan.

Al-Qāʾim came to the caliphate amid the customary splendour expected for the office by the mid-fifteenth century and rode in a grand procession to his house preceded by the qadis and notables. Medieval authors characterise Ḥamza as a stickler for classical Abbasid traditions who later acted to introduce even greater caliphal pomp into ceremonial procedures. Few contemporaries likely anticipated that the later intrigues of his brief reign would shatter nearly forty years of political quietism in the Abbasid Caliphate of Cairo.[66]

The Affair of Abū al-Khayr al-Naḥḥās

Scarcely a year into his caliphate, al-Qāʾim waded into politics in Shaʿbān 856/August 1452, attempting to use his influence to intercede for the disgraced administrator, Muḥammad Abū al-Khayr al-Naḥḥās (d. 864/1459). By 853/1449, al-Naḥḥās had risen quickly through Jaqmaq's government to wield power as a close confidant of the sultan. In his quest for influence, al-Naḥḥās made many enemies, while nevertheless ingratiating himself in some circles, including that of the caliph al-Qāʾim. Eventually, the sultan exiled him to Ṭarsūs.[67] In 856/1452, news reached al-Qāʾim that the sultan had ordered al-Naḥḥās to sustain regular beatings in captivity. Using his sway with the sultan, the caliph encouraged Jaqmaq to allow al-Naḥḥās a secret return to Cairo to answer for himself. However, al-Qāʾim's interest in the matter may not have been motivated by mere camaraderie, as al-Sakhāwī had it on the authority of al-Naḥḥās himself that the disgraced courtier had bribed the caliph by offering him rights to some of his properties (*khāṣṣ*) in exchange for influence with Jaqmaq.[68]

Perhaps wishing to distance himself from the controversial figure, al-Qāʾim recruited his nephew Abū al-ʿIzz ʿAbd al-ʿAzīz (the future caliph al-Mutwakkil II) to intercede for al-Naḥḥās and accompanied him as he entered the Duhaysha Hall (*Qāʿat al-Duhaysha*) in the Citadel. The shamed bureaucrat kissed the feet of Jaqmaq, but the sultan, not wishing to be exposed, denied knowledge of approving the visit and instead cursed al-Naḥḥās and reminded those present of his many offences. Perhaps hoping to appear sensitive to *Abbasid* interest in the matter, Jaqmaq commuted al-Naḥḥās' sentence to imprisonment in the tower of the Citadel and, according to

Ibn Taghrībirdī, discussed with ʿAbd al-ʿAzīz the impact his eminent uncle had on the matter: 'I intended to bisect [al-Naḥḥās], but for the sake of the caliph I have pardoned him.' ʿAbd al-ʿAzīz received a gift of 100 dinars and the meeting adjourned. Jaqmaq's change of heart may have stemmed from pressure applied by the powerful enemies of al-Naḥḥās who wished for him to remain imprisoned in Ṭarsūs and would have paid the sultan to keep him there.[69] On the surface, the caliph's intercession was sufficient to grant al-Naḥḥās a second hearing, though not powerful enough to secure the sultan's pardon, even if it spared the fallen bureaucrat future beatings and execution.

The Death of Jaqmaq and Rise of Īnāl

At the end of Jaqmaq's life contemporary observers assumed that the sultan would name his son ʿUthmān successor. A number of amirs wished to discourage the selection, but the sultan could not be dissuaded. At an assembly on 21 Muḥarram 857/1 February 1453, Jaqmaq revisited the illusion that the final decision would be in the hands of the caliph and qadis. Playing his part, al-Qāʾim recognised the fitness of ʿUthmān, based on his aptitude and maturity, which facilitated a speedy same-day caliphal affirmation. The remaining attendees joined in the *bayʿa*, after which ʿUthmān, dressed in traditional black caliphal robes, paraded with the amirs and notables to the sultan's castle. The new sultan robed al-Qāʾim and the senior member of the court, amir Īnāl, as *amīr kabīr*. The pair also received double robes of gold-spun satin and gold-saddled horses. Al-Qāʾim received a cash gift of 1,000 dinars alongside generous land grants for the Abbasid family.[70]

As Jaqmaq sank deeper into illness, al-Manṣūr ʿUthmān took up affairs of state. On 3 Ṣafar 857/13 February 1453 al-Qāʾim led funerary prayers for the only Egyptian ruler acknowledged by Ibn Taghrībirdī as having held the distinct honour of receiving *bayʿa* by three Abbasid caliphs.[71] Some weeks later, notables read ʿUthmān's investiture document aloud during a ceremony in the sultan's castle in the Citadel. Al-Qāʾim oversaw the investiture, but much to his alleged vexation, found himself seated unceremoniously on the ground beside the dais. Nevertheless, according to Ibn Taghrībirdī's narrative, the caliph refrained from displaying outrage at the sultan's disregard for caliphal prestige and ignoring the pageantry that al-Qāʾim had supposedly worked hard to reintroduce during the early years of his caliphate. The ceremony continued undisturbed and after the completion of the reading, al-Manṣūr ʿUthmān invested the caliph and other dignitaries.[72]

Shortly after ʿUthmān began his sultanate, the seventy-three-year-old *amīr kabīr* Īnāl, firm in his position thanks to experience and the accumulation of resources, prepared to seize power and conflict erupted in Rabīʿ I 857/March 1453. The Ashrafiyya *mamlūk*s joined forces with the Muʾayyadiyya and Sayfiyya factions. After adding some of the important Ẓāhirī amirs of Jaqmaq and the treasurer to their ranks, they gathered at Īnāl's residence on Elephant Island. The majority of amirs pledged support to Īnāl, renounced al-Manṣūr ʿUthmān and donned battle gear. To challenge the sultan they applied for Abbasid sanction and beckoned al-Qāʾim to join their coup in its final stages of preparation. The caliph offered encouragement for Īnāl and was said to have required little convincing, seizing the moment as a timely opportunity to exact revenge against al-Manṣūr ʿUthmān.[73]

The coup began with a battle at Rumayla Square during which many of the sultan's *mamlūk*s closed ranks with Īnāl. On 2 Rabīʿ I/13 March, the caliph, who enjoyed a spike in authority (*wa-ṣārat al-kalima lil-khalīfa*), addressed the public several times on the necessity and legality of deposing al-Manṣūr ʿUthmān.[74] Emboldened by the caliph's public blessing, supporters of Īnāl besieged the Citadel and attempted to cut the young sultan's supply lines. After two days of stalemate, al-Qāʾim emerged to enthusiastically announce the deposition of ʿUthmān in favour of Īnāl. Nevertheless, the sultan stubbornly held fast in the Citadel while his cannon pounded Īnāl's men. For his part, the caliph attempted to gather all of his family members for fear that they might fall into the clutches of ʿUthmān, who was likely advised to invest a new anti-caliph from their ranks.[75]

Three days later, Īnāl invited al-Qāʾim, the chief qadis and the *kātib al-sirr*, and listened at length to their strategies for legally deposing ʿUthmān. The religious elite requested a scribe to take dictation from the head Shāfiʿī qadi ʿAlam al-Dīn al-Bulqīnī (d. 868/1464) on the censure and deposition of the sultan. The resulting document, read before amirs and supporters, became the centrepiece of a rally for Īnāl as al-Qāʾim and the qadis led cries for his nomination as sultan. Al-Bulqīnī questioned the assembly on the nomination of Īnāl as sultan, which they unanimously accepted.

After the Friday sermon at which special prayers were offered for 'the caliph and the army of the Muslims', the qadis departed from the prayer hall as renewed fighting against ʿUthmān commenced. Al-Qāʾim remained with Īnāl and together the pair entered the Ḥarrāqa pavilion after Īnāl's soldiers stormed the royal stables and captured important Ẓāhirī amirs. Once ʿUthmān's fall seemed imminent, Īnāl, joined by the caliph at his side, rode out with the army in grand procession. Onlookers gathered as Īnāl passed and ascended the Ḥarrāqa pavilion.[76]

Three days later prominent government officials and soldiers gathered at the royal stables in ceremonial dress to witness al-Qāʾim invest Īnāl as al-Malik al-Ashraf. In black caliphal robes and emblems, Īnāl rode to the sultan's palace and took the throne in the Columned Hall. The amirs kissed the ground before him and he invested the caliph with a reversible green and white outer robe, a decorative brocaded Yalbughāwī band and a gold-saddled horse. Four days of festivities continued in the sultan's castle. By Rabīʿ II 857/April 1453, the sultan ordered the caliph and his family to relocate to the Citadel to avoid political disquiet until fallout from the revolt ended.[77]

Īnāl honoured the caliph again in the Citadel later that month and al-Qāʾim received a *kāmiliyya* overcoat lined with sable fur and forty bushels of sugar. Some weeks later, al-Qāʾim and the qadis witnessed a reading of Īnāl's diploma in the palace of the Citadel on 5 Jumādā I 857/14 May 1453. Īnāl sat on a large pillow on the ground without a throne, while al-Qāʾim sat on his right with the qadis in their assigned seats. After completion, the sultan robed al-Qāʾim and the group disbanded.[78]

Al-Ashraf Īnāl, grateful for the lead role the caliph had played in deposing ʿUthmān, rewarded al-Qāʾim financially and granted him unprecedented influence as an unofficial adviser at a level far beyond any attained by his recent Cairene ancestors.[79] According to Ibn Taghrībirdī, al-Qāʾim enjoyed enormously the fruits of his collaboration with Īnāl, but quickly fell prey to his own ambitions.

The Revolt of the Jaqmaqī Ẓāhirīs and the Sultan's Purchased *Mamlūks*

In Jumādā II 859/April–May 1455, some 500 of the sultan's *julbān* (purchased *mamlūk* recruits) were ordered to travel to the al-Buḥayra region of the Western Delta (northwest of Cairo) but refused, complaining that Īnāl had neglected to equip them with camels and other supplies. Frustration drove the contingent to renounce the sultan and make common cause with a group of Jaqmaq's disgruntled Ẓāhirī *mamlūk*s. The Ẓāhirīs begrudged Īnāl his deposition of their master ʿUthmān, and their subsequent demotion in favour of Īnāl's Ashrafī *mamlūk*s. Likewise, the disenfranchised *mamlūk*s of al-Ashraf Barsbāy (also called Ashrafīs) turned out to join the Ẓāhirī mutineers. The Ẓāhirīs advised Īnāl's unhappy *julbān* that any lasting political change could prevail only by way of armed rebellion against Īnāl blessed by the very Abbasid caliph who had legitimised him.[80]

To this end, Ẓāhirī agents secretly visited the residence of al-Qāʾim with the aim of courting caliphal sanction for the cause. The caliph mulled over possible outcomes and considered it prudent to betray Īnāl, perhaps hopeful that the gambit would deliver even greater influence through the new group. With part of his army in open revolt in the streets of Cairo, Īnāl, fearing the danger, ordered the caliph and his family to remain in confinement until the threat dissipated. Al-Qāʾim refused, and went out to meet the rebels when they called for him.[81]

Their morale bolstered by the caliph's assent, the rebels finished arming themselves in his presence. Various displaced *mamlūk*s, starving peasants and urban riffraff (*awbāsh* and *ḥarāfish*) came out to lend a hand. Gradually, the mutinous *julbān* who had instigated the affair, whether fretful of the consequences or doubtful in the ability of their Ẓāhirī allies, slowly began deserting and abandoned the latter to battle the forces of Īnāl, which easily scattered them after a brief confrontation. The victors promptly arrested al-Qāʾim and brought him before the sultan and an assembly of dignitaries in the Rudaynī mosque. Expecting the worst, the caliph was reportedly surprised by Īnāl thrice repeating that he had forgiven him, though the sultan's true attitude proved unsympathetic. Observers claim the awkwardness of the situation combined with anxiety over his imminent deposition, left the caliph mute from shock for almost an hour. Once he had composed himself, after the gravity of his predicament had set in, al-Qāʾim, perhaps feeling that the game was up, made a last ditch attempt at revenge by blurting out before the assembly, 'I resign myself and [therefore] depose you! (*khalaʿtu nafsī wa-ʿazaltuka*).' The attending courtiers clamoured as they digested the thorny implications now posed for the sultan's socio-political standing. The chief Shāfiʿī qadi al-Bulqīnī came to Īnāl's rescue, however, by reminding the court that the caliph, by joining with rebels, had forfeited his caliphal authority, including his (theoretical) right to remove the sultan. Legally, according to al-Bulqīnī's on-the-fly jurisprudence, the dishonoured caliph was therefore able to be dismissed.[82]

The sultan harshly rebuked the caliph who abdicated in disgrace. Al-Qāʾim was then compelled to openly testify that he had no right or power to remove Īnāl. The sultan ordered the caliph to be incarcerated in the Citadel's Fountain Hall (*Qāʿat al-Baḥra*) and terminated his caliphate. Left with a sudden vacancy in the holy office, the sultan summoned several prominent Abbasid family members, including two sons of al-Mutawakkil: Mūsā al-Hāshimī (d. 891/1486) and his younger brother Abū al-Maḥāsin Yūsuf, to assess their suitability. At the outset Yūsuf's chances were greatly improved by his father-in-law, al-Bulqīnī (likely owed a favour by Īnāl due to his quick thinking), who advocated on behalf of the Abbasid prince. Thus, the choice landed on Yūsuf, who received *bayʿa* as al-Mustanjid bi-llāh Abī al-Muẓaffar before the sultan, qadis, amirs and notables on 3 Rajab 859/19 June 1455.[83]

Several days later, Īnāl's entourage removed al-Qāʾim from Citadel imprisonment and sent him on horseback to begin a long journey into exile in Alexandria, wherein the ex-caliph would ultimately remain confined for several years before being shifted to a fortress residence that granted him unrestrained movement throughout the city. The deposed caliph lived in Alexandria until his death following a brief illness on 17 Shawwāl 862/28 August 1458. Al-Qāʾim was interred near his full brother al-Mustaʿīn and one of their sisters. Contemporary observers did not fail to notice the coincidence that both brothers had been exiled to Alexandria for respective interferences in Cairene politics.[84]

Al-Qāʾim in the Sources

Ibn Taghrībirdī's coverage of the reign of al-Qāʾim is rife with speculation and hearsay. We must accept that the caliph's true motivations for joining the revolt against Īnāl are murky at best, but were likely facilitated by the uncertain nature of Cairene politics. However, if Ibn Taghrībirdī's interpretation is reliable, it seems that after weighing the risks, the caliph believed that his political venture would have gained him something. But what? Slightly later sources suggest the caliph was anxious to infuse his office with more ceremonial importance.[85] One wonders if he was likewise interested in restoring some of its influence in temporal affairs. Garcin understood al-Qāʾim's participation in the revolt as a final attempt at independence for the caliphate after which the caliphs never again had opportunity to depart from their ceremonial role and residences in the Citadel, near the Nafīsī shrine, or in al-Kabsh.[86]

The ambitious al-Qāʾim was not well-remembered by contemporary historians who depicted him in an unflattering light. Even al-Suyūṭī, champion of the Abbasid cause, viewed al-Qāʾim as impetuous and driven by arrogance. Ibn Taghrībirdī dismissed him as short-sighted and ungrateful for the gains he had made under Īnāl. In his remarks on the career of al-Qāʾim, Ibn Taghrībirdī noted that the caliph had started in the service of Jaqmaq and later played a prominent role in the coup that had helped Īnāl to power. Because of the latter event, al-Qāʾim enjoyed an elevation in material wealth and influence at court. More importantly, he had the sultan's respect and confidence, but in the end his thirst for power clouded his judgement and hastened his downfall.[87]

Al-Mustanjid bi-llāh, 859–84/1455–79

Born in approximately 798/1396, Abū al-Maḥāsin Jamāl al-Dīn Yūsuf became the fifth and final son of al-Mutawakkil to hold the caliphate as al-Mustanjid bi-llāh in Rajab 859/June 1455. Raised in his father's household, Yūsuf spent much of his childhood immersed in contemplative studies of the Qurʾān. Before receiving *bayʿa* as caliph, al-Sakhāwī claims al-Mustanjid experienced a 'true vision' (*ruʾya*) that the prophet Abraham had guaranteed his place in the caliphal succession. After his investiture as caliph on 3 Rajab 859/19 June 1455, al-Mustanjid participated in the usual ceremonial rituals after being invested with the symbols of office: atop a decorated mount and surrounded by notables, the new caliph followed a great procession down to his residence.

Before his death in mid-Jumādā I 865/February 1461, Īnāl left al-Mustanjid with the task of religiously authorising the selection of his heir Aḥmad as sultan. The political order established by Īnāl appeared to be steady enough for his supporters to maintain power through Aḥmad, but it was quickly unravelled by rivals gathering behind the elderly *amīr kabīr* Khushqadam, who invited al-Mustanjid and the qadis to the Citadel and seated them in the tented pavilion (*dihlīz*) of the Duhaysha Hall. Al-Mustanjid and Khushqadam sat together in the upper part of the assembly room, while the qadis occupied their traditional seats before the caliph in the forecourt.

After the pledge, the amirs and leading officials rose donning *kalafta* caps and white *ṭaṭar* coats. The young sultan proceeded to the palace on horseback, al-Mustanjid riding at his side. The amirs and qadis walked before them until it became apparent that the caliph's horse was too powerful for him to control. The sultan later robed al-Mustanjid in a resplendent, reversible white and green silk overcoat with lavish embroidery. The caliph was also assigned revenues from the small village of Inbāba (or Minbāba) in Giza, while Khushqadam received a similar robe and over-cloak along with a horse and gold saddle. The caliph led other dignitaries in offering their prayers and final respects to Īnāl at his bier in the Citadel. With Aḥmad at his side, al-Mustanjid participated in the late sultan's funeral procession.

Al-Mustanjid and the qadis attended the reading of Aḥmad's diploma on 13 Jumādā II 865/26 March 1461 in the Qaṣr al-Ablaq. The caliph received more gifts from the sultan, including another similar robe with a brocaded sleeve and a gold-saddled horse.[88]

Khushqadam, 865–72/1461–7

Few may have expected the young son of Īnāl to enjoy a long sultanate. By Ramaḍān 865/June 1461, Khushqadam had amassed formidable support, including even followers of the sultan who feared the loss of their stipends. Moreover, important religious personnel such as al-Mustanjid and the qadis, as well as principal administrative officials, abandoned al-Mu'ayyad Aḥmad. Barely opposed, Khushqadam seized the sultanate on 18 Ramaḍān 865/27 June 1461, which, after investiture by the caliph, he maintained until his death in 872/1467.[89]

Wishing to be named sultan in the presence of his amirs, Khushqadam ordered al-Mustanjid and others to repeat the *bay'a* ceremony the next day at the Ḥarrāqa Pavilion. After the ceremony, the new sultan ascended the Citadel in a black robe with the emblems of power; the soldiers marching before him and the caliph mounted at his side. Later al-Mustanjid again received a silk robe and gold-saddled horse. The sultan ordered a reading of his investiture deed at the palace before the caliph, qadis and amirs in Shawwāl 865/July 1461. Later that month, Jānim al-Ashrafī (d. 867/1462), the viceroy of Damascus, challenged Khushqadam's rule and mobilised his forces towards the Siryāqūs monastery. Using the pretext of a robing ceremony, the sultan ordered al-Mustanjid, along with the qadis and important amirs, to remain in the Citadel to prevent Jānim from luring them away. Deprived of the caliph and unable to intimidate Khushqadam, Jānim ultimately obeyed the sultan's order to depart. The qadis and amirs returned to their typical quarters, but Khushqadam refused to allow al-Mustanjid to return to his family residence and forced the caliph to remain a permanent resident of the Citadel where he lived in the vacated house of al-Manṣūr ʿUthmān ibn Jaqmaq for nearly twenty years until his death, confined largely to the sultan's royal court (*ḥawsh*). The caliph was denied access to the city, but Khushqadam ordered that rations of chicken, lamb, sugar and watermelon be delivered to the Abbasid household each day until the sultan's death. Later sources speculated that the caliph's mandatory residence in the Citadel dated from this incident and that subsequent sultans maintained the practice for reasons of preventing access to the caliph in the event that challengers arose to threaten the incumbent.[90]

Amidst a harsh Egyptian drought in Shawwāl 866/July 1462, Khushqadam's adviser *shaykh* Amīn al-Dīn al-Āqṣarāy directed the sultan to assemble all living members of the Abbasid family, regardless of age; give them water with which to rinse their mouths, then spit into an empty vessel. The collected water, now containing Abbasid *baraka*, should then be poured into the well of the Nilometer (*fasqiyyat al-miqyās*). The sultan gathered the Abbasids on the Nile at the Old Cairo home of al-Mustanjid's brother ʿAbd al-ʿAzīz. After the 'Abbasid water' was emptied into the well, Cairenes claimed the river's level rose by two finger-lengths.[91]

After initially sending gifts to the sultan and caliph of Cairo, the sultan of Malwa, Maḥmūd Shāh Khaljī (839–73/1436–69) in Jumādā I 870/January 1466 received a return embassy from the caliph al-Mustanjid (Indian sources make no mention of Khushqadam), including a Qurʾān, a sword, a ring, a caliphal robe, and an investiture deed dated 8 Shaʿbān 869/5 April 1465. The caliphal embassy to Malwa proved important locally, and after receiving acknowledgement, Maḥmūd Shāh struck coins the next year naming himself the 'right-hand' and 'supporter' of the caliph (*yamīn al-khalīfa, nāṣir amīr al-muʾminīn*). Thrilled to be a lieutenant of the caliph, Maḥmūd Shāh wrote again to the court of Khushqadam, though both rulers died before a return embassy could be sent.[92]

The caliph maintained the ceremonial role attached to his family and in Dhū al-Ḥijja 870/July–August 1466 the sultan ordered him to lead funerary prayers for his eldest daughter.[93] After Khushqadam himself died two years later, the amir Yilbāy seized power for two months in 872/1467. Although summoned to provide investiture, harsh travel conditions delayed the arrival of al-Mustanjid and the qadis during their journey from the Columned Hall to the palace of the sultan. Few details of the ceremony have survived, though Yilbāy sat on the throne and invested the amir Timurbughā as commander in chief before robing and investing the caliph and other notables. The sultanate of Yilbāy proved to be brief, as the army lost patience with him after two months and installed Timurbughā in his place on 7 Jumādā I 872/4 December 1467. Al-Mustanjid and two of the chief qadis (the remaining two had fallen ill) extended their hands thereby granting *sharīʿ* approval to the deposition of Yilbāy. In a black robe and sultanic emblems Timurbughā left the Ḥarrāqa Pavilion with only the caliph riding before him. From the throne in the sultan's castle, Timurbughā invested the caliph with a robe and also invested the amir Qāyitbāy, head of the guards, as commander of the army in his place. Timurbughā seemed an agreeable candidate for the religious and political elite but was sacked shortly after by his executive secretary Khāyrbak al-Khushqadamī, who with the help of other conspirators, arrested the sultan on 5 Rajab 872/30 January 1468. Unsure how to proceed, some of the purchased *mamlūk*s went to the barracks and armed themselves, others wanted to secure access to the Abbasid caliph, and still others sought to plunder the sultan's quarters.[94]

Al-Ashraf Qāyitbāy, 872–901/1468–96

Although poised to take the throne, Qāyitbāy restrained himself until notaries testified to the abdication, involuntary or not, of Timurbughā. Although Timurbughā's resignation was likely made under duress, al-Mustanjid and the qadis testified that it had been tendered of his own free will and thus the *bayʿa* to his successor was valid. The caliph proclaimed the dismissal of Timurbughā and requested that allegiance be sworn to Qāyitbāy as al-Malik al-Ashraf.[95]

In a ceremony at the Ḥarrāqa Pavilion, the religious dignitaries, including the caliph, pledged allegiance to Qāyitbāy on 6 Rajab 872/31 January 1468. The new sultan, dressed in black Abbasid robes, mounted a horse and rode through the streets with the emblems of his office. He confirmed al-Mustanjid as caliph before the noon-time call to prayer and accepted the *bayʿa* of his amirs.[96] It is worth mentioning that by the later fifteenth century, particularly during the reigns of Qāyitbāy and later Qāniṣawh al-Ghawrī, Abbasid robing ceremonial received less attention from contemporary chroniclers. Carl Petry writes that robing no longer appeared to be

> central to the sultan's own enthronement, which underscored the derivation of his legitimacy from the caliph's administration of an oath to rule justly [as well as] pledges of obedience (*bayʿa*) to him from the four qāḍīs and senior amirs. The sultan swore his oath on a Koran held out to him by the caliph while the former was seated under the Abbasids' black banner. He wore a black *jubba* or sleeved tunic of cotton and/or silk rather than wool.[97]

The ongoing struggle for domination in eastern Anatolia intensified during the reign of Qāyitbāy. After the Ottoman sultan Meḥmed II conquered Qarāmān in 880/1475, Dulqadirid-controlled Elbistan acquired strategic importance as a buffer zone between the two empires. The Cairo-backed candidate Shāh Budāq had been installed by Khushqadam, but was ousted in 870/1465 when his Ottoman-backed brother Shāh Sūwār took control. Shortly after ordering a retributive campaign, Khushqadam passed away, ultimately leaving unfinished affairs in the hands of Qāyitbāy.[98]

On 14 Dhū al-Qaʿda 872/5 June 1468, after an initial defeat by Shāh Sūwār some months earlier, Qāyitbāy convened a council in the *ḥawsh* area of the Citadel to discuss his empty treasury. The caliph al-Mustanjid, seated at the sultan's right, was joined by the four chief qadis, along with the *shaykh al-islām* Amīn al-Dīn al-Āqṣarāy and other important amirs and *ʿulamāʾ*. Speaking on behalf of the sultan's cause, the *kātib al-sirr* pointed out that many of the Citadel elite (*al-nās*) had extra funds that ought to have been transferred to the treasury to finance a campaign against Shāh Sūwār in northern Syria. The sultan and his spokesmen argued that 'surplus' funds must also be extracted from other subjects, local merchants, as well as money tied up in pious endowments (*awqāf*) if the army was to be successful. The caliph and qadis consented after the argument had been couched in religious terms with the pretext of defending the Muslims in the sultan's realm. However, the *shaykh al-islām* remained adamant over the illegality of seizing funds and his arguments forced an exasperated Qāyitbāy to abandon the idea. Ultimately, to the relief of those amirs who stood to lose funds, nothing was decided. A short time later the sultan met again with the amirs and religious authorities, emphasising the importance of fighting Shāh Sūwār, which the caliph and qadis together decried as something harmful to the greater interest of the Muslims.[99]

Finally, after successfully freeing up funds by denying stipends to older soldiers, orphans and widows, Qāyitbāy was able to send an expedition towards Elbistan. The campaigns against Shāh Sūwār proved to be highly expensive and by the end of his first year in power, Qāyitbāy, in the hope of raising funds, committed several arbitrary and unpopular acts. Among them, the sultan stripped al-Mustanjid of revenues from Inbāba in Dhū al-Qaʿda 872/May–June 1468, a holding that the caliph had received seven years earlier from the son of Īnāl. A short time later, the sultan also confiscated Ṣābūnī Island from the caliph and redistributed sections of it to his *mamlūk*s. Qāyitbāy's dispute with Shāh Sūwār was still unresolved by 877/1472, causing the sultan again to seek the approval of the religious authorities to seize merchants' revenues, after a congratulatory session with the caliph and qadis. Ultimately, Shāh Sūwār was not subdued until Rabīʿ I 877/August 1472, with damage done to Qāyitbāy's coffers and prestige.[100]

Despite his confiscation of several caliphal *iqṭāʿ*s from the family, Qāyitbāy continued to enjoy the reputation of a fervent ally and loyal defender of the Abbasid Caliphate. Later courtiers of the sultan Qāniṣawh al-Ghawrī discussed Qāyitbāy's respect for the Abbasids, and the Iranian jurist Faẓlullāh ibn Rūzbihān Khunjī-Iṣfahānī (d. 928/1521) visited Qāyitbāy's Egypt and commented on the lofty position of the Abbasid caliph and his protection by the sultan of Cairo. Indeed, much of the Sunni world recognised Qāyitbāy as one of the strongest rulers alongside his Ottoman counterpart.

In Jumādā II 876/November–December 1471 Cairo received a visit from an ambassador of the new ruler of Malwa, Ghiyāth al-Dīn Shāh Khaljī (873–906/1469–1501), who requested a *taqlīd* from the Abbasid caliph for his master's enthronement.[101] The Indian embassy presented gifts to both Qāyitbāy and al-Mustanjid. The sultan draped the ambassador in a robe and received recognition as suzerain. Qāyitbāy then sanctioned the caliph's confirmation of Ghiyāth al-Dīn's succession and al-Mustanjid signed a decree. After receiving acknowledgement, Ghiyāth al-Dīn struck coins describing himself as 'the one upon whom authority has been conferred by the caliph of the age in the worlds'.[102]

Later Years, Death and Succession

Al-Mustanjid lived quietly in the Citadel investing sultans and accepting their gifts.[103] His reign marked a change in Abbasid living conditions, as forced occupancy in the Citadel became mandatory for the caliphs, allowing them to be held under close watch and kept away from the sultan's enemies.[104] The specific extent to which Qāyitbāy's confiscations affected Abbasid family income remains unclear, though the ongoing donations made at the shrine of Sayyida Nafīsa surely eased some financial burdens. ʿAbd al-Bāsiṭ al-Malaṭī, in addition to mentioning al-Mustanjid's great wealth, described the caliph as modest and well-mannered, though criticising him for being ignorant of scholarly Islam, and, most tellingly, prone to family squabbles stemming from excessive greed.[105]

The caliph wed his only daughter to the Syrian amir Khushqaldī al-Baysuqī.[106] Unmentioned events forced Khushqaldī's exile to Syria and al-Mustanjid attempted to use his court connections to expedite an annulment. The caliph negotiated at length with the qadis who, although they had the power to dissolve the marriage, withheld support. The caliph used his monthly access to Qāyitbāy in Dhū al-Qaʿda 876/April 1472 to receive a proper hearing for the case and seek the sultan's intervention, which he obtained some time thereafter.[107]

At peace with his restricted powers and remembered elsewhere for modest simplicity,[108] the Abbasid caliph passed away in his late eighties or nineties on 24 Muḥarram 884/17 April 1479 after suffering two years of paralysis. Following funerary prayers members of the Citadel elite laid the caliph to rest in the family crypt. When news of his death reached Syria a month later, special prayers were offered on the caliph's behalf at the Umayyad mosque in Damascus.[109]

The Scholar-Caliph: Al-Mutawakkil ʿalā Allāh II, 884–903/1479–97

With no male heirs, al-Mustanjid had turned to his extended family to select a successor. The most senior Abbasid at the time was his uncle Mūsā al-Hāshimī, a wealthy son of al-Mutawakkil respected for his lineage, but rumours of his questionable business dealings and alleged mental instability disqualified him from office.[110] The grandsons of al-Mutawakkil, notably from the line of his son Yaʿqūb (who had never held the caliphate), were considered next. These included Abū al-ʿIzz ʿAbd al-ʿAzīz, Ismāʿīl and Nāṣir al-Dīn Muḥammad. The latter commanded respect but also failed to secure the appointment.[111]

Ultimately, al-Mustanjid appointed his sixty-two-year-old nephew ʿAbd al-ʿAzīz, who had previously represented Abbasid interests in 856/1452 in the court of Jaqmaq during the hearing of Abū al-Khayr al-Naḥḥās. ʿAbd al-ʿAzīz received *bayʿa* as caliph from Qāyitbāy and his amirs. The caliph had initially sought the regnal title of al-Mustaʿizz bi-llāh, but when the name tested unfavourably with courtiers, he considered calling himself al-Mustaʿīn bi-llāh before ultimately settling on the *laqab* of his well-remembered grandfather. Thus, he received investiture as al-Mutawakkil ʿalā Allāh on 26 Muḥarram 884/19 April 1479 by the qadis and other notables. After the pledge ceremony al-Mutawakkil II, dressed in caliphal finery atop a gold-saddled horse, led a solemn parade with Abbasid heraldry on display. He left the Citadel and headed towards the caliphal residence preceded by the four qadis and major officials, though he later returned to his uncle's lodging in the Citadel.[112]

Diplomatic Relations

The majority of al-Mutawakkil's caliphate fell within the last two decades of Qāyitbāy's rule during an escalation of pressure placed on the Cairo Sultanate by the Ottoman Sultanate of Bāyezīd II (886–918/1481–1512). Relations deteriorated as the ongoing rivalry in the Anatolian marches accelerated over Qāyitbāy's interference in the Ottoman succession struggle that followed the death of Meḥmed II in 886/1481. The sons of the Ottoman sultan quarrelled over the sultanate until Bāyezīd II, the choice of the army, bested his father's intended successor Cem and forced his flight to the court of Qāyitbāy which fuelled enduring suspicion on the part of Bāyezīd.[113]

Relations between Cairo and Istanbul were strained once again over the Dulqadir principality when the Ottoman-backed candidate, Bāyezīd's own father-in-law, ʿAlāʾ al-Dawla was successfully installed in 884/1479 and the Ottomans supported his fight against Qāyitbāy in early 889/1484. In response, the sultan of Cairo sent a party of *mamlūk*s to Aleppo to survey the Anatolian frontier and bolster the Syrian garrison. When it was confirmed that the Ottomans had undermined Qāyitbāy's interests in the region, the sultan sent his special envoy, the amir Jānibak Ḥabīb, with gifts for Bāyezīd II in the hope of restoring peace. To further impress the Ottoman sultan, Qāyitbāy ordered al-Mutawakkil II to draft a special diploma recognising *de facto* Ottoman authority over territory conquered from the Byzantine Empire in Asia Minor and naming Bāyezīd II as the sultan in Anatolia (*sulṭān ʿalā bilād al-Rūm*). The document 'confirmed that which God had entrusted to his hand from the land of disbelief (*bilād al-kufriyya*)' and implied that the Ottomans would not receive Abbasid approval for gains made at the expense of fellow Muslims, particularly the sultan of Cairo and his Turkmen allies in Anatolia.[114] Drawing heavily on allusions to classical Islamic sources, the document extolled the benefit of cooperation between the two powers. In his presentation at the Ottoman court, Jānibak Ḥabīb was instructed to emphasise important precedents. Qāyitbāy's chancery attached a written memorandum from al-Mutawakkil II to the document, the tone of which was meant to reconcile Cairo and Istanbul.[115] Despite the warm reception and robe of honour draped upon the shoulders of Jānibak Ḥabīb, diplomacy fizzled out as the two sides descended into several years of conflict from 890 to 896/1485 to 1491.[116]

After a short stay at Qāyitbāy's court, the Ottoman prince Cem left his family behind in Cairo and joined his remaining forces to make war on his brother Bāyezīd II. The campaign came to naught. Finding all return access to the territories of the Cairo Sultanate blocked by his rival, Cem accepted an invitation from the Grand Master of the Knights Hospitallers of St John, Pierre d'Aubusson, to come to the island of Rhodes, so beginning a lengthy period during which the defeated prince became a political pawn for various European rulers in their dealings with the Ottomans.

Some years later, Qāyitbāy, urged by Cem's surviving family in Egypt, began negotiations to recover Cem, who was now in France, and bring him back to Cairo. The sultan also hoped to use him for his own purposes against the interests of Bāyezīd II amid ongoing tensions between them. The various rulers of France, however, as well as the pope, persevered with their own designs on Cem, complicating his extraction. Nevertheless, Qāyitbāy selected Lorenzo de Medici, the duke of Florence, to be his mediator with the rulers of Europe.[117] In late 892/1487, Qāyitbāy sent a messenger to Florence and presented Lorenzo with a request that Cem be returned to Cairo, and, if not, that the Ottoman prince should instead be given to the pope or other rulers who could ensure he would be kept away from Bāyezīd II. According to Shai Har-El:

> [Cairo's] ambassador also asked Lorenzo to intercede with the Pope, to whom he brought a letter from the ʿAbbasid Caliph in Cairo. In the letter, the Caliph reminded the Pope that the detention of Cem was a breach of the agreement between d'Aubusson and Cem, concluded when the latter had taken refuge in Rhodes and asked him to set Cem free and allow him to join his family in Egypt.[118]

Lorenzo presented the request to the pope, though Qāyitbāy's wishes were ignored. The Christian rulers, who ultimately wanted to see Cem convert to Christianity and lead a new anti-Ottoman crusade, clearly understood the great value of a pretender to the Ottoman throne. Thus, Qāyitbāy may have sought, though in vain, to use the highest office in Islamdom (the Abbasid Caliphate) to negotiate with the papacy. After having spent time at Rhodes, various castles in France, and later in Rome as a guest of the pope, Cem died in Naples in 900/1495.[119]

Ceremonial in the Court of Qāyitbāy

By the end of the fifteenth century, Cairene court culture expected the five chief religious functionaries (the caliph and the four chief qadis) to make monthly visits to the Citadel to pay respects to the sultan. This was especially important for the major milestones of the political order such as religious festivals, moon sightings or congratulating the sultan on a triumphant return to his capital. The practice had begun in the reign of al-Mustanjid and continued with some regularity until the end of the sultanate in Cairo. On most occasions, the caliph arrived at the Citadel from his residence and upon his entry into the sultan's sitting room, the sultan would descend his throne to sit briefly beside the caliph before the latter departed and the qadis stayed behind to attend to religious business or offer their counsel.[120] In addition to paying formal respect to the sultanate, such visits offered the caliph an opportunity to hold the sultan's attention and bring personal issues to his attention. The sultan could also question the caliph alongside the qadis on legal matters such as the legality of securing funds from questionable sources.

The caliph held the symbolic duty of serving as a living 'seal' to agreements and thus became indispensable to the sultan in matters of authenticating agreements with amirs or *mamlūk*s. In Rabīʿ II 894/March 1489, the sultan's *mamlūk*s threatened to revolt over pay concerns. Qāyitbāy mediated the affair with the help of the *ʿulamāʾ*. After the parties reached a settlement, the sultan ordered al-Mutawakkil II to come from his residence near the *ḥawsh* to seal the agreement. Before the caliph and the qadis, the *mamlūk*s pledged a new oath of allegiance to Qāyitbāy. Qāniṣawh al-Ghawrī continued the practice in his sultanate, often in rituals involving the supposed Qurʾān of the 'rightly-guided' third caliph ʿUthmān ibn ʿAffān (r. 23–35/644–56).[121]

Despite the dignity of his office, the Abbasid caliph of Cairo remained an accessible and assailable target for other courtiers. A rather curious incident in Rabīʿ II 894/March 1489 found al-Mutawakkil II accused of gross misconduct (*ʿaẓāʾim*) by an unnamed plaintiff (or plaintiffs) who had complained to the sultan about what had been described as the caliph's 'humbling and heinous' actions. Nevertheless, the mysterious matter was settled without further commentary from the sources.[122]

Family Properties and Landholdings

By the time al-Mutawakkil II assumed the caliphate, Qāyitbāy had already significantly reduced Abbasid landholdings by reassigning Inbāba and Ṣābūnī Island. The caliph's finances suffered yet another major blow at the end of the fifteenth century when Qāyitbāy's government removed the Nafīsī shrine and related *waqf*s from Abbasid administration. Although earlier caliphs had used most of the revenue generated by access to the shrine, al-Suyūṭī depicts al-Mutawakkil II as a faithful servant of Sayyida Nafīsa, disinterested in the accompanying financial benefits, too humble to take its resources and quick to redistribute profits elsewhere for upkeep, maintenance, and alms for the poor. The shrine was restored to Abbasid control, however, at the end of the fifteenth century, when al-Mutawakkil II was nearing death and remained in the family until the Ottoman conquest.[123]

Qāyitbāy was an enthusiastic participant in *mawlid* festivals celebrating the birth of the Prophet as well as saintly figures such as Sayyida Nafīsa. The caliph al-Mutawakkil II, at the behest of the sultan, participated in lively celebrations at the shrine in 889/1484 and 890/1485. The four chief qadis and Cairene notables attended each year, and the Nafīsī *mawlid* was also referred to as the caliph's *mawlid* (*mawlid al-khalīfa*) as the presence of the Commander of the Faithful in his capacity both as host and 'cousin of the messenger of God', proved useful at popular celebrations dedicated to members of the Prophet's family.[124]

By the end of the fifteenth century, the Nafīsī shrine generated heavy revenues which were available to the Abbasid family. In addition to regular pious donations from pilgrims and profits from the sale of devotional items (oil, candles, incense, etc.), income also came from opportunities to participate in nearby functions. Prominent funerals, for example, proved to be lucrative for the family. In one instance after the burial of a wealthy notable close to the tomb, the caliph, his family, the caretaking personnel of the shrine, and local students all received generous offerings during a lavish funeral for which they offered graveside blessings and prayers.[125]

Other Abbasid landholdings attracted the interest of the political elite when the small village annex (*manshiyyat*) of Dahshūr, officially an ongoing charitable trust bequeathed to the caliph's family as part of the inheritance of his aunt Maryam bint al-Mutawakkil I, became the focus of unwanted attention.[126] Maryam had held the land for several decades until it fell under the supervision of her nephew al-Mutawakkil II. In 892/1487, the amir Asanbāy al-Ashrafī claimed to have a legal basis to encroach upon a portion of the estate. Asanbāy, who enjoyed influence in both military and religious circles, became more vociferous in his claims and a public hearing on the matter took place in which the qadis, after having surveyed the disputed section of Dahshūr to assess its resources and suitability for hunting, listened to the testimony and proofs provided by Asanbāy's deputy Ibn Muẓaffar, and ultimately concluded that the claim was lawful. For his part, al-Mutawakkil II deliberately kept a low profile at the initial hearing, perhaps for fear of inviting reprisals from Asanbāy and his supporters. The chief qadis determined the matter in Jumādā I 892/May 1487, and almost unanimously sided in favour of the amir, save for the Mālikī qadi who, according to al-Sakhāwī, may have harboured personal reasons for resenting Asanbāy. Al-Mutawakkil II kept silent once again, we are to believe, because of his indifference towards the property in question, and also due to wariness concerning the political pull of Asanbāy.[127]

Some years later, in Jumādā II 899/March 1494, a kitchen fire broke out in the Abbasid living quarters in the Citadel which ultimately spread to the sultan's storehouse and incinerated most of Qāyitbāy's prized and costly war tents. Enraged, the sultan evicted al-Mutawakkil II from his residence in the *ḥawsh* near the Baḥra Hall of the Citadel, and ordered him to live elsewhere in the city. The caliph had no choice but to move with his family into another residential living space (*qāʿa*) near the Nafīsī shrine. According to Ibn Iyās, the caliph himself had not been involved in the fire and rather fell victim to a rumour started by jealous rivals.[128]

Death of Qāyitbāy

The reign of Qāyitbāy had included moments of cultural, economic and political prosperity, particularly in the 1470s. With the onset of increased old age, however, the sultan's faculties began to falter and the acting *atābak* Timrāz al-Shamsī hoped to install the sultan's adolescent son Muḥammad for long enough to secure the sultanate for himself. Before Timrāz could act, however, a group of conspirators led by the amir Qāniṣawh al-Khamsī swiftly recognised the boy, who reigned as al-Nāṣir Muḥammad (901–4/1496–8), as a compromise candidate.[129] Muḥammad received investiture as sultan by al-Mutawakkil II and the qadis the day before his father's death on 26 Dhū al-Qaʿda 900/18 August 1495.[130]

The reign of the adolescent Muḥammad, which unfolded during the political crisis following Qāyitbāy's death, proved to be brief and troubled, though he, unlike many other sultans appointed by their fathers, briefly managed to establish effective rule. The young sultan also interacted with al-Mutawakkil II after his accession to the sultanate. Forced to live outside the Citadel as a *persona non grata* after the kitchen fire that destroyed Qāyitbāy's property, al-Nāṣir Muḥammad reversed his father's policy, and after three years of living near the Nafīsī shrine, recalled the caliph and his family to reside within the Citadel once more.[131]

Machinations in the Scholarly World

Like his father and recent ancestors, al-Mutawakkil II had sat at the feet of reputable experts in the Islamic sciences. The caliph proved to be an avid student of religious studies and a master calligrapher possessing a style of his own. A *dawādār* was even assigned to assist the caliph.[132]

Continuing the tradition of Abbasid and Suyūṭī family ties that had begun with al-Mustakfī II and Abū Bakr Kamāl al-Dīn al-Suyūṭī, the celebrated scholar Jalāl al-Dīn al-Suyūṭī personally tutored al-Mutawakkil II in Islamic sciences and the two developed a close bond.[133] In Ṣafar 902/October 1496, amid the atmosphere of chaos and confusion following the death of Qāyitbāy and the succession of al-Nāṣir Muḥammad, al-Suyūṭī used his ties to the caliph to increase his own religious authority. Al-Suyūṭī, a long-time critic of the four grand qadiships established by Baybars, famously put forward the idea of a newly-created post of executive qadi (*qāḍī kabīr*) and persuaded al-Mutawakkil to name him to the office with his caliphal sanction and issue a document to that effect. In theory, the post would have granted al-Suyūṭī power to appoint and dismiss magistrates all over Islamdom.[134]

Betrayed by the proposal, the four chief qadis voiced their outrage and derided the caliph for what they perceived as his ignorance and treachery. Al-Mutawakkil II defended himself against detractors: 'What part did I have in this? It was *shaykh* Jalāl al-Dīn [al-Suyūṭī] who showed me that this position harkened back to antiquity when the caliphs chose to [fill positions] with the wise man they considered most capable.'

Pressure from the scholarly establishment forced al-Mutawakkil II to rescind the document. Modern historians read the incident as a shrewd power-play by al-Suyūṭī with the aim of securing more strength for the caliphate, while bolstering his own power during a weak moment for the sultanate. As it played out, neither the qadis (who stood to lose a great deal) nor the caliph (reluctant to face scrutiny and major responsibility) supported al-Suyūṭī's attempt to reinvigorate caliphal authority.[135]

Already in his sixties at the start of his nineteen-year caliphate, al-Mutawakkil's health steadily deteriorated until by Muḥarram 903/August 1497 he was scarcely able to leave his bed. The caliph no longer attended monthly salutations for the sultan and was transported on a litter (*maḥaffa*) whenever he left his home. As he grew frailer, al-Mutawakkil II turned his attention to the issue of succession. The caliph's union with an Abyssinian slave had produced al-Ruknī ʿUmar (d. 913/1508), who, although an esteemed prince at court, was not selected to hold the family office. Among the wives of al-Mutawakkil II was Amīna (d. 915/1510), daughter of his uncle al-Mustakfī II and together in 851/1447–8 the cousins begat a full-blooded Hāshimī son whom they named Sharaf al-Dīn Yaʿqūb. Contemporary observers made much of the child's lineage and watched his career with interest.[136] The elderly caliph al-Mutawakkil II summoned his son Yaʿqūb, by then a fifty-something, greying man with poor eyesight, to designate him as *walī al-ʿahd* with a testament authenticated by the four qadis. Yaʿqūb, and his uncle, Muḥammad (817–81/1414–76),[137] were consecutively named as the heirs to the caliphate, but when the latter died, some in the family held that the claim of Muḥammad transferred to his son Khalīl. Al-Mutawakkil II passed away in Old Cairo (Miṣr al-ʿAtīqa) several days later aged about eighty-four. The night before his solemn funeral, presided over by al-Nāṣir Muḥammad and his late father's amirs, the caliph's body was transferred to his residence adjacent to the mosque of Ibn Ṭūlūn. The young sultan prayed for the caliph at the Muʾminī fountain before his interment. Late fifteenth-century Arabic sources resoundingly praised both his erudition and public persona.[138]

Diverse Fifteenth-century Readings of 'Caliphate'

Most of the fifteenth-century sources used to construct the current chapter were written by historiographers who were also legal scholars. As such, they were part of a tradition that favoured a specific Sunni juristic reading of 'Caliphate'. Thus, within the broader background and discursive context of competing claims to sovereignty among the Ottomans, Timurids, Aqquyunlu (as well as the Safavids and Mughals later in the sixteenth century), the image of the 'Caliphate' espoused by the Sunni historians and scholars of the Cairo

Sultanate often appears to us almost fleeting or ephemeral: one voice among many, lost in the din of debate.

Other strands across Muslim west Asia, however, argued differently about the nature of sovereignty and the relationship between the creation and the divine which did not always include a caliph (or one that was necessarily an Abbasid) within their arguments. In the context of the early fifteenth century, it is worthwhile to examine other simultaneous claims of sovereignty which sought to move beyond more traditionalist understandings of 'Caliphate', especially in the early Timurid cultural milieu. Tracing the intellectual lineage of the mystical philosopher Muḥyī al-Dīn ibn ʿArabī (d. 638/1240), later authors and actors in Iran and Central Asia such as Iskandar ibn ʿUmar Shaykh (d. 818/1415) and Sharaf al-Dīn ʿAlī Yazdī (d. 858/1454) broadened the discourse through their excursus on the dual nature of the caliphate in regard to its more external/manifest side (*khilāfat-i ṣūrī*) and its more esoteric/hidden (*bāṭinī*) side (*khilāfat-i maʿnavī*). In the model proposed by Evrim Binbaş, for example, Yazdī understood the Timurid ruler Shāh Rukh to be the temporal and external '*khalīfa ṣūrī*', which also implied a necessary and complementary spiritual side in the form of the *khilāfat-i maʿnavī*. Both dimensions of the *khilāfat* thus set him forth as a more universalist ruler. The two sides of the model in which the caliphate comprises external and internal/spiritual compartments follows the line of Ibn ʿArabī's thought which suggests the caliph as the pole (*quṭb*) for political and religious authority.[139]

The Abbasid Caliphate of Cairo was not without its mystical implications, and, indeed, most members of the Syro-Egyptian religious elite also had ties to Sufi networks.[140] If Cairene social practices involving the Abbasid Caliphate did not take direct influence from Sufism, they at least shared some commonalities. In Cairo, the word *khalīfa* itself referred to the Commander of the Faithful's position as successor to the Prophet or of God on Earth. The *ʿulamāʾ* clung to one image of idealised unity represented by a *khalīfa* charged with rule over a human empire, while in the Sufi context, *khalīfa* suggested man as a perfected microcosm.[141] Islamic mysticism retained the title *khalīfa* as a position of vice-regency to the spiritual knowledge of the Prophet (or as the subordinate or representative of a Sufi *shaykh*), with relevance on the esoteric plane, upon which the *khilāfat al-bāṭina*, which implied access to the hidden or secret knowledge of Islam, was the more important caliphate (*khilāfat al-kubrā*). Several of the investiture deeds discussed in Chapters 8 and 9 reference the Abbasid caliph as the repository for the Muḥammadan secret or mystery (*sirr Muḥammadī*), implying that the caliph was privy to an unspecified aspect, essence or element of prophetic knowledge and spiritual heritage.[142] As a technical term in Sufism, *sirr* refers to notions of inner consciousness or being. Sufis protected the intrinsic knowledge of Islam (as well as their *silsila* links to the Prophet), just as according to the investiture deeds, the Abbasids protected a unique spiritual and familial bond with the Prophet. *Wilāya*, a term used by investiture deeds to discuss the assignment of the caliph's duties when the powers of the caliphate are delegated to another party, can be thought of as a kind of divine election that bestows power upon an office holder. The authority of the caliphate is divinely sanctioned and sanctified by God, just as the caliph's delegation is to the sultan. In the Sufi context, *wilāya* refers to the very idea of sainthood itself, which, like a delegated office, shares in the idea of sanctified power. Chapter 1 briefly discussed the *futuwwas* with strong links to Sufi networks. The idea of melding the Abbasid Caliphate to the *futuwwa* intrigued Baybars perhaps as a means to tap into even more powerful symbols of spiritual authority.[143]

The five Abbasid caliphs of the later fifteenth century presented in this chapter demonstrate the continuity established and perpetuated for the office by the political and religious elites of the Cairo Sultanate. The caliphs continued to symbolise order and good Islamic governance to the subject population.[144]

As for the duties left to the Commander of the Faithful in the fifteenth century, at the start of each new month when the moon was sighted, the caliph would join the qadis to pay respects to the sultan and, on rare occasions, offer his own counsel.[145] This was important on the two Muslim festival days, *ʿĪd al-Fitr* and *ʿĪd al-Aḍḥā*. The caliphs were also expected to participate in the funerals of important officials, amirs, *ʿulamāʾ* and even members of the sultans' families.[146]

Apart from having the caliphs appear at investiture ceremonies, certain sultans emphasised the religious role of the caliphs by making them the centrepiece in public rituals seeking relief from drought and plague as well as denouncing the infidelity of official enemies. Beginning in the late fourteenth century the caliphs also frequently appeared by request at a sultan's deathbed and solemnly swore to oversee their final dreams of dynastic succession.[147]

Perhaps evolving naturally from his role as an interlocutor and representative of the sultan in the type of political conflicts discussed in Chapter 3, the caliph in the fifteenth century was often called upon (or bribed) to mobilise his accrued social and symbolic capital to intercede for troubled amirs and disgraced courtiers such as Baybars ibn Baqar and Abū al-Khayr al-Naḥḥās. Al-Qāʾim bi-Amr Allāh, during his brief caliphate, attempted to restore some of the earlier honours and pageantry of the caliphal office while also demonstrating his own agency in cultivating a role as one of the sultan's political advisers. The fifteenth century witnessed the return of the caliph and his family to confinement in the Citadel to protect them against the enemies of the ruling political elites. It was also the time when new traditions were introduced such as amiral escorts for the caliph on campaign and war stipends. Financially, it appeared to be a time of some strain compared with the mid-fourteenth century. Al-Muʿtaḍid II struggled in comparison with his father al-Mutawakkil, and the sultan Qāyitbāy substantially decreased the revenue-producing landholdings of the family.

Helping to perform the caliphate at Cairene investiture ceremonies kept the family relevant and maintained their symbolic capital in the public eye. For some sultans, providing the Abbasid family with generous sources of economic capital was seen as a questionable priority and their revenue streams could be reassigned whenever the need arose. This was also a period of growth in the size and branches of the family and rival contenders began to appear and present difficulties for succession practices, as we will see in Chapter 5.

Notes

1. Van Steenbergen, Wing and D'hulster, 'Mamlukization Part II', 564.
2. Van Steenbergen and Van Nieuwenhuyse, 'Truth and Politics', 151–2; Van Steenbergen, Wing and D'hulster, 'Mamlukization Part I', 551–3; Van Steenbergen, Wing and D'hulster, 'Mamlukization Part II, 560; Loiseau, *Les Mamelouks*, 193–4.
3. Van Steenbergen, Wing and D'hulster, 'Mamlukization Part II', 564–6; Loiseau, *Les Mamelouks*, 128–9.
4. Onimus, *Les maîtres du jeu*, 207–15; Loiseau, *Les Mamelouks*, 196–200.

5. Van Steenbergen, 'Appearances of *dawla* and Political Order', 79–80; Van Steenbergen and Van Nieuwenhuyse, 'Truth and Politics', 151–2.
6. Al-Qalqashandī, *Maʾāthir*, 2:211; al-Maqrīzī, *Sulūk*, 4:282, 288; Ibn Ḥajar, *Inbāʾ al-ghumr*, 3:35; Ibn Taghrībirdī, *Nujūm*, 14:19–21, 35–6; Ibn Taghrībirdī, *Manhal*, 6:295–6, 302–3, 397–8; al-Ṣayrafī, *Nuzhat*, 2:340; al-Sakhāwī, *Wajīz*, 2:437; al-Malaṭī, *Rawḍ*, 1:236. According to al-ʿAynī, the sultan excused the caliph from this mission, see *ʿIqd* (1985–9), 1:234
7. Van Steenbergen and Van Nieuwenhuyse, 'Truth and Politics', 151–2.
8. Adriaenssens and Van Steenbergen, 'Mamluk Authorities', 4–5.
9. Van Steenbergen and Van Nieuwenhuyse, 'Truth and Politics', 174–5.
10. Adriaenssens and Van Steenbergen, 'Mamluk Authorities', 5, 14n.49.
11. Al-Maqrīzī, *Sulūk*, 4:384–5; Ibn Ḥajar, *Inbāʾ al-ghumr*, 3:126–8; Ibn Taghrībirdī, *Nujūm*, 14:46–56.
12. Adriaenssens and Van Steenbergen, 'Mamluk Authorities', 5; Har-El, *Struggle for Domination*, 27–59; al-Maqrīzī, *Sulūk*, 4:422; Ibn Taghrībirdī, *Nujūm*, 14:60.
13. Al-Maqrīzī, *Sulūk*, 4:459–60; Ibn Ḥajar, *Inbāʾ al-ghumr*, 3:171–2; al-ʿAynī, *ʿIqd* (1985–9), 1:319, 384; Ibn Taghrībirdī, *Nujūm*, 14:68, 99–100; Ibn Iyās, *Badāʾiʿ*, 2:39–40. See also Schimmel, 'Some Glimpses', 360.
14. Al-Maqrīzī, *Sulūk*, 4:535; Ibn Ḥajar, *Inbāʾ al-ghumr*, 3:222; Ibn Taghrībirdī, *Nujūm*, 14:99–100.
15. Al-Maqrīzī, *Sulūk*, 4:487–8, 549–50; Ibn Ḥajar, *Inbāʾ al-ghumr*, 3:198–9; Ibn Taghrībirdī, *Nujūm*, 14:77–80; Ibn Iyās, *Badāʾiʿ*, 2:45–6.
16. Al-Maqrīzī, *Sulūk*, 4:563–4, 587; Ibn Ḥajar, *Inbāʾ al-ghumr*, 3:227, 237; al-ʿAynī, *ʿIqd* (1985–9), 2:117; Ibn Taghrībirdī, *Nujūm*, 14:103, 107–9, 167; Ibn Taghrībirdī, *Manhal*, 6:308–9; al-Sakhāwī, *Dhayl*, 1:521; al-Sakhāwī, *Wajīz*, 2:465; al-Suyūṭī, *Taʾrīkh*, 407.
17. Van Steenbergen and Van Nieuwenhuyse, 'Truth and Politics', 151–2.
18. Al-Maqrīzī, *Sulūk*, 4:569, 572; Ibn Ḥajar, *Inbāʾ al-ghumr*, 3:240–1; al-ʿAynī, *ʿIqd* (1985–9), 2:118–19; Ibn Taghrībirdī, *Nujūm*, 14:176, 180–1; Ibn Iyās, *Badāʾiʿ*, 2:63–4.
19. Al-Maqrīzī, *Sulūk*, 4:576, 582; Ibn Ḥajar, *Inbāʾ al-ghumr*, 3:243–7; al-ʿAynī, *ʿIqd* (1985–9), 2:135–44, 158–9; al-Ṣayrafī, *Nuzhat*, 2:503–4, 509; al-Sakhāwī, *Dhayl*, 1:522; al-Sakhāwī, *Wajīz*, 2:466; Ibn Taghrībirdī, *Nujūm*, 14:186, 198; Ibn Taghrībirdī, *Manhal*, 6:399, 402; al-Suyūṭī, *Taʾrīkh*, 407; al-Malaṭī, *Nayl*, 4:88, 94–5; Ibn Iyās, *Badāʾiʿ*, 2:67, 70–1.
20. Al-Maqrīzī, *Sulūk*, 4:587; Ibn Ḥajar, *Inbāʾ al-ghumr*, 3:446; Ibn Taghrībirdī,

Nujūm, 14:205–6; Ibn Taghrībirdī, *Manhal*, 6:403, 7:63; al-Sakhāwī, *Ḍaw'*, 4:20; Ibn Iyās, *Badā'i'*, 2:74.

21. Adriaenssens and Van Steenbergen, 'Mamluk Authorities'; Ibn Ḥajar, *Inbā' al-ghumr*, 3:250, 254; Ibn Taghrībirdī, *Nujūm*, 14:205–6, 211; Ibn Taghrībirdī, *Manhal*, 3:258–62; al-Ṣayrafī, *Nuzhat*, 2:516; al-Malaṭī, *Nayl*, 4:101; Ibn Iyās, *Badā'i'*, 2:74, 76.
22. Al-Maqrīzī, *Sulūk*, 4:593, 607–9; Ibn Ḥajar, *Inbā' al-ghumr*, 3:269–70; al-'Aynī, *'Iqd* (1985–9), 2:180; Ibn Taghrībirdī, *Nujūm*, 14:221; Ibn Taghrībirdī, *Manhal*, 3:261–2; al-Ṣayrafī, *Nuzhat*, 3:5–6; Ibn Iyās, *Badā'i'*, 2:79.
23. Adriaenssens and Van Steenbergen, 'Mamluk Authorities', 5; Van Steenbergen and Van Nieuwenhuyse, 'Truth and Politics', 152–4.
24. Woods, *Timurid Aristocratic Order*; Binbaş, *Intellectual Networks*, 260–1; Dekkiche, 'New Source', 268–9; Kennedy, *Caliphate*, 250; Loiseau, *Les Mamelouks*, 128; Arnold, *Caliphate*, 112; Becker, 'Barthold's Studien', 380. See also Markiewicz, *Crisis of Kingship*, 159–65.
25. Ibn Taghrībirdī, *Manhal*, 6:199–203.
26. Becker, 'Barthold's Studien', 383.
27. Dekkiche, 'New Source', 249–51; Ibn Ḥajar, *Inbā' al-ghumr*, 3:342; Ibn Taghrībirdī, *Nujūm*, 14:368.
28. On the relation between the two in this period, see Laoust, *Essai*, 46, 65–6.
29. Binbaş, *Intellectual Networks*, 260; Broadbridge, *Kingship and Ideology*, 199; Manz, 'Temür and the Problem of a Conqueror's Legacy'; Arnold, *Caliphate*, 105–6; Becker, 'Barthold's Studien', 378.
30. Irwin, 'Political Thinking', 46–7. See also Woods, *Aqquyunlu*, 103.
31. Wing, 'Submission, Defiance', 5; Van Steenbergen and Van Nieuwenhuyse, 'Truth and Politics', 158–9.
32. For further comment on the so-called 'Baghdad style' of caliphal turbans, see Ibn Iyās, *Badā'i'*, 5:41. Leo Aryeh Mayer describes the caliph's turban as follows: 'The caliph's headgear consisted of a fine round turban with a trailing end piece (*rafraf*) at the back, about two feet long and one foot wide, reaching from the top to the bottom of the turban . . . [At the time of investiture the caliph might receive] a black head shawl (*ṭarḥa*).' See Mayer, *Mamluk Costume*, 13; Fuess, 'Sultans with Horns', 75; Mājid, *Nuẓum*, 1:34; Schimmel, 'Kalif und Kadi', 117.
33. Al-'Aynī, *'Iqd* (1985–9), 2:428–30.
34. Ibn Taghrībirdī reports that the sultans of Cairo had made it a long-standing practice for the Abbasid caliph to be escorted by an amir over lengthy journeys.

35. Al-Maqrīzī, *Sulūk*, 4:891; Ibn Ḥajar, *Inbāʾ al-ghumr*, 3:492–500, 510; Ibn Taghrībirdī, *Nujūm*, 15:8–9, 13–35; al-Ṣayrafī, *Nuzhat*, 3:259; al-Sakhāwī, *Dhayl*, 1:579; al-Sakhāwī, *Wajīz*, 2:524; al-Suyūṭī, *Taʾrīkh*, 327; al-Malaṭī, *Rawḍ*, 1:236; Ibn Iyās, *Badāʾiʿ*, 2:146, 151; Van Steenbergen and Van Nieuwenhuyse, 'Truth and Politics', 178–81; Wing, 'Submission, Defiance', 5–10; Woods, *Aqquyunlu*, 50–4.
36. Al-Maqrīzī, *Sulūk*, 4:1044–5, 1053; Ibn Ḥajar, *Inbāʾ al-ghumr*, 4:73–4, 79; al-ʿAynī, *ʿIqd* (1985–9), 2:499–501; Ibn Taghrībirdī, *Nujūm*, 15:102–3, 106–7; al-Ṣayrafī, *Nuzhat*, 3:415–17; al-Sakhāwī, *Dhayl*, 1:608; al-Sakhāwī, *Wajīz*, 2:554; al-Suyūṭī, *Taʾrīkh*, 407; Ibn Iyās, *Badāʾiʿ*, 2:188.
37. Ibn Taghrībirdī, *Nujūm*, 15:222, 227, 235; al-Sakhāwī, *Wajīz*, 2:554; al-Malaṭī, *Nayl*, 5:40; Ibn Iyās, *Badāʾiʿ*, 2:191–2. On the caliph as a guarantor in the late fifteenth century, see Banister, 'Naught Remains', 232–4; Holt, *Age of Crusades*, 189; Petry, *Twilight of Majesty*, 18.
38. In Ṣafar 842/August 1438, the caliph had also been an important symbol for the Ashrafiyya supporters of Yūsuf during the rivalry with supporters of Jaqmaq (*Sulūk*, 4:1073–4; *Nujūm*, 15:233–9).
39. Al-Maqrīzī, *Sulūk*, 4:1086–7, 1096–7; Ibn Ḥajar, *Inbāʾ al-ghumr*, 4:94; al-ʿAynī, *ʿIqd* (1985–9), 2:515; Ibn Taghrībirdī, *Nujūm*, 15:256, 261, 276; Ibn Taghrībirdī, *Manhal*, 4:283–4; al-Ṣayrafī, *Nuzhat*, 4:19, 38; al-Sakhāwī, *Dhayl*, 1:615; al-Sakhāwī, *Wajīz*, 2:562; Ibn Iyās, *Badāʾiʿ*, 2:197, 199.
40. Yüksel Muslu, *Ottomans and Mamluks*, 102, 185; Loiseau, *Les Mamelouks*, 45.
41. Al-Ṣayrafī identifies him as Baybars ibn Nuʿayr, see *Nuzhat*, 4:154.
42. Al-Maqrīzī, *Sulūk*, 4:1165; al-ʿAynī, *ʿIqd* (1985–9), 2:546; al-Ṣayrafī, *Nuzhat*, 4:322; al-Malaṭī, *Nayl*, 5:97. On the social practice of intercession in the Cairo Sultanate, see Eychenne, *Liens personnels*, 52–5; Chamberlain, *Knowledge*, 97.
43. Al-Malaṭī, *Rawḍ*, 1:236; Garcin, 'Histoire', 63.
44. Ibn Taghrībirdī, *Manhal*, 4:304; Ibn Taghrībirdī, *Mawrid*, 1:258; al-Suyūṭī, *Ḥusn*, 2:90; al-Suyūṭī, *Taʾrīkh*, 407; al-Sakhāwī, *Ḍawʾ*, 3:215; al-Sakhāwī, *Dhayl*, 1:634; al-Sakhāwī, *Tibr*, 25; al-Sakhāwī, *Wajīz*, 2:581; al-Malaṭī, *Nayl*, 5:144; al-Malaṭī, *Rawḍ*, 1:235-7; al-Qaramānī, *Akhbār*, 2:218.
45. See the discussion of Ibn Ḥajar in Chapter 7. Other scholars dedicated praise poetry to al-Muʿtaḍid II, including the Shāfiʿī qadi Nūr al-Dīn ʿAlī ibn ʾĀqbars (d. 862/1458), see al-Biqāʿī, *ʿUnwān*, 4:58.
46. Hassan, *Longing for the Lost Caliphate*, 126–7, 131–3.

47. Al-Qalqashandī, *Maʾāthir*, 1:1–5, 3:375–81; Ibn Taghrībirdī, *Manhal*, 4:305; Ibn Taghrībirdī, *Ḥawādith*, 137; Ibn Taghrībirdī, *Mawrid*, 1:258; al-Sakhāwī, *Ḍawʾ*, 3:215; al-Sakhāwī, *Wajīz*, 2:581; al-Sakhāwī, *Tibr*, 26.
48. Al-Malaṭī, *Rawḍ*, 1:236.
49. Banister, 'Naught Remains', 238–9.
50. Al-Maqrīzī, *Sulūk*, 4:787; Ibn Ḥajar, *Inbāʾ al-ghumr*, 3:417; al-Ṣayrafī, *Nuzhat*, 2:481, 3:140; Ibn Taghrībirdī, *Nujūm*, 15:151–2; al-Sakhāwī, *Jawāhir*, 1195; al-Sakhāwī, *Ḍawʾ*, 1:314–15; Petry, *Civilian Elite*, 208–9.
51. Al-Maqrīzī, *Sulūk*, 4:756, 924–5; Ibn Taghrībirdī, *Nujūm*, 15:192–3. A series of embassies were also exchanged between 832 and 836/1428 and 1433 until the death of the sultan of Gujarat and the succession of his fourteen-year-old son al-Muẓaffar Aḥmad Shāh (836–40/1433–7). See Behrens-Abouseif, *Practising Diplomacy*, 46–7; al-Mashhadānī, *Al-ʿAlāqāt*, 51. According to John Meloy, Ibn Taghrībirdī identifies six 'notable kings' of India: Delhi, Cambay, Bengal, Gulbarga, Jawnpur and Bijankar (Vijayanagara), which he calls '*wilāyāt*' or appointed governorates of the Abbasid caliph. See Meloy, 'Aggression', 610–11.
52. Ibn Taghrībirdī commends al-Muʿtaḍid II for his handling of the family's debts and attributes the caliph's determination to get free of usury to his Islamic piety, see *Manhal*, 4:304–5; Ibn Taghrībirdī, *Ḥawādith*, 137; Ibn Taghrībirdī, *Mawrid*, 1:258.
53. Ibn Ḥajar, *Inbāʾ al-ghumr*, 3:520; al-Suyūṭī, *Rafʿ*, 28–9; al-Malaṭī, *Nayl*, 4:343; al-Sakhāwī, *Ḍawʾ*, 1:50; al-Sakhāwī, *Wajīz*, 2:533.
54. Ibn Ḥajar believed the caliph's age at death was close to ninety (*Inbāʾ*, 4:79, 189), while al-Suyūṭī had it on the authority of the caliph's niece that al-Muʿtaḍid II died aged sixty-three, see *Taʾrīkh*, 407. See also al-Malaṭī, *Rawḍ*, 1:235.
55. Ibn Ḥajar, *Inbāʾ al-ghumr*, 4:189; Ibn Taghrībirdī, *Nujūm*, 15:489; Ibn Taghrībirdī, *Ḥawādith*, 1; Ibn Taghrībirdī, *Manhal*, 6:53; Ibn Taghrībirdī, *Dalīl*, 1:296; Ibn Taghrībirdī, *Mawrid*, 1:258–61; al-Ṣayrafī, *Nuzhat*, 4:236, 241; al-Sakhāwī, *Ḍawʾ*, 3:215, 269; al-Sakhāwī, *Dhayl*, 1:634; al-Sakhāwī, *Wajīz*, 2:581; al-Sakhāwī, *Tibr*, 13, 359; al-Suyūṭī, *Ḥusn*, 2:91; al-Suyūṭī, *Taʾrīkh*, 407; al-Malaṭī, *Nayl*, 5:144, 328–9; al-Malaṭī, *Rawḍ*, 1:237; Ibn Iyās, *Badāʾiʿ*, 2:230; al-Qaramānī, *Akhbār*, 2:218.
56. Al-ʿAynī, *ʿIqd* (1985–9), 2:570; Ibn Taghrībirdī, *Nujūm*, 15:349; Ibn Taghrībirdī, *Dalīl*, 1:320; al-Sakhāwī, *Tibr*, 13, 359; al-Malaṭī, *Nayl*, 5:144; Ibn Iyās, *Badāʾiʿ*, 2:230.

57. Ibn Taghrībirdī, *Nujūm*, 15:532–3; Ibn Iyās, *Badāʾiʿ*, 2:230.
58. Al-Suyūṭī's father later received the honour of composing the caliph's investiture deed. See al-Suyūṭī, *Taʾrīkh*, 410; al-Suyūṭī, *Taḥadduth*, 9.
59. Al-Suyūṭī, *Ḥusn*, 2:91.
60. Ibn Taghrībirdī, *Manhal*, 6:52; al-Sakhāwī, *Ḍawʾ*, 3:269.
61. Ibn Taghrībirdī, *Ḥawādith*, 87; al-Sakhāwī, *Tibr*, 310–11. On the Ribāṭ al-Athār, see al-Maqrīzī, *Khiṭaṭ*, 4:2:801–2; Taymūr, *Āthār*, 27–36.
62. Al-Sakhāwī, *Dhayl*, 2:53–4; Ibn Taghrībirdī, *Wajīz*, 2:646; al-Sakhāwī, *Tibr*, 310–11; al-Malaṭī, *Nayl*, 5:315–19; Ibn Iyās, *Badāʾiʿ*, 2:282. See also Ibn Taghrībirdī, *Nujūm*, 15:424–5.
63. Ibn Taghrībirdī, *Nujūm*, 16:1; Ibn Taghrībirdī, *Ḥawādith*, 101; Ibn Taghrībirdī, *Manhal*, 6:52–3; Ibn Taghrībirdī, *Mawrid*, 1:260–1; al-Biqāʿī, *Iẓhār*, 1:67, 405; al-Sakhāwī, *Ḍawʾ*, 3:269; al-Sakhāwī, *Tibr*, 344, 359; al-Sakhāwī, *Wajīz*, 2:657; al-Suyūṭī, *Taʾrīkh*, 410; al-Suyūṭī, *Ḥusn*, 2:91; al-Malaṭī, *Nayl*, 5:328–9; Ibn Iyās, *Badāʾiʿ*, 2:287–8. It is unclear which disease claimed the life of the caliph, though he had at least one daughter that died of the plague in 853/1449, see *Ḍawʾ*, 12:165.
64. Garcin, 'Histoire', 63.
65. Al-ʿAynī, *ʿIqd* (1985–9), 2:573; Ibn Taghrībirdī, *Manhal*, 6:52; Ibn Taghrībirdī, *Mawrid*, 1:261; al-Suyūṭī, *Taʾrīkh*, 410; al-Sakhāwī, *Dhayl*, 2:65; al-Sakhāwī, *Wajīz*, 2:657; al-Malaṭī, *Nayl*, 5:328–9; Ibn Iyās, *Badāʾiʿ*, 2:287.
66. Ibn Taghrībirdī, *Nujūm*, 15:432, 16:1, 89, 193–4; al-Biqāʿī, *Iẓhār*, 1:68–77, 405; al-Malaṭī, *Nayl*, 5:329; al-Sakhāwī, *Ḍawʾ*, 3:166; al-Suyūṭī, *Ḥusn*, 2:90; al-Suyūṭī, *Taʾrīkh*, 410; Ibn Iyās, *Badāʾiʿ*, 2:287–8; Garcin, 'Histoire', 63.
67. Ibn Taghrībirdī, *Nujūm*, 15:440–1; al-Biqāʿī, *Iẓhār*, 1:226–8; al-Sakhāwī, *Tibr*, 389. For an overview of the whole affair, see *Nujūm*, 15:375–8, 16:210–11; al-Sakhāwī, *Ḍawʾ*, 7:63–6; al-Malaṭī, *Nayl*, 5:364–5; Ibn Iyās, *Badāʾiʿ*, 2:296; Mortel, 'Decline'.
68. Al-Sakhāwī, *Tibr*, 390.
69. Ibn Taghrībirdī, *Nujūm*, 15:441–2; al-Sakhāwī, *Tibr*, 389–90; Ibn Iyās, *Badāʾiʿ*, 2:296. See also Mortel, 'Decline', 185–6.
70. Ibn Taghrībirdī, *Nujūm*, 15:452–4, 16:23; Ibn Taghrībirdī, *Ḥawādith*, 381; al-Biqāʿī, *Iẓhār*, 1:288–90; al-Sakhāwī, *Tibr*, 423–4; al-Sakhāwī, *Wajīz*, 2:674–5; al-Sakhāwī, *Dhayl*, 2:85; al-Malaṭī, *Nayl*, 5:377–9; Ibn Iyās, *Badāʾiʿ*, 2:301. According to Mayer, the caliph's coat was likely woven from material very similar to watered silk, which was used during much of the period. See Mayer, *Mamluk Costume*, 14.

71. Ibn Taghrībirdī, *Nujūm*, 15:455, 459; Ibn Taghrībirdī, *Ḥawādith*, 349; Ibn Taghrībirdī, *Manhal*, 4:299–300.
72. Ibn Taghrībirdī, *Nujūm*, 16:35; al-Biqāʿī, *Iẓhār*, 1:320; al-Sakhāwī, *Ḍawʾ*, 3:166–7; al-Suyūṭī, *Ḥusn*, 2:90; al-Suyūṭī, *Taʾrīkh*, 410; al-Malaṭī, *Nayl*, 5:385–6; Ibn Iyās, *Badāʾiʿ*, 2:304.
73. Ibn Taghrībirdī, *Nujūm*, 16:35, 40–1, 193–4; Ibn Taghrībirdī, *Ḥawādith*, 169, 381–2; Ibn Taghrībirdī, *Mawrid*, 1:263; al-Biqāʿī, *Iẓhār*, 1:322–9; al-Sakhāwī, *Wajīz*, 2:676–7; al-Sakhāwī, *Tibr*, 426; al-Suyūṭī, *Taʾrīkh*, 410; Ibn Iyās, *Badāʾiʿ*, 2:304; Ibn al-Ḥimṣī, *Ḥawādith*, 1:121.
74. Al-Sakhāwī, *Wajīz*, 2:677. On the ceremonial significance attached to the Rumayla Square, see Onimus, *Les maîtres du jeu*, 310–14.
75. Ibn Taghrībirdī, *Nujūm*, 16:44–5; Ibn Taghrībirdī, *Ḥawādith*, 169–70; al-Biqāʿī, *Iẓhār*, 1:327–31; al-Sakhāwī, *Ḍawʾ*, 3:166; al-Sakhāwī, *Dhayl*, 2:88–9; al-Sakhāwī, *Tibr*, 426; Ibn Iyās, *Badāʾiʿ*, 2:304.
76. Ibn Taghrībirdī, *Nujūm*, 16:45–53; Ibn Taghrībirdī, *Ḥawādith*, 169; al-Sakhāwī, *Wajīz*, 2:677; al-Malaṭī, *Nayl*, 5:386.
77. Ibn Taghrībirdī, *Nujūm*, 16:57–8; Ibn Taghrībirdī, *Ḥawādith*, 182, 739; Ibn Taghrībirdī, *Mawrid*, 1:263; al-Biqāʿī, *Iẓhār*, 1:336–7; al-Sakhāwī, *Wajīz*, 2:677; al-Sakhāwī, *Tibr*, 430; al-Suyūṭī, *Taʾrīkh*, 410; al-Malaṭī, *Nayl*, 5:387–9. See also Mayer, *Mamluk Costume*, 14.
78. Ibn Taghrībirdī, *Nujūm*, 16:67; Ibn Taghrībirdī, *Ḥawādith*, 184; al-Biqāʿī, *Iẓhār*, 1:354–5; al-Sakhāwī, *Wajīz*, 2:677; al-Malaṭī, *Nayl*, 5:396, 398; Ibn Iyās, *Badāʾiʿ*, 2:312.
79. Ibn Taghrībirdī, *Nujūm*, 16:89–90, 194; Ibn Taghrībirdī, *Ḥawādith*, 382; Ibn Taghrībirdī, *Mawrid*, 1:264; al-Biqāʿī, *Iẓhār*, 1:354; al-Sakhāwī, *Ḍawʾ*, 3:166.
80. Ibn Taghrībirdī, *Nujūm*, 16:87–9; Ibn Taghrībirdī, *Ḥawādith*, 232–8; al-Suyūṭī, *Taʾrīkh*, 410; al-Malaṭī, *Nayl*, 5:441; al-Qaramānī, *Akhbār*, 2:220.
81. Ibn Taghrībirdī, *Nujūm*, 16:89; Ibn Taghrībirdī, *Ḥawādith*, 382; Ibn Taghrībirdī, *Mawrid*, 1:264; al-Biqāʿī, *Iẓhār*, 2:131–2; al-Suyūṭī, *Ḥusn*, 2:90; Ṭarkhān, *Miṣr*, 67; Ḍāḥī and Mizbān, *al-Raʾy al-ʿāmm*, 64.
82. Ibn Taghrībirdī, *Nujūm*, 16:90–1, 194; Ibn Taghrībirdī, *Ḥawādith*, 233, 235, 382; Ibn Taghrībirdī, *Mawrid*, 1:265; al-Biqāʿī, *Iẓhār*, 2:132; al-Sakhāwī, *Ḍawʾ*, 3:166; al-Sakhāwī, *Dhayl*, 2:102; al-Sakhāwī, *Wajīz*, 2:689; al-Suyūṭī, *Ḥusn*, 2:90; Marʿī ibn Yūsuf Karmī, *Nuzha*, 75; Ṭarkhān, *Miṣr*, 67.
83. Ibn Taghrībirdī, *Nujūm*, 16:90–1, 194; Ibn Taghrībirdī, *Ḥawādith*, 233–8, 382; Ibn Taghrībirdī, *Manhal*, 5:184; Ibn Taghrībirdī, *Mawrid*, 1:265–7;

al-Biqāʿī, *Iẓhār*, 1:398n.3, 2:132; al-Ṣayrafī, *Inbāʾ*, 365; al-Sakhāwī, *Ḍawʾ*, 3:166; al-Sakhāwī, *Wajīz*, 3:988; al-Sakhāwī, *Dhayl*, 2:103; al-Suyūṭī, *Ḥusn*, 2:90–1; al-Suyūṭī, *Taʾrīkh*, 411; al-Malaṭī, *Nayl*, 5:443, 7:226; al-Qaramānī, *Akhbār*, 2:221. See also Garcin, 'Histoire', 63–4; Ṭarkhān, *Miṣr*, 67.

84. Ibn Taghrībirdī, *Nujūm*, 16:90, 126, 193–4; Ibn Taghrībirdī, *Ḥawādith*, 233, 238, 380–3; Ibn Taghrībirdī, *Manhal*, 5:184; Ibn Taghrībirdī, *Mawrid*, 1:265; al-Biqāʿī, *Iẓhār*, 2:379; al-Sakhāwī, *Ḍawʾ*, 3:166; al-Sakhāwī, *Dhayl*, 2:131; al-Sakhāwī, *Wajīz*, 2:689, 718; al-Suyūṭī, *Ḥusn*, 2:90; al-Suyūṭī, *Taʾrīkh*, 411; al-Malaṭī, *Nayl*, 5:444, 6:43–4; Ibn Iyās, *Badāʾiʿ*, 2:349; al-Qaramānī, *Akhbār*, 2:220.
85. Al-Qaramānī, *Akhbār*, 2:221.
86. Garcin, 'Histoire', 63; Garcin, 'Circassian Mamlūks', 303.
87. Ibn Taghrībirdī, *Nujūm*, 16:89–90, 194; Ibn Taghrībirdī, *Ḥawādith*, 236; Ibn Taghrībirdī, *Manhal*, 5:183–4.
88. Ibn Taghrībirdī, *Ḥawādith*, 235, 382; Ibn Taghrībirdī, *Nujūm*, 16:218–20, 226; Ibn Taghrībirdī, *Mawrid*, 1:266–7; al-Sakhāwī, *Ḍawʾ*, 10:329; al-Sakhāwī, *Dhayl*, 2:150–1, 326; al-Sakhāwī, *Wajīz*, 2:689, 734–5; al-Biqāʿī, *Iẓhār*, 3:209–12, 214–15, 233–4; al-Malaṭī, *Nayl*, 5:443–4, 6:100–2, 105; al-Malaṭī, *Rawḍ*, 2:34–6, 47; Ibn Iyās, *Badāʾiʿ*, 2:367, 369–71. See also Schimmel, 'Kalif und Kadi', 95–6.
89. Ibn Taghrībirdī, *Nujūm*, 16:246; Ibn Taghrībirdī, *Ḥawādith*, 398–9; al-Biqāʿī, *Iẓhār*, 3:277–89; al-Sakhāwī, *Dhayl*, 2:151–2; al-Sakhāwī, *Wajīz*, 2:738; al-Suyūṭī, *Taʾrīkh*, 411; al-Malaṭī, *Nayl*, 6:111; al-Malaṭī, *Rawḍ*, 2:63–78; Ibn Iyās, *Badāʾiʿ*, 2:377.
90. Ibn Taghrībirdī, *Nujūm*, 16:253–4, 259; Ibn Taghrībirdī, *Ḥawādith*, 398–9, 406–7; al-Ṣayrafī, *Inbāʾ*, 1, 115, 183, 316, 427; al-Sakhāwī, *Ḍawʾ*, 10:329; al-Sakhāwī, *Dhayl*, 2:151–2, 154; al-Suyūṭī, *Ḥusn*, 2:91; al-Suyūṭī, *Taʾrīkh*, 411; al-Malaṭī, *Nayl*, 6:119, 121, 7:227; al-Malaṭī, *Rawḍ*, 2:78–80; Ibn Iyās, *Badāʾiʿ*, 2:378–9, 382–4, 457, 3:151. See also Haarmann, 'Al-Mustandjid'.
91. Al-Malaṭī, *Nayl*, 6:145–7; al-Malaṭī, *Rawḍ*, 2:163–4; Ibn Iyās, *Badāʾiʿ*, 2:395.
92. Meloy, 'Aggression', 613–14.
93. Ibn Taghrībirdī, *Ḥawādith*, 593.
94. Ibn Taghrībirdī, *Nujūm*, 16:357, 365, 373, 387–8; Ibn Taghrībirdī, *Ḥawādith*, 602, 614–17; al-Sakhāwī, *Wajīz*, 2:790–1; al-Sakhāwī, *Dhayl*, 2:209; al-Suyūṭī, *Taʾrīkh*, 411; al-Malaṭī, *Nayl*, 6:280, 294–7; al-Malaṭī, *Rawḍ*, 3:269–73, 296–300; Ibn Iyās, *Badāʾiʿ*, 2:459, 468.
95. Al-Malaṭī, *Nayl*, 6:306–9; Ibn Iyās, *Badāʾiʿ*, 3:4.

96. Ibn Taghrībirdī, *Nujūm*, 16:394; Ibn Taghrībirdī, *Ḥawādith*, 617–18; al-Suyūṭī, *Taʾrīkh*, 411; al-Malaṭī, *Nayl*, 6:310; al-Malaṭī, *Rawḍ*, 3:347–8; Petry, *Twilight of Majesty*, 37.
97. Petry, 'Robing Ceremonials', 360. See also al-Malaṭī, *Rawḍ*, 3:342–4, 346-9; Ibn Iyās, *Badāʾiʿ*, 4:3.
98. Har-El, *Struggle for Domination*, 39–42.
99. Ibn Taghrībirdī, *Ḥawādith*, 635–7. Al-Ṣayrafī dates a similar meeting to 16 Rabīʿ II 873/3 November 1468, see *Inbāʾ*, 33–5; Ibn Iyās, *Badāʾiʿ*, 3:14–15; Lev, 'Symbiotic Relations', 23–4; Amīn, *Awqāf*, 326–7; Schimmel, 'Kalif und Kadi', 98.
100. Ibn Taghrībirdī, *Ḥawādith*, 633; al-Malaṭī, *Nayl*, 6:327; al-Malaṭī, *Rawḍ*, 3:397; Ibn Iyās, *Badāʾiʿ*, 3:13, 85–6. See also Har-El, *Struggle for Domination*, 86–92; Petry, *Twilight of Majesty*, 57–72; Amīn, *Awqāf*, 328; Holt, *Age of Crusades*, 196–7.
101. An initial request had been sent to Khushqadam by his predecessor, Maḥmūd Shāh Khaljī and a second request to Qāyitbāy, to which he responded to Ghiyāth al-Dīn Shāh. See Meloy, 'Aggression', 604.
102. Al-Ṣayrafī, *Inbāʾ*, 362; al-Suyūṭī, *Taḥadduth*, 157; Ibn Iyās, *Badāʾiʿ*, 3:65; Meloy, 'Aggression', 613–14; Petry, *Twilight of Majesty*, 74; Margoliouth, 'Caliphate', 337.
103. Garcin, 'Histoire', 64.
104. Ibn Taghrībirdī, *Nujūm*, 16:259.
105. Al-Malaṭī, *Nayl*, 7:226. Further evidence of al-Mustanjid's affluence comes in the form of a badly preserved 869/1465 *waqf* document listed in Muḥammad Amīn's catalogue of the Dār al-Wathāʾiq collection naming the caliph and the amir Aḥmad ibn al-Khiṭāʾī as co-administrators. See *Fihrist wathāʾiq al-Qāhira*, 34 No. 155.
106. Al-Malaṭī, *Nayl*, 8:69–70; al-Sakhāwī, *Ḍawʾ*, 12:54–5; al-Sakhāwī, *Dhayl*, 2:269, 456; al-Sakhāwī, *Wajīz*, 3:1026–7; Ibn Iyās, *Badāʾiʿ*, 3:151, 240; Ibn Ṭūlūn, *Mufākahat*, 1:77.
107. Al-Suyūṭī, *Taʾrīkh*, 336; al-Sakhāwī, *Dhayl*, 2:456; al-Sakhāwī, *Wajīz*, 2:874; al-Malaṭī, *Nayl*, 7:62, 79; Ibn Iyās, *Badāʾiʿ*, 3:85, 240–1. For a discussion of Cairene Abbasid marriage unions, see Banister, 'Princesses born to Concubines'.
108. Ibn Iyās, *Badāʾiʿ*, 3:151. Al-Ṣayrafī frequently states that 'he had nothing of the caliphate but its name/title (*ism*)'. See *Inbāʾ*, 1, 115, 183, 316.
109. Al-Malaṭī, *Nayl*, 7:185, 221; al-Sakhāwī, *Ḍawʾ*, 10:330; al-Sakhāwī,

Dhayl, 2:301, 326; al-Suyūṭī, *Ḥusn*, 2:91; al-Suyūṭī, *Taʾrīkh*, 411–12; Ibn Iyās, *Badāʾiʿ*, 3:151; al-Qaramānī, *Akhbār*, 2:221; Rāġib, 'Al-Sayyida Nafīsa', 52.

110. Al-Sakhāwī, *Ḍawʾ*, 10:188; al-Sakhāwī, *Dhayl*, 2:413; al-Sakhāwī, *Wajīz*, 3:988; Ibn Iyās, *Badāʾiʿ*, 3:151, 225. Five of Mūsā's brothers had held the caliphate, and when he was snubbed in favour of a nephew, we are told 'he nearly died of the insult'.
111. Ibn Iyās, *Badāʾiʿ*, 3:125. Muḥammad ultimately succumbed to plague in Dhū al-Ḥijja 881/March–April 1477, though his own descendants survived as contenders for the family office.
112. Al-Sakhāwī, *Ḍawʾ*, 2:309, 4:236–7, 10:86; al-Sakhāwī, *Dhayl*, 2:320; al-Sakhāwī, *Wajīz*, 3:877–8, 897; al-Suyūṭī, *Ḥusn*, 2:92; al-Suyūṭī, *Taʾrīkh*, 412; al-Malaṭī, *Nayl*, 7:227; Ibn Ṭūlūn, *Mufākahat*, 1:5, 51, 59, 63; Ibn Iyās, *Badāʾiʿ*, 3:151–2, 378–9; al-Qaramānī, *Akhbār*, 2:222; Quṭb al-Dīn, *Chroniken*, 3:184. See also Ṭarkhān, *Miṣr*, 68.
113. Al-Suyūṭī, *Taʾrīkh*, 413; Ibn Iyās, *Badāʾiʿ*, 3:215.
114. Ibn Iyās, *Badāʾiʿ*, 3:213, 215–16. See also Behrens-Abouseif, *Practising Diplomacy*, 29–30; Irwin, 'Political Thinking', 46; Broadbridge, *Kingship and Ideology*, 199; Har-El, *Struggle for Domination*, 128; Petry, *Twilight of Majesty*, 93; Holt, *Age of Crusades*, 197.
115. The document itself has not survived and is only described by Ibn Iyās.
116. Ibn Iyās, *Badāʾiʿ*, 3:214–76; Yüksel Muslu, *Ottomans and Mamluks*, 1–2, 134–55; Har-El, *Struggle for Domination*, 133–51, 163–214; Petry, *Twilight of Majesty*, 93.
117. Adriaenssens and Van Steenbergen, 'Mamluk Authorities', 35–7; Har-El, *Struggle for Domination*, 152–3.
118. Har-El, *Struggle for Domination*, 156.
119. Finkel, *Osman's Dream*, 83–9.
120. Al-Suyūṭī, *Taʾrīkh*, 327; Ibn Iyās, *Badāʾiʿ*, 3:361, 4:244, 269, 295–6; Banister, 'Naught Remains', 234–5. On the role played by the chief religious functionaries at public festivals, see Schimmel, 'Kalif und Kadi', 77–9. One of the earliest instances of the caliph's presence concerns al-Mustanjid's visit with the qadis to negotiate a divorce for his daughter in Dhū al-Qaʿda 876/April 1472, see Ibn Iyās, *Badāʾiʿ*, 3:85.
121. Al-Sakhāwī, *Wajīz*, 3:1079; Ibn Iyās, *Badāʾiʿ*, 3:262; Banister, 'Naught Remains', 232–4; Schimmel, 'Kalif und Kadi', 72.
122. Al-Malaṭī, *Nayl*, 8:150.

123. Al-Sakhāwī, *Ḍaw*ʾ, 3:31, 4:237; al-Suyūṭī, *Ḥusn*, 2:92; Ibn Iyās, *Badāʾiʿ*, 1:2:378, 5:192; Rāġib, 'Al-Sayyida Nafīsa', 42–3.
124. Al-Malaṭī, *Nayl*, 6:372–3; Ibn Iyās, *Badāʾiʿ*, 3:206. See also Schimmel, 'Kalif und Kadi', 77–8; Schimmel, 'Some Glimpses', 371; Rāġib, 'Al-Sayyida Nafīsa', 39.
125. Al-Sakhāwī, *Ḍaw*ʾ, 7:54, 12:164; Schimmel, 'Some Glimpses', 354; Rāġib, 'Al-Sayyida Nafīsa', 41–2.
126. Al-Sakhāwī refers to it alternately as philanthropic land (*khayriyya*) or as a continuing charity (*ṣadaqa jāriyya*), see *Dhayl*, 2:422; al-Sakhāwī, *Wajīz*, 3:998. For a succinct biography of Maryam bint al-Mutawakkil, see al-Sakhāwī, *Ḍaw*ʾ, 12:125.
127. Al-Sakhāwī likewise made no secret of his high regard for Asanbāy, see *Dhayl*, 2:422–3; al-Sakhāwī, *Wajīz*, 3:998–9.
128. Al-Sakhāwī, *Dhayl*, 3:132; Ibn Iyās, *Badāʾiʿ*, 3:300–1. See also Behrens-Abouseif, *Cairo of the Mamluks*, 9; Sartain, *Al-Suyūṭī*, 88–90.
129. Ibn Iyās, *Badāʾiʿ*, 3:321–34; Ibn Ṭūlūn, *Mufākahat*, 1:167; Petry, *Twilight of Majesty*, 116–17.
130. Ibn al-Shiḥna, *Badr al-zāhir*, 35–45.
131. Sartain, *Al-Suyūṭī*, 13–14.
132. Al-Sakhāwī, *Ḍaw*ʾ, 4:326–7; al-Suyūṭī, *Ḥusn*, 2:92; Ibn Iyās, *Badāʾiʿ*, 3:379, 4:101; al-Qaramānī, *Akhbār*, 2:222; al-Ḥaṣkafī, *Mutʿat al-adhhān*, 1:432.
133. On the close relations between the Suyūṭī and Abbasid families, see al-Sakhāwī, *Ḍaw*ʾ, 4:69, 11:72–3; al-Suyūṭī, *Taʾrīkh*, 410; al-Suyūṭī, *Taḥadduth*, 8–10; al-Shādhilī, *Bahja*, 57–8; Banister, 'Casting the Caliph in a Cosmic Role', 102; Hassan, *Longing for the Lost Caliphate*, 136–7; Sartain, *Al-Suyūṭī*, 22, 81–2; Garcin, 'Histoire', 34–7, 65–6.
134. For the text of the document, see al-Shādhilī, *Bahja*, 172–4.
135. Banister, 'Casting the Caliph in a Cosmic Role', 109–12; Hassan, *Longing for the Lost Caliphate*, 137; Saleh, 'Al-Suyūṭī', 78; Schimmel, 'Kalif und Kadi', 31–2; Garcin, 'Histoire', 65; Margoliouth, 'Caliphate', 335.
136. Al-Suyūṭī, *Taʾrīkh*, 413; Ibn Iyās, *Badāʾiʿ*, 3:379; al-Ḥaṣkafī, *Mutʿat al-adhhān*, 1:431.
137. Al-Sakhāwī, *Ḍaw*ʾ, 10:86. In his obituary for Muḥammad, Ibn Iyās used titles suitable for an Abbasid crown prince or heir apparent: *al-jannāb al-nāṣirī*, see *Badāʾiʿ*, 3:125. On the *jannāb* title for use with heirs to the caliphate or sultanate, see Ibn Nāẓir al-Jaysh, *Tathqīf*, 8, 189.

138. Al-Suyūṭī, *Taʾrīkh*, 412–13; al-Sakhāwī, *Ḍawʾ*, 10:86, 285; Ibn Iyās, *Badāʾiʿ*, 3:376, 378–9, 4:128, 171, 5:389; Quṭb al-Dīn, *Chroniken*, 3:184; al-Qaramānī, *Akhbār*, 2:222; al-Ḥaṣkafī, *Mutʿat al-adhhān*, 1:431.
139. Binbaş, *Intellectual Networks*, 258, 265–74; Markiewicz, *Crisis of Kingship*, 160–5. For the Ottoman branch of the debate and the Sufistic caliphate in general, see Yılmaz, *Caliphate Redefined*, 89–90, 115, 206–17.
140. Homerin, 'Sufism in Mamluk Studies', 191. For further discussion of the Cairene Abbasid Caliphate's links to Sufism, see Chapter 10.
141. Casale, 'Tordesillas', 493; Moin, *Millennial Sovereign*, 6; Hodgson, *Rethinking World History*, 187.
142. For some examples, see al-Qalqashandī, *Ṣubḥ*, 10:48; Ibn Ḥijja, *Qahwat al-inshāʾ*, 74. See also Hassan, 'Poetic Memories', 10–12.
143. Ibn ʿAbd al-Ẓāhir, *Rawḍ*, 111, 145–7.
144. Hassan, *Longing for the Lost Caliphate*, 13–14, 64–5.
145. The caliph was frequently excluded from the advisory portion of the monthly meetings with the sultan beginning in the later fifteenth century. Nevertheless, some succession documents indicate that the caliph was expected to advise the sultan and his circle. See al-Qalqashandī, *Ṣubḥ*, 9:372–3. See also Schimmel, 'Kalif und Kadi', 74.
146. Ibn Iyās, *Badāʾiʿ*, 5:27–8, 30-1; Schimmel, 'Kalif und Kadi', 68, 75; Chapoutot-Remadi, 'Une institution', 17; Sümer, 'Yavuz Selim', 346–7.
147. On these and other ceremonial functions of the Cairo caliphs, see Banister, 'Naught Remains', 227–37.

5

The Last Abbasids of Cairo, 903–22/1497–1517

Introduction

The caliphs of the late fourteenth and fifteenth centuries studied in Chapters 3 and 4, likely hoped that the position and perks of their family, as stewards of the caliphate, would weather the tumult of changing political orders in Cairo and continue on into the foreseeable future. In addition to enjoying reverence and ceremonial deference, they were also the holders of a number of revenue-producing *iqṭāʿ*s and estates that provided a substantial living. The caliphal office, which had persisted largely undisturbed until the reign of the sultan Qāyitbāy, would ultimately end in confusion and disarray after the Ottoman conquest of the Cairo Sultanate. The early sixteenth century would prove to be a period of heightened tension within the family as squabbles over wealth, resources and the future of the caliphal office itself led to public embarrassments and the intervention of authorities.

The last two Abbasids to reign with pomp in Cairo, the father and son al-Mustamsik and al-Mutawakkil III, witnessed the collapse of the Cairo Sultanate and the loss of much of their family fortune and prestige to the invading Ottomans. In a unique development, they also reigned together simultaneously for a brief period. During the transition to Ottoman rule in Cairo the caliphate persevered as a status quo symbol, but ended in relative obscurity. As had been the case during the reign of Qāyitbāy discussed in the previous chapter, in the context of war preparations, a cash-strapped sultan had to make the difficult choice of whether to use dwindling funds to maintain the caliphate at full ceremonial strength, or to pay for the loyalty of his own military forces. As problems mounted, the Abbasid caliph seldom received high priority and often had to fend for himself.

The Reign of al-Mustamsik bi-llāh, 903–14/1497–1508 and 922–3/1516–17

The religious and political elite invested the Abbasid prince Yaʿqūb as Abū al-Ṣabr al-Mustamsik bi-llāh on 26 Muḥarram 903/24 September 1497. There had been opposition to his assumption of office from within the family and squabbles disrupted his caliphate from the outset. A month after al-Mustamsik had been named successor, his cousin Khalīl, a grandson of al-Mutawakkil II, challenged his caliphate at the inaugural ceremony at the Citadel on 13 Ṣafar 903/11 October 1497. Over the din Khalīl loudly heckled his cousin: 'This fellow has bad eyesight which invalidates his accession to the caliphate!' Puzzled by the outburst, and presumably unaware of the classical stipulations for the caliphate, the young son of Qāyitbāy, sultan al-Nāṣir Muḥammad defended the new caliph arguing that al-Mustamsik's father had been caliph and no better proof of his entitlement to the office was necessary. Other amirs likewise came forward to support al-Mustamsik, claiming that he was the most suitable member of the Abbasid family, and the challenger left the Citadel frustrated. Undaunted, the qadis deemed a second performance of the *mubāyaʿa* superfluous and members of the sultan's entourage adorned the caliph with family heraldry as he departed from the Citadel meeting, dressed in a robe of honour and was escorted back to his living quarters in a solemn procession.[1]

Ultimately, al-Nāṣir Muḥammad was betrayed by his *atābak* Qāniṣawh al-Khamsī when his officers seized the Gate of the Chain, held it, and summoned the caliph and qadis to invest him as sultan and announced the deposition of al-Nāṣir Muḥammad. The young sultan was murdered by a group of his father's *mamlūk*s in Giza on 15 Rabīʿ I 904/31 October 1498. Qāniṣawh al-Khamsī was thereafter deposed by al-Nāṣir Muḥammad's uncle and former leader of his entourage, al-Ẓāhir Qāniṣawh. Qāniṣawh was merely the nominee of the more powerful amir Ṭūmānbāy who hoped to seize power at an opportune time. His plans came to naught, however, and instead another contender, Jānbalāṭ al-Ashrafī, became sultan in Dhū al-Ḥijja 905/July 1500. After his investiture, Jānbalāṭ persuaded al-Mustamsik to continue living at his father's former residence in the Citadel. In Jumādā I 906/November 1500, Jānbalāṭ, aware of the fragility of his political order, attempted to swear his officers to fidelity over the supposed relic, the 'Qur'ān of 'Uthmān', in the presence of al-Mustamsik and the four qadis. The pageantry proved to be insufficient to safeguard Jānbalāṭ's reign, and Ṭūmānbāy staged his return to Cairo from Damascus in Jumādā I 906/November 1500. Worried over reports of his impending return to the city with a large army, the sultan hung his own standard from the Gate of the Chain and called soldiers and officers to the Citadel, along with various members of the Abbasid family and the chief qadis. In the end, Jānbalāṭ could do little to stop the arrival of al-'Ādil Ṭūmānbāy, who began a brief reign after securing a public endorsement from al-Mustamsik in Jumādā II 906/December 1500.[2]

After the rapid turnover of several short-reigning sultans following the death of Qāyitbāy, politics shifted once again at the end of 906/1501 when some of the amirs pushed the reluctant *dawādār* and veteran Qāniṣawh al-Ghawrī forward as the next sultan. The religio-political community once again summoned al-Mustamsik and the qadis to invest him and draw up the necessary documents. The Shāfi'ī and Ḥanafī qadis had been hesitant to participate before a firm consensus had been reached, but the caliph came prepared to perform his duty.[3]

In a solemn ceremony in Dhū al-Qa'da 906/May–June 1501, al-Mustamsik and the four qadis presided over an official reading of Qāniṣawh al-Ghawrī's investiture deed. The five men ascended the Citadel early the next month to congratulate the sultan at the start of the Islamic lunar year. At the time, Qāniṣawh al-Ghawrī had been wrestling with the issue of how to raise funds to pay his *mamlūk* recruits. He wanted to manipulate *waqf* yields and proposed a system to the qadis, which, after some discussion, they unanimously condemned.

Cash shortages often increased anxiety among the troops and Qāniṣawh al-Ghawrī, fearing rebellion and disorder from the recent escape of *mamlūk* prisoners, continued the earlier practice of ordering amirs to swear fealty over the Qur'ān of 'Uthmān in the presence of the Abbasid caliph until the end of his reign. The sultan hoped that his officers would not break faith based on the relics of the sacred past, and the watchful gaze of the Abbasid caliph to whom all owed allegiance.[4] The 'sacred presence' of the caliph, qadis and the ʿUthmānī Qurʾān served the sultan as an important symbol of religious accountability.[5]

To bolster his religious credentials and ward off accusations of greed, Qāniṣawh al-Ghawrī laid the foundation for a number of pious structures and highlighted the caliph and qadis as guests of honour. In late 908/1503, he invited them to a banquet to celebrate the completion of his mosque and mausoleum complex at the time of the *ʿĪd al-Aḍḥā* festival. The five chief religious authorities likewise attended a formal ceremony as the sultan's honoured guests the next year.[6]

Some years later in mid-1507 the German nobleman, Martyn von Baumgarten (d. 1535) visited Christian holy sites in the Syro-Egyptian territories of the sultanate and twice encountered and described al-Mustamsik bi-llāh. On the first occasion, at the celebrated Cairene homecoming of Baumgarten's guide, the amir 'Tongobardin' (Taghrībirdī?) who the caliph had come to visit with other dignitaries in Jumādā I 913/September 1507:

> All the great men came thronging in to pay their compliments to Tongobardin; among the rest the Calif, that is, their pope, with a very white, and as 'twere horned crown on his head, and a long black beard, came with a numerous train, and in great pomp to welcome Tongobardin, who received him very honourably.[7]

Baumgarten comments on the caliph's horned-headgear three days later when he again observed al-Mustamsik as part of a ceremonial procession at the sultan's palace. He describes the sultan al-Ghawrī as wearing a pointed diadem on his head with pure white robes, while 'next to him, but to a degree lower, sat the caliph of the same visage and complexion, and distinguished by his diadem'.[8] Baumgarten's description of the caliph in pointed-head gear resembling the sultan's appears unique and may indicate an alternative form of ceremonial garb to the Baghdādī-turban style donned by the Cairene Abbasids on other occasions.[9]

The Deposition of al-Mustamsik

For the duration of his caliphate, al-Mustamsik dutifully served as a pious officiator of Qāniṣawh al-Ghawrī's ceremonies and remained aloof from politics. Although his possible illiteracy and poor vision distanced him from the

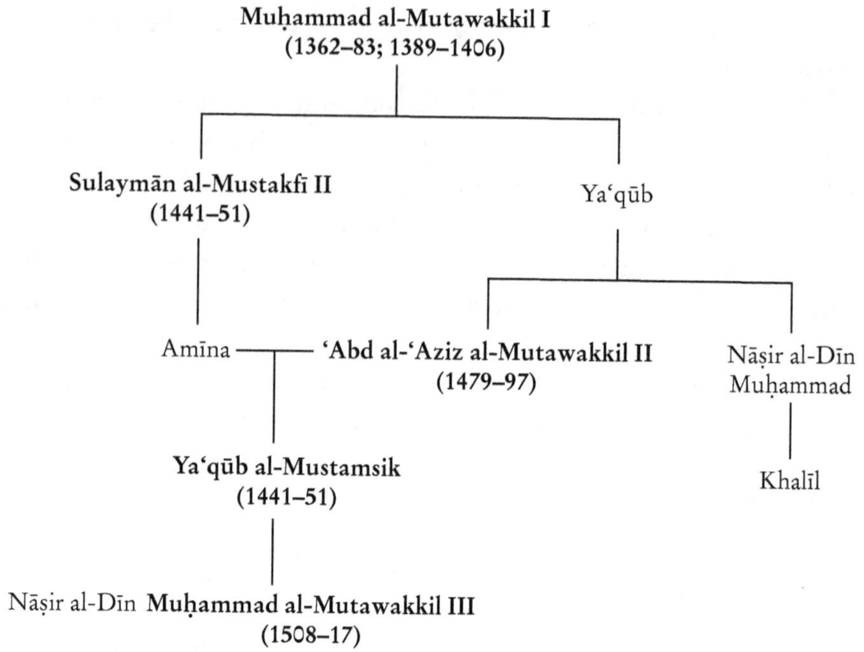

Table 5.1 Disputed succession to al-Mustamsik, 1508.

academic legacy of his father, the issue provided fodder for continued attacks by his cousin Khalīl who had grown no less covetous of the family office in the years since his cousin's caliphal inauguration.

In Sha'bān 914/November 1508 Khalīl vigorously renewed his efforts to contest the suitability of al-Mustamsik to hold the caliphate, which ended in an embarrassing altercation in the sultan's court during the caliph's monthly greetings to Qāniṣawh al-Ghawrī. Khalīl, long aware of al-Mustamsik's failing eyesight, again challenged his cousin publicly and pulled no punches the second time: 'Your caliphate is invalid due to your blindness.' The forty-four-year-old son of al-Mustamsik, Nāṣir al-Dīn Muḥammad, rushed to his father's defence by deflecting attention to a speech impediment that prevented Khalīl from properly pronouncing the Arabic letter *rā'*, thereby invalidating his prayer due to his inability to correctly recite the opening chapter of the Qur'ān (*al-fātiḥa*) integral to Muslim prayer. No doubt amused, Qāniṣawh al-Ghawrī demanded a public demonstration of Khalīl's performance before the qadis, and after several moments of awkward stammering, Khalīl proved unable to reach the final verse. The historian Ibn Iyās described the ordeal as deeply agonising for all who observed.

Qāniṣawh al-Ghawrī declared a recess and announced that the qadis would adjourn for several days to resolve the question of the caliphate. Authorities added the name of Muḥammad, son of al-Mustamsik, to the running and many presumed that the elderly caliph would step aside no matter the outcome. This was because Qāniṣawh al-Ghawrī accepted the criticisms of Khalīl, particularly when the jilted cousin was heard to remark to the caliph, 'Your eyesight is failing . . . and your authority over the Muslims no longer has legal basis.' The sultan also had a vested financial interest in seeing al-Mustamsik deposed: to prevent future difficulties, it was, according to Ibn Iyās, the prerogative of the sultan to banish a deposed caliph, in the case of al-Mustamsik perhaps to Damietta or Jerusalem. If the former caliph wished to remain near his family, property and the streams of revenue he had accumulated in Cairo, Qāniṣawh al-Ghawrī would have occasion to extract money in exchange for granting al-Mustamsik permission to reside in the city.[10]

Proceedings resumed on 4 Shaʿbān 914/28 November 1508. The humiliating exposure of Khalīl's speech impediment had damaged his candidacy, though not nearly as much as new documents al-Mustamsik had prepared in the interim, the first of which named his son Muḥammad as his formal heir and *walī al-ʿahd* to the caliphate. The caliph presented the document to the chief Shāfiʿī qadi Kamāl al-Dīn al-Ṭawīl along with an earlier document attributed to the caliph's father al-Mutawakkil II, which designated al-Mustamsik as his successor followed by 'Nāṣir al-Dīn Muḥammad' (no copy of which has survived).

On the surface, the dispute concerns the identity of the latter 'Nāṣir al-Dīn Muḥammad'. Both Khalīl's father as well as al-Mustamsik's son shared the name. Schimmel argued that it clearly referenced Muḥammad ibn al-Mustamsik, while Ṭarkhān later suggested that the purpose of the second council was to ratify a formal break with the earlier document naming al-Mustamsik's brother Muḥammad ibn al-Mutawakkil II as the second successor in line.[11] Khalīl pressed his claim based on the idea that he had inherited his father's birth right. Al-Mustamsik, on the other hand, presented the document to strengthen his delegation of the caliphate to his son Nāṣir al-Dīn Muḥammad. Whether or not the document was authentic, if Muḥammad ibn al-Mustamsik was in his forties at the time of the dispute, he may have been legally named as the second heir to the caliphate by his grandfather al-Mutawakkil II. The document that named Yaʿqūb successor also proposed that the caliphate go to his son Muḥammad (the future al-Mutawakkil III) instead of Khalīl which the latter unsuccessfully contested, fully expecting that he would succeed his uncle ʿAbd al-ʿAzīz in place of his late father. Ibn Iyās provides the details of Khalīl's outburst upon receiving news of the unfavourable ruling:

> [Khalīl] felt despair and the world closing in on him, for he was awaiting the caliphate after his uncle ʿAbd al-ʿAzīz, and had received no consideration. Seeing power slipping away from him, he lashed out with profanity, urged on by a fire in his heart against Sharaf al-Dīn [Yaʿqūb al-Mustamsik]; but little good came of it. No qadi listened to his charges, and the sultan cared even less.[12]

After the qadis ruled on the validity of the documents, al-Mustamsik came forward, formally abdicated the caliphate, and requested that Qāniṣawh al-Ghawrī recognise his son. The sultan thus oversaw the unprecedented Cairene succession of an Abbasid son during the lifetime of his father while sharing the same residence.

The amirs accepted the decision and members of the elite confirmed Muḥammad ibn Yaʿqūb as caliph after an eloquent speech. The qadis bore witness to the events and al-Mustamsik was retired to his own dwelling in style, surrounded by decorations and robed in one of the sultan's own white linen tunics with sable lining. Khalīl, on the other hand, having been denied the caliphate despite an extensive campaign of bribes, received only a tunic of his own as consolation.[13] Muḥammad received the caliphal insignia and became the third Cairene Abbasid to reign as al-Mutawakkil ʿalā Allāh. Donning his emblems of office, he sat on a throne opposite the sultan, and before the meeting ended he re-affirmed the caliphal authority that al-Mustamsik had granted eight years earlier.

Those on hand praised Qāniṣawh al-Ghawrī for maintaining the caliphate in the same line of the Abbasid family. Khalīl, whose various kickbacks were not returned, left the Citadel bitterly disappointed and embarked upon a self-imposed exile to lick his wounds in the holy cities of the Hijaz.[14] Al-Mutawakkil III left the Citadel accompanied by the qadis and notables in a solemn street procession to his residence which was lavishly decorated with flags and candles. As for al-Mustamsik, just as Qāniṣawh al-Ghawrī had eagerly expected, the elderly caliph agreed to pay the 12,000 dinar ransom to remain in Cairo.

Later Years in Cairo, 914–27/1508–21

Returning to the life of a quasi-elite civilian, Yaʿqūb al-Mustamsik was a man in his seventies at the start of his son's caliphate. In the months immediately following his abdication, the former caliph was confined to his residence. By 917/1512, however, after having contributed to the coffers of Qāniṣawh al-Ghawrī, he enjoyed the freedom to ride without restraint from his residence to attend Friday prayers and to visit the graves of the Qarāfa cemetery. He was also assigned a personal assistant (*bardadār*) named Ḥājj ʿAlī.[15]

Al-Mustamsik faded into the background as his son assumed the monthly visits to the sultan and other ceremonial duties. Ironically, Qāniṣawh al-Ghawrī's thoughts returned to the former caliph some years later in 919/1513 after suffering a disease that damaged his own eyesight. The sultan may have reflected empathetically on his own lack of sympathy and sent the amir and *nāʾib* of the Citadel, Ṭuqṭubāy, to present the retired caliph with a gift of 500 dinars. Ṭuqṭubāy delivered a special message soliciting the prayers of the ex-caliph and apologising for the sultan's past conduct. Qāniṣawh al-Ghawrī pleaded with the caliph not to hold him in ill-regard. Al-Mustamsik sent a reply indicating that he had no reason to bear a grudge for his deposition and that he recalled the sultan with affection.[16]

Meanwhile, the caliph's cousin Khalīl had grown increasingly ill during his sojourn in Mecca, and, sporting a long white beard, returned finally to Cairo as part of a caravan in early 920/1514. Khalīl died not long after in his seventies and despite the upheaval he had inflicted on his family, received a lavish funeral and interment in the Abbasid mausoleum. Ibn Iyās dismissed Khalīl as frivolous and rash, and wrote that he had left a bad taste in the mouth of the people by embarrassing al-Mustamsik and waging an ugly campaign for the caliphate, which, by comparison, had made the caliph and his son appear virtuous for patiently weathering the abuse.[17]

By Ramaḍān 922/September–October 1516, Qāniṣawh al-Ghawrī, engulfed in the frenzy that accompanied preparations to do battle with the Ottomans, subjected many to confiscations with the goal of financing the campaign. This, in spite of earlier repentant overtures, extended to al-Mustamsik bi-llāh from whom he confiscated a substantial amount of property. The sultan claimed that the former caliph was in his debt and provided him with an itemised invoice. As had been the case with Qāyitbāy, Egyptian sources interpreted confiscations from the Abbasid caliph as one of the sultan's many grave abuses of power.[18] As will be discussed below, unforeseen circumstances forced al-Mustamsik to reprise his role as caliph and re-enter politics in 922–3/1516–17 after the defeat of the Cairo Sultanate by the Ottomans.

Like his mother Amīna, al-Mustamsik was completely blind by the end of his nearly eighty years. He died on 19 Rabīʿ II 927/29 March 1521 and was subsequently eulogised by Cairene poets and literati. Qadis and military officers attended his funeral and observed the caliph's burial the next day in proximity to his Hāshimī parents near the shrine of Sayyida Nafīsa. One eulogy described the caliph as 'simultaneously majestic and humble, a man of deep piety, who since his teens until [his accession to the caliphate] never behaved in a blameworthy or childish manner'.[19]

Cairo's Last Abbasid: Al-Mutawakkil III, 914–22/1508–17

Ibn Iyās lauded the abdication of al-Mustamsik in favour of his son al-Mutawakkil III as the most noteworthy event of the year 914/1508–9.[20] Nevertheless, the early years of al-Mutawakkil's caliphate proved somewhat uneventful. The new caliph made his debut at a monthly meeting with Qāniṣawh al-Ghawrī in Ramaḍān 914/December 1508, crowned with Abbasid headgear wrapped in the 'Baghdad style' with its two characteristic flaps of train (*rafraf*) dangling from the turban. The caliph's presence remained ceremonial and al-Mutawakkil tended to avoid the sultan and qadis' monthly theological and ethical discussions.[21] Nevertheless, al-Mutawakkil, like many of his predecessors, received some formal Islamic training, having memorised the Qurʾān and studied with scholars including Fakhr al-Dīn al-Ṭanbāwī and Jamāl al-Dīn al-Armawī.[22]

A decade after the Portuguese arrived in India and threatened the

Cairo–Venetian Mediterranean monopoly on the spice trade, Qānişawh al-Ghawrī called on the Muslim rulers of Calicut and Gujarat to block the Portuguese from their markets. After customs revenues fell in Cairo and enemy corsairs entered the Red Sea, the sultan sent a fleet of mostly Turkmen mercenaries to surprise the Portuguese near Cochin. The Portuguese counterattacked Gujarat at the 914/1509 Battle of Diu and subsequently acquired control over the Indian Ocean. Wishing to keep ties with Cairo strong after the conflict in the hope of ousting them, Indian ambassadors sent by the ruler Muẓaffar Shāh reached Cairo in 916/1510 bringing gifts and a formal request for investiture by al-Mutawakkil III. Qānişawh al-Ghawrī expressed his support and returned the ambassadors with a caliphal robe.[23]

Some years later in 918/1513, while inspecting dyke and canal maintenance outside Cairo, Qānişawh al-Ghawrī visited the Abbasid estate established at Dahshūr.[24] The sultan had spent time near the pyramids of Giza, hunting and inspecting fortifications in Fayyūm. Before embarking on the return journey, Qānişawh al-Ghawrī made a final stop to pay respects to the Commander of the Faithful. The sultan honoured his host by presenting al-Mutawakkil III with a wool tunic (*silārī*) lined with sable fur worth nearly 300 dinars. Together, sultan and caliph reviewed the ceremonial cavalry units adorned with saddles of gold and bridles with embedded crystal. The caliph presented al-Ghawrī with racing camels, sheep, cattle, numerous geese and chickens, as well as containers of honey, wax and milk. The sultan's officers also received robes lined with ermine, sable and Russian squirrel to commemorate the occasion.[25] This was a public demonstration of the sultan's patronage of the Abbasid family in a mutual exchange of honour and ceremonial submission to publicise the alliance between the caliph and the sultan.[26]

To welcome the sultan back to Cairo after one of his many excursions in Shaʿbān 919/October 1513, members of the political elite lavishly decorated the city. Amid the festivities al-Mutawakkil III decorated the door of the Nafīsī shrine and the qadis decorated their own doors.[27]

By the end of the next year, the sultan and his advisers could no longer postpone an impending diplomatic collision with the Ottomans. In late 920/1514, the sultan had been preoccupied with tactical preparations during his monthly congratulatory session with the caliph and qadis, and briskly dismissed them to resume his plans. Fond of leaving Cairo and its politics at difficult moments for short getaways to Fayyūm or Alexandria, Qāniṣawh al-Ghawrī, upon returning from the latter, arranged to camp at Raydāniyya. Perhaps hoping to curry sultanic favour in their proactive enthusiasm, the caliph and qadis arrived at the sultan's camp and found him preparing to parade through Cairo. Although they had not been expected the five men joined in: al-Mutawakkil III rode to the right of the sultan in his customary black Baghdadī turban and a robe spun of white and green wool, while the qadis stayed in the rear.[28]

By 921/1515, the long brewing threat of Ottoman invasion became an imminent reality. Early the next year, al-Ghawrī busied himself with examining weapons inventories and other preparations to meet the forces of the Ottoman Sultan Selīm the Grim (918–26/1512–20).

At the monthly congratulatory session for Ṣafar 922/March 1516, Qāniṣawh al-Ghawrī ordered al-Mutawakkil III and the qadis to prepare themselves to travel on campaign against the Ottomans, for which the sultan expected them to pay their own way. According to Ibn Iyās, no sultan, since the time of Barsbāy's expedition to subdue Āmid in 836/1433, had brought the caliph and qadis on campaign beyond Syria without providing their expenses. Qāniṣawh al-Ghawrī, perhaps oblivious to or uninterested in the tradition, made no such provisions much to the dismay of his chief religious functionaries.[29]

Qāniṣawh al-Ghawrī, accused in his own time of greed and financial malfeasance by Ibn Iyās, suffered bad publicity when former officials fled to the Ottoman sultan to complain of his questionable practices in Cairo. The sultan had to answer for the charge that he had corrupted the judiciary by prohibiting qadis from collecting funds from their deputies to subsidise their travel expenses. In an apparent attempt at damage control, al-Ghawrī cancelled arbitrary monthly and weekly taxes despite the blow to his coffers.[30]

Although burdened by travel expenses, al-Mutawakkil III quickly prepared for the expedition. When word spread that the caliph had been forced to pay his own way, members of the sultan's court reminded him of the customary responsibility to arrange the transport of caliphal baggage on campaign. On 5 Rabīʿ I 922/8 April 1516, the sultan sent his deputy *kātib al-sirr*, the qadi Shihāb al-Dīn al-Jīʿān, to inspect the caliph's luggage. Al-Mutawakkil prepared an estimate that set his overall expenses between

5,000 and 10,000 dinars. Weeks later, the caliph, in the hope of receiving financial assistance from the sultan, attended a gathering in which Qāniṣawh al-Ghawrī dispersed funds to amirs of various rank. When no assistance came from the sultan, however, al-Mutawakkil III set about the humiliating task of seeking loans from high-level amirs who often expected usurious rates of interest upon return, which the caliph was ultimately unable to pay back.[31]

The issue remained unresolved when tragedy struck the sultan with the death of his consort, the Circassian slave Jān Sukkar. Al-Mutawakkil and the qadis ascended the Citadel with other officials to pay respects. The caliph was also approached to preside over the religious service, oversee funerary prayers at the Sitāra Gate, and lead the procession convoy from the Citadel to the sultan's college.[32] On 28 Rabīʿ I 922/1 May 1516, Qāniṣawh al-Ghawrī held a grand evening reception at his *madrasa* complex attended by the caliph and important notables to mourn the one-week anniversary of Jān Sukkar's death. Perhaps softened by the passing of a wife, the sultan relented and on 6 Rabīʿ II 922/9 May 1516 sent al-Mutawakkil another 1,000 dinars to defray some of his travel costs. Some days later, Qāniṣawh al-Ghawrī sent the caliph an assortment of new tents and a gold-inlaid sword.[33]

Cairene authorities sent forth the caliphal luggage with great pomp, accompanied by an honour guard and a band of drums and horns as Cairo celebrated the crossing of the battalion on its way to camp at Raydāniyya. Visiting notables participated in the procession along with key members of the sultan's entourage, followed by the religious officials and finally the Abbasid caliph in a black tunic of Baʿlabakkī cloth with a silk band. According to Ibn Iyās, although he wore the distinctive Baghdadī turban, al-Mutawakkil III and al-Ghawrī's elite omitted some of the pageantry associated with Abbasid Baghdad that some of the fifteenth-century caliphs had again popularised, most notably the conspicuous absence of a special caliphal standard displayed above the caliph as he set out with the sultan.[34]

To manage affairs in Cairo during his absence, Qāniṣawh al-Ghawrī deputised his nephew Ṭūmānbāy to rule as caretaker regent. After almost two weeks of travel, the sultan permitted al-Mutawakkil III and the qadis to ride ahead towards Gaza. Rejoining them the next week, the sultan and his chief religious officials enjoyed a sumptuous feast prepared by the governor of Gaza before the sultan, led by caliph and qadis, paraded through the city.[35]

Earlier that month, the Ottoman sultan Selīm had sent a confusing message to al-Ghawrī, referring to him as 'father' and revealing his intention to kill the Safavid Shāh Ismāʿīl (r. 907–30/1501–24) based on a fatwa composed by Ottoman religious authorities. Having already dealt the Safavids a crushing defeat at the Battle of Chāldirān in 920/1514, Selīm urged the Cairo Sultanate to remain neutral.[36] Suspicious of Ottoman intentions in the region, al-Ghawrī continued to advance his defensive expedition.

As the sultan's forces and entourage travelled northeast from Gaza, they paused briefly outside Damascus. It was at this point that the Damascene historian Ibn Ṭūlūn claims to have spent time reciting ḥadīth collections to al-Mutawakkil III in the latter's tent in Barza on 20 Jumādā I 922/21 June 1516.[37] After passing Damascus, the sultan reached Aleppo on 10 Jumādā II/11 July, the caliph and qadis having preceded his entrance. After a celebratory welcome to the city, Qāniṣawh al-Ghawrī received emissaries from Selīm, including the qadi of the Ottoman army and a high-ranking officer.[38] These ambassadors claimed that the Ottoman sultan was at Caesarea preparing to confront the Safavids, and presented al-Ghawrī and the caliph with lavish Ottoman gifts. The sultan received, among other things, forty *mamlūk*s in sable jackets, velvet cloth, wool and Baʿlabakkī fabric, while the caliph collected two sable jackets, a velvet costume with gold-stitched hems and two suits of fine wool. The qadi of the Ottoman army also gave the caliph two serge suits, a prayer carpet and a mule. Al-Ghawrī likewise sent Selīm gifts, and plans for peace seemed to be in the offing. However, the Ottoman sultan was convinced of Cairo's collusion with the Safavids and, although al-Ghawrī sent an emissary to Selīm's camp reassuring him of his neutrality, the messenger was badly abused and returned with Selīm's abrupt message: 'Meet me at Marj Dābiq!'[39]

By Rajab 922/August 1516, the bulk of Qāniṣawh al-Ghawrī's forces had arrived in Aleppo. Before their battle with the Ottomans, both sides demonstrated a keenness to cast their respective causes as a struggle for the faith and used banners decorated with religious slogans. Selīm secured fatwas from his *ʿulamāʾ* denouncing al-Ghawrī as a Safavid proxy who could legally be attacked as the ally of an infidel, while the sultan of Cairo, who had sworn many of his amirs to fidelity over the Qurʾān of ʿUthmān, engaged in special prayers led by al-Mutawakkil III in the sultan's tent in the centre of the Hippodrome of Aleppo (*al-maydān*) in the hope that the caliph's favour might secure divine victory for the Egyptian army. Before the battle in Aleppo, al-Ghawrī gathered all his religious personnel and spiritual guides. Among other demonstrations of his piety and munificence, the sultan paid the caliph 400 dinars and gave him 100 sheep. As he rode into battle, al-Ghawrī positioned the caliph at his right, with a flag above his head along with forty *sharīfs* with Qurʾāns (including the ʿUthmānī Qurʾān) encased in yellow silk.[40]

As Selīm led the Ottoman advance, Qāniṣawh al-Ghawrī ordered his own army to deploy at Ḥaylān, outside Aleppo, to meet the Ottomans on 17 Rajab/16 August. Al-Mutawakkil III wrote news of the impending battle to his father in a letter that also discussed dire economic conditions such as the rising prices for foodstuff and animal fodder in Aleppo.[41] Prior to his departure, the sultan sought to make a final showing of his dedication to Islam before engaging the enemy. He left Aleppo joined by prominent *ʿulamāʾ* and Sufi *shaykhs* who had been ordered to display the insignias of their *ṭarīqas* on parade alongside the banners of the Abbasid Caliphate.[42]

The Battle of Marj Dābiq

Both sides faced off near the tomb of King David, north of Aleppo on the plains of Marj Dābiq. Beginning early on 25 Rajab 922/24 August 1516, the battle proved to be a swift, decisive Ottoman victory due, in large part, to their military superiority and mastery of firearm technology. The Ottomans were also aided by the last-minute defection of key units of al-Ghawrī's forces, notably those of Khāyrbak, the *nāʾib* of Aleppo, at a critical moment.[43] The sultan of Cairo collapsed in battle and his body was never recovered. Al-Mutawakkil III and the qadis were quickly collected among Selīm's high-profile prisoners.[44]

While the majority of the defeated survivors fled to Damascus, the Abbasid caliph, cognizant of his own symbolic capital, lingered in the nearby village of Ḥaylān, perhaps, in part, to curry an advantageous reception from the victor as he entered Aleppo.[45] Despite a report that the caliph, filthy from travelling through dusty battlefields, entered the sultan's presence (with three of the four chief qadis) in a shabby state (*hum fī ḥāl riththa*), the Ottoman sultan still rose to greet al-Mutawakkil when he entered Selīm's chamber.[46] Hoping to portray himself as a servant of the caliphate, Selīm bade the caliph sit, and pledged to restore all customary rights to the office. Selīm inquired about al-Mutawakkil's place of origin, promising to return the caliph to his ancestral seat of Baghdad, a place in which no Cairo-born Abbasid had ever set foot. As a life-long resident of Cairo with no ties to Baghdad, al-Mutawakkil III could hardly have been enthusiastic about 'returning' to a city, which, in the early sixteenth century, was an unimportant backwater in the hands of competing Turkmen tribal groupings.

When al-Mutawakkil expressed his desire to leave, the Ottoman sultan robed him in a silk, Turkish-style caftan tunic (*dolama*), presented him with an immense cash gift, and authorised the caliph's return to Aleppo under Ottoman escort both to monitor and frustrate any possibility of escape.[47] Shortly after his reception with the caliph and qadis in Ḥaylān, Selīm set up camp in the hippodrome of Aleppo and seized the treasury, weapons and provisions abandoned in the Citadel by the fleeing forces of al-Ghawrī.[48] Modern scholars debate whether al-Mutawakkil and the qadis offered *bayʿa* to Selīm as the new sultan of the Syrian territories of the Cairo Sultanate. Faruk Sümer argues that an administrative log book (*rûznâme*) of the Ottoman bureaucrat Ḥaydar Çelebi written after Marj Dābiq makes no such claim and that Selīm would not have bothered to ask Egyptian *ʿulamāʾ* if he needed the caliph's permission (*icâzet* or *ijāza*) to take the sultanate. Benjamin Lellouch, on the other hand, suggests that religious officials, including the caliph, offered *bayʿa* to the Ottoman sultan.[49]

When al-Ghawrī failed to return from the battlefield and authorities could recover no body, mosque orators throughout Egypt and Syria were left with the delicate but weighted question of *who* to pray for in the Friday *khuṭba*. Some preachers refrained from naming any sultan and instead only mentioned al-Mutawakkil, while others prayed for God's deliverance.[50] In the great mosque of Aleppo, however, the congregation prayed for Selīm 'the just *imām*' (*al-imām al-ʿādil*) and 'sultan of the two noble sanctuaries [of Mecca and Medina]' (*sulṭān al-ḥaramayn al-sharīfayn*), an Ayyubid-era title that had survived into the sixteenth century.[51]

Al-Mustamsik Returns to Office

The remaining amirs in Cairo coaxed Ṭūmānbāy, the *nāʾib* of Egypt, to assume the sultanate and continue the resistance. Traditional Cairene ceremonial demanded an Abbasid to preside over sultanic investiture, and with al-Mutawakkil and the qadis detained in Ottoman custody a stand-in was required. There was initial speculation that one of the sons of Khalīl would serve due to al-Mustamsik's formal abdication in 914/1508, but in Ramaḍān 922/October 1516 the amirs brought the former caliph out of retirement. Al-Mustamsik approached the Gate of the Chain with family members including his grandson Hārūn and some of the sons of his rival Khalīl. After formalities, the court accepted a document al-Mustamsik had produced granting him legal ability to represent his son.[52] Since al-Mustamsik had already been ceremoniously removed from office, there may have been less fear that he would be unwilling to surrender the office in the event that al-Mutawakkil returned.

The council of surviving amirs and *ʿulamāʾ* in Cairo ratified al-Mustamsik's *bayʿa* and delegation of sultanic powers to Ṭūmānbāy as a deputy (*niyāba*) acting on behalf of al-Mutawakkil III. The deputy qadis, themselves filling in for the chief qadis in Selīm's custody, prepared an investiture deed testifying to Ṭūmānbāy's delegation by the presiding Abbasid caliph.

Few resources remained in Cairo to perform a lavish ceremony or parade. Thus, Ṭūmānbāy rode out in black garb after his investiture, on a parade horse without a gilded saddle or parasol. Preceded by al-Mustamsik, the sultan ascended the Ḥarrāqa Pavilion and entered the grand palace to sit upon the throne. The amirs paid homage and news of the succession spread through Cairo. After the ceremony, grandees robed al-Mustamsik and solemnly returned him to the Abbasid residence. Later that month, he attended the ceremonial reading of Ṭūmānbāy's investiture deed, along with the deputy qadis and amirs commanding 1,000. As a commemorative gift, al-Mustamsik received some partial *iqṭāʿ*s including more land adjoining Dahshūr.[53]

A two-month period of sustained diplomatic correspondence ensued between Selīm, now garrisoned in Damascus, and the fledgling government of Ṭūmānbāy, as the Ottoman sultan planned his next move and wrestled with the prospect of invading Cairo or returning to Istanbul. In a letter sent to the Citadel of Cairo in 922/1516, Selīm forwarded a mixture of claims and threats to Ṭūmānbāy's entourage:

> God revealed to me that I would possess the universe, I would be the master of all the regions of the earth, east to west, as they were once possessions of

> Alexander Dhū al-Qarnayn . . . You [i.e., Ṭūmānbāy] are a slave to be sold and bought, power does not suit you, whilst I am a king – the son of a king for twenty generations. **I hold power by *ʿahd* from the caliph and the qadis of the religious law.** These territories are mine thanks to my sword and by the death of al-Ghawrī. For this reason it is to me that you send the tax (*kharāj*) that was previously sent to the caliphs of Baghdad. I am the caliph of God on earth and my rank is above yours in the service of the two Sacred Cities (*ḥaramayn al-sharīfayn*). If you wish to preserve your power which cannot resist us, strike your coins in our name, pronounce the *khuṭba* on our behalf and govern the territory from Gaza to Egypt as our governor (*wālī*). If you disobey me, I will come to Egypt and I will not spare the life of your companions or your soldiers.[54]

If the text of this letter is authentic, it presents a rare opportunity to examine Selīm's perception of the Abbasid Caliphate of Cairo. A key un-vowelled Arabic phrase (translation in bold above) has afforded scholars some room to interpret the words attributed to the Ottoman sultan: *tawallay**tu** al-mulk bi-ʿahd min al-khalīfa wa-min quḍāt al-sharʿ*. Among the translators of this letter, Barthold, Schimmel and Gaston Wiet understood Selīm to be claiming investiture by the Abbasid caliph and qadis in accordance with existing Cairene ceremonial norms.[55] Sümer, however, read the Arabic instead as *tawallay**ta** al-mulk bi-ʿahd min al-khalīfa*, and stated that the Ottoman sultan, far from lowering himself to any such appeal to local traditions, was merely *criticising* Ṭūmānbāy for being obliged to seek authority from the caliph.[56] Given Selīm's apparent interest in local political precedents during his early time as an occupier of their territory, it should not seem odd that he would have initially projected himself as a symbolic deputy of the Abbasid caliph akin to any incoming sultan of Cairo.[57]

Preparing to make his last stand against the Ottomans, Ṭūmānbāy, reportedly distressed by the letter, began negotiating with Selīm from his base at al-Bahnasā in Middle Egypt, seeking the intercession of al-Mutawakkil and proclaiming his interest in ruling as an Ottoman vassal. In need of impartial representatives, the parties tapped al-Mutawakkil III and the qadis to mediate between them. Like his recent predecessors, the caliph had no real negotiating power and was merely a messenger relaying official positions. Initially unopposed to the idea of recognising Ṭūmānbāy as governor, Selīm seemed anxious to make peace and dispatched the caliph and qadis to negotiate a settlement. The Ottoman sultan used the caliph and qadis to deliver an affirmative response to the former sultan. Both sides were interested in a Cairo-based government with Ṭūmānbāy at the helm, as long as he paid proper respect to the Ottoman sultan on his coinage and in the weekly *khuṭba*. Growing weary of ongoing dialogues, al-Mutawakkil sent his *dawādār* secretary Bardbak (or Birdī Beg) with the qadis in his place to relay messages. It all came to naught, however, when hawkish Cairene amirs sabotaged Ṭūmānbāy's overtures for peace and forced Selīm's ambassadors to flee. Angered by the insult, Selīm promptly executed a number of high-ranking enemy officers in his captivity and prepared to overpower Egypt.[58]

After an hour of battle, the Ottomans overwhelmed the surviving fighters at Raydāniyya in early 923/1517. Ṭūmānbāy attempted a short-lived guerrilla resistance, but a final showdown with the Ottomans at Giza secured Ottoman control over Egyptian territory, although Ṭūmānbāy and his loyal veterans remained at large for several months. The day after the battle at Raydāniyya, mosque orators in Cairo, making no mention of the Abbasid caliph, proclaimed: 'Oh God, grant victory to the sultan, son of the sultan, the king of the two continents and the two seas, the destroyer of the two armies, the sultan of the two 'Irāqs, the servant of the two holy sanctuaries, the victorious king, sultan Selīm Shāh.'[59]

Abbasid Caliph of Ottoman Cairo

Some days before the Battle of Raydāniyya, al-Mutawakkil III had entered Cairo with Selīm and his officers and grandees. According to Ibn Iyās, who initially regarded the caliph favourably, al-Mutawakkil used the goodwill he had established with the Ottoman sultan to curb plundering of the city as well as to spare members of the defeated elite from summary execution. As ambassador to the Ottomans and as 'the last political representative of independent Egypt',[60] the Abbasid caliph may have managed to increase his value as an intermediary between the previous political order and the new Ottoman one. Heralds ushered the caliph through the city with torches, charged with preparing Cairo for Selīm's entry and to declare a general amnesty.[61] The caliph's words emphasised general security, the notion that trade should resume unhindered, and that the sultan's troops must not molest the population. Nevertheless, Ottoman troops ignored the caliph's calls for restraint and ravaged Cairo for three days, often ransacking houses under the pretext of hunting fugitive enemy officers. On 3 Muḥarram 923/26 January 1517, al-Mutawakkil III and the qadis solemnly led Selīm through the streets of Cairo.[62]

Selim's attempts at enforcing Ottoman policies in Syria and Egypt caused chaos and brought the judicial administration to a halt. After having dismissed the deputy qadis in Cairo, Selim ultimately summoned the four chief qadis of Egypt who he had seized after Marj Dābiq and returned them to their positions in Rabīʿ I 923/March 1517.[63] Selīm, needing to capitalise on the reputation of the caliph in the chaotic climate, indulged al-Mutawakkil III as an administrator as no Cairo sultan had ever done. Ibn Iyās, perhaps in exaggeration, claimed that the caliph enjoyed 'unlimited power' at this time and described him as chief disposer of affairs (*al-ṣāḥib al-ḥāl wa-l-ʿaqd*) in early Ottoman Cairo. The caliph's city residence became a hub for dispossessed members of the old elite. In a clear reversal of fortune, many notables of the previous regime wandered aimlessly in the caliph's corridors or sat idly in his parlour.[64]

According to Ibn Iyās, parts of Cairo reportedly felt the influence of al-Mutawakkil III for several months as he executed local tasks at his own discretion. The caliph's duties in Cairo primarily involved intercession for members of the population who had become the recipients of unwanted Ottoman attention. As if seeking protection, some Cairene households displayed Abbasid flags on their doors. Petitioners flocked to the caliph's residence in search of intervention with Ottoman administrators and in exchange bestowed lavish gifts the like of which earlier caliphs in Cairo had never seen. Such rapid wealth accumulation piqued Selīm's interest, and he demanded a share for the Ottoman treasury, although al-Mutawakkil III successfully persuaded the sultan to content himself with a small amount. The caliph had collected tribute and received bribes in the form of the many women and slave-girls brought to his abode, 'strewn so numerously about the house that the caliph barely took notice of them. Even princesses who had been married to Ṭūmānbāy sat around his house like slave women.' One such 'princess', the daughter of the prominent *dawādār* Āqbirdī, had taken refuge with the caliph after the Ottomans executed Ṭūmānbāy and left her with a heavy fine. Taking pity on the young woman or perhaps sensing an opportunity, al-Mutawakkil III regularly petitioned Selīm on her behalf until he achieved a substantial reduction. In return for his chivalry, many women of the former sultan's court offered him fancy gifts, resulting in, what seemed to Ibn Iyās, an unseemly atmosphere that clouded the caliph's judgement, contributed to his vainglorious sense of self-importance, and ultimately led to his political unravelling.[65] It is problematic that contemporary Ottoman sources make little mention of al-Mutawakkil III at this important time and modern historians are right to question whether Ibn Iyās greatly exaggerated the caliph's influence during the period and to what end.[66]

Thanks largely to authority invigorated by the Ottoman sultan, the Abbasid caliph served Cairo as an arbitrator able to provide tentative rulings to the populace (which could later be appealed after review by Ottoman authorities). Naturally, the caliph's rulings failed to please every plaintiff. In the days of Qāniṣawh al-Ghawrī, a disgraced deputy qadi convicted of adultery, Nūr al-Dīn al-Mashālī along with his mistress, and al-Zankalūnī, a colleague who had come to their defence, were stoned and hanged on the sultan's orders. The families of both men harboured lasting grievances against the qadi Shams al-Dīn ibn Wuhaysh whom they blamed for wrongfully inciting the sultan against their patriarchs. When the Ottomans took power in Cairo, a proclamation encouraged such injured parties to seek out the justice of the new conquerors. The Ottomans appointed al-Mutawakkil III as arbiter in the case of the two families against Ibn Wuhaysh. The caliph, perhaps sympathetic or wary of alienating the religious establishment, ruled that the qadi should not die but instead pay blood money of 300 dinars to the family of al-Zankalūnī and 200 to the family of al-Mashālī. Both sides, unsatisfied by the caliph's ruling, dismissed it in favour of a direct referral to the Ottoman sultan in Muḥarram 923/January–February 1517.[67]

According to the log book attributed to Ḥaydar Çelebi (preserved by the Ottoman chancery chief Ferīdūn Beğ (d. 991/1583)), rare among contemporary Ottoman sources for its mention of the caliph of Cairo, al-Mutawakkil played a minor role in settling affairs with Ṭūmānbāy who had been confined to Upper Egypt in the weeks after Raydāniyya.[68] Wishing to court another offer from Selīm, Ṭūmānbāy wrote of his interest in accepting the initial offer to govern Egypt.[69] He sent a messenger to Selīm's headquarters on 10 Ṣafar 923/4 March 1517 asking for a trustworthy man to conduct negotiations:

> One of the qadis returned from [initial negotiations with] Ṭūmānbāy and asked for safe passage and a trustworthy man [from the Ottoman side]. On [11 Ṣafar 923/5 March 1517] the pashas gathered in their council (*dīvān*) to arrange for embassies to and from Ṭūmānbāy. Even the caliph and qadis of the four schools went to the sovereign [Selīm] to speak, [after which, the Ottoman sultan] granted them authorizations of safe conduct (*amān*) [to engage in negotiations with Ṭūmānbāy's camp unmolested]. [On 12 Ṣafar/6 March] the Abbasid caliph al-Mutwakkil . . . the last representative of the Abbasid dynasty in Egypt, along with his men and the four qadis, met with Muṣṭafā Çelebi, the former finance minister (*defterdar*) of Anatolia, who had been appointed ambassador,[70] as well as Ṭūmānbāy's appointee qadi Abū al-Salām. After coming together and taking their seats, a royal order (*ḥukm-i sharīf*) was composed and letters were sent on behalf of Khāyrbak and the caliph.[71]

In the days that followed, the delegation of Muṣṭafā Çelebi, including the four qadis and the caliph's secretary Bardbak, set out to meet Ṭūmānbāy and swear him to the conditions of Selīm. The ambassadors were ambushed, however, resulting in the murders of Muṣṭafā Çelebi and the Ḥanafī qadi, though the others escaped. Ṭūmānbāy was eventually captured and executed; the Ottomans hung him from the Zuwayla gate on 21 Rabī' I 923/13 April 1517.[72]

Sürgün to Istanbul

It is difficult to discuss Selīm's long-term intentions for al-Mutawakkil III, but after two months the sultan included the caliph in a forced exile (*sürgün*) of former Egyptian aristocrats to the Ottoman capital after the ex-general Khāyrbak, rewarded for his defection in favour of the Ottomans at Marj Dābiq, took power formally as the new Ottoman governor of Egypt.[73] In Rabī' II 923/May 1517, al-Mutawakkil III, on Selīm's orders, prepared his luggage for Istanbul. The exile of the caliph was part of an extraction that often included artisans, and notables, as well as potential troublemakers. Select Abbasid family members were chosen to accompany al-Mutawakkil including his son-in-law as well as his second cousins Aḥmad and Abū Bakr, the sons of Khalīl.[74] Ibn Iyās claims that Cairenes bitterly resented the removal of the caliph from Egypt under such harsh circumstances and little apparent regard for his person.[75] At this time, the Ottomans also relieved the Abbasid family of stewardship of the shrine of Sayyida Nafīsa. The loss of income presented the caliph's father al-Mustamsik with a great financial burden, dependent as he was on the shrine's collected revenue, and he protested through the appropriate channels without success.[76] No doubt adding to the injury, the Ottomans also removed valuable heirloom swords (including the alleged blade of the last Baghdad caliph al-Mustaʿṣim) from the private treasury of al-Mustamsik.[77] Combined with the caliph's part in the failure to broker a peace with Ṭūmānbāy, the confiscation of family heirlooms and Nafīsī shrine revenues widened the growing cleft between Selīm and the Abbasid Caliphate.[78]

After completing his preparations, the caliph left his residence for Istanbul on 12 Jumādā I 923/2 June 1517. Joined by his kinsmen, he boarded a boat on the bank of Būlāq, a Nile port just beyond the walls of the old city.[79] After a week's confinement, al-Mutawakkil's party followed the river to Rosetta and Alexandria. This allowed Selīm to join the exiles after he completed his affairs in Cairo.[80]

Before his departure from Cairo on 26 Shaʾbān 923/13 September 1517, Selīm ordered that another 800 exiles be shipped to Istanbul.[81] The earlier deportees remained sequestered prisoners in caravansaries and fortified towers in Jumādā I 923/May–June 1517 with the plan that all detainees would leave at the same time with the sultan's permission. Ibn Iyās describes abysmal conditions for the *sürgün* exiles. Things worsened in Alexandria due to a water shortage brought about in part by the influx of Ottoman troops to the city. News reached Cairo in Ramaḍān 924/September 1518 that as many as eighty deportees had died though the Abbasids were not said to be among them.

Selīm returned leisurely to his capital through Syria and southwestern Anatolia, his prisoners having arrived in Istanbul some time before him. Details on prisoner conditions are sparse, though we might wonder whether al-Mutawakkil III and other high-ranking prisoners may have enjoyed some degree of respect as hostages of distinction. Once he learned of Selīm's imminent arrival, al-Mutawakkil rode to greet the sultan with his family members and other important exiles, anxious to learn their fate. The caliph moved to dismount from his horse in the presence of Selīm, but the Ottoman sultan bade him remain saddled and lavished special marks of honour on him. The sultan ignored other Egyptian notables that had come to welcome him. Selīm immediately embarked on procession through Istanbul and sojourned for a week before moving on to inspect the old Ottoman capital at Edirne (Adrianople). The Ottoman sultan was far more worried about the plague and food shortages threatening his army and capital than the lives of has-beens from a vanquished and scattered political order.[82]

The Fabled 'Transfer of the Caliphate' in Istanbul

In later times, a legend developed that al-Mutawakkil III formally transferred his office and all his rights to the Ottoman dynasty. The earliest versions of the story to appear in western sources include the works of Georg Fabricius and Johannes Rosinus, who claimed in the late seventeenth century that Selīm forced al-Mutawkkil III to abdicate, yet did not state that the sultan made any claim to the office for himself. According to Bernard Lewis, the most widely referenced story that al-Mutawakkil III transferred his title to Selīm appeared in 1788 in Mouradgea D'Ohsson's *Tableau général de l'Empire othoman*, which collected popular versions of the story circulating at the end of the eighteenth century. D'Ohsson's work was widely accepted and cited in later historical accounts without further question.[83]

In later years, Halil Inalcik pointed out that Arabic sources of the time frequently identify al-Mutawakkil III as *al-khalīfa* or *amīr al-muʾminīn*, while Selīm is merely *malik al-Rūm*.[84] Legends about the transfer became current when the Ottomans felt the need to respond to Russian aspirations to 'protect' Ottoman Christians with a counter-claim of spiritual authority over Muslims newly integrated into Russia after the conquest of Crimea and the treaty of Küçük Kaynarca in 1188/1774.[85] Such authority was largely based on the myth that the last Abbasid had relinquished caliphal authority to the Ottomans.

Finally, Holt found a minor clue in the annals of the Syrian chronicler Ibn Ṭūlūn, who introduces each year of his *Mufākahat al-khillān* with the names of the reigning caliph and sultan and continues this practice during the early Ottoman period of Egypt and Syria until 926/1519–20, at which point the manuscript ends abruptly. At the start of 924/1518, Ibn Ṭūlūn, having mentioned al-Mutawakkil III as *amīr al-muʾminīn*, adds 'and he has been sent under escort from Egypt to Istanbul by sea'. When the chronicle picks up again in 926/1519–20, he mentions that al-Mutawakkil III is living in Istanbul yet says nothing about a transfer of the caliphate. Thus, according to Holt, 'Ibn Ṭūlūn (and doubtless others) saw no break in al-Mutawakkil's reign when power passed from Ṭūmānbāy to Selīm'.[86]

In early sixteenth-century Istanbul, however, the caliph continued to receive special treatment and was able to access a portion of the gifts and payments he had accumulated in Cairo. Cairenes remained eager for news of their caliph, and on 2 Dhū al-Qaʿda 925/26 October 1519 an Ottoman ambassador arrived with news that there had been a great falling out between al-Mutawakkil III and his second-cousins Abū Bakr and Aḥmad. Hoping to gain the upper hand, the sons of Khalīl had sought Selīm's intervention after accusing the caliph of extortion and having hoarded a fortune in cash, property and luxurious fabrics from the widowed families of fallen Cairene officers, particularly a vulnerable widow of Ṭūmānbāy and her mother.

Selīm listened to the charges and the sultan's ministers publicly voiced support for Abū Bakr and Aḥmad and advised the sultan to distance himself from al-Mutawakkil III. Any faith the Sublime Porte had placed in the Abbasid Caliphate seemed to evaporate. Ibn Iyās added his own inventory of the caliph's misdeeds and corruption, which included gluttony, depravity and excess, not to mention the caliph's penchant for singing slave girls often financed through the misappropriation of *waqf* properties in his care. The primary reason for the family quarrel, however, was al-Mutawakkil's suspension of the allowances of Abū Bakr and Aḥmad. Selīm had earlier determined that the caliphate's endowment would be divided into three equal shares and administered by al-Mutawakkil to his relatives.[87]

Now interested in auditing Abbasid holdings in Cairo, the sultan dispatched an ambassador to subpoena the caliph's staff and carry out an inventory of remaining family properties in the city. The ambassador interviewed the caliph's *dawādār* Bardbak and requested a full accounting of all sums received by Abū Bakr and Aḥmad in the five years since their father's death in 920/1514. Faced with resistance and evasion from the caliph's staff and family in Cairo, the officer hounded them until he obtained the figures for the Ottoman sultan to uphold the rights of the sons of Khalīl.[88] Although the caliph received a temporary lease on his office within the Ottoman capital, his apparent transgression ultimately cast him into confinement in the heavily guarded Ottoman fortress of Yedikule, the 'Castle of the Seven Walls' in Istanbul.[89] Rumours circulated that the sons of Khalīl had petitioned Selīm to confiscate at least one-third of the caliphal allowance which al-Mutawakkil III had withheld. The standing of the caliph likewise suffered from attacks by Ottoman ministers who pledged support to Khalīl's sons.[90]

News of Selīm's death reached Cairo by courier in Dhū al-Qaʿda 926/ October 1520. A letter from al-Mutawakkil III to his father also reported the event. The caliph eventually obtained freedom under that sultan's more magnanimous successor, Süleymān the Magnificent (d. 973/1566), who released the caliph from imprisonment but failed to include him in the initial return of exiles to Cairo. According to the later account of Evliyā Çelebi, the Abbasid caliph was rumoured to have played a ceremonial role in the investiture rituals for Süleymān and was on hand when the latter received decorative swords including the sword of Osman at the Eyüp mosque in Istanbul.[91] Süleymān allowed the caliph to remain in the city for an unspecified amount of time during which he received a daily pension of 60 dirhams.[92] The caliph remained in Istanbul for some time on this meagre stipend before returning to Egypt. Evliyā claims that al-Mutawakkil III stayed in the Ottoman capital until the death of his father al-Mustamsik on 19 Rabīʿ II 927/29 March 1521, after which Süleymān allowed him to return to Cairo where he quietly 'reclaimed' the family office.[93] Michael Winter suggests that Süleymān's release of al-Mutawakkil III was further proof that the myth of the caliphal transfer was a later invention, considering that if the Abbasid caliph were a person of importance and authority, the Ottomans would hardly have allowed him to slip through their fingers.[94]

The chronicle of Ibn Iyās concludes in the lunar year 928/1521–2, after which details on al-Mutawakkil III and his descendants are sparse. After his return to Egypt, the caliph, having never been officially divested of office by Ottoman or local Egyptian authorities, continued using the caliphal title.[95]

After his betrayal at Marj Dābiq, Khāyrbak had governed Egypt as an obedient Ottoman governor until his death in 929/1522. The next year, his replacement, Aḥmad Pasha, attempted to proclaim himself sultan also based

Figure 5.1 Sketch of Yedikule hisarı fortress, Istanbul. Image courtesy of François Charles Hugues Laurent Pouqueville, *Voyage en Morée, à Constantinople, en Albanie, et dans plusieurs autres parties de l'Empire othoman, pendant les années 1798, 1799, 1800 et 1801*, vol. 2. Ghent University Library MS BIB.HIST.005154.

on the old model model of caliphal investiture. On 6 Rabīʿ II 930/12 February 1524 he summoned an Abbasid (perhaps al-Mutawakkil)[96] and the four chief qadis (whom he had reinstated after their dismissal by the Ottomans) and pressured them for an endorsement of his sultanate. 'Al-Malik al-Manṣūr' Aḥmad, as pseudo-sultan acting with a caliphal mandate, briefly attempted to buck Ottoman authority by minting coins and ordering the *khuṭba* to be given in his name, though he was ultimately thwarted by mutineers in his own ranks shortly before the arrival of a force sent by Süleymān to crush the revolt. The Abbasid in question escaped without consequence.

The Meccan historian Quṭb al-Dīn al-Nahrawālī (d. 990/1583) claims to have met al-Mutawakkil in 933/1536–7, and notes that after again 'becoming caliph in Egypt' (*ṣāra khalīfa bihā*), remained there until his death during the reign of the Ottoman governor Dāvud Pasha on 12 Shaʿbān 950/10 November 1543. Quṭb al-Dīn describes al-Mutawakkil III in later life as well-mannered and generous, a cultured man with a propensity and aptitude for verse.[97]

The date of the caliph's death, like that of his return to Cairo, however, remains uncertain. Two alternate death dates for al-Mutawakkil III are 945/1538 and 950/1543. Little is known about the status and numbers of the Abbasid house in Cairo by the mid-sixteenth century, although we know, according to the historian al-Qaramānī, that at least some of the sons of al-Mutawakkil, including Yaḥyā, ʿUmar and ʿUthmān, remained in Istanbul enjoying lucrative careers as Ottoman financial administrators. According to the Ottoman historian Muṣṭafā Cenābī (d. 999/1590), the young men continued to draw pensions from the Ottoman treasury for some time.[98]

Historians writing many years after Marj Dābiq, including Quṭb al-Dīn al-Nahrawālī, al-Qaramānī, Cenābī and Marʿī ibn Yūsuf Karmī (d. 1033/1623–4), believed that after the death of al-Mutawakkil III, the Abbasid Caliphate truly 'became extinct from the world'. Nevertheless, Ottoman era sources demonstrate some awareness of the descendants of al-Mutawakkil at the end of the seventeenth century. Abbasid lineage and descent continued to be viewed with prestige. Yemen welcomed one 'son' of al-Mutawakkil with great ceremony as the '*amīr al-muʾminīn*' and granted him a brief residency. We know that an Abbasid descendant in Yemen was on hand as late as 1112/1701 to welcome emissaries sent by the last Safavid Shāh Ḥusayn (1105–35/1694–1722).[99] The famous historian and first-hand observer of Napoleon's conquest of Egypt, ʿAbd al-Raḥmān al-Jabartī (d. 1240/1825), included the obituary of the last known Abbasid descendant residing in Egypt in 1220/1805–6; a certain ʿUthmān Effendi ibn Saʿd al-ʿAbbāsī [al-Anṣārī], who was a mildly successful Ottoman financial administrator in the eighteenth century, and whose father was a direct descendant of al-Mutawakkil III.

Besides the line of the family that remained in Cairo, living quietly among the populace until it went extinct, little else is known about the Abbasid descendants scattered across history. Some seem to have gone further south as Holt traced Abbasid claimants in Nubia and northern Sudan among the Jaʿaliyyūn, suggesting that local dynasties may have attempted to exploit Abbasid symbolic capital in their local politics. Barthold found that in addition to strains of the Abbasid family that he identified in Yemen, others survived in an unknown capacity elsewhere in the Ottoman Empire.[100]

By the dawn of its second century in Cairo, the Abbasid Caliphate had achieved levels of political prestige, if not actual power, that neither sultans, nor those who coveted the office, could ignore.[101] By virtue of its complicated and at times reactive development, the history of the Abbasid Caliphate in Cairo is difficult both to map and effectively periodise. Nevertheless, the positive narrative produced by medieval Arabic chronicles and biographical literature, further explored in Chapter 7, demonstrates the continuing evolution of what was already a centuries-old Islamic institution and idea for socio-political organisation. Whether it was the nominal delegator of authority for sultans and other appointees, the liaison between various social groupings among the ruling elite, or as the figurehead of popular protest and revolt, the Abbasid caliph retained significance because many in society *perceived* that he did.[102]

Part One of the book has demonstrated that there was no singular version of the caliphate, and that with every new Abbasid office holder and context came a new relationship between the representative(s) of the caliphate and the historical actors engaging with it. The history of the caliphate on the micro-level therefore appears different in every period, even as it was performed and recreated in each new sultanic reign or *dawla*. Although the early sixteenth-century Ottoman conquest of Egypt ended both the sultanate and caliphate of Cairo, the different timelines leading up to that era starting with the investiture of al-Mustanṣir by Baybars, have demonstrated many important differences and transformations.

The preceding chapters of Part One have also sketched a contextual framework of reference by which we can further analyse the role of the office and the office holders in the politics of the Cairo Sultanate. As we have seen from the dynastic history, the classical prerogatives of caliphal officeholders could be omitted at the whim of a sultan or ruling magnate. Nevertheless, the caliphs had certain rarely discussed responsibilities. In detailing the lives and duties of the caliphs as units of study, the details, expectations, evolution and full expanse of the office during the mid-thirteenth to the early sixteenth century can come into clearer focus. The second section of this book will more completely examine the functions of the caliphal office as well as its associated expectations shaped by authors of various genres of medieval Arabic literature, along with the courts and political elites linked to the sultans of Cairo.

Notes

1. Al-Suyūṭī, *Taʾrīkh*, 413; Ibn Iyās, *Badāʾiʿ*, 3:141, 380; al-Qaramānī, *Akhbār*, 2:222; al-Ḥaṣkafī, *Mutʿat al-adhhān*, 1:431. The *kātib al-sirr* al-Ashraf al-Badrī ibn Maẓhar and the *shaykh al-islām* Zakariyyāʾ al-Shāfiʿī advocated in favour of al-Mustamsik's claim with the sultan, arguing that the late caliph's 'son is better than his nephew'.
2. Ibn Iyās, *Badāʾiʿ*, 3:342, 401–5, 438-9, 453–7, 463–4, 4:2–4; Ibn Ṭūlūn, *Mufākahat*, 1:230; 108–11, 117; Garcin, 'Circassian Mamlūks', 297; Petry, *Twilight of Majesty*, 125–32; Holt, *Age of Crusades*, 198.
3. Ibn al-Ḥimṣī, *Ḥawādith*, 1:121–2; Petry, *Twilight of Majesty*, 129.
4. Ibn Iyās, *Badāʾiʿ*, 4:8–9, 14–15, 18. See also Amīn, *Awqāf*, 337; Petry, *Twilight of Majesty*, 146. On oath-swearing as part of the political culture, see Onimus, *Les maîtres du jeu*, 351–3; Van Steenbergen, *Order Out of Chaos*, 24.
5. Banister, 'Naught Remains', 232–4; Chapoutot-Remadi, 'Liens et relations', 48.
6. Ibn Iyās, *Badāʾiʿ*, 4:52–3, 58; Ibn al-Ḥimṣī, *Ḥawādith*, 1:175; Petry, *Twilight of Majesty*, 169.
7. Baumgarten, 'Travels', 396.
8. Ibid., 398.
9. Fuess, 'Sultans with Horns', 75–83.

10. Ibn Iyās, *Badāʾiʿ*, 4:139–41, 323–4.
11. Ṭarkhān, *Miṣr*, 68–70; Schimmel, 'Kalif und Kadi', 18.
12. Ibn Iyās, *Badāʾiʿ*, 3:378.
13. Ibn Iyās, *Badāʾiʿ*, 4:140–1. For details on these squirrel- or sable-lined garments, see Mayer, *Mamluk Costume*, 14.
14. Ibn Iyās, *Badāʾiʿ*, 4:140–1, 360–1. The Hijaz was not unfamiliar to Khalīl, who had previously made the pilgrimage in Shawwāl 897/August 1492, during which he spent considerable time engaged in solitary acts of worship as well as communal practices with the noted Shāfiʿī scholar al-Shihāb al-Qasṭalānī (d. 923/1517), to whom he inaccurately boasted that no other member of the Cairo Abbasid family (save for Yaḥyā ibn al-Mustaʿīn) had undertaken the Islamic pilgrimage rite. See al-Sakhāwī, *Ḍawʾ*, 3:205.
15. Ibn Iyās, *Badāʾiʿ*, 4:252, 5:389–90. For use in fifteenth-century Egypt, Popper translates *bardadār* as a 'bailiff' or 'usher' (*Systematic Notes*, 1:116). By the early sixteenth century, however, the office appears to have had some secretarial functions in addition to aiding the daily life of the elderly caliph in an unknown capacity.
16. Ibn Iyās, *Badāʾiʿ*, 4:323–4.
17. Ibid., 4:360–1. Al-Sakhāwī, who penned a brief biography of Khalīl before the succession debacle, described the Abbasid as a humble and devoted worshipper consumed with good works, see *Ḍawʾ*, 3:205.
18. Ibn Iyās, *Badāʾiʿ*, 5:87, 90–1; Petry, *Twilight of Majesty*, 121.
19. Ibn Iyās, *Badāʾiʿ*, 3:380, 388–9; al-Qaramānī, *Akhbār*, 2:225; Quṭb al-Dīn, *Chroniken*, 3:184.
20. Ibn Iyās, *Badāʾiʿ*, 4:149. The Damascene chronicler Ibn Ṭūlūn still associated al-Mustamsik with the caliphate as late as 917/1511 (annals from 918–20/1512–16 are in some cases missing or incomplete), though he later acknowledged the succession of al-Mutawakkil III in 921 (1515), see Ibn Ṭūlūn, *Mufākahat*, 1:352, 379.
21. Ibn Iyās, *Badāʾiʿ*, 4:143. Ibn Iyās does not mention the caliph in his account of the sultan seeking legal counsel from the qadis on the legality of acquiring funds to pay the army (*Badāʾiʿ*, 4:211–12). Nevertheless, Ibn Iyās often mentions the meetings at the top of each new month. On one occasion the caliph and qadis even braved torrential rain and hail to deliver New Year's greetings to the sultan (*Badāʾiʿ*, 4:295–6).
22. Al-Ḥaṣkafī, *Mutʿat al-adhhān*, 2:756. On the learning practices of the Cairene Abbasids, see Banister, 'ʿ*Ālim*-Caliph'.

23. Al-Mashhadānī, *Al-ʿAlāqāt*, 59; Inalcik and Quataert, *Economic and Social History*, 1:319–21.
24. On Dahshūr as an Abbasid property in Egypt, see al-Sakhāwī, *Wajīz*, 3:998–9.
25. Ibn Iyās, *Badāʾiʿ*, 4:290–93; Petry, *Twilight of Majesty*, 172; Petry, 'Robing Ceremonials', 363. On the sultans' love for furs, see Loiseau, *Les Mamelouks*, 147.
26. See Onimus's remarks on the 'economy of honour' in *Les maîtres du jeu*, 94–7.
27. Ibn Iyās, *Badāʾiʿ*, 4:334; Schimmel, 'Kalif und Kadi', 110–11.
28. Ibn Iyās, *Badāʾiʿ*, 4:413, 417–18; Schimmel, 'Kalif und Kadi', 114; Petry, *Twilight of Majesty*, 191, 194. According to Mayer, in the late period of the sultanate, when deprived of typical 'Abbasid' dress, the caliphs sometimes donned the garb of the military aristocracy. See Mayer, *Mamluk Costume*, 14.
29. Ibn Iyās, *Badāʾiʿ*, 5:30, 33.
30. Petry, *Twilight of Majesty*, 121, 215; Schimimel, 'Kalif und Kadi', 116.
31. Ibn Iyās, *Badāʾiʿ*, 5:23, 30; Schimmel, 'Some Glimpses', 355.
32. Ibn Iyās, *Badāʾiʿ*, 5:27–8. See also ʿAbd ar-Rāziq, *La femme*, 7.
33. Ibn Iyās, *Badāʾiʿ*, 5:30–1, 33.
34. Ibid., 5:37, 40–1; Winter, 'Ottoman Occupation', 496.
35. Ibn Iyās, *Badāʾiʿ*, 5:51; Schimmel, 'Kalif und Kadi', 117.
36. Ibn Iyās, *Badāʾiʿ*, 5:60; Petry, *Twilight of Majesty*, 222–3.
37. Al-Ḥaṣkafī, *Mutʿat al-adhhān*, 2:756.
38. Ibn Ṭūlūn, *Mufākahat*, 2:13–14.
39. Ibn Iyās, *Badāʾiʿ*, 5:60–1; Behrens-Abouseif, *Practising Diplomacy*, 92; Winter, 'Ottoman Occupation', 497; Schimmel, 'Kalif und Kadi', 118.
40. Ibn Iyās, *Badāʾiʿ*, 5:63; Becker, 'Barthold's Studien', 392. Special prayers were also offered for the sultan at the Umayyad mosque, see Ibn al-Ḥimṣī, *Ḥawādith*, 1:285–6.
41. Ibn Iyās, *Badāʾiʿ*, 5:64–5.
42. Ibid., 5:68–9. Other notable members of the Cairo religious landscape were in attendance, such as the servant (*khādim*) of the shrine of Sayyida Nafīsa, masters (*khulafāʾ*) of the shrines of Aḥmad al-Badawī and Aḥmad ibn al-Rifāʿī, and members of the Qadariyya *ṭarīqa*. See also Lellouch, *Ottomans en Égypte*, 1–2; Petry, *Twilight of Majesty*, 224 Sümer, 'Yavuz Selim', 347–8.
43. Finkel, *Osman's Dream*, 108; Irwin, 'Gunpowder Reconsidered'.
44. Ibn al-Ḥimṣī, *Ḥawādith*, 1:286–7. Little is known as to how the caliph and qadis came into Ottoman custody. Arabic sources are largely silent, and

Turkish sources do not even use the word 'caliph' according to Faruk Sümer, see 'Yavuz Selim', 349.

45. Ibn al-Ḥimṣī, *Ḥawādith*, 1:288. Although he had not participated in the fighting, the Abbasid caliph was present at the battlefield to administer *bayʿa* pledges and safeguard the fidelity of the sultan's fighting men, see Lellouch, *Ottomans en Égypte*, 5.
46. Ibn Ṭūlūn, *Mufākahat*, 2:32.
47. Ibn Iyās, *Badāʾiʿ*, 5:74, 77. Ottoman authorities prohibited the caliph and three qadis from leaving Aleppo. See Petry, *Twilight of Majesty*, 229; Sümer, 'Yavuz Selim', 348n.17; Schimmel, 'Kalif und Kadi', 25.
48. Ibn Iyās, *Badāʾiʿ*, 5:74.
49. Lellouch, *Ottomans en Égypte*, 9; Sümer, 'Yavuz Selim', 344.
50. Ibn Iyās, *Badāʾiʿ*, 5:81.
51. On prayers for Selīm in Damascus, see Ibn al-Ḥimṣī, *Ḥawādith*, 1:290–1. Mosque orators prayed for the Ottoman sultan in all the new Arab lands he conquered after Marj Dābiq, see Becker, 'Barthold's Studien', 402–6; Arnold, *Caliphate*, 140, 144–8; Schimmel, 'Kalif und Kadi', 82; Inalcik, *Ottoman Empire*, 33–4; Holt, *Egypt and the Fertile Crescent*, 42; Veinstein, 'Les Serviteur', 229–46; Lellouch, *Ottomans en Égypte*, 9.
52. Ibn Iyās, *Badāʾiʿ*, 5:104. It is noteworthy that two Abbasid caliphs, a father and son, were used to simultaneously legitimise the authority of two hostile rulers. See Schimmel, 'Kalif und Kadi', 120; Becker, 'Barthold's Studien', 397–8.
53. Ibn Iyās, *Badāʾiʿ*, 5:104–5, 110.
54. Ibid., 5:124–5.
55. See Wiet, *Journal*, 2:117; Schimmel, 'Kalif und Kadi', 25–6; Becker, 'Barthold's Studien', 397. In another translation of the passage, W. H. Salmon interprets Selīm's statement as follows: 'I . . . have taken possession of the country by agreement with the Khalīfah and the judges.' See Salmon, *An Account of the Ottoman Conquest of Egypt*, 91.
56. Sümer, 'Yavuz Selim', 349.
57. Indeed, Selīm sought to project his image as legitimate sovereign in acceptable terms to Syro-Egyptian audiences and communities. See Yılmaz, *Caliphate Redefined*, 147.
58. Ibn Iyās, *Badāʾiʿ*, 5:125, 147–58, 169–70; Ferīdūn Beğ, *Münşeʾātü s-selāṭīn*, 1:487; Lellouch, *Ottomans en Égypte*, 17; Holt, *Egypt and the Fertile Crescent*, 39–40; Schimmel, 'Kalif und Kadi', 121–2; Arnold, *Caliphate*, 141.
59. Ibn Iyās, *Badāʾiʿ*, 5:147–8; Finkel, *Osman's Dream*, 110; Sümer, 'Yavuz Selim',

349; Inalcik, 'Appendix: The Ottomans and the Caliphate', 1:321; Schimmel, 'Kalif und Kadi', 26–7; Arnold, *Caliphate*, 140.

60. Lellouch, *Ottomans en Égypte*, 14.
61. Ibn Iyās, *Badāʾiʿ*, 5:147. See also Becker, 'Barthold's Studien', 398. According to Ibn Ṭūlūn, al-Mutawakkil and the qadis entered Egypt in Ramaḍān 922/ October 1516, see Ibn Ṭūlūn, *Mufākahat*, 2:32.
62. Ibn Iyās, *Badāʾiʿ*, 5:147–8, 150; Winter, 'Ottoman Occupation', 503.
63. Markiewicz, *Crisis of Kingship*, 138–9.
64. Ibn Iyās, *Badāʾiʿ*, 5:157–8.
65. Ibid., 5:158.
66. Becker, 'Barthold's Studien', 396; Sümer, 'Yavuz Selim', 349–50.
67. Ibn Iyās, *Badāʾiʿ*, 4: 344–47, 355; 5:158; Ibn al-Ḥimṣī, *Ḥawādith*, 2:252; Banister, 'Naught Remains', 235–7. This case has received some attention in recent scholarship, see Rapoport, 'Women and Gender', 1–3; Petry, *Criminal Underworld*, 140–1; Petry, 'Royal Justice'; Petry, *Protectors or Praetorians?* 149–51.
68. Ferīdūn Beğ, *Münşeʾātü s-selāṭīn*, 1:487; Sümer, 'Yavuz Selim', 350n.27. It is strange that Ottoman sources mention so little of al-Mutawakkil III. Barthold suggested that the Ottomans wished to conceal the caliph among their own supporters as it is difficult to believe that Ottoman participants in Marj Dābiq would have been unaware of the caliph's presence, see Becker, 'Barthold's Studien', 396.
69. Lellouch, *Ottomans en Égypte*, 34.
70. Ibn Iyās names the Ottoman ambassador Muṣliḥ al-Dīn, see *Badāʾiʿ*, 5:164.
71. I thank Victor Ostapchuk and Lale Javanshir for assistance in the translation of this passage. The text of the *rûznâme* is found in Ferīdūn Beğ, *Münşeʾātü s-selāṭīn*, 1:487, also partially quoted in Sümer, 'Yavuz Selim', 350n.27. See also Schimmel, 'Kalif und Kadi', 121–2.
72. Ibn Iyās, *Badāʾiʿ*, 5:166–8; Ferīdūn Beğ, *Münşeʾātü s-selāṭīn*, 1:487; Sümer, 'Yavuz Selim', 350; Winter, 'Ottoman Occupation', 500–4.
73. Quṭb al-Dīn, *Chroniken*, 3:184.
74. Ibn Iyās, *Badāʾiʿ*, 5:183–5, 229. See also Becker, 'Barthold's Studien', 398.
75. Ibn Iyās, *Badāʾiʿ*, 5:185, 352; Sümer, 'Yavuz Selim', 350–1; Lellouch, *Ottomans en Égypte*, 17.
76. Ibn Iyās, *Badāʾiʿ*, 5:192; Rāġib, 'Al-Sayyida Nafīsa', 43.
77. Alexander, 'Swords from Ottoman and Mamluk Treasuries'.
78. Lellouch, *Ottomans en Égypte*, 19; Tetsuya, 'Cairene Cemeteries', 102.

79. Al-Maqrīzī, *Khiṭaṭ*, 3:430–5.
80. Ibn Iyās, *Badāʾiʿ*, 5:184; Becker, 'Barthold's Studien', 398.
81. Inalcik, 'Selīm'.
82. Ibn Iyās, *Badāʾiʿ*, 5:185, 272.
83. For an overview, see Hassan, *Longing for the Lost Caliphate*, 9; Casale, 'Tordesillas', 487–90; Asrar, 'Myth about the Transfer', 116; Veinstein, 'La question du califat ottoman'; Lewis, 'ʿAbbāsids'; Arnold, *Caliphate*, 146–7.
84. Inalcik, 'Selīm'.
85. Hassan, *Longing for the Lost Caliphate*, 145–8; Finkel, *Osman's Dream*, 111; Casale, 'Tordesillas', 486–7, 490; Sourdel, 'Khalīfah'; Becker, 'Barthold's Studien', 408–12.
86. Holt, 'Some Observations', 507.
87. Ibn Iyās, *Badāʾiʿ*, 5:317–18; al-Qaramānī, *Akhbār*, 2:226; Becker, 'Barthold's Studien', 399; Arnold, *Caliphate*, 142.
88. Ibn Iyās, *Badāʾiʿ*, 5:317–18; Sümer, 'Yavuz Selim', 351–2.
89. Finkel, *Osman's Dream*, 54. The precise duration of al-Mutawakkil's stay at Yedikule (Arabic: al-Sabʿa Qilliyyāt) is unclear. Another reason for his internment there was the rumour that many Egyptian prisoners had escaped, and the Ottomans were interested in monitoring the caliph's whereabouts. See Becker, 'Barthold's Studien', 399.
90. Ibn Iyās, *Badāʾiʿ*, 5:352–3; al-Qaramānī, *Akhbār*, 2:226.
91. Evliyā Çelebi, *Seyahatnâmesi*, 10:30.
92. Ibn Iyās, *Badāʾiʿ*, 5:360, 365; al-Qaramānī, *Akhbār*, 2:226. It is unclear whether Selīm or his son Süleymān ordered the daily stipend and subsequent release of al-Mutawakkil. Ibn Iyās and Cenābī state that the caliph received 60 dirhams, though Sümer argues that the caliph would have been paid in *akçes*.
93. Evliyā Çelebi, *Seyahatnâmesi*, 10:30. The Ottoman historian ʿAbdüʾṣ-Ṣamed Diyārbekrī claims that al-Mutawakkil III returned some years later on 4 Ṣafar 934/30 October 1527 accompanied by other members of the former Cairene civilian elite given leave to return by Süleymān. See Ibn Iyās, *Badāʾiʿ*, 5:394–403; Lellouch, *Ottomans en Égypte*, 49, 62; Sümer, 'Yavuz Selim', 352; Becker, 'Barthold's Studien', 400.
94. Winter, *Egyptian Society*, 11.
95. Sourdel, 'Khalīfah'; Becker, 'Barthold's Studien', 400.
96. While most secondary scholarship assumes the caliph on hand was al-Mutawakkil III, based on the uncertainty of the caliph's precise date of return from Istanbul, it is unclear which member of the Abbasid family invested

Aḥmad Pasha. Lellouch discovered a contemporary Jewish source, the *Megillat Miṣrayim*, a commentary on a Cairene purim scroll written during Aḥmad Pasha's revolt, which claims that a son or possibly a half-brother of al-Mutawakkil invested Aḥmad Pasha. See Lellouch, *Ottomans en Égypte*, 59n.284; Becker, 'Barthold's Studien', 401.

97. Quṭb al-Dīn, *Chroniken*, 3:185; Evliyā Çelebi, *Seyahatnâmesi*, 10:30; Lellouch, *Ottomans en Égypte*, 59; Holt, *Egypt and the Fertile Crescent*, 48–51; Sümer, 'Yavuz Selim', 353; Arnold, *Caliphate*, 142; Becker, 'Barthold's Studien', 400–1.
98. Becker, 'Barthold's Studien', 400. Al-Qaramānī (*Akhbār*, 2:226) names 12 Shaʿbān 945/3 January 1539 as the caliph's date of death. However, other historians claim al-Mutawakkil died in Egypt in Shaʿbān 950/November 1543.
99. See Quṭb al-Dīn, *Chroniken*, 3:183–5; Marʿī ibn Yūsuf Karmī, *Nuzha*, 67; Becker, 'Barthold's Studien', 400–1; Sümer, 'Yavuz Selim', 353; Yılmaz, *Caliphate Redefined*, 105.
100. Al-Jabartī, *Taʾrīkh*, 3:75-6; Holt, 'Some Observations', 507. See Becker, 'Barthold's Studien', 401.
101. Banister, 'Naught Remains', 242; Berkey, 'Mamluk Religious Policy', 12; Garcin, 'Histoire', 61.
102. Hassan, *Longing for the Lost Caliphate*, 31, 84, 88; Banister, 'Naught Remains', 245.

PART TWO

THE LEGAL, HISTORIOGRAPHICAL AND CHANCERY DIMENSIONS OF THE ABBASID CALIPHATE OF CAIRO

6

Normative Perspectives on the Caliphate of Cairo: Jurisprudential, Advice and Courtly Literature

Introduction

The chapters of Part One have demonstrated that the overall character of the institutional caliphate can be gleaned through an examination of the careers of the Abbasid family members appointed to office for nearly three centuries in late medieval Cairo. Muslim intellectuals have imagined politics from a variety of perspectives. The scope of this chapter is limited to the primarily elite views of scholars, courtiers and jurists from the mid-thirteenth to early sixteenth centuries. In addition to engaging with scholarship of the period contemporary to the Abbasid Caliphate of Cairo, it analyses the views of the intellectual elite (often with relational ties to the political elites of the amirs and the sultan) and is thus not the place to reflect on the opinions of the masses or scholars beyond the world of normative Sunni Islam.

To better contextualise the narrative history of the Abbasid caliphs of Cairo presented in the previous chapters, the current chapter, in five chronological sections, discusses authors of different backgrounds and genres who engaged with the contemporary Abbasid Caliphate directly and indirectly. Authors addressing the intrinsic workings of government and contemporary politics often found it necessary to acknowledge the special arrangement between the sultans and caliphs of Cairo. Mona Hassan discovered ample evidence suggesting that many of the important jurists of the period, at the very least, recognised the Abbasid caliph of Cairo in the hierarchical structure of government as the theocratic source of the sultan's power.[1] Indeed, Muslim scholars residing in late medieval Egypt and Syria had no shortage of opinions on the re-imagined caliphate rooted in history and tradition.

Naturally, discussions of the caliphate and the production of texts dealing with the imamate did not occur in a vacuum. To better understand late medieval scholarly discourses on leadership and religio-political organisation, some remarks on the wider intellectual environment will be useful to contextualise the status of the texts as well as the scholars and debates that produced them.[2] Following the Mongol conquests, Sunni scholars identified closely with the four legal schools of jurisprudence which accepted creeds associated with the intellectual visions of Traditionalism, as well as Ashʿarī and Māturīdī theology.[3]

Down to the end of the Cairo Sultanate, Traditionalism (and its adherents known to the Islamic tradition as *aṣḥāb al-ḥadīth* or *ahl al-ḥadīth*) with its prioritisation of Qurʾān and revealed tradition over reason, had, since the late eighth century, remained an important intellectual trend juxtaposed against the growing influence of its more rationalist (*ahl al-raʾy*) Ashʿarī counterpart. The Sunni-Islamic identity and nuanced debates around the Traditionalist and Ashʿarī outlooks informed the writing and conceptualisation of most of the authors and historians discussed in Chapters 6 and 7, influencing the way they wrote about the imamate and caliphate. Many were involved in *fiqh* and ḥadīth studies, which is indicative of their proficiency for understanding the arguments, methodologies and subtleties of legal debates rooted in the types of knowledge transmission that were influenced by Traditionalist and Ashʿarī debates and ideas by the late fifteenth and early sixteenth centuries.[4] When considering some authors' conceptions of leadership it seems likely that their texts were framed in part by their own background and socio-political context in relation to religious thought. Traditionalism, Ashʿarism, and the areas both in between and beyond, influenced the intellectual frameworks which the authors inherited and defended. Thus, references to the administrative and legal systems, with all of their hierarchies including caliphs, sultans and other functionaries, appear weighted with great significance in many of their works.

This chapter examines normative and prescriptive literature comprising jurisprudential works, advice literature and commentary on governing institutions taken from scribal manuals. Much of it demonstrates ways in which one particular strand of juristic thinking on the Sunni caliphate was constructed and reconstructed within certain types of textual material. Taken on its own, this corpus of 'political literature' presents some problems. Azfar Moin has warned intellectual historians against attempts at understanding the institutions of Muslim kingship solely via elite prescriptive texts rather than through an engagement with the performative elements, social practices and cultural embeddedness of pre-modern kingship. Indeed, caliphs, sultans and their courts interacted less with elite genres of writing and more with everyday life and the popular imagination.[5] Moin argues that such texts are best understood as a supplement to writings from other genres including historiography.[6] Thus, it is in combination with the historiographical literature assessed in Chapter 7, chancery documents and literature examined in Chapters 8 and 9 that Part Two of this book contributes to a holistic understanding of the Cairene caliphate as our source material presents it.

Contextualising the Abbasid Caliph in Late Thirteenth-century Cairo: the Anonymous *Miṣbāḥ al-hidāya fī ṭarīq al-imāma* and Shihāb al-Dīn al-Qarāfī

An anonymous thirteenth-century treatise on the imamate, *Miṣbāḥ al-hidāya fī ṭarīq al-imāma*, was dedicated to Baybars and, according to Wilferd Madelung, emerged from a Sufi context just after the investitures of the first Abbasids in Cairo.[7] The treatise represents an early attempt to set down a juristic interpretation in the light of Baybars' successful Abbasid restoration. The author of the *Miṣbāḥ* argues for the necessity of the imamate to ward off usurpers and to ensure the continuation of 'Islamic' rule, mainly by imposing order in both religious and temporal matters. Although the author refers to both *sulṭān* and *imām* (quite likely embodied in a single person) he stipulates that the *imām*, in addition to having sound mind, maturity, freedom and probity, must possess knowledge of the *sharīʿa* and be able to engage in *ijtihād* to produce sound Islamic rulings.[8]

The author of the *Miṣbāḥ* departs from the classical requirement that the *imām* be a descendant of the Prophet's tribe of Quraysh, thus opening the way for the legitimisation of Baybars' rule. The treatise further asserts that if the imamate is taken by force, necessity dictates that the act be accepted, even if the *imām* is ignorant of legal norms.[9]

From what little information seems apparent about the author, Madelung suggests that a member of Baybars' entourage with strong Sufi leanings wrote the work. It is thus that the *Miṣbāḥ* seems concerned with clearing the way for the reign of the sultan, a former slave, who ruled by virtue of his competence, power and ability to protect the religion. No Qurayshī blessing was necessary to furnish the imamate with religious legitimisation; in its place was a stronger role for learned Sufis and *ʿulamāʾ* in advisory and ruling affairs.[10]

Another late thirteenth-century perspective on the revived imamate comes from the Mālikī jurist Shihāb al-Dīn al-Qarāfī (d. 684/1285), originally of Sanhāja Berber origin, who grew up in Old Cairo and later held important positions in city *madrasa*s. Like earlier Ashʿarī authors, he allowed rationalism to enter his thought on the imamate and sought to protect the minority positions of independent scholars who did not enjoy the support of the ruling elite in Shāfiʿī-dominated Cairo prior to Baybars' institution of the four chief qadiships. Al-Qarāfī wrote his *Kitāb al-iḥkām fī tamyīz al-fatāwā ʿan al-aḥkām wa-taṣarrufāt al-qāḍī wa-l-imām* around 661/1262. Like the *Miṣbāḥ*, it offers a potential snapshot of religious and political tensions at the time of Baybars' early sultanate and investiture of two Abbasid caliphs.[11]

As Sherman Jackson indicates, the legalistic ramifications of inserting an Abbasid caliph into the religio-political landscape had yet to appear. Wariness may well have urged al-Qarāfī, already writing from an embattled minority position, to define and limit the role of important positions in the religious structure such as caliph, qadi and mufti, which he apparently understood to be mutually inclusive. Balancing the three authorities was important to al-Qarāfī, who discussed the degree to which new caliphal decrees should be binding. The issue was pressing: never before had Egypt been subject directly to an Abbasid caliph in its midst; and the caliphs of Baghdad had operated within the confines of a unique arrangement with local scholars under a political framework distinct from that of late thirteenth-century Egypt.[12]

Above all, in with regard to the caliph, al-Qarāfī wished to illustrate that any of the caliph's actions, whether a discretionary injunction, binding decision or fatwa, differed significantly from a (legally binding) fatwa of the Prophet since the opinion of the caliph was subject to human error. In his bid to secure equal footing, al-Qarāfī advised contemporaries to take the fatwas of caliphs and qadis as nothing more than individual opinions.[13] In this way, writing in anticipation of the caliph and expecting the worst, al-Qarāfī may have wished to limit Abbasid power in Cairo. He identified two categories of the caliph's jurisdiction: various religious practices and other matters outside of that which scripture dictated such as prosecuting *jihād*. If the caliph's fatwa contradicted the popular consensus of the jurisprudents, the fatwa of the latter could be accepted as an endowment of legal right and the caliph's fatwa ignored as non-binding.[14]

The work of al-Qarāfī, like the *Miṣbāḥ*, presents an interesting early glimpse of the religious landscape of Cairo shortly after the establishment of Baybars' political order which included a freshly invested Abbasid caliph. In it, we find some of the *ʿulamāʾ* who did not enjoy strong influence attempting to preserve their interests from the reintroduction of a caliph into the socio-political landscape. It may have been important to some jurists that the religious leadership could mute the caliph if he made a controversial or unpopular decree.

Early Fourteenth-century Political Literature: Advice Texts and Encyclopaedic Writings on Government

In the context of the medieval Middle East, different forms of wisdom and advice literature date back to Arabic translations of Pahlavi originals. After the Abbasid revolution of the mid-eighth century, writings of the so-called 'mirrors for princes' genre appeared with some regularity in Arabic and Persian to moralise on just government and promise guidance to rulers by way of maxims, aphorisms and anecdotes. Secretaries, courtiers and even religious scholars penned works of advice literature at the behest of one patron or another in an Islamic sovereign's court. Many works tended to offer timeless political wisdom rather than situation-specific counsel.[15]

Little is known about the life of the fourteenth-century Egyptian courtier Ḥasan ibn ʿAbdallāh al-ʿAbbāsī (d. after 716/1316), allegedly a descendant of the Abbasid caliph Hārūn al-Rashīd and the author of *Āthār al-uwal fī tartīb al-duwal*, an early fourteenth-century Arabic 'mirror' dedicated to the short-reigning sultan Baybars al-Jāshinkīr (r. 709/1308–9).[16]

Divided into four sections covering the mandates of kingship, the important personnel and machinery of the king's polity, court ceremonial and war, the *Āthār* provides protocols of governance based on past examples. Ḥasan al-ʿAbbāsī follows many of the themes associated with Perso-Islamic advice literature such as commentary on a king's obligations to his subjects and the overall importance of justice and obedience, which cites the so-called 'sovereignty verse' of the Qur'ān (4:59)[17] and discusses various interpretations of the 'holders of power' (*ulū al-amr*).[18] The *Āthār* discusses notions of divine election and asserts that God chooses rulers based on proofs from the Qur'ān and prophetic traditions.[19] Concerning the caliphate, the author's presentation as a whole assumes the status quo of fourteenth-century Cairene politics, namely, that the caliph has formally delegated the sultan with authority to act as the classical Islamic sovereign who must now be treated with the old trappings of caliphate and kingship.[20] Ḥasan al-ʿAbbāsī thus leaves little room for the caliph, and focuses on the realities of the sultanate, a term he makes interchangeable with caliphate and imamate.

The author examines two relevant and oft-quoted verses of the Qur'ān concerning the caliphate: the verse of the Davidian caliphate (38:26),[21] and an earlier verse which states that God makes caliphs (deputies in charge) of mankind on the Earth to see how they will act (7:129). He then concludes that the purpose of the caliphate is for the acting ruler to hold divine appointment over the people and rule amongst them in truth and justice.[22]

While the words '*malik*', '*sulṭān*' and '*khalīfa*' appear interchangeably in the *Āthār*, the first two appear most regularly. In his chapter on the king's relations with neighbouring rulers, Ḥasan al-ʿAbbāsī acknowledges that the Franks have their pope, while the Muslims have their caliph.[23] Because the title of caliph had taken on a sensitive meaning in the early fourteenth century, especially at a time when the rule of Baybars al-Jāshinkīr had grown unpopular, Ḥasan al-ʿAbbāsī may have been conscious of overusing the word, or allowing it to overshadow the importance of Baybars as the legitimate merit-based sultan against the resurgent dynastic threat of al-Nāṣir Muḥammad.

The first two sections of the *Āthār* deal with the king's behaviour with his subordinates, emphasising that he must respect and heed their advice. Ḥasan al-ʿAbbāsī thus comments on the state of the sultan's relationship with the religious leadership (of which the Abbasid caliph was a member *ex officio*). The seventh chapter later addresses the sultan's relationship with the scholarly class of his *dawla*. Ḥasan al-ʿAbbāsī calls upon the king, if he wished to lead a mighty empire, to respect his resident scholars, just as the

Greeks and Persians honoured their men of wisdom. The author writes that in the days when prophets such as David and Solomon had been kings, they were constantly engaged in the religious sciences, but in times when rulers were no longer adept in religious learning, they needed to be great patrons of the scholars.[24] For Ḥasan al-ʿAbbāsī, the prestige of the *ʿulamāʾ* derived from their protection of the holy law, which, incidentally, was also one of the charges of the king. He cites the Abbasids of Baghdad who built famous *madrasas* as a concerted effort to promote an official understanding of Islam, as well as the caliph al-Maʾmūn (189–218/813–33) who engaged directly in the religious debates of his time and, for better or worse, even attempted to promulgate his own favoured version of the faith.[25]

Among those who must be protected and honoured by the king are the noble descendants of venerable houses. Ḥasan al-ʿAbbāsī divides these into two groups: the first, progeny of the prophets and their companions, saints and notable aesthetes; and the second group, the descendants of just or noble kings. Quoting the ḥadīth, 'whomever honours the Quraysh is honoured by God', Ḥasan al-ʿAbbāsī, himself of Abbasid stock, affirms that the Quraysh were to be honoured in Egypt, which was a nod to the resident line of caliphs as well as the other local *sharīf* descendants of the Prophet. Since the scholars were famously described by Muḥammad as 'heirs of the prophets', the *Āthār* extended protection to them as well. It was thus the mark of a good king and a just kingdom that people of noble descent within its territory would be respected and cared for by the authorities.[26]

The *Āthār* discusses the role of other members of the king's ruling apparatus, including the wazir, the importance of *shūra* counsel, the various bureaus (*dīwāns*), postal riders and messengers, the *maẓālim* courts, and those who protect access to the king, such as the chamberlains (*ḥujjāb*) as well as a variety of associates and boon companions.[27] Ḥasan al-ʿAbbāsī emphasises the importance of capable advisers for the king among his intimates and the *ʿulamāʾ*. Overall, the work reinforces the concept of a multifaceted sultanate–imamate where many role-players and position-holders cooperate to run a classical state comparable with the lauded Persian, Greek and Islamic models. The king or sultan is in effect a divinely selected *primus inter pares* who directs matters with the resources of the state at his disposal. The wazir shares his burdens, advises him based on religious sources and helps to organise his realm. The bureaucrats and secretaries are the king's tongue. In order for the government to function, there can be no disconnect between the king and his advisers and messengers. The *maẓālim* provides the means through which the king dispenses justice, the proper execution of which serves as evidence of royal integrity.[28]

Many modern scholars have identified a distinct encyclopaedic tendency in the fourteenth- and fifteenth-century lands of the Cairo Sultanate. Several fields of knowledge underwent change in this period, which resulted in the production of comprehensive works intended to provide scholars and laymen with a complete image of the past and the contemporary state of knowledge.[29]

The scribe and encyclopaedist Shihāb al-Dīn Aḥmad al-Nuwayrī (d. 733/1333), the compiler of one such work in early fourteenth-century Egypt, worked as a clerk during the reign of al-Nāṣir Muḥammad, managing the sultan's lands in the *dīwān al-khāṣṣ* and tending to chancery affairs. Government service furnished al-Nuwayrī with access to the sultan of Cairo as well as to important documents which the author used in the historical and administrative sections of his 9,000-page encyclopaedia, *Nihāyat al-arab fī funūn al-adab*, compiling all the knowledge needed by a gentleman scribe.

Al-Nuwayrī's idealised discussion of rulers and their governments makes up the fifth and final section in the second book (*fann*) of the *Nihāya* which deals with mankind. After having treated heaven and Earth in the first *fann*, al-Nuwayrī covers living beings in the next three books: mankind, animals and plants. His exploration of the human experience discusses physiology, love poetry, genealogy, wine, music and other elements before examining the governance of human beings, which the author subdivides into fourteen chapters devoted to administrative organisation.

Al-Nuwayrī's treatment of imamate and kingship is divided into fourteen *abwāb*, covering familiar topics such as the conditions for the imamate, mutual obligations between the ruler and his subjects, what constitutes superior statecraft, the men around the ruler, the importance of advice and consultation (*shūra*), amirs, wazirs, chamberlains, and the keeping of secrets, warfare and its leaders, judiciary, *maẓālim* courts, *ḥisba* and the bureaucracy.[30]

As a master encyclopaedic compiler, al-Nuwayrī composed a section on administration that drew on numerous earlier works, including the eleventh-century Shāfiʿī jurist Abū ʿAbdallāh al-Ḥusayn al-Jurjānī al-Ḥalīmī (d. 403/1012) (d. 403/1012) whose *al-Minhaj* the author quoted alongside the influential eleventh-century Baghdādī theorist and Shāfiʿi *faqīh* ʿAlī al-Māwardī (d. 450/1058) as an important foundational archetype. Al-Nuwayrī's compilation on government is unique by virtue of the author's selections (throughout the *Nihāya*) from classical Arabic *adab* compilations. On the subject of government administration, al-Nuwayrī draws on the work of Ibn al-Muqaffaʿ (*al-Adab al-kabīr* and *Rasāʾil Ibn al-Muqaffaʿ*), Ibn Qutayba (*ʿUyūn al-akhbār*), Abū al-Faraj al-Iṣfahānī (*Kitāb al-aghānī*) and the *ʿIqd al-farīd* of Ibn ʿAbd Rabbih, amongst others, to provide examples for his discussion of leadership and government.[31]

The first chapter (*bāb*) on administrative organisation deals with the conditions for the imamate, in which al-Nuwayrī distinguishes between the legal (*sharʿiyya*) conditions of the *imām* and the traditional (*ʿurfiyya*) conditions concerning the king (*malik*). Regarding the legal qualities, al-Nuwayrī favours the traditionalist opinions of al-Ḥalīmī for their brevity and clarity. Al-Ḥalīmī has three requirements: that the *imām* be of Qurayshī stock; that he be knowledgeable enough to make rulings on matters of prayer, alms distribution, the appointment of qadis, the proper execution of *jihād* and the dispersal of war booty; and, finally, that he have sufficient probity for matters of religion, thereby immersing himself in works of religious piety, for he is accountable to God and the Muslim community.[32] As for the shorter section on the traditional or conventional conditions for the imamate (the author having swapped the word '*imām*' for '*malik*'), al-Nuwayrī does not name explicit stipulations, rather he compiles a number of anecdotes supposedly from the first Umayyad caliph Muʿāwiya, the early Abbasid-era secretary and litterateur Ibn al-Muqaffaʿ, and a number of popular sayings which enumerate the things a king should *not* be (i.e., excessively angry, dishonest, miserly, severe in temperament, envious or cowardly).[33]

That al-Nuwayrī differentiates between *imām* and *malik*, implies that there are certain prerequisites for the imamate which preclude that the office holder must be free from the less favourable qualities of a ruler engaged in secular kingship (*mulk*). This interpretation lends itself to the idea that there was a Quraysh-descended Abbasid *imām* engaged in religious practices, who had delegated authority to the sultan al-Nāṣir Muḥammad, who, although a 'traditional' king (one thoroughly engaged in the unsavoury and impious tasks of ruling), was also presented as a paragon of just rule and piety.

In the second chapter on administrative organisation, al-Nuwayrī begins discussing the office of the 'sultan' whom, through an excerpt from Ibn ʿAbd Rabbih, he describes as 'the reins of power, the organisation of rights, the upholder of the punishments (*qawām al-ḥudūd*), and the axis upon whom the undertaking of worldly and spiritual [affairs is hung] (*quṭb qiyyām al-dunyā wa-l-dīn*), and who is God's sanctuary on His earth, His shadow extended over His slaves'.[34]

The third chapter deals with that which the subjects owe to the king (*malik*), namely, obedience, advice and reverence. Muslims had to advise their sultan, and whosoever befriended the sultan was obliged to advise him in a friendly way so he may discreetly learn of his faults. For his part, the sultan or king must not suppress the advice of his subjects. The basis for the reverence of the subjects is the king's status as God's shadow (*fay*ʾ or *ẓill*) on earth or God's pole or spear (*raml*) on the earth.[35]

In the fifth chapter concerning kingly obligations to subjects, al-Nuwayrī stresses justice, which is an important theme throughout the section of the *Nihāya* devoted to administration. In addition to the eight sentences on justice written by Aristotle to Alexander the Great,[36] al-Nuwayrī quotes sayings on justice attributed to the mythical Iranian kings Jamshīd and Ardashīr and devotes several pages to the characteristics of the just *imām*.[37] While al-Nuwayrī's presentation recognises the premise that the Abbasid caliph endowed the broader 'imamate' with its obligatory Qurayshī connection and religious sanctity, it was of course his own master al-Nāṣir Muḥammad who truly wielded power in the sultanate of Cairo, and to whom al-Nuwayrī addressed in his presentation of just government.

Fourteenth-century Hierarchical Recognition of the Abbasid Caliphate

The Shāfiʿī chief qadi Badr al-Dīn Muḥammad ibn Jamāʿa (d. 733/1333) produced one of the most famous works of Islamic political theory during the fourteenth century. His *Taḥrīr al-aḥkām fī tadbīr ahl al-Islām* has long been consulted in theoretical studies of the caliphate and is a mainstay in contextual analyses of late medieval Egyptian politics.[38] *Taḥrīr al-aḥkām* revisits the subject matter of previous treatises such as the legal requirements for the imamate, the obligatory nature of the institution, as well as legal sources of revenue, the means of selecting a caliph and, perhaps most importantly, as Ovamir Anjum argues, the legality and importance of *jihād* against the Mongols, and dispersing provisions among troops.[39] Ibn Jamāʿa wrote on the imamate not only because the scholarly tradition he was brought up in had bearing on it, but also because of its relevance to his own socio-political context. He composed the *Taḥrīr al-aḥkām* in the 710s/1310s for al-Nāṣir Muḥammad following the brief sultanate of Baybars al-Jāshinkīr when the caliph al-Mustakfī had been used to issue a document challenging Qalawunid legitimacy by claiming that kingship was childless (*al-mulk ʿaqīm*).[40] Although the caliphate and sultanate underwent an awkward period of reconciliation in the months and years that followed, the relationship remained tense. Because al-Mustakfī lived in Cairo, Ibn Jamāʿa thus had to position his text to include the caliph as well as the sultan.

Many modern studies have seized upon a key passage of Ibn Jamāʿa's treatise which claims that an imamate can be conferred to a possessor of force and military might. In the eleventh century, even al-Māwardī recognised *de facto* amirates seized forcibly, but Ibn Jamāʿa, writing as each amiral household and faction competed to establish a new political order with one of its own as sultan, went further to maintain that coercive power alone secured legally binding authority. In other words, any man capable of seizing authority held it by right.[41] Some modern scholarship casts Ibn Jamāʿa as the originator of the idea that accepted the absorption of the caliphate and sultanate into a single *imām* by way of coercive power.[42] The idea was already extant in the anonymous *Miṣbāḥ* treatise on the imamate.[43] More recently, however, Hassan has identified earlier strains of Ḥanbalī law originating with Imām al-Ḥaramayn ʿAbd al-Mālik al-Juwaynī (d. 478/1085) that recognised the seizure of power as a legitimate means of acquiring the imamate/caliphate, an idea that had precedence in Ibn Jamāʿa's own Shāfiʿī tradition.[44]

The sultan had seized power forcibly and used an Abbasid caliph to delegate control over affairs to him in order to preserve order and ensure the obedience of the community. The *imām* was expected to spread and defend Islam in consultation with the *ʿulamāʾ* and by prosecuting *jihād* and upholding justice which Ibn Jamāʿa counted among his most significant duties. Ibn Jamāʿa's second chapter on the delegation of duties opens with the argument that political demands and the vast nature of empire had required caliphs to delegate matters to deputies and governors. He observed that by his own time, kings and sultans received delegation to undertake important government functions such as appointing qadis, organising armies, and collecting and dispersing revenues.[45] As Hassan indicates, Ibn Jamāʿa acknowledged that the sultan acted in the place of the caliph, which in itself carried the implication that the sultan met every criterion of the classical imamate save Qurayshī lineage which was delivered via Abbasid delegation.[46]

As Aziz Al-Azmeh points out, in describing the *imām*'s duties Ibn Jamāʿa continues the trend of earlier treatises in making 'sultan' synonymous with '*imām*'.[47] In his discussion of the mutual obligations between the sultan and caliph, on the one hand, and the Muslim community, on the other, it seems plain that he viewed the two leadership entities as a dyad. The nature of the duties addressed in *Taḥrīr al-aḥkām*, however, could refer only to the sultan, who alone had the strength to defend the frontiers, organise warfare, maintain (forcibly if need be) the precepts of *sharīʿa*, and appoint others to uphold prayers.[48] Ibn Jamāʿa's blurring of the sultanate and caliphate into a single entity is analogous to the way in which the wazirate and the magistrate were classically understood as separate jurisdictions which all fell under the broader notion of imamate as a functional whole.[49] This interpretation suggests the reality that in the fourteenth century, the caliphate was an annex of the sultanate that the political elite were expected to keep on retainer in order to supply the sultan with access to Qurayshī lineage and through it, a link to God, the Prophet and perpetual blessings for the polity.[50] Emphasising the importance of a Qurayshī *imām* allowed Ibn Jamāʿa to remain vague about that *imām*'s rights, perhaps in fear of the repercussions he may face for explicitly defining any imperative relationship between the caliph, the sultan and the populace.[51]

In *Taḥrīr al-aḥkām*, Ibn Jamāʿa advanced a view that was wholly complimentary with the original ideology that Baybars and his successors sought to promote: that the sultan had subsumed the former role of the caliph while receiving his continuous recognition and cooperation. Because the sultan (with the help of the *ʿulamāʾ* on the religious front) could execute the former duties of the caliph and satisfy all the conditions of the office besides Qurayshī descent, Ibn Jamāʿa – as Hassan's analysis confirms – maintains the stipulation of a Qurayshī descendant to bestow *sharī*ʿ legitimacy on the project and satisfy any cultural or traditional demands of the community at large by referring to the resident Abbasid caliph.[52] Thus, at least in Ibn Jamāʿa's conceptualisation of a functioning Islamic political entity, the sultan carried out the caliph's traditional duties while the caliph, despite having little else to do, had a guaranteed role.

In Ḥarrān, Syria, not long after the Mongols ended the Abbasid Caliphate of Baghdad, the prominent Banū Taymiyya clan had been among the first notables to offer the *bayʿa* pledge to the caliph al-Ḥākim brought to the city by the amir Āqqūsh al-Barlī.[53] Later, after fleeing the Mongols to Damascus, the clan would produce one of the most influential thinkers in Islamic history, Aḥmad Taqī al-Dīn ibn Taymiyya (d. 728/1328).

Scholarly interpretations of Ibn Taymiyya's position on the caliphate are varied to say the least. Recent research suggests that the wide array of conflicting positions stem from an often selective reading of the source material.[54] Until recently, much of the modern scholarship faithfully repeated the notion that Ibn Taymiyya advocated a full abolition of the caliphate, which in the light of historical changes and the rise of sultans, he declared no longer obligatory (*wājib*). As Hassan argues, however, the conclusion itself seems an abrupt departure from the tradition of Sunni juristic treatises on the caliphate that sought to affirm its mandatory nature and define its power. The genesis of this confused interpretation of Ibn Taymiyya appears to have originated with the work of the French scholar Henri Laoust.[55] To arrive at his conclusions, Hassan argues that Laoust misinterpreted at least two key passages of Ibn Taymiyya's *Minhāj al-sunna* written in the context of the author's refutation of the Shiʿite concept of the occulted *imām*, and interpreted them instead as a rejection of the Sunni caliphate. Instead, Ibn Taymiyya appears to have consistently considered the caliphate and all of its classical (i.e., pre-Māwardī) stipulations to be an obligation on the *umma* to regulate itself, because the Prophet had named the caliphate as a model in the so-called 'thirty years' ḥadīth.[56] In his compendium of fatwas, *Majmūʿ al-fatāwa*, Ibn Taymiyya writes:

> In our view, kingship (*mulk*) is essentially unlawful, and the obligation is to set up a Prophetic Caliphate (*khilāfat al-nubuwwa*). This is because the

> Prophet said, 'You must follow my practice and the practice of the rightly-guided caliphs after me; stick to it and hold it fast. Refrain from innovation, for every innovation is an error.' . . . This *ḥadīth* is therefore a command; it exhorts us to follow by necessity the practice of the Caliphate (of the Prophet), enjoins us to abide by it and warns us against deviation from it. It is a command from him and makes the establishment of the caliphate a definite duty . . . Again, the fact that the Prophet expressed his dislike for kingship that will follow the Prophetic Caliphate proves that kingship lacks in something which is compulsory in religion . . .[57]

Any study of Ibn Taymiyya's thought on politics and the caliphate requires that several works be consulted and that the reader make a number of inferences. Hassan argues that Ibn Taymiyya addressed the subject with consistency in the context of wider discussions of authority and obedience in works such as *Majmūʿ al-fatāwa*, *Minhāj al-sunna*, and what amounts to a work of *fiqh*/advice literature for medieval Syro-Egyptian elites, *al-Siyāsa al-sharʿiyya*.[58] Anjum identified further delineation of Ibn Taymiyya's position from the author's chief epistemological and philosophical work, *Darʾ taʿāruḍ al-ʿaql wa-l-naql*.[59]

Ibn Taymiyya understood the caliphate as an instrument to apply the *sharīʿa* with the aim of safeguarding the interests (*maṣlaḥa*) of the Muslim community.[60] He favoured the caliphate above *mulk* and held it as an idealised form of government, though, as prophesised in the 'thirty years' ḥadīth, one which might never re-emerge. He saw the caliphate as 'a moral and legal necessity for the community's welfare and well-being'.[61] Ibn Taymiyya insisted that all rulers be held to the standards of the rightly-guided caliphs while also accepting that circumstances had made it impossible for modern rulers to do so. For Ibn Taymiyya, dire need had forced the permissibility of *mulk*, which was not comparable with the caliphate.[62] On the other hand, Caterina Bori argues that while Ibn Taymiyya does not deny the symbolic value or obligatory nature of the caliphate (whenever the issue arises), he nevertheless embraces a more pragmatic view in which the caliphate is not necessarily central to his political vision.[63]

Several aspects of Ibn Taymiyya's conceptualisation of authority in Islamic government are worthy of mention. Ibn Taymiyya did not see one single office as the repository for political authority; instead, it was divided among several offices.[64] Based on revelation and reason, Ibn Taymiyya brought the focus from the caliphate to the community and *sharīʿa*.[65] It is possible that Ibn Taymiyya, who, like many authors of advice and leadership literature, valued *shūra* consultation, cooperation and mutual advice between the ruler and the ruled, sought to promote the idea that Islamic society was meant to command the good and forbid the wrong, and that all political offices were merely a politicisation of this Quranic notion. The substance of the government and how closely the rulers followed the Rāshidūn model were also of greater importance to Ibn Taymiyya than the individual person of the ruler.[66]

Ibn Taymiyya's treatise on politics, *al-Siyāsa al-sharʿiyya*, while containing no direct passage addressed to the Abbasid Caliphate of Cairo, speaks collectively to various contemporary office holders. The work itself deals with the actual performance and execution of Islamic governance, which, as Hassan argues, has led many scholars to point to its lack of direct engagement with the caliphate as sufficient evidence of the author's wholesale dismissal of the institution.[67]

Recognised as a gifted religious scholar even in his own time, Ibn Taymiyya, like other contemporaries, was aware of what the caliphate had become in the hands of the late medieval sultans of Egypt and Syria.[68] He viewed the caliphate as a 'formal position and rational obligation', and felt it essential that modern rulers closely followed the models of Rāshidūn-style governance. The caliphate, having been endorsed by the Prophet, thus outweighed any competing form of government.[69] However, no ruler, no matter how well-suited or virtuous, could be a *prophetic* caliph until he satisfied the classical criteria and had acquired tangible power. Any ruler incapable of enforcing his own power was, for Ibn Taymiyya, simply not a ruler.[70] This included an *imām* with a reputable claim to legitimacy, which could only be seen as relevant if he were the actual ruler. For Ibn Taymiyya, 'rule', which required the ability to bring justice and peace to the realm, was impossible for one as feeble as the powerless Abbasid caliph of Cairo.[71]

As Anjum argues, Ibn Taymiyya may well have thought that the *umma* focused too closely on formalities, practices, symbols and images when it came to the caliphate, and sought instead to direct the focus of political thought towards reality and practicality, and opined that the divine protection of society stemmed from the *umma* itself rather than the individual *imām*. For Ibn Taymiyya, the community was the real source of legitimacy, and the caliphate was merely one of its needs.[72]

Where, then, did all of this leave the Abbasid line of Cairo? Hassan's examination of *al-Siyāsa al-sharʿiyya* suggests that the author acknowledged the legitimacy of the existing political order by adopting a view of the caliph of Cairo as one of the symbolic chiefs of the political and military hierarchy. In the course of his broad advice to non-specific public servants as to how best to serve the state, Ibn Taymiyya addresses functionaries whether caliph, sultan, *wālī*, qadi or *nāʾib*. Hassan points out that Ibn Taymiyya's arrangement suggests his acknowledgement of the existing hierarchical structure with the Abbasid caliph as the symbolic head of all elites.[73] Although Ibn Taymiyya believed the caliphate to be obligatory, he may not have accepted that the powerless Abbasid caliph of Cairo was a *true* caliph in the classical sense of the *khilāfat al-nubuwwa*. Nevertheless, he was uninterested (or merely concluded that nothing would be gained) by discrediting the sitting Abbasid caliph who was merely superfluous in his ideal conceptualisation of Islamic politics. If Ibn Taymiyya's thought critiqued the political situation that he encountered, its essence was that the caliph, if he were to lead on the classical model, should behave more like his 'rightly-guided' early predecessors.[74]

A final fourteenth-century recognition of the caliph's place in the socio-political hierarchy appears in the writings of the Shāfiʿī Ashʿarī and Damascene qadi Tāj al-Dīn al-Subkī (d. 771/1370). Although best known for his encyclopaedia of scholars sharing his legal rite, *Ṭabaqāt al-Shāfiʿiyya*, al-Subkī also authored the more curious *Muʿīd al-niʿam wa-mubīd al-niqam*, an advice manual treating over 100 positions and offices in fourteenth-century Egypt and Syria.[75] Dealing with the theme of good intentions and gratitude (*shukr*), the *Muʿīd* offers an occasionally sharp critique of the Cairo-based government and members of the *ʿulamāʾ* which al-Subkī viewed as having strayed from historic ideals. The work focuses on how religious and political elites in medieval Egypt and Syria, by expressing thanks, might best curry God's favour.

Observing that the first public office to be treated by the *Muʿīd* was the caliphate, Hassan again recognised implicit significance in the author's decision to treat the caliphate as the most symbolically important position.[76] Al-Subkī directs his remarks generally to the occupant of the caliphal office, though his instructions for the caliph do not reflect the contemporaneous Abbasid Caliphate with its inability to adjudicate the affairs of litigants. Instead, al-Subkī assumes that *any* caliph ought to possess some modicum of power to dispense justice. The *Muʿīd* warns the caliph against approximating the deplorable judicial behaviour of the fourteenth-century Turkish ruling elite (*al-Atrāk*), who the author accuses of blind partiality for whichever litigant first presented them with a complaint or grievance. He diagnoses the hearts of the Turkish rulers as drowned in heedlessness, likening their corrupt justice system to dry arid land, so desperate to absorb water that it would not differentiate between cool, clear water and hot, viscous swill.[77]

Tāj al-Dīn al-Subkī stresses that the caliph did not owe his divine appointment of office (*wilāya*) to his intellect or virtue, but purely to God's will for which he must have perpetual gratitude. The only true demands on the caliph are that he must equally exercise justice among his people and also engage in actively cultivating God's pleasure through acts of worship such as fasting and night prayer. It is imperative that the caliph should not neglect either of these corollaries lest he risk the displeasure of God and be made to forfeit his *wilāya*.[78]

It is thus that the author's idealised demands on the caliphate do not reflect entirely the classical caliphate of the treatises on political theory, or the realities of the Cairene incarnation of the Abbasid Caliphate. Tāj al-Dīn al-Subkī's configuration acknowledges that the caliphate has been stripped of certain prerogatives such as military leadership, which is formally the domain of the sultan, but insists that the caliph be someone able to ensure impartiality and righteousness for the population.[79]

Wilāya for all positions of authority stems from God and the author clearly lays out the caliph's obligations to religion and justice. For al-Subkī, divine decree alone has mandated the caliph's position and time in office. The author sees the caliph foremost as a religious leader, directly responsible to God, yet one who should dispense justice in some capacity as an adjudicator between disputing parties, a role the sultans and their entourages would occasionally leave to the caliphs of the fifteenth century.

While, as Hassan has shown, the caliph is an important authority in the hierarchy of the *Muʿīd*, al-Subkī leaves no doubt that the sultan is the true source of strength in the government. The author similarly demands that the sultan upholds justice, but includes more sharpened criticism that underscores the sultan's primary duty of making war on the enemies of faith and overseeing the military infrastructure, which also included the proper distribution of *iqṭāʿ*s to responsible amirs who would not hoard wealth or deprive the central government of revenue.[80] That the sultan is the chief authority is also indicated by al-Subkī's bold opening declaration that he is the 'great *imām*' (*al-imām al-aʿẓam*), a title previously reserved exclusively for the Abbasid caliph, to which modern scholars have rightly called attention to as a unique development in the history of Islamic political theory.[81]

Early Fifteenth-century Cairene Scholarship on the Caliphate: Ibn Khaldūn and al-Qalqashandī

A nuanced perspective on the caliphal office and its implications in late fourteenth-century Egypt emerges from the work of the philosopher, political theoretician and social historian ʿAbd al-Raḥmān ibn Khaldūn (d. 808/1406). Active in the mid-fourteenth century at various courts across North Africa and Spain, the author of the celebrated *Muqaddima* ultimately moved to Cairo for an appointment as chief Mālikī qadi at the behest of the sultan Barqūq beginning in 784/1382–3.[82] Although many scholars consider Ibn Khaldūn to be a historian, his idealised views in the *Muqaddima* (which might be read as advice literature),[83] supplemented by his historical and autobiographical writing, are pertinent to the aims of the present chapter.

Ibn Khaldūn spent his later years in Egypt refining the prolegomena to his history, perhaps in the light of his experiences in court service.[84] The *Muqaddima* begins with a general discussion of human civilisation, followed by a detailed discourse on Bedouin life, tribal politics and the rise of party spirit or group solidarity (*ʿaṣabiyya*). The third chapter of the *Muqaddima* focuses on the nature of rule, particularly in cases of dynasty, royal authority (*mulk*), the caliphate and other ranks of government.[85] The wealth of theory and historical example in Ibn Khaldūn's writing facilitates an examination of the author's excursus on the classical caliphate and its implications for politics.

As Hamilton Gibb observed, Ibn Khaldūn's thought regards the caliphate as the pinnacle of human leadership and social organisation. Ibn

Khaldūn's ideas on justice and ideal governance come at the end of a lengthy presentation, culminating in the discussion of social and political organisation in the context of mankind's need for cooperation and civilised urban society. Ibn Khaldūn's understanding of the caliphate contained a powerful component of the ruler's responsibility to protect religion alongside the best interest(s) (*maṣlaḥa*) of the public, as well as to govern the world through Islamic *sharīʿa*.[86] The eleventh-century work of al-Māwardī also proved an important authority for Ibn Khaldūn, who used the *Aḥkām al-sulṭāniyya* in discussions of the laws and conditions pertaining to the governing functions which formerly fell under caliphal jurisdiction.[87]

For Ibn Khaldūn and his predecessors, the most vital period was encapsulated by the 'rightly-guided' caliphs who reigned free of the less honourable concept of *mulk*. Arab *ʿaṣabiyya* demanded that rulers continued to be styled as 'caliphs', which facilitated a period of coexistence between caliphate and *mulk*.[88] The presentation in the *Muqaddima* confirms that the Abbasids, the quintessential 'destroyed dynasty', was, by the author's time, so far along the road of decay that any discussion of their political or military power whatsoever was a non-starter. Ibn Khaldūn clearly expresses his theory that the Abbasids had lost what little had remained of the caliphate by the latter half of the ninth century, and although the office had persisted as *mulk* for many centuries, even that had vanished prior to the Mongol invasions.

Indebted to the good graces of Barqūq, Ibn Khaldūn wrote glowingly of the 'Dawlat al-Atrāk' and the sultans' legacy as protectors of Islam, expressing his belief that the previous political orders established by subsequent sultans possessed a unique efficacy capable of transcending what he perceived as the rise and fall of dynasties. The *Kitāb al-ʿibar* contains an oft-cited description of the classical Abbasid Caliphate, mired in centuries of corruption, on the eve of the rise to power of the 'Dawlat al-Atrāk'. In it, the historian depicts the Baghdad Abbasids as a dynasty 'drowned in decadence and luxury' until its overthrow by the Mongols and rebirth in Cairo under the *mamlūk*s who God sent to rescue Islam, preserve order and defend the lands they had entered through slavery.[89]

Despite a lengthy treatment of the classical caliphate, Ibn Khaldūn remains vague about the status of the institution in his own time. The *Muqaddima* contains only sparse references to the Cairo caliphs, though Ibn

Khaldūn mentions them in relation to the difficulty with which dynasties are established in heterogeneous social groupings fraught with tension due to competing forms of *ʿaṣabiyya*. He presents contemporary Egypt as the antithesis to such situations and depicts his contemporary political landscape as free of such disunited group feeling:

> In Egypt *mulk* is established at the height of tranquillity, as there are few dissenters (*khāwarij*) or tribal groups (*ʿaṣāʾib*), rather there is the sultan and his subjects. Egypt's ruling dynasty is comprised of Turkish kings and their factions who seize power consecutively among themselves, while the caliphate is named to an Abbasid descendant of the caliphs of Baghdad.[90]

Without defining the relationship or outlining a political structure that included the sultanate and caliphate, Ibn Khaldūn conveys the powerlessness of the latter while acknowledging its institutional persistence. Rule changed hands only among the sultans, the amir, and other elites, while the sultanate and caliphate existed as two isolated phenomena in society.

The sultans of Egypt and their political elite, unlike earlier rulers who wished to distance themselves from the caliphal figureheads under their tutelage, sought a more direct absorption of Abbasid attributes in their attempt to present Cairo as the new bulwark of Islamdom. Keenly aware that the caliphate had been depreciated by his own time, Ibn Khaldūn was a careful self-censor of his remarks on political practices in Cairo. In an analysis of what happens when a leader's control is usurped by unauthorised advisers or underlings, Ibn Khaldūn mentions Turkish, Buyid and Seljuk domination of the Abbasid caliphs, along with the eunuch Kāfūr's power over two Ikhshīdid princes in tenth-century Egypt.[91] To be sure, there were parallels with the seizure of classical Abbasid prerogatives upon the establishment of Barqūq's political order. It is unsurprising that Ibn Khaldūn avoids direct comparison with the contemporary situation of Egypt and instead praises his patrons.

The *Muqaddima* sidestepped controversial topics in recent history, such as the end of the Ayyubid *dawla* in the thirteenth century or the late fourteenth-century rise of Barqūq and his Circassian allies at the expense of other Qalawunid amiral households. Addressing such topics to illustrate theories of usurpation could prove just as seditious as an unflattering interpretation of the sultanate's 'protection' of Abbasid survivors. Instead, Ibn Khaldūn downplayed the significance of the Abbasid Caliphate of Cairo and presented a positive image of sultanic deeds done on behalf of Islam.

In *Kitāb al-ʿibar*, the chronicle adjoined to the *Muqaddima*, Ibn Khaldūn's narrative is broken into sections arranged with separate headings devoted to battles, coups and affairs of great importance.[92] Despite an awareness of the marginal role of the caliphate by his own time, Ibn Khaldūn afforded the Abbasids of Cairo significance enough in his historical presentation, devoting no fewer than five breakaway sections to discuss events of interest, particularly deaths and successions in the contemporary Abbasid family.[93] In these sections on the Cairo caliphs, Ibn Khaldūn covers the seven Abbasid family members of the thirteenth and fourteenth centuries who received *bayʿa* in Egypt down to the caliph al-Mutawakkil in his own time. His decision to order events around the Abbasid Caliphate, as well as separate passages devoted to its incumbents, represents an attempt to follow the conventions of earlier historians that closely followed caliphal milestones and the family succession.[94]

Ibn Khaldūn offers little indication as to the significance of the re-establishment of the caliphate in Egypt, although he describes the lands as 'destitute without the caliphate until Baybars renewed and reconstructed its throne'.[95] Ibn Khaldūn's treatment of the 'Dawlat al-Atrāk' ends during the so-called 'Nāṣirī revolt' in 791/1389 by the two amirs who ousted Barqūq. Upon gaining prominence over his partner Yalbughā al-Nāṣirī, the amir Minṭāsh used the caliph and chief qadis to legitimise himself by forcing them to sign a document declaring Barqūq an outlaw and enemy of Islam. Ibn Khaldūn, Mālikī qadi at the time, chafed at the experience, feeling himself little better than a powerless caliph.[96]

It is somewhat difficult to ascertain Ibn Khaldūn's explicit position on the Abbasid Caliphate of Cairo in the light of his indifference and self-censorship. There is no doubt that he understood Abbasid *ʿaṣabiyya* to have been destroyed by the late ninth century with only vestiges of it remaining to account for the ceremonial practices he observed in Barqūq's Cairo. He acknowledged the reigning Abbasid al-Mutawakkil as caliph in name, and even emphasised the caliphate's traditional importance in his famous conversation with Temür.[97] Nevertheless, Ibn Khaldūn believed in the legitimate authority and entitlement of the group with the strongest *ʿaṣabiyya*:

Barqūq and his entourage in his own time.[98] As a pragmatist he saw the Abbasid Caliphate of Cairo as acutely irrelevant pageantry that pandered to an outmoded *ʿaṣabiyya* yet one that still mattered to the designs of the contemporary and dominant group solidarity. While praising his patrons directly in his *Kitāb al-ʿibar* and indirectly in the *Muqaddima*, he legitimised the government while subliminally pointing to its flaws in comparison with the classical caliphate.

Ibn Khaldūn's thought expands upon two important themes: the gradual erosion of Abbasid *ʿaṣabiyya* along with the need for a true caliphate. There is some contradiction in this presentation. As a historian, he flatters Barqūq and his predecessors by casting them as rescuers of an Abbasid dynasty mired in corruption. He likewise projects acceptance of the notion that the Abbasid caliph formally delegates the sultan with all of the caliphal prerogatives.[99] It is unclear if the author thought that the 'Turks' were sent by God to restore the caliphate, or whether they absorbed and remade it in their own image with the sultan as acting *imām* of the Muslim community.

We can argue that Ibn Khaldūn's admiration for the legacy of his patrons came complete with its element of Abbasid legitimacy. While his pragmatic impulse may have been to ignore the Abbasid Caliphate of Cairo, its place in tradition and its significance to the political culture and socialisation of military elites in the context of the Cairo Sultanate forced him to accept it as part of a functioning whole and he relegated it to its proper place in the background. The *Muqaddima* contains Ibn Khaldūn's longing for the resurrection of an Arabo-Islamic *ʿaṣabiyya* to revive the classical Rāshidūn-style caliphate, and, like Ibn Taymiyya, the author interpreted the Abbasid Caliphate of Cairo as a symbolic placeholder until the time that such a situation might arise.[100]

Some writers of the period chose to de-emphasise the stipulation that the caliph or *imām* be a Qurayshī descendant or that the acting leader receive delegation of power from such an *imām*.[101] Al-Nuwayrī and later al-Qalqashandī passively compiled the statements of earlier scholars who argued for Qurayshī descent and implied that it was the widespread expectation of the scholarly community. Ibn Khaldūn, on the other hand, perhaps writing in favour of his patron Barqūq (whose difficult relationship with the caliph al-Mutawakkil was well known), delivered an important refutation of the need for Qurayshī descent on the ground that it had become superfluous.[102] Nevertheless, it is important to remember that Ibn Khaldūn was something of an outsider, and often even reminded of his status by contemporaries. He therefore fails to serve as a 'true voice' of his times, although modern scholars occasionally present him as such.[103]

Islamic sentimentality, cultural affinity and regard for his patrons stopped Ibn Khaldūn from arguing that the contemporary caliphate failed to serve a purpose. Instead, he tiptoed around it, acknowledged its nominal nature, and moved on. It had no bearing on his theories and, having no wish to discredit it, he merely chose not to engage it without explicitly advocating that it had no practical place in politics.

A contemporary of Ibn Khaldūn who likewise served the government of Egypt was the court scribe Shihāb al-Dīn Aḥmad al-Qalqashandī (d. 821/1418), perhaps best known to modern scholars for secretarial works, notably his scribal encyclopaedia *Ṣubḥ al-aʾshā fī ṣināʿat al-inshā* completed in about 814–15/1412. His final six years were committed to preparing a shorter compilation of documents from the *Ṣubḥ* pertaining to the caliphate which he dedicated to the reigning Abbasid caliph al-Muʿtaḍid II of Cairo. Titled *Maʾāthir al-ināfa fī maʿālim al-khilāfa*, the author prefaced the collection with a brief treatise on the caliphate and a caliphal history covering the men that had held the office down to the incumbent. Providing the caliph, as well as aspiring courtiers, with a holistic view of the caliphate, both the *Ṣubḥ* and the *Maʾāthir* approach everything from the etymology and grammatical history of the Arabic word *khalīfa* to the history of titulature chosen by the caliphs.[104]

Interested in the titular nomenclature of high office, al-Qalqashandī considered '*khalīfa*' to be the highest title among the military class or lords of the sword (*arbāb al-sayf*), denoting a great leader who upholds the affairs of the *umma*. In his discussion on the delegation of office (*wilāya*), al-Qalqashandī writes that Abbasid regnal names were selected in part to announce the splendour of the caliph and elevate his position as leader of the community.[105]

Among the designations surviving to the fifteenth century which the caliph could bestow upon his *de jure* subordinates, al-Qalqashandī identified a quintet of titles, arranged from highest to lowest rank, made by annexing the phrase 'commander of the faithful' to a noun implying nearness or sincerity. The intent of such titles was to lend prestige to the highest officials by asserting their intimacy with the caliph. The first, and most important, was *qasīm amīr al-muʾminīn*, reserved for sultans and meaning one who shared the caliph's authority and power.[106] The more ambiguous *khalīl amīr al-muʾminīn* was, according to the author of the *Ṣubḥ*, a title given to the sultan's children or other miscellaneous rulers, often in distant realms but still suggesting a close bond with the caliph. Among the highest honours a governor (*nāʾib*) could hope to obtain was the title *ʿaḍud amīr al-muʾminīn*, which implied that he lent his support as a pillar to the commander of the faithful. Additionally, two slightly lower titles, both of which connote swords, *sayf amīr al-muʾminīn* and *ḥusām amīr al-muʾminīn*, were bestowed on amirs as men of the sword. As for caliphal titles for the bureaucratic and religious classes, or men of the pen, qadis and *ʿulamāʾ* could attain the titles *walī amīr al-muʾminīn*, *khāliṣatu amīr al-muʾminīn* and *ṣafiyu* or *ṣafwat amīr al-muʾminīn* among their honours.[107]

Al-Qalqashandī's *Maʾāthir al-ināfa* reflects on a century and a half of Abbasid tradition in Cairo, while instructing the reader in early caliphal history, propriety and customs associated with the office. The author recognises a distinct place for the Abbasid Caliphate in Cairo, and although he treats the reigning caliph with a degree of pomp, he does not overstate the reality of the caliphate's (fifteenth-century) role in his theoretical writing, which, like the writing of al-Nuwayrī and Ibn Khaldūn, draws on al-Māwardī's paradigmatic *Aḥkām al-sulṭāniyya* of the eleventh century.[108]

Al-Qalqashandī opens his *Maʾāthir* by praising God for bringing the Abbasid Caliphate to Cairo which he identifies as the Heartland of Islam (*Bayḍat al-Islām*). The notion that Egypt had emerged as the heart of the Sunni world was an important theme for religious scholars and bureaucrats, who understood the sultanate of Cairo as having attained distinction and regional dominance over other polities, due to the transformation of Egypt into the abode of the Abbasid Caliphate.[109] Al-Qalqashandī's remarks demonstrate contentment with Cairo as the functional successor to Abbasid Baghdad:

> [The caliphate's] pavilion was entrusted to Egypt and thus was no longer in need. [The Abbasid Caliphate] set down its baggage and walking staff

> at [Egypt's] elegant courtyard and [Egypt] offered its shade and became the abode of the imamate (*Dār al-Imāma*) and the dome of tranquillity (*Qubbat al-Salām*) for it was known that Egypt was the best destination and that [the caliphate] had no further need of Baghdad.[110]

Echoing the sentiments of bureaucratic forerunners like Aḥmad ibn Faḍlallāh al-ʿUmarī (d. 749/1349) and Taqī al-Dīn ibn Nāẓir al-Jaysh (d. 786/1384), al-Qalqashandī attached considerable importance to the traditional caliphal investiture even as late as the early fifteenth century. He described the position of the sultanate as analogous to 'a delegated vizirate and [declared] that it consisted of a combination of (al-Māwardī's) *imārat al-istīlāʾ* with the *wizārat al-tafwīḍ*'.[111] In al-Māwardī's conception, the *wazīr al-tafwīḍ*, who enjoyed omnipotent authority to act on the caliph's behalf, cleared the way for the position of the *amīr al-umarāʾ* to seize power and leave the caliphs of tenth- and eleventh-century Baghdad as mere figureheads. Although the sultan of Cairo occupied a role similar to an *amīr al-umarāʾ* in this regard, an important difference was the legal veneer his entire political order received by virtue of the caliph's general delegation of authority.[112]

Al-Qalqashandī composed his own treatise on the imamate in the *Maʾāthir* which drew on al-Māwardī and other authors. The section covers the obligatory nature of the caliphate, the conditions required to hold it, the social and political practices through which the *bayʿa* is established, as well as the mutual responsibilities that the caliph and his Muslim subjects could expect from each other.[113] Like other authors, al-Qalqashandī may have been skittish about describing his own political reality in the late fourteenth/early fifteenth century,[114] and instead made the choice to revisit al-Māwardī's classical exposition of the caliphate.

In regard to those who had the power to elect the caliph in his own time, al-Qalqashandī recognises the electorate as members of the *ʿulamāʾ*, the military leadership (*riʾāsa*) and other notables (*wujūh*) who gather to select an *imām* capable of satisfying al-Māwardī's criteria. Without the people of authority, who al-Qalqashandī identifies in association with 'those in authority' referenced in Qurʾān 4:59, the author claims there can be no legitimate contract (*ʿaqd*) between the caliph and the community.[115]

The final section of the treatise deals with ten functions (*waẓāʾif*) al-Qalqashandī identifies as having been associated with the caliphate of earlier times. The section acknowledges a transformation of the prerogatives of the caliphate by the fourteenth century in the light of the formal caliphal designation of authority to the sultan in Cairo.[116] The duties evoke al-Māwardī's discussion of the wazirate, various types of amirate and the judiciary – upholding the rulings of *sharīʿa* and appointing qadis, the holding of the *maẓālim* court, upholding the five daily prayers, organising *ḥajj* leadership, distributing alms, market inspection (*ḥisba*), and a general application of the Islamic notion of enjoining good and forbidding evil. By the early fifteenth century, these functions of leadership were the jurisdiction of the sultan who appointed office holders to carry them out. Nevertheless, in the context of the classical caliphate, the duties imply that the caliphate encapsulated a great deal more than the single man who held the office.[117] Rather, it was an entire apparatus designed for enabling coherent rule.[118] The caliphate and later sultanate consisted of lower levels through which the ruler publicly displayed authority and upheld his end of the contract by presiding at *maẓālim* courts or delegating a *muḥtasib* that allowed the ruler to ensure that important duties were carried out initially by himself and later by appointees.[119]

Whether grounded in reason or religion, al-Qalqashandī bases his discussion of the necessity of the imamate on earlier scholars.[120] He closely follows al-Māwardī's seven stipulations that the *imām* should possess probity, knowledge sufficient for *ijtihād*, functioning faculties of sight, speech and hearing, freedom, the ability to offer judgement, courage, and Qurayshī descent. Al-Qalqashandī himself does not explicitly demand that the caliph or *imām* be of Qurayshī stock, but rather restates al-Māwardī's unswerving position in favour of it as well as the opinion of other earlier Shāfiʿī scholars.[121] Al-Qalqashandī also recognises a special position for the descendants of al-ʿAbbās and identifies them as rightful holders of the caliphate for all time.[122]

We must exercise caution when weighing the influence of al-Māwardī on later medieval Arabic authors, as the socio-political conventions of the Buyid period did not share the same ethos as that of the early fifteenth-century sultanate of Cairo. Despite some surface-level similarities, the powerless Abbasid caliph kept by the Shiʿite Buyids of the tenth century was not the same as his equally powerless late medieval Cairene counterpart. In the earlier case, al-Māwardī and his ilk considered the Buyids a temporary nuisance that would be swept away by the return of the classical caliphate. While military rulers essentially used the caliph for their own legitimating purposes in thirteenth–sixteenth-century Egypt, the expectations and social institutions evolved in entirely different contexts.[123] Indeed, al-Qalqashandī's scribal encyclopaedias drew influence from the earlier work of al-ʿUmarī, and in the nearly sixty years between their deaths many official positions in Egypt had changed considerably. Both authors tended to describe idealised practices at the expense of reality. However, at least one portion of the *Ṣubḥ*, composed just after the accession of the caliph al-Mustaʿīn to the sultanate in 815/1412, demonstrates al-Qalqashandī's belief (or perhaps hope) that the Cairo Caliphate had opened a new and exciting chapter which might prove permanent. He observes that until the arrest of the sultan Faraj in Syria that year, the caliphs of Cairo had done little more than delegate control over affairs to the sultans. With the sultanate of al-Mustaʿīn, however, '[the caliph] became the caliph of the age in the matter of the caliphate in regard to writing contracts, assigning *iqṭāʿ*s, *taqlīd*s, *tawqīʿ*s and other correspondence. His name [was mentioned] alone in the *khuṭba* and struck on dinars and dirhams . . .'[124]

Al-Qalqashandī's brief treatise in the *Maʾāthir* provides an overview of theoretical aspects of the *bayʿa* and the caliphal succession reminiscent of the author's discussion of the *bayʿa* in the *Ṣubḥ*.[125] In discussing the historic legality of the *bayʿa*, al-Qalqashandī appeals again to Shāfiʿī authorities by recapitulating that the contract between the caliph and members of the community is best fulfilled when the people who control affairs assemble to witness the *mubāyaʿa* ceremony. As in previous examples given by the author, the number of assembled members is not set, nor is it mandatory for all the distant religious and military notables to personally provide their assent. It is merely enough for someone in a distant province to hear news of the investiture to make his obedience and allegiance binding upon him.[126] This is why news of the investiture of a new caliph or sultan in Cairo was also sent to the important cities of Syria.

Al-Qalqashandī's writing encourages the caliph to assume an inflated sense of importance that might appear as mere flattery for a caliph with hardly any political power. As Hassan indicates, however, the *Maʾāthir* and relevant sections of the *Ṣubḥ* seem to have been composed with the intention of strengthening the theoretical foundations of the Abbasid Caliphate of Cairo.[127] Despite his awareness of the rich history of documents of the Islamic world, al-Qalqashandī's theoretical expressions of the caliphate and preservation of its norms appear to reflect the classical work of al-Māwardī more than the actual contemporary social practices and performance of the caliphate in Cairo.[128] It may not have been the intention of the author to describe the existing duties or power relationship of the sultan of Cairo and the Abbasid caliph, or to detail the theoretical significance of the latter. Although he fails to insist on the Qurayshī descent of the leader in clear terms and recognises the legitimacy of rule by usurpation, al-Qalqashandī emphasises the caliph's social and symbolic importance, while leaving the way clear for rule by the sultan and his elites. Like earlier writers, al-Qalqashandī's work lends stability to the status quo, but also demands respect for the contemporary Abbasid caliph, whose mere presence allows the fifteenth-century incarnation of the Cairo Sultanate to attain and maintain true distinction as the new heartland of the Muslim world.[129]

Late Fifteenth-/Early Sixteenth-century Articulations of Caliphate and Kingship: Khalīl ibn Shāhīn al-Ẓāhirī, Faḍlullāh ibn Rūzbihān Khunjī-Iṣfahānī and the Sixteenth-century *majālis* sessions of Sultan Qānişawh al-Ghawrī

As the son of a *mamlūk* amir, Khalīl ibn Shāhīn al-Ẓāhirī (d. 872/1468) went on to distinction as an administrator under the sultans Barsbāy and Jaqmaq. His *Zubdat kashf al-mamālik wa-bayān al-ṭuruq wa-l-masālik* is all that remains of a longer work providing glimpses of government structure in late fifteenth-century Egypt. The work itself is a collection of ideals and advice appropriate to various positions in the court such as the sultan, the caliph and the qadis, as well as military personnel and other royal functionaries.[130]

Acknowledging his master Jaqmaq, Khalīl al-Ẓāhirī discusses the duties of the sultanate in the second chapter. Much of the text concerns the obligations which make a ruler suitable for the throne. In the case of the sultan, military responsibilities such as providing defence, upholding justice and protecting the weak are among the chief duties.[131] Khalīl al-Ẓāhirī vigorously praises

Jaqmaq, who, according to the author, more than satisfies the kingly criteria and emphasises his ability to protect the weak and project his supremacy over Muslim rivals. Khalīl al-Ẓāhirī then shifts to the sultan's role as the great protector who oversees and guarantees the law of God and the Prophet, who protects the realm from rebellion, sedition, unbelief and polytheism. The sultan deflects injustice against the oppressed (*manṣaf al-maẓlūmīn min al-ẓālimīn*), acts as the refuge of widows, orphans and the impoverished, and finally serves as protector and intimate of the Commander of the Faithful (*walī amīr al-muʾminīn*). It is interesting not only that Khalīl al-Ẓāhirī presents protection of the caliph as a formal expectation and duty of the sultan, but also that he has placed the caliph at the end of a list of social groupings in need of protection including widows, orphans and the poor.[132]

Khalīl al-Ẓāhirī concludes his chapter on the sultanate with a discussion of public ceremony, showing that as late as the mid-fifteenth-century reign of Jaqmaq, Abbasid involvement maintained its central legitimising position. The author notes that investiture occurs

> when the electors (*ahl al-ḥall wa-l-ʿaqd*), gather in the presence of the Commander of the Faithful, along with amirs, state dignitaries (*arkān al-dawla al-sharīfa*) and the military assemble to kiss the ground before the sultan after he sits upon the throne of the kingdom following the conclusion of the mutual pledge (*mubāyaʿa*) and the sultan's handclasp (*muṣāfaḥa*) with the Commander of the Faithful.[133]

The author treats the caliphate in more detail during a brief third chapter on the men of religion, dealing first with the caliph and then the chief qadis and other *ʿulamāʾ*.[134] While he chose to discuss the sultan first, it is clear that Khalīl al-Ẓāhirī understands the caliph as an office holder with influence and importance as a nominal ruler over the lands of Islam. His description begins with allusions to the caliph's traditional prestige as God's representative on earth; a 'cousin' of the Prophet whom 'God Almighty has made ruler over the whole land of Islam'.[135] The author states that without a caliph placed in the governing structure with whom the sultan and his entourage could form an alliance, there could be no legitimate sovereignty nor any appointments, judicial rulings or marriages, all of which would be invalid in the absence of a caliph.[136] It is thus that Khalīl al-Ẓāhirī's presentation carries the implication that the caliph bears more importance than the sultan, considering good government cannot persist without him, no matter how skilled or powerful the sultan may be.

Court propriety likewise expected the caliph to be seen at the sultan's side at other times of crisis, whether castigating the latter's foes or praying for the perpetuation of his rule against plague and famine.[137] In return, the caliph could expect placement in the government hierarchy and maintenance of his family and lifestyle, although Khalīl al-Ẓāhirī mentions only that the properties allotted to the caliph would be enough to meet his needs without offering specific information.

Khalīl al-Ẓāhirī's *Zubda* presents the caliphate in line with the realities of the later fifteenth century, especially during the reign of Jaqmaq. The work presumes that the reader is both aware and familiar with the respective positions of caliph and sultan in Cairene politics by affirming the caliph's traditional place as chief of religion, while acknowledging that he has been effectively subordinated to the sultan and the historical traditions associated with his court. Thus, the *Zubda* legitimises the socio-political practices of late fifteenth-century Egypt based on contemporary courtly protocol instead of juristic precedent.

The migration of scholars from Iran and Central Asia during the fourteenth and sixteenth centuries altered the intellectual landscapes of key medieval scholarly hubs like Cairo and Damascus.[138] Having visited the territories of the Cairo Sultanate at least twice during the late fifteenth century as part of two pilgrimages to the Hijaz, the Iranian Shāfiʿī jurist and historian Faḍlullāh ibn Rūzbihān Khunjī-Iṣfahānī (d. 926/1520) wrote admiringly of the sultan of Cairo and the Abbasid caliph under his protection. The scion of a notable family who had enjoyed Aqquyunlu patronage, Khunjī-Iṣfahānī was greatly concerned with the application and preservation of the *sharīʿa* in society.[139] Falling under the influence of the Egyptian ḥadīth scholar Muḥammad al-Sakhāwī (d. 902/1497) while in the holy cities, Khunjī-Iṣfahānī appears to have cultivated respect and admiration for both the Abbasid Caliphate of Cairo and the sultans that maintained it.

A staunch Sunni traditionalist theologian, Khunjī-Iṣfahānī abhorred the advent of the Safavid Shāh Ismāʿīl in 907/1501, and from later exile in Kāshān wrote polemics against the fourteenth-century Shiʿite theologian

ʿAllāma al-Ḥillī (d. 726/1326) and the Safavid family in his Persian chronicle, *Taʾrīkh-i ʿālam-ārā-yi amīnī*.[140] Having visited the lands of the sultanate on at least two occasions to perform the *ḥajj* in 878–9/1473–4 and 886–7/1481–2, Khunjī-Iṣfahānī sought out the chiefs of the religious establishment and even met with Qāyitbāy in Cairo. He saw the sultan as a righteous ruler and bulwark against the peril of Safavid Shiʿism.[141]

In his account of 907/1501, the year that Shāh Ismāʿīl defeated the Aqquyunlu Turkmen and took Tabrīz, Khunjī-Iṣfahānī writes that the sultans of Cairo had inherited the former lands of the Ayyubids and were the rightful rulers from greater Syria to the border of the Euphrates and the lands of northeast Africa, effectively making them heirs to the Abbasid caliphs, particularly on account of their possession of the holy cities of Mecca and Medina.[142] Moreover, he describes the ruling government of Egypt as distinct from other Islamic rulers in that its 'Islamic soldiers' served as the vanguard regiments of the Abbasid caliphs in protecting the borders of Islam against the accursed unbelievers.[143]

Early Safavid victories forced Khunjī-Iṣfahānī to flee to the protection of Muḥammad Shībānī Khān in Uzbek Bukhara in the hope that the latter would rout Shāh Ismāʿīl. It came to naught, however, after the Safavid shāh killed the Uzbek ruler in 916/1510, causing Khunjī-Iṣfahānī to flee again, this time to Babur's Samarqand.[144]

At the end of his life, commissioned by an Uzbek patron, Khunjī-Iṣfahānī compiled a 'mirror for princes' manual for good Islamic government, applying *sharīʿa* to the tribal realities of Central Asia. Written more than a decade after his *Taʾrīkh*, the author's *Sulūk al-mulūk* revisits his earlier idealisation of Cairo as the home of the Abbasid Caliphate. The work revisits Khunjī-Iṣfahānī's theme of Egypt as the 'Islamic heartland' and refers to Cairo as 'the exalted abode of Islam'.[145] It is in the course of a discussion on legal penalties (*ḥudūd*) in the *Sulūk*, that one finds an interesting caricature of the position of the sultan in Egypt *vis-à-vis* the Abbasid caliph. Acquainted with the mechanics of pilgrimage by virtue of his own experience, Khunjī-Iṣfahānī mentions the various pilgrimage caravans of Syria and Iraq before claiming that 'the caravan sent by the sultan of Egypt is called the *maḥmal* of the Egyptians and is the greatest. The master (*ṣāḥib*) of the great *imārat* within the pilgrimage is the amir of the Egyptian caravan because the Abbasid caliphs in the land of Egypt are independent in their caliphate, and the sultans of Egypt are their deputies.'[146] It was clear to Khunjī-Iṣfahānī that in an Islamic world fragmented at its peripheries the Abbasid Caliphate ought to receive precedence at least during the *ḥajj* because the holy cities were in the hands of the sultans of Cairo who enjoyed Abbasid legitimacy.[147]

Ulrich Haarmann argued that Khunjī-Iṣfahānī's fundamental misrepresentation of the Abbasid Caliphate of Cairo stemmed from nostalgia and idealism fuelled by the author's desire for a Sunni champion to stand against the Safavids in the form of an independent caliphate protected by the righteous sultans of Cairo.[148] Nevertheless, Khunjī-Iṣfahānī's time in Egypt and his training with the *ʿulamāʾ* likely exposed him to a courtly culture that respected the caliph, especially before foreign visitors. Thus, Khunjī-Iṣfahānī's remarks may have been the result of his exposure to the culture of the court of Qāyitbāy, which posited the sultan's protection of the caliphate as a sign of his just rule.[149]

A final sixteenth-century perspective on the caliphate emerges from the sessions (*majālis*) recorded during the scholarly salons of one of Qāyitbāy's successors, the sultan Qāniṣawh al-Ghawrī, held several times a week in the Citadel's Duhaysha Hall. A series of meetings in 910–11/1505–6 were preserved as *Nafāʾis al-majālis al-sulṭāniyya*[150] by Ḥusayn ibn Muḥammad al-Ḥusaynī who, along with other Persian and Turkish intellectuals, held favour at al-Ghawrī's court.[151] The slightly later and anonymous *Kawkab al-durrī*, completed in 919/1513, offers highlights of the sultan's discussions and debates arranged by subject matter rather than by session as in the case of the *Nafāʾis*.[152]

Often beginning with a question posed by the sultan on a variety of topics, the *Nafāʾis* provides notable moments from the proceedings of each meeting. The comments ultimately offer idealised explanations and advice to the sultan. As Robert Irwin observed, the caliphate, in both its classical and contemporary incarnations was a starting point for many discussions at court and was addressed in both the *Nafāʾis* and the *Kawkab*. To shed light on the position of the contemporary caliphate, one seeming proponent of caliphal primacy, a courtier identified as 'Umm Abī al-Ḥasan', served as a kind of 'devil's advocate' in the text.[153] Umm Abī al-Ḥasan encouraged discussion of ḥadīth such as the Prophet's alleged statement that the caliphate would remain in the line of al-ʿAbbās until the Day of Judgement, as well as the so-called 'thirty years' ḥadīth in which the Prophet predicted the longevity of the 'true caliphate' until its devolution into *mulk* kingship.[154]

A general sampling of the meetings indicates an effort by several intimates of the sultan, including al-Ḥusaynī, to downplay the importance of the caliphate in favour of Qāniṣawh al-Ghawrī. The sultan himself raised questions about his own status and authority in relation to the caliph, and in one instance asked attendees to comment on who ought to march first in a funeral procession. Al-Ḥusaynī claimed that books of *fiqh* were unanimous that the sultan, followed by the qadis, must precede other dignitaries. Umm Abī al-Ḥasan, meanwhile, insisted on the caliph's priority.

Indeed, Umm Abī al-Ḥasan, after provocatively suggesting that the marriages and children of Muslims inhabiting lands in which rulers *did not* recognise the Abbasid Caliphate of Cairo were illegitimate, launched the company into a lengthy debate (*munāqisha*) on the caliphate and sultanate which occupied several sessions in Jumādā II-Rajab 911/November–December 1505. Hailing from the non-Arab lands of Greater Iran which knew no formal recognition of the Cairo caliph, al-Ḥusaynī was accused by some members of the court of being a child born of such fornication who should be ejected from the sultan's presence. The status of Muslim children and marriage conducted in lands that spurned or ignored the Cairene Abbasids consumed the discussion for some time. A fatwa was presented to the gathering, ruling that for any child or marriage to be legally recognisable by the *sharīʿa*, the king of that land must recognise the contemporary caliph of Cairo, al-Mustamsik bi-llāh. Several of the qadis found the fatwa objectionable, however, and suggested penalties for any strict adherents of it. The issue later irked Qāniṣawh al-Ghawrī when his courtiers suggested that even the marriages and children of Egypt could be considered invalid without the *baraka* and perpetual blessings secured by the presence of the Abbasid caliph. The sultan angrily demanded to know if the court considered *him* an inferior to the other sultans of the world.[155]

Concerning the caliphate, the sessions also treated the issue of whether the sultan derived glory (*fakhr*) from his position as deputy (*nāʾib*) of the caliph. Al-Ḥusaynī argued that although the ruler of Yemen was not formally the caliph's deputy, he still enjoyed glory and that the same should apply to the sultan of Egypt, who as possessor of the two holy shrines, derived authority and respect not from proximity to the caliph, but rather from the *sharīʿa*. Seeking clarity, al-Ghawrī asked about the status of Baybars after he received his robe of honour from the Abbasid caliph in the thirteenth century. Al-Ḥusaynī replied that Baybars had wished to strengthen the weakened position of the descendants of al-ʿAbbās and wore their robe to lend them his charisma, and that the glory of the caliph came from the fact that the sultan of Egypt honoured him by donning his robe. Umm Abī al-Ḥasan then remarked that if such a statement had been uttered in the presence of Qāyitbāy, that sultan would have promptly beheaded the offender – an assertion al-Ghawrī found exasperating.[156]

It is worth mentioning that numerous meetings adjourned with concluding words (*khātima*), in which the sultan received 'Commander of the Faithful' and 'Caliph of the Muslims' among his titles. In one instance, after the sultan had distributed bread to the poor, al-Ḥusaynī publicly addressed al-Ghawrī with the titles before calling him the best of the kings of the world.[157] In discussing the attributes of a noble ruler attributed to the theologian and jurist Abū Ḥāmid al-Ghazālī (d. 504/1111), al-Ḥusaynī gives thanks to God that 'these characteristics are present in the sultan of the world, caliph of the Arabs and non-Arabs . . . the sun of the caliphate . . . Commander of the Faithful and *imām* of the Muslims, Qāniṣawh al-Ghawrī'.[158] The *Nafāʾis* itself concludes with a special prayer for the sultan, identifying him as 'caliph of all who inhabit the world'.[159] The *Kawkab* similarly opens with praise for al-Ghawrī as both Commander of the Faithful and caliph of the Muslims.[160]

The question of addressing the king with caliphal titles is addressed later in the latter book when, after receiving a book of Mongol history from the Safavid Shāh Ismāʿīl containing a biographical notice naming a certain Shāhīn Beg Khān '*khalīfat al-raḥmān*', the sultan's court debated the issue of whether one could address a king as 'caliph'.[161] The consensus was that it was acceptable to refer to a king as Commander of the Faithful or *khalīfat al-rasūl*, but impermissible to use any appellation implying successorship to God, such as *khalīfat Allāh* or *khalīfat al-raḥmān*.[162]

Although later sultans of Cairo fantasised about using the titles associated with the caliphate or listened to courtly discussions that sought to restructure the hierarchy of caliphate and sultanate for their self-pride, Abbasid legitimacy remained an important part of sultanic investiture and ceremonial until the end of the sultanate in 1516–17. In his own dealings with the two caliphs of his reign, Qāniṣawh al-Ghawrī exercised ceremonial deference along with caution. He was certainly aware of the social pressure to behave generously with the caliph and provide monetary retribution to al-Mustamsik and financial aid for al-Mutawakkil III for fear, perhaps, that the former caliphs might publicly convey their displeasure with him. Nevertheless, it appears that when the sultan was alone with his court, he did not mind absorbing a great deal of caliphal pomp and listening to his courtiers expound upon the caliph's irrelevance for his own satisfaction. While we must take seriously the use of the caliphal titles by the sultan and his courtiers, to delete the Abbasid caliph from the political scene would have created more problems than it would have solved.

According to Laoust, the very presence of the caliph in Cairo might be explained as the result of a compromise among the jurisprudents, who, through *ijmā*ʾ consensus, adopted the necessity of a caliph of Qurayshī descent at the head of the community.[163] Although an office/idea of sometimes conflicted legitimacy, the caliphate held particular importance as an office to which the sultans themselves could never aspire due to the prerequisite of Qurayshī (or even Arab) descent, while an office such as the sultanate posed no such problems.[164] The centrality of discussions around the caliphate and sultanate thus ensured that both offices/ideas were in perpetual states of renegotiation between Traditionalist and Ashʿarī jurists of most Sunni schools: Shāfiʿīs (Ibn Jamāʿa, al-Subkī, al-Nuwayrī and al-Qalqashandī); Ḥanbalīs (Ibn Taymiyya); Mālikīs (al-Qarāfī and Ibn Khaldūn).[165] In these discussions, the authors presented a variety of positions, arguments, strategies and layouts for the mechanisms of power. Many of these interpretations were highly flexible and readily available to political actors to select the most useful presentation that best suited contemporary contexts according to wider conceptions of what was deemed morally and religiously acceptable.

Awareness of attitudes among the contemporary intelligentsia is essential to understanding how the caliphate had evolved by the fourteenth and fifteenth centuries and its ongoing evolution in Cairo. Many of the authors discussed in this chapter transmitted normative or prescriptive understandings of what the caliphal office *ought* to be along with the functions it should fulfil. Thirteenth-century works by al-Qarāfī and the unknown author of the *Miṣbāḥ al-hidāya* had not yet experienced the newly resurrected caliphate in the context of the Cairo Sultanate, and their authors wrote standard treatises reflecting concerns that the caliphate should not disrupt the burgeoning cooperation between the *dawla* of the sultan and the learned class of *ʿulamāʾ* and Sufis. Later authors wrote ambiguously of an undefined '*imām*' and recapitulated various views about the necessity of his descent from the Quraysh. Indeed, the treatises of the period seem to say more about the lasting paradigmatic influence of al-Māwardī than the true position of the modern caliphate in relation to the sultanate.[166]

That the caliph should bestow his powers on a strongman and continue as the nominal head of the religious community was an old idea by the late thirteenth century, and in many ways, the sultans of Cairo resembled a logical continuation of earlier Sunni political traditions predicated on Abbasid delegation.[167] As an office, the sultanate had developed at the height of eleventh-century Seljuk power and 'coexisted with [a] much reduced caliphate, intertwining loyalties and forcing a re-assessment of the purpose and structure of political power'.[168] In the late eleventh/early twelfth century, Abū Ḥāmid al-Ghazālī (d. 505/1111) believed that the caliph should no longer rule his subjects politically, and recognised that Muslims belonged to two communities: the first, led by the caliph, was the modern incarnation of the Prophet's *umma*; while the second, under the sultan, was the secular or political community that paid taxes and enjoyed military protection.[169] The sultan supplied the power, while the caliph symbolised the moral *raison d'être*. The sultan 'lent' power to the caliph and served as his executive (through *tafwīḍ*), thereby acknowledging that power came from beyond the religious institution.[170]

While it is impossible to argue that the caliph enjoyed more influence than the sultan, or indeed much practical influence at all, the *ʿulamāʾ* supported the notion that the caliphate must occupy *some* place in the government, though seldom did they venture into specifics. Scholars such as Ibn Taymiyya, Tāj al-Dīn al-Subkī and al-Qalqashandī were somewhat accommodating of the caliphal metamorphosis while also conscious of the demands of past ideals.[171] In short, they were interested in structuring their political visions around the caliphate, but not without it.

Writers linked to the political elites through official appointments might also have felt pressure to avoid an explicit definition of the caliph's role, lest it challenge the sultan's own prestige or position. As a result, many authors often enshrined the traditional investiture ceremony into their treatises and accepted the premise of the caliph's delegation of authority to the sultan as a point of departure. Few jurists or writers openly challenged the legitimacy of the Abbasid Caliphate so critical to the sultan's projection of himself as protector of Islam, Muslims and the caliphate.[172] There is no doubt that the *ʿulamāʾ* outfitted the sultans of Cairo with legitimacy, and in the context of their rule, the caliph was partially recast as a scholar and private individual, rather than the traditional '*imām*' described in the treatises of al-Māwardī or even Ibn Jamāʿa.[173] The relationship of terminology, particularly the subtle differences between 'imamate' and 'caliphate', deserves further attention from future studies. Although on the surface level, the words appear interchangeable in some texts of advice literature, '*imām*' tends to be a more ambiguous open term that sometimes has a one-on-one relationship with the caliphate and elsewhere does not. In terms of the 'imamate by coercion', it is sometimes unclear whether authors such as Ibn Jamāʿa address the position of the caliph or the sultan. In most cases it appears to be the latter, but '*imām*', a somewhat peculiar and open signifier, is deeply meaningful while simultaneously flexible.[174]

Few religious scholars believed that the contemporary caliph should lead in the temporal sphere; most expressed their great satisfaction, or at least their resignation, to the status quo that formally delegated caliphal duties to the sultan. The imamate, as it had been understood in classical times, had been theoretically reconfigured as a sultanate and caliphate working as separate parts of a single mechanism, a schema tolerable to many scholars including Ibn ʿAbd al-Ẓāhir, Ibn Jamāʿa and Ibn Taymiyya, as long as Islamic obligations were serviced by the arrangement. Earlier authors such as al-Māwardī and Nāṣir al-Dīn al-Ṭūṣī (d. 672/1274) conceived of a far more complex and far-reaching image of an imamate that managed an apparatus including the wazirate, the judiciary, leadership in prayer, organisation of warfare, tax collection, alms distribution, public order (*ḥisba*), redress of grievance courts (*maẓālim*), various delegated functionaries among the men of the sword, men of the pen, and men of the turban, the networks of advice and intelligence available to the ruler, as well as the merchants and farmers, all of whom played a part.[175] The various *dīwān*s at the ruler's disposal were also an aspect of his imamate/caliphate, and the chancery likewise contributed to the wider notion of caliphate.[176] This inclusive vision was maintained in the fourteenth and fifteenth centuries by later compilers and historians such as al-Nuwayrī, al-Qalqashandī, Ibn Khaldūn and Ibn Taghrībirdī who had accepted the reduced status of the caliphate as an ongoing reality in their own time and continued to endow the term with meaning whenever they used it.[177]

Another Taymiyyan position, seemingly favoured by newly arrived outsiders or quasi-independents such as Ibn Khaldūn or al-Maqrīzī (see Chapter 7), was that unless the caliph was a participant in actual power, the institution as it stood in Cairo, was not a caliphate in the classical sense, a position no doubt enjoying broader support at times when the political order established by the sultan was seen to have stumbled or become oppressive. Such authors observed the caliphs from a cautious distance and took a pragmatic stance towards them in their writing. Historians like Ibn Khaldūn and al-Maqrīzī who idealised the Rāshidūn-era caliphate remained ambivalent about the Cairo Caliphate, implying in their writings that such a caliphate, while acceptable, was not the most desirable situation. For such thinkers the status quo sufficed only until a better form of Islamic leadership (presumably one in line with 'prophetic caliphate' or the ideals and practices of the Rāshidūn caliphs) might manifest itself.[178]

Legal texts and juristic literature were intended to communicate rules and norms for ideal Muslim behaviour, and as a result, could often impact the ways in which the caliphate was represented and written about in historiography.[179] It is this presentation of the Abbasid Caliphate of Cairo in contemporary historical writing that the next chapter treats in further detail.

Notes

1. Hassan, *Longing for the Lost Caliphate*, 108–41.
2. For an overview of some of the issues at stake, see Bori, 'Theology, Politics, Society'.
3. Crone, *God's Rule*, 220.
4. Berkey, *Transmission of Knowledge*; Holtzman, *Anthropomorphism in Islam.*

On these debates in the thirteenth and fourteenth centuries, see Mirza, 'Ibn Kathīr', 6–156; Fancy, *Science and Religion*, 20–7, 30–5.

5. Hassan, *Longing for the Lost Caliphate* 19, 259.
6. Moin, *Millennial Sovereign*, 14–17.
7. Madelung, 'Treatise'.
8. Ibid., 92–7.
9. Ibid., 95.
10. Ibid., 101–2.
11. Al-Qarāfī, *Iḥkām fī tamyīz al-fatāwā*, 13–14; al-Qarāfī/Fadel, *Criterion*, 4–9; Jackson, 'Shihāb al-Dīn al-Ḳarāfī'; Jackson, 'Primacy of Domestic Politics', 58.
12. Jackson, 'Prophetic Action', 81–2.
13. Ibid., 83.
14. Ibid., 85–6. Mohammad Fadel has recently challenged Jackson's thesis that al-Qarāfī sought to limit the caliph's power, see al-Qarāfī/Fadel, *Criterion*, 38–45.
15. Fouchécour, *Moralia*, 357–453; Crone, *God's Rule*, 153.
16. Ḥasan al-ʿAbbāsī, *Āthār al-uwal*, 22–3.
17. 'O you who believe: Obey God and obey the Messenger, and those among you who are in authority. (And) if you differ in anything amongst yourselves, refer it to God and His Messenger, if you believe in God and in the Last Day. That is better and more suitable for final determination.'
18. Ḥasan al-ʿAbbāsī, *Āthār al-uwal*, 90–4.
19. Ibid., 57.
20. Hassan, *Longing for the Lost Caliphate*, 110–11.
21. 'O David, verily we have made you caliph on the earth, so judge between the people in truth and do not follow [your own] desire, as it will lead you astray from the path of God.'
22. Ḥasan al-ʿAbbāsī, *Āthār al-uwal*, 67. For a discussion of Ḥasan al-ʿAbbāsī's views on succession, a sensitive issue in the light of Baybars al-Jāshinkīr's usurpation of the Qalawunid household by his displacement of al-Nāṣir Muḥammad, see Bauden, 'Sons of al-Nāṣir Muḥammad', 56–7; Marlow, 'Kings, Prophets, and the ʿUlamāʾ'.
23. Ḥasan al-ʿAbbāsī, *Āthār al-uwal*, 100.
24. Ibid., 111.
25. Ibid., 116–18.
26. Ibid., 130–3.
27. Ibid., 144–95.

28. Ibid., 144–7, 150, 168–76.
29. Hirschler, 'Islam', 277–8; Muhanna, 'Fourteenth Century'.
30. On the contents and arrangement of the work see Muhanna, *World in a Book*, 1, 29–42, 145–52.
31. Al-Nuwayrī likewise appropriates the wisdom of Aristotle, the Sasanian kings and the *Nahj al-balāgha* attributed to ʿAlī ibn Abī Ṭālib. For a comprehensive listing of sources used by al-Nuwayrī in books (*funūn*) 1, 3 and 4 of the *Nihāya*, see Muhanna, *World in a Book*, 65–70.
32. Al-Nuwayrī, *Nihāya*, 6:1–2.
33. Ibid., 6:4–5.
34. Ibid., 6:5.
35. Ibid., 6:9–10, 12.
36. Ibid., 6:16.
37. Ibid., 6:33–9.
38. Ibn Jamāʿa, *Taḥrīr al-aḥkām*. On Ibn Jamāʿa's scholarly contribution and the career of his family, see Nielsen, *Secular Justice*, 68–71; Salibi, 'Banū Jamāʿa'; Lambton, *State and Government*, 138–43.
39. Anjum, 'Ibn Jamāʿah'.
40. See Chapter 2 above.
41. Ibn Jamāʿa, *Taḥrīr al-aḥkām*, 6:355–74; Jackson, *Mongols and the Islamic World*, 322.
42. Tezcan, 'Hanafism and the Turks', 71.
43. Madelung, 'Treatise', 102.
44. Hassan, *Longing for the Lost Caliphate*, 103–7, 109–10; Jackson, *Mongols and the Islamic World*, 322.
45. Ibn Jamāʿa, *Taḥrīr al-aḥkām*, 6:358–9, 369–74; Hassan, *Longing for the Lost Caliphate*, 110.
46. Hassan, *Longing for the Lost Caliphate*, 110–11; Jackson, *Mongols and the Islamic World*, 322.
47. Ibn Jamāʿa, *Taḥrīr al-aḥkām*, 6:359–63; Al-Azmeh, *Muslim Kingship*, 185.
48. Ibn Jamāʿa, *Taḥrīr al-aḥkām*, 6:360–1; Hassan, *Longing for the Lost Caliphate*, 110.
49. Hassan, *Longing for the Lost Caliphate*, 111.
50. Ibid., 14, 17.
51. Ibid., 111.
52. Ibid., 110.

53. Al-Dhahabī, *Ta'rīkh*, 48:81; al-Ṣafadī, *Wāfī*, 6:318; al-Suyūṭī, *Ta'rīkh*, 383; Hassan, *Longing for the Lost Caliphate*, 76; Heidemann, *Kalifat*, 21, 25.
54. Bori, 'Pensiero politico', 65; Malkawi and Sonn, 'Ibn Taymiyya', 121.
55. Hassan, *Longing for the Lost Caliphate*, 111–12; Hassan, 'Modern Interpretations', 340–3. Cf. Laoust, *Essai*, 282–3.
56. Hassan, *Longing for the Lost Caliphate*, 112; Hassan, 'Modern Interpretations', 339–40; Anjum, *Politics*, 28, 253, 257; Bori, 'Pensiero politico', 61–2; Bori, 'Théologie politique,' 10–15; Khan, *Political Thought*, 129.
57. Translation from Anjum, *Politics*, 257.
58. Hassan, 'Modern Interpretations', 342, 346, 354; Bori, 'Pensiero politico', 58; Malkawi and Sonn, 'Ibn Taymiyya', 121; Lambton, *State and Government*, 144.
59. Anjum, *Politics*, 26.
60. Malkawi and Sonn, 'Ibn Taymiyya', 112; Khan, *Political Thought*, 41.
61. Hassan, 'Modern Interpretations', 339; Bori, 'Théologie politique', 21–2.
62. Hassan, *Longing for the Lost Caliphate*, 112–13; Hassan, 'Modern Interpretations', 345; Anjum, *Politics*, 265; Hoover, *Ibn Taymiyya*, 96.
63. Bori, 'Pensiero politico', 65.
64. Ibid.; Anjum, *Politics*, 246.
65. Anjum, *Politics*, 27, 196.
66. Ibid., 244–9.
67. Hassan, *Longing for the Lost Caliphate*, 114–15; Hassan, 'Modern Interpretations', 346; Bori, 'Pensiero politico', 62–4. For an application of Ibn Taymiyya's thought to the performance of the caliphate and sultanate in Egypt, see Bori, 'Théologie politique', 30–8.
68. Khan, *Political Thought*, 107.
69. Hassan, *Longing for the Lost Caliphate*, 112–14; Anjum, *Politics*, 259.
70. Anjum, *Politics*, 258–60, 265. For Ibn Taymiyya, legitimacy was linked to the practical ability to uphold the *sharīʿa*. See also Hirschler, *Medieval Arabic Historiography*, 111–12.
71. Anjum, *Politics*, 250, 258–60, 265; Bori, 'Pensiero politico', 60.
72. The authority of the Sunni caliph originated from the community he ruled, because of his ability to provide law, order and defence. See Anjum, *Politics*, 261–4; Woods, *Aqquyunlu*, 5–6; Gibb, 'Constitutional Organization', 3–4.
73. Hassan, *Longing for the Lost Caliphate*, 114–15; Hassan, 'Modern Interpretations', 349–50; Bori, 'Théologie politique', 31; Khan, *Political Thought*, 145–6.

74. Hassan, *Longing for the Lost Caliphate*, 112–13; Anjum, *Politics*, 255–7; Hoover, *Ibn Taymiyya*, 93–4.
75. See Hassan, *Longing for the Lost Caliphate*, 118–20; Khalidi, *Arabic Historical Thought*, 187; Marmon, 'Quality of Mercy', 133–4. Further evidence of the enduring influence of earlier eastern advice literature in medieval Cairo comes from the curious binding of an eleventh-century manuscript ascribed to al-Māwardī together with an original manuscript of al-Subkī's *Muʿīd*, see Marlow, 'A Samanid Work'.
76. Hassan, *Longing for the Lost Caliphate*, 119.
77. Tāj al-Dīn al-Subkī, *Muʿīd*, 23.
78. Ibid., 24.
79. Hassan, *Longing for the Lost Caliphate*, 119.
80. Tāj al-Dīn al-Subkī, *Muʿīd*, 25–7.
81. Hassan, *Longing for the Lost Caliphate*, 119–20; Khalidi, *Arabic Historical Thought*, 196; Mājid, *Nuẓum*, 1:29; Laoust, *Essai*, 46.
82. Ibn Khaldūn, *Taʿrīf bi-Ibn Khaldūn*, 254; Ibn Taghrībirdī, *Manhal*, 7:207–8.
83. Irwin, *Ibn Khaldun*, 58.
84. Ibid., 92–3; Hassan, *Longing for the Lost Caliphate*, 123–4; Fischel, *Ibn Khaldūn in Egypt*, 4.
85. Ibn Khaldūn, *Muqaddima*, 156–7, 184–333. See Cheddadi, *Ibn Khaldûn*, 297–357.
86. Ibn Khaldūn, *Muqaddima*, 73–5, 221–62, 417–68; Gibb, 'Islamic Background', 30; Hassan, *Longing for the Lost Caliphate*, 124; Cheddadi, *Ibn Khaldûn*, 341.
87. Cheddadi, *Ibn Khaldûn*, 338, 343–4.
88. Ibn Khaldūn, *Muqaddima*, 219; Cheddadi, *Ibn Khaldûn*, 342–4.
89. Ibn Khaldūn, *Taʾrīkh*, 5:438–42; Martinez-Gros, *Ibn Khaldûn*, 222–3. For lengthier treatments of Ibn Khaldūn's remarks on slavery and the *mamlūk* training process, see Van Steenbergen, ''Aṣabiyya, Messiness'; Irwin, *Ibn Khaldun*, 87–8; Little, 'Religion under the Mamluks', 165–7; Ayalon, 'Mamlūkīyyat', 340–9; Ayalon, 'Mamlūks and Ibn Xaldūn', 11–13.
90. Ibn Khaldūn, *Muqaddima*, 195–6.
91. Ibid., 217–18.
92. On the work's structure, see Martinez-Gros, *Ibn Khaldûn*, 107–10.
93. Ibn Khaldūn, *Taʾrīkh*, 5:454–5, 493, 524.
94. Hassan, *Longing for the Lost Caliphate*, 85–7; Cobb, 'Al-Maqrīzī', 69.
95. Ibn Khaldūn, *Taʾrīkh*, 5:454–5.

96. Ibn Khaldūn, *Taʿrīf bi-Ibn Khaldūn*, 329–31; Ibn Taghrībirdī, *Nujūm*, 11:360–1; Onimus, *Les maîtres du jeu*, 134, 185–7, 306; Irwin, *Ibn Khaldun*, 91; Hassan, *Longing for the Lost Caliphate*, 92, 124–5. For analysis of Ibn Khaldūn's post-Ayyubid coverage of the sultanate of Cairo down to his own time, see Martinez-Gros, *Ibn Khaldûn*, 222–30.
97. Hassan, *Longing for the Lost Caliphate*, 125–6; Banister, 'Sword in the Caliph's Service', 10–11; Fischel, *Ibn Khaldūn in Egypt*, 57–8.
98. Hassan, *Longing for the Lost Caliphate*, 124–5.
99. Ibid., 92–3, 125.
100. Ibid., 125–6; Anjum, *Politics*, 255–7.
101. Berkey, 'Mamluk Religious Policy', 12.
102. Ibn Khaldūn, *Muqaddima*, 225–7.
103. Irwin, *Ibn Khaldun*, 95, 103–7; Cheddadi, *Ibn Khaldûn*, 344–5.
104. Al-Qalqashandī, *Ṣubḥ*, 5:444–7; al-Qalqashandī, *Maʾāthir*, 1:8–12, 17–29; Hassan, *Longing for the Lost Caliphate*, 127; Broadbridge, 'Diplomatic Conventions', 105; Bosworth, 'al-Ḳalḳashandī'.
105. Al-Qalqashandī, *Ṣubḥ*, 5:444, 9:263.
106. Ibid., 6:47, 65, 108, 113. On this title see the discussion in Chapter 8.
107. Ibid. 6:47, 108–9, 113–14.
108. Al-Qalqashandī, *Maʾāthir*, 1:29–80; Hassan, *Longing for the Lost Caliphate*, 128–31.
109. Al-Qalqashandī, *Ṣubḥ*, 1:31; al-Qalqashandī, *Maʾāthir*, 1:1. Before al-Qalqashandī, the chancery chief Ibn Faḍlallāh al-ʿUmarī identified Cairo, because of the presence of the caliph and the righteous scholars, with such epithets as '*umm al-mamālik*', '*ḥāḍirat al-bilād*' and '*dār al-khilāfa*'. See *Taʿrīf*, 2:247. The theme of Egypt's pre-eminence as the seat of the caliphate is revisited in the late fifteenth century by al-Suyūṭī as well as Abū Ḥāmid al-Qudsī (d. 888/1483) who identifies Egypt, thanks to the presence of the Abbasid caliph, as 'Heartland of Islam'. See Van Steenbergen, 'Mamlukisation', 18; Irwin, *Ibn Khaldun*, 85–7; Hassan, *Longing for the Lost Caliphate*, 127; Broadbridge, 'Diplomatic Conventions', 101, 106; Chapoutot-Remadi, 'Liens et relations', 60 ; Haarmann, 'Rather the Injustice', 63–4; Laoust, *Essai*, 46.
110. Al-Qalqashandī, *Maʾāthir*, 1:3.
111. Al-Qalqashandī, *Ṣubḥ*, 11:72–3. See also Hassan, *Longing for the Lost Caliphate*, 129; Sourdel, 'Khalīfah'; Tyan, *Institutions du droit public musulman*, 2:220–1.
112. Northrup, 'Baḥrī Mamlūk Sultanate', 255; Gaudefroy-Demombynes, *La Syrie à l'époque des mamelouks*, xxix.

113. Hassan, *Longing for the Lost Caliphate*, 128–9.
114. Vermeulen, 'La *bay'a* califale', 301.
115. Al-Qalqashandī, *Ma'āthir*, 1:39–48.
116. Ibid., 1:74–80.
117. Hassan, *Longing for the Lost Caliphate*, 107.
118. Al-Qalqashandī, *Ṣubḥ*, 3:273–4.
119. See Al-Azmeh, *Muslim Kingship*, 145–6, 149, 151–2.
120. Al-Qalqashandī, *Ma'āthir*, 1:29–30. For al-Māwardī's conditions for the imamate, see *Al-Aḥkām al-sulṭāniyya*, 5–24.
121. Hassan, *Longing for the Lost Caliphate*, 128.
122. Al-Qalqashandī, *Ma'āthir*, 1:2, 37–9.
123. I thank Ovamir Anjum for sharing this observation. See also Bori, 'Pensiero politico', 51–6; Broadbridge, 'Diplomatic Conventions', 105–6; Al-Azmeh, *Muslim Kingship*, 180–3; Haarmann, 'Rather the Injustice', 63; Holt, 'Structure of Government', 52–3; Lambton, *State and Government*, 139. For comment on Roy Mottahedeh's discussion of loyalty in the Buyid period compared with late medieval Syro-Egypt, see Irwin, 'Factions in Medieval Egypt', 237.
124. Al-Qalqashandī, *Ṣubḥ*, 3:275–6.
125. On the selection of the caliph, see *Ṣubḥ*, 9:252. On the *bay'a* in general, see *Ṣubḥ*, 9:273–319; Vermeulen, 'La *bay'a* califale', 296–300.
126. Al-Qalqashandī, *Ma'āthir*, 1:42–5.
127. Hassan, *Longing for the Lost Caliphate*, 128.
128. Vermeulen, 'La *bay'a* califale', 301.
129. Hassan, *Longing for the Lost Caliphate*, 127.
130. Khalīl al-Ẓahirī, *Zubdat*, 3–7. On Khalīl al-Ẓāhirī's contribution to medieval Egyptian cultural and administrative history, see Herzog, *Geschichte und Imaginaire*, 344–5; Bori, 'Théologie politique', 37–8, 45; Holt, 'Some Observations', 504–5; Holt, *Age of Crusades*, 150; Becker, 'Barthold's Studien', 370–1.
131. Khalīl al-Ẓāhirī, *Zubdat*, 58–9.
132. Ibid., 66–7.
133. Ibid., 86.
134. Ibid., 89–92.
135. Ibid., 89.
136. On this popular anxiety of the times, see Hassan, *Longing for the Lost Caliphate*, 102–3, 135; Crone, *God's Rule*, 238–9; Chapoutot-Remadi, 'Liens et relations', 51; Holt, 'Structure of Government', 44.

137. Al-Maqrīzī, *Sulūk*, 4:487–8; Ibn Taghrībirdī, *Nujūm*, 14:77–8; Ibn Iyās, *Badāʾiʿ*, 2:46, 282, 395.
138. Binbaş, *Intellectual Networks*, 114–64; Markiewicz, *Crisis of Kingship*, 106–10.
139. Haarmann, 'Khundjī'. On Khunjī-Iṣfahānī's role as the court historian of Yaʿqūb ibn Uzun Ḥasan, see Woods, *Aqquyunlu*, 220. On the influence of al-Māwardī and Ibn Jamāʿa on Khunjī-Iṣfahānī, see Markiewicz, *Crisis of Kingship*, 243–6.
140. Haarmann, 'Khundjī'.
141. Haarmann, 'Yeomanly Arrogance', 112–13, 120.
142. Ibid. See also Khunjī-Iṣfahānī, *Taʾrīkh*, 187–8.
143. Haarmann, 'Yeomanly Arrogance', 120; Khunjī-Iṣfahānī, *Taʾrīkh*, 191.
144. Haarmann, 'Yeomanly Arrogance', 112, 119; Haarmaan, 'Khundjī'.
145. Haarmann, 'Yeomanly Arrogance', 117–20; Lambton, *State and Government*, 179–200; Khunjī-Iṣfahānī, *Taʾrīkh*, 191; Khunjī-Iṣfahānī, *Sulūk al-mulūk*, 214.
146. Haarmann, 'Yeomanly Arrogance', 120.
147. Lambton, *State and Government*, 199.
148. Haarmann, 'Yeomanly Arrogance', 120.
149. Irwin, 'Political Thinking', 47.
150. Through his use of the title '*Nafāʾis al-majālis*' al-Ḥusaynī may have been engaging in a shared literary exchange with the '*Majālis al-nafāʾis*', an earlier compendium of poetry written by rulers and other notables compiled by the Timurid adviser, poet and cultural figure, Mīr ʿAlī Shīr Navāʾī (d. 906/1501). Numerous works from the period referred directly or indirectly to other works through their text and titles. For a general discussion of intertextuality in late medieval Syro-Egypt, see Bauer, 'Mamluk Literature as a Means of Communication'; Van Steenbergen, *Caliphate and Kingship*, 82.
151. Markiewicz, *Crisis of Kingship*, 108–10; Irwin, 'Political Thinking', 37–8.
152. Partial editions of both works have been published together (and paginated separately) as *Majālis al-Sulṭān al-Ghawrī: ṣafaḥāt min taʾrīkh Miṣr fī qarn al-ʿāshir hijrī*, ed. ʿA. ʿAzzām (Cairo, 1941). For an extensive study of the *majālis* literature and court of sultan al-Ghawrī, see Mauder, 'In the Sultan's Salon'.
153. I thank Christian Mauder for sharing this observation.
154. Al-Ḥusaynī, *Nafāʾis*, 103–4, 107.

155. Ibid., 100–13.
156. Ibid., 110–11; Irwin, 'Political Thinking', 47.
157. Al-Ḥusaynī, *Nafāʾis*, 55, 66, 69.
158. Ibid., 86–7.
159. Ibid., 145.
160. *Kawkab*, 2.
161. There is no further information about this 'Shāhīn Beg', though it may be a reference to the Özbek ruler Muḥammad Shaybānī Khān (d. 915/1510). See also Irwin, 'Political Thinking', 47.
162. *Kawkab*, 73–4.
163. Laoust, *Essai*, 45.
164. Chamberlain, *Knowledge*, 49–50; Bulliet, 'History of the Muslim South', 63; Bulliet, 'Neo-Mamluk Legitimacy', 63; Brinner, 'Struggle for Power', 233.
165. Cf. Hassan, *Longing for the Lost Caliphate*, 108–41; Hirschler, *Medieval Arabic Historiography*, 110–14.
166. Markiewicz, *Crisis of Kingship*, 246; Al-Azmeh, *Muslim Kingship*, 93, 106–7, 170; Lambton, *State and Government*, 139, 142. See also Hassan, *Longing for the Lost Caliphate*, 111, 122, 128–9, 134–5.
167. Hassan, *Longing for the Lost Caliphate*, 23, 110, 129–30, 203; Lev, 'Symbiotic Relations', 12–13; Holt, 'Structure of Government', 46; Tyan, *Institutions du droit public musulman*, 2:219–21; Gaudefroy-Demombynes, *La Syrie à l'époque des mamelouks*, xxix.
168. Khalidi, *Arabic Historical Thought*, 183.
169. Crone, *God's Rule*, 240–4. See also Hassan, *Longing for the Lost Caliphate*, 102.
170. Ibid. See also Lambton, *State and Government*, 112.
171. Hassan, *Longing for the Lost Caliphate*, 111–15, 118–20, 126–31.
172. Aigle, *Mongol Empire*, 245; Bori, 'Théologie politique', 31–2; Holt, 'Position and Power', 247.
173. Banister, 'ʿ*Ālim*-Caliph'; Hassan, *Longing for the Lost Caliphate*, 111; Broadbridge, *Kingship and Ideology*, 14.
174. An interesting case in point is Van Steenbergen's study of the panegyric for the sultan al-Ṣāliḥ Ismāʿīl, in which the scribe Ibn al-Qaysarānī identifies the sultan as 'the imam, son of the imam, son of the imam'. See 'Qalāwūnid Discourse', 8.
175. Al-Māwardī, *Al-Aḥkām al-sulṭāniyya*, 25–33, 43–67, 83–119, 299–322; al-Ṭūsī, *Nasirean Ethics*, 226–42.
176. Hassan, *Longing for the Lost Caliphate*, 126–31.

177. Cf. Ibn Taghrībirdī, *Nujūm*, 14:369.
178. Hassan, *Longing for the Lost Caliphate*, 112–13; Anjum, *Politics*, 255–7; Al-Azmeh, *Muslim Kingship*, 165
179. Van Steenbergen, *Caliphate and Kingship*, 55, 58.

7

The Cairo Caliphate in Medieval Arabic Historiographical Literature

Introduction

The 'political literature' addressed in the previous chapter is typically approached by modern historians as the main source for the political thinking of jurists and authors of advice literature. As Konrad Hirschler has demonstrated, however, many chronicles and works of historiography, although typically avoiding explicit legalistic statements, nevertheless regularly offer relevant insights, normative statements on politics and even advice for rulers.[1]

Building on the perspectives of authors of the prescriptive literature surveyed in Chapter 6, the current chapter further engages with contemporary scholarly opinions in order to enhance the history of the Cairene Abbasid dynasty covered in Part One. By examining an array of descriptions composed by the professional classes, yet another multifaceted perception of the Cairo Caliphate emerges. Members of both the military and civilian elite wrote on a multitude of topics whether discussing the organisation of government or chronicling the history of Islam down to their own times. It is therefore difficult to distinguish between so-called *ʿulamāʾ* and bureaucrats, since it was commonplace for a 'bureaucrat' working in the administration to have formal training in Islamic sciences, just as a doctor of the religious law might hold an official government posting.[2] Authors of historical works described the social practices involved in the performance of the caliphate and occasionally offered commentary. Encyclopaedists and authors such as al-Nuwayrī and Ibn Khaldūn discussed the imamate and caliphate within broader works that also included historical writing. The line between religious scholar and court secretary was thus frequently blurred and vocational overlap was routine. Scholars and litterateurs from all vocations and backgrounds wrote historical works, which forces any categorisation to remain tentative at best.

Later Medieval Arabic Historical Writing

For a variety of reasons, the Syrian, Egyptian and Hijazi territories of the Cairo Sultanate experienced an explosion in the creation and consumption of Arabic historiographical texts during the late fourteenth and fifteenth centuries. The works themselves were often intended to serve a performative purpose that went beyond mere attempts at preserving the past in narrative forms.[3] According to Tarif Khalidi, chroniclers compiled their texts against the backdrop of increased self-consciousness and cooperation between the *ʿulamāʾ* and the political class. Authors of historical works scrutinised the governing classes and allowed the *ʿulamāʾ* to figure prominently in the historical narrative through biography. Histories penned by the religious elite permitted a version of their proper, *sharīʿ* worldview, while Khalidi's '*siyāsa*-oriented' historiography, characterising the Arabic historical writings of the eleventh to fifteenth centuries, remained distinct for its tendency to focus heavily on issues of governance and a ruler's ability to preserve the polity. Such historical writing may have been predisposed towards de-emphasising the theological considerations at the core of '*sharīʿa*-oriented' historiography. Historians of the latter category often took pains to burnish immediate moral or didactic (or *ʿibar*) meanings from the historical narrative to 'provide a moral service and also entertain', all while underscoring God's authority and Islam's veracity before the political elites as well as the community at large.[4]

Hirschler argues that the social profile of historians underwent changes during the Islamic Middle Period, and historiography thus became increasingly self-conscious and self-confident. An increased authorial presence became the norm in historical texts of the period as authors, engaging with increasingly presentist concerns, began to realise that they were chronicling the events of an unprecedented present.[5] Late medieval Syro-Egyptian historians, steeped in the Islamic tradition, frequently composed annals of events in their own lifetimes that were subsequently appended to larger universal histories or general histories of Islam. Many historians became interested in chronicling everyday life and different sectors of the population. Indeed, regardless of the caliph's diminished public role, medieval Arabic historians seldom failed to demonstrate awareness of the Abbasid Caliphate in their coverage of contemporary events. The chroniclers and historians of the Cairo Sultanate were the heirs of classical Arabic historiography with its wide array of interests, literary forms and subjects, including both justification for the caliphate and celebration of its longest-reigning family. Joining with the religious scholars, they picked up and elaborated upon the discourses and debates of their predecessors as well as the rich tradition of Abbasid hagiography carried forward into their own time. [6]

In his discussion of architecture and a 'Mamluk collective memory', Nasser Rabbat commented upon the subtle influence that the establishment of the Cairo Caliphate, along with other early political milestones, may have had upon historical writing:

> [The Mamluk state] had very swiftly defeated the Crusaders and Mongols, asserted its rule over all the Syro-Egyptian territories, and devised a new caliphal legitimacy with the installation of an Abbasid caliph in Cairo after the annihilation of the Baghdadi caliphate by the Mongols in 1258. The culture reacted to these Mamluk victories with renewed hope of recapturing the glorious past and reviving the true caliphate after two centuries of uncertainty, a feeling which lasted well into the fifteenth century. It was reflected in the reorientation of Mamluk historical writing towards a pan-Islamic outlook reminiscent of the writing of the eighth- and ninth-century historians who lived under an at least nominally unified Islamic world. Thus, an entire generation of Mamluk historians – including al-ʿUmarī and al-Nuwayrī in Cairo and Ibn Kathīr and al-Dhahabī in Damascus – adopted a universal and upbeat approach and covered the entire Islamic world in their writing.[7]

By further utilising the analytical concept of collective memory in regard to the Abbasid Caliphate in historiography, Mona Hassan found that historical writing was crucial for the preservation of communal memories and that four interconnected forms of history: narrative, discursive, embodied and artistic, comprised the main vehicle of Muslim collective memory. Combining the mundane with the religious, the caliphate's cultural history gathered sacred, secular and metaphysical elements to bestow the institution with a potent symbolism and profound cultural resonance that spanned regions and centuries.[8]

Indeed, among the long-standing forms and structures inherited by fourteenth- and fifteenth-century Arabic historiography, the Abbasid Caliphate often proved to be vital as a precondition for organisation. Several chroniclers, including Ibn Khaldūn, frequently broke their continuous narrative format to devote separate sections to the detailing of events connected to the caliphate or simply to announce the succession of a new caliph. Beginning new annals by naming the reigning Abbasid caliph was a well-known convention among Muslim historians long before the late medieval sultanate of Cairo. In many ways, the Abbasid Caliphate imposed order on the way historiographers approached their craft. Like their predecessors, many Syro-Egyptian chroniclers were committed to recording trivia and minutiae about the contemporary caliphs, such as disparities in lineage, the establishment of various precedents, unique given names, origins for regnal titles, and the longest and shortest caliphal reigns.[9]

Even in instances in which historians described a caliph as little more than a prisoner of the Citadel, no author ever explicitly expressed the situation in terms of the caliphs, as representatives of an anachronistic institution, merely providing a crass legitimisation of newcomers to the sultanate. Indeed, only in modern times are scholars at liberty to surmise that insecure slave-kings exploited the Abbasid family to provide a faith-based gloss to their oligarchy. Whether or not the scholars of medieval Egypt and Syria privately *agreed* with this estimation, all but a few refrained from even approaching the subject. To their dismay, many fourteenth- and fifteenth-century writers fully recognised that the contemporary caliphs were very different from their distant idealised predecessors of the early Islamic period. Even so, as authors of historical works, they could scarcely ignore the prevailing socio-political climate.

If the sultan and his entourage sought to acquire a theocratic nature for their authority through courting the religious class, the latter were likewise aware that they had much to gain from lending their support, whether lucrative careers, new opportunities to please God by serving the *umma* or a combination of both.[10] Ripples of a possible symbiosis emerge in the historiography of bureaucrats, military men and religious scholars. Many writers, intentionally or not, disseminated a somewhat official view of history the sultans sought to promote, or one that cast them above all as 'protectors' of Islam and the caliphate which deliberately connected them to previous political orders.[11]

Finally, lists of late medieval rulers and officials, preserved in Arabic historiographical sources from the thirteenth to sixteenth centuries and examined by Jo Van Steenbergen, reveal a 'careful hierarchical construction around the sultanate of Cairo, and very often also the Abbasid Caliphate of Cairo', which present the sultanate as an integrated time and space rather than as perpetually changing groups and network configurations in flux.[12] It is in repeating these lists at the start of each year, often beginning with the caliph and sultan, that authors spoke to a specific audience of power-holders and conveyed intentional meanings.

Regional and Occupational Considerations

As a cultural practice, late medieval Arabic historiography is characterised by its high degree of intertextuality. Numerous groups of interrelated authors and texts appear to be in dialogue with each other, share and refer to each other's work, and attempt to provide correctives and supplements to earlier works. Clusters of historians emerged in geographic locales, typically urban centres, and sometimes among students of the same master. Organising studies of fourteenth- and fifteenth-century Arabic historiography into regional groupings has proven to be useful in mapping similarities in the works that suggest the influence of similar backgrounds. In Cairo, the heart of the sultanate, claims and propaganda involving the Abbasid Caliphate were the most vociferous. Modern scholars have pinpointed a distinct Egyptocentrism to the works produced by the Cairo-based Arabic-speaking historians of the later fifteenth century.[13] For these authors, Cairo was nothing less than the *umm al-dunyā*, the 'mother of the world', dwarfing all other competing centres in Islamdom. Close coverage of the Abbasids among later Cairo-based historians suggests that by the late fifteenth century, public appearances made by the caliphs were a natural part of urban life in Egypt.

Despite a wealth of contemporary source material, it remains more challenging to gauge the tone of Abbasid symbolism in early fourteenth-century Syrian historiography. Religious scholars who also wrote history were more oriented towards the totality of Islamic history, particularly its origins, and their interests often transcended the immediate realities of Cairene politics. Nevertheless, their works betray many hints of how people in their region accepted and received the performance of the caliphate and its Abbasid office holders in Cairo.

Of increased importance to gauging the role and agency of historiographical works is the historicising of both authors and texts to understand the context in which the text was produced and the social worlds in which the author participated.[14] The organisation of this chapter reflects socio-economic and geographic contexts among a select group of authors. It is difficult to shoehorn authors into watertight categories or assume that a shared vocation or environment implied identical attitudes about religio-political institutions such as the contemporary Abbasid Caliphate. The following survey places focus on a sampling of authors who present discernible insight into the Cairo Caliphate from the late thirteenth to the early sixteenth centuries. While many authors offer little if any such insight into the institution, others have written enough on the contemporary caliphate to make their collective writings, whether historical asides or specialised biographical entries, a worthwhile object of analysis.

Discipline, geography and chronology are points of departure in a search for patterns amongst groupings of authors. Later writers certainly had the advantage of hindsight, nostalgia and first-hand experience of the Cairo Caliphate to ruminate upon, whereas the majority of authors who died prior to or during the 730s/1330s tended to discuss only Baybars and the first two Abbasid investiture ceremonies in Cairo. By the early sixteenth century, however, authors such as al-Suyūṭī and Ibn Iyās had the potential to provide wide-ranging analyses spanning nearly two and a half centuries of a uniquely Cairene Abbasid tradition.

In view of the paucity of material, it is difficult to undertake a true *Gesellschaftgeschichte* of late medieval Egypt and Syria. While it is true that our only sources were penned by elite members of the bureaucratic class and religious intelligentsia who seldom spoke for the masses, their wide array of vocations offers a valuable variety of perspective and presentation. Nevertheless, our information on the existing caliphate must be filtered through the lens of their (somewhat) privileged world. To transcend such a limiting notion, however, it is worth remembering that many Syro-Egyptian

Figure 7.1 Dedication page of al-Baghawī's *al-Maṣābīḥ* made for the caliph al-Mutawakkil in 778/1376–7 by Muḥammad b. Salmān b. Dāwūd al-Khabbāz. Image Courtesy of Nur Osmaniye 1264, fol. 2a, provided in the context of Frédéric Bauden's *Ex(-)Libris ex Oriente* project.

chroniclers were also privy to unique sources of information. The factoids and stories which worked their way into late medieval Arabic historiography reflect the exclusive experience and proximity to real power enjoyed by members of the scholarly, administrative and military classes.

Bureaucrat Historians

Bureaucrats working in the ruling structures of Cairo, particularly the chancery, were in an excellent position to write histories supplemented by direct access to both rulers and documents pertaining to their rule. In some cases, a former *kātib al-sirr* who had drafted the relevant documents might insert them into a work of history to illustrate the career of a given sultan or remind the reader of his own involvement or prestigious achievement.

Historians of the Ayyubid period had been overwhelmingly Syrian, but a spike in Egyptian historiography occurred in the late thirteenth and early fourteenth centuries and yet again in the mid-fifteenth century. Chancery officials serving the earliest sultans had the opportunity to serve as court historians and occasionally penned royal biographies (*sīra*s) in praise of the rulers. Later writers drew heavily on the work of these authors for coverage of the late thirteenth century. Such regnal histories, inclining towards favourable depictions of the sultan while suppressing unflattering information, often sought to present their subjects as paragons of Islamic leadership.[15]

Ibn ʿAbd al-Ẓāhir, d. 692/1292

No other early courtier could boast of the intimacy Muḥyī al-Dīn ibn ʿAbd al-Ẓāhir, as official historian and chancery chief, enjoyed with the early post-Ayyubid sultans. His *Rawḍ al-zāhir fī sīrat al-Malik al-Ẓāhir* presents the investiture of al-Mustanṣir as a good deed linked to the munificence of the sultan Baybars.[16] Presenting Baybars as a pillar of Islamic morals and comportment, Ibn ʿAbd al-Ẓāhir praises the sultan for his good behaviour in the presence of the caliph, and even makes use of a topos describing the eyes of the sultan filled with joyful tears at the investiture ceremony. It was important for Ibn ʿAbd al-Ẓāhir to stress the physical and spiritual proximity of Baybars to the caliph in his narrative presentation. The *Rawḍ* emphasises that Baybars was the first to extend his hand to offer *bayʿa* and rode off beside the caliph to Syria.[17] The *Rawḍ* harbours no doubts about al-Mustanṣir's right to assume the caliphate and depicts the caliph as eager to work with Baybars to retake Baghdad, just as later on, the caliph al-Ḥākim would enthusiastically endorse the sultan's wish to restore the *futuwwa* brotherhood.[18] The narrative of the proposed Iraq counterattack emphasises the sultan's generous support of the caliph with men and money.[19] Ibn ʿAbd al-Ẓāhir does not mention the details of the campaign though he discusses its outcome. The *Rawḍ* never betrays the author's sculpted image of an open-handed sultan and as a result the caliph is represented as fatally deficient in common sense.[20] Ibn ʿAbd al-Ẓāhir's assessment of the failed mission would rather assign blame to al-Mustanṣir's impetuousness than on Baybars' miscalculation or naiveté when his forces were withdrawn:

> The caliph was rash and failed to summon the army that had gone to the Euphrates with the amir Sayf al-Dīn al-Rashīdī, so God ordained his death as a warrior in His cause . . . One cannot oppose the fates, and victory lies with God. When God intends a thing, He accomplishes it, and 'it may be that you dislike a thing, while it is good for you'.[21]

Ibn ʿAbd al-Ẓāhir's fatalist pragmatism may have been a reflection of the sultan's own position on the affair, though elsewhere we are told that Baybars was profoundly troubled by what befell the caliph in Mongol Mesopotamia.[22] Despite his vantage point as head of the chancery by 661/1262 and his direct participation in the investiture of al-Ḥākim, Ibn ʿAbd al-Ẓāhir's reports on the second Abbasid of Cairo tend to be lopsided. Due to a conflict of interests noted by Stefan Heidemann, we cannot expect an author closely linked to the political programme of Baybars to comment on al-Ḥākim's period of 'political vagabondage' and previous investitures as caliph by the sultan's competitors. Ibn ʿAbd al-Ẓāhir likewise fails to mention the caliph's participation in the Baghdad campaign (under the direction of Āqqūsh al-Barlī). Instead, the *Rawḍ* abruptly opens a section on the new caliph's mysterious arrival in Cairo, followed directly by a description of his investiture ceremony in 661/1262. The author fails to mention that al-Ḥākim, previously recognised as caliph in Aleppo, languished in confinement for nearly a year after his arrival in Cairo before Baybars needed him.[23]

An observer of extraordinary events in his own time, Ibn ʿAbd al-Ẓāhir wrote of the 665/1266 re-establishment of Friday congregational prayers at the mosque of al-Azhar, one of the three important Cairene mosques from which orators declared the ruler's sovereignty from the *minbar* each Friday, after an extended absence due in part to restorations dating back to the early Ayyubid *dawla*. The author declared that it had been God's wish to leave the mosque dormant until prayers could be restored specifically in the name of the Abbasid caliph of Cairo and the noble sultan that had come to his aid.[24]

For the remainder of the reign of Baybars, Ibn ʿAbd al-Ẓāhir provides little information on the sequestration of al-Ḥākim. Suppression of the caliph extended through the reign of Qalāwūn covered by the author's *Tashrīf al-ayyām wa-l-ʿuṣūr fī sīrat al-Malik al-Manṣūr*. Although Ibn ʿAbd al-Ẓāhir died several months before the death of Qalāwūn's successor al-Ashraf Khalīl, the surviving portion of his third and final royal history, *al-Alṭāf al-khafiyya min al-sīra al-sharīfa al-sulṭāniyya al-Malakiyya al-Ashrafiyya*, covers a substantial part of Khalīl's three-year reign. The author devotes a lengthy passage to the sultan's reinvigoration of the caliph's career in 690/1291. As had been done for Baybars and Qalāwūn, there was every attempt to cultivate a favourable image of Khalīl. The depiction of a filial relationship between the young sultan and the elderly caliph may have been an attempt to show that al-Ashraf Khalīl came to power steeped in the traditions and legacy of the political order established by Baybars, including the religious symbolism embodied by the Abbasid Caliphate.[25]

Ibn ʿAbd al-Ẓāhir's sweeping metaphors imply a privileged relationship between caliphate and sultanate. Dichotomies of black and white represent an important leitmotif in his treatment of the caliphate. As an illustration, the author of the *Rawḍ*, describing the sultanic investiture ceremony in a garden outside Cairo, compares the sultan, dressed in black turban and white robe of honour, to a full moon rising on a dark night. The narrative recounts the sultan upon a white horse with a black sash and trappings. Likewise, Baybars' investiture document, preserved though not composed by Ibn ʿAbd al-Ẓāhir, states that *jihād* is a deed that turns the black-lettered record of sins into pure white.[26] Later in his *Alṭāf*, the author revisits the theme when comparing the aged caliph al-Ḥākim, dressed in his black Abbasid gown, to the dark iris of an eye. The caliph is juxtaposed with the young, white-clad sultan, who becomes the eye's sclera providing protection to the iris from all sides, as parts of a single eye.[27] This metaphor is striking for its implication that the two men thus comprised an inseparable dyad in which there was no disconnect. In the sultan, the caliph had a strong right arm leading the armies, while in return, the sultan received the *baraka*, wisdom and divine blessings linked to the caliphate.[28] In Ibn ʿAbd al-Ẓāhir's construction, neither of the two individuals was supposed to oppose the will of the other, acting instead as a harmonious whole.

Elsewhere, Ibn ʿAbd al-Ẓāhir likens al-Ashraf Khalīl to Alexander the Great with the caliph al-Ḥākim at his side, whom he describes as a modern-day Khiḍr. The purpose of comparing the sultan, preparing to undertake *jihād*, with the greatest known world conqueror is clear enough.[29] On the other hand, comparing the caliph with Khiḍr, the mystical guiding figure of divine wisdom and mentor to Moses in the Islamic tradition, is likely an allusion to advisory sessions in which al-Ḥākim counselled al-Ashraf Khalīl. It also demonstrates recognition of the caliph's sanctity and spiritual power, a power deemed capable of summoning divine protection for the state in times of existential threat.[30]

Ibn ʿAbd al-Ẓāhir also sketches out what he considered to be an ideal relationship between a sultan and caliph. Above all, the sultan, formally acting on his behalf as his deputy, should protect the caliph and treat him generously, examples being Baybars furnishing al-Mustanṣir with wealth and a household, as well as al-Ashraf Khalīl's restoration of al-Ḥākim's caliphal honour and upgrading of his living conditions.[31]

In his remarks on the contemporary Abbasids one can always note Ibn ʿAbd al-Ẓāhir's deference to the idea of caliphate, combined as it was with a cautious acknowledgement that his first priority was extolling the virtues of his immediate patrons, the sultans of Cairo. Simply put, there was no better way to project a sultan's piety and respect for Islamic tradition than discussing his proximity to the Abbasid caliph. While it is tempting to dismiss Ibn ʿAbd al-Ẓāhir as a panderer before power, he nonetheless offers what we might describe as a somewhat formal and quasi-official delineation of the caliphate.[32]

By the time of Baybars, the office of the sultanate represented the symbolic centre of gravity for the political order. Ibn ʿAbd al-Ẓāhir, attuned to his task as spokesman for the governance of Baybars and his successors, advances the idea that there can be no caliphate without a sultanate to protect it. Once the caliph entrusts responsibility to the sultan, the residual caliphate can exist with the sultanate as a combined entity. It is thus that Ibn ʿAbd al-Ẓāhir encourages a reconfiguration of the schema which demands that the caliphate and sultanate be two alternating or even competing moieties rather than a singly-bound authority.[33]

Shāfiʿ ibn ʿAlī, d. 730/1330

Ibn ʿAbd al-Ẓāhir's nephew, the bureaucrat and chancery scribe Shāfiʿ ibn ʿAlī, similarly penned royal histories of Baybars, Qalāwūn, and his sons al-Ashraf Khalīl and al-Nāṣir Muḥammad. Writing as a scribe for Qalāwūn's chancery, Shāfiʿ ibn ʿAlī loyally defended his patron from allegations that he had usurped the sultanate from his wards, the two sons of Baybars.[34] The restoration of the Abbasid Caliphate had been a watershed moment in the early reign of Baybars, but later languished for the duration of Qalāwūn's reign. Shāfiʿ avoided explaining *why* the caliphate had remained on the sidelines, but with Baybars safely dead he allowed himself the luxury of critically reviewing the former sultan's legacy.[35]

Discussing Baybars' decision to arm al-Mustanṣir against the Mongols, Shāfiʿ ibn ʿAlī does not disguise his amazement that the sultan should send the caliph at the head of an inferior force, claiming that all the armies of Egypt and Syria would scarcely be sufficient. Such remarks, however, came in the 690s/1290s, long after the Mongols had consolidated their domain in Iran and Iraq. This led Holt to the conclusion that Shāfiʿ had assumed, with only slight justification, that Mongol strength was as formidable thirty years earlier as it was in his own day.[36]

In his history of Qalāwūn, *al-Faḍl al-maʾthūr min sīrat al-Sulṭān al-Malik al-Manṣūr*, Shāfiʿ ibn ʿAlī sought to establish the sultan as an exemplary Muslim ruler and to absolve him of wrongdoing in his ascent to power.[37] The work scarcely mentions the reigning caliph al-Ḥākim apart from documents used by Qalāwūn to appease rebellious Syrian amirs discussed in Chapter 1. The absence of the Abbasid Caliphate in the *Faḍl,* and indeed in the reign of its subject, may have been connected to Qalāwūn's desire to inflate his own spiritual significance as sultan.[38] Through the author's own activities as an administrator for Qalāwūn, Shāfiʿ may well have sensed that his master's neglect of the Abbasid Caliphate was linked to its association with the lauded career of Baybars.

In spite of potential constraints placed on his writing, Shāfiʿ ibn ʿAlī's greatest contribution to the historiography of the Cairo Caliphate is a literary snapshot of the Abbasid family that glosses over some thirty years of seclusion from the political scene. In it, the author shares their living conditions, income and what he perceives as their abasement resulting from fraternisation with common Cairenes:

> In the beginning, the caliph had been permitted to come and go as he pleased . . . The sultan grew apprehensive about the situation and barred him from attending gatherings and guarded his door for two years. When Malik al-Manṣūr Lājīn took power [in 696/1296], he removed the caliph from the Citadel and settled him in the district of al-Kabsh where he and his children became one with the common folk, riding in the markets, gathering with the masses, and otherwise debasing their sanctity (*tahalhalat ḥurmatahum*). The caliph married the daughter of Malik al-Nāṣir Dāwūd, master of al-Karak, known as 'Dār Dīnār' and who had acquired many landholdings on the shore of the canal (*shāṭiʾ al-khalīj*) known to have belonged to [her previous husband] amir Jamāl al-Dīn Āqqūsh al-Muḥammadī.[39] The caliph rode out to see her, passing through throngs of common folk (*yushaqqa al-ʿawwām*) until the end of his days.[40]

If anything, this passage, while possibly functioning as a contemporary critique, also indicates an abiding concern about the way the caliph and his household presented themselves in society. Moreover, it is a sign that the author's primary audience, the religious and political elite of the time, had an abiding interest in the sayings and doings of the 'Commander of the Faithful' that went well beyond his mere presence at investiture ceremonies.[41] Baybars and Qalāwūn might have hidden the caliphate behind a screen for different reasons, but significantly never abolished it.[42] In subsequent times, however, when comparatively weaker men came to the sultanate, there would be efforts among the elite authorities to remove the caliphate from its obscurity and restore the prominence and splendour it had enjoyed in the early years of Baybars.

Military Historians

The work of two members of the political-military class who counted historical writing among their interests, permits another perspective on the Abbasid Caliphate. They are the military officer Baybars al-Manṣūrī and the Ayyubid scion, delegated by the Abbasid caliph of Cairo as 'sultan' of Ḥamā, Ismāʿīl Abū al-Fidāʾ.

Baybars al-Manṣūrī, d. 725/1325

Both a military man and an exceptional student of knowledge, Baybars al-Manṣūrī represents a distinctive voice in early fourteenth-century Arabic historiography. Access to the inner workings of the government and military made Baybars al-Manṣūrī an authority on political affairs. Moreover, he was a known Qurʾān exegete, and much of his work retains a tone of piety informed by an admiration for Sufism.[43] For his coverage of events in late thirteenth-century Syro-Egypt, Baybars al-Manṣūrī closely followed the writing of Ibn ʿAbd al-Ẓāhir and mirrored the tone and presentation of that author in his universal chronicle, *Zubdat al-fikra fī Taʾrīkh al-hijra*, as well as his shorter work, *al-Tuḥfa al-mulūkiyya fī al-dawla al-Turkiyya*. While relying a great deal on *al-Rawḍ al-zāhir*, Baybars al-Manṣūrī frequently departs from its narrative to introduce his own experiences and eyewitness accounts, adding depth to coverage of later years.[44] Like Ibn ʿAbd al-Ẓāhir, Baybars al-Manṣūrī describes the caliphal investiture as a testament to the piety and righteousness of the sultan Baybars, which influenced later chroniclers.[45] The author of the *Zubda* depicts the caliphate as an important link to the legacy of the Prophet:

> The caliphate had fallen vacant since the murder of the *imām* al-Mustaʿṣim bi-llāh so the sultan was pleased to rekindle its *raison d'être* (*bi-itiṣāl asbābihā*), renew its garments (*athwāb*), erect its beacon (*manār*), and display its emblems in order to solidify its foundation and link it to the Abbasid family as has been related in the prophetic promises to ensure that [the caliphate] remain time-honoured and everlasting in this [Abbasid] lineage.[46]

Baybars al-Manṣūrī portrays the sultan as an emotional figure, bound by duty to the caliphate, claiming that Baybars had viewed the slaughter of al-Mustanṣir by the Mongols as a horrible calamity and a personal failure that he had been unable to prevent.[47] Whereas Ibn ʿAbd al-Ẓāhir chastised the impetuousness of the caliph to protect the reputation of the sultan and Shāfiʿ questioned the decision-making of the sultan, Baybars al-Manṣūrī judiciously avoided judging either historical actor, limiting himself to musing how al-Mustanṣir calculated that an assault on Mongol territory might be feasible despite his reduced forces. The author then offers praise to both caliph and sultan for their service to the greater cause of religion.[48]

Competing interests and loyalties influenced the authorial voice of Baybars al-Manṣūrī. At different times he could be a dedicated Muslim recognising God's involvement in historical events, a soldier committed to the effectiveness of the sultan's forces, and an accomplished courtier loyal to the house of Qalāwūn.[49]

As a pious commentator of contemporary events, Baybars al-Manṣūrī repeatedly concerned himself with the caliphate and the Abbasid family, emphasising the relationship between the caliph as 'commander' and the contemporary Muslim community as 'the faithful'.[50] He even composed a history of caliphs and rulers, *al-Laṭāʾif fī akhbār al-khalāʾif*, which has not survived.[51] Baybars al-Manṣūrī seldom fails to mention the caliphate without offering a short prayer of thanks for its restoration or for the well-being of the current caliph, his father and their virtuous ancestors.[52]

For modern historians, Baybars al-Manṣūrī has value for his vantage point as a senior *mamlūk* officer who occupied the lofty rank of amir of 100 and commander of 1,000.[53] Like most classical Muslim historians, his historical writing understands the outcome of battles as the result of God's intervention. The caliph occasionally accompanied the army during military campaigns, and the author depicts him as a living representation of the prophetic legacy.[54] The Abbasid caliph, emulating his pious ancestors, rides at the sultan's side at the head of numerous soldiers. Later they confront the enemy head-on in the company of hosts of angels (recalling Muslim accounts of the Battle of Badr) at an auspicious and divinely determined hour.

For the author, the Abbasid caliph was a kind of pennant representing *dīn*, *dawla* and God's favour for the 'army of the Muslims'. It is in this sense that Baybars al-Manṣūrī transforms the caliph into a talisman of piety embedded in the army, the latter's mere presence vouchsafing divine blessing and victory. Having the caliph in the sultan's civilian retinue among his army likewise added grace, legitimacy and *sharīʿa* morality to the cause. Concerning *jihād*, there is never a hint here that the Abbasid caliph is a parasite, camp follower or hanger-on. Rather, Baybars al-Manṣūrī emphasises that the military had been highly fortunate to have such a resource in their company, for the caliph ensured God's assistance, no matter who the sultan of the day was.[55]

This image is consistent with an understanding that Baybars al-Manṣūrī, though he was a loyal servant of the reigning sultan and his *dawla*, held a broader, transcendent loyalty to the ruling elite and its army, as an institution fundamentally committed to Islam no matter who was in charge.[56] This may in part help to explain the author's unabashed commemoration of the legacy of the late sultan Baybars as restorer of the caliphate, even though he himself had been in the service of Qalāwūn and his sons. As a veteran of early engagements against the Franks, Baybars al-Manṣūrī esteemed the sultanate and interpreted Baybars as a figure whose governance was guided by Islamic piety.[57]

Though the Mongols were nominally Muslim by 702/1302, their rival ideology refused to allow the acceptance of caliphal authority in Cairo.[58] Baybars al-Manṣūrī mentions the caliph al-Mustakfī's participation in the campaign of the young al-Nāṣir Muḥammad, recollecting a pre-existing prayer of acknowledgement that the caliph is

> cousin of our master the Messenger of God, peace and blessings be upon him, whom every Muslim is obliged to follow and in so doing, we are following the regulations of God and the Prophet in carrying out *jihād* . . . Whoever follows the obligations of God [follows] the obligations of the Commander of the Faithful, because God has protected him and made him our ruler and whoever refuses or is stubborn in submitting to him, will be humiliated by God.[59]

Equally trained in Islamic sciences and secretarial arts, the erudition of Baybars al-Manṣūrī strongly informs his historiography. As a soldier, he was certain that military victory and the success of the state depended on the perpetuation of the Abbasid Caliphate and its good treatment by the ruling elite.[60] In his historical presentation, it is clear that the author believed that the Egyptian sultans brought the caliph on campaigns to curry God's favour and secure success for the army. As it had for Ibn ʿAbd al-Ẓāhir, the contemporary Abbasid Caliphate played an important role in Baybars al-Manṣūrī's characterisation of the contemporary political and military orders as highly functional machines of coherent Islamic governance.

Abū al-Fidāʾ, d. 732/1331

The historical writing of Ismāʿīl Abū al-Fidāʾ, an Ayyubid prince and vassal of al-Nāṣir Muḥammad, offers a slightly different perspective. The abbreviated version of his universal chronicle, *al-Mukhtaṣar fī Taʾrīkh al-bashar*, written about 718/1318, covers events in Cairo from his seat in Syria. The *Mukhtaṣar* shares similarities with the writing of Baybars al-Manṣūrī and both authors may have worked from similar sources.[61]

A long-standing collaborator in the sultan of Cairo's military operations from as early as 684/1285, Abū al-Fidāʾ was well-placed to offer his unique take on affairs in the sultanate thanks to the resources afforded by his high-born position.[62] His coverage of the Abbasid investitures lacks, to say the least, the panache of his recent predecessors and contemporaries who took great pains to affirm the lofty titulature of caliphal office. In a section of his narrative devoted to the first two caliphs of Cairo, he describes al-Mustanṣir as somebody (*shakhṣ*) who merely received the pledge of the caliphate and whose lineage was authenticated. Indeed, Abū al-Fidāʾ seems almost cavalier in his report that 'a group of Bedouin approached Egypt and among them was a black-coloured fellow called Aḥmad whom they claimed to be the son of the [Abbasid] *imām* al-Ẓāhir bi-llāh'. He appears to be the first historian to style the dark-complexioned al-Mustanṣir as 'the black caliph', an epithet adopted by later historians.[63]

In his coverage of the later investiture of al-Ḥākim in Cairo, Abū al-Fidāʾ writes that Baybars invited this 'person of Abbasid descent named Aḥmad' to appear at a general audience and named him caliph after confirming his claim. It is here that the author notes that by his own time, nearly half a century later, the dispute over the official Abbasid genealogy had continued.[64] While Abū al-Fidāʾ never went as far as to *reject* the genealogical claims of either al-Mustanṣir or al-Ḥākim, he did imply that questions lingered in some circles regarding their authenticity, at least in centres at a further radius from Cairo. It suggests likewise that a rival interpretation diverging from ongoing trends in contemporaneous historiography actually existed.

Abū al-Fidāʾ scarcely mentions al-Ḥākim until his death in 701/1302, when he again discusses the lineage dispute and the succession of al-Mustakfī bi-llāh.[65] The author's scepticism towards the early Cairo Caliphate, combined with its eventual mothballing by Baybars and Qalāwūn, may have caused him to lose interest after the initial investiture of al-Ḥākim. Unlike Baybars al-Manṣūrī, the surviving text of Abū al-Fidāʾ makes no mention of the caliph accompanying the sultan's forces into Syria to battle the Mongols. While Abū al-Fidāʾ may have harboured mildly suspicious feelings towards the caliphate, there could be other reasons for his lack of coverage. Having been born in 673/1273, he had missed Baybars' caliphal investitures. Later, as a military man whose primary concern was recording the history of the environs outside Ḥamā, the caliphate in Cairo occupied less immediate interest.[66] Although a well-liked hunting partner and boon companion of al-Nāṣir Muḥammad, Abū al-Fidāʾ remained a Syrian-based non-*mamlūk*, perhaps left uninformed of the political tensions surrounding the Abbasid Caliphate in the early fourteenth century.

The unique position and background of Abū al-Fidāʾ raises questions about the sources of caliphal legitimacy. He was on good terms with earlier Cairo-based sultans who considered him an ally despite his family connection to the Ayyubids, most of whom had failed to accept the new political order that ended their dynastic reign.

Awlād al-Nās Historians

The sons of trained *mamlūk* officers, the 'sons of the people' or *awlād al-nās*, comprised a social grouping sometimes (though never formally or officially) barred from military service in the late thirteenth and early fourteenth centuries.[67] Nevertheless, many went on to later occupy military as well as other positions among the civilian elite in the bureaucracy or in the scholarly echelons.[68] Having close family ties to the sultan or members of his entourage granted special access to a world unseen by all but a minority of Arab historians. Some historical sources composed by the *awlād al-nās* tended to sympathise with the sultans and their courts. Like others, they wrote conventional chronicles, biographies and handbooks, though not always with the same intense training as their contemporaries, which is evident in the colloquialisms, vernacular prose and departure from literary Arabic often apparent in their work as many writers took to inventing dialogues, adding gossip and fomenting a literary quality in their historiography.[69] Their knowledge of Turkish languages and shared background instilled in them a 'close affinity to the ruling elite's outlook'.[70]

Al-Ṣafadī, d. 763/1363

As the son of an amir and former *mamlūk*, Khalīl ibn Aybak al-Ṣafadī easily secured access to careers in government and the arts. After studying with the likes of Ibn Taymiyya and al-Dhahabī in Syria, al-Ṣafadī travelled to Cairo and wrote on linguistics and literature, though he is best known for his biographical dictionaries. Several biographies of the contemporary caliphs provide exceptional coverage. His observations, thanks in part to earlier historians, often include detailed information on the financial standing of the Abbasid caliphs and offer a candid view of disquiet among the subject populations whenever the sultans attempted to disrupt harmony in the caliphate.

In addition to his meticulous chronology, the true value of al-Ṣafadī's approach to biography is his variety of interests. He did not limit his entries to particular classes or professions; instead, al-Ṣafadī covers a wide assortment of notables and professionals. Caliphal military involvements, stipends, living conditions and scholarly prowess are among his interests, allowing the author to compose multifaceted portraits of several Cairo caliphs.[71]

Likely based on the slightly earlier writing of al-Dhahabī, some of al-Ṣafadī's most detailed observations concern al-Mustakfī, the reigning caliph for much of his lifetime. Candid glimpses of the caliph include the battle finery he wore beside the sultan. One can also find a poetic description of the caliph's 737/1337 exile to Qūṣ in al-Ṣafadī's commentary on the mourning throngs that tearfully witnessed the departure of al-Mustakfī.[72] Concerning the events that followed, the author offered subtle criticism of the sultan's misdealing with the caliphs by contrasting al-Ḥākim II's open *bayʿa* to the hurried and secretive pledge ceremony for al-Wāthiq bi-llāh.[73] By comparison, al-Ṣafadī's entries on the two sons of al-Mustakfī; al-Ḥākim II and al-Muʿtaḍid, merely recount their genealogies and enumerate their years in office.[74]

Such details provide a sketch of the caliphs in the mid-fourteenth century as members of the court observed them. They were easily accessible to some visitors, usually courtiers, bureaucrats, *ʿulamāʾ* and litterateurs, while the sultans remained cautious about their receiving amirs or members of the military class.[75] The account of the caliph al-Mustakfī provides an excellent description of the author's own casual interactions with the caliph. Also displayed are various sides of the caliph's life, including military involvements, personal finances and household, as well as clues about the caliph's reception among the masses.

Ibn Taghrībirdī, d. 874/1470

Access to a diverse grouping of scholarly mentors and sultans, as well as his own forays into the contemporary military culture, furnished Abū al-Maḥāsin Yūsuf ibn Taghrībirdī, an Egyptian-based courtier, commander and historian, with a vista covering numerous social strata – including the household of at least one contemporary Abbasid caliph.[76] In chronicling each new political order of the Cairo Sultanate, Ibn Taghrībirdī valued the heritage of the High Caliphate, and although aware of the limitations of the office in his own time, he acknowledged its primacy as the highest position in Islam.[77] He also occasionally presents the Umayyad and Abbasid caliphs as paragons of virtuous leadership that the sultans of Cairo as their practical successors, ought to emulate.

Throughout his regnal history of Egypt, *al-Nujūm al-zāhira fī mulūk Miṣr wa-l-Qāhira*, Ibn Taghrībirdī alludes to stories of great men of the Islamic golden age, including Hārūn al-Rashīd, often using them to take the measure of contemporary sultans. It is clear that for Ibn Taghrībirdī the sultans he served, particularly Jaqmaq, Khushqadam, Timurbughā and briefly Qāyitbāy, are the true heirs of the Umayyad and early Abbasid caliphs, comparable to them in power and position in the Islamic world.[78]

Notwithstanding the practical pre-eminence of the sultans of his day, Ibn Taghrībirdī occasionally suggested that even the contemporary Abbasid caliphs were still worthy models: he drew attention, for example, to the piously abstemious (although apparently impoverished) living of the caliph al-Muʿtaḍid II, juxtaposed against the opulence of the sultans.[79]

Demonstrating presentist concerns for the caliphs of his own time, Ibn

Taghrībirdī wrote frankly of the predicament of earlier caliphs in the fourteenth century. In his biography of the caliph al-Ḥākim II, the historian remarked upon the way that '[al-Ḥākim] approached the caliphate in the manner of these caliphs of our time, nothing remaining to him from the caliphate save for its title'.[80]

Any further discussion of Ibn Taghrībirdī's vision of the late fifteenth-century sultanate of Cairo requires an understanding that the historian, despite years of formal Islamic training, was first and foremost the product of a Turkish military and court culture. His social status and position as a leading member of the court of Jaqmaq was linked to a number of factors (i.e., his connection to his prestigious father the amir Taghrībirdī, his own personal relationships with various sultans of Cairo, and his network of fellow courtiers) rather than his default status as a member of the so-called '*awlād al-nās*'. His father's household understood a universal loyalty to the Abbasid house as a secondary part of the socio-political ethos or amiral milieu, but individual amirs could often do little to shield the caliph from the animus of the sultan.[81] Similarly, the narrative of Ibn Taghrībirdī readily turned on individual caliphs the moment they overstepped political or religious expectations of the office.

The journey of the caliph al-Wāthiq to the family office proved to be a touchy subject for some later chroniclers. Ibn Taghrībirdī was aware of the historiographical controversy surrounding al-Nāṣir Muḥammad's interference with the caliphal succession after the death of the caliph al-Mustakfī in 740/1340 and mentions in his history of caliphs and kings, the *Mawrid al-laṭāfa fī man waliya al-salṭana wa-l-khilāfa*, that historians differ over al-Wāthiq's caliphate because it had been established by the sultan rather than by caliphal *ʿahd* from a predecessor. Unlike al-ʿUmarī and al-Suyūṭī, who did not hide their disdain for the sultan's 'interference' and the subsequent behaviour of al-Wāthiq, for Ibn Taghrībirdī it was for the individual observer, upon learning the details of the matter, to determine whether 'to affirm [al-Wāthiq as a legitimate holder of office] or reject him if one so desires'.[82]

Ibn Taghrībirdī's account of the alleged 785/1383 plot by the caliph al-Mutawakkil and two amirs to depose and murder Barqūq presents the case against the caliph without comment, suggesting that the issue of the caliph's guilt or innocence may have been sensitive in official circles.[83] Three decades later, Ibn Taghrībirdī used the contentious deposition of the caliph al-Mustaʿīn from the sultanate in 815/1412 as an occasion to discursively weigh in on the legitimacy of his successor, al-Muʾayyad Shaykh. For the historian, it was clear that al-Mustaʿīn was never intended to exercise the sultanate for long, and was merely a compromise appointee agreed upon by Syro-Egyptian amirs to prevent discord in the interim.[84] Some Islamic legalists, on the other hand, found it difficult to accept that al-Mustaʿīn's deposition had been lawful. According to *sharīʿa* norms, removing a caliph from power required proof that he had deviated from Islam or no longer met the qualifications for the caliphate. Until then, the selected caliph could remain in office indefinitely, provided he fulfilled his contract. Commentators such as al-Maqrīzī doubly accused Shaykh of illegally deposing the caliph without religious proof and, worse still, creating a vacancy in the caliphate.[85] Rising to defend Shaykh against such 'wicked fabrications',[86] Ibn Taghrībirdī argued that the sultan had been preoccupied with battling his rival Nawrūz and therefore delayed settling the caliphate issue. Regarding the ouster of the caliph, Ibn Taghrībirdī appealed to the presence of other authorities at court:

> Al-Muʾayyad Shaykh discussed the situation before the qadis, eminent amirs and others on the given day, and what greater proof is there than that? As for the vacancy in the caliphate, it was brief; indeed, deposition and appointment can be accomplished within a single hour![87]

Elsewhere, Ibn Taghrībirdī echoes the alleged view of the sultan Shaykh that discord and bloodshed among Muslims would be the outcome of a dysfunctional sultanate under al-Mustaʿīn. As consolation, the historian restates al-Maqrīzī's observation that al-Mustaʿīn had been suited for the caliphal office, but fortune was simply not on his side.[88]

Thus, an unwritten rule became manifest: a caliph reaches for the powers of the sultanate at his dire peril. Nevertheless, Ibn Taghrībirdī recognised that it was still to the advantage of the sultans to give the Abbasid caliph his due, just as he reported that al-Ẓāhir Ṭaṭar's later reconciliation with al-Mustaʿīn endeared the former to political elites in Cairo.[89]

Forty years after al-Mustaʿīn, the author was appalled by the political opportunism of his brother, the caliph al-Qāʾim bi-Amr Allāh. At that time,

Ibn Taghrībirdī's narrative scolds the caliph for disruption after suffering the indignity of being seated unceremoniously on the floor by the son of Jaqmaq, al-Manṣūr ʿUthmān.[90] Once again, the historian defended the sultan and his political order by conceding that '[Jaqmaq] did as such with [al-Qāʾim's predecessor] al-Muʿtaḍid bi-llāh on the day [the sultan's] investiture document was read. Perhaps it was a custom of the bygone kings . . . for al-Ẓāhir Jaqmaq always treated the *ʿulamāʾ* and doctors of the law respectfully [by seating them at his feet], so why not the caliphs[?]'[91]

After al-Qāʾim's attempt to aid the 859/1455 coup against Īnāl (the sultan he had helped invest), Ibn Taghrībirdī portrays the caliph as a traitor who failed to do his part in supporting the incumbent (and thereby rightful) sultan. Ibn Taghrībirdī chastised what he interpreted as al-Qāʾim's shallow opportunism:

> The caliph was frivolous and foolish and thus inclined toward [the rebels], thinking that if he was with [them], one of their number might triumph as sultan, and his own position would be strengthened, becoming even more important than before . . . When this *fitna* occurred he thought he might make common cause with its promoters and if one of them became sultan he would raise [al-Qāʾim's] position above that which Īnāl had done and complete control would come into his hands, heedless that the 'voice of the ages' would speak to him thusly:
>
> The best of ways is the middle path,
> for love of the extreme is faulty.
>
> Birds seldom take flight and soar so high –
> without tumbling as they fly.[92]

Rather than execute the caliph, Īnāl exiled him to Alexandria, presenting Ibn Taghrībirdī with the occasion to praise the sultan for having done no harm during his reign save for banishing the caliph for his part in the rebellion. He commented that '[Īnāl] is to be excused for that, and if it had been any other of the leading kings he would have done many times [worse than] that [to the caliph]'.[93] In this statement, the historian again makes a case for the legality of Īnāl's political order in the controversy attached to the exile of a caliph, a deeply divisive act for any sultan.

Ibn Taghrībirdī's diligence in reporting the Abbasid presence at official functions, although by no means unique, suggests a keen awareness of the caliph's symbolic capital. In mentioning the caliph at key moments the historian demonstrated that the political order in question venerated the caliph by referring to him as a vital officiator alongside the four chief qadis. If his historical writing was indeed intended for other courtiers, consistent mention of the caliph at notable occasions may have been an attempt to shield the sultan and his entourage from rivals.[94]

As a pragmatist in touch with the complex realities of courtly life, Ibn Taghrībirdī understood the caliphs as public figures whose powers were severely restricted by the political elites and subject to their whims. His view of the caliphate carried the notion that individual caliphs were replaceable should the need arise, but he was attuned to the *ʿulamāʾ*'s historical reverence for the caliphate, which certainly mattered considering their collective approval legitimised the political order of each sultan and his new *dawla*.[95] Nevertheless, for Ibn Taghrībirdī, veneration of an Abbasid caliph could never come at the expense of a sultan's reputation, and this remained a central tenet in the author's historical outlook.

Void of scepticism, Ibn Taghrībirdī describes the practice of most fifteenth-century sultans who at the end of their lives made ineffective attempts to establish their dynasties by bequeathing their powers to their sons under the auspices of helpless caliphs. It was peculiar that the sultans persevered in the custom despite the realities of historical precedent; few of them seemed to remember that they too had sidestepped a predecessor's son on the way to power, a son whose birth right had been 'guaranteed' by the same caliph whom they now approached for help.[96]

At times inconsistent, Ibn Taghrībirdī presents himself as a pious Muslim sensitive to Islamic social mores, though one who tacitly approved flagrant infractions of the *sharīʿa* by the ruling elite as well as newly-recruited *mamlūk*s.[97] As a high-placed Turkish scholar and historian, he certainly had his share of jealous rivals among Arab classical religious scholars.[98] Despite criticisms for failing to abandon his Turkish connections, Ibn Taghrībirdī maintained many of the cultural values of his non-Turkish colleagues. Any affinity he felt for the contemporary caliphate seems more influenced by its use in late fifteenth-century ceremonial than by personal religious upbringing or visits to the household of al-Muʿtaḍid II. It was the political order of his own day which he understood as rightful successor to the historical caliphate, the legacy of which the sultanate was obliged to uphold.[99] Although he occasionally charged members of the military elite with corruption, his sympathies were planted firmly in the camp of the rulers, thereby colouring his moral pronouncements on individual caliphs which were frequently made in the service of defending and representing the legacy of the rulers he served. It is through Ibn Taghrībirdī, as a keen social observer and critic, that we achieve, along with Ibn ʿAbd al-Ẓāhir and Baybars al-Manṣūrī, a near image of how the political elite interpreted the idea of the caliphate as well as the caliphs confined in their capital and the role they played in their court culture.[100]

Ibn Iyās, d. 930/1524

Born, like Ibn Taghrībirdī, into a military family, Muḥammad ibn Iyās held an *iqṭāʿ* that afforded him enough financial freedom to compose historical works. Although descended from the military class, his family had lost much of the influence it had enjoyed at court in previous generations, losing its place among the elite amirs. As a compiler of history, however, Ibn Iyās maintained some contacts and counted several officers among his informants.[101]

A condensed universal history and important local history of Cairo during the years of the author's life, the later annals of the *Badāʾiʿ al-zuhūr fī waqāʾiʿ al-duhūr* are largely based on eyewitness reports. Sami Massoud claims that the historiography of Ibn Iyās coincides with two important phenomena: the changeover from the *dawla* of Qāniṣawh al-Ghawrī and Ṭūmānbāy to Ottoman rule in Egypt and Syria and a growing dearth in Islamic historiography written in Arabic.[102] Modern scholars characterise him as 'deeply identified with the people of Cairo and the fallen regime' and as 'a mouthpiece of the medium strata of society'.[103] The author of the *Badāʾiʿ*, by virtue of his survival to 930/1524, was able to cover the entire span, including the vivid finale of the Cairo Sultanate and the transformation of its Syrian, Egyptian and Hijazi territories into Ottoman provinces. He was in a unique position to evaluate the legacy of sultanic policies, including the Abbasid Caliphate, which remained a prevailing concern to him. As a source for the final six Abbasid caliphs of Cairo, Ibn Iyās is without equal.

The *Badāʾiʿ* is full of first-hand reports from the years 870–928/1467–1522 that include lengthy asides on the affairs of the caliphate and a marked respect for the men who held that office. For the two centuries prior to his own lifetime, Ibn Iyās consistently recapitulates caliphal issues mentioned by slightly earlier sources. For the author, the Abbasid Caliphate remains a vital concern, a viewpoint that may have remained consistent among his own social circles as well as the everyday Cairenes on behalf of whom he was thought to be writing.[104] Nevertheless, some modern historians have accused Ibn Iyās of falsifying and grossly embellishing reports of the caliph's relevance in early Ottoman Cairo.[105]

Although it frequently interjects anecdotes about the caliphs into Cairene history, as a historical source on the contemporary Abbasid Caliphate, the latter-day vantage point of the *Badāʾiʿ* offers little retrospective consideration of the institution. The author informs us of precedents and some evolution in caliphal practices by the fifteenth century, such as the practice established under Barsbāy that made the sultans responsible for granting funding for a caliph's campaign expenses to Syria and beyond.[106]

Like most late medieval Arabic chroniclers, Ibn Iyās often notes the caliph's presence at official events, particularly in matters of legitimating sultans, occasionally augmenting earlier reports with anecdotes or rumours. Concerning the caliphs' monthly visits in the company of the qadis to congratulate the sultans, Ibn Iyās first mentions the practice in the reign of al-Mustanjid (859–84/1455–79), and for the remainder of the *Badāʾiʿ* mentions whether the meeting occurred at the start of each new month.[107]

Regarding the nature of the data, the *Badāʾiʿ* includes a great deal of inter-familial politics, gossip, and comment on the complex relationships between competing branches of the Abbasid family. In matters of succession for both the caliphs al-Mutawakkil II (884/1479) followed by al-Mustamsik (903/1497 and 914/1508), Ibn Iyās presents the schemes of rival Abbasid cousins as a subplot to the succession, hinting at its interest for contemporary Cairenes.[108] He likewise devotes space to notable female members of the Abbasid family and reports minor changes in custom such as the way caliphs wore turbans or received gifts including properties and extravagant robes. So important to the author was the status of the caliph, that he even recounts details of the caliph's belongings, finery and luggage as they travelled separately on campaign, and later describes the unpleasant conditions of the caliph's passage to Istanbul in spring 923/1517.[109]

Ibn Iyās makes use of Egyptian vernacular in his writing and his history suggests the concerns of a man with an ear tuned to the streets. If Ibn Taghrībirdī, in part, had been a courtier who wrote history for other courtiers, Ibn Iyās was aware of the discussions of the *ʿāmma* and committed a degree of common knowledge and rumour to his chronicle. The author received information on the Abbasid Caliphate from two important groups: the Citadel elite and everyday Cairenes. Ibn Iyās remained conscious of the 'public persona' of the caliphs and how various Cairene social groupings responded to members of the Abbasid family.

In instances involving perceived victimisation of individual caliphs by political elites, Ibn Iyās alludes to outrage among a population that he unfortunately does not define well. With his non-specific use of the Arabic word *al-nās*, he frequently complicates matters by not distinguishing the attitudes of the Citadel elite (also referred to as '*al-nās*') from the collective mood of the masses in his writing.[110] In regard to the sultan Qāyitbāy's relieving the caliph al-Mustanjid of family properties, Ibn Iyās wrote that the Citadel elite (*al-nās*) 'regarded [the sultan's policies] as nasty actions' and also counted them among the sultan's bad deeds (*dhālika min masāwiʾhi*).[111] According to the author, religious and political elites were likewise scandalised by al-Manṣūr ʿUthmān's coarse treatment of the caliph al-Qāʾim and quietly prayed for his downfall;[112] a statement in stark contrast to Ibn Taghrībirdī's justification for the caliph being denied the honours of his high office based on recent precedent. Ibn Taghrībirdī was likewise more candid about the restriction of the caliphs to the Citadel beginning with the reign of al-Mustanjid, whereas Ibn Iyās decried it as bald-faced injustice.[113] The author of the *Badāʾiʿ* also notes that the relationship between al-Mutawakkil II and the public (*al-nās*) was marked by copious intimacy (*kathīrat al-ʿishra*).[114] For the reigns of the last caliphs that he witnessed himself, Ibn Iyās admits to gathering information from rumour, 'that which was widely spread among the populace' (*fa-alladhī istifāḍa bayna al-nās*), and hearsay from Syria about the caliph in Ottoman custody, noting that 'talk on the matter [concerning the caliph] was abundant' (*al-aqwāl fī dhālik kathīra*).[115] When the Ottoman sultan decided to expel the last caliph from Cairo, Ibn Iyās wrote that 'the population bitterly regretted the departure of the Commander of the Faithful from Egypt: "The caliphate has left Egypt to settle in Istanbul," they said. These were gloomy circumstances.'[116] Subsequent information included in the *Badāʾiʿ* concerning that caliph's detention in Istanbul likewise derives from gossip circulating among the population during the visit of an Ottoman ambassador in late 925/1519 as well as letters the caliph wrote to his father.[117]

A secondary image of the author's interest in the caliphate is punctuated by popular poetry preserved throughout the *Badāʾiʿ*. Through previously existing verse or new lines inspired by current events, Ibn Iyās showcases contemporary perceptions of the Cairo caliphs. Poets often wrote verses containing witticisms that emphasised caliphal honour or lamentations in the wake of a caliph's death or exile. It is through his reports interspersed with verse that Ibn Iyās, himself perhaps more of a belletrist than a historian, reflects the thoughts of the literary and educated classes regarding the Abbasid caliphs of their city.[118]

In his coverage of the first Abbasid investitures by the sultan Baybars, Ibn Iyās cites anonymous verses celebrating the sultan and emphasising that something broken had been restored through great difficulty:

> O lion of the Turks; O you who are their pillar!
> O taker of vengeance after the horror!
>
> You broke the tyranny and restored that which had been obliterated.
> You crossed the Euphrates and restored the caliphate.[119]

Similarly, Barqūq's unpopular 785/1383 deposition of the caliph al-Mutawakkil inspired the verses of Shihāb ibn al-ʿAṭṭār, which highlight the virtue of the Abbasid family and draw attention to its spiritual autonomy from the sultanate:

> Rejoice Commander of the Faithful; for that which has happened
> is the strongest proof of your enduring honour.
>
> Fear not inactive aggression
> for 'no hand can extend beyond the hand of the caliphate'.[120]

Fond of the added tone that embedded verse could lend to his text, Ibn Iyās included poetry that encouraged reflection about what had befallen the Abbasid caliphs. Like many chroniclers, his work interpreted the caliphs as quiet characters of dignity often persevering against unbridled aggression at the hands of the sultans.[121] Veneration of the Abbasid family was also a powerful motif in poetry preserved by the *Badāʾiʿ*. The Abbasid presence in Cairo was widely viewed as hallowed subject matter, exemplified in verses commemorating the accession of the caliph al-Mustaʿīn in 808/1406:

> Our caliph must be allowed to feel pride in his family
> for it is through his family that all people come together.[122]

When Yaʿqūb Ibn ʿAbd al-ʿAzīz ascended the caliphate as al-Mustamsik in 903/1497, verses reminding him to fear God and remember his virtuous ancestor were part of Ibn Iyās' account of the investiture:

> O Commander of the Faithful, approach but do not
> make request of any save for [God] who honoured you.
>
> Were al-ʿAbbās ever to return, surely he would say:
> 'God have mercy on he who sired you'.[123]

Drama and indignity drew the attention of many to the Abbasid succession squabble of the early sixteenth century. Concerning the first struggle between the Abbasid prince Khalīl and the newly invested al-Mustamsik, Ibn Iyās included verses in support of the authority of the caliph and his son against his cousin, 'the envier' (*al-ḥāsid*), claiming that something unique in the soul of al-Mustamsik granted him victory in securing the caliphate.[124] The poetry chosen by Ibn Iyās personifies the caliphal office, which, portrayed as an anthropomorphic, sentient being, does not wish to be defiled by the spiteful Khalīl. The verses also allude to the Quranic Jacob (namesake of the caliph Yaʿqūb al-Mustamsik) and affirm that the divine election of the caliph could not be set aside on the whim of a challenger:

> The lofty place [i.e., the caliphate] says to the one who aims for it:
> 'The master (*mawla*) has already solved the problem'.
>
> They claim that the envious one burned to be in that place
> but '[it was] a desire within the soul of Jacob, which [God] satisfied'.[125]

When Khalīl failed to win the caliphate a second time in 920/1514, Ibn Iyās informs us that Cairenes rallied around al-Mustamsik and his son al-Mutawakkil as the rightful caliphs abused at the hands of conniving relatives. Popular poetry directed at the caliph again rang true for the author:

Have patience in the face of the enemy's torment –
Surely your patience gives him battle.

Flames turn inwards, consuming themselves
if they do not find something to devour.[126]

The death of a caliph, like any great public figure, was an occasion for poets to commiserate and give voice to widespread mourning. Poets often called upon mourners to be patient and advised cautious and sober remembrance of a 'national treasure' in modern parlance, such as these verses accompanying the death of al-Muʿtaḍid II in 845/1441:

O soul, be patient lest you die in misery
Verily the age is built upon all that which you despise.

Believe not in the happiness of abiding amenities
For each one holds the key to doors of despair.[127]

On the death of the caliph Yaʿqūb al-Mustamsik in 927/1521, Ibn Iyās recorded a lengthy elegy (*marthiyya*) by the laureate Nāṣir al-Dīn Muḥammad ibn Qāniṣawh.[128] The verses open by stating that arrows of grief had found their bullseyes in the hearts of the people. The author laments the bygone era of al-Mustamsik's caliphate as a golden age and bemoans the death of the caliph as the inauguration of a period of lawlessness wherein heroes and great kings have vanished from the earth:

Where are the good people among us, the great families, the companions
and where are the kings and warriors?

God has wanted them all to pass on
Just as He has ordained upon Yaʿqūb.[129]

For the people, the elegy likens the calamity of the caliph's passing to the trials faced by the Biblical prophet Job (Ayyūb). Ibn Qāniṣawh claims that the caliph died unhappy because the Ottomans had taken his son al-Mutawakkil. He then lists the caliph's good deeds, emphasising his kindness to orphans and widows, whom the poet now calls upon to weep and pray for the caliph's entry into the highest paradise (*jannat al-firdaws*) and for God to return his son, the exiled Abbasid caliph al-Mutawakkil III, to Egypt to reside in felicity with his people.[130] The poem closes with Ibn Qāniṣawh's own aspiration to die with the same lofty reputation as al-Mustamsik and a restatement of profound despair.

Ibn Iyās' interest in the Abbasid caliphs suggests an almost voyeuristic obsession with a royal family of Islamic notables in the public eye. On several occasions he describes the Abbasid presence in Cairo and its 'great prestige' (*ghāyat al-ʿizz*) servicing a long string of sultanates.[131] The author even extends his admiration to minor members of the Abbasid family, irrespective of whether they held office. When discussing elder family members, the historian refers to them as 'our master' (*mawlā-nā*) or 'my master' (*sīdī* or *sayyidī*), perhaps reflecting their social stature in civilian as well as military circles.[132] The author describes 'my master Mūsā', an elder son of al-Mutawakkil who never secured the family office, as 'a respected man whose wrongdoings cost him the caliphate'.[133] Despite his affection for the family, Ibn Iyās by no means concealed reports of bad behaviour among individual members as in the case of the Abbasid prince Khalīl, who sought to secure the family office by waging an ugly public campaign that embarrassed the Abbasid clan.

The career of the final Cairo caliph al-Mutawakkil III after the battle of Marj Dābiq received an enthusiastic treatment in the *Badāʾiʿ*. Ibn Iyās' narrative first presents the caliph as a hero and intercessor for everyday Cairenes, then as a deportee to Istanbul unleashing profound sorrow among the masses, and, finally, as a sad pawn corrupted by wealth who 'lost his head and thought that the advantageous situation would endure, [heedless that] the balance beam (*al-qabbān*) was at its end'.[134] Shortly afterwards, Ibn Iyās sketches the caliph's fall from grace in Ottoman custody, complete with family quarrels over money, accusations of embezzlement and an unpleasant Ottoman audit of Abbasid assets in Cairo.

In sum, Ibn Iyās provides a valuable image of the Abbasid Caliphate at the end of the Cairo Sultanate and many of the traditions that developed around it.[135] Most importantly, he confirms the visibility of the caliphs at important socio-political moments, demonstrating the leadership's links to higher power. In the first decades of transition into Ottoman rule, Ibn Iyās portrays the caliphate as a bridge between two political orders. At first, one learns, the Anatolian Turks accept the local importance of the Abbasid Caliphate and appear ready to incorporate it. But as the career of al-Mutawakkil III slowly crumbled into disappointment, the Ottomans, perhaps inexorably, disposed of the Abbasid Caliphate in favour of their own dynastic legitimacy and inheritance of the lofty titles associated with becoming caretakers of the holy shrines of the Hijaz.

Syrian *ʿUlamāʾ* Historians

The best prospects for examining the textual traces of the Abbasid Caliphate in medieval Syrian historiography come from the cluster of histories composed by religious scholars, some of them former students and colleagues of Ibn Taymiyya, active in the traditionalist scholarly milieu of late thirteenth-/early fourteenth-century Damascus.[136] The authors embraced and emulated the historical tradition started by the *Mirʾāt al-zamān fī Taʾrīkh al-aʿyān*, a universal chronicle attributed to the Iraqi historian Sibṭ ibn al-Jawzī (d. 654/1256).[137] Among the important historians writing in the late thirteenth/early fourteenth centuries were ʿAbd al-Raḥmān Abū Shāma (d. 665/1268) and Muḥammad ibn Wāṣil (d. 697/1298); followed some decades later by Mūsā al-Yūnīnī (d. 726/1326), Muḥammad al-Jazarī (d. 739/1338), al-Qāsim al-Birzālī (d. 739/1339), Muḥammad al-Dhahabī (d. 748/1348), ʿUmar ibn al-Wardī (d. 749/1349), Muḥammad al-Kutubī (d. 764/1363) and Ismāʿīl ibn Kathīr (d. 774/1373).[138] Historiographical works produced in Syria became less abundant in the later fourteenth and fifteenth centuries, making way for a new wave of Cairene historiography that drew heavily from the Syrian annals but focused firmly on events in Cairo.[139]

Defining characteristics of this group of authors include a great deal of mutual borrowing and adherence to a format dividing historical works into annals that included obituaries, often of notables and religious scholars, as well as information about their teachers, appointments and scholarly careers. Overall, the Syrian *ʿulamāʾ* historians preferred an holistic view of Islamic history and looked for a broader significance beyond the current socio-political realities of the Cairo Sultanate. Syrian scholars kept abreast of events involving the caliph and included them in their histories.[140]

The earliest authors of Arabic historical works from the mid-thirteenth century witnessed the end of the Ayyubid era and were contemporary with the dramatic sack of Baghdad and murder of the last Abbasid caliph in 656/1258.[141] In his *Tarājim rijāl al-qarnayn al-sādis wa-l-sābiʿ*, the Damascene scholar ʿAbd al-Raḥmān Abū Shāma (d. 665/1267) provided a contemporary account of the first two caliphal investitures, and from his post in Syria described an important mass celebration of the first Abbasid investiture in Cairo. The Syrian magistrate Jamāl al-Dīn Muḥammad ibn Wāṣil (d. 697/1298) served in the administration of Baybars and wrote a detailed history of the early sultanate beginning with the *dawla* of the Ayyubid family, *Mufarrij al-kurūb fī akhbār Banī Ayyūb*, which ended in the year 659/1261 and detailed the first Abbasid investiture in Cairo.

Abū Shāma provided a contemporary account of Baybars' investitures of the first two caliphs in his *Dhayl ʿalā al-rawḍatayn*, and his *Tarājim al-rijāl* provides an important glimpse of the widespread jubilation among Damascenes upon learning of the restored caliphate. Abū Shāma captures the reaction as the qadi of Damascus read the communiqué from Baybars at the ʿĀdiliyya *madrasa*:

> The people were immensely happy with this and thanked God for the return of the Abbasid Caliphate after the disbelieving Mongols had cut it off by killing the Caliph al-Mustaʿṣim ibn al-Ẓāhir, who was the nephew of the one given *bayʿa* in Egypt . . .[142]

Abū Shāma's account was particularly important to later Syrian historians such as al-Dhahabī and al-Yūnīnī, who cited it extensively, as well as historians in Egypt like Ibn Iyās and even al-Suyūṭī, who may even have absorbed and re-imagined Abū Shāma's words.[143]

In his comparative contextual analysis of the historical works of Abū Shāma and Ibn Wāṣil, Konrad Hirschler discovered rich commentary on the sultanate and caliphate embedded in the texts. Hirschler argues that Ibn Wāṣil, like al-Māwardī and Ibn Jamāʿa, accepted the status quo of the seizure of power by military force. Ibn Wāṣil's involvement with several prominent figures at different courts perhaps made him reluctant to present one single legitimate mode of rule. The ruler alone could not preserve good rule which instead was shared by elites at different courts. The rise of one amir to power over the others in the creation of a new localised dynasty was thus not problematic for the author. The opposite was true in the case of Abū Shāma, who opposed the status quo and sought reform. A contemporary of the Abbasid Caliphate of Baghdad, Abū Shāma understood the caliphate as an important symbol and form of legitimation. As Hirschler argues, the caliphate played an important symbolic role in the text of Abū Shāma which served as a point of reference for his general outlook.[144]

The Syrian Circle of the Early Fourteenth Century

Syrian historians working in the century after the death of Abū Shāma tended to be religious scholars with a secondary interest in historiography. Many shared similar backgrounds, lived in Damascus and were expert in ḥadīth transmission. Unlike their Egyptian counterparts, they had relatively fewer entanglements with the sultan's court and were often predisposed towards covering the activities of local urban notables and other religious scholars in Syria.[145]

This 'Syrian cluster', particularly al-Jazarī, al-Birzālī and al-Yūnīnī, are also noteworthy for the level at which they shared, copied and edited each other's works. Slightly later Syrian authors such as al-Kutubī, al-Dhahabī and Ibn Kathīr took information from the earlier three, perpetuating a great similarity among the works and complicating the process of discovering the origins of common information.[146]

Al-Yūnīnī's *Dhayl al-mirʾāt al-zamān*, a supplement (*dhayl*) to Sibṭ ibn al-Jawzī's *Mirʾāt al-zamān*, continues from the year 654/1256. It is fortunate that al-Yūnīnī covered the years (659/1261 and 661/1262) in which Baybars invested the two caliphs in Cairo, as copies of those corresponding annals in al-Jazarī's *Ḥawādith* have not survived, and al-Birzālī's *Muqtafī*, a *dhayl* of Abū Shāma's history, begins with the Islamic year 665/1266–7. Based on modern intertextual studies, it is likely that al-Jazarī's coverage of the investiture ceremonies closely resembles that of al-Yūnīnī.[147]

The real value of the information preserved in al-Yūnīnī's *Dhayl* derives from the testimony of Zayn al-Dīn Ṣāliḥ ibn al-Bannāʾ, a close confederate of the caliph al-Ḥākim whose account may well have appeared in al-Jazarī's lost annals. Ibn al-Bannāʾ accompanied the caliph during his escape from Baghdad, witnessed his seeking of support among the Bedouin tribes, the investiture in Aleppo, skirmishes with the Mongols, and ultimately his arrival at Cairo in 660/1262. These reports of Ibn al-Bannāʾ also became a source valuable to later historians such as al-Suyūṭī and centuries later al-Jabartī.[148]

Interest in all matters religious and Syrian guided al-Yūnīnī's coverage of the Abbasid investitures in Cairo. In addition to the details and text of the subsequent announcement sent to Syria, the author provides extensive details on the first caliphal visit to Damascus with Baybars, campaigns fought on the outskirts of Syria and Mesopotamia, and the alliance between al-Mustanṣir and al-Ḥākim intended to 'erect the *dawla* of Banī ʿAbbās'.[149] Al-Yūnīnī's *Dhayl* places more focus on Syria, including the caliph al-Ḥākim's period of vagabondage with Bedouin tribes, as well as his brief public appearance at Friday prayer in Damascus and many of the details involving al-Mustanṣir's campaign to retake Baghdad, which launched from Syria.[150]

The *Muqtafī li-Taʾrīkh* attributed to the Shāfiʿī traditionalist al-Birzālī, a continuation of Abū Shāma, adopts a strict chronological framework that includes more biographies and obituaries than historical events. An early report on the caliphate concerns a 676/1277 marriage connection between the lines of al-Mustanṣir and al-Ḥākim.[151] Since, like al-Yūnīnī, much of his interest lay in Syria and its religious scholars, al-Birzālī's coverage of caliphal issues tends to be sparse, brief and similar in content to al-Yūnīnī.

After several 'missing' annals, al-Jazarī's coverage of the Abbasid Caliphate resumes in 737/1336 amid the deteriorating relationship between sultan al-Nāṣir Muḥammad and the caliph al-Mustakfī, who was relocated to quarters within the Citadel along with his family, then returned to a private residence the following year.[152] While al-Jazarī died before the caliph's expulsion to Qūṣ, he still prays for the victory of al-Nāṣir Muḥammad (*ʿizza naṣruhu*) against his foes, even if that included the Abbasid caliph.

Al-Dhahabī, another prominent Shāfiʿī traditionalist and Syrian historian, known largely for his religious scholarship, sat in the scholarly circles of Ibn Taymiyya and al-Birzālī and accessed the works of al-Jazarī and al-Yūnīnī.[153] According to Heidemann, al-Dhahabī's works serve as the repository for what is known about the caliph al-Ḥākim's time in Aleppo, preserving information on the Banū Taymiyya's involvement in the Syrian *bayʿa* in Ḥarrān, perhaps through his interactions with Ibn Taymiyya.[154] Al-Dhahabī simultaneously acknowledged the widely accepted position of al-Mustanṣir as the thirty-eighth Abbasid caliph,[155] and repeated reports of his courage and fitness for office.[156] Upon describing the investiture of the caliph of his own time, al-Ḥākim II (741–53/1341–52), al-Dhahabī writes, '[The caliph] received the pledge of allegiance and sat with the sultan atop the throne of sovereignty as the qadis and others pledged allegiance; God be praised!'[157]

Another younger student of Ibn Taymiyya and al-Dhahabī, the Shāfiʿī traditionalist Ibn Kathīr, wrote an important universal history, *al-Bidāya wa-l-nihāya fī al-Taʾrīkh*, in which he offered frank images of sultans and caliphs.[158] Like al-Dhahabī, Ibn Kathīr recognised al-Mustanṣir as the thirty-eighth caliph of his line and also hinted that the ill-fated Baghdad campaign had been the caliph's own idea.[159] Mohammad Gharaibeh's study of the *Bidāya* has also examined Ibn Kathīr's view of the Abbasid Caliphate in the light of his ideological and eschatological pre-commitments. Ibn Kathīr saw the Abbasids, based on dubious traditions of the Prophet, as the rightful rulers who would rule until the Day of Judgement. For Ibn Kathīr, who had a strong inclination towards religiously interpreting events, history was only on track when it conformed to the predictions of the Prophet, which strengthened Abbasid legitimacy. Ibn Kathīr believed that the *mahdī*, the end-time eschatological deliverer of the Islamic tradition, would eventually arise from the Abbasid line and rule until the return of Jesus. It is thus that while the Abbasid Caliphate lost control of its territory and played only a muted political role, the author of the *Bidāya* gave it a powerful theological role down to the present and into the future.[160]

Hassan has demonstrated that geographic distance from the seat of power in Cairo made little difference to the bond the scholars of greater Syria felt with the Abbasids.[161] Wiederhold's study of the Ẓāhirī movement in late fourteenth-century Damascus likewise provides evidence that the caliphate was central to religious identity and public life, not to mention a *cause célèbre* among disaffected members of the religious leadership.[162] While the caliphs maintained a potent importance in historiography as authors wrote of locals rejoicing over the investiture of new caliphs and mourning their exiles or deaths, Syrian authors, in reality, would have encountered the Abbasid caliph through his infrequent visits to Damascus or Aleppo embedded in the sultan's army. Under such circumstances, the caliph, with the four chief qadis nearby, would be one member among many of the official civilian retinue: in that situation, the caliph would appear as merely another reminder of sultanic sovereignty. In short, any physical Syrian connection to the performance of the Abbasid Caliphate in the fourteenth century, compared with Cairo, was perhaps far less immediate (though symbolically no less important).

Although their geographical separation from Cairo rendered Syrian religious scholars somewhat provincial, it behoved most of them to recognise the legitimacy of the Abbasid line in Cairo. After all, the perpetuation of the caliphate partially underwrote their own authority as *ʿulamāʾ* involved in patronage relationships with local political elites, just as it did their Cairene counterparts.[163] Thus, whatever their true feelings, the Syrian historians clearly had a vested interest in showing that the political elite of Cairo (and by extension the rest of Egypt and Syria) had done right by reviving and maintaining the caliphate in the line of al-ʿAbbās after the events of 656/1258.

Later Fifteenth-century Egyptian Historical Writing

The fifteenth century was a unique time for the production and consumption of historical texts. Amid a contextual background of major social transformation brought about by plagues, the invasion of Temür and the collapse of the political order during the reign of sultan Faraj, many historians such as al-Maqrīzī, Ibn Ḥajar and al-ʿAynī, as 'survivors', had to reinvent themselves in order to participate in the new socio-political order after 815/1412. As important judges, market inspectors and *manṣab* position-holders, they all sought patrons and opportunities for employment, and in their historical writing helped to construct 'a cultural order that aligned itself with the new social and political orders of the times'.[164]

It is difficult to identify distinct 'schools' among the Egyptian and Syrian writers of historical works, though later chroniclers tended to focus more heavily on events in Egypt. Claims of the Abbasid caliph's sanctity and universal authority were met with the greatest acceptance and immediacy in Cairo, the locus of the Citadel and political centre of the sultanate which vigorously proclaimed its access to the caliphs. Later histories penned by Egyptian-based historians, like any denizens of an imperial capital, tended to envision Cairo as the centre of the world.[165] Thus, as Hassan and Wiederhold have made clear, the religious authority of the Abbasid Caliphate, such as it was, was *accepted* in scholarly circles, even if it was often downplayed or ignored outright. Egyptian historians came from all walks of society: political elites, religious scholars, chancery clerks, many of whom blended a style mixing colloquial with high-class literary Arabic.[166]

Al-Maqrīzī, d. 845/1442

Resoundingly considered *the* iconic Egyptian historian of the fifteenth century, the so-called '*shaykh al-mu'arrikhīn*' Aḥmad al-Maqrīzī, despite his official capacities as a market inspector (*muḥtasib*), deputy qadi, mosque orator and teacher, was not particularly favourable towards the sultans of Cairo of his day. Al-Maqrīzī's reputation has preceded him both inside and outside the modern field of 'Mamluk Studies'. The 'fame' of al-Maqrīzī may be attributable to the fact that his chronicle was among the first to become widely available to modern scholars. Presenting a civilian point of view in much of his historical writing, al-Maqrīzī's historiography focuses on Egypt. His love for Cairo and its past allows him to embrace even earlier dynasties living there, such as the Fatimids and the sultans of Cairo dating back to the Ayyubids.[167] Employed by the chief secretary and administrator Fatḥ al-Dīn Fatḥ Allāh (d. 816/1413) in the early fifteenth century, al-Maqrīzī closely witnessed (and worked for) the brief pseudo-sultanate of al-Mustaʿīn bi-llāh (815/1412).[168] He had contempt for later sultans such as Shaykh and Barsbāy, and after the loss of his official position enjoyed a life of writing and apparent freedom to express his opinions.

Familiar with bygone centuries of Islamic history, al-Maqrīzī, as a chronicler of his own age, commented frequently on the status of the Abbasid Caliphate of his time and seldom shied away from criticising the reigning political order whenever he thought it fell short. Indeed, as a trained public official and scholar, al-Maqrīzī's moral vision of an ideal Islamic state demanded a role for the *ʿulamāʾ* in guiding the community, as well as their inclusion in the important task of advising sultans on the most efficient application of *sharīʿa*.[169]

Al-Maqrīzī's introduction to the history of mankind, *Al-khabar ʿan al-bashar*, while written late in his life, serves as a political introduction to world history leading up to the birth of the Prophet.[170] In it, al-Maqrīzī discusses the perfection of the Hashemite line and the Prophet's appearance within it, sentiments which appear in four earlier treatises of varying length that touched on the legacy of the Abbasid Caliphate in the context of the author's views on rule in Islam.[171] These treatises on the caliphate provided space for the author to grapple with lingering questions about earlier epochs of Islamic history and what constituted proper leadership of the Muslim community. His lengthy biographical work on the Prophet, *Kitāb Imtāʿ al-asmāʿ bi-mā lil-rasūl min al-anbāʾ wa-l-amwāl wa-l-ḥafada wa-l-matāʿ*, contained biography as well as essays on claims to leadership after the death of Muḥammad.[172] A work emphasising support for the Hashemite clan (comprising the Alids and Abbasids) came in the form of his *Kitāb maʿarifat mā yajibu li-Āl al-Bayt al-Nabawī min al-ḥaqq ʿalā man ʿadāhum*, written in 841–2/1438 after the historian returned to Cairo from a sojourn in Mecca. *Kitāb maʿarifa* parses five verses of the Qurʾān on their significance to the caliphate and prefaces the author's defence of the historical right of the Hashemites to leadership of the Muslim community.[173]

Al-Maqrīzī tackled the early caliphs of the Umayyad and Abbasid dynasties in his most famous work on the subject, *Kitāb al-nizāʿ wa-l-takhāṣum fī mā bayna Banī Umayya wa-Banī Ḥāshim*. He discussed the historical rivalries between the families and, while he never portrayed the Umayyads positively, al-Maqrīzī likewise denounced Abbasid atrocities committed during their early eighth-century revolutionary period.[174] *Kitāb al-nizāʿ* traces the Abbasids from pre-Islamic times, with little elaboration, to the mid-thirteenth century. A truncated version of the work appeared as *Kitāb fī dhikr mā warada fī Banī Umayya wa-Banī al-ʿAbbās*, possibly composed in Mecca for a patron of Abbasid descent, which takes a decidedly pro-Abbasid tone. After a harsh section on the Umayyads, al-Maqrīzī praises members of the Abbasid family from al-ʿAbbās to al-Saffāḥ and champions their claims, emphasising Abbasid pre-eminence in Islamic history.[175]

Al-Maqrīzī's treatises on the early age of Islam are understandably removed from his work on the contemporary Abbasid Caliphate detailed in the later annals of his *Kitāb al-sulūk li-maʿrifat duwal al-mulūk*. Similar in many ways to his former teacher Ibn Khaldūn, al-Maqrīzī read a practical ending to the Abbasid Caliphate in its eradication by the Mongol conqueror Hülegü. Although Baybars restored the line in Cairo, al-Maqrīzī failed to see its 'return' as a true restoration that went beyond the caliphate's nominal nature in his own time.[176] Al-Maqrīzī's discussion of the caliphate in *Kitāb al-nizāʿ* remains pragmatic and cognizant of long-standing institutional problems dating back to the Umayyads and worsening under the early Abbasids. For al-Maqrīzī, as for many authors of the period, the notion that leadership ought to remain in the hands of a Qurayshī *imām* is an important proposition for which he gives much support in the form of prophetic traditions.[177] While defending the historical right of the Abbasids as Hashemites, the historian does not shy away from listing their faults, including violent purges of the Umayyads, the Muʿtazilī innovations of al-Maʾmūn and al-Mustaʿṣim, as well as the latter's fatal over-reliance on Turkish slave soldiers, an error revisited in Egypt, in the view of the author.[178]

In *Kitāb al-nizāʿ*, al-Maqrīzī clarifies that the Abbasid family had long since inherited a troubled office that had 'grown weak, and its supports had become shaky, and people had successively seized power over the Muslim community by force of arms'. The Abbasids, through the help of the Persians and Khurāsānīs, seized office by force. During the dynasty's tenure in Baghdad, their rule from the centre deteriorated until 'all political power transferred from the Banū ʿAbbās (Abbasids) to the Banū Buwayh (Buyids) of Daylam, and all that was left to the Banū al-ʿAbbās of the caliphate was the name, without any freedom of executive action'. While symbolic heads of Islam, the caliphs remained subject to the Buyids and Seljuks who retained true power over the caliphs 'as a master (*mālik*) does over his slave (*mamlūk*)' until Hülegü's conquest.[179]

It is at this point in the *Kitāb al-nizāʿ* that al-Maqrīzī, a versatile Muslim historian with a working knowledge of Old Testament lore, finds parallels between the fortunes of the post-Mongol Abbasid caliphs and the Children of Israel in the wake of Nebuchadnezzar.[180] He wrote that foreign invasions spelled the end for both lines, and neither Jews nor Muslims ever united under a single man as leader of their religion amid a tremendous loss of political power that saw the rise of numerous regional rulers, including the ruling sultans of Syro-Egypt:

> Likewise after Nebuchadnezzar's destruction of the Children of Israel's power, the Israelites acquired a regime in which they were under the domination of the Greeks and others, whilst Jerusalem was being rebuilt and

> after their return from the captivity. Similarly, the Turkish rulers of Egypt set up one of the Banū ʿAbbās as caliph, but he had no power to command or forbid, nor was any decree of his effective in any way.[181]

In his historical output concerning his own times, al-Maqrīzī sets forth a view of the Abbasid Caliphate as a ruined institution comprising little more than its name. A now famous passage of the *Sulūk* which closes a section on the Abbasids of Baghdad while demonstrating the author's presentist concerns about the caliphate has been cited by numerous modern historians as the final 'smoking gun' of Abbasid irrelevance to late medieval Egyptian politics and governance:

> The Turkish sovereigns of the 'Mamluk dynasty' installed a man as caliph to whom they gave the name and titles suitable to the caliphs. He had no authority and not even the right to express his opinion. He passed his time among the amirs, the major officers, the scribes, the qadis, and made visits to them to thank them for the dinners and pleasantries to which they invited him.[182]

In two of his other works, al-Maqrīzī took the career of the caliph-sultan al-Mustaʿīn as a point of departure from which to sketch the Abbasid dynasty of Cairo. The possibly earlier of the two narratives appeared in his topographical study of Cairo, *al-Mawāʿiẓ wa-l-iʿtibār bi-dhikr al-khiṭaṭ wa-l-āthār fī Miṣr wa-l-Qāhira* (hereafter the *Khiṭaṭ*), during the course of a history of the 'Kings of Egypt since the building of the Citadel'.[183] After discussing the early thirteenth- and fourteenth-century sultans of Cairo (as al-Akrād and *dawlat al-mamālik al-baḥriyya*, respectively), the historian discusses the Circassian line of sultans (*dawlat al-mamālīk al-jarākisa*)[184] beginning with Barqūq until he arrives at the brief reign of al-Mustaʿīn, after which he embarks on the 'origin of those caliphs in Egypt . . . [after] the world had been void of a caliph and the people deprived of a Qurayshī *imām*'.[185] Al-Maqrīzī asserts that the caliphs, save for a few, were imprisoned: a situation that 'continued for [al-Ḥākim] and the caliphs who came after him'. The author argues that during his forty years in office, al-Ḥākim 'had no authority (*amr*) or ability to prohibit (*nahy*); rather, his only portion [of the caliphate] is that he was called "Commander of the Faithful"'.[186]

The brief caliphal history in the *Khiṭaṭ* also conveys interesting details about Abbasid stewardship of the shrine of Sayyida Nafīsa, but it is largely a summation of the standard milestones involving the Cairo Caliphate contained in the *Sulūk* and other contemporary sources. In the *Khiṭaṭ*, the history of the Abbasids ends with the termination of al-Mustaʿīn's sultanate by al-Muʾayyad Shaykh and his successors.[187]

In al-Maqrīzī's encyclopaedia of contemporaries, *Durar al-ʿuqūd al-farīda fī tarājim al-aʿyān al-mufīda* written almost a year later, the entry devoted to al-Mustaʿīn again reviews all of the Cairene Abbasids.[188] The text here resembles the earlier one in the *Khiṭaṭ*, save for two digressions. The *Durar* biography includes a longer history of the caliph al-Ḥākim's earlier adventures in Syria with the Āl Faḍl Bedouin, his recognition by Quṭuz and his competition with the caliph al-Mustanṣir for investiture in Cairo.[189] Al-Maqrīzī also includes further details of the career and later life of al-Mustaʿīn which do not appear in the *Khiṭaṭ* version.

Covering his own ninth century of the Islamic lunar calendar, al-Maqrīzī adopts the editorial convention among other contemporary chroniclers of mentioning the caliph presiding over each year.[190] This does not hinder him from reminding readers of the impotence of the Abbasid caliph in his own time. At the start of his organisational list of position-holders for the Islamic year 801/1398–9, the author of the *Sulūk* reiterates:

> At the commencement of this ninth century the caliph of the age was the Commander of the Faithful al-Mutawakkil . . . who while garbed in authority, is prohibited from it: his order commands no influence (*lā nufūdh kalima*) – rather he shares the status (*manzila*) of one of the notables.[191]

In *al-Dhahab al-masbūk fī dhikr man ḥajja min al-khulafāʾ wa-l-mulūk*, al-Maqrīzī's treatise on caliphs and kings that attempted the pilgrimage to Mecca, the author, according to Van Steenbergen, may have used the troubled narrative of the caliph al-Ḥākim's 697/1298 *ḥajj* to engage with the robust contemporary discourse on the caliphate and sultanate by subtly addressing the weakened position of caliphal authority and the contested legitimacy of the caliph in Cairo. Al-Maqrīzī, positioning the narrative at the end of a sequence of more powerful caliphs (thus resembling a cycle of rise, decline and fall in the caliphal line), may have read a practical end to traditional caliphal authority and used it to transition into his third chapter on non-caliphal rulers who embarked on the pilgrimage. Al-Maqrīzī cites disagreements over al-Ḥākim's lineage and points out the failure of the modern caliphs to be prayed for in Mecca (save for the caliph-sultan al-Mustaʿīn) 'against a background of powerlessness and defunct authority that reads as an anticlimactic moment in the text'.[192]

Nevertheless, al-Maqrīzī acknowledged that the Abbasid Caliphate carried some weight on the political stage, particularly when eastern ambassadors visited Cairo, though he differentiates between the ability to issue orders that are obeyed and the more abstract religious authority residually invested in the caliphs of his day.[193] Ever the hard-nosed historian, al-Maqrīzī did not sugar-coat his judgement of the Abbasid Caliphate of his own time, thus shaping an attitude seemingly all his own. His general dislike of the political orders constructed by the supporters of Shaykh and Barsbāy may also have coloured his perception of the caliphate as empty pageantry manipulated by the insufferable government.[194] Nevertheless, abiding respect for the Banū ʿAbbās as a historical force ensured al-Maqrīzī's continued interest in the family's fortunes in Cairo in spite of himself.[195] Although he harboured little love for the later fifteenth-century sultans of his day, al-Maqrīzī was a great admirer of the Seljuks, Fatimids and early sultans of Cairo. One noteworthy passage of the author's eulogy for Baybars in the *Sulūk*, an unattributed reworking of earlier sentiments expressed by Ibn ʿAbd al-Ẓāhir,[196] puts forth the contemporary caliphate as a literary device connecting them all:

> [Just as the Seljuk sultan] **Rukn al-Dīn** Ṭughril Beg returned the caliphate to the Abbasids after the tumult [brought about by the Buyid commander] al-Basāsīrī, **Rukn al-Dīn** Baybars is the one who returned the caliphate to the Abbasids after that of Hülegü. [Likewise] in Egypt after the *khuṭba* [was made in the name of] the Fatimid caliph **al-Ḥākim** [it was made for his successor] **al-Ẓāhir** li-Iʿzāz Dīn Allāh, while [in the thirteenth century] after the name of the Abbasid caliph **al-Ḥākim**, al-Malik **al-Ẓāhir** Baybars [was mentioned in the *khuṭba*].[197]

In frank terms, al-Maqrīzī interprets the reality of the Abbasid Caliphate as many modern historians have come to assess it.[198] However, like most authors of historical works in late medieval Cairo, he accepted the caliphs as true Abbasids descended from the caliphs of Baghdad. Moreover, his later writings do not dispute the idea that the world needed a Qurayshī *imām* lest it go spiritually astray.[199] Al-Maqrīzī's absorption of a long tradition of pro-Abbasid attitudes may have encouraged his recognition of the men of the Cairo line as Abbasids, but not as caliphs or *imām*s in the classical sense[200] and certainly not worthy of his veneration.

Al-Maqrīzī's proximity to the so-called Ẓāhirī movement of the late fourteenth/early fifteenth century deserves more scrutiny based on his biographies of Ẓāhirīs in the *Durar al-ʿuqūd al-farīda* and his ties to the Egyptian scholar Abū Hishām Aḥmad ibn al-Burhān al-Ẓāhirī (d. 808/1405).[201] Al-Maqrīzī's position that rule had to return to the Alids and the Hashemite line may well have been influenced by his movement in Ẓāhirī circles in the late fourteenth/early fifteenth centuries.

The varied nature of al-Maqrīzī's writing over the years demonstrates that one must be aware that an author's position on socio-cultural or political issues did not always remain static throughout their life. The modern undertaking of Brill's *Bibliotheca Maqriziana* project (directed by Frédéric Bauden) to contextualise each surviving work of the author opens the possibilities of considering a chronological evolution of al-Maqrīzī's worldview including his perspective on notions of caliphate and kingship which have survived in both his short treatises as well as his longer works of history.

Ibn Ḥajar al-ʿAsqalānī, d. 852/1449

In his biographies of the Abbasid caliphs of the eighth Islamic century, the noted religious scholar Ibn Ḥajar al-ʿAsqalānī preserved examples of the political elite's desires to encourage the caliphs to pursue academic pastimes as the dynamics of the sultan–caliph relationship played out in Cairo. The historical writing of Ibn Ḥajar also carries a sense of sanctity for the caliphal *bayʿa* as a hallowed Islamic tradition, the gravity of which was not to be disrupted by petty politics in Egypt and Syria. He wrote that al-Nāṣir Muḥammad, a century earlier, had illegally forced the issue of succession and trespassed against what should have been the sole prerogative of the caliph al-Mustakfī to name his own successor.[202] In a later discussion of the deposition of al-Mutawakkil, Ibn Ḥajar implies that he was the true caliph and that Barqūq, cowed by impending revolt, had been forced to restore him under duress.[203]

Ibn Ḥajar al-ʿAsqalānī covered caliphal issues with interest, and for the year 800/1397–8 noted that while the Abbasid Commander of the Faithful was al-Mutawakkil, his title was disputed by the Zaydī *imām* and various rulers of North Africa and Yemen. In the latter region, mosques delivered Friday prayers in the name of the last caliph of Baghdad, al-Mustaʿṣim, who had been dead for well over a century.[204]

We can also derive an intriguing image of the contemporary caliphate from poetry attributed to Ibn Ḥajar al-ʿAsqalānī. While he was a contemporary, Ibn Ḥajar's precise role in the saga of the caliph-sultan al-Mustaʿīn is unknown at best.[205] He would later describe the doomed caliph-sultan as thinking he had 'a free hand in appointing and dismissing, but in reality had only the emblems [of the sultanate] and [mention in] the *khuṭba*',[206] the author, like al-Qalqashandī and doubtless others, nevertheless got caught up in initial optimism at the investiture of the caliph in 808/1406. Ibn Ḥajar sought to commemorate the occasion with a lengthy *qasīda*[207] that opens with praise:

> Dominion (*mulk*) among us is firm of foundation
> through al-Mustaʿīn, the just, al-ʿAbbās.
>
> The position of the family of the Prophet's uncle returned
> to its place after prolonged disregard.[208]

Ibn Ḥajar al-ʿAsqalānī notes the date of the caliph's accession, then comments on widespread rejoicing over the investiture. Using a floral analogy he likens al-Mustaʿīn to a luscious branch growing forth from the garden of the Prophet's Hāshim family.[209] He lauds the great qualities of past leaders, whether powerful caliphs or sultans, and claims that God exalted the religion of Islam after it had been in desolation by fortifying it through noble leaders with the ability to exact vengeance on behalf of the community. He also refers to military leaders capable of decimating their enemies as sublime supports, though it is apparent that for Ibn Ḥajar, the divine significance of the caliphate dwarfs military prowess. After all, it is the caliph's presence in Cairo that plainly perpetuates all political and social order:

> Their *imām* through his splendour (*bi-jalālihi*) precedes them,
> as '*bismillāh*' takes precedence atop the document (*fī al-qirṭās*).

If not for the ordering of the state under his direction (*niẓām al-mulk fī tadbīrihi*),
the condition (*ḥāl*) of men in the kingdom could not persist.[210]

And later:

The hands of kings obey him, in submission
[just as] the fingers of the Nilometer [obey] the Nile of Egypt.

For he is the one who has repelled from us misery,
evil would abound in the world were it not for him.

He has alleviated the all-embracing oppression (*ẓulm*)
of every remaining type and kind.[211]

Through poetry Ibn Ḥajar expressed his understanding of the caliph as a supernatural actor with God-given privileges to command the hearts of men as well as the retention of divine influence in matters of climate and ecology. In this context, the 'powerlessness' of the caliph may have been seen positively as he was less inclined to fall prey to the temptations and impurities of actual worldly power. That Ibn Ḥajar read untold blessings from the presence of the caliph is clear in the poem which also states that the caliph brought immeasurable favours from God (*naʿmāt* or *niʿmāt*).[212] Reminding the reader/listener to cherish the incumbent caliph, Ibn Ḥajar recounts all the good that the caliphate brought to Cairo, for it is in the Abbasid caliph that God grants the people a ruler whose days are exalted and prosperous:

None shall seek to disparage the signs of his glory
among men, save for the wicked fool.

The virtues (*manāqib*) of al-ʿAbbās have never been united
except in his descendant, king of mankind, ʿAbbās [al-Mustaʿīn].

Deny not to al-Mustaʿīn leadership
in dominion after the evasion of forgetfulness.[213]

Ibn Ḥajar closes his inaugural *qaṣīda* with a solemn prayer effectively offering fealty to al-Mustaʿīn as his liege lord:

My master, your servant (*ʿabduka*) has come to you, seeking
acceptance from you, that it not be taken deficiently.

And were it not for awe of you, his praises would be longer,
to where he has brought them in a balance.

May the God of mankind make your glory endure,
guarded in justice by the God of mankind.

And may you live to hear praises from your servant (*khādim*),
for were it not for you he would endure sorrow.[214]

The realities of Syro-Egyptian politics that brought about the swift dismissal of al-Mustaʿīn by al-Muʾayyad Shaykh did not prevent Ibn Ḥajar from continuing, in his chronicle at least, to formally recognise the caliphate of al-Mustaʿīn, who became an exile in Alexandria until his death in 833/1430.[215] As chief Shāfiʿī qadi, however, Ibn Ḥajar also recognised al-Mustaʿīn's successor, al-Muʿtaḍid II and met with him many times officially and at scholarly sessions. Ibn Ḥajar enjoyed a patronage tie with the caliph al-Muʿtaḍid II and composed an ode thanking him for gifts he had received on the caliph's departure for Āmid to campaign against the Aqquyunlu with Barsbāy in 836/1433:

O master who gained lordship over the people of the world (*banī al-dunyā*),
for they are under his war banner, generous and enduring.

You bestowed on me largesse and my thanks are insufficient
So if you seek my thanks, [know] they are inadequate.

You resemble ʿAbbās who summoned the rain in time of drought –
as the abundant rain obeyed him when all seemed lost.

[True] generosity ended with Abī al-Faḍl [al-ʿAbbās], but among
his offspring it remains; ask and you will find.

None succeeded in the generosity of his ancestor –
save for the Commander of the Faithful al-Muʿtaḍid![216]

Clearly, the poem uses strong imagery to link al-Muʿtaḍid II to his ancestor al-ʿAbbās, alluding to the year 17/638 in which a major drought threatened the Hijaz during the reign of the second caliph ʿUmar ibn al-Khaṭṭāb (d. 23/644).[217] Precedent for the Muslim *tawassul* prayers for rain began with the Prophet's request to God to send rain. Scholars such as Ibn Ḥajar, al-Suyūṭī and Ibn Iyās drew attention to the story's cultural bearing and the role it had on casting the contemporary Abbasid caliphs as descendants of a holy man obeyed by the elements.[218] Extra magnitude attributed to prayers made by the caliph as a descendant of al-ʿAbbās brought more integration of the caliphate into Cairene life at public gatherings for prayer to alleviate plague, bring rain or increase the Nile inundation in years of drought, all of which were important performances of the Abbasid Caliphate before the public in Cairene society.

But could it be that there was a residual element of pagan thinking too, as well as poetic hyperbole? We have the notion that al-Muʿtaḍid, like all other Abbasid caliphs, was the *true* heir of the Prophet's uncle al-ʿAbbās who, according to tradition, 'brought the rain in a time of drought'. This appears to be an ascription of supernatural powers to the caliph, who by his ancestry alone was said to be a lightning rod for *baraka* or favour with God to the extent that even the rain obeyed him. We know that this concept of the caliph as rain-bringer was important to the ruling elite, who periodically made use of the caliph by asking him to pray for rain or sufficient levels at the well of the Nilometer.[219]

It is of little surprise that Ibn Ḥajar al-ʿAsqalānī, a man who so loved the Abbasids of his own time, was attended in his funeral bier by the brother and successor of al-Muʿtaḍid, al-Mustakfī II, a celebrated participant amongst the estimated 50,000 attendees at the funeral for a notable Cairene scholar eulogised as the '*amīr al-muʾminīn fī 'l-ḥadīth*' in 852/1448.[220]

Jalāl al-Dīn al-Suyūṭī, d. 911/1505

Although the scholarly interests of al-Suyūṭī cover an array of subjects related to the sciences and humanities, he wrote at great length about history and Islamic governance. Modern scholars have described his worldview as consistently representing a Sunni piety at odds with sultanic usurpation of classical caliphal rights.[221] His works, *Ḥusn al-muḥāḍara fī Taʾrīkh Miṣr wa-l-Qāhira* and *Taʾrīkh al-khulafāʾ*, showcase a unique image of the Abbasid Caliphate in the socio-political order of the sultanate of Cairo. In the latter, a chronologically arranged history of every caliphal successor since the death of the Prophet, the author includes documents and noteworthy events such as battles or natural disasters that occurred during a caliph's time in office. The *Ḥusn*, on the other hand, was a localised history of Egypt that drew attention to the relationship of its rulers with the caliphate. For al-Suyūṭī it was clear that in the years since Baybars resurrected the Abbasid Caliphate, Egypt had undergone a profound cultural efflorescence and emerged as a devoutly Islamic capital.[222]

The histories of al-Suyūṭī exude the indignation of a staunch traditionalist who frequently bristled at what he perceived as the insults of sultans aimed at the contemporary caliphs, as well as their wrongfully diminished station in society. It remains difficult to speak of the author's aspirations for the caliphate beyond general terms, though some clues emerge from his historical works. At the outset, it seems clear that the Abbasid Caliphate, as traditional guarantor of the *sharīʿa*, must underwrite the legitimacy of government. For al-Suyūṭī, sultans were only as good as their treatment of the Commander of the Faithful.[223]

Al-Suyūṭī's failed 902/1496 scheme to advance the political power of his ally al-Mutawakkil II and get himself named executive qadi (*qāḍī kabīr*) offers more insight into the author's conception of the contemporary caliphate. Aware as he was of the limitations that religious and political elites had placed on the caliphate, al-Suyūṭī nevertheless cited historical example and, according to Ibn Iyās, wished to be named as the *qāḍī kabīr* on the precedent that previous caliphs had appointed meritorious men as they saw fit.[224] In this case, al-Suyūṭī did not seek more power for the caliph beyond naming delegates. While this posed no immediate threat to the ruling elite, it frightened the *ʿulamāʾ*, particularly the four chief qadis who viewed it as an existential threat to their own positions. This implied trouble for the *dawla* of Qāyitbāy whose *actual* authority over the land derived more from the *ʿulamāʾ* than the caliph; if the *ʿulamāʾ* were unhappy with the rulers for some reason, the sultan and his men would have the choice of either appeasing them or potentially facing their castigation in the public sphere.

As Garcin puts it, al-Suyūṭī may have wished to 'restore the natural order', as he longed to see at least some power restored to the caliphate, certainly more than it had enjoyed in previous years in Cairo. He also was an opponent of the system of four chief qadiships, wishing instead to gather their authority in the hands of one man, whether himself or the Abbasid caliph aided by a learned adviser.[225] It was not just a matter of al-Suyūṭī playing for a high position; his suggestion was based on the Ayyubid precedent that Tāj al-Dīn ibn Bint al-Aʿazz appointed and dismissed all the magistrates of the empire.[226] Moreover, past history clearly demonstrated that a caliph also had the right to appoint whom he saw fit to office. Baybars' decision to create four chief qadiships in the 660s/1260s had no history behind it, though it facilitated the efforts of the Cairo sultan to control the religious leadership by divide and rule.[227]

Although al-Suyūṭī disapproved of the caliph as a powerless figurehead, he paradoxically may have been wary of a caliphate with too much power. If, in fact, the caliph received advice, selected fatwas and potentially engaged with military policy, it is difficult to envisage where such an arrangement would have left the sultan. Such an image of the caliphate was focused on the religious sphere, seeking to maintain the caliph as the symbolic heart of Islam albeit with the power of selecting religious policies and making appointments in the world of the *ʿulamāʾ* through informed counsel (*shūra*).[228]

For their part, the caliphs of the later fifteenth century had not sought out a larger role.[229] Even if they had been interested in more power, they rarely had opportunities to seize it and had no practical means of maintaining it. Al-Suyūṭī believed not only in the legitimising force of the Abbasid family for a political elite comprising former slave-soldiers, dynastic princes and usurpers, but viewed it as the caliph's privilege to recognise whomever he wished.

In his historical works, al-Suyūṭī forces a distinction between caliphs and sultans, and his choice of composing Islamic history in the medium of a caliphal history speaks to his understanding that the caliph was central to the organisation and efficiency of the natural world and that history incessantly occurred within the reign of the caliph of the age.[230]

The survey in this chapter demonstrates varying degrees of interest in the Abbasid Caliphate of Cairo among historians of dissimilar backgrounds. In several cases, the background and vocation of a writer influenced his engagement with discourses on the caliphate. It is important to be aware of the different contexts that produced these different textual perspectives. The authors chosen for Chapters 6 and 7 present different normative and narrative conceptions of the caliphate/imamate that engage with the contemporary caliphate in their writings. The textual elements connect to the ritual and symbolic presentations of the Abbasid Caliphate in Cairo that not only represent the discourse[231] but also contribute to making and guiding that discourse in deliberate directions.

Administrative insiders and religious scholars with interests at court tended to speak highly of the Abbasid Caliphate as a reflection of the ruling political order and its commitment to Islam.[232] On the other hand, relatively more independent authors such as al-Maqrīzī watched the caliphs from a cautious distance and took a pragmatic or even ambivalent stance towards them in their writing. Which voices in society were represented by the historical views on the caliphate expressed by the historians discussed in this chapter? While many of the authors seem to be converging on the idea that the caliphate retained relevance, the fact that some historians such as Badr al-Dīn al-ʿAynī had comparatively less to say on the topic is equally important.

Royal histories of the late thirteenth/early fourteenth centuries adopted and projected the idea that the re-establishment of the caliphate had been a good deed of Baybars, helping in part to explain his authority and overlook his complicity in the murder of his predecessor. Court historians were obliged to portray their patrons in the best possible light, sometimes emphasising the esteem of the sultans towards the idea of the caliphate.[233]

Many scholars and administrators who wrote history such as al-Ṣafadī, Ibn Ḥajar, Ibn Taghrībirdī and al-Suyūṭī enjoyed patronage, relational and/or familial ties with the Abbasid caliphs, and were often, though not always, inclined towards sympathy with their family. Proximity and sentimentality could influence the biography of a well-liked caliph, although historians with complex identities and pre-commitments such as Ibn Taghrībirdī or even pragmatists like al-Maqrīzī and Ibn Khaldūn remained aloof or dismissive towards the caliphs. It is difficult to diagnose the precise reasons *why* an author presented the caliphal role in recent history as he did, though background and position played no small part in their explanations of recent and ongoing events.[234]

The caliph and the development of his office remained an important concern to many authors.[235] Nevertheless, beyond traditional reverence for the descendants of the Prophet's uncle al-ʿAbbās, the realities and limits of the contemporary caliphal office seemed to escape few historians. The position of the caliphs of Cairo resembled that of the later Abbasids of Baghdad under the Turkish amirs, Buyids, and Seljuk rulers who seized power in succession. The primarily ceremonial role of bestowing authority on an incoming temporal ruler was nearly identical, although no contemporary historian admitted this explicitly, beyond pointing out the presentist observation that in his particular time, the caliphate was void of independent temporal power. Later fifteenth-century historians such as Ibn Khaldūn, al-Maqrīzī and al-ʿAynī, while fully recognising the continuity between the Baghdad and Cairo lines of the family,[236] simultaneously reinforced notions of a practical disconnect between the political landscape of the previous Abbasid capital and that which had emerged in the new one.

As a cultural practice, Arabic historiography endured as a venue providing a diverse grouping of authors with space to culturally produce the state according to an underlying social logic.[237] Like the late medieval jurists and authors discussed in Chapter 6, historians of the fourteenth and fifteenth centuries demonstrated a 'shared imagination of the hierarchies of power that structured their wider Muslim worlds and their closer Syro-Egyptian surroundings'.[238] As a result, there was an extant relationship between historiographical writing and the social and political orders produced (and perpetually in a state of flux) around the different sultans and their courts.[239]

As Hirschler, Van Steenbergen and others have demonstrated, many of the works produced in this period were meant to accomplish specific purposes, thereby endowing the texts and narrative stories with agency as 'actors' in their own right. Historiographical texts coordinated an author's meaning-making process and oriented them towards spaces where meaning was performed through writing and re-performed through reading.[240] The current chapter has engaged with questions of how context and social standing may have influenced an author's individual recreation and performance of the Cairene Abbasid Caliphate in their texts. By putting narrative sources at the centre of historical action, however, a question for future consideration remains: what did an author's presentation of the Cairo Caliphate contribute to the overall agency of their text? This remains an important consideration given that many such texts went on to live a life of their own beyond the author's intentions down to our own time.[241]

Notes

1. Hirschler, *Medieval Arabic Historiography*, 109–11.
2. Muhanna, *World in a Book*, 3–4, 83–104; Van Steenbergen, Wing and D'hulster, 'Mamlukization Part I', 552; Guo, 'Mamluk Historiographic Studies', 29–30; Little, 'Historiography', 413.
3. Van Steenbergen, *Caliphate and Kingship*, 60–1; Hirschler, 'Studying Mamluk Historiography', 161, 177.
4. Khalidi, *Arabic Historical Thought*, 191–2; Irwin, *Ibn Khaldun*, 4–6; Hirschler, 'Islam', 276–8; Lev, 'Symbiotic Relations', 24–6; Robinson, *Islamic Historiography*, 100–1; Guo, 'Mamluk Historiographic Studies', 34; Humphreys, *Islamic History*, 187–208; Little, 'Historiography', 413.
5. Hirschler, 'Islam', 267, 279–82.
6. Hassan, *Longing for the Lost Caliphate*, 31–3, 86; Elbendary, *Crowds and Sultans*, 90–1, 94; Hirschler, 'Islam', 267; Bosworth, *Book of Contention*, 9–12; Cobb, 'Al-Maqrīzī', 69–71.
7. Rabbat, 'Perception of Architecture', 162.
8. Hassan, *Longing for the Lost Caliphate*, 19, 29–33.
9. Ibid., 85–7; Holt, 'Some Observations', 507. For some examples, see al-Yūnīnī, *Dhayl*, 2:187; Ibn Kathīr, *Bidāya*, 13:231–2; al-Qalqashandī, *Ṣubḥ*, 1:439–45; al-Qalqashandī, *Maʾāthir*, 3:334–74; al-ʿAynī, *ʿIqd*, 1:349; al-Malaṭī, *Rawḍ*, 1:266.
10. On the relationship between piety and *baraka* with knowledge and official religious service, see Talmon-Heller, 'ʿIlm, Shafāʿah and Barakah', 26–9, 40–1.
11. Hassan, *Longing for the Lost Caliphate*, 67; Aigle, *Mongol Empire*, 245; Berkey, 'Mamluk Religious Policy', 8; Lev, 'Symbiotic Relations'; Broadbridge, *Kingship and Ideology*, 12–16; Holt, 'Position and Power', 247; Bori, 'Théologie politique', 31–2; Rapoport, 'Royal Justice'; Lapidus, *Muslim Cities*, 167.
12. Van Steenbergen, 'Appearances of *dawla* and Political Order', 57–62; Van Steenbergen, 'ʿAṣabiyya, Messiness'.
13. Hirschler, 'Studying Mamluk Historiography', 169–71.
14. Hassan, *Longing for the Lost Caliphate*, 17, 19, 85–6, 108–10, 115, 116, 118; Hirschler, *Medieval Arabic Historiography*, 15–62.
15. Little, 'Historiography', 412; Guo, 'Mamluk Historiographic Studies', 30. See also Holt, 'Chancery Clerk'; Holt, 'Sultan as Ideal Ruler'.
16. Ibn ʿAbd al-Ẓāhir, *Rawḍ*, 99–101; Hassan, *Longing for the Lost Caliphate*,

72–3; Elbendary, 'The Sultan', 140–4; Holt, 'Virtuous Ruler'; Holt, 'Three Biographies'.
17. Ibn ʿAbd al-Ẓāhir, *Rawḍ*, 100–1.
18. Ibid., 145–7.
19. Ibid., 110–12.
20. Heidemann, *Kalifat*, 156; Amitai-Preiss, *Mongols and Mamluks*, 58–9.
21. Ibn ʿAbd al-Ẓāhir, *Rawḍ*, 112.
22. Baybars al-Manṣūrī, *Zubdat al-fikra*, 68.
23. Ibn ʿAbd al-Ẓāhir, *Rawḍ*, 141. See also Hassan, *Longing for the Lost Caliphate*, 79–80; Heidemann, *Kalifat*, 156–60.
24. Ibn ʿAbd al-Ẓāhir, *Rawḍ*, 279–80.
25. Ibn ʿAbd al-Ẓāhir, *Alṭāf*, 1–19. On this point see Hassan, *Longing for the Lost Caliphate*, 72–3; Broadbridge, *Kingship and Ideology*, 45; Heidemann, *Kalifat*, 187–8.
26. Ibn ʿAbd al-Ẓāhir, *Rawḍ*, 101, 107.
27. Ibn ʿAbd al-Ẓāhir, *Alṭāf*, 18.
28. Hassan, *Longing for the Lost Caliphate*, 17, 83–4, 102, 104–5, 110, 114–15, 119.
29. Ibid., 5. On the use of 'Alexander' as a title in the late thirteenth century, see De Polignac, 'Un "nouvel Alexandre" mamelouk'; Aigle, 'Les inscriptions de Baybars', 73–7; Aigle, *Mongol Empire*, 234–5; Eddé, 'Baybars et son double'.
30. Hassan, *Longing for the Lost Caliphate*, 17, 37, 45, 80, 83, 127; Laoust, *Essai*, 47.
31. Ibn ʿAbd al-Ẓāhir, *Rawḍ*, 110–12; Ibn ʿAbd al-Ẓāhir, *Alṭāf*, 3–6.
32. Although some authors had proximity to power, many retained their authorial agency and proved to be capable of moving beyond mere legitimisations of the powerful. See Hirschler, 'Islam', 277, and in particular for the cases of Ibn ʿAbd al-Ẓāhir and Shāfiʿ ibn ʿAlī, see Van Den Bossche, 'Past, Panegyric'.
33. Ibn ʿAbd al-Ẓāhir, *Rawḍ*, 110–12; Ibn ʿAbd al-Ẓāhir, *Alṭāf*, 18. See also Hassan, *Longing for the Lost Caliphate*, 86, 108, 120.
34. Holt, 'Presentation of Qalāwūn', 143–4.
35. Holt, 'Three Biographies', 26–7.
36. Shāfiʿ ibn ʿAlī, *Ḥusn*, 45; Holt, 'Some Observations', 502; Holt, 'Sultan as Ideal Ruler', 136.
37. Holt, 'Presentation of Qalāwūn', 143, 148.
38. Northrup, *From Slave to Sultan*, 175–6.

39. Heidemann, *Kalifat*, 34, 191. On Āqqūsh al-Muḥammadī, an interesting chronicler in his own right, see Hassan, 'Loss of Caliphate', 273–4.
40. Shāfiʿ ibn ʿAlī, *Ḥusn*, 55.
41. Hassan, *Longing for the Lost Caliphate*, 83–95, 108–41.
42. Heidemann, *Kalifat*, 174–5, 194.
43. Little, *An Introduction*, 6; Ashtor, 'Baybars al-Manṣūrī'; Baybars al-Manṣūrī, *Zubdat al-fikra*, xx; Irwin, 'Mamluk History', 163.
44. Northrup, *From Slave to Sultan*, 36–7, 39; Little, 'Historiography', 423–4; Guo, 'Mamluk Historiographic Studies', 16–17.
45. Hassan, *Longing for the Lost Caliphate*, 86–8.
46. Baybars al-Manṣūrī, *Tuḥfa*, 47–9, 60. For further discussion of this passage as an indication of the caliphate's resonance in society, see Hassan, *Longing for the Lost Caliphate*, 88.
47. On Baybars al-Manṣūrī's coverage of the Mongol sack of Baghdad, see Hassan, *Longing for the Lost Caliphate*, 46, 56.
48. Baybars al-Manṣūrī, *Zubdat al-fikra*, 68.
49. It is perhaps for these latter reasons that Rabbat described Baybars al-Manṣūrī as 'the closest representative we have of a Mamluk viewpoint'. See 'Mamluk History through Architecture', 6.
50. Hassan, *Longing for the Lost Caliphate*, 56.
51. This work comprised several volumes, some passages having survived in the work of al-ʿAynī. See Baybars al-Manṣūrī, *Zubdat al-fikra*, xx; Richards, 'A Mamluk Amir's Mamluk History', 38.
52. Baybars al-Manṣūrī, *Zubdat al-fikra*, 82, 359–60, 372.
53. Guo, 'Mamluk Historiographic Studies', 30; Little, *An Introduction*, 4.
54. Hassan, *Longing for the Lost Caliphate*, 22, 97–9.
55. Baybars al-Manṣūrī, *Zubdat al-fikra*, 372, 375.
56. Ibid., 375.
57. Ibid., 67.
58. Broadbridge, *Kingship and Ideology*, 42, 68–70; Hassan, *Longing for the Lost Caliphate*, 117; Amitai-Preiss, 'Fall and Rise', 488; Becker, 'Barthold's Studien', 374–5.
59. Baybars al-Manṣūrī, *Zubdat al-fikra*, 359–60.
60. Hassan, *Longing for the Lost Caliphate*, 86–8.
61. Little, *An Introduction*, 43.
62. Ibid., 42.
63. Abū al-Fidāʾ, *Mukhtaṣar*, 3:253–4. The history of Abū al-Fidāʾ harbours some

doubt concerning the veracity of the caliph's identity which did not escape the notice of later historians. See Van Steenbergen, *Caliphate and Kingship*, 296–7; Heidemann, *Kalifat*, 71–5; Chapoutot-Remadi, 'Liens et relations', 30–1; Tyan, *Institutions du droit public musulman*, 2:208–9.

64. Abū al-Fidā', *Mukhtaṣar*, 3:255–6. Although many accepted him as a true Abbasid, medieval historians never fully arrived at an agreement on the genealogy of al-Ḥākim. See Hassan, *Longing for the Lost Caliphate*, 87; Van Steenbergen, *Caliphate and Kingship*, 16, 96; Heidemann, *Kalifat*, 73; Schimmel, 'Some Glimpses', 354; Becker, 'Barthold's Studien', 367–8.
65. Abū al-Fidā', *Mukhtaṣar*, 4:59.
66. Little, *An Introduction*, 45.
67. The '*awlād al-nās*' designation is worthy of far more scholarly interest. In historiographical practice, contemporary authors appear to have applied it inconsistently. See Van Steenbergen, 'Revisiting the Mamlūk Empire', 85; Van Steenbergen, 'Qalāwūnid Discourse', 11n.32. Modern research suggests a far more structural or institutionalised understanding of the '*awlād al-nās*' notion than may have actually been the case.
68. Onimus, *Les maîtres du jeu*, 71–3; Eychenne, *Liens personnels*, 34, 173–5; Loiseau, *Les Mamelouks*, 93, 140–1.
69. Elbendary, *Crowds and Sultans*, 81–4; Hirschler, 'Studying Mamluk Historiography', 168; Little, 'Historiography', 425; Robinson, *Islamic Historiography*, 100; Khalidi, *Arabic Historical Thought*, 188; Haarmann, 'Arabic in Speech', 104–5; Lapidus, *Muslim Cities*, 116–17.
70. Hirschler, 'Islam', 276. On linguistic concerns of the period, see Eychenne, *Liens personnels*, 153–88; Loiseau, *Les Mamelouks*, 181–90.
71. The richest examples come in al-Ṣafadī's two biographies of the caliph al-Mustakfī; see *A'yān al-'aṣr*, 2:419–21; al-Ṣafadī, *Wāfī*, 15:349–50.
72. Al-Ṣafadī, *A'yān al-'aṣr*, 2:420–1. See also Hassan, *Longing for the Lost Caliphate*, 89.
73. Al-Ṣafadī, *A'yān al-'aṣr*, 1:220.
74. Al-Ṣafadī, *Wāfī*, 10:235, 30:103–4, 148–9; al-Ṣafadī, *A'yān al-'aṣr*, 1:220–1.
75. Banister, '*'Ālim*-Caliph'.
76. As a boy, Ibn Taghrībirdī frequented the household of the caliph al-Mu'taḍid II whose wife had been a concubine in the household of his father. See Ibn Taghrībirdī, *Manhal*, 4:305; Ibn Taghrībirdī, *Ḥawādith*, 137–8.
77. Ibn Taghrībirdī acknowledges the caliphate as such in the context of a discussion of the wazirate's devolution by his own time. See *Nujūm*, 16:85.

78. Ibn Taghrībirdī, *Nujūm*, 13:149, 14:369; Ibn Taghrībirdī, *Mawrid*, 2:158–86.
79. Ibn Taghrībirdī, *Manhal*, 4:305.
80. Ibid., 1:308.
81. On this 'amiral milieu', see Onimus, *Les maîtres du jeu*, 63, 71–86.
82. Ibn Taghrībirdī, *Mawrid*, 1:244.
83. Ibn Taghrībirdī, *Nujūm*, 11:234–5.
84. Ibn Taghrībirdī, *Manhal*, 7:61.
85. Ibid., 4:303. See also al-Maqrīzī, *Sulūk*, 4:273–4.
86. Ibn Taghrībirdī, *Manhal*, 4:303.
87. Ibid., 4:304.
88. Ibid., 7:64. See al-Maqrīzī, *Durar*, 2:215.
89. Ibn Taghrībirdī, *Nujūm*, 14:205–6.
90. Ibid., 16:35.
91. Ibn Taghrībirdī, *Ḥawādith*, 184.
92. Ibn Taghrībirdī, *Nujūm*, 16:89–90.
93. Ibid., 16:158.
94. Massoud, *Chronicles*, 65; Little, 'Historiography', 208.
95. Hassan, *Longing for the Lost Caliphate*, 67, 83–5, 259.
96. Banister, 'Naught Remains', 234. The sultans were indeed sincere in their 'dynastic impulse' to establish their sons in power after them. See Onimus, *Les maîtres du jeu*, 394–8; Loiseau, *Les Mamelouks*, 131–2; Sievert, 'Family, Friend or Foe', 109–12, 116–17; Van Steenbergen, 'Appearances of *dawla* and Political Order', 75; Van Steenbergen, 'The Mamluk Sultanate'; Broadbridge, 'Sending Home', 1–2; Holt, 'Position and Power', 239–41.
97. Berkey, 'Mamluks as Muslims', 166.
98. For modern and pre-modern critiques of Ibn Taghrībirdī as a historian, see al-Sakhāwī, *al-Ḍaw*ʾ, 10:305–8; Popper, 'Sakhāwī's Criticism of Ibn Taghrībirdī'; Massoud, *Chronicles*, 60–5. On the bias of Arab *ʿulamā*ʾ towards Turkophone scholars, see Haarmann, 'Arabic in Speech', 82–5.
99. Van Steenbergen, 'Appearances of *dawla* and Political Order', 66.
100. Perho, 'Al-Maqrīzī and Ibn Taghrī Birdī', 117–20. Notions of elite identity and 'loyalty' to the sultan and his 'state' have been noted and discussed by Reuven Amitai. See 'Mongol Occupation of Damascus', 36. On Ibn Taghrībirdī's use and understanding of the term '*dawla*', see Van Steenbergen, 'Appearances of *dawla* and Political Order', 63–6.
101. Little, *An Introduction*, 92; Massoud, *Chronicles*, 69.
102. Massoud, *Chronicles*, 69–70.

103. Winter, 'Ottoman Occupation', 490–1; Havemann, 'Chronicle of Ibn Iyās', 88.
104. Hassan, *Longing for the Lost Caliphate*, 133, 138–41; Winter, 'Ottoman Occupation', 494.
105. See Becker, 'Barthold's Studien', 396, 399; Sümer, 'Yavuz Selim', 351.
106. Ibn Iyās, *Badāʾiʿ*, 5:30, 33.
107. Ibid., 3:85.
108. Ibid., 3:151, 378–9, 4:139–41.
109. Ibid., 5:37, 352.
110. Ibid., 1:2:205. On this distinction, see Eychenne, *Liens personnels*, 34; Perho, 'The Sultan and the Common People', 147.
111. Ibn Iyās, *Badāʾiʿ*, 3:13.
112. Ibid., 2:304.
113. Ibid., 2:457.
114. Ibid., 3:379.
115. Ibid., 5:74.
116. Ibid., 5:185.
117. Ibid., 5:317–18.
118. Irwin, 'Mamluk History', 170. On the role of poetry in creating historical narrative in this period, particularly in the work of Ibn Iyās, see Guo, 'Ibn Iyās, the Poet'; Guo, 'Songs, Poetry, and Storytelling'.
119. Ibn Iyās, *Badāʾiʿ*, 1:1:314.
120. Ibid., 1:2:333–4.
121. Ibid., 1:2:399.
122. Ibid., 1:2:747.
123. Ibid., 3:380.
124. Ibid., 3:378–9.
125. Ibid. See Q. 12:68.
126. Ibid., 4:361.
127. Ibid., 2:12.
128. Ibid., 5:389–90.
129. Ibid., 5:389.
130. Ibid., 5:390.
131. Ibid., 3:151.
132. Ibid., 3:225, 5:104; Hassan, *Longing for the Lost Caliphate*, 87.
133. Ibn Iyās, *Badāʾiʿ*, 3:151, 225. See also al-Sakhāwī, *Ḍawʾ*, 10:188; al-Sakhāwī, *Wajīz*, 3:988; al-Malaṭī, *Nayl*, 8:16.

134. Ibn Iyās, *Badāʾiʿ*, 5:158.
135. For his comments on Abbasid ritual innovated during the fifteenth century, see Ibn Iyās, *Badāʾiʿ*, 1:2:124, 2:395.
136. Mirza, 'Ibn Kathīr', 14–63.
137. Guo, 'Mamluk Historiographic Studies', 32; Humphreys, *Islamic History*, 240–1; Little, *An Introduction*, 57.
138. Li Guo has underscored the importance of the late medieval Syrian historiographical tradition, see *Early Mamluk Syrian Historiography*, 1:1–96; Guo, 'History Writing', 451–3.
139. There was still a tradition of Syrian historiography in the works of Ibn Ṣaṣra, Ibn Ḥabīb, Ibn Qāḍī Shuhba and Ibn Ṭūlūn, but never again a close cluster of chroniclers similar to the fourteenth-century scholars.
140. I thank Stephen Humphreys for these observations.
141. Hassan, *Longing for the Lost Caliphate*, 73; Lev, 'Symbiotic Relations', 11n.34; Little, 'Historiography', 418–19.
142. Translation from Hassan, *Longing for the Lost Caliphate*, 73.
143. Cf. Ibn Iyās, *Badāʾiʿ*, 1:1:321; al-Suyūṭī, *Ḥusn*, 2:94.
144. Hirschler, *Medieval Arabic Historiography*, 112.
145. Elbendary, *Crowds and Sultans*, 92–3; Humphreys, *Islamic History*, 187–8; Guo, 'Mamluk Historiographic Studies', 29–31; Northrup, *From Slave to Sultan*, 43.
146. The extent and nature of the sharing has been analysed in modern scholarship, see Little, *An Introduction*, 46–73, 92, 94–8; Haarmann, *Quellenstudien*, 92–118; Humphreys, *Islamic History*, 240–1; Guo, *Early Mamluk Syrian Historiography*, 41–86, 94–6; Guo, 'Mamluk Historiographic Studies', 25.
147. Guo, *Early Mamluk Syrian Historiography*, 1:42–59; Haarmann, *Quellenstudien*, 22–6; Little, *An Introduction*, 57–61.
148. Al-Yūnīnī, *Dhayl*, 1:484–7, 2:153. See Hassan, *Longing for the Lost Caliphate*, 69 and notes; Heidemann, *Kalifat*, 22–3.
149. Al-Yūnīnī, *Dhayl*, 1:451–3, 455, 2:106–11, 153.
150. Ibid., 1:453–4, 2:95, 124–5.
151. Al-Birzālī, *Muqtafī*, 1:404. Cf. al-Yūnīnī, *Dhayl*, 3:235; Ibn Kathīr, *Bidāya*, 13:277.
152. Ibid., 3:875, 929.
153. Little, *An Introduction*, 62.
154. Heidemann, *Kalifat*, 25; Hassan, *Longing for the Lost Caliphate*, 117–18.

155. Al-Dhahabī, *ʿIbar*, 5:259. See also Hassan, *Longing for the Lost Caliphate*, 117; Tyan, *Institutions du droit public musulman*, 2:212–13.
156. Al-Dhahabī, *Siyar*, 23:169.
157. Al-Dhahabī, *Duwal*, 2:188.
158. For a study of Ibn Kathīr's positions and contributions, see Mirza, 'Ibn Kathīr', 44–60, 94–125.
159. Ibn Kathīr, *Bidāya*, 13:231.
160. Gharaibeh, 'Geschichtsschreibung', 116–22. A strikingly similar presentation of arguments made by al-Suyūṭī over a century later has been explored by Mona Hassan, see *Longing for the Lost Caliphate*, 140–1.
161. Hassan, *Longing for the Lost Caliphate*, 4, 17, 29, 31, 68, 94, 98, 108, 111–20.
162. Wiederhold, 'Legal-Religious Elite', 224–6.
163. Hassan, *Longing for the Lost Caliphate*, 102, 135; Elbendary, *Crowds and Sultans*, 93–4.
164. Van Steenbergen and Van Nieuwenhuyse, 'Truth and Politics', 153–4; Van Steenbergen, *Caliphate and Kingship*, 2, 129–31.
165. Elbendary, *Crowds and Sultans*, 92–3.
166. Guo, 'Mamluk Historiographic Studies', 39; Robinson, *Islamic Historiography*, 102.
167. Holt, *Age of the Crusades*, 208–9; Perho, 'Al-Maqrīzī and Ibn Taghrī Birdī', 120.
168. Al-Maqrīzī, *Sulūk*, 4:207–44; al-Maqrīzī, *Durar*, 2:211–15, 3:13–14.
169. Levanoni, 'Al-Maqrīzī's Account', 103–4. On the advisory role of one of his works, *Dhahab al-masbūk*, see Van Steenbergen, *Caliphate and Kingship*, 82, 103–4.
170. Bauden, 'Al-Maqrīzī', 392–4.
171. On al-Maqrīzī's pro-Hashemite views, see Cobb, 'Al-Maqrīzī'; Bosworth, 'Al-Maqrīzī's Exposition'; Bosworth, 'Al-Maqrīzī's Epistle', 39–45.
172. Cobb, 'Al-Maqrīzī', 71.
173. Ibid., 71–3, 80.
174. Bosworth, 'Al-Maqrīzī's Epistle', 41–4; Cobb, 'Al-Maqrīzī', 70, 78.
175. Bosworth, 'Al-Maqrīzī's Epistle', 40–5; Cobb, 'Al-Maqrīzī', 72, 79–80.
176. Bosworth, *Book of Contention*, 32–3.
177. Hassan, *Longing for the Lost Caliphate*, 5, 122, 128, 138.
178. Bosworth, *Book of Contention*, 32.
179. Al-Maqrīzī, *Kitāb al-nizāʿ*, 95–6, 109; Bosworth, *Book of Contention*, 87–8, 102.

180. Cobb, 'Al-Maqrīzī', 78. Other medieval historians made these connections as well, see Hassan, *Longing for the Lost Caliphate*, 46.
181. Al-Maqrīzī, *Kitāb al-nizāʿ*, 115–16; Bosworth, *Book of Contention*, 107.
182. Several historians have cited this passage, originally translated into English by Thomas Arnold (*Caliphate*, 102) from the French of E. Blochet (*Histoire d'Égypte de Makrizi*, 76): Schimmel, 'Some Glimpses', 355; Garcin, 'Histoire', 34n.1; Chapoutot-Remadi, 'Une institution', 15–16; Chapoutot-Remadi, 'Liens et relations', 59.
183. Al-Maqrīzī, *Khiṭaṭ*, 3:750–88.
184. It is perhaps an interesting point that this usage in the *Khiṭaṭ* is one of the only contemporary medieval Arabic references to a 'Mamluk' *dawla* or sultanate.
185. Al-Maqrīzī, *Khiṭaṭ*, 3:783. Alternately in the caliphal history recorded in the *Durar*, al-Maqrīzī substitutes *al-dunyā* with *al-amṣār* and *al-nās* with *al-muslimūn*. See al-Maqrīzī, *Durar*, 2:207.
186. Al-Maqrīzī, *Khiṭaṭ*, 3:784.
187. Ibid., 3:786–7.
188. Al-Maqrīzī, *Durar*, 2:206–15.
189. Ibid., 2:207–8.
190. Hassan, *Longing for the Lost Caliphate*, 85–6; Holt, 'Some Observations', 507.
191. Al-Maqrīzī, *Sulūk*, 3:915. Al-Maqrīzī likewise states that al-Mustaʿīn's promotion to sultan did not allow the caliph to accrue any additional influence (*nufūdh*) or power over affairs (*tadbīr al-amūr*). See *Khiṭaṭ*, 3:203. In his treatise on caliphs and kings who completed the Islamic pilgrimage, al-Maqrīzī observed that the caliph al-Ḥākim 'remained a caliph, without any [power to] command and forbid and without any effective authority (*lā nufūdh kalima*), until he died', see Van Steenbergen, *Caliphate and Kingship*, 298–9.
192. Van Steenbergen, *Caliphate and Kingship*, 65–6, 69, 100–2.
193. Al-Maqrīzī, *Sulūk*, 3:645, 4:756.
194. Levanoni, 'Al-Maqrīzī's Account', 95–103.
195. On the strength and pervasiveness of this current in late medieval Syro-Egyptian society and scholarship, see Hassan, *Longing for the Lost Caliphate*, 66–141.
196. Van Den Bossche, 'Past, Panegyric', 196–7.
197. Al-Maqrīzī, *Sulūk*, 1:639.
198. Berkey, 'Mamluk Religious Policy', 11.
199. Hassan, *Longing for the Lost Caliphate*, 80, 87, 91, 104–5, 110, 117, 122, 128.

200. Bosworth, *Book of Contention*, 23.
201. Rabbat, 'Who Was al-Maqrīzī?', 12–16; Wiederhold, 'Legal-Religious Elite', 207, 209–15, discusses Ibn al-Burhān though apparently without awareness of al-Maqrīzī's biography (*Durar*, 1:297–303) or Ibn al-Burhān's manifesto, *Ṭarīq al-istiqāma li-maʾrifat al-imāma*, both of which include many of his possible motivations.
202. Ibn Ḥajar, *Durar*, 1:62, 159.
203. Ibn Ḥajar, *Inbāʾ al-ghumr*, 1:275, 2:343–4.
204. Ibid., 2:36.
205. Jaques, *Ibn Hajar*, 55.
206. Ibn Ḥajar, *Inbāʾ al-ghumr*, 3:445–6.
207. Al-Suyūṭī, *Taʾrīkh*, 404–6 (abridged version: Ibn Iyās, *Badāʾiʿ*, 1:2:823–4). For a recent study of the poem's text and reception, see Hassan, 'Poetic Memories', 18–24.
208. Al-Suyūṭī, *Taʾrīkh*, 404; Ibn Iyās, *Badāʾiʿ*, 1:2:824. Cf. Hassan's edition/translation in 'Poetic Memories', 21–4.
209. Ibid. See also Hassan, 'Poetic Memories', 14–15.
210. Al-Suyūṭī, *Taʾrīkh*, 405.
211. Ibid.
212. Hassan, 'Poetic Memories', 16–17.
213. Al-Suyūṭī, *Taʾrīkh*, 405–6.
214. Ibid., 406.
215. Ibn Ḥajar, *Inbāʾ al-ghumr*, 2:344.
216. Al-Malaṭī, *Rawḍ*, 1:236; al-Sakhāwī, *Ḍawʾ*, 3:215; al-Sakhāwī, *Dhayl*, 1:634; al-Sakhāwī, *Wajīz*, 2:581 al-Sakhāwī, *Jawāhir*, 197.
217. Al-Suyūṭī, *Taʾrīkh*, 104.
218. Banister, 'Casting the Caliph in a Cosmic Role', 98–104; Hassan, *Longing for the Lost Caliphate*, 58–9, 138–40.
219. Banister, 'Naught Remains', 228–31; Al-Azmeh, *Muslim Kingship*, 78.
220. Ibn Taghrībirdī, *Nujūm*, 15:532–3; Ibn Taghrībirdī, *Manhal*, 2:22. Before his death, Ibn Ḥajar had been one of the qadis on hand to officiate at the caliph's *bayʿa* ceremony, see Ibn Iyās, *Badāʾiʿ*, 2:230.
221. Most notably, see Garcin, 'Histoire'.
222. Khūlī, *ʿUlamāʾ*, 71–2.
223. Garcin, 'Histoire', 55.
224. Ibn Iyās, *Badāʾiʿ*, 3:339; al-Shādhilī, *Bahja*, 172–4.
225. Garcin, 'Histoire' 64, 66; Hassan, *Longing for the Lost Caliphate*, 138.

226. Al-Suyūṭī, *Taʾrīkh*, 384; Ibn Iyās, *Badāʾiʿ*, 3:339. See also Jackson, 'Primacy of Domestic Politics', 61–5.
227. Arjomand, 'Legitimacy', 252; Garcin, 'Histoire', 64–5.
228. On al-Suyūṭī's conception of *ijtihād* and the caliph's role among the *ʿulamāʾ*, see Banister, '*ʿĀlim*-Caliph'; Hassan, *Longing for the Lost Caliphate*, 137–8.
229. Garcin, 'Histoire', 62–3.
230. See Banister, 'Casting the Caliph in a Cosmic Role'; Hassan, *Longing for the Lost Caliphate*, 58–9.
231. Hassan, *Longing for the Lost Caliphate*, 16–17, 30–1, 44–6, 72, 86.
232. Ibn Taghrībirdī, *Nujūm*, 14:369.
233. Hassan, *Longing for the Lost Caliphate*, 66–7; Broadbridge, *Kingship and Ideology*, 14–15; Holt, 'Three Biographies', 24–5.
234. Hirschler, 'Islam', 268–9; Hirschler, 'Studying Mamluk Historiography', 167; Perho, 'Al-Maqrīzī and Ibn Taghrī Birdī', 120.
235. Hassan, *Longing for the Lost Caliphate*, 83–8, 108–41; Hirschler, *Medieval Arabic Historiography*, 110.
236. Ibid.
237. Chamberlain, *Knowledge*, 175; Van Steenbergen, 'Appearances of *dawla* and Political Order', 60–1; Hirschler, 'Studying Mamluk Historiography', 177.
238. Van Steenbergen, 'Appearances of *dawla* and Political Order', 60–1.
239. Van Steenbergen, 'Appearances of *dawla* and Political Order', 57–62; Van Steenbergen, 'ʿAṣabiyya, Messiness'.
240. Van Steenbergen, *Caliphate and Kingship*, 105–33; Van Steenbergen and Van Nieuwenhuyse, 'Truth and Politics', 154, 182; Muhanna, *World in a Book*, 123–40; Hirschler, *Medieval Arabic Historiography*, 115–21; Van Den Bossche, 'Past, Panegyric', 255–301; Hassan, 'Poetic Memories', 18–24.
241. Ibid.

8

Caliphal Investiture Documents and the Ideality of a Cairo Caliphate

Introduction

In the light of the varied opinions of the authors and historians presented in Chapters 6 and 7, it is clear that the Abbasid caliphs, divested of genuine power, played only a marginal role in politics and day-to-day administration. To refine the analysis of the caliph's position in the political, administrative and social systems of the period, it is necessary to conduct a thorough survey of the surviving documentary evidence in the form of documents, sermons, coins and inscriptions. Complementing the normative texts discussed in Chapter 6, the investiture deeds and succession contracts, composed by chancery scribes, offer a genre-specific view of the theoretical position of the Abbasid Caliphate in politics, ceremonial and society at large. Many of the documents surveyed in Chapters 8 and 9 contain lengthy *ḥamdala* sections which, in the context of bestowing praise on God and the Prophet, offer opportunities to examine Abbasid legitimacy alongside conceptual representations of the caliphate's authority in society.

Administrative documents such as investiture deeds and succession contracts focused on defining and affirming the rights (*ḥuqūq*) of the caliph and his 'partner' the sultan. Allusions to the reigning Abbasid imparted a classical caliphal authority to official writs from the sultan's seat of power. The documents counted among a small number of venues in which the theoretical power and authority of the Abbasid Caliphate could be presented as far-reaching and authentic, thereby providing a basis for Citadel ritual. Chapters 8 and 9 seek to explain the gap between the ideality and reality of the Abbasid

Caliphate in late medieval Syro-Egypt. Although many fourteenth- and fifteenth-century succession documents produced by the Cairo chancery were based on existing templates and language from earlier Seljuk and Ayyubid models, this is not the place for a comparative discussion.[1]

While documents such as bills of sale or endowment deeds (*waqfiyya*) often serve modern historians as unintentional historical sources, the documents analysed in the current chapter sought to capture the performative essence of Islamic ritual and ceremonial and project them for posterity. Many investiture deeds are composed with a sense of historical consciousness, which may help to explain their frequent injection into formal historical narratives, encyclopaedias and anthologies. Documents prepared by the chancery tended to be a collaborative effort among professional scribes adhering to a well-defined protocol.[2] Documents referred to specific rulers, but the clerks composing them conformed to particular rhetorical and ideological concerns, often under the guidance of the head of the chancery (*ṣāḥib dīwān al-inshāʾ*) or the confidential secretary (*kātib al-sirr*). Executing more than mundane state procedures, chancery scribes used the composition of important ceremonial documents to exhibit their erudition and skill as well-trained literati.[3] As Elias Muhanna points out, however, in addition to a scribe's proficiency in high-class Arabic, work in the chancery also required detailed awareness of the 'social and professional landscapes of the civilian elite'.[4]

It is useful to consider and evaluate late medieval Syro-Egyptian documents, including official and private correspondence as a legitimate genre of literature. Many chancery documents included rhymed prose text (*sajʿ*) and, as Thomas Bauer points out, were often considered worthy of inclusion in literary anthologies allowing them to live a 'second life' beyond their initial pragmatic communicative purposes. Ceremonial documents sought to convey that an important transfer of power had taken place.[5] It is no coincidence that many of these documents were read publicly before members of the military and educated elite as part of a grand performance.[6] Thus analysing documents involving the Abbasid Caliphate as a form of *de facto* literature may further elucidate the symbolic relationship connecting the caliph, the sultan and the *dawla*. Investiture deeds and caliphal succession contracts are understandably rich in allusions to the lofty graces associated with the Prophet's family and the descendants of his uncle al-ʿAbbās.[7] Many of the deeds and contracts appear formulaic, including a flowery introduction, appeals to the Qur'ān, praise for God, the Prophet and the Abbasid house. To understand them merely under the vague rubric of 'documents' is rather misleading as their composition frequently implies the intent for performance and grand spectacle.

Documents pertaining to the caliphate in late medieval Cairo provide a supplement to our literary historical sources, even, if as Urbain Vermeulen has observed, they fail to reflect or convey the functional impotence of the Abbasid caliphs.[8] Much of the rhetoric of the documents was directed at the Cairene elite, both to appease the *'ulamā'* and assure them that the existing order preserved important Islamic institutions, while promoting a culture of acceptance and obedience to the organisation of the latest political order established by the sultan, amirs, religious elites and other military and civilian personnel.

Documents have survived for our study in several ways. Historians such as Ibn 'Abd al-Ẓāhir, Shāfi' ibn 'Alī and Ibn al-Furāt often held chancery positions and selectively incorporated documents into their histories. Original and model documents have also been preserved in chancery manuals and administrative encyclopaedias, notably in the *Ṣubḥ al-a'shā fī ṣinā'at al-inshā'* and *Ma'āthir al-ināfa fī ma'ālim al-khilāfa* of al-Qalqashandī, as well as other works such as Ibn Faḍlallāh al-'Umarī's *al-Ta'rīf bi-al-muṣṭalaḥ al-sharīf*, al-Nuwayrī's *Nihāyat al-arab fī funūn al-adab*, Ibn Nāẓir al-Jaysh's *Tathqīf al-Ta'rīf bi-al-muṣṭalaḥ al-sharīf*, the *munsha'āt* manual of Abū Bakr ibn Ḥijja al-Ḥamawī (d. 837/1434), *Kitāb qahwat al-inshā'*, an anthology of models and documents dealing largely with writs of investiture, and the *Thaghr al-bāsim fī ṣinā'at al-kātib wa-l-kātim* of Muḥammad al-Saḥmāwī (d. 868/1464).[9]

In the absence of a systematic archive for the period, it is impossible to study investiture documents chronologically or completely. While documents preserved by our literary sources are invaluable, they cannot supplant the importance of an organised archive. Without documents that observe the entire breadth of the sultanate, it is difficult to map the evolution of ceremonial practices involving the Abbasid Caliphate. With only a small portion of what remains, we may draw only tentative conclusions from isolated moments that survived.

As a high-ranking bureaucrat, al-Qalqashandī had access to the then existing archives of the sultanate of Cairo, though his level of fidelity to the original documents is unknown and his primary purpose in including full documents in his scribal encyclopaedia was didactic and intended to transmit bureaucratic knowledge. Al-Qalqashandī frequently copied authentic documents, though without important elements such as marks of registration or more generally the non-textual and material elements of each original document that tell its story.[10]

Interpreting medieval documents is a treacherous enterprise. Medieval Arabic stylists frequently composed documents in an exceedingly ornate vernacular as many documents were intended to be read aloud before the sultan's entourage or during state processions. The assumption may have been that one must be a cultured person of the period to understand much of the intertextuality, allusions, puns, double entendres (*tawriyya*), and other contemporary references and devices in the text. This poses little concern for this study, however, as the rhetoric is frequently couched in straightforward Islamic terminology.

How, then, does a study of the Abbasids of Cairo benefit from the examination of documentary evidence that only enshrines contemporary political pageantry? Caliphal and sultanic investiture documents demonstrate an important convergence of the religious and political and an intersection between the various social groupings of men of the pen, the turban and the sword.[11] As will be explored in Chapter 9, such documents also reveal formal expectations for the caliphate at court and in society, while shedding light on social practices central to religious ideology in the Cairo Sultanate such as the *bayʿa* and the primordial covenant (*ʿahd* or *mīthāq*) between God and man. The documents, in addition to their instructions about issues of succession and legal designation, reveal the importance of the caliphate in the Cairene chancery and its role in the composition of letters of state, appointments to high office and other business.[12]

While largely confined to matters of investiture and succession, the documents touch upon a wide range of information. An initial classification of the various texts helps to formulate a thematic framework suitable for a thorough examination of the subject matter. The current study focuses on: deeds of investiture (*ʿahd, taqlīd, taqrīr*) issued on behalf of the caliphs for the sultans or to announce the advent of a new caliph; testamentary designations (*ʿahd, taqlīd, ʿaqd*) in which a reigning caliph duly named his designated successor (*walī al-ʿahd*); letters sent to and from the caliphs to local amirs and foreign princes; the texts of sermons allegedly given by caliphs; and a brief discussion of relevant coins and inscriptions.

Deeds of Investiture

Contracts in the sultanate of Cairo were often limited to political enactments, civil engagements or treaties, though they could also be used by a ruler to appoint a successor.[13] In the context of the present chapter, the *ʿahd* (pl. *ʿuhūd*) was the contract between the caliph and the man who stood to obtain the plenary powers of the classical Abbasid Caliphate, the sultan of Cairo.

The Arabic verbal noun *taqlīd* as a convention of appointment has a long history in Islamic juristic discourses, often used for high officials such as wazirs and qadis, though by the late thirteenth/early fourteenth centuries it was largely confined to high-ranking officials such as sultans, caliphs or the head of the chancery. The *taqlīd*, in sources of the period, functions interchangeably with other terms including *tawqīʿ*, *taqrīr*, *ʿahd* and *ʿaqd*, which all refer to diplomas of appointment to high office.[14]

Physical copies of the documents themselves comprised a valuable part of Abbasid ceremonial in the creation of new political formations under each new Cairo sultan. After the ceremony of Baybars, almost every new ascending sultan had his *ʿahd* or *taqlīd* read publicly and paraded through the streets of Cairo with great pomp. The *mubāyaʿa* ceremony and festivities surrounding Baybars' mutual investiture with the caliph al-Mustanṣir set important precedents to which we can trace both the tenor and composition of subsequent investiture documents.[15]

Most medieval Arabic administrative documents are divided into at least three components: the initial elements (*ṭirāz* or *iftitāḥ*); the main body of the text (*matn*); and the concluding protocols (*khawātim*). Investiture deeds or letters of appointment from the Cairo Sultanate regularly contain three key elements: the *ḥamdala*, a customary section which begins with a doxology praising God, the Prophet, his companions and the family of al-ʿAbbās; followed by the *tafwīḍ* – often a short clause within the body of the document delegating authority from the caliph to the sultan; and, finally, the *waṣiyya* which contains ethical and religious counsel, advice and the duties of the officeholder.[16]

The *ḥamdala* sections are primarily concerned with praising God and the Prophet with familiar Islamic formulas and pious expressions. Even though many investiture deeds were performed before an audience, some employed a standard phraseology that was likely intelligible to the average person; whether an *ʿālim*, an amir or even a Cairene bystander. It is in the delegation of affairs to the sultan that earlier ideas of the East manifested in late medieval Cairo. Similar to the jurists and authors discussed in Chapter 6, many chancery secretaries of the time wrote with a subliminal reading of al-Māwardī in mind, largely taking his positions in *al-Aḥkām al-sulṭāniyya* for granted and often presenting them as the way of the world. Both the political theory and the investiture documents of the period suggest a far-reaching dissemination of al-Māwardī's presentation.[17]

Delegation and Caliphal Authority

The most noteworthy feature of sultanic investiture documents is the delegation of powers from the Abbasid caliph to the sultan of Cairo. Following tradition, the caliph typically affixed his own marker or sign (*ʿalāma*) to the bottom of the document confirming the delegation of power with a short written formula stating that he had indeed delegated power to the sultan. The four chief qadis would then sign the document demonstrating that they had been witnesses.[18]

The concept of delegation of powers in Islamic political theory provided a means for the political and military leader or sultan to legally usurp or otherwise alter the prerogatives of the caliphate. Works of so-called public or constitutional law such as *Aḥkām al-sulṭāniyya* enjoyed a long-lasting influence in the sultanate of Cairo as many jurists simply understood the idea of an amir or governor's usurpation of power and ad hoc delegation by the Abbasid caliph as a given.[19] The caliph, thought to embody divine sovereignty, acted as a unique source of authority bestowing legitimacy on the sultan through his delegation attested to by an *ʿahd* that permitted the sultan to rule in his name.[20]

The later medieval investiture deed that has garnered the most scholarly attention is the *taqlīd* for Baybars.[21] Its composer, the *kātib al-sirr* Fakhr al-Dīn

Luqmān establishes a theme of the caliph's gratitude for having received sanctuary in Cairo. According to the document, preserved by Ibn ʿAbd al-Ẓāhir, a kind of enlightened wisdom drove al-Mustanṣir to delegate sovereignty over Egypt and Syria, Diyar Bakr, the Hijaz, Yemen and the Euphrates territory along with future conquests to Baybars. The author assures the sultan that the caliph is grateful for his tremendous service to Islamdom:

> The Commander of the Faithful shows his gratitude for these favours, and recognizes that in the absence of your concern [in his affair], things would become damaged beyond repair . . . Thus he has entrusted to you, in a unique instance of generosity, care of the armies and subjects; excluding from this not one single city or fortress . . .[22]

The remainder of the document emphasises Baybars' duty to uphold justice before God, and the necessity to appoint governors and subordinates in his lands, both former prerogatives of the Abbasid caliph. Another key theme of the document is restoration, an important task delegated to the sultan that transformed him into a divinely appointed instrument charged with securing prosperity.

An explicit clause delegating authority mirroring those found in later documents appears to be absent and instead the *taqlīd* states that there is no one nobler than Baybars to receive the obedience of the people. The delegation implied by the caliph's ceremonial handclasp is reflected in the document by the acknowledgement that Baybars had elevated the Abbasid caliph and selected him as a spiritual director. The document explains that Baybars is the true leader and the caliph is on hand to lend spiritual support and ease any misgivings among the populace on submitting to the sultan.[23] Shortly after the ceremony in Cairo, Baybars, apparently following Fatimid tradition, issued another document announcing his *bayʿa* in Damascus, notifying the *ʿulamāʾ* of Syria that his *mubāyaʿa* with the caliph had been in full observance of the *sharīʿa*. The document labels it 'the affair of happy splendour for the community' (*amr bahj al-umma*) in which the caliph has been treated well and unity preserved.[24]

It is noteworthy that the caliph's name is absent from Muḥyī al-Dīn ibn ʿAbd al-Ẓāhir's '*taqlīd*' for the son of Baybars, al-Saʿīd Berke, who had been named successor by his father early in Shawwāl 662/August 1264 when

Baybars abruptly planned to confront a Mongol delegation.[25] The document was read, and in the voice of Baybars, made use of the tropes that Berke was a righteous branch from the tree of his family and a new full moon.[26] The document, removing any allusion to the Abbasid Caliphate, says notably that:

> there is no administration – in whole or in part – of a kingdom except through us or through our son. There is neither sword nor sustenance (*rizq*) without our command . . . There is no throne of sultanate (*dastu salṭana*) save for ours alone, the like of which brings clarity to radiance . . . There is no *minbar* whose sermon does not reverberate with our two names. There are no kinds of dirhams or dinars except those that shine with [our names] . . .[27]

The document names Berke heir to power solely on the legitimating authority of Baybars and claims that the young prince satisfies the demands for leadership. It is apparent from the document that Baybars, the rightful delegate of the caliph, no longer needs the caliph's approval to make appointments or even to establish a dynasty of his own.[28] Before this, only caliphs could legitimate sultans. In the eleventh century, al-Māwardī had posited that the sultan, once he had attained the caliph/*imām*'s authority as acting *amīr*, was thereafter free to appoint whomever he wished, with or without the explicit approval of the caliph/*imām*. Even so, this particular selection (and the document itself) appears to leave the caliph's position in theoretical limbo.

Nevertheless, the forty-year reign of the caliph al-Ḥākim (661–701/1262–1302), a crucial participant in the investitures of no fewer than eight Cairo sultans, witnessed the composition of at least six writs of investiture preserved by contemporary Arabic sources. Once Baybars had secured the Abbasid Caliphate in his capital, the developing religio-political culture demanded that later sultans undergo similar investiture ceremonies involving caliphal delegation and symbolic robes of honour.[29] Investiture documents for Qalāwūn, his three sons, al-Ṣāliḥ ʿAlī, al-Ashraf Khalīl and al-Nāṣir Muḥammad, as well as the non-Qalāwūnid sultans Kitbughā and Lājīn, provide further possibility for understanding the joint legitimisation and delegating capabilities of the Abbasid Caliphate.

Due perhaps to disparities in training and practice between Fakhr al-Dīn Luqmān and his successor Ibn ʿAbd al-Ẓāhir, differences are apparent in the composition of the *taqlīd* of Baybars and the *ʿahd* of Qalāwūn.[30] Chancery officials likely tailored Qalāwūn's *ʿahd* document to the sultan's specifications. In clearer language than the investiture deed of Baybars, the *tafwīḍ* delegation clause in Qalāwūn's document establishes that the sultan has been invested with all the former prerogatives of the classical caliphate:

> The command of our master the Commander of the Faithful – may God honour him – went forth that all that God had entrusted to [him] should go hence to the sublime position of the sultan al-Malik al-Manṣūr [Qalāwūn] in [all] matters of sovereignty . . .[31]

It is in this wide and vague delegation of authority that Linda Northrup has attempted to expose the injury done to both the symbolic and theoretical value of the caliphate by the wording of the clause. Qalāwūn was cautious to avoid having the limits of his authority spelled out, instead calling for a 'general, complete, perfect, intact, regular, and systematic sovereignty'.[32] The *tafwīḍ* clause thus accurately depicts the existing relationship between al-Ḥākim and Qalāwūn, as the latter was simply in search of a blanket legitimacy to cover his authority before distancing himself from the caliph. Like Baybars, Qalāwūn based his legitimacy on management of the Abbasid Caliphate, and allowed the symbolic value of the caliph to continue from the shadows.[33]

Ibn ʿAbd al-Ẓāhir likewise penned the investiture documents of Qalāwūn's son and desired successor, al-Ṣāliḥ ʿAlī, as well as his eventual successor al-Ashraf Khalīl. Unlike the previous documents, the *ḥamdala* of al-Ṣāliḥ ʿAlī's *ʿahd* does not follow praises of God and the Prophet with praise for the line of al-ʿAbbās or the caliphate established by his descendants. Nevertheless, Ibn ʿAbd al-Ẓāhir writes that there were men around the Prophet who laid the foundations of religion and maintained the army.[34] Perhaps the logical progression from his own disregard for the caliphate, Qalāwūn's personal charisma and reputation are at the heart of al-Ṣāliḥ ʿAlī's document.[35] As had been the case in the earlier *taqlīd* naming Berke the heir of Baybars, the *ʿahd* of al-Ṣāliḥ ʿAlī does not cite the caliph as the reason for the delegation of power and authority in Egypt and Syria; rather 'the reigns of affairs were bestowed upon him for these noble lands, and he was made successor of the sultanate by his father . . . so that the *umma* could see [at the same time, one] sultan and [one] caliph'.[36] Interested as Qalāwūn was in establishing dynastic succession, this sentiment was likely an attempt to remove the caliph from traditional legitimating duties and instead focus on the tanistric reproduction of his polity.[37] The *tafwīḍ* clause replaces the caliph's name with that of Qalāwūn, who has 'issued the order' (just as the caliph had done in Qalāwūn's own document) delegating the great sultanate along with full and complete authority to al-Ṣāliḥ ʿAlī, the holder of the contract (*walī al-ʿahd*).[38] When compared with Baybars' practice concerning the accession of his own son Berke, we may conclude that the early sultans were happy to set aside the Abbasid Caliphate when it came to dynastic aspirations, and al-Māwardī's earlier understanding of the nature of caliphal delegation freed them to do so. That Qalāwūn and not the Abbasid caliph was the major legitimating force within the document is clear, and the understanding is that once the caliph delegated his deputy (Qalāwūn), the deputy became free to assume caliphal prerogatives such as naming his successor.[39]

By overturning his father's policy of containing the caliphate, al-Ashraf Khalīl consciously grasped at Abbasid legitimacy. In the *ḥamdala* of his investiture deed, we find that its author, again Ibn ʿAbd al-Ẓāhir, assumes that the listener/reader is already aware of Khalīl's assumption of power.[40] As important as Khalīl later made the Abbasid Caliphate during his brief reign, reference to the institution is strangely meagre in the deed itself. There appears to be no clear caliphal clause of delegation and although the document acknowledges that Khalīl honoured the institution, it remains unclear as to *who* bestowed the son of Qalāwūn with his authority. The document merely implies that the time to name the sultan was getting late, and the collective counsel of the ruling assembly (*naṣāʾiḥ al-jumhūr*) agreed upon Khalīl.[41]

Upon succeeding his elder brother Khalīl in 693/1293, al-Nāṣir Muḥammad twice witnessed his own reign disturbed by the ambitions of his father's amirs. One year later the Manṣūrī *mamlūk* of Mongol origin, al-ʿĀdil Kitbughā seized the sultanate until 696/1296, driving al-Nāṣir Muḥammad into exile at al-Karak. Kitbughā himself was forced from power that same year by another of Qalāwūn's former *mamlūk*s, Ḥusām al-Dīn Lājīn (696–8/1296–8). Investiture deeds for al-Nāṣir Muḥammad's dispossessors have survived in the pages of al-Qalqashandī's *Ṣubḥ al-aʿshā*.[42]

During his time in the Cairo chancery, the Syrian scribe Shihāb al-Dīn Maḥmūd al-Ḥalabī (d. 725/1325) authored Kitbughā's *ʿahd* (694/1294), which opened with the claim that the family of the Prophet (i.e., the Abbasids) had imbued the noble contract (*ʿahd sharīf*) with their authority. After stating that the document had been composed on behalf of the Cairo caliph al-Ḥākim to Kitbughā, the *ʿahd*, offering little in the way of a *ḥamdala*, abruptly shifts to the matter of delegation, addressing the would-be sultan with the caveat that concomitant with his new power, was divinely ordained obligation to the caliphate:

> God made you sultan to protect the caliph, and through your sovereignty established for the caliph that which was delegated to him from the affairs of God's creation as aid and support. The caliph bestowed you with everything beyond his throne in the interests of Islam upon the thrones and pulpits of all lands. God brought you to the caliph to assist him in everything that [God] has made [the caliph] successor to among the affairs of His slaves in power for your Lord is powerful. To you, God has gathered all the wayward hearts of the *umma* after some had deviated. He has aided you in upholding his imamate with the pious souls (*awliyāʾ*) of your land.[43]

In what would become an oft-repeated expression in sultanic deeds of the era involving the caliph, Shihāb al-Dīn Maḥmūd described the delegation of power to Kitbughā with the observation that 'the caliph has now covenanted to [the sultan] everything which is beyond his holy caliphate, and all that is incumbent in the rulings of his imamate which is founded in Godly piety (*taqwā*)'.[44] It is then the duty of the sultan (delegated with Abbasid authority) to establish the symbols of Islamic sovereignty divinely entrusted to him. According to the document, God and the caliph al-Ḥākim have delivered the reins of power (*maqālīd*) to Kitbughā along with public and private sovereignty in all lands of Islam.[45]

In much the same way, Shihāb al-Dīn Maḥmūd's investiture document for Lājīn (696/1296) states that the caliph delegates 'those requirements of the caliphate of God on His earth' while claiming that the advent of Lājīn has restored blessings to the community. The document characterises the caliph as swift to yield to God's commandments in all matters delegated to him with respect to the affairs of the faithful.[46]

Shortly after the overthrow of Lājīn, reference to al-Ḥākim appeared in one final document, the *ʿahd* written for al-Nāṣir Muḥammad (at the behest of the ruling amirs) by the qadi and court scribe Shams al-Dīn Ibrāhīm ibn al-Qaysarānī.[47] The document beseeches the young prince to return to Cairo from exile in al-Karak to assume the sultanate and initiate what was to become his second reign as sultan (698–708/1299–1309).

The document begins by assuring the young sultan of his value to the government and his role in preserving order. The document informs al-Nāṣir Muḥammad that control is in his hands, particularly over *jihād* and the enforcement of the Qurʾān and *sunna*. Drawing allusion to God's delegation of prophethood to John the Baptist in the Qurʾān, as well as the trope that authority is hoisted upon the unwilling servant, the *ʿahd* instructs al-Nāṣir Muḥammad to take the Qurʾān 'in his hand with strength'.[48] Elsewhere the document reiterates the delegation with emphasis on the sultan's duty to the caliphate:

> The Commander of the Faithful desires victory to be upheld for monotheism (*al-dīn al-ḥanīf*) so he has established you in his position and set you forth among the peoples of obedience and rebellion [to extend and exact] his generosity and revenge. So praise God who returned you to sovereignty . . . and has made you an aid of the caliph in [governing] creation. He made you a strong support for the caliph in the world and raised you first to the sultanate, second to the caliphate, and of the two moons (i.e., the sun and the moon), made you the third.[49]

Despite the prestige of having been 'hand-picked' by the caliph himself, the claims laid out in the document failed to protect the sultan from a second expulsion by magnate amirs. During the brief decade of al-Nāṣir Muḥammad's second sultanate, the caliph al-Ḥākim passed away in 702/1302 and his son Sulaymān al-Mustakfī bi-llāh inherited the family office. With al-Nāṣir Muḥammad exiled to al-Karak in 709/1309, al-Mustakfī had no choice but to recognise the sultanate of Baybars al-Jāshinkīr. In all, two investiture deeds survive from the few months of Baybars' reign: the first at his initial inauguration,[50] and the second, an eleventh-hour declaration of authority meant to influence the people and composed in the face of al-Nāṣir Muḥammad's triumphal return to Cairo.[51]

The first investiture deed for Baybars al-Jāshinkīr, composed by Muḥyī al-Dīn ibn ʿAbd al-Ẓāhir's grandson ʿAlāʾ al-Dīn, concedes that great authority remains invested in the caliphate, but necessity urged the selection of another party to carry out the obligation of *jihād*. Careful to ensure that the caliph's surrogate was indeed worthy of the dignity, the document names Baybars al-Jāshinkīr, 'the sultan of Islam and the Muslims, master of kings and sultans, victor of the Muḥammadan community, reviver of the Abbasid state, Abū al-Fatḥ Baybars, associate of the Commander of the Faithful, [may] God strengthen and protect the caliphate through his abiding and [indeed] has done so'.[52] The document establishes the primacy of *jihād*, while observing that, incapacitated by crisis the caliph found himself over-extended and unable to oversee his commitments and was thereby obliged to delegate authority to Baybars.[53] The document thus explains delegation of power to the sultan as a necessary reality to implement warfare against the caliph's enemies, whether Mongol battalions or resurgent forces loyal to al-Nāṣir Muḥammad.

Before beginning the advisory *waṣiyya* section, the document describes a number of the sultan's duties, such as fighting the enemies of religion, constructing mosques and caring for the *dhimmī* population. The author then assures listeners/readers that the caliph has completed prayers for

> God to make the caliphate an enduring authority in the lineage [of al-ʿAbbās], and bless Islam and the Muslims with honour by virtue of [the caliph's] station and lineage (*ḥasab wa-nasab*), covenanting to the lofty position of the sultan, everything that is beyond the throne (*sarīr*) of his caliphate and investing [the sultan] with everything invested to [the caliph] from the ordinances (*aḥkām*) of his imamate . . . as well as everything ascribed to the caliphate of the Commander of the Faithful in the regions comprising his imamate.[54]

On the eve of al-Nāṣir Muḥammad's final return to Cairo, Baybars al-Jāshinkīr requested a second investiture deed from al-Mustakfī emphasising the illegitimacy of hereditary kingship. The resulting document contained a delegation composed from the first-person perspective of the caliph, used for its inherent urgency:

> I am pleased with the slave of God Most High, al-Malik al-Muẓaffar Rukn al-Dīn [Baybars al-Jāshinkīr], as my representative in the sovereignty of the Egyptian and Syrian territories, I have set him in place of myself in consideration of his religion, competence, aptness, and because he has pleased me as leader for the faithful. I deposed his predecessor [al-Nāṣir Muḥammad] after I learned that he had abdicated from power. I considered this my duty, and the four qadis concurred in favour of that. Know – may God have mercy upon you – that kingship is without heir (*al-mulk ʿaqīm*), and cannot be inherited from predecessor to successor or from a noble ancestor to a peer. I have besought the choice of God most high, and appointed al-Malik al-Muẓaffar as governor over you. Whoever obeys him, obeys me; and whoever disobeys him, disobeys me; and whoever disobeys me, disobeys my cousin Abū al-Qāsim [i.e., Muḥammad] (God's peace and blessings upon him).[55]

Despite the public involvement of al-Mustakfī, popular demand for the return of al-Nāṣir Muḥammad outweighed even the orders of the caliph, and Baybars al-Jāshinkīr was ultimately exiled and executed. After al-Nāṣir Muḥammad's final reign concluded with his death in 741/1341, the well-organised political elite he left behind shortly installed his son Abū Bakr (741–2/1341) in the name of al-Mustakfī's heir, the caliph Aḥmad al-Ḥākim II. Abū Bakr's investiture deed, succinct in its delegation, merely marks the transfer of power 'from one powerful one (the caliph) to another (the sultan)'.[56]

Three sultanic investiture deeds from the fifteenth century uphold many of the themes and rhetoric discussed above, as well as similar clauses of delegation. Examples include the 815/1412 investiture deed for al-Muʾayyad Shaykh in the name of the caliph al-Mustaʿīn composed by the chancery chief Nāṣir al-Dīn Muḥammad al-Bārizī (d. 823/1420),[57] as well as documents for the sultans al-Ẓāhir Ṭaṭar and al-Ashraf Barsbāy in the name of that caliph's brother and successor, Dāwūd al-Muʿtaḍid II (r. 816–45/1414–41), composed by Abū Bakr ibn Ḥijja al-Ḥamawī.

Although the caliph al-Mustaʿīn had received the sultanate after the death of Faraj in 815/1412, he relinquished it unhappily to Shaykh. The subsequent investiture document for Shaykh cited al-Mustaʿīn as the

Commander of the Faithful and caliph of the age who bestowed powers on the new sultan. The religious leadership had attested to the document to appease Shaykh.[58] Composed by Shaykh's close confidant and *kātib al-sirr*, Muḥammad al-Bārizī, the *ʿahd* enshrines the formal acclamation by elite amirs, qadis and *ʿulamāʾ*, along with the masses, which precedes its *tafwīḍ* clause of delegation:

> The caliph, may God strengthen religion through him, with *baraka* gathered auspiciously (in his right hand), rallied the totality of Islam and the Muslims, uniting [them] on the delegation of authority amongst them and upon the holder of their contract, the one responsible for the noble sultanate and the grand imamate; to you – may God make your sultanate last forever and subordinate the age to you, with the angels as your helpers. The caliph, having sought the best of outcomes [from God] (*istikhāra Allāh*) sets forth this investiture (*taqlīd*) and that which is deemed noble *sunna*.[59]

Elsewhere al-Bārizī addresses justice and enjoining the good, while informing the new sultan that the Abbasid caliph

> covenants to you all that which is beyond the throne of his caliphate, and in everything associated with the ordinances (*aḥkām*) of his imamate. Thus he invests you both in east and west, near and far, land and sea, over smooth and rough terrain, and in all of his sovereignty, lands and henceforth all that which God opens for him by your hand. [It is] a total delegation, a complete investiture, a finished contract and general ascription . . . It is founded upon Godly piety (*taqwā*) and God's pleasure.[60]

That delegations of authority were often in reality forced upon the caliph is nowhere more evident than the delegation to Shaykh by the reluctant caliph who gave up the sultanate and was ultimately ordered to vacate both Cairo and the caliphate in favour of his brother al-Muʿtaḍid II. Among the first to receive an investiture document in the name of the latter was al-Ẓāhir Ṭaṭar.

After having been 'selected' by the caliph, 'the sultan thus became the protector (*walī*) of this *umma* and God aided him in that which he took over and allowed him to fulfil the conditions of the *ʿahd* and the *bayʿa* . . .'[61] A clearer delegation follows with the recognition that the caliph delegates to Ṭaṭar everything God had entrusted to his office, including responsibility over lands and worshippers, and then assigned to the sultan everything both 'in his hand and beyond his throne'. The document then affirms that the caliph has accepted the legal conditions which oversaw the assignment of authority to Ṭaṭar, and declares that God is merciful upon the one who takes the caliph's place and enables his enjoyment of widespread support.[62]

The final investiture deed, for the sultan Barsbāy, dates to 825/1422 and survives in the *inshāʾ* collection of Ibn Ḥijja. The *tafwīḍ* clause goes beyond a commonplace caliphal delegation, employing the familiar trope that Barsbāy, reluctant to assume leadership, had to be forced by al-Muʿtaḍid's *demand* that he take power. The delegation for Barsbāy is noteworthy in its attempt to trace the theoretical sources of caliphal authority:

> Our master the caliph urged that which was incumbent upon him from his obligations to God and cast the staff of his selection (*ʿaṣan ikhtiyārihi*), and discerned the choice of God (*khīrat Allāh*) in the delegation of the affairs of the Muslims to [Barsbāy], honoured him thusly, but he refused, so the *imāms* of religion made a fatwa forbidding him to abstain from [taking care of] the interests of the Muslims . . . So when the breezes of assent blew and veils lifted from the countenance of delegation, the lightning which accompanies dazzling guidance shimmered for our master the caliph and he delegated to our sultan al-Malik al-Ashraf that which God had entrusted to [the caliph] from the affairs of the Muslims, a divine designation appointing its order (*isnād*) to him and enforcing its obligation, and confirming the validity of this order with the chief qadis of Islam and they ruled upon it with reason. Thus [Barsbāy] was put forth for the imamate, and the Muslims became aware that he was the *imām* of every *miḥrāb* and they said 'God is great'![63]

Barsbāy's *tafwīḍ* concludes with the observation that in his bestowal of authority to the sultan, the caliph has empowered every aspect of faith. As in earlier documents, the caliph delegates everything beyond his throne (i.e., the caliphate itself) to Barsbāy, thereby honouring the sultanate through his wide-encompassing authority, now legally and publicly wielded by the sultan of Cairo.

Finally, it is worth comparing the caliphal delegations of power made to the sultans above with one made to a religious scholar. A document dated 9

Ṣafar 902/17 October 1496, allegedly composed by the caliph al-Mutawakkil II, delegated full powers over the judiciary to Jalāl al-Dīn al-Suyūṭī based solely on caliphal authority. Al-Suyūṭī, well acquainted with the many caliphal and sultanic investiture deeds that appear in his historical works, encouraged the caliph to name him grand qadi (*qāḍī kabīr*) and likely participated in the composition of the document. The delegation resembles al-Mustanṣir's full delegation of power to Baybars over all the Muslim lands and those yet to be 'opened' from infidel control in 659/1261, as well as al-Ḥākim's 'total' delegation of power to Qalāwūn in 678/1279:

> [The caliph al-Mutawakkil II] delegates to [al-Suyūṭī] rule and judgement over Egypt and the rest of the noble Islamic lands, east and west, and that which God opens for the Muslims from the lands of unbelief; a general and absolute delegation (*tafwīḍan ʿāmman muṭlaqan*) without condition or exception. The Commander of the Faithful – may God prolong his honour – delegated to the *shaykh al-Islām* Shaykh Jalāl al-Dīn supervision (*al-naẓar*) over the affairs of the qadis, so that he may appoint those among them who are righteous, and depose those who are not. In this, the Commander of the Faithful – may God bring glory to his reign – models his ancestor the Commander of the Faithful Hārūn al-Rashīd bi-llāh [who delegated similar authority] to the great *imām* al-Layth bin Saʿd. May God renew His *baraka* upon the Commander of the Faithful and the rest of the Muslims.[64]

There is no question that the sultans, delegated with the powers and authority of the Abbasid Caliphate, are the true gravitational centre of these documents. The investiture deed itself became an important symbol of the political order, as it enshrined the caliph's transfer of authority to the sultan. As such, the sultanate of Cairo upheld the norms of the holy law and symbolically preserved the integrity of the community's pledge to God and the Prophet.[65]

Caliphal Succession Contracts (*ʿahd* or *ʿaqd walī al-ʿahd*)

In the context of succession documents, the term *ʿahd* (which proves quite versatile), refers to the contract between the Abbasid caliph and his designated dynastic successor. Al-Qalqashandī considered many such documents preserved in the *Ṣubḥ* as formal appointments. It is no coincidence that the term *ʿahd* was used to denote both the document enshrining the caliphal delegation to the sultan, as well as the caliph's selection of his own successor to the caliphate, as the *ʿuhūd* were reserved to refer to contracts of appointment for the highest office holders in the sultanate.[66]

Dominique Sourdel traced the origin of the caliphal practice of leaving a written designation for the presumptive heir to the reign of the Umayyad caliph ʿAbd al-Malik (65–86/685–705). As a title, *walī al-ʿahd* referred to the successor of a caliph or other ruler by virtue of a contract concluded between the heir, his delegator and the community. As they had been in Baghdad, heirs to the Abbasid Caliphate in Cairo tended to be sons of the reigning caliph, though there was no formalised means of succession and nothing barred brothers or cousins from assuming the caliphal dignity.[67] Position as heir to the caliphate was not without prestige and al-Qalqashandī lists several honorifics associated with the title of the *walī al-ʿahd*, such as 'noble excellence' (*al-jānib al-sharīf*),[68] the 'exalted master' (*al-sayyid al-jalīl*) and the 'armoury of religion' (*dhakhīrat al-dīn*).[69] A caliph's selection was often ratified by a council of the regime's notables including the sultan, qadis and important amirs.

The present investigation in Chapters 8 and 9 benefits from the fifth chapter (*maqāla*) of the *Ṣubḥ al-aʿshā*, which concerns documents of appointment for public offices (*wilāyāt*) and includes al-Qalqashandī's discussion of the theoretical position of the *bayʿa*, in which the author discusses popular motifs used in the standardisation of caliphal *bayʿa* documents.[70] Based on first-hand knowledge of classical investiture deeds and normative caliphal documents from his own time, al-Qalqashandī instructs aspiring chancery secretaries to use the full name of the caliph, discuss the circumstances which led to the *bayʿa* ceremony, mention the nobility and necessity of the office, praise the candidate and state his suitability for office above and beyond all contemporaries, mention that the choice had been made by the electoral community and witnessed by important officials, and, lastly, affirm that the candidate had accepted the contract freely without rival claimants. All that ensured that the new *imām* would be rightfully owed the trust and obedience of the entire community. Al-Qalqashandī went on to advise future scribes-in-training that condolences should be offered if the previous caliph had died, and that removal of an incumbent *imām* was unlawful without good reason.[71]

Finally, there must be mention of the reigning sultan performing the *bayʿa*, as well as prominent notables in attendance, as well as the great quality of the oath itself.[72] These requirements suggest that many of the documents were unique reflections of specific socio-political contexts. In what remains of the current and following chapter, we will see that many chancery clerks indeed strove to include these points in their rhetoric on the *bayʿa* and the caliphate.

Succession and Perpetuation of the Abbasid Caliphate

Caliphal succession contracts are principally concerned with the perpetuation of the Abbasid Caliphate. The idea of preserving and strengthening the succession was crucial to scribal secretaries who took pains to assure their listeners/readers that the latest caliphal succession had been legal (*sharīʿ*), sound (*ṣaḥīḥ*), and explicitly the product of an outgoing caliph's wilful participation.[73] In reality, however, the sultan and his entourage discussed suitable successors when an incumbent caliph was thought to be near death, and although they favoured an Abbasid candidate who had been previously named successor in an *ʿahd*, maintained their prerogative over any final decisions.[74]

The first such contract issued for a Cairo caliph is attributed to al-Ḥākim bi-Amr Allāh and was composed for his heir Sulaymān al-Mustakfī in Jumādā I 701/January 1302.[75] This document, if it is authentic, attests to al-Mustakfī's aptitude and fitness for office, claiming that the soundness of the contract led to the divine gathering of Islamic authority for bestowal upon the new caliph coupled with the powerful charisma (*baraka*) of his noble ancestors to assist with imposing restraint on tyrants. By praising al-Ḥākim as 'cousin of the master of the prophets' and 'carrier of God's mercy, strength, and his own virtuous life example (*ḥusn sīratihi*) to the gardens of paradise', the document attempts to vouchsafe the caliphal succession based on the idea that the caliph and his son, in their knowledge and demeanour, were like students who sat at the feet of the prophets, the companions and other rightly-guided caliphs.[76]

When the time came for al-Mustakfī to name his own successor in the 730s/1330s, he initially chose his son Baraka al-Mustawathiq, named in a partial, perhaps model, *walī al-ʿahd* document preserved by al-Qalqashandī. The *ḥamdala* begins by indicating God's interest in supporting the Abbasid Caliphate by consistently supplying it with the best fathers and sons, and ensuring that its abiding authority remained in the lineage. God's protection and preservation of the caliphal succession is considered evident even in ominous times, as certain as 'light comes from darkness'.[77]

Events in the wake of al-Mustakfī's 740/1340 death in exile in Upper Egypt gave rise to one of the most remarkable and revealing Abbasid documents of the fourteenth century. After the unpopular caliphate of al-Wāthiq bi-llāh, a caliph purportedly chosen by al-Nāṣir Muḥammad as a posthumous snub to the *ʿahd* contract concluded by the caliph al-Mustakfī, the *ʿulamāʾ* ultimately secured the succession of the latter's selected heir, al-Ḥākim II. It was not until al-Ḥākim II came to Cairo, that the chancery secretary Ibn Faḍlallāh al-ʿUmarī, a vociferous advocate for the ouster of al-Wāthiq, composed a new and highly celebratory deed of appointment. A joyful vindication that the caliphate had resumed and the harmony of the universe restored, this document reflects the ways in which a courtier and chief of the chancery, delighted to be rid of a court pariah (al-Wāthiq), envisaged the caliphal idea through a lens of unbridled idealism. Al-ʿUmarī, who personally toiled to rehabilitate the tarnished reputation of al-Mustakfī and his family at court, wrote that God had selected the late caliph as an honoured servant, relocated him to Cairo from Baghdad, and rewarded him for an exemplary life by placing him amongst excellent recipients of divine favour such as prophets, trustworthy companions, martyrs and the pious.[78]

Later succession documents justified a caliph's selection of his son based on the candidate's hypothetical fulfilment of the classical requirements of the imamate: knowledge of religion, probity, generosity, good intentions and a general suitability for office, as was the case when the caliph al-Muʿtaḍid I named his son al-Mutawakkil heir in 763/1362. The author of the document establishes that the caliphal transfer was concluded in accordance with *sharīʿa*, praying that God champion and support the holy law through Islamic authority.[79]

In a document dating to roughly 800/1397–8, several years before his death, al-Mutawakkil bestowed the caliphate upon his son al-Mustaʿīn and thus 'established through [his son] the well-spring (*ʿayn*) of the Abbasid Caliphate as he had done with his father [before him]'.[80] Through the affirmation of his son's qualities, the document preserves the legality of the succession and defends the Abbasid legacy. We are told that the caliph al-Mutawakkil chose his son al-Mustaʿīn because he had suitable characteristics for the caliphate and that it was his mercy to the community that such a young man, in truth the *only* acceptable candidate, became designated as the heir apparent.[81]

After al-Mustaʿīn's acceptance of the family office and implied entry into the pantheon of his excellent ancestors, the document attests to the strength of the succession by likening the caliphs to the prophets and employing the leitmotif of equating Abbasid descent to a tree with the best roots developing into fine branches bearing great quantities of fruit. Al-Mustaʿīn, as incoming caliph who has absorbed all the goodness and knowledge of his father, is described as having been 'created with [his father's] noble temperament, benevolent ethics (*akhlāquhu al-karīma*), and having obtained the caliph's good manners which nourished him in the cradle (*fī mahdihi*)'.[82]

Finding the succession unchallenged, the caliph repeatedly prayed to God for the best outcome (*istikhāra*) and reached the epiphany that the only satisfactory recourse was to name his son to the caliphate. Al-Mutawakkil thus left the family office to his son 'in the fashion of the past caliphs and the basis of his predecessors among the rightly-guided *imāms* and delegated to him that which he had of its ordinances and requirements, foundations, and nobilities, from covenant and decree (*ʿahd wa-waṣāya*), deposition and delegation'.[83]

To further strengthen the legitimacy of the succession and to provide rationale for keeping the caliphate within a select household, the document reasons that growing up in the household of the caliph al-Mutawakkil, who had 'directed the face of the caliphate to its *qibla*', made the young al-Mustaʿīn the supreme choice for the office. Indeed, the Abbasid prince had been 'suckled at the breast of the caliphate and reared in its chambers; prophecy [mandated that] he belonged to it and thus it pressed him to its bosom; and *why should it not* cling to his beauty, hang from the trails of his robe, and covet nearness to him, loving him excessively, inclining towards his sociability and tempting him, sufficient as he was for all of its conditions?'[84]

The implication is that the caliphate, described here poetically as a living, motherly, sentient being, *chose* al-Mustaʿīn, even longing for him to 'give the *khuṭba*', a metaphor describing the caliph's traditional ascent to the *minbar*. The author, al-Qalqashandī, appears to appreciate that 'caliphate' was an idea that went far beyond the man given the office. It also embodied the roles of the sultanate, the judiciary and the hierarchy of amirs, with the ensemble depicted as a single free entity, guided by divine justice, self-aware and eternally coveting the best men to occupy its offices.[85] This emphasises the point that many at court saw the caliphate and the man who held it as different entities – one charged with the defence and upkeep of the other.

Defending the integrity of the succession proved to be equally important in several later documents that linked mismanagement of the caliphate to social chaos. Some forty-five years later, when al-Mustaʿīn's brother and successor the caliph al-Muʿtaḍid II left the caliphate to their brother al-Mustakfī II in 845/1441, the succession document proclaimed that, if care of the government had been left to anyone else trouble would have unavoidably fallen upon the electoral community (*ahl al-ḥall wa-l-ʿaqd*).[86] Thus, in his final act of defending the caliphate by selecting the best successor, al-Muʿtaḍid II chose with alacrity to spare the sultan's government the burden of having to choose a caliph themselves. The document informs us that his selection of al-Mustakfī II left his mind at ease knowing that one worthy of advising the sultan and his circle would assume office.

In the case of succession documents written for the incoming caliph and attributed to his outgoing predecessor, one would rightly expect the documents in question to contain florid praise for both the Abbasid family and their position in society. Like the investiture deeds for the sultans, *ʿahd* documents for the caliphal succession emphasised the major themes of protecting Islam and Muslims and upholding the *sharīʿa*. Focused on the incumbent caliph, his successor and occasionally the sultan who protected them, caliphal succession deeds of the period centred on the figure of the Commander of the Faithful, his investiture in the capital, the legacy of his position, his ties to natural order, and sought to define his theoretical place in the hierarchy of the current social order. The documents demonstrated, in the context of ceremonial, that the caliphate continued to be properly upheld and its integrity preserved under the supervision of the sultan's court. While the *ḥamdala* and *tafwīḍ* closely resembled those of sultanic investiture deeds, caliphal succession documents ventured to present an Abbasid Caliphate steeped in tradition to closely observing scribes, courtiers and religious scholars.[87]

Other Documents Alluding to Caliphal Authority

Chancery workers in medieval Cairo treated Abbasid authority with the same ceremonial reverence in letters pertaining to domestic affairs and in issues involving relatively distant clients, as they did in affairs of (caliphal or sultanic) succession. A letter issued in 708/1308 by the Cairo chancery to the Rasulid leader al-Muʾayyad Ḥizabr al-Dīn Dāwūd sought to reprimand the ruler of Yemen and remind him of Cairo's hegemony.[88] Vermeulen speculates that the letter, though written in the caliph's voice, was largely the product of a chancery team urged by a young al-Nāṣir Muḥammad, anxious to exert authority in a theatre that had escaped the attentions of his guardians Salār and Baybars al-Jāshinkīr.[89]

Quickly establishing that he had invested the sultan with theocratic authority, in the document the caliph declared that caliphal delegation enabled success in the world and the interests of the afterlife, and allowed the sultan to publicise the traditional symbols of Islamic sovereignty such as minting coins and naming himself and the caliph in the *khuṭba*.[90] The caliph claims to have chosen the sultan because of his familiarity with the Muslim provinces and expert fiscal management of the empire. Indeed, the Rasulid court receives a reminder that al-Nāṣir Muḥammad is 'the best guide and organiser of the lands' with whom true power resides.[91]

The *Ṣubḥ* also preserves a Shawwāl 813/February 1411 investiture deed in the name of the Abbasid caliph al-Mustaʿīn presented in Damascus to representatives of the sultan of Gujarat, Muẓaffar Shāh (810–14/1407–11).[92] By the early fifteenth century, investiture deeds involving the Abbasid Caliphate were routinely issued to sultans in Delhi. Al-Qalqashandī makes note of the document's rarity, describing it as the only surviving investiture deed issued by a Cairo caliph to a foreign king. The document provides a view into the delegation of caliphal authority to rulers beyond the territories of the sultanate of Cairo. Like the earlier delegation to Qalāwūn by al-Ḥākim, the transfer of power concluded for the sultan of Delhi by al-Mustaʿīn is 'full, total and complete' in all remaining lands of India along with its regions, ports, lands and armies, in all matters of its subjects, patrons, lesser rulers, governors, and qadis far and wide. The document states that the *ʿahd* is covenanted through the caliph al-Mustaʿīn, God's slave and cousin of the Prophet.[93]

At least two surviving documents invoke the caliphate in domestic affairs unrelated to sultanic investiture. The first involves the caliphal authority of al-Ḥākim II in a dispute over the use of pellet-shooting crossbows in Syria in the 740s/1340s. The petition appears in a section of the fourth chapter of the *Ṣubḥ* on correspondence and letters (*al-mukātabāt*) with various members of the civilian and military personnel that present the proper etiquette illustrating how petitioners must address the reigning rulers of Egypt.[94] The document cites a continuing use of the weapon despite an earlier writ demanding that they be discontinued in the name of the caliph.[95]

The petition, according to protocol, blesses the chancery with a number of epithets including *imāmī* and *ḥākimī*. This indicates that documents depending on the authority of the Abbasid caliph must emanate from the 'noble *dīwān*', thereby presenting the chancery as a formal extension of the caliph's authority.[96] It also addresses the failure of a certain Nāṣir al-Dīn ibn al-Ḥimsī, and quite a few of his associates, to comply with an official order forbidding the use of the weapons in Syria.[97]

The petitioners 'kiss the ground of the sublime gate' of the caliphal chancery and take refuge with its position, which, through its proximity to the caliph, enjoys a similarly close relationship to the religious legitimacy of the Ka'ba. The author, possibly al-'Umarī, appears to chastise the 'shooters' for being in breach of a ruling 'strengthened and aided by the opinion of the *imām* al-Ḥākim bi-Amr Allāh', cousin of the Prophet, to which, at least initially, the offending party had shown some deference and even prayed for the Commander of the Faithful whose rulings 'increased their happiness'. Contemporaries understood the document, read publicly 'in every place of hearing', to be 'that which God had ruled upon [through] the speech (*lisān*) of the caliph al-Ḥākim'.[98]

The second document involves the sanction of a domestic office in 822/1419, when the sultan al-Mu'ayyad Shaykh named Muḥammad ibn al-Bārizī orator and manager of the library (*khazīn al-kutub*)[99] of his Mu'ayyadiyya mosque during al-Bārizī's tenure as *kātib al-sirr* (815–23/1413–20), making him overseer of the building in the name of the Abbasid caliph al-Mu'taḍid II.[100] The investiture deed, composed by Ibn Ḥijja, affirms that authority resides in the *umma*, and that an office holder need not fear the collective wrath of the community of believers lest 'he tread on the carpet of obedience in their mosques'.

After fulsome praise for al-Bārizī, the document sets about the task of linking the esteemed *kātib al-sirr* to Abbasid prestige as 'the chosen pillar (*al-rukn al-sāmī*) in the foundations of [the caliph's] noble house, the one firmly planted to raise his Abbasid banner so that it might provide shade with its extensive shadow, observing with the eye of felicity that which is in our most amazing lineage, and the Muḥammadan secret (*al-sirr al-Muḥammadī*) which remains to Banū ʿAbbās in full'.[101] For its part, the document lauds al-Bārizī for his service to Islam, notably for causing the *masjid* to flourish by creating an atmosphere of calm tranquillity within its walls. Al-Bārizī and his suitability for the position are the true focus of the document, but the piece itself confirms that court culture in the time of Shaykh considered it acceptable for the Abbasid Caliphate to honour other (non-military) members of the sultan's entourage.

Khuṭbas

Medieval Muslim societies attached great significance to the ruler named in the Friday sermon. The mention of the Abbasid caliph in Friday mosques occurred in the late thirteenth century, but was not consistent and seems to have been sporadic at best after the mid-fourteenth century.[102] With the exception, perhaps, of the Citadel mosque, the larger congregational mosques throughout the Cairo Sultanate named the Abbasid caliphs with some regularity until the dismissal of al-Wāthiq and the succession of al-Ḥākim II in 741/1341.[103] The name of the caliph was rarely heard in the *khuṭba* for many years until the brief sultanate of the caliph al-Mustaʿīn began in 815/1412, though only because he was sultan.[104] A century later in the confusion following Marj Dābiq in 923/1516, some Egyptian mosques made Friday prayers in the name of the Abbasid caliph after the death of Qāniṣawh al-Ghawrī.[105]

On some occasions, the political elite invited the caliph to deliver the Friday sermon. Donald Little described the transcribed versions of several sermons of the caliph al-Ḥākim (along with treaties and other diplomatic scripts) as 'internal documents' embedded within historical texts.[106] The sultans Baybars and al-Ashraf Khalīl commissioned al-Ḥākim to address elite audiences at the Citadel in 662/1263 and 691/1291–2, respectively, and on both occasions the caliph delivered the same *khuṭba*.[107] Focused on themes of *jihād* and defence, the original *khuṭba* opens with the description of the Abbasid house, supported and defended by Baybars.[108] Like many of the investiture documents, the *khuṭba* includes praise for the Abbasid house and the virtues of the Prophet's uncle al-ʿAbbās, who joins the four Rāshidūn caliphs as an archetype of high merit. The caliph's homily stresses the imamate itself as an obligation of Islam in the same breath with *jihād* as the Commander reminded the Faithful of Mongol atrocities against the people of Baghdad, which he had himself survived. The sultan and the importance of his support was a cornerstone of the speech, and the caliph emphasised that Baybars had protected and secured the victory of the imamate, scattered infidel armies and arranged for the *bayʿa* of a new caliph. The importance of *jihād* is paramount in the original *khuṭba*, recited to attending amirs, dignitaries and emissaries from Berke Khān of the Golden Horde only a few years after the battle of ʿAyn Jālūt. The sultan is again praised as the conductor of holy war and the pillar of faith and the world (*rukn al-dunyā wa-l-dīn*). Baybars' interest in the affairs of the Abbasid Caliphate moved him to set the imamate on a secure footing, and the caliph claims that the Abbasid dynasty has thus 'secured numerous soldiers'.[109]

Al-Ashraf Khalīl also commissioned a series of fresh *khuṭba*s from the caliph in 691/1292 to be read at the Citadel and at his father's tomb to drum up morale for his movements against Armenian and Mongol positions. After praising the sultan, the first half of the only surviving *khuṭba* states that *jihād* is an obligation upon the believers. The words of the caliph portray holy war as an eternal struggle between good and evil with spiritual rewards that awaited the military elite.[110]

Likely addressing his remarks to a politically savvy audience of *mamlūk*s and upper-level amirs (many of whom may have had designs on the sultanate), the caliph did not promise booty or earthly rewards. Words of piety and religious obligation would be easier to digest coming from the caliph as opposed to al-Ashraf al-Khalīl, the son of their master.[111] We may also consider this the expression of a leader wishing to wage holy war in the same style as his predecessors which had concrete political advantages. This *khuṭba* presents an image of the ideal caliph for the late thirteenth century, one who summons the believers to God's pleasure through fighting enemies of the faith. However, despite the meagre amount of evidence available, it is clear that a universal messenger such as the Abbasid caliph would have been listened to with more admiration than a sultan ruling through dynastic legitimacy who many in the hall may already have been scheming to thwart or replace.

The second part of the *khuṭba* includes the requisite praise for the Prophet, his family and companions before evoking the Abbasid mystique and the symbol of al-ʿAbbās as 'the one who prayed for rain, face turned towards the clouds (*al-mustasqā bi-wajhhi al-ghamām*)', followed by al-Ḥākim's communal prayer to God:

> O Lord, grant me gratitude for the blessing which you have bestowed upon me and upon my ancestors. Answer my prayer that seeks to do good for Islam, for myself, the sultan al-Malik al-Ashraf the most glorious lord, salvation of the world and religion (*ṣalāḥ al-dunyā wa-l-dīn*), master of kings and sultans, king of the earth and sultan of the world, Abū Fatḥ al-Khalīl. Lord, grant him influence over the planets and make him king wherever he goes . . . bring down upon him that assistance which opens the doors of the kingdoms of the earth saying 'come on in', (*hayta lak*) . . . and through him make the land of Islam a place of peace [filled with] *minbar*s of the caliphate . . . Make his army victorious and fulfil for him his promise and satisfy his father al-Malik al-Manṣūr [Qalāwūn] who battled the unbelievers in his *jihād*.[112]

The prayer of the Abbasid caliph, complete with its elliptical statements, was no doubt well suited for the Citadel audience. The astrological auspiciousness of the hour of departure for battle remained an important concern throughout the long history of the Cairo Sultanate, and it is only natural that the *khuṭba* of the caliph, one of the chief spiritual figures in the land and its adjoining regions, would touch upon it in a public address. Again this provides an image of what the social and political orders expected the caliph to be: a holy man who could divine the future – leading the government and its military support to the best outcome, or else an astrologer, or magus-type adviser, many of whom were similarly called upon to select the best and most cosmically auspicious dates for military engagements.

Inscriptions and Coinage

The Syro-Egyptian lands of the Cairo Sultanate are well known for the epigraphy of the later medieval period. Inscriptions on new and restored buildings serve historians as vital documents in their own right. Important inscription inventories and resources such as the *Répertoire chronologique d'épigraphie arabe* (RCEA) and the *Thesaurus d'épigraphie islamique* supplement our study of Abbasid documents. Coins of the mid-thirteenth century also reflect a strong involvement with the Abbasid Caliphate of Cairo in its earliest years, followed by a later period of disuse beginning in the early fourteenth century. The scope of the current chapter limits its discussion to inscriptions and coins that contribute to a titulary repertoire involving the Abbasid Caliphate of Cairo.

Inscriptions

After Baybars had installed two successive Abbasid princes in his capital, caliphal protocol figured prominently in his inscriptions and coinage.[113] Based on its frequency and consistency, the most important title he used was 'Associate of the Commander of the Faithful' (*qasīm amīr al-muʾminīn*) which the sultan employed heavily in his titulary in inscriptions in important locations in Cairo and throughout Syria,[114] including the tomb of the early Muslim general and companion of the Prophet, Khālid ibn al-Walīd in Ḥims,[115] the mosque of al-Azhar in Cairo,[116] Baybars' own mosque complex in that city,[117] the *maqām* Nabī Mūsā near Jericho[118] and the citadel of Damascus.[119] Reuven Amitai has divided the titles of Baybars into three categories: those that show him as a *jihād* warrior; those that present him as a just and powerful Muslim ruler; and those that reflect his power and majesty. In the light of its legitimating potential, *qasīm amīr al-muʾminīn* is arguably the most important title because of its placement immediately after the sultan's proper name and appearance in many of his inscriptions and coins.[120]

Another important title used by Baybars in the inscription at the tomb of Moses (Nabī Mūsā) is 'he who commanded the taking of the *bayʿa* to two caliphs' (*al-āmir bi-bayʿat al-khalīfatayn*).[121] Certainly, the latter was a title of distinction, though one connoting executive direction and free of the notion of being an 'associate' or underling of the caliph. Qalāwūn continued the use of the *qasīm* title at his *madrasa* and added it to his restorations at the Ḥisn al-Akrād fortress.[122] Qalāwūn completed the work on Baybars' mausoleum in Damascus and had an inscription declaring that the project had reached its termination thanks to 'al-Malik al-Manṣūr Qalāwūn, Associate of the Commander of the Faithful, may God extend his kingdom'.[123] Al-Ashraf Khalīl likewise continued to use *qasīm amīr al-muʾminīn* inscribed with his name at the citadel of Aleppo.[124] In addition, Khalīl also introduced a different title, notably on one of the bands of the citadel of Aleppo which names him 'restorer of the noble Abbasid state, the defender of the Muḥammadan community, may his victory be glorious!'[125]

The title is then inscribed sporadically, on the *madrasa* of al-Ashraf Shaʿbān (770/1368–9),[126] and later by al-Ashraf Barsbāy at the Bāb al-Nabī in Mecca (825/1421–2) as well as in his *madrasa* (827/1423–4),[127] followed by an absence of almost sixty years until it reappears in regard to Qāyitbāy on a chandelier in the mosque of Aṣālbāy in the Fayyūm.[128]

Few other inscriptions involving the Abbasid caliphs of Cairo survived save for the caliph-sultan al-Mustaʿīn's proclamation outside Gaza in 815/1412.[129] It is unfortunate that the inscriptions in the Abbasid mausoleum in Cairo appear to offer little beyond the names, regnal titles and dates of death of the nearly two dozen interred there, only two of whom appear to have been caliphs in Cairo.[130]

Coinage and Numismatic Evidence

As it had in monument inscriptions, *qasīm amīr al-muʾminīn* retained importance on coinage struck by the same early sultans, Baybars, Qalāwūn and Khalīl. Beginning in 659/1261, Baybars named the caliphs on the reverse of his coins and first took the title '*al-sulṭān al-malik*'.[131] On at least one coin struck that year, Baybars had the sultanic titles on one side, and the full name and *laqab/kunya* of the caliph on the other.[132] Some dirhams dated 659–61/1261–3 also include the title *qasīm amīr al-muʾminīn* directly after the name of Baybars.[133] In the early days, both the names of al-Mustanṣir and then al-Ḥākim appeared on the reverse of coins that named Baybars.[134] It is interesting that both full titles appear in some cases: the caliph as *amīr al-muʾminīn* on one side, and Baybars as *qasīm amīr al-muʾminīn* on the other.[135] Baybars did not always make use of the *qasīm* title and later coins replaced it with his insignia of a large feline (possibly a lion or panther).[136] While the caliph's full name was eventually removed from the coins, Baybars named himself *qasīm amīr al-muʾminīn* as late as 666/1267 and 668/1269.[137] The two sons of Baybars likewise maintained the title popularised by their father on their own coins during their brief reigns.[138] Qalāwūn struck it on his coins and inscriptions without ever naming the reigning caliph.[139] Al-Ashraf Khalīl's coins also match the pretensions of his inscriptions, naming himself the victor or helper (*nāṣir*) of the Muslim *umma* and the reviver of the Abbasid state (*muḥyī al-dawla al-ʿabbāsiyya*).[140] Similarly, the usurpers of Khalīl's younger brother al-Nāṣir Muḥammad, Kitbughā (694/1294) and Baybars al-Jashnakir (709/1309) employed the *qasīm* title in their coinage.[141] According to Paul Balog, al-Nāṣir Muḥammad may not have used the title until his third reign in which several undated silver dirhams name him 'Sultan al-Malik al-Nāṣir Nāṣir al-Dunyā wa-l-Dīn, Muḥammad ibn Qalāwūn, *qasīm amīr al-muʾminīn*'.[142]

During the later Qalāwūnid period the title seems to have vanished from the coinage never to return. For many of the subsequent rulers until Barqūq, it was more important to be identified as a descendant of Qalāwūn, who himself had been known widely as *qasīm amīr al-muʾminīn*. It is noteworthy that the religious formula proclaiming the Islamic profession of faith remained constant on coins of the era after the caliph's name was removed. This may have been sufficient to remind the population that the sultans and the socio-political orders established around them were helping to uphold the *sharīʿa*, protect the caliph and maintain the classical image of Arabo-Islamic government.

As for the coins of later vassals of the Cairo Sultanate such as the Jalayrids, Qaramanids, Artuqids, Eretnayids and early Ottomans, none, save for the Jalayrid Sulṭān-Aḥmad (784–813/1382–1410), minted coins hinting at fealty to the Abbasid caliph of Cairo.[143] While the remaining Circassian sultans do not appear to have used caliphal protocols in their coinage, it is worth mentioning that during his brief 'sultanate', the caliph-sultan al-Mustaʿīn had time enough to mint coins naming himself '*amīr al-muʾminīn*' and '*al-imām al-aʿẓam*'.[144]

Caliphal Titulary and Protocol in Late Medieval Egypt

The widely disseminated sultanic epithet, 'associate' or 'partner' of the caliph, affirmed that the caliph invested the sultan with the 'affairs of the lands and subjects and made him manager of creation (*wakala ilayhi tadbīr al-khalq*) and his associate (*qasīm*) in enacting rights, delegating to him the rest of the matters [of rule] and entrusting him with bringing prosperity to the public'.[145] This naturally left the caliphate with a role not easily defined. As a designation, *qasīm amīr al-muʾminīn*, one of the loftiest additions to the Commander of the Faithful title, meant that the sultan or ruler shared in the caliph's authority and sovereignty, or that the caliph looked upon him as an equal in power.[146]

An early usage of '*qasīm amīr al-muʾminīn*' dates to the Buyid ruler of Fārs and Iraq, Abū Nāṣr al-Malik al-Raḥīm (440–7/1048–56). Although the title was perhaps unknown to the Fatimids, it was used by the Ghurid rulers of Afghanistan and the Seljuks of Rūm, who exploited it until at least 659/1260–1.[147] By resurrecting the title, or bringing it to his territory, Baybars demonstrated his appreciation of the gravitas of his watershed restoration of the caliphal institution.[148]

In reality, the power of the sultan eclipsed that of the Abbasid caliph and had replaced it in most practical respects. Nevertheless, titles involving the caliphate in this period are indicative of more than mere propaganda. Combined with the ideology expressed in the *ʿahd* of Qalāwūn, the sultan was interested in setting up his office as a seat of absolute power independent from the caliphate, though one that continued to share and absorb aspects of its authority.[149]

The title *khalīfa* appears with some regularity in contemporary Arabic chronicles, though it shared importance with *amīr al-muʾminīn*, the unique caliphal epithet associated with notions of the Qurayshī, Hashemite caliphate.[150] Early sultans and amirs, some of whom may have been hesitant to adopt the title because of its potent symbolism, often chose instead to append it to their own titles such as *qasīm amīr al-muʾminīn* or *sayf amīr al-muʾminīn*.

The term *khalīfa* was a more ambiguous inter-regional title in the later medieval period, used frequently as a title of courtesy for many rulers outside the territories of the Cairo Sultanate. Thus, it is somewhat difficult to delineate a precise meaning for the term during the mid-thirteenth to the early sixteenth centuries.[151]

In their own experiments with Abbasid legitimacy and the legacy of its titulature, the sultans and amirs of Cairo could explore two interpretations in the hope of capitalising on universal caliphal legitimacy. The first was the idea of the caliph as *khalīfat Allāh*, God's deputy or chosen 'successor' on the earth which implied divinely-guided theocratic authority.[152] Alternately, the caliph could be *khalīfat rasūl Allāh*, which implied successorship to Muḥammad's religio-political authority. Arguably, both understandings (which associated the authority of the caliph to that of God or the Prophet) had equal importance. The image of the caliph, as an important descendant and family member of the Prophet, was especially important in sultanic/caliphal investiture deeds composed by the *ʿulamāʾ* and scribal classes.

Nevertheless, some titulature blurred the lines between the paradigms of caliphate and sultanate. Van Steenbergen observed that in a panegyric for the Qalawunid sultan al-Ṣāliḥ Ismāʿīl (743–6/1342–5), the sultan, in addition to being called '*imām*', is described as 'elevator of the head of the faithful' (*rāfiʿ raʾs al-muʾminīn*), which may be a synonym for the caliph as it subsumes his role as 'commander' of the faithful.[153] This was not an impossibility, however, as Baybars had been referred to as 'Commander of the Faithful' in popular fourteenth-century *sīra* literature, Qalāwūn likewise on coins and, by the early sixteenth century, Qāniṣawh al-Ghawrī, at least in courtly sessions, appropriated caliphal epithets including *amīr al-muʾminīn* and *khalīfat al-Islām*.[154] Sultanic investiture deeds, which highlighted the caliph's delegation of power to the sultan, also provided a venue in which the role of the caliph (including his titles and office) were also occasionally 'borrowed' on behalf of the sultan. Such strategic experiments, however, were done primarily to flatter the sultan's position and to experiment with new ways of re-imagining sultanic and caliphal authority in more symbolically advantageous ways for the sultan.

Some sources allege that the Cairo caliphs were occasionally mentioned with some form of *taṣliyya*, or succinct prayers following their names. This may have been done in imitation of Fatimid practice in Cairo, in which, after mentioning the reigning imam-caliph in public, it was common to say '*ṣalawāt Allāh ʿalayhi wa ʿalā abāʾihi al-ṭāhirīn wa abnāʾihi al-akramīn*'.[155] We cannot assume, however, that the Cairo sultans blindly incorporated the practice from Fatimid times, if they did so at all. Although the genealogy of the practice deserves further inquiry, modern studies, making use of Ibn Khaldūn and al-Qalqashandī, claim that the Abbasids of Cairo could be mentioned with the formula (typically reserved for Muḥammad): '*ʿalayhi salām*' or for his companions '*raḍīya Allāhu ʿanhu*', which, while not used in Abbasid Baghdad, had again been used in Fatimid times to indicate that the imamate was divinely inherited from ʿAlī ibn Abī Ṭālib via the Prophet.[156]

Documents and protocol allowed all members of the elite 'to receive crucial messages about status and the relations of power that underlay the ceremonies'.[157] Acting as the 'public relations' men of their times, scribal secretaries often forged titulature and protocol in chancery manuals. Al-Qalqashandī's *Ṣubḥ* deliberately includes numerous references to the history of the caliphate, its accompanying titles, dignities and protocol, as a way to perpetuate the institution and instruct future secretaries on how to make use of it in official settings.[158]

Deeds of investiture are useful in helping to ascertain elite expectations for both the men and the office of the contemporary Abbasid Caliphate, which the next chapter explores at greater length.

Much of the official protocol associated with investiture ceremonies, Abbasid and otherwise, was 'codified, reinforced, and perpetuated' by chancery scribes who provided a link between protocol and politics.[159] It would not make sense for scribal secretaries to diminish the Abbasid Caliphate or to call attention to its practical weaknesses. Instead, many *kuttāb* accepted the reality to a certain degree, but continued to bolster and project the caliphate in documents, insisting on its proper protocol and appealing to important precedents as a way to boost the power of the bureaucracy; the grand *dīwān* that represented itself as the 'gates of the caliphate'.[160] Chapter 9 continues the discussion by isolating the important themes and recurring motifs that appear in the text of the documents including the social ramifications of the *bayʿa*, caliphal succession, Abbasid lineage and perpetuation, and delegation of caliphal authority to the sultan.

Notes

1. See Northrup's comparative discussion of earlier investiture documents in *From Slave to Sultan*, 167–72.
2. Broadbridge, *Kingship and Ideology*, 17; Petry, *Civilian Elite*, 313–14.
3. Bauer, 'Mamluk Literature as a Means of Communication', 32.
4. Muhanna, *World in a Book*, 93–5; Van Den Bossche, 'Past, Panegyric', 49–83.
5. Bauer, 'Mamluk Literature: Misunderstandings', 108, 119, 125–6; Bauer, 'Mamluk Literature as a Means of Communication', 23, 50.
6. Contemporary historical sources frequently mention that deeds of investiture (*taqlīd* or *ʿahd*) were read aloud as an important part of late medieval Cairene ceremonial. Van Steenbergen suggests that the later sultans of Cairo appropriated Fatimid processions and the overall presentation of a public face connected to copious ceremonial rituals. See 'Ritual, Politics', 229–31.
7. Hassan, *Longing for the Lost Caliphate*, 80–3, 139–40.
8. Vermeulen, 'Une lettre du Calife', 370–1.
9. Humphreys, *Islamic History*, 40–9; Little, 'Use of Documents', 6; Bauden, 'Mamluk Era Documentary Studies', 20–1.
10. Reinfandt, 'Mamlūk Documentary Studies', 301.
11. On the various branches and subdivisions of these three social groupings, see al-ʿUmarī, *Masālik*, 3:304–12; al-Qalqashandī, *Ṣubḥ*, 4:14–43; Nielsen, *Secular Justice*, 56; Holt, 'Structure of Government', 51–60; Gaudefroy-Demombynes, *La Syrie à l'époque des mamelouks*, lv–lxiv.
12. Hassan, *Longing for the Lost Caliphate*, 126–31.
13. Schacht, 'ʿAhd'.
14. This is not unanimously the case, however, as Shāfiʿ ibn ʿAlī identifies the investiture document for Baybars as a *taqrīr* (*Ḥusn*, 38). See also Tyan, *Institutions du droit public musulman*, 2:219–20.
15. Schimmel describes the public reading of investiture deeds as an important verbal homage to the sultan (to which the caliph and qadis testified). The choice to describe the deed of designation as a '*taqlīd*' in itself suggests blind acceptance and obedience. See Schimmel, 'Kalif und Kadi', 16; Aigle, *Mongol Empire*, 246–7; Holt, 'Structure of Government', 44–5.
16. Northrup, *From Slave to Sultan*, 167; Richards, *Mamluk Administrative Documents*, 18–31; Björkman, 'Diplomatic'.
17. Cf. Al-Saḥmāwī, *Thaghr*, 577, 584–6, 588. For a similar discussion of the lasting influence of al-Māwardī's theory in regard to the *maẓālim* court in late

thirteenth-/early fourteenth-century Egypt, see Nielsen, *Secular Justice*, 27–33, 133.

18. Tyan, *Institutions du droit public musulman*, 2:223–4.
19. In his section on the wazirate, al-Māwardī discusses two kinds of wazirs tapped to shoulder the burdens of the *imām* or caliph: executive (*wizāra tanfīdh*) and delegative (*wizāra tafwīḍ*), see *Al-Aḥkām al-sulṭāniyya*, 25–33.
20. Hassan, *Longing for the Lost Caliphate*, 74; Bori, 'Théologie politique', 33–4; Northrup, *From Slave to Sultan*, 166; Tyan, *Institutions du droit public musulman*, 2:215–19, 223–8.
21. For discussions of the entire document, see Aigle, *Mongol Empire*, 251–4; Hassan, *Longing for the Lost Caliphate*, 74; Holt, 'Position and Power', 244; Arnold, *Caliphate*, 94.
22. Ibn ʿAbd al-Ẓāhir, *Rawḍ*, 104.
23. Ibid., 104–8.
24. Al-Yūnīnī, *Dhayl*, 1:451.
25. Ibn ʿAbd al-Ẓāhir, *Rawḍ*, 203–10.
26. Ibid., 207.
27. Ibid., 208. For the coins of Baybars and his son, which made use of similar titulature, symbols and slogans, see Balog, *Coinage*, 85–109.
28. Holt, 'Succession', 146.
29. Hassan, *Longing for the Lost Caliphate*, 88–95; Berkey, 'Mamluk Religious Policy', 12; Heidemann, *Kalifat*, 194.
30. Hassan, *Longing for the Lost Caliphate*, 130.
31. Al-Qalqashandī, *Ṣubḥ*, 10:118; al-Qalqashandī, *Maʾāthir*, 3:133.
32. Northrup, *From Slave to Sultan*, 169.
33. Ibid., 166, 174; Broadbridge, 'Mamluk Legitimacy', 104.
34. Al-Qalqashandī, *Ṣubḥ*, 10:173.
35. Holt, 'Succession', 146.
36. Al-Qalqashandī, *Ṣubḥ*, 10:174–5.
37. Van Steenbergen, 'Appearances of *dawla* and Political Order', 75–9.
38. Al-Qalqashandī, *Ṣubḥ*, 10:175.
39. Shāfiʿ ibn ʿAlī likewise makes note of the parallel between Qalāwūn's designation of al-Ṣāliḥ ʿAlī as heir to the sultanate with al-Ḥākim's appointment of Qalāwūn as sultan. See *Faḍl*, 163.
40. Al-Nuwayrī, *Nihāya*, 8:111–12; al-Qalqashandī, *Ṣubḥ*, 10:166.
41. Al-Nuwayrī, *Nihāya*, 8:115–16; al-Qalqashandī, *Ṣubḥ*, 10:168.
42. Al-Qalqashandī, *Ṣubḥ*, 10:46–58; al-Qalqashandī, *Maʾāthir*, 3:39–60.

43. Al-Qalqashandī, *Ṣubḥ*, 10:47–8; al-Qalqashandī, *Maʾāthir*, 3:39–40.
44. Al-Qalqashandī, *Ṣubḥ*, 9:327, 10:49; al-Qalqashandī, *Maʾāthir*, 3:43; al-Suyūṭī, *Taʾrīkh*, 397.
45. Al-Qalqashandī, *Ṣubḥ*, 10:49; al-Qalqashandī, *Maʾāthir*, 3:43.
46. Al-Qalqashandī, *Ṣubḥ*, 10:58; al-Qalqashandī, *Maʾāthir*, 3:59–60.
47. Al-Ṣafadī, *Aʿyān al-ʿaṣr*, 1:83–4. See also Van Steenbergen, 'Qalāwūnid Discourse', 4–6.
48. Al-Qalqashandī, *Ṣubḥ*, 10:59; al-Qalqashandī, *Maʾāthir*, 3:60–1; al-Saḥmāwī, *Thaghr*, 651. The document references verse Q. 19:12, instructing John the Baptist (Yaḥyā ibn Zakariyyāʾ) to 'take hold of the book with strength', and poses it to al-Nāṣir Muḥammad as a command for the sultan to take the message (*kitāb*) from the caliph with strength just as John was ordered to hold fast to the biblical scripture (*kitāb*) and prepare himself for accountability on the Day of Judgement.
49. Al-Qalqashandī, *Ṣubḥ*, 10:65; al-Qalqashandī, *Maʾāthir*, 3:71.
50. Al-Nuwayrī, *Nihāya*, 8:128–35; al-Qalqashandī, *Ṣubḥ*, 10:68-75. Ibn Taghrībirdī claims the initial document came from the *inshāʾ* of the qadi ʿAlāʾ al-Dīn ibn ʿAbd al-Ẓāhir. See *Manhal*, 6:19.
51. Al-Maqrīzī, *Sulūk*, 2:65–6; Ibn Taghrībirdī, *Nujūm*, 8:263. See also Shoshan, *Popular Culture*, 52.
52. Al-Nuwayrī, *Nihāya*, 8:130; al-Qalqashandī, *Ṣubḥ*, 10:70.
53. Al-Nuwayrī, *Nihāya*, 8:130–1; al-Qalqashandī, *Ṣubḥ*, 10:71.
54. Al-Nuwayrī, *Nihāya*, 8:132–3; al-Qalqashandī, *Ṣubḥ*, 10:72.
55. Al-Maqrīzī, *Sulūk*, 2:65–6; Ibn Taghrībirdī, *Nujūm*, 8:263; Holt, 'Some Observations', 505–6.
56. Al-Shujāʿī, *Taʾrīkh*, 1:127–8.
57. Shaykh appointed Nāṣir al-Dīn Muḥammad al-Bārizī as *kātib al-sirr* in Ramaḍān 815/December 1412 to replace Fatḥ Allāh. See Ibn Ḥajar, *Inbāʾ al-ghumr*, 2:519. On al-Bārizī, see Ibn Taghrībirdī, *Nujūm*, 14:161–2; al-Sakhāwī, *Ḍawʾ*, 9:137–8. On al-Bārizī as an agent loyal to Shaykh's interests during the sultanate and deposition of al-Mustaʿīn, see Jaques, *Authority*, 94–7. On the role of the Bārizī family in Syro-Egyptian politics, see Hirschler, 'Formation of the Civilian Elite', 106–8, 124–9; Martel-Thoumian, *Les civils*, 249–66.
58. Al-Qalqashandī, *Ṣubḥ*, 10:121; al-Saḥmāwī, *Thaghr*, 594–604. Indeed, al-Qalqashandī's didactic preface to the document overlooks the brief sultanate of al-Mustaʿīn, instead writing that Shaykh came to power on the death of Faraj after resolving a brief contest for the sultanate with a rival.

59. Al-Qalqashandī, *Ṣubḥ*, 10:123–4; al-Saḥmāwī, *Thaghr*, 598.
60. Al-Qalqashandī, *Ṣubḥ*, 10:124–5; al-Saḥmāwī, *Thaghr*, 599. See also Ibn Taghrībirdī, *Nujūm*, 13:205–7.
61. Ibn Ḥijja, *Qahwat al-inshā'*, 338.
62. Ibid., 339–40.
63. Ibid., 370.
64. Al-Shādhilī, *Bahja*, 173. See also Sartain, *Al-Suyūṭī*, 92–3.
65. Hassan, *Longing for the Lost Caliphate*, 84; Lev, 'Symbiotic Relations', 10–14.
66. Björkman, 'Diplomatic'.
67. Sourdel, 'Khalīfah'.
68. On the various uses of *jānib* or *janāb* to refer to the 'nobility' of the heir to the caliphate (as well as others), see Al-'Umarī, *Ta'rīf*, 15–18; Ibn Nāẓir al-Jaysh, *Tathqīf*, 8, 187–9; al-Saḥmāwī, *Thaghr*, 512; Yüksel Muslu, *Ottomans and Mamluks*, 76, 181, 190; Broadbridge, 'Diplomatic Conventions', 108.
69. Al-Qalqashandī, *Ṣubḥ*, 6:123, 9:263.
70. For an overview of the fifth *maqāla*, see *Ṣubḥ*, 1:24–6. For al-Qalqashandī's discussion of the historical *bay'a*, see *Ṣubḥ*, 9:273–347. See also Ibn Nāẓir al-Jaysh's earlier discussion on the mandatory nature of caliphal *bay'a*: *Tathqīf*, 138–40. On popular motifs used in *bay'a* documents, see *Ṣubḥ*, 9:276–9. For al-Qalqashandī's description of fourteenth-century investiture ceremonies involving the Abbasid Caliphate, see *Ṣubḥ*, 3:276–7. On *bay'a* ceremonies and oaths of allegiance in the Cairo Sultanate, see al-'Umarī, *Ta'rīf*, 209–15; al-Qalqashandī, *Ṣubḥ*, 13:216–20; al-Saḥmāwī, *Thaghr*, 567–8.
71. In the event that the caliph died in office, al-Qalqashandī provided a document template for how the next succession deed should be composed. See *Ṣubḥ*, 9:308–13.
72. Vermeulen, 'La *bay'a* califale', 297–300.
73. Al-Suyūṭī, *Ḥusn*, 2:64–5, 66.
74. Mājid, *Nuẓum*, 1:39; Sartain, *Al-Suyūṭī*, 1:12; Tyan, *Institutions du droit public musulman*, 2:252–3.
75. Al-Suyūṭī, *Ḥusn*, 2:67.
76. Ibid., 2:64–5.
77. Al-Qalqashandī, *Ṣubḥ*, 9:389–90; al-Qalqashandī, *Ma'āthir*, 2:337–8; al-Saḥmāwī, *Thaghr*, 578–80.
78. Al-Qalqashandī, *Ṣubḥ*, 9:322–3; al-Suyūṭī, *Ta'rīkh*, 394; Garcin, 'Histoire', 57.
79. Al-Saḥmāwī, *Thaghr*, 583; al-Suyūṭī, *Ḥusn*, 2:83.

80. Al-Qalqashandī, *Ṣubḥ*, 9:370; al-Qalqashandī, *Maʾāthir*, 3:340–1. The Arabic word *ʿayn* can also be translated as 'soul' or 'eye'. On this document, see also Hassan, 'Poetic Memories', 9–11.
81. Al-Qalqashandī, *Ṣubḥ*, 9:374; al-Qalqashandī, *Maʾāthir*, 3:347.
82. *Mahd* in this context can refer to a child's cradle or, more generally, to childhood or the period of princely rearing. See Hassan, 'Poetic Memories', 10.
83. Al-Qalqashandī, *Ṣubḥ*, 9:374; al-Qalqashandī, *Maʾāthir*, 3:348–9.
84. Al-Qalqashandī, *Ṣubḥ*, 9:373; al-Qalqashandī, *Maʾāthir*, 3:346.
85. Ibid.
86. Al-Suyūṭī, *Taʾrīkh*, 409–10.
87. Hassan, *Longing for the Lost Caliphate*, 84–8.
88. Baybars al-Manṣūrī, *Zubdat al-fikra*, 396–9; al-Nuwayrī, *Nihāya*, 8:152–8; al-Qalqashandī, *Ṣubḥ*, 6:421–6; al-Qalqashandī, *Maʾāthir*, 3:256–64; al-Saḥmāwī, *Thaghr*, 649.
89. Vermeulen, 'Une lettre du Calife', 365, 370–1. See also Flinterman and Van Steenbergen, 'Al-Nasir Muhammad', 93.
90. Al-Nuwayrī, *Nihāya*, 8:152; al-Qalqashandī, *Ṣubḥ*, 6:422; al-Qalqashandī, *Maʾāthir*, 3:258.
91. Al-Nuwayrī, *Nihāya*, 8:154; al-Qalqashandī, *Ṣubḥ*, 6:423; al-Qalqashandī, *Maʾāthir*, 3:259–60.
92. Al-Qalqashandī, *Ṣubḥ*, 10:129–34; Ibn Ḥijja, *Qahwat al-inshāʾ*, 428–34; al-Saḥmāwī, *Thaghr*, 604; Spies, 'Ein Investiturschreiben'. On Abbasid investiture deeds issued to Indian rulers during the fourteenth and fifteenth centuries, see Auer, *Symbols of Authority*, 108–16; al-Mashhadānī, *Al-ʿAlāqāt*, 46–56; Hassan, *Longing for the Lost Caliphate*, 95–7.
93. Al-Qalqashandī, *Ṣubḥ*, 10:129.
94. Ibid., 7:119–34. On the processing of petitions by the *kātib al-sirr* and the *maẓālim* court, see Nielsen, *Secular Justice*, 63–73.
95. Al-Qalqashandī, *Ṣubḥ*, 7:130–4; al-Qalqashandī, *Maʾāthir*, 3:324–31.
96. Ibid. In the early thirteenth century, the government of Baghdad had styled itself the High Diwan (*dīwān ʿazīz*) implying that the sultan's power, at its source, was akin to that of the caliph. See al-ʿUmarī, *Taʿrīf*, 6–14; Ibn Nāẓir al-Jaysh, *Tathqīf*, 7–8; al-Saḥmāwī, *Thaghr*, 512; Barthold, 'Caliph and Sultan', 133.
97. Al-Qalqashandī, *Ṣubḥ*, 7:130; al-Qalqashandī, *Maʾāthir*, 3:324.
98. Al-Qalqashandī, *Ṣubḥ*, 7:130–1, 133; al-Qalqashandī, *Maʾāthir*, 3:325–6, 330.

99. On the duties of the *khāzin al-kutub*, see Petry, *Civilian Elite*, 253–5.
100. Al-Qalqashandī, *Maʾāthir*, 3:194–8; Ibn Ḥijja, *Qahwat al-inshāʾ*, 73–5; Ibn Taghrībirdī, *Nujūm*, 14:91. See also Martel-Thoumian, *Les civils*, 251; Levanoni, 'Salt of the Earth', 66–7. Al-Bārizī was named as overseer of Shaykh's mosque.
101. Al-Qalqashandī, *Maʾāthir*, 3:195–6; Ibn Ḥijja, *Qahwat al-inshāʾ*, 74.
102. Al-Qalqashandī, *Ṣubḥ*, 3:279; al-Maqrīzī, *Khiṭaṭ*, 3:763; Chapoutot-Remadi, 'Liens et relations', 44–5.
103. Mājid, *Nuẓum*, 1:34–5.
104. Van Steenbergen, *Caliphate and Kingship*, 65–6.
105. The distinction made by Ibn Iyās suggests that the *khuṭba* had previously been given only in the name of the sultan. See Tyan, *Institutions du droit public musulman*, 2:230.
106. Little, 'Use of Documents', 6–7. On the social significance of the Friday *khuṭba* in the early modern world, see Casale, 'Tordesillas', 494–500; Berkey, *Popular Preaching*, 12–14.
107. For the caliphal sermon for Baybars, see Ibn ʿAbd al-Ẓāhir, *Rawḍ*, 143–5; for al-Ashraf Khalīl, see Ibn ʿAbd al-Ẓāhir, *Alṭāf*, 8–10. Slightly later fourteenth-century sources identify the original *khuṭba* as a work attributed to the *inshāʾ* of the qadi Sharaf al-Dīn Aḥmad ibn al-Maqdisī. See al-Jazarī, *Ḥawādith*, 1:56; al-Dhahabī, *Taʾrīkh*, 51:57; al-ʿAynī, *ʿIqd*, 3:87; Chapoutot-Remadi, 'Liens et relations', 49–50; Becker, 'Barthold's Studien', 369.
108. Ibn ʿAbd al-Ẓāhir, *Rawḍ*, 143. For further analysis of the *khuṭba*, see Aigle, *Mongol Empire*, 249–50; Hassan, *Longing for the Lost Caliphate*, 84–5; Heidemann, *Kalifat*, 164–5.
109. Ibn ʿAbd al-Ẓāhir, *Rawḍ*, 142–4.
110. Ibn ʿAbd al-Ẓāhir, *Alṭāf*, 12–13; Broadbridge, *Kingship and Ideology*, 48.
111. Ibid.
112. Ibn ʿAbd al-Ẓāhir, *Alṭāf*, 14.
113. Balog, *Coinage*, 85–106.
114. Aigle, *Mongol Empire*, 225.
115. *RCEA*, 12, No. 4556.
116. Ibid., No. 4562.
117. Ibid., Nos 4563 and 4586.
118. Ibid., No. 4612. See also Amitai, 'Some Remarks', 47–51.
119. Ibid., No. 4690; Al-Bāshā, *al-Alqāb al-Islāmīyya*, 206; Aigle, 'Les inscriptions de Baybars', 63.

120. Amitai, *Holy War*, 56–9, 95; Amitai, 'Some Remarks', 50–1; Loiseau, *Les Mamelouks*, 107.
121. Amitai, 'Some Remarks', 47–51. On this title, which appears to suggest that the caliphs were subsequently under obligation to the sultan, see Aigle, *Mongol Empire*, 225–6.
122. *RCEA*, 12, No. 4623, 13, Nos 4844, 4845, 4846, 4848, 4852 and 4857.
123. *RCEA*, 13, No. 4884. Qalāwūn used the *qasīm* title in a few other inscriptions, including the grand mosque of Baʿlabak (4824), the *markab* of the Citadel (4858), the mosque of Acre (4886) and the Ashrafī *madrasa* (4895).
124. *RCEA*, 13, No. 4957.
125. Ibid., No. 4959.
126. *RCEA*, 17, No. 770 005.
127. *Thesaurus d'épigraphie islamique*, No. 11460.
128. Ibid., No. 13489.
129. Sharon, *CIAP*, 4:147–8; Sadek, *Architektur*, 98–9; Mayer, 'Decree of the Caliph', 27–9.
130. Only two caliphs appear to be buried within the structure itself; the other Abbasids are the sons and grandsons of al-Ḥākim and al-Mustakfī, many of whom were small children. Nevertheless, many of the children received honorary Abbasid regnal names and recognition as '*imāms*' even in death.
131. Balog, *Coinage*, 85; Schultz, 'Mamluk Coins', 253; Chapoutot-Remadi, 'Liens et relations', 45–6. For the most comprehensive study of early Cairene Abbasid coinage, see Heidemann, *Kalifat*, 205–323.
132. Balog, *Coinage*, 89, 91. The coins identify the caliph as: '*al-imām al-Mustanṣir bi-llāh Abū al-Qasīm Aḥmad ibn al-Imām al-Ẓāhir amīr al-muʾminīn*'.
133. Ibid., 87–8, 92, 94, 97, 99–101, 105.
134. Ibid., 85. The name of al-Ḥākim only appeared on silver and copper coins, not on the gold as al-Mustanṣir's had.
135. Ibid., 92 (Nos 44 and 46).
136. Loiseau, *Les Mamelouks*, 152–3.
137. Balog, *Coinage*, 97.
138. Ibid., 107–11.
139. Ibid., 112, 114. Some numismatic evidence suggests that Qalāwūn named himself Commander of the Faithful on coinage. An anomalous coin minted in Damascus in 678/1279 names Qalāwūn the *amīr al-muʾminīn*, perhaps due to a lack of space for '*qasīm*'. Likewise an undated silver dirham names al-Nāṣir Muḥammad 'son of the *amīr al-muʾminīn*'. See Balog, *Coinage*, 141, No. 191.

140. Balog, *Coinage*, 120–2; Schultz, 'Mamluk Coins', 254, 265. Aigle found evidence of a similar title used by Baybars, 'the reviver of the great caliphate' (*muḥyī al-khilāfa al-muʿaẓẓama*), see *Mongol Empire*, 225.
141. Balog, *Coinage*, 127–8, 135–6.
142. Ibid., 141; Schultz, 'Mamluk Coins', 254.
143. Sultan Aḥmad, perhaps in fear of Temür, struck coins as the '*mughīth amīr al-muʾminīn*' implying his vassal status to the sultan Barqūq. See Broadbridge, *Kingship and Ideology*, 149–50nn.53 and 56.
144. In addition to Balog's remarks (*Coinage*, 296–8), coinage minted in the name of the caliph-sultan al-Mustaʿīn has received some attention, see Ilisch, 'Inedita', 39–41; Schultz, 'Silver Coinage', 210–19; Schultz, 'Mamluk Coins', 253.
145. Ibn ʿAbd al-Ẓāhir, *Rawḍ*, 141–2.
146. Aigle, 'Les inscriptions de Baybars', 64; Amitai, *Holy War*, 56–7, 95.
147. Al-Bāshā, *al-Alqāb al-Islāmīyya*, 204–5. Eleventh-century Seljuk sultans also made use of other titles suggesting fealty to the caliph such as Alp Arslan (*nāṣir amīr al-muʾminīn*) and Malik Shāh (*yamīn amīr al-muʾminīn*). On Ayyubid understandings of the sultanate, see Humphreys, *From Saladin to the Mongols*, 365–9.
148. Hassan, *Longing for the Lost Caliphate*, 71–4; Northrup, *From Slave to Sultan*, 174.
149. Northrup, *From Slave to Sultan*, 174–5.
150. Hassan, *Longing for the Lost Caliphate*, 87; Mājid, *Nuẓum*, 1:35.
151. Many rulers including the Timurids, Aqquyunlu, Delhi Sultans, Rūm Seljuks, Ozbegs and Ottomans used the terms '*khalīfa*' and '*khilāfa*' in their panegyrics, official correspondence, etc. See Hodgson, *Venture of Islam*, 2:453; Becker, 'Barthold's Studien', 379–87; Arnold, *Caliphate*, 107–20; Sourdel, 'Khalīfah'.
152. This title had been objectionable to the majority of Sunni *ʿulamāʾ* since the Umayyad period. It is explored at length in Crone and Hinds, *God's Caliph*, as well in the Ottoman and Timurid contexts: Yılmaz, *Caliphate Redefined*, 108–12; Markiewicz, *Crisis of Kingship*, 245, 252, 282. For al-Māwardī's discussion of caliphal titles, see *Al-Aḥkām al-sulṭānīya*, 17–18.
153. Van Steenbergen, 'Qalāwūnid Discourse', 8.
154. Al-Ḥusaynī, *Nafāʾis*, 86–7. See also Markiewicz, *Crisis of Kingship*, 108–10.
155. Hassan, *Longing for the Lost Caliphate*, 63, 73, 138–40; Tyan, *Institutions du droit public musulman*, 2:241–2.
156. Hassan, *Longing for the Lost Caliphate*, 87; Mājid, *Nuẓum*, 1:36.
157. Broadbridge, 'Diplomatic Conventions', 115.

158. Hassan, *Longing for the Lost Caliphate*, 129–31; Al-Azmeh, *Muslim Kingship*, 152.
159. Broadbridge, 'Diplomatic Conventions', 115.
160. Al-Qalqashandī, *Ṣubḥ*, 7:130; al-Qalqashandī, *Maʾāthir*, 3:324. Al-Qalqashandī, *Ṣubḥ*, 6:122, 10:6, 11:72. For an example, see *Ṣubḥ*, 7:130, in which a petitioner in Syria responds to a chancery letter from Cairo by praying for God to lengthen the days of the noble *dīwān*, adding to it a string of titles reflecting the Abbasid Caliphate: *al-mawlawī, al-sayyidī, al-nabawwī, al-imāmī, al-ḥākimī*. See also Ibn ʿAbd al-Ẓāhir, *Rawḍ*, 103; Ibn Nāẓir al-Jaysh, *Tathqīf*, 7–8.

9

Beyond the Throne of the Caliphate: Analysing Caliphal Documents

Introduction

Chapter 9 continues the discussion of the sultanic and caliphal documents introduced in the previous chapter. Whenever historiographical sources describe investiture ceremonies, chroniclers often include mention of an ostentatious reading of the investiture deed by chancery personnel followed by many members of the court parading through town. Such power rituals defined the political culture of the late medieval sultanate of Cairo and, in paying close attention to detail, governed official relationships between the ruler and his elite.[1] It was in these grandiose public displays that the sultans and their courts 'reinvented the Abbasid Caliphate of Cairo through elaborate rituals and ceremonies reminiscent of a glorious past'.[2]

The event itself was a social practice in which listeners/readers among the populace became engaged in a communal discourse about leadership and authority. The documents are neither solely pragmatic nor solely literary, as they were composed with the specific purpose of communicating an official change at the highest levels of government. They were intended to send a message, be it a restatement of the government's *raison d'être*, or a reminder that *jihād* would continue, or merely the notion that everyone in society (including the caliph and sultan themselves) would receive the rights they were entitled to under the *sharīʿa*.

The Caliph as Conduit to the Prophet's Family

As Mona Hassan has argued, reverence for the Prophet, his family and, in particular, the 'august lineage of al-ʿAbbās' was at the heart of Abbasid legitimacy in Cairo.[3] Indeed, following praise for the family and companions of Muḥammad, many document stylists transitioned into praise for al-ʿAbbās and his descendants.[4] Reverence for the Prophet dominated Sunni piety in late medieval Egypt, and the idea of intercession of God's Last Messenger for the Muslim community was important and undisputed.[5] One premise of the documents was the ability of the caliph's lineage to connect administrators instantaneously to the legacy of the Prophet. After all, it was the caliph's status as 'cousin of the Prophet' that defined his right in society.[6] Indeed, the *taqlīd* for Baybars blesses the family of the Prophet (*ālihi*) 'whose noble qualities are everlasting and without perish'.

In the 741/1341 caliphal deed of al-Ḥākim II, al-ʿUmarī described the caliph as a member of a noble house that enjoyed 'sovereignty until the Day of Judgement, [and whose] magnificence puts clouds to shame . . .'[7] In caliphal succession documents, kinship remained a central theme which emphasised traditions of the Prophet's calls for amity and friendship among family members, and that the best affinity resided among his own family and associates, making them 'the most just creatures in matters of ruling'.[8] Ibn Ḥijja's succession deed for al-Muʿtaḍid II thus acknowledges the present-day Abbasid as the rightly-guided caliph of the age whose noble house draws both the mercy and blessings of God, and employs the motif of the House of al-ʿAbbās as budding foliage.[9]

Ibn Ḥijja's *ʿahd* for the sultan Barsbāy alludes to the caliph's pre-eminence as a descendant of the Quraysh and declares that 'if the ages had claimed the existence of another *imām* of his calibre, they would be lying'. Despite such exaggeration, the scribe cautions against over-confidence in the assumption that the caliph's noble ancestry was sufficient on its own, and that while righteous families often enjoyed higher status, all would be equals on the Day of Judgement, even those as lofty as the Abbasid family.[10] Ibn Ḥijja reprises the family-as-foliage leitmotif in the investiture deed of Barsbāy by claiming that blessings came from the house of the caliph, to whom all in Cairo must pay heed, as 'it has been proven that [the caliph's] house and speech owe to his pure ancestors, for he is the successor of the caliphs and there is no dispute in his nobility which has done good and has grown in the earth. Verily he is from the house which resides in the garden and of the tree whose roots are solid and whose branches are in the heavens.'[11]

In the deed for his investiture over India, Muẓaffar Shāh is informed that God deliberately placed one family (the Abbasids) in distinction and honour above all others and sent them to witness, spread good news, warn and call others to God, acting as a guiding light by His leave.[12] God granted the Abbasids knowledge of the caliphate and favoured them by sending them forth as *imāms*. The Abbasids are the 'first house' for the caliphate and it remained God's will that the caliphs be from the 'watering place' (*siqāya*) of al-ʿAbbās, an allusion to the former task of the Hashemite clan and later the Prophet's uncle of distributing water or 'watering' pilgrims who came to the Hijaz, and poetically evoking it as a spring from which his descendants and relatives drink up distinguished honour.[13]

The caliph's symbolic position linked the lofty character of an already respected office holder such as the qadi and *kātib al-sirr* Muḥammad al-Bārizī with the honour of the Prophet's family by way of a Quranic insinuation that he shares 'protected status' (Q. 59:9). In the investiture deed naming al-Bārizī overseer of al-Muʾayyad Shaykh's mosque complex, Ibn Ḥijja likens the *kātib al-sirr* to the family of al-ʿAbbās 'whose tree has solid roots and its branches in the heavens [. . . which is] the furthest extent of nobility, so whoever takes ḥadīth from [the Abbasids] is successful in [conducting] good oversight and [managing the] bounty of the *masjid*, for verily their house and ḥadīth are without dispute'.[14] The implication is that al-Bārizī is as fit to hold his position as mosque overseer as the caliph is for the caliphate. His speech is eloquent and hearing his advice, wisdom or ḥadīth narration is on par with hearing it from the descendants of al-ʿAbbās with their indisputable Islamic credentials.[15]

The Prophet's uncle al-ʿAbbās, as the originating founder of the fount of *baraka* embodied by his living descendants, is celebrated in the documents. Maḥmūd al-Ḥalabī likens the Prophet's uncle to a fatherly figure with the maxim, 'a man's uncle is the twin of his father'.[16] The deed of al-Nāṣir Muḥammad praised God's selection of 'the Commander of the Faithful from among the descendants of the uncle of his Prophet, al-ʿAbbās, and [who] chose his house from the best of the *umma* . . . God permitted privilege and favour to reside in his line, and through it, protected Islamic lands [. . . so that . . .] hands [clenched tight] became white in thanks'.[17]

The name of al-ʿAbbās is particularly germane to the succession of the Cairo caliph al-Mustaʿīn who had been named after the dynasty's eponymous ancestor. Al-Mustaʿīn, having been the only caliph to be named al-ʿAbbās, was thus blessed by God, raised to the loftiest degree, and distinguished by having 'his ancestor al-ʿAbbās in his name and *kunya*, thereby making him successful with something with which none of the forty-six caliphs before him had succeeded'.[18] For his part, the caliph is described as profoundly appreciative of his noble lineage and the good roots and noble branches from which he himself had sprung.[19]

The Fall and Rise of the Caliphate in History and Society

Late thirteenth-century investiture deeds for Baybars and Qalāwūn acknowledge that recent historical events had degraded the traditional standing of the Abbasid Caliphate and thus it fell to the sultan to restore it to its rightful place. The triumphant restoration of Islam's most sacred office provided the Cairo Sultanate with its crowning achievement, and with it the chance to aggrandise the sultan's own position. Any disturbance in the caliphate provided the sultan with the opportunity to intercede and enter history as both hero and divine agent. To that effect, the investiture deed of Baybars explains that:

> whereas [so many] noble qualities are particular to the [lofty] position of al-Malik al-Ẓāhir [Baybars . . .] (may God increase his loftiness!) the noble, prophetic, *imāmī, mustanṣirī* [*dīwān*] (may God honour its power!) emphasises his noble destiny and acknowledges his favour . . . because he has established the Abbasid *dawla* after the evil affections of time crippled it and eliminated its beauties and beneficence. [Baybars] dispatched evil to its fate, and has [instead] extinguished the tragedy that had attacked [the Abbasid Caliphate] with the tyranny of one enraged.[20]

For his service to the caliphate, and through his restoration of order to the confused state of spiritual and worldly affairs, Baybars thus received the authority of the sultanate. Though the *taqlīd* of Baybars also lauds his excellence in *jihād*,[21] the document takes pains to underline the sultan's yearning for God's reward (*thawāb*) as the prime motivation behind his support and generosity in favour of the Abbasid caliph:

> Upon the advent of the caliph, [Baybars] allotted compassion and affection, and in his desire for God's reward, made known [his] unconcealed loyalty. He has revealed his interest in the matter of the *bayʿa*, [an affair which] if any other [than Baybars] had desired it, he would be denied . . . God has preserved this good deed so that it weighs heavily on the scale of his reward and lightens [the severity of] his reckoning on the Day of Judgement.[22]

Taking up the caliphate question from its outset, the later *ḥamdala* of Qalāwūn's *ʿahd* opens with three separate segments focused on the revived caliphate. The first section highlights Qalāwūn's connection to *jihād* by virtue of the Quranic 'verse of the sword',[23] implying that his reign will see a pursuit of holy warfare more fervent even than that of Saladin's family.[24] The next two sections address the Abbasid Caliphate.

Qalāwūn's investiture deed recognised that God had reversed the fortunes of the Abbasid Caliphate and 'allowed it to smile after it had been made to frown and restored its beautiful characteristics after they had grown sickly and emaciated. After the dispersal [of caliphal unity by the Mongols] every land of Islam became greater for [the Abbasid Caliphate] than Baghdad (*kullu dār Islām lahā aʿẓamu min dār al-salām*)'. Ibn ʿAbd al-Ẓāhir's composition praises God for making the Abbasid Caliphate the vanquisher of its foes. After having sunken to profound depths for a time, the 'broken pieces' of the caliphate were restored, amid widespread fear that nothing of it would remain in the eyes and hearts of the people but the distant legacy and symbolism of its iconic black banners.[25]

None of the successors to Baybars could boast of being first to install an Abbasid in Cairo; they could only claim to be a protector, preserver or perpetuator of the caliphate. Indeed, Qalāwūn's document makes clear that part of the sultan's role included raising the caliph and projecting his authority throughout the sultanate. In the third section of the *ḥamdala*, after praise and prayers for the Prophet, the *ʿahd* praises God for presenting Qalāwūn to the community, and for establishing the Abbasid Caliphate in his time with victory or assistance (playing on his regnal title al-Manṣūr), as it had been established in the recent past. It is at the inauguration of Qalāwūn's reign that God

> who brought life to [the caliphate's] landmarks after they had been obliterated and all vestiges made extinct, chose to announce [the caliphate's] call (*daʿwa*) [from the *minbars*], and gathered to it all that which had been gathered before . . . and dispersed its authority throughout the lands of the exalted realm with the goodness of a sharp and resolute sword [i.e., Qalāwūn's]. Obedience [to the caliphate] in the hearts [of the people] intermingled with its mention upon their tongues, and how not while al-Manṣūr [Qalāwūn] is the ruler (*al-ḥākim*)?[26]

The final sentence contains a subtle but significant play on words. Qalāwūn is the reason that the caliphate *continues* to enjoy authority in Cairo and beyond. It is not a coincidence that Ibn ʿAbd al-Ẓāhir chose to describe Qalāwūn's station as ruler with the *laqab* of the sitting Abbasid caliph. This wordplay suggests commentary on the notion that al-Manṣūr *is* al-Ḥākim, or at the very least that he has subsumed the latter's importance and is now preparing to distance his authority from the caliphate.

Having established the Abbasid Caliphate's link to the sultanate, the document shifts its focus to Qalāwūn, notably his ability and duty to protect the realm. The later ʿ*ahd* of his son al-Ashraf Khalīl makes little reference to the caliph or caliphal delegation, though it revisits the motifs of honour restored to the office.[27]

The Caliphate in Religion: God and the ʿ*Ulamā*ʾ

Emphasising the religious role of the caliphate was an obvious way to supplement the deficit left in the classical position. With most discussion of the caliphate confined to the *ḥamdala* of investiture documents, it follows that mention of the caliphate was a necessary appendage to the central theme of praising God. Because God was believed to have chosen the caliph by way of divine election, many documents conceived a special relationship between the two. The *ḥamdala* of the succession contract for al-Mustakfī, for example, states that by preserving the Abbasid Caliphate in Cairo, God ensured that the line of Qurayshī *imāms* would abide forever, commanding the obedience and allegiance of the people. After establishing that the authority of God and the Prophet must be firmly obeyed, the *ḥamdala* states that God's prerogative includes assigning power to whomever He wills. The document alludes to the death of al-Mustakfī's father and states that until his final days, the caliph had feared God, ever-mindful of his secret actions and private relationship with his creator.[28]

In 741/1341, al-ʿUmarī's investiture deed viewed the son of al-Mustakfī, al-Ḥākim II, as exceedingly fit for office, which inspired his explanation of the theoretical position of the caliph in relation to God and the sultan:

> [The caliph is one who] only ascends the lower portion of the *minbar* in the presence of the sultan of his age, to speak of him as protector and to establish him in his standing. [The caliph] does not sit atop the throne of the caliphate, without it being known that his satisfactory character (*mustakfihu*) was not confounded nor his judgement (*ḥākimuhu*) absent. He is the deputy (*nāʾib*) of God on His earth, and the one who stands in the position of the Messenger of God (peace and blessings be upon him), is his caliph, his cousin, the follower of his virtuous deeds, and the inheritor of his knowledge. Our master (*sayyid*) and *mawla*, God's slave and intimate, 'Aḥmad Abū al-ʿAbbās' al-Ḥākim bi-Amr Allāh [II], may God Most High strengthen the religion through his abiding, and fasten the clasp of his sword onto the necks of the heretics (*al-mulḥidīn*) and subdue the transgressors beneath his banners, assigning him victory until the Day of Judgement. [May God] hinder corrupt transgressors through [the caliph's] *jihād*, thereby sanctifying the earth from those who revile religion.[29]

Evoking both the primeval covenant (*mīthāq*) between God and mankind (Q. 7:172) and the famous *mirāj* night-journey of the Prophet, al-ʿUmarī depicts al-Ḥākim's primordial incarnation before God and describes him as a son of heaven who beheld his predecessors. The document claims that although prophecy ended with Muḥammad, the caliph al-Ḥākim II was cut from similar cloth alongside his most praiseworthy ancestors.[30]

The notion of God as divine selector of caliphs and the effect of supernatural intervention in earthly affairs is addressed in the *ḥamdala* of al-Muʿtaḍid's 763/1362 *walī al-ʿahd* document for his son al-Mutawakkil. The author praises God as the one 'who honoured the sons of the caliphs in adornments of justice, dressing whomever He desired among them in robes of decency and humility, raising his ability (*qadr*) above his peers as he traversed paths of righteousness laid out before him'.[31]

The rhetoric of the documents emphasises God's involvement in producing the best caliphs to hold office. After all, it was God who arranged for the Abbasids to hold authority as *imāms* of the Muslims and favoured the family by increasing their power, intellect, liberality and good judgement.[32] Regarding the *walī al-ʿahd* on the verge of accession, God illuminates his eyesight, favouring him with purity, awarding him dominion and wisdom, and establishing him as a preserver of the interests of the subjects (*raʿiyya*) and the defence of the *umma*, privy to knowledge of divine will.[33]

The *ḥamdala* of a remaining fragment of the succession deed for the caliph al-Muʿtaḍid II (*c.* 816/1414) thanks God for strengthening the *umma* by providing a caliph 'who remains as *shaykh* of the kings, [thus] setting forth his noble house [to serve the sultan as] a *mujtahid* and to erect the Abbasid flag after [the fashion] of Abū Muslim with Abī Naṣr'.[34]

Clerks and document stylists of the Cairo chancery also evoked the connection between God and the caliphate to make an impression on foreign supplicants to the sultanate and caliphate of Cairo. The *ḥamdala* of the fifteenth-century investiture deed for Muẓaffar Shāh of India, after praising God 'who strengthened the *ʿahd* of he who asks for help [i.e., al-Mustaʿīn]', mentions that God grants victory to those who seek it (from beyond the Syro-Egyptian territories). The document establishes that for one to request caliphal recognition (since many contemporary Muslim rulers did not) assures victory and 'decorates the skies of the world with bright lamps and sends out onto the far reaches of the earth the garbs of the noble caliphate'.[35] The sultan of India courted classical Abbasid legitimacy, which may suggest that he had domestic rivalries brewing in his own capital, and caliphal approval was no small matter.[36] The *ḥamdala* acknowledges that those who recognised the Abbasid caliph protected by the Cairo Sultanate were few and far between, but nevertheless blessed with the observation that 'one who knows the family of this noble house is like the ark of Noah and we thank him with the thanks of one who receives wealth upon entering beneath the Abbasid standard'.[37]

As far as the broader religious hierarchy was concerned, the documents could afford to rhetorically inflate the caliph's position. Thus, juxtaposed against the military resources and arsenal at the dawn of the eighth/fourteenth century, the caliph al-Ḥākim is described as the armoury of religion (*dhakhīrat al-dīn*),[38] while by the end of the century his great-grandson al-Mutawakkil was also dubbed the 'instrument of religion (*'uddat al-dīn*) and its armoury'.[39]

Prayers inaugurating the reign of al-Mustakfī in 701/1302 associated the caliph with the success of Islam and the sultan's *dawla*. The qadis who witnessed the succession of al-Mustakfī all signed a testament asserting that the ailing caliph al-Ḥākim, as *imām*, had been 'the gatherer of authority to the faith (*īmān*), organiser of the unity of Islam, master of the learned caliphs, *imām* of the Muslims, defender of the *sharī'a* of the master of the prophets, through whose abiding, God strengthened religion and blessed Islam and the Muslims'.[40]

The language of the 763/1362 *walī al-'ahd* document for al-Mutawakkil similarly suggests that the candidate's good character should be common knowledge among the *'ulamā'* and any pious people that had access to the Abbasid family. The implication being that al-Mutawakkil was in fact a person of such character. The document for the incoming caliph begins with commentary on the status of his office within the religious hierarchy:

> The caliphate is the noblest garment for the people of religion, and the clearest garment of protection, and it is the source of every authority (*aṣl kulli al-siyāda*) connected to it – the confidence of leadership growing exalted upon it. It is the most splendid of positions and it grew nobler, higher, and most splendid . . . Among its requirements is that its designation must only be given to one who satisfactorily possesses its characteristics, adorns the sweetness of its pasture, and encourages, through his goodly life example, [the ascent] to lofty ranks.[41]

In a later succession document issued in the name of the ailing al-Mu'taḍid II to his brother al-Mustakfī II, Abū Bakr al-Suyūṭī described the outgoing caliph as 'our master possessed of dignities – noble, pure, wholesome, [being of] the great imamate, Abbasid, prophetic, God-strengthened (*al-mu'taḍidiyya*)'. The document is strictly a testament proclaiming that al-Mu'taḍid had made the covenant in favour of his brother, and his predecessor's testimonial that '[al-Mustakfī] is the most god-fearing and trustworthy of any he has seen'.[42]

Explicit Exposition of Caliphal Authority in Society

That, in practice, the Abbasid caliphs were instead powerless inferiors to the mighty sultans of Cairo is clear from the wording of contemporary historical annals. The caliph and qadis were 'summoned' and compelled to invest the sultan.[43] A different image of the caliph's authority plays out in the documents and we are fortunate that many bureaucratic professionals saw fit to outline their interpretation of the caliphate's ideal functionality in an Islamic polity. To demonstrate the 'power' of the caliphate in the early fourteenth century, the Cairene chancery adopted the voice of al-Mustakfī so that the caliph might explain his own authority and *de facto* relationship to his office to the ruler of Yemen:

> The religion (*dīn*) which God has imposed upon all men, from which suns of guidance rise forth in the east and west; God in His wisdom has entrusted it to our command and rulings; He girded us with a great sword to serve the great caliphate, and increased His helpers and supporters and delegated us with command in the realms of Islam and for us to gather their fruits to our sanctuary, and raised to our great office (*dīwān*) our rejection or approval (of taxation and other financial practices) . . . God delegated the garment of the caliphate (*ḥullat al-khilāfa*) upon us, and made it a noble position of mercy and clemency, and sat us at the seat of the caliphate (*suddat khilāfa*) as long as it was supervised by the heirs of our forefathers, and rejoiced in the great leadership of the great nobles among our predecessors, and dressed us in robes of dominion dyed black . . . and used us to direct public and private affairs, establishing [our authority] in each region . . . making us sufficient . . . and we took Egypt as the abode (*dār*) of our position thereby making it the *seat* of our position in this age [thus allowing it to become] the Dome of Islam (*Qubbat al-Islām*) . . .[44]

As Vermeulen has made clear, it is interesting that the above passage underscores the *physical* person of the caliph. Scribes and scholars, speaking to the wider contemporary understanding of the caliphate, appear to have forced a necessary distinction between the caliphate and the position of the caliph. The caliph has received a sword from God to protect his office, effectively making him caretaker of the institution. The caliph and sultan thus appear here as distinct poles of power, both expected to defend a greater notion of the caliphate. Thus, the roles of sultan and caliph are blurred and not presented as separate positions. Although the historical reality reinforced the idea that they were two different people with a vast disparity in actual power, the idea expressed in this letter represented something different, forcing the notion that the caliph in the early fourteenth century was far more than an empty title.

Courtly Expectations, Duties and Advice for the Caliph

In the different courts of the many Cairo sultans, the mere presence of the Abbasid caliph exuded sanctity, leading to a widespread expectation that the docile men elevated to the dignity ought not to degrade themselves by interfering in politics for personal gain. As Chapters 4 and 7 have shown, in writing about the cases of various caliphs drawn into politics many chroniclers attempted neutrality, but the notable case of the caliph al-Qāʾim bi-Amr Allāh (855–9/1451–5) left some authors too shocked by the idea of a caliph failing to act as a detached man of piety to conceal their repugnance.[45]

The political and religious elite were cognizant of the inherent religious authority of the institution, which could be manipulated for their own interests. Investiture document rhetoric regularly suggests that prosperity and government stability depended on a caliph's prayers for the promulgation of the state. Many authors perceived this as fact and wrote of the caliphs as fixtures integral to the maintenance and functionality of the political order established by and around the sultan and his supporters.

Investiture deeds and caliphal succession contracts, necessarily involving the Abbasid caliphs of Cairo, were a place for scholars and scribes not only to advise but also to reveal the socio-religious expectations of appointees to the holiest office in Syro-Egypt.[46] Unlike the *waṣiyya* sections of many investiture deeds which offered detailed advice to the sultan concerning the expectations and duties attached to his office, no similar section existed for the Abbasid caliph. Therefore, many contemporary scholars have concluded that the caliph, after having bestowed his authority on the sultan, was responsible for little else. The opposite seems true, however, as advice and expectations for the position of the caliph are sprinkled throughout many of the documents, often, again, within the *ḥamdala* section.[47] Indirectly and largely confined to the world of rhetoric, document composers provided insight into the perception of the caliphate at court and how, in theory, courtiers conceived it to function alongside sultans, amirs and the *ʿulamāʾ*. The following thematic categories, as may be expected, are not mutually exclusive.

The Caliph is the Living Symbol of Jihād

In the classical caliphate, the caliph had formally been recognised as chief leader of *jihād* and the organiser of annual raids, albeit often merely for show in the later Abbasid period, against non-Muslim positions. The role of the caliph as principal cheerleader for holy war persisted during the late thirteenth century, as is evident in the fierce *jihād-khuṭba*s given by al-Ḥākim in 661/1262 and 690–1/1291 which praised the sultan as one who 'permits religion to be supported by his sword, who stands firm in *jihād* and gathers the kings of unbelief beneath his feet'.[48] As the chapters of Part One demonstrated, the sultans brought the caliphs on military expeditions often to boost troop morale, emphasise the religious superiority of the polity and challenge the authority of Muslim enemies. In the late fourteenth/early fifteenth centuries, as Clément Onimus argues, the caliph and sultan both served as guarantors of symbolic authority on the battlefield and their visibility was a crucial part of that authority.[49] The sultan Faraj, for example, systematically travelled with the caliph each time he went on expedition to Syria in the early fifteenth century. As a symbol of legitimisation linked in part to anti-Mongol *jihād* in the late thirteenth and early fourteenth centuries, the Abbasid caliph likewise strengthened the image of the sultan as his delegate, and as a true warrior for the faith.[50] The involvement of the Abbasid caliph was thought to secure heavenly intervention for the army. Up to the Battle of Marj Dābiq, the caliph often stood by the sultan as the standard-bearer for holy war.[51]

In the investiture deed for al-Nāṣir Muḥammad, the scribe Ibn al-Qaysarānī depicted the caliph as one who emboldened both the army and the people to take up the cause against enemies of the faith.[52] By selecting the caliphs from the house of the Prophet's uncle and choosing them from the best of the *umma*, God strengthened the heart (*jāsh*) of the Muslim and monotheist forces (*juyūsh al-muwaḥḥidīn*) against the unbelieving heretics (*al-mulḥidīn*), 'granting [the caliph] the command (*siyāda*) and good fortune (*saʿāda*) of his ancestor . . . and through [the caliph], protecting the believers and producing a leader for the fervent adherents (*al-muttaqīn*), increasing him in the dual honours: station and lineage (*ḥasab wa-nasab*)'.[53]

As a status quo symbol, the caliph was moreover expected to stand against all challengers of the established socio-political order. Faced by the threat of al-Nāṣir Muḥammad's return to Cairo in 709/1310, the second document confirming the authority of Baybars al-Jāshinkīr threatened the ousted sultan in the voice of the caliph al-Mustakfī: 'I will go out and lead an army against [al-Nāṣir Muḥammad] if he persists in this. I will defend the sanctity of the Muslims and their souls and children in this great matter and I will fight him until he returns to the order of God.'[54] The document, challenging hereditary kingship, states that sovereignty is God's to bestow, and that the reins of power fall to whoever can suppress the people of rebellion and protect the religion from misfortune.[55]

In his succession testament for al-Ḥākim II, al-ʿUmarī saw a clear resemblance between the caliph and the Prophet in his dual capacities as a soldier (*ʿaskarī*) during the day followed by entire nights engaged in worship (*huwa fī layl al-sajjād*), 'perpetually in supplication to God for success (*tawfīq*)'. For al-ʿUmarī, it was the job of the caliph to seek out divine blessings (*niʿmāt*) to overthrow God's enemies.[56]

As for the practical application of warfare, al-ʿUmarī naturally left day-to-day command of *jihād* to remain with the sultan, formally the caliph's deputy, who, having been delegated with authority beyond the caliphate, is appointed by God 'as an eye that never sleeps'.[57] By ordering the sultan to engage in *jihād*, the caliph is expected to restore any disruptions caused by the regime's enemies. Despite al-ʿUmarī's acknowledgement that the sultan had been delegated to undertake *jihād* in the caliph's name, it is still the latter who restores order to the world via holy war:

> [The caliph's] decree to continue military expeditions (*ghazw*) on land and by sea has already gone forth. He will not hesitate to kill or capture those over whom he gains victory, nor will he free them from their fetters and bonds. [The caliph will not] relent in sending crow-like vessels by sea and eagle-like steeds on land; all of them bearing falcon-like riders. He will protect the domains (*mamālik*) against any whose feet dare to breach them. He will oversee the reparations of citadels, fortresses, and

> frontiers (assessing their need in regard to weapons and all they require to weaken the ruse (*al-muḥtāl*) of the enemies), as well as the capital cities which are the stations of the troops . . . He will inspect their conditions for review [including] everything they have between the heavens and the earth: their closely-quartered horses, their chain-mail, and their swords sheathed in gold, as if they were beautiful, wide-eyed maidens hidden from view.[58] Through all of this, the caliph wants to gladden your hearts and lengthen the elongated coat tail (*dhayl al-taṭwīl*) over your desires. Your blood, wealth, and honour (*aʿrāḍ*) will be protected save for that which is prohibited by the pure *sharīʿa*.[59]

In practice, however, sultans expected the ceremonial participation of the caliph and the qadis on larger campaigns, though in some cases the religious officials merely stayed behind at the edge of nearby towns, clutching copies of the Qurʾān and assuring participants that Muslim martyrs would reside in paradise while the enemy was destined for torment in hell.[60]

The Caliph Summons God's Assistance through Constant Prayer for the State

In Cairo, the caliph's informal religious duties likewise included public and private prayers for the perpetuation and success of the realm.[61] The first document that alludes to the significance of caliphal prayers is the *ʿahd* of Lājīn, which declares that the caliph had engaged in the supplication ritual of *istikhāra*, offering prayers for the *dawla* of the sultan to obtain the best outcomes and advantages.[62] Indeed, the document describes the start of Lājīn's reign as a blessing (*niʿma*) to the *umma* attributable to the caliph's prayers. It was the caliph, in search of someone to carry out his own duties, who prayed that God send someone to take up Islamic sovereignty and thereby appoint Lājīn to uphold the trust (*amāna*), as he was best suited to enforce that which was religious obligation (*farḍ*).[63] In the 'search process' that led to the delegation of power to Lājīn, the caliph offered copious prayers for guidance on behalf of the community and sought refuge with God, relying on His support (*tawfīq*) to uphold correctness, offer guidance and protect governance (*ḥukm*).[64]

In the fragment of al-Mustakfī's succession deed for his son Baraka al-Mustawathiq, the author explains that caliphal power stems from the office holder's fear of God in every matter, including delegation to his successor. The caliph seeks the best outcome from God in every matter, including even his own decision to become caliph or leave it to another.[65] In the investiture deed for Baybars al-Jāshinkīr, before delegating power to the sultan, the author[66] religiously fortifies the selection by stating 'our lord and master, the *imām* al-Mustakfī bi-llāh, Commander of the Faithful . . . beseeches God Most High for the best outcome (*istikhāra Allāh ta ʿāla*)'.[67]

Similarly in the succession contract left to al-Mustaʿīn by his father al-Mutawakkil, the caliph is told that the purpose of his office is to 'seek the face of God' [through prayer]:

> Whoever looks to God for victory and help worries not, aware of the certain truth that the goodness of the *imām* is multiplied on account of everything he is charged with concerning the interests [of Islam and Muslims] or in renewing the means for obtaining them [just as] his badness or evil is multiplied.[68]

Al-Bārizī's investiture deed for al-Muʾayyad Shaykh, while appealing to caliphal authority, mandates that the caliph alone must beseech God for the best outcome for the Muslims and their lands.[69] Thus, Shaykh's document used the authority of the caliphate for little more than the delegation of authority combined with the understanding that the caliph would continue to pray for the best outcomes. At the end of the document, al-Bārizī again conjures an image of a devout caliph, determined to honour the contract, ever engaged in sincere prayer:

> The caliph seeks the forgiveness of God in every circumstance and seeks the refuge of God from heedlessness. The caliph seals his words with that which God has ordered of justice and beneficence (*iḥsān*) and he praises God as He is the most praiseworthy (i.e., Aḥmad) and God has granted him Solomonic kingship (*mulk Sulaymān*), and God Most High grants the caliph enjoyment with that which He has given him, He makes him possessor of the regions of the land . . . may his seat never cease to be on the elevated seats of loftiness and may the garb of the caliphate through him be the splendour of eminence . . .[70]

Most documents that allude to the caliph's delegation also state that the decision to delegate the affairs of Islamic lands or otherwise deliver the reins of power to the next sultan, comes hand in hand with the caliph asking God for proper guidance in the exchange of power made in the *ʿahd.*

The Caliph 'Selects' Sultans in Accordance with Divine Decree

In the practical realm of Cairene power politics, the start of a sultan's reign was complicated by amiral household politics in the fourteenth century and by long and difficult paths to power in the fifteenth century. The outcome appears in historiographical sources to be an endless series of usurpations and coups which then receive the caliph's blessing. In the theoretical world of caliphal documents, however, the prayers of the Abbasid caliph are linked to yet another task, that of selecting the best candidate to take up his former duties. The caliph's prayers reach God, who then directs him towards the best man for the job.[71] Thus, the caliph becomes the catalyst (or even a lightning rod) for the divine election of the sultan. Most documents include no other intermediary between God and the sultan. The Prophet is not involved other than to serve as the famous ancestor of the caliph. Thus, the Abbasid caliph emerges with the most important tasks of prayer, *istikhāra*, and of serving as the recipient of a unique revelatory epiphany regarding the sultan's suitability for rule.

Some documents attribute divine wisdom to the caliph, a gift used for the betterment of society through the installation of outstanding leaders. In his counsel for al-Nāṣir Muḥammad, Ibn al-Qaysarānī assures the sultan, that even though the caliph al-Ḥākim had initially testified unfavourably to his minority, he had known that al-Nāṣir Muḥammad's rule would bring great benefit, based on reports of his probity and noble deeds. The author claims that the caliph felt both a longing and a closeness to the young sultan and although al-Nāṣir Muḥammad had been an exile in distant Karak, the caliph, an ever-watchful admirer from afar, kept his love of the rightful ruler close, never feeling the sting of his absence. After extensive praise and flattery for al-Nāṣir Muḥammad, Ibn al-Qaysarānī writes that the sultan had been tried and found in possession of the many noble characteristics of his father Qalāwūn. It is thus news of his good character that inspires a message from Cairo:

> The caliph has observed the ways in which your opponents have tested you and he is aware of your accountability, your dignity in conducting affairs,

> and your good deeds, so he has chosen you according to his knowledge of the worlds (*ʿalā ʿilm ʿalā al-ʿālamīn*) and selected you to defend Islam and the Muslims. He seeks the proper guidance of God (*istikhāra Allāh*) in these matters and delegates to you from his blessed *bayʿa* . . . He concludes a testament with you in all that is encompassed in the invocation (*daʿwa*) of his grand imamate, and the ordinances (*aḥkām*) of his caliphate which the regions remain bound to in obedience and organisation and he delegates to you the sultanate of the Islamic territories: land and sea, Egypt and Syria, near and far, lowland and highland and all that which will be conquered in the future.[72]

Before embarking upon the *waṣiyya* advising al-Nāṣir Muḥammad about the duties of his office, Ibn al-Qaysarānī revisits the theme of the caliph selecting the sultan to act in his stead:

> Glad tidings to you! The caliph chose you with great care and established you in his place in all good pleasantry and realised that the felicity of his reign continues from you [by virtue of his] ancestors and descendants.[73]

The overall message of the document is a statement of reassurance directed to the sultan on the honours implicit in his divine election facilitated by the Abbasid caliph, a holy man with celestial favour and access to God. Ibn al-Qaysarānī urges al-Nāṣir Muḥammad, in the caliph's name, to carry out the duties of an Islamic ruler.

The later diploma for Baybars al-Jāshinkīr named al-Mustakfī as chief executor of affairs, portraying him as the one who establishes a new sultan and then summons the secretaries to confirm the *bayʿa*.[74]

Some of the fifteenth-century documents composed by Ibn Ḥijja including the investiture deed for al-Ẓāhir Ṭaṭar, which states, 'our master the Commander of the Faithful has cast the staff of his selection (*ʿaṣan ikhtiyārihi*) to choose the *imām*, and the real chooser in the matter was God',[75] mention the caliph's figurative 'staff of selection'. Elsewhere the caliph 'cast his staff on [Ṭaṭar's] selection as sultan, and carried out *ijtihād* to the utmost of his ability until Ṭaṭar sat atop the throne to 'purify the land (against mischief-makers) with good deeds'.[76] The implication here is that by recognising the sultan, the caliph transformed into the vessel or instrument of God's selection of the sultan and a mode for divine intervention in political affairs. In both his copious practice of *istikhāra* and the metaphorical 'casting of his staff for decision' the caliph was expected to serve as the diviner and compass of the *umma*'s spiritual path, shape, and direction.[77]

*Grounded in Godly Piety (*taqwā*), the Caliph upholds the* Sharīʿa

An oft-repeated proposition in the investiture documents is that Godly piety (*taqwā*) is at the heart of the caliphate, serving the caliph both as a source of guidance and as the basis for his commands. A number of the documents described in Chapters 8 and 9 reinforce the idea that the caliph's authority stems equally from his piety (*taqwā*) as well as his ability to inculcate the commandments and prohibitions (*awāmir wa-nahy*) of God.

The documents frequently reiterate the proposition that *taqwā* resides at the heart of the caliphate, a source of guidance and the basis for orders and opinions given by the caliph, reinforcing the notion that in the context of Egypt during the fourteenth to sixteenth centuries, the caliph was primarily interpreted as a man of religion.[78] A second factor in caliphal authority was the idea that the caliph demands that knowledge of God's commandments and prohibitions must be made widespread. It is thus foremost amongst his duties to uphold the *sharīʿa* and remind the faithful that God's commands were inescapable.

Al-ʿUmarī, in solidifying the succession of al-Ḥākim II in 742/1341, recommends that his listeners/readers disregard any outstanding quarrels with (the previous controversial) caliphate so that the present caliph might be left to the important task of 'passing among the people with the Qurʾān and *sunna*; acting in accordance with that which God has bestowed and sent'.[79]

Revisiting the importance of piety, the document reminds the new caliph that *taqwā* is vital to his supervision of affairs. As kingship and religion had once been described in the famous maxim attributed to the Sasanian monarch Ardashīr, the Qurʾān and *sunna* (the sources of *sharīʿa*) were likewise to be two inseparable and indispensable 'brothers' for the caliph.[80]

The image of the caliph's unswerving loyalty to the *sharīʿa* had the same lineaments at the advent of Barsbāy in 825/1422. Ibn Ḥijja strengthened the caliphal foundations through his claim that the caliph, leader of the people, is invincible; never deviating from leadership or yielding to the corrupting forces of popular knowledge, non-revelation and folk wisdom, even if threatened with physical force.[81]

The image of the caliphate that emerges in fourteenth- and fifteenth-century investiture documents is one grounded in Godly piety and fidelity to the *sharīʿa* and its sources. The notion of *taqwā* in the documents goes beyond Quranic notions of fearing God and takes on the original social dimensions associated with the word. The implication is that the caliph had the role of caretaker of society (as a macrocosm of the tribe) as well as his classical role as a dutiful enforcer of religious law and *sharīʿ* morality.[82]

The Caliph Represents the Contemporary Political Order

Defining the precise authority of the Abbasid caliph throughout the long history of the Cairo Sultanate was problematic for many jurists as classical Islamic doctrine, in Holt's words, 'knew of only one sovereign (under God) over the Muslim community, namely, the caliph'.[83] The understanding was essentially that the caliph made himself available to receive the obedience of the people, commanding their allegiance and wielding it for the cause of *jihād*.[84]

The second (presumably more frantic) investiture document for Baybars al-Jāshinkīr from 708/1310 contains fewer references to *jihād*, and more justifications for the sultan as a bulwark against the corrosive influence of hereditary kingship. Tellingly, the second document wastes no time in addressing 'the amirs of the Muslims and their armies'.[85] After urging all listeners/readers to obey God and the Prophet, the document continues in the voice of the caliph and catalogues the offences of al-Nāṣir Muḥammad whom he labels a blood-shedding destroyer of Islamic unity and enabler of the enemies of Islam. The document presents the caliph as a universal symbol committed to enforcing harmony and protecting Islamdom, even against a popular sultan.

An unmistakable depiction of the caliph as personification of the status quo appears in al-ʿUmarī's 742/1341 contract for al-Ḥākim II. The head of the chancery did not expect the caliph to embroil himself in the mundane affairs of Cairo's government, then in the hands of the amir Qawṣūn. Rather, according to the document, the caliph should silently watch over affairs, serving as a magnet for *baraka* and interested in little more than accumulating blessings:

> The caliph witnesses before God and His creation that he has established every man among the holders of Islamic authority (*kulla amri' min wullāt al-umūr al-islāmiyya*) in his present position and that [the office holder] may continue in office under the [protection of] the shade of the caliph's shadow (*taḥta kanafi ẓilālihi*), according to the ranks of those in authority, divided amongst the dominions and frontiers on land and sea, east and west, near and far. All of them, be they . . . king, slave or amir . . . those who are wazirs, qadis and secretaries, those who work as scribes or accountants (*taḥqīq ḥisāb*), postal riders, tax collectors . . . teachers and students in the *ribāṭ*s, *zāwiya*s and *khānqāhs* . . . and the rest of the office holders and stipendiaries. Those who receive a portion of their sustenance from the wealth of God, whether [their] right is known or unknown; every matter will continue according to precedent (*kull amrin ʿalā mā huwa ʿalayhi*), so that the caliph can beseech God for the best outcome and have it made clear to him what is before him . . . The caliph seeks only the face of God, favouring none in terms of religion or legal right (*ḥaqq*) . . . Everything which has come to pass thus far, is established according to the rule of God from that which God has instructed [the caliph] in, as well as [his father] Sulaymān [al-Mustakfī]. The caliph is unable to change any part of this, and continually expresses thanks to God for His blessings and thus the one who gives thanks receives reward.[86]

The caliph's responsibility to society thus spelled out, al-ʿUmarī moves on to the obligation of the faithful towards their commander:

> For you, O people, from the caliph, is right-guidance (*rushd*) and the clear proof [which he provides], and that which he summons you to is the path of his lord as wisdom and good counsel. Owed to the caliph [on your behalf] is obedience, for if the subjects did not uphold it, God would not accept their deeds, nor would the ocean be held back, nor the earth spread out or its mountains firmly fixed. There would be no agreement of opinion as to whom was the proper holder of rights, and the caliphate would come [to anyone] dragging the tails [of its robes].[87]

The document explains that as caliphs come and go, the social order is to remain unchanged. Those who remain supporters of the caliph will be rewarded and those who abandon him will be forgotten. Regardless of rank, loyalty to the caliph is mandated upon all, and all men stand in truth before him, in what appears to be a reflection of the ethos of the contemporary court culture and chivalry as well as the presiding socio-political order of which the caliph and chief qadis were prime representative agents.[88]

The Caliph Transmits the Will of the Cairo Sultanate Abroad

Investiture deeds and letters addressed to faraway lands are the best place to gauge the ways by which the caliphate figured in the external relations of the Cairo-based Syro-Egyptian sultanate. In the early fourteenth-century letter to the Rasulid al-Muʾayyad Dāwūd, the chancery presents the caliph as spokesman and admonisher, warning the Yemeni ruler that his infractions have angered Cairo and that he faces the threat of military invasion.[89] These shortcomings included his failure to send annual tribute to Cairo as his father had done. Moreover, Dāwūd had stopped sending grain supplies to Mecca, detained Egyptian merchants and, perhaps most damning from the supposed point of view of the caliph, 'no longer mentioned the name of the Abbasid caliph from atop the *minbar*s during the Friday *khuṭba* and barred the caliph from "tying and untying"'.[90] The voice of al-Mustakfī offers the possibility of reconciliation and warns against the grievous misstep of abandoning the pledge of loyalty that Yemen had entered into with the Abbasid Caliphate of Cairo:

> It is not our intent to unleash an attack against whoever the tongue and heart pronounce the two testaments of faith, nor against whoever the reason and the heart obeys the imperious commandments of God . . . we are not of a mind to unsheathe swords except against those who have abandoned obedience to us, refused the book of God, and withdrawn from our *mubāyaʿa*.[91]

The caliph orders, first, that Yemen and its people be made aware of his leniency, and, second, that Dāwūd send a messenger to Cairo, who in deference to caliphal authority, will represent the Rasulid ruler, provide a satisfactory report of the situation in Yemen, and effectively restore relations with Cairo, 'caring for the fruits of his compassion and mercy, after having planted the tree of obedience to the caliph, accompanied by large provisions . . . that should be sent annually to the public treasury'. The caliph likewise urges Dāwūd to send support and military aid in the struggle against the Mongols and to arrange for his troops to be at the disposal of the sultan of Cairo.[92]

Similarly, the investiture deed for Muẓaffar Shāh of India affirms that the Abbasid caliph al-Mustaʿīn, after much prayer, found the Delhi sultan suitable to receive control of affairs as the caliph's guide and helper in India. Muẓaffar Shāh's subjects, in distant India, are thus duty-bound to obey him as the rightful deputy of the Abbasid caliph.[93] The 824/1421 letter sent by the Cairo chancery announcing the commencement of Ṭaṭar's sultanate in Cairo to the Rasulid ruler of Yemen, al-Nāṣir Aḥmad (803–27/1400–24), reaffirms Cairo's regional dominance via the caliph. The document describes al-Muʿtaḍid II as having elevated the foundations of the faith by forcing the sultan to embark upon the *sharīʿ* path of religious law, following the precepts agreed upon by Muslims. The document demands that local rulers uphold the rules of belief and makes clear that support for the caliph's designation of Ṭaṭar is unanimous in Egypt and Syria, and that Yemen must thus rightfully be among their client polities.[94]

Classical Expectations of the Caliph

Based on the preceding tradition of Sunni discourse on the imamate and its classical understanding of caliphal prerogatives, al-ʿUmarī's succession deed attributed several privileges to the caliph, including the commanding of mosque orators to publicly name the reigning sultan from the *minbars* so that the day would 'ring with prayers for them both'.[95] Al-ʿUmarī ascribes duties to the caliph from earlier times, though these were not carried out in the fourteenth century:

> Every year, during the *ḥajj* season, the caliph is in charge of [God's] worshippers. He encloses (with his kindness) the residents of the two holy cities and the gatekeeper of the Kaʿba (*sidānat bayt Allāh al-ḥaram*). He prepares the path according to habit and wishes to restore it to its initial state from times past. He will pour forth an overwhelming abundance onto these two *masjids*, and he will send to the third of them (in) Jerusalem a flowing cloud (*sākib al-ghamām*). He will be in charge of erecting (or maintaining)

> the tombs of the prophets – blessings of God be upon them – wherever they may be, and most are in Syria. Friday prayer and daily congregational prayers will continue among you according to their previous traditions. Whoever joins with the caliph during his reign will see an increase [in prosperity], and that which is delivered from the lands of the unbelievers will be placed securely into his hands.[96]

Despite the gusto of al-ʿUmarī's document, surely no one at court was surprised to see that after the investiture, the actual duties of al-Ḥākim II were again limited to bestowing his theocratic authority and Abbasid legitimacy on the sons of al-Nāṣir Muḥammad and the most powerful amirs during the next decade. For the sake of exuberance, al-ʿUmarī could ascribe limitless religious duties to the caliph, but the constraints remained the same as they had been for al-Māwardī: as Commander of the Faithful, the caliph could merely delegate the heavy lifting for such matters to his subordinates. It was considered far more important that he endure as a nexus, both to the glorious past and to divine power, ensuring that such tasks would be achieved by his formal deputies in a broader notion of 'caliphate' that also included the sultan and the larger religious establishment – a condominium of political and religious authority.[97]

Advice for the Abbasid Caliph

Although many of the documents alluded to contemporary expectations of the Abbasid caliph in the socio-political order, few offered explicit advice. The succession document for al-Mustaʿīn, for example, contained sections of counsel for the newly seated caliph that tell us more about caliphal decorum than anything else. Its author warns al-Mustaʿīn that affairs can only be set right through good sense; deeds alone are useless if deemed inappropriate for the situation.[98]

Al-Mustaʿīn receives the recommendation that the best way for him to serve his subjects is to regularly seek the advice of those who ratified his selection as caliph: the electoral community of qadis, amirs, wazirs, *ʿulamāʾ*, the notables of the age, as well as his own relatives, the general population and the governing assembly. The author also advises the caliph against relying solely on his lineage, and warns that only those obedient to God can enter paradise, and even a Hashemite is vulnerable to the flames of hell. The caliph must seek God as helper for guidance in accordance with the Qur'ān.[99]

Most interestingly, al-Mustaʿīn as *walī al-ʿahd* is instructed, even before his caliphate, to begin work on a worthy legacy. The document informs the caliph-to-be that his objective is to seek the face of God, and that he must be more than the prince of a noble house, and therefore do something the like of which will bring good thoughts of him to the minds of all who hear his mention. His deeds must be better than those of his predecessors, and be well known enough to leave a mark on posterity so that he would be remembered along with the great caliphs.

In explaining the duties of office to al-Mustaʿīn, the succession document states that as caliph he is responsible for the land and subjects. The document advises him to follow the good behaviour of his ancestors, the rightly-guided caliphs, and not deviate from it in the hope that his caliphate will lead him to be among the righteous *imāms* shaded beneath God's throne on the Day of Judgement.[100]

Medieval Arabic documents and chancery manuals have left us a great deal of information with which to speculate on the expectations that the *ʿulamāʾ* and sultans had for the caliphs. To be sure, the sultans required caliphs to be of great personal *baraka*, or better still, charisma, who would constantly offer prayers for the state as their highest calling.

Demonstrating Links to Tradition

To supplement Hassan's discussions of caliphal continuity between the Baghdādī and Cairene Abbasids, we find that many investiture documents sought to present a relationship of both analogy and continuity between the contemporary Abbasid caliphs and the Biblical prophets and earlier generations of caliphs.[101] It is worth mentioning that in most cases, if a sitting caliph or sultan named in the documents shared a proper name such as Dāwūd or Abū Bakr, the authors then provided various puns, allusions and levels of meaning associated with the historical names.

In the case of the caliph Sulaymān al-Mustakfī, several authors were quick to draw reference to the way in which the Biblical Solomon, a prophet in the Islamic tradition, had begun his letter to the Queen of Sheba (Q. 27:30): 'verily (this document comes) from Sulaymān in the name of God the Most

Compassionate, Most Merciful'.[102] The second clause of the *ḥamdala* of the investiture deed for Baybars al-Jāshinkīr praises God in His arrangement of divine fate and for making manifest the secret (*sirr*) of sovereignty with the Abbasid imamate with sufficient testing from the two chosen ones, in this instance a likely reference to the Biblical David and Solomon.[103]

To bridge the gap between Solomon as a Judeo-Islamic prophet and Sulaymān al-Mustakfī of Cairo, al-ʿUmarī suggests that Muḥammad's uncle al-ʿAbbās had received special portions of the prophetic heritage (*mīrāth al-nubuwwa*), which itself had been granted as an extension of Solomonic kingship (*al-mulk al-sulaymānī*).[104] In the Qurʾān, Solomon received special dominion over the winds and was taught the language of the birds (*manṭiq al-ṭayr*) to control them, which no prophet received after him.[105] For al-ʿUmarī, this is comparable to the Abbasid caliph of Cairo receiving news of remarkable events by way of carrier pigeons and postal riders (*al-barīd*), and that he inherited or absorbed some of the greatness of his father which helped to unite creation under his obedience. The robes of the Abbasid house (*libās Banī al-ʿAbbās*) furnished him with that which fulfils their symbols of his noble ancestry and extends his shadow over the earth, over all the lands under [Muslim] sovereignty, including even Baghdad in its entirety.[106]

In three documents displaying the authority of the caliph al-Muʿtaḍid II, Ibn Ḥijja evokes the caliph's namesake, Dāwūd, by citing the Quranic verse of the Davidian caliphate. Ibn Ḥijja opened the investiture deed of Ṭaṭar with the verse:

> Praise be to God who opened every door of justice by means of Abī al-Fath [al-Muʿtaḍid II] and rectified and made manifest every hidden thing and said: 'O David, verily we have made you caliph on the earth', and this (verse) indicates the nobility of the Davidian caliphate (*khilāfat dāwūdiyya*) both in posterity and at present, and connects to the Abbasid role of watering the pilgrims which has continued into the reign of al-Muʿtaḍid.[107]

When succession of the caliphate passed from al-Mutawakkil to al-Mustaʿīn in 808/1406, al-Qalqashandī, as author of the testamentary document, described the caliph as 'wrapped in the mantle (*burda*) of the office' by his father, and continued the allusion to prophecy in Islam with the Biblical succession of Moses, Aaron and John the Baptist:

> [The caliph al-Mustaʿīn] followed the life example of his father [al-Mutawakkil] in knowledge, followed his honourable legacy, and was comparable to him in nobility; whoever resembles his father engages not in wrongdoing (*man yushābih abahu fa-mā ẓalama*). God accepted the prayers of his father, granted [his request] and made [al-Mustaʿīn] *walī* thereby making it possible for him to be set upon the earth to receive power (*ḥukm*) [as God gave to John the Baptist (Yaḥyā) in Q. 19:12] and making it obligatory that there be for the Muslims at that time, a *walī* for their *ʿahd*, a *walī* over their affairs to loosen and bind them, vouchsafing authority near and far, appointed as caliph during the lifetime of his father [to inherit the office] after him, and to proclaim and clarify the succession, reciting to him in the speech of delegation [as Moses said to Aaron]: 'Take my place among my people and keep things right'.[108]

Scribes similarly found avenues to evoke the glorious past if a reigning caliph (or sultan) shared his given name with a well-regarded Muslim ruler. In his deed for al-Ḥākim II, al-ʿUmarī prays for a long reign for the caliph and for the increase of God's mercies on his predecessors.[109]

Eager to draw powerful comparisons to symbolise the transfer of power between caliph and sultan in 741/1341, one chancery stylist, upon observing that the name of the incoming sultan was Abū Bakr, and the caliph, Aḥmad (in Arabic, a synonym for Muḥammad), reached for the analogy that the caliph Aḥmad al-Ḥākim II, in stepping aside to bestow power on the young sultan Abū Bakr mirrored the Prophet Muḥammad handing power and authority to the first caliph Abū Bakr on his death in 11/632.[110] Another pairing of Muḥammad and Abū Bakr can be found in the succession document that named Muḥammad al-Mutawakkil the *walī al-ʿahd* of his father, Abū Bakr al-Muʿtaḍid. The *ḥamdala* lingers on the name Abū Bakr, who was 'intimate [to the Prophet] in the cave (*anīs sayyid al-mursalīn fī al-ghār*)'. The *ḥamdala* then praises the uncles of the Prophet, Ḥamza and al-ʿAbbās, 'two pure figures free of blemish or foulness'.[111]

The Arabic literary device of drawing analogy (*tashbīh* or *kināya*), in this case between prophets and non-prophets, may have been unsettling to more conventional Muslims who revered the prophets as inimitable bearers of God's commands and messages, a far cry from the powerless caliphs of late medieval

Cairo. It is clear in the context of the pomp of the documents, however, that the authors saw nothing objectionable in likening the contemporary caliphs and sultans to the prophets and prestigious early companions of Muḥammad, who they sought to represent as the superior notables of their age, worthy of lofty and exclusive comparisons. Nevertheless, many people could appreciate a link, if only nominal, between contemporary caliphs and ancient prophets as chosen men of God.[112] Although the remaining text of the document confirming the transfer of the caliphate from Dāwūd al-Muʿtaḍid II to his brother Sulaymān al-Mustakfī II in 845/1441 makes no mention of either prophetic/Biblical namesake, Ibn Iyās claims that contemporaries revelled in the fact that in respect to the Abbasid Caliphate of their day, 'Solomon [had] inherited from David'.[113]

Bayʿa and Ceremonial

The social practice of the *bayʿa*, the oath of allegiance between the caliph or king and any Muslim, became an Islamic institution partially adopted from the predecessors of the *umma*.[114] In later times through universal acceptance, it became the act of showing homage to the caliph whose election was ratified by a select electoral body (often consisting of a single member), and then confirmed by the masses.[115] The invaders who supplanted the Abbasids of Baghdad, from the Buyids to the Seljuks, adapted the *bayʿa* as an important means by which to ensure loyalty among their supporters.[116]

Bayʿa ceremonies for the Fatimid caliphs of Cairo had been dazzling affairs, reports of which were sent to the provinces, and influenced later investiture ceremonial in the fourteenth- and fifteenth-century sultanate of Cairo.[117] For all intents and purposes, *bayʿa* ceremonies in late medieval Cairo, often concluded at the accession of a new sultan or caliph, were the ritual expressions of a mutual pledge of allegiance (*mubāyaʿa*) carried out for public recognition in the form of a traditional handclasp between investor and investee, and accompanied by an investiture document produced by the chancery. For the actors involved, the repetition and perpetuation of the practice indicated its value and as a custom (*al-ʿāda*) had the force of law. Undeniably, historians like al-Maqrīzī and Ibn Taghrībirdī often observe that a caliph invested the sultan over the affairs of the people according to custom (*qallada-hu al-khalīfa umūr al-nās ʿalā ʾl-ʿāda*), implying that if certain customs were not respected it might invalidate the reign of the ruler.[118]

In the fifteenth century Khalīl al-Ẓāhirī wrote that the *bayʿa* had prophetic origins which represented a chain linking the contemporary caliph and his deputy, the sultan, to the legacy of Muḥammad's leadership. In that sense, the *bayʿa* offered notions of a physical connection to the Prophet by virtue of a symbolic handshake:

> The Prophet (God's peace and blessings be upon him) was truly the master of the world; then, the caliphate passed to the *imām* Abū Bakr al-Ṣiddīq, then the companions and caliphs (may God be pleased with all of them) inherited it in succession, until the present time when it is now [passed] through *mubāyaʿa* from the Commander of the Faithful, with the concurrence of the electoral community, the *ʿulamāʾ*, the pillars of the noble state, notable amirs in good standing, and the divinely-assisted armies.[119]

Peter Holt's reading of this passage suggested that sultans were invested with the entirety of the caliphate based on a lack of reports of the caliphs *receiving* pledges from the sultans after the mid-fourteenth century. Instead, according to Holt, most contemporary chronicles mention that caliphs offered *bayʿa* to the rulers as sultans. In the passage above, however, Khalīl al-Zahirī uses 'caliphate' as a synonym for 'imamate'. Jurists and historians understood that the reigning sultans sought to establish themselves as successors to the imamate in the vein of the Rāshidūn, Umayyad and early Abbasid caliphs. Reading it as a transfer of the 'caliphate' in the classical sense is problematic, as the incarnation of the Abbasid Caliphate which evolved in Cairo had long ceased to be a caliphate based on the prophetic model (*khilāfat al-nubuwwa*).[120]

After Baybars' watershed re-establishment of the caliphate in Cairo, an Abbasid caliph was on hand at the accession of nearly every subsequent sultan. So vital to the socio-political order was the *bayʿa*, that if a caliph was deposed or died in office, the *bayʿa* to the sultan had to be promptly renewed by the successor.[121] Nevertheless, if Holt's hypothesis is correct, historical caliphal investiture changed over the decades and by the mid-eighth/fourteenth century the dual, mutually exchanged oaths (*mubāyaʿa*) may have given way to a new development: the sultan, as acting *imām*, receiving the oath of allegiance from the Abbasid caliph.[122] Beginning with the investiture of the Qalawunid al-Nāṣir Aḥmad in 742/1342, the caliph, according to the sources, in a one-way transfer of power, is described as giving the sultan authority through *bayʿa* (*bāyaʿuhu al-khalīfa bi-l-salṭana*). Holt isolated instances of the phrase used in various sources, observing that most chronicles of the period, with some regularity from the reign of the Qalawunids through to the later fifteenth-century sultans, only record that the caliph offered homage to the sultan.[123] The chroniclers, aware of the sultan's authority as acting *imām*, likely recorded it as convenient shorthand for the ceremony rather than saying both caliph and sultan exchanged power as they had in the late thirteenth century.

Holt appears to have misinterpreted the use of the phrase as the embodiment of a new doctrine: namely, that the caliphs, in a surprising turnaround of their 'constitutional positions' now invested the sultan with the *totality* of the caliphate. Even if the caliph only gave *bayʿa* to the sultan, the relationship of delegation occurring in the later fifteenth-century documents maintained the notion that the caliph delegated everything 'beyond the throne of his caliphate' (though never the office itself) to the sultan. From the Arabic of the chronicles cited by Holt, it is also evident that the caliph granted the sultan only the sultanate (*bāyaʿuhu bi-l-salṭana*) through the *bayʿa*.[124] The developing pageantry of the investiture ceremonies, which may well have devolved into a one-way *bayʿa* for the sultan, comprised a different though interrelated symbolic world than that of the documents. The language of the clauses of delegation contradict any notion that the sultan received the entire caliphate through the *bayʿa*. While the caliphate was notoriously stripped of all power, the notion of completely depriving the caliph of his office, which was more like a trust given to the Abbasid family, would have been objectionable to the *ʿulamāʾ*, amirs and bureaucrats who supported the routines and protocols of late medieval Cairene ceremonial.[125]

The later fifteenth-century annals of Syro-Egyptian Arabic historiography mention little concerning *bayʿa* ceremonies, and authors note only that they occurred in the presence of the caliph and qadis, though not infrequently that the caliphs continued to offer homage to the sultans. This was little more than the enactment of the formal delegation of caliphal powers encapsulated by every sultanic investiture deed.[126] If indeed the ruling elites dispensed with the mutual *mubāyaʿa*, while a different approach from their early tradition, it became implicit in the formal transfer of authority and seems to have caused little alarm among the jurists or historians who wrote about it.

The symbolic position of the *bayʿa* is heavily weighted in many of the documents examined in Chapters 8 and 9, particularly Ibn al-Qaysarānī's investiture deed for al-Nāṣir Muḥammad and al-ʿUmarī's succession deed for al-Ḥākim II. Recurring themes in investiture document rhetoric are the obligatory nature and social ramifications of the *bayʿa*/*mubāyaʿa* between the caliph and the sultan, as well as the sultan and the community. Formally, the *ʿulamāʾ* and bureaucrats presented the existing *bayʿa* as a prerequisite that guaranteed the protection and supportive intervention of God in society.[127]

In his *ʿahd* for Qalāwūn, Ibn ʿAbd al-Ẓāhir portrays the *mubāyaʿa* as an act of worship (*ʿibāda*) in which the recipient of the community's allegiance (in this case Qalāwūn) occupies the position of the Prophet. God bestowed control over the affairs of creation to the Prophet's lineage (i.e., the Abbasids) and the caliph had invested his control in another to uphold and regulate the affairs of Islam. Nevertheless, the caliph retains relevance as the petitioner of divine assistance:

> It is necessary that the one who has the satisfactory *mubāyaʿa* on the necks of the Community of Muslims . . . has, as his right, the inherited position of prophethood, and whoever rectifies through it every lawful [delegation of] office (*wilāyat sharʿiyya*), takes its contract in hand with strength. Whomever is the caliph of the age and time, from whose prayers descend victory upon you [in the form of] the companions of Islam (*muʿāshir al-Islām*) – the angels of divine assistance, from [the caliph's] lineage is the lineage of your Prophet.[128]

In his later deed for al-Ashraf Khalīl, Ibn ʿAbd al-Ẓāhir asserts a widespread acceptance for the arrangement and comments on the new roles of caliph and sultan:

> The *bayʿa* [of al-Ashraf Khalīl] took place engulfed in [divine] acceptance, while enemies decried [the *bayʿa* as] one made through submission and fear [of the sultan]. Thanks was given for this deed, which, after the caliphs had made sultans of the kings, one of the sultans then appointed the designated successors (*wulāt al-ʿahd*), caliph after caliph.[129]

It is clear that many authors and scribes saw an enormous significance in the *bayʿa* ceremony, particularly in the interests of coherent governance. The first investiture deed for Baybars al-Jāshinkīr states that its purpose was to organise the 'pearl necklaces' of the interests of sovereignty and the dominions (*ʿuqūd maṣāliḥ mulk al-mamālik*).[130]

The richest discourse on the ties of both the *bayʿa* and *ʿahd* to natural order and society appears in the introductory protocol of al-ʿUmarī's deed for al-Ḥākim II. Most investiture deeds emphasise the notion of enforcing rights, and al-ʿUmarī opens by citing God's commandment that trusts must be delivered to those who are entitled to them and that all Muslims must fulfil contracts.[131] Like the earlier deed of al-Nāṣir Muḥammad, the *ʿahd* for al-Ḥākim II cites Qurʾān 48:10, which references the so-called 'Pledge of Good Pleasure' (*bayʿat al-riḍwān*) made between the Prophet and 1,400 of his followers beneath a tree prior to the Treaty of al-Ḥudaybiyya in 6/628.

In praise of the *bayʿa* between the caliph and the *umma*, al-ʿUmarī describes it as:

> a *bayʿa* of good pleasure or acceptance (*riḍwān*), beneficence (*iḥsān*), and contentment[132] testified to by the group (*al-jamāʿa*) [of electors representing the *umma*] just as God (*al-raḥmān*) testifies to it. [It is] a *bayʿa*, the contents of which are compulsory upon the necks [of those concerned], and the good news of which hovers above the horizon . . . It is a *bayʿa* the lineage (*nasab*) of which will improve the *umma*,[133] and which bestows blessings . . . Kindness (*al-rifāq*) flows through [the *bayʿa*], and groups of heavenly bodies compete in the basin of the galaxy (*ʿalā ḥawḍ al-majarra*) to be in proper concord with it.

Civilian elites comprising the so-called 'men of the pen' and 'men of the turban' viewed the existing contract between the ruler and the community as a sign of the community's divine protection. As al-ʿUmarī observed, '[The] *bayʿa* guarantees tranquillity (*al-salāma*) in religious and worldly affairs (*fī-l-dīn wa-l-dunyā*), [as it is] a *bayʿa* sound (*ṣaḥīḥa*) [and carried out in accordance with the] *sharīʿa*'.[134] The conclusion of the latest *bayʿa* also announced the moment at which God renewed blessings (*niʿmāt*) for the subjects, thus perpetuating His original mercy of bestowing divine guidance on the community by establishing power among the children of the Prophet's uncle. For al-ʿUmarī, the role of God in caliphal and community affairs is undeniable, as it is God who selected the caliph and raised his position high enough to receive the *bayʿa*, and then ordered every subservient holder of power to obey the *ʿahd* by upholding the *imām*'s contract, according to the tradition of the Prophet, 'even if [the *imām* were to be] a black slave'.[135]

Praised for its unmistakable power to unite disparate groups of society around common (religious) goals, the *bayʿa* obtained its authority from the consensus of the group (*ijmāʿ*), and was thus binding upon all believers.[136] The electors (*arbāb al-ʿaqd wa-l-ḥall*), often referring to amirs and various members of the *ʿulamāʾ*, united on the *bayʿa* to represent a spirit of inclusiveness among the *umma*. As an act of worship, knowing that God had control, society was meant to place trust in the *bayʿa*.

In hyperbolised rhetoric, al-ʿUmarī makes the case for the supreme spiritual significance of the *bayʿa*, which asserted Cairo's primacy as the capital of the Islamic world; eclipsing even Mecca itself, in which even pilgrims, he claims, are preoccupied with thoughts of the caliphate and the blessings of the *ʿahd* as they circumambulate the Kaʿba.[137] In al-ʿUmarī's conception, the covenant is concluded with the denizens of the heavens and the Earth acting in concert. The will of God is manifested through the *bayʿa,* which the author makes no effort to disguise as the most dire interest of Islam. If nothing else, the attitude of bureaucrats such as al-ʿUmarī and al-Qalqashandī towards post-1258 caliphal delegation proves that the matter was hardly a trivial one by the late fourteenth/early fifteenth century.

Ibn Ḥijja's investiture deed for Ṭaṭar discusses the relationship between the sultan, as deputy and proxy of the caliph, and the people. Again, it was no small concern for the sultan's amanuensis:

> Our master the sultan receives [universally obligatory obedience] with the perfumed breezes of acceptance and heeds the advice of the caliphal contract (*ʿahd al-khilāfa*) 'humbled and nearly bursting through the fear of God'.[138]

Ibn Ḥijja's subsequent investiture deed for Barsbāy revisits the primacy of the *bayʿa*, noting that the companions of the Prophet had abandoned commercial and other interests on the day of the *bayʿa* in order to purchase the hereafter through the good deeds implicit in their participation.

Concluding a sound agreement with the caliph granted the sultan power to protect his government. After the *ḥamdala*, the deed of Barsbāy states that the *ʿahd* emanates from the caliph al-Muʿtaḍid II, who was so beloved by God that no one was permitted to fight him, obstruct him from receiving his dues or even live in a land that failed to recognise him. Ibn Ḥijja spells out the arrangement: 'the sun of the *ʿahd* does not shine except with the light of the caliphate, and the sultan is shielded by the unassailable Davidian armour of the *ʿahd*, assigned to him by the caliph and guaranteed by God'. In praising the *ʿahd* of Barsbāy, Ibn Ḥijja writes of the influence it will carry as it is announced to distant rulers whom he lists by name: the Rasulid al-Nāṣir Aḥmad of Yemen, Temür's heir Shāh Rukh, and even various unnamed rulers of China and other locales east and west.[139]

For client rulers interested in Cairo's blessing, document writers presented fidelity to the *bayʿa* and the *ʿahd* as inarguably binding. The investiture deed for Muẓaffar Shāh of Gujarat is full of Quranic reminders (Q. 2:177, 3:77) about the dangers of withdrawing from his agreement with the Abbasid caliph of Cairo.[140]

The document indicates that later generations emulating the Prophet's *bayʿa* will be duly honoured by his successor, the caliph. The document again emphasises the importance of the contract by asserting that one of the kings of Earth is invited to participate in the prophetic *ʿahd* only once the honour of his *dawla* has become common knowledge. Essentially, in the theoretical world of the investiture deeds, both God and the caliph (as his agent on Earth) decide which foreign rulers might be worthy of entering into the contract.[141]

In the classical theory of the caliphate, authority was believed to emanate from the community at large, though by the fourteenth and fifteenth centuries this proposition had grown complicated and difficult to maintain.[142] The structure of most sultanic investiture documents immediately divested the caliphate of its authority while making it clear that only those powers 'beyond the throne of the caliphate' had been reassigned, and that an imprecise residual authority remained for the Abbasid caliphs. The documents perpetuate a somewhat fluid understanding of sultanate and caliphate that does not seem to abide by the classical conceptions of those offices. The offices are clearly separate from the individuals and it was possible for a sultan named in the document to be understood as the *imām* of the time.[143] Indeed, investiture deeds for sultans imply that the caliph has vacated the imamate in favour of the sultan, while succession documents for the caliphs still allude to the idea that the imamate and its 'throne' are only vacant for a caliph selected from the Abbasid family.

In the ideality described by the documents and contracts examined in Chapters 8 and 9, chancery stylists largely presented and theoretically conceived the Abbasid caliph as a source of authority powerful enough to place a check on the influence of the sultan and his entourage and provide an authority to whom they were answerable. It was not that the caliph out-ranked the sultan, rather, they were meant to represent separate parts of a single entity, each meant to advise the other. Most importantly, the caliph had bestowed his powers upon the sultan as a trust.[144]

Through their composition, as well as their performance at public assemblies, investiture and succession documents – while always shaped by the context of the court and produced by the bureaucracy – addressed amirs and *ʿulamāʾ*, as well as the masses, conveying the message that the basic tenets of Islam were being upheld by the *dawla* of the sultan. Thus, all audiences were in theory reminded that the administration remained on solid foundations, and the religious class in particular would be reassured that regardless of the individual occupying the sultan's throne, the criteria which made the government both theocratic and recognisably 'Islamic' would endure.[145]

Alluding to the caliphate in their documents allowed chancery scribes to make their own contributions to an ongoing dialogue on authority in Islamic society. The documents also provided a way for each new iteration of the political order of the 'Dawlat al-Atrāk' to announce its importance to the participants. The documents, which contained so much about the duties, rights and respect owed to the sultan, were particularly aimed at his former peers who now had to be subordinates or rebels. The *ʿulamāʾ* in their turn were occupied with organising and supervising *bayʿa* ceremonies, thereby injecting the government with its religious authenticity.[146] The chancery, responsible for the documents themselves, received a platform to present itself as the mouthpiece or the 'noble gates' of the caliphate or the sultanate. In some cases, scribes exploited the illusion that the caliph himself had composed the document conferring recognition or disapproval on subjects and petitioners.[147] If scribes addressed how the change in the caliphal or sultanic office had come to pass, it was also in their power to spin recent political events and present truth claims in favour of or on behalf of the new political order they sought to support or otherwise seek benefits from.

Notes

1. Van Steenbergen, 'Ritual, Politics', 227; Broadbridge, 'Diplomatic Conventions', 97.
2. Hassan, *Longing for the Lost Caliphate*, 17.
3. Ibid., 63, 73, 80–1, 84–8, 108–41, 134, 138–40; Hassan, 'Poetic Memories', 9–10; Al-Azmeh, *Muslim Kingship*, 162.
4. The deed of al-Ashraf Khalīl, for example, praises al-ʿAbbās and his descendants 'whose ranks produced caliphs to govern creation'. See al-Nuwayrī, *Nihāya*, 8:112; al-Qalqashandī, *Ṣubḥ*, 10:166–7.
5. Marmon, 'Quality of Mercy', 126–8.
6. Al-Qalqashandī, *Ṣubḥ*, 9:390; al-Qalqashandī, *Maʾāthir*, 2:338; Hassan, *Longing for the Lost Caliphate*, 136–41; Tyan, *Institutions du droit public musulman*, 2:251–2.
7. Al-Qalqashandī, *Ṣubḥ*, 9:324; al-Suyūṭī, *Taʾrīkh*, 394.
8. Al-Suyūṭī, *Ḥusn*, 2:63.
9. Ibn Ḥijja, *Qahwat al-inshāʾ*, 336.
10. Ibid., 368.
11. Ibid., 370.
12. Al-Qalqashandī, *Ṣubḥ*, 10:130; Ibn Ḥijja, *Qahwat al-inshāʾ*, 428–9.
13. Ibid.
14. Al-Qalqashandī, *Maʾāthir*, 3:197–8; Ibn Ḥijja, *Qahwat al-inshāʾ*, 75.
15. Al-Qalqashandī, *Maʾāthir*, 3:195; Ibn Ḥijja, *Qahwat al-inshāʾ*, 74. Ibn Taghrībirdī described al-Bārizī as a skilled orator capable of reducing his congregation to tears, see *Nujūm*, 14:96–7.
16. Al-Qalqashandī, *Ṣubḥ*, 10:48; al-Qalqashandī, *Maʾāthir*, 3:40–1.
17. Al-Qalqashandī, *Ṣubḥ*, 10:61; al-Qalqashandī, *Maʾāthir*, 3:63–5.
18. Al-Qalqashandī, *Ṣubḥ*, 9:370; al-Qalqashandī, *Maʾāthir*, 2:202, 3:340–1. See also Hassan, 'Poetic Memories', 9–11.
19. Al-Qalqashandī, *Ṣubḥ*, 9:371; al-Qalqashandī, *Maʾāthir*, 3:342–3.
20. Ibn ʿAbd al-Ẓāhir, *Rawḍ*, 103.
21. Ibid., 107–9.
22. Ibid., 103–4.

23. Q. 9:5.
24. Northrup, *From Slave to Sultan*, 169.
25. Al-Qalqashandī, *Ṣubḥ*, 10:116; al-Qalqashandī, *Maʾāthir*, 3:130.
26. Al-Qalqashandī, *Ṣubḥ*, 10:117; al-Qalqashandī, *Maʾāthir*, 3:131.
27. Al-Nuwayrī, *Nihāya*, 8:115; al-Qalqashandī, *Ṣubḥ*, 10:167. The document mentions the cleansing of the besmirched countenance of the caliphate, and its re-establishment based on important precedents.
28. Al-Suyūṭī, *Ḥusn*, 2:63–4.
29. Al-Qalqashandī, *Ṣubḥ*, 9:324; al-Suyūṭī, *Taʾrīkh*, 394-5.
30. Al-Qalqashandī, *Ṣubḥ*, 9:324–5; al-Suyūṭī, *Taʾrīkh*, 395.
31. Al-Suyūṭī, *Ḥusn*, 2:81.
32. Al-Qalqashandī, *Ṣubḥ*, 9:371; al-Qalqashandī, *Maʾāthir*, 3:342–3.
33. Al-Qalqashandī, *Ṣubḥ*, 9:372; al-Qalqashandī, *Maʾāthir*, 3:345.
34. This may be a reference to Naṣr ibn Sayyār, the last Umayyad governor of Khurāsān, who failed to halt the spread of the Abbasid propaganda (*daʿwa*) and nascent revolution, which, with Abū Muslim at its helm, ousted Naṣr from Khurāsān in 130/748.
35. Al-Qalqashandī, *Ṣubḥ*, 10:130; Ibn Ḥijja, *Qahwat al-inshāʾ*, 428.
36. Jackson, *Delhi Sultanate*, 296–8.
37. Al-Qalqashandī, *Ṣubḥ*, 10:131; Ibn Ḥijja, *Qahwat al-inshāʾ*, 430; Yüksel Muslu, *Ottomans and Mamluks*, 9–10.
38. Al-Suyūṭī, *Ḥusn*, 2:63.
39. Al-Qalqashandī, *Ṣubḥ*, 9:370; al-Qalqashandī, *Maʾāthir*, 3:340–1.
40. Al-Suyūṭī, *Ḥusn*, 2:64–6.
41. Ibid., 2:82–3.
42. Al-Suyūṭī, *Taʾrīkh*, 409.
43. Berkey, 'Mamluk Religious Policy', 12.
44. Al-Nuwayrī, *Nihāya*, 8:153–4; al-Qalqashandī, *Ṣubḥ*, 6:423; al-Qalqashandī, *Maʾāthir*, 3:258–9.
45. Ibn Taghrībirdī, *Nujūm*, 16:35, 158, 194; Ibn Taghrībirdī, *Mawrid*, 1:264–5; Ibn Taghrībirdī, *Ḥawādith*, 232–8; al-Sakhāwī, *Ḍawʾ*, 3:167; al-Malaṭī, *Nayl*, 5:442–3; Ibn Iyās, *Badāʾiʿ*, 2:327–8.
46. For expectations of the caliph in the Cairo Sultanate, see Laoust, *Essai*, 46.
47. See, for example, Hassan, 'Poetic Memories', 10.
48. Broadbridge, *Kingship and Ideology*, 45–9; al-Qalqashandī, *Ṣubḥ*, 10:55; al-Qalqashandī, *Maʾāthir*, 3:53.
49. Onimus, *Les maîtres du jeu*, 153, 333–6.

50. Broadbridge, *Kingship and Ideology*, 16; al-Qalqashandī, *Ṣubḥ*, 10:55; al-Qalqashandī, *Maʾāthir*, 3:53.
51. Tyan, *Institutions du droit public musulman*, 2:242–3.
52. This had been true of al-Ḥākim at the time of the document's composition and it was also true four years later in 702/1303 when al-Mustakfī accompanied the sultan to Shaqḥab to lend his prayers on campaign. See al-ʿAynī, *ʿIqd*, 4:233–4; al-Maqrīzī, *Sulūk*, 1:933.
53. Al-Qalqashandī, *Ṣubḥ*, 10:61; al-Qalqashandī, *Maʾāthir*, 3:1:63–5.
54. Al-Maqrīzī, *Sulūk*, 3:66; Ibn Taghrībirdī, *Nujūm*, 8:263. The last line alludes to Q. 49:9 which addresses conflict among two factions of believers.
55. Al-Nuwayrī, *Nihāya*, 8:128–9; al-Qalqashandī, *Ṣubḥ*, 10:69; al-Suyūṭī, *Ḥusn*, 2:113.
56. Al-Qalqashandī, *Ṣubḥ*, 9:326; al-Suyūṭī, *Taʾrīkh*, 395–6.
57. Al-Qalqashandī, *Ṣubḥ*, 9:329; al-Suyūṭī, *Taʾrīkh*, 398. This resembles the caliph al-Ḥākim's *khuṭba* in which he describes the vigilance of the sultan al-Ashraf Khalīl to his subordinates: 'When you sleep, he is awake', see Broadbridge, *Kingship and Ideology*, 47–8.
58. *Bayḍ maknūn*. This Quranic allusion (Q. 37:48–9) compares the women of paradise to eggs hidden by feathers.
59. Al-Qalqashandī, *Ṣubḥ*, 9:329–30; al-Suyūṭī, *Taʾrīkh*, 398.
60. Schimmel, 'Some Glimpses', 361.
61. Banister, 'Naught Remains', 228–31.
62. See Fahd, 'Istikhāra'.
63. Al-Qalqashandī, *Ṣubḥ*, 10:55; al-Qalqashandī, *Maʾāthir*, 3:54.
64. Al-Qalqashandī, *Ṣubḥ*, 10:58; al-Qalqashandī, *Maʾāthir*, 3:59–60.
65. Al-Qalqashandī, *Ṣubḥ*, 9:390; al-Qalqashandī, *Maʾāthir*, 2:338.
66. Most likely ʿAlāʾ al-Dīn ibn ʿAbd al-Ẓāhir.
67. Al-Nuwayrī, *Nihāya*, 8:132; al-Qalqashandī, *Ṣubḥ*, 10:72.
68. Al-Qalqashandī, *Ṣubḥ*, 9:376; al-Qalqashandī, *Maʾāthir*, 3:352.
69. Al-Qalqashandī, *Ṣubḥ*, 10:123.
70. Ibid., 9:331; al-Suyūṭī, *Taʾrīkh*, 399.
71. Al-Qalqashandī, *Ṣubḥ*, 10:56–7; al-Qalqashandī, *Maʾāthir*, 3:56–7.
72. Al-Qalqashandī, *Ṣubḥ*, 10:63–4; al-Qalqashandī, *Maʾāthir*, 3:68–9.
73. Al-Qalqashandī, *Ṣubḥ*, 10:66; al-Qalqashandī, *Maʾāthir*, 3:72.
74. Al-Nuwayrī, *Nihāya*, 8:133; al-Qalqashandī, *Ṣubḥ*, 10:73.
75. Ibn Ḥijja, *Qahwat al-inshāʾ*, 338.
76. Ibid., 346–7.

77. On the caliph's role as a source of guidance, see Hassan, *Longing for the Lost Caliphate*, 90, 93.
78. Numerous documents reference *taqwā* in connection to the Abbasid Caliphate of Cairo: al-Nuwayrī, *Nihāya*, 8:129–30; al-Qalqashandī, *Ṣubḥ*, 10:49, 56–7, 70, 124–5; al-Qalqashandī, *Maʾāthir*, 3:43, 56–7; al-Suyūṭī, *Ḥusn*, 2:82–3.
79. Al-Qalqashandī, *Ṣubḥ*, 9:328–9; al-Suyūṭī, *Taʾrīkh*, 397.
80. Al-Qalqashandī, *Ṣubḥ*, 9:372, 376; al-Qalqashandī, *Maʾāthir*, 3:350–1.
81. Ibn Ḥijja, *Qahwat al-inshāʾ*, 368–9.
82. See Lewisohn, 'Taḳwā'.
83. Holt, 'Structure of Government', 44.
84. Laoust, *Essai*, 46.
85. Al-Maqrīzī, *Sulūk*, 2:65–6; Ibn Taghrībirdī, *Nujūm*, 8:263.
86. Al-Qalqashandī, *Ṣubḥ*, 9:327; al-Suyūṭī, *Taʾrīkh*, 397.
87. Al-Qalqashandī, *Ṣubḥ*, 9:328–9; al-Suyūṭī, *Taʾrīkh*, 397.
88. Al-Qalqashandī, *Ṣubḥ*, 10:133; Ibn Ḥijja, *Qahwat al-inshāʾ*, 433.
89. Al-Nuwayrī, *Nihāya*, 8:154–5, 157; al-Qalqashandī, *Ṣubḥ*, 6:423–4, 425; al-Qalqashandī, *Maʾāthir*, 3:259–60.
90. Al-Nuwayrī, *Nihāya*, 8:156; al-Qalqashandī, *Ṣubḥ*, 6:425; al-Qalqashandī, *Maʾāthir*, 3:262.
91. Al-Nuwayrī, *Nihāya*, 8:157–8; al-Qalqashandī, *Ṣubḥ*, 6:425; al-Qalqashandī, *Maʾāthir*, 3:262–3.
92. Ibid. See Vermeulen, 'Une lettre du Calife', 369–70.
93. Al-Qalqashandī, *Ṣubḥ*, 10:133; Ibn Ḥijja, *Qahwat al-inshāʾ*, 433.
94. Ibn Ḥijja, *Qahwat al-inshāʾ*, 346–7.
95. Al-Qalqashandī, *Ṣubḥ*, 9:327–8; al-Suyūṭī, *Taʾrīkh*, 397.
96. Al-Qalqashandī, *Ṣubḥ*, 9:329; al-Suyūṭī, *Taʾrīkh*, 398.
97. Hassan, *Longing for the Lost Caliphate*, 17, 67–70; Levanoni, 'Al-Maqrīzī's Account', 104.
98. Al-Qalqashandī, *Ṣubḥ*, 9:372–3; al-Qalqashandī, *Maʾāthir*, 3:345–6.
99. Al-Qalqashandī, *Ṣubḥ*, 9:376; al-Qalqashandī, *Maʾāthir*, 3:352. See Q. 25:31, 'Sufficient is your Lord as a guide and helper'.
100. Al-Qalqashandī, *Ṣubḥ*, 9:376; al-Qalqashandī, *Maʾāthir*, 3:351. See Q. 40:51–2.
101. Hassan, *Longing for the Lost Caliphate*, 83–8, 127; Hassan, 'Poetic Memories', 10–11.
102. Al-Maqrīzī, *Sulūk*, 2:65; Ibn Taghrībirdī, *Nujūm*, 8:263.
103. Al-Nuwayrī, *Nihāya*, 8:129; al-Qalqashandī, *Ṣubḥ*, 10:69.

104. Al-Qalqashandī, *Ṣubḥ*, 7:130, 9:326; al-Qalqashandī, *Maʾāthir*, 3:324; al-Suyūṭī, *Taʾrīkh*, 396.
105. Q. 27:16–7.
106. Al-Qalqashandī, *Ṣubḥ*, 9:326; al-Suyūṭī, *Taʾrīkh*, 396. On the convention of linking historical actors to prophets, see Hirschler, *Medieval Arabic Historiography*, 81–2.
107. Ibn Ḥijja, *Qahwat al-inshāʾ*, 336.
108. Al-Qalqashandī, *Ṣubḥ*, 9:373–4; al-Qalqashandī, *Maʾāthir*, 3:347. See Q. 7:142.
109. Al-Qalqashandī, *Ṣubḥ*, 9:329; al-Suyūṭī, *Taʾrīkh*, 397–8.
110. Al-Shujāʿī, *Taʾrīkh*, 1:127.
111. Al-Suyūṭī, *Ḥusn*, 2:82.
112. Hassan, *Longing for the Lost Caliphate*, 87.
113. Ibn Iyās, *Badāʾiʿ*, 2:230.
114. Bori, 'Théologie politique', 23; Watt, *Islamic Political Thought*, 6–9, 35–42; Tyan, *Institutions du droit public musulman*, 1:36–43, 93–7; Tyan, 'Bayʿa'.
115. Hodgson, *Rethinking World History*, 148.
116. Mottahedeh, *Loyalty and Leadership*, 51–2.
117. Van Steenbergen, 'Ritual, Politics'; Sanders, *Ritual*, 58, 63; Sanders, 'Robes of Honor', 225–39.
118. Onimus, *Les maîtres du jeu*, 130–2.
119. Khalīl al-Ẓāhirī, *Zubda*, 54.
120. Holt, 'Position and Power', 244–5; Holt, 'Structure of Government', 46. See also Al-Azmeh, *Muslim Kingship*, 185–6.
121. Al-Qalqashandī, *Ṣubḥ*, 9:308–13; Tyan, *Institutions du droit public musulman*, 2:225–6.
122. Van Steenbergen, *Order Out of Chaos*, 24n.26; Herzog, *Geschichte und Imaginaire*, 343–5; Holt, 'Some Observations', 504–5n.9; Holt, 'Structure of Government', 44–7; Holt, 'Succession', 147.
123. Holt, 'Some Observations', 504. See also Tezcan, 'Hanafism and the Turks', 70–1.
124. Holt, 'Some Observations', 504n.9; Kennedy, *Caliphate*, 249. Mounira Chapoutout-Remadi also argues that the oft-used phrase '*ʿaqada baynahumā*' underscores the contractual and mutual nature of the *bayʿa* between caliph and sultan, see 'Liens et relations', 40–1.
125. Broadbridge, 'Diplomatic Conventions', 115. See also Northrup's discussion of caliphal delegation to Qalāwūn, *From Slave to Sultan*, 166–74.

126. On the practical and theoretical nuances of how caliphal delegation worked in the Cairo Sultanate, see Tyan, *Institutions du droit public musulman*, 2:223–8, 231–8.
127. According to al-ʿUmarī, God provided direct leadership to the Muslims, by guiding the community towards realising the *bayʿa*, thereby participating in the affairs of the community. See al-Qalqashandī, *Ṣubḥ*, 9:321; al-Suyūṭī, *Taʾrīkh*, 393.
128. Al-Qalqashandī, *Ṣubḥ*, 10:118; al-Qalqashandī, *Maʾāthir*, 3:132.
129. Al-Nuwayrī, *Nihāya*, 8:117–18; al-Qalqashandī, *Ṣubḥ*, 10:169.
130. Al-Nuwayrī, *Nihāya*, 8:128; al-Qalqashandī, *Ṣubḥ*, 10:69.
131. Q. 4:58. See al-Qalqashandī, *Ṣubḥ*, 10:60; al-Qalqashandī, *Maʾāthir*, 3:63.
132. Al-Suyūṭī's version has *wa-jamʿiyya riḍā* instead of *bayʿa riḍā*.
133. The version of the document preserved by al-Suyūṭī records it as 'a *bayʿa* which God uses to make the community righteous' (*bayʿa yaṣliḥ Allāh bi-hā al-umma*).
134. Al-Qalqashandī, *Ṣubḥ*, 9:320–1; al-Suyūṭī, *Taʾrīkh*, 392.
135. Al-Qalqashandī, *Ṣubḥ*, 9:370–1; al-Qalqashandī, *Maʾāthir*, 3:341–3.
136. This idea follows the classical juristic theory, but Anjum has argued that following the conception of al-Māwardī, the wider community was entirely removed from the equation until its reintroduction in the political thought of Ibn Taymiyya, see Anjum, *Politics*, 121, 133–4.
137. Al-Qalqashandī, *Ṣubḥ*, 9:320–2; al-Suyūṭī, *Taʾrīkh*, 392–4.
138. Ibn Ḥijja, *Qahwat al-inshāʾ*, 340; Q. 59:21.
139. Ibid., 368–9.
140. Al-Qalqashandī, *Ṣubḥ*, 9:325–6; al-Suyūṭī, *Taʾrīkh*, 395.
141. Al-Qalqashandī, *Ṣubḥ*, 10:132; Ibn Ḥijja, *Qahwat al-inshāʾ*, 432.
142. Woods, *Aqquyunlu*, 4–6; Yılmaz, *Caliphate Redefined*, 1–4.
143. Al-Qalqashandī, *Ṣubḥ*, 10:65; al-Qalqashandī, *Maʾāthir*, 3:71. See also Al-Azmeh, *Muslim Kingship*, 183.
144. Ibn ʿAbd al-Ẓāhir, *Rawḍ*, 102–3.
145. Talmon-Heller, ''Ilm, Shafāʿah and Barakah', 26–9, 40–1.
146. Hassan, *Longing for the Lost Caliphate*, 84; Lev, 'Symbiotic Relations', 14.
147. Notable examples include: al-Qalqashandī, *Ṣubḥ*, 6:421–6; al-Maqrīzī, *Sulūk*, 2:65–6; al-Shādhilī, *Bahja*, 172–4. However, al-Ṣafadī suggests that some caliphs were capable of producing acceptable documents, see *Wāfī*, 6:318.

10

Re-constructing a Nuanced Caliphate

Introduction

Synthesising the findings of the previous chapters, this final chapter discusses the nuances and evolution of the caliphal office within its uniquely Cairene context. Attention to the evolution of the caliphate in late medieval Egypt and Syria demonstrates the ways in which the classical model of the office had to deal with the vulnerability created when the caliph became a sheltered 'son of heaven' often isolated from the Muslim community.[1]

The nominal authorities of the caliphate and sultanate endured and went uncontested for much of the thirteenth to the sixteenth centuries, suggesting that they were normative (though largely symbolic) state institutions.[2] It is thus that the Abbasid Caliphate serves as a somewhat static point of analytical entry into the complex social configurations and realities of the Cairo Sultanate.

Through figures like the caliph, late medieval Muslim polities, often sacral kingships with a theocratic Islamic colouring, were able to employ an arsenal of repertory full of 'persistent institutions, metaphors, iconographies, and propositions concerning power, and especially power relating to the sacred'.[3] Nevertheless, few authors of the period seemed interested in reconciling the theory of the caliphate with the evolving socio-political practices of the caliphate performed by the sultans of Cairo and their supporters. Upon bestowing all powers 'beyond the throne' of his office to the sultan, the residual authority invested in the Abbasid caliph has proven to be difficult to extract and define in its medieval context.

The Caliphate between Idea and Institution

In discussing the collective image of the later Abbasid Caliphate that emerges from medieval Arabic chronicles, biographical dictionaries, and deeds of investiture fashioned from the elite views of religious scholars, historians and chancery scribes, we find a multi-layered construct, which, like the office itself, transcended the singular descendants of al-ʿAbbās living in Cairo. In taking a wide definition of the Abbasid Caliphate as both an idea and an institution, we can argue that its flexibility allowed it to transform according to political needs. It was occasionally a locus of struggle in which familial squabbles played out on the micro-level and social conflict unfolded on the macro-level. Aided by the religio-political office of the caliph, the political elite tried to embed their own political practices into a religious arena where the representatives had traditionally been the *ʿulamāʾ*. The office was very much a cultural form, which, through manipulation, the elite and their subordinate social groups represented competing interests.[4] Able to traverse various socio-political intersections, the caliph embodied a neutral focal point capable of masking or even deflating pressure from the real power struggles taking place around him. The caliphate at times could reflect tension between individuals and social groupings, and over time it enabled stabilisation and reduced uncertainty for those political actors that interacted with it.[5]

Normative jurisprudential literature and historiographical texts kept alive the idea that contemporary Cairene culture demanded that the reigning caliph be a member of the Abbasid family installed by Baybars. Despite this, the intelligentsia disagreed over some characteristics of the caliphate. For some, it mattered little that the caliph lacked power to 'command, forbid, and be obeyed' as long as the work of the symbolic caliphate (as it embraced hierarchies topped by caliph and sultan) occurred through labour delegated to the sultan and dispersed among his entourage and throughout the political order.[6]

Nevertheless, the historical record of relations between the Abbasid caliphs and the courts of the sultans in late medieval Cairo makes it difficult to argue that the political elite respected individual caliphs. The *office* of the caliphate, on the other hand, could always be manipulated or reassigned to a favourable candidate.[7] There is thus a powerful disconnect between the virtue of the office and what it represents as opposed to the office holders who, while honoured during their tenure, were ultimately expendable. This was likewise true of the chief qadiships, and, indeed, most public offices.

The Syro-Egyptian ruling elite stayed in power through constantly renegotiated power relationships and social networks that linked individuals and social groups to the ruling class.[8] The prestige and influence that the caliphs were able to yield and exert can be linked to Pierre Bourdieu's notion of different forms of individual capital in the fields of social interaction: in this case, social and economic, as well as symbolic.[9] By virtue of their membership in the Abbasid family, the caliphs benefited from an institutionalised form of social capital which was further augmented by weekly, monthly or annual participation in scholarly salons and continued learning with renowned teachers.[10] The Abbasid household (which included family members and servants) was integrated into the complex social world of the ruling political and religious elites, and alongside them, competed for resources and revenue-producing properties for family funding and engaged in other social practices such as competition, patronage, the pursuit of capital and the means for social reproduction. Individual caliphs and other Abbasid family members forged relationship ties and created networks which they navigated via the powerful and residual symbolic and accumulated social capital made available by virtue of their family's historical reputation and traditional standing.[11] The goal of the caliphs in each generation was to make it possible to transmit their symbolic capital, their economic capital (in the form of stipends and landholdings), as well as their social capital (of network and relational ties) for their heirs to inherit in the future.

After the caliphate had been established and an Abbasid family member firmly lodged in Cairo, the symbolic value of the institution itself grew, and unrest could be stoked across all social groupings if ever the office or the man holding it was disturbed or perceived to have been insulted. As scions of old Arabo-Islamic nobility, many elites watched Abbasid family members with wonderment and expectation.[12]

As Van Steenbergen, Wing and D'hulster have argued, the traditional social categories defined by Ira Lapidus' model of medieval Syro-Egyptian society as the 'Mamluk' political elite, the *ʿulamāʾ* and the masses, by the fifteenth century had become far more permeable as relational changes unfolded in the social order. The military involved itself in roles from which it had been previously removed, as social divisions became penetrable between the 'men of the sword' and 'men of the pen'. The sultan and his representatives began encroaching on the traditional rights of the *ʿulamāʾ* in areas such as the dispensing of judicial rulings.[13] The caliph, in most cases, as a figure with transferable symbolic and social capital relevant to nearly all social groupings, was able to pass through many divisions and remain a near universal figure of interest.[14]

In the context of late medieval Cairo the political, legal and theological idea of the caliphate manifested as a historical phenomenon in the way it was performed, reproduced and made meaningful by and for the actors and social groupings that engaged with it through a variety of practices and connected institutions. As Hugh Kennedy has illustrated, the iteration of the caliphate in late medieval Cairo is but one realisation of the rich and varied tradition of the caliphate as an idea of leadership connected to premodern Muslim notions of kingship and understandings of ideal social organisation.[15] In effect, the caliphate was a 'master symbol' of sacred kingship and divine election for the sultans of Cairo largely for purposes of political reproduction.[16]

The caliphate as it was performed alongside the sultanate, created the appearance of normative order and continuity in both the texts of the period as well as the realities those texts sought to influence and normalise.[17] The caliphal idea was a part of the social order in the minds of the participants and failed to exist – in a tangible way – outside those who participated in its performance. Its existence was connected to how participants imagined themselves belonging to one integrated and organised social order which was produced anew each time based on the perceptions and understandings of the actors engaging with it.[18]

The idea of the 'Caliphate' existed in the minds of Muslims looking to their caliph to be the centre of cultural activities and to produce the aura of splendour and magnificence.[19] If reality is based on expectation and perception, the times and the political culture of each new sultanic court demanded importance for the idea of the caliphate, elites perceived it as such, and thus meaning was attached.[20] Just as the relics of Catholic or Muslim shrines enjoyed importance based on the expectations of the people making pilgrimage to them, the caliphs similarly manifested a great power in court ceremonial and chancery documents simply because, as Hassan has also argued, the expectations (derived from collective memory) expected no less. It was certainly theatre, but the beholders saw far more than the crass legitimisation of the new sultan's brute force. In essence, the caliphate and the *bayʿa* it produced mattered because the people of the time *believed* that it did.[21]

We can best understand the caliphate, both institution and idea, along with the sultanate, as a symbolic form of authority that became meaningful within particular imaginations of order taking origin from social practice. In other words, its meaning was linked to that which historical actors thought and did. The caliphate was thus socially constructed and continuously reproduced via ceremonial practices, rituals, generated documents, and strengthened and reinforced by its depiction in ongoing historiographical practices. The idea was thus made into an institution based on repeated actions. Expectations of the court, based on recent past examples dictated what the caliphate was supposed to be in its Cairene context. In addition to being flexible and dynamic, the caliphate, by its repeated performance, also had its own ongoing effect on social practices.[22]

Although it appears to us in the sources as Heidemann's 'hereditary court office',[23] the longer the Abbasid Caliphate persisted as a viable idea in the political culture, the stronger its social claims became and the more the idea transformed into an institution and abstraction of power. We can attach the office to Bourdieu's interpretation of institutions as formalising processes which lend form and represent norms and practices as bounded units. Institutions like the caliphate thus appear as fields of contending social forces that, over time, produce stability and define boundaries.[24] The Abbasid Caliphate was established, supported and developed by the state as a long-lasting institution important to perceptions of power and hierarchy. It was given shape by the expectations of its participants and its institutional continuity characterised both the political and social order. Its persistence as a symbolic source of political legitimacy, theocratic authority, and sovereignty made its absence difficult to imagine from perceptions of power and social order in the Cairo Sultanate for much of the fourteenth and fifteenth centuries. This contributed to the ongoing requirement that a caliph remain on retainer even if he represented little 'beyond the throne' of his office.[25]

Political Realities in the Cairo Sultanate

Like the idea of the 'Dawlat al-Atrāk' itself, which was continuously recreated and reinvented based on the needs of particular times and contexts,[26] the caliphate, on the micro-level, could change, subtly or overtly, over the course of each new sultanic reign or *dawla*. The needs of every political order were different and thus the caliphate adapted (or was made to adapt) accordingly. The late thirteenth-century political solutions required by al-Ashraf Khalīl, naturally, were not the same as those of Qāyitbāy's reign nearly two centuries later.

Modern scholars such as Hassan and Berkey have remarked upon an 'enduring salience' of both caliphal office and office holder after its initial installation, noting that it remained 'technically indispensable' in Cairo at major state occasions.[27] The fact remains that although the caliph appears to have been stripped of some privileges and significance in day-to-day matters at court he remained rooted in political culture. Berkey claimed a kind of political lethargy mandated the caliph's frequent public appearances and dictated his social role. According to William Popper, although the Abbasid caliph of Cairo 'was usually treated by the court with great respect and generosity, his position was rather social than official, with certain personal influence at times as the nominal head of the religious-legal system'.[28] It is unclear what Popper meant by the caliph's 'social' position, though we may take steps towards a clarification by recalling al-Maqrīzī's description of the caliphs of his day as socialites, flitting from one honorary dinner to the next. The caliph was also an important personality able to transcend and move freely between different social formations whenever restraints were not too severe as a uniquely universal figure enjoying a fair degree of mobility.[29]

The caliphs' occasional function as an interloper or mediator between parties in the aftermath of conflict warrants further scrutiny. By sending the caliph to relay official messages or appear to negotiate with rebels, the sultan could use caliphal authority to exert influence in difficult places by providing a more subtle pressure in instances in which the sultan's own influence might have been excessive. It is in this way that the sultans may have used the caliphs for symbolic or 'soft power' in politics as defined in the modern sense by Joseph Nye. The Abbasid caliph of Cairo was theoretically neutral and usable by any political actor who could gain access, so the caliph had the potential to appear as a bargainer in good faith. Wearing the cultural mask of a universal Islamic figure, the caliph could act on behalf of the political order. Thus, sending the caliph to vanquished enemies might also have provided a moral high ground in negotiation, especially when the defeated party had claimed to be acting on behalf of wounded Abbasid honour.

Despite the privileged relationship between caliphate and sultanate, there seems to have been more political tension between the caliphs and sultans than meets the eye. Several office holders had famously complicated relationships that demonstrate some of the strain between their offices: Baybars and al-Mustanṣir, al-Nāṣir Muḥammad and al-Mustakfī, Barqūq and al-Mutawakkil, Shaykh and al-Mustaʿīn. The latter instance of al-Mustaʿīn's ascent to the sultanate remains an instructive moment, as it shows the existence of factions among the political elite, the religious elite, and the masses of common people who came out to support the caliph during his brief sultanate of 815/1412. Political elites had to walk a delicate line between appearing close to the caliph while also distancing the Abbasids from the spotlight because of their mass appeal and for the political and ecclesiastical currents which periodically demanded a 'return of the caliphate'.[30]

On his own the caliph symbolised an agent capable of transforming military slaves and freedmen soldiers (and their sons) into divinely-appointed rulers. Although the sultan thus ruled by divine election in turn as a figurative agent of the caliph, he was not the spiritual guide or religious leader. The caliph's facilitation of rule for the political elite transformed him into a symbol for sacred kingship in Egypt.[31] As Azfar Moin has argued, the sultans would have relied less on sacred texts or normative treatises, and more on broad processes of social memory and the performative aspects of kingship such as the *bayʿa* and investiture ceremonies. The public acts of the sultans involving the caliphs allowed them to exercise their sovereign agency by engaging with social institutions through the manipulation of an important early symbol of Muslim kingship.[32]

The theocratic authority of the caliphate was used to mark transitions and transformations of power, and to help to construct and define each new sultanic political order.[33] The presence of the caliph often punctuated moments of social or political change and helped to bring order and stability to make sense of upheaval. In the socio-political order represented by the 'Dawlat al-Atrāk', the sultanate and amirate were the primary institutions of political military leadership, while the caliph and qadis were the main representatives 'of a defining value system for the contemporary political order'.[34]

This was particularly crucial if the sultan proved to be unable to attach himself to the previous political order in any other meaningful way. In contrast to the distant Ayyubid family members forced to petition the caliphs of faraway Baghdad for investiture deeds, the Abbasid caliph of Cairo lived locally and was even the guest of honour at investiture ceremonies. Access to a local caliph provided convenience and lent an air of immediacy to royal court proceedings and pageantry that few other previous or contemporary Muslim sultans could boast of save for those that had enjoyed direct control of the caliph through a military presence in Baghdad. While the caliphs appear to have been used by the sultans in a way resembling the political practices of earlier Daylamī or Turkic dynasts, the context was indeed different. The sultans were establishing and normalising the Abbasid Caliphate in Cairo, where no 'caliph' had reigned since the Fatimids (297–567/909–1171).

In the light of the symbolic and social capital on offer from an endorsement or relational tie to the Abbasid Caliphate, the most important function filled by the caliphs was the 'caliphal honour' (*al-tashrīf al-khalīfatī*): the on-demand performance of the caliphal *bayʿa* or mutual *mubāyaʿa* (often including an honorary robe or *tashrīf*) for whichever amir was successful in securing the resources needed to seize power and thereafter request Abbasid recognition as the finale.[35]

Rituals designed to showcase and demonstrate power were a defining feature of political culture in the sultanate of Cairo.[36] As Aziz Al-Azmeh indicates, ceremonial is constituted by different languages of power, including formal dress, decoration, ordered ritual movement, spatial and temporal disposition of bodies and other objects in special spaces.[37] The political elite understood the caliphate as an opportunity to embed political practices in a particular conception of the socio-religious order linked to the unique legitimacy claims associated with caliphal power. Thus, 'Caliphate' was connected to a wide variety of social practices, including ceremonies, processions, public prayers and references made to the office holders in texts.[38]

Despite an occasionally muted role, the caliphs retained an almost talismanic power that had its most potent expression in the rituals of court ceremonial and political pageantry surrounding the investiture of each new sultan. This ensured that the holders of political power had to approach the caliphate as a resource and carefully keep the office holder under guard. For participants, the repeated and ongoing performance of the practices reinforced their significance and, as repeated customs (*al-ʿāda*), became authoritative. Indeed, if certain customs, such as those involving caliphal recognition, failed to be observed or respected it could later invalidate the reign of the ruler.[39]

It is worthwhile to point out the socialising role that many of these oft-repeated caliphal practices – though by no means the main cultural phenomena in the life of *mamlūk* recruits – nevertheless played in their identity formation as political and military elites.[40] The symbolic capital of the caliph remained a highly valuable commodity/resource pursued by all who engaged in the political sphere, and for members of the military elite loyalty to the caliphate, *prima facie*, was never a point of dispute. A rebel amir could easily argue that the current sultan had failed to do the job that the caliph had appointed him to do, while he, as the new challenger, would surely do better. Although individual *mamlūk* recruits were loyal both to their peers and to the *ustādh* that had trained and manumitted them, in theory, all were socialised with an ingrained allegiance to the caliphal idea.

Over time, however, the caliph and his office may have become slightly removed from the traditional religious understanding and gone on to represent the basis for a brand of universal loyalty with the potential to transcend more localised loyalties. Any actor engaging with the performance of the caliphate would have been made to understand that loyalty to it was a given part of any political order. Sultans who only considered the caliph's presence in their entourage a matter of *realpolitik* would still have seen the caliph as an object that lent specific meanings capable of reminding rivals of an incumbent's pre-eminence. It was certainly one thing for military elites to *pretend* to be allegiant to the caliph for the sake of the religious leadership or the *ʿāmma*, and quite another to continue the 'charade' (if indeed it was one) alone in the context of the highly competitive amiral milieu.

An important and unanswered question remains: why did the amirs lack the ability to show disloyalty to the caliph? Was the caliphate a real rallying point, or just a convenient excuse to legitimately take up arms against a powerful rival?[41] It was part of a normative political language, and at least in theory (though seldom in practice), loyalty to the caliphate ought to have trumped allegiance to the reigning sultan. It may have been easier to turn one's back on a beleaguered and embattled ruler like Aynabak al-Badrī, Barqūq in 791/1389 or his son al-Nāṣir Faraj (in which case the amirs and the people favoured the caliph against the sultan in 815/1412), rather than a popular sultan like al-Nāṣir Muḥammad in 709/1310 (in which case the amirs and the people favoured a popular sultan at the expense of the caliph al-Mustakfī bi-llāh).

Thus, this trope of 'defending the caliphate' went deeper in political culture than merely paying lip-service to a normative Islamic institution to appease the *ʿulamāʾ* and secure their support. Instead, 'protecting the caliph', an utterly helpless holy man (sometimes even mentioned in the same context as widows and orphans), may also have been linked to courtly notions of honour, virility, chivalry and pride of place in Cairo in a way that was neither simply or strictly 'Islamic'. A unique and abiding interest in the caliphate was important to their elite identity formation as well as to the construction and perception of their own customs distinct from Islamic norms. Supported by decades of ceremonial reinforcement, the importance of the caliphate became firmly established in the political culture until it was eventually taken for granted and interpreted as an innocuous reality in tune with historical precedent.

Thus, for the amirs, the caliph represented a 'guarantor of power' and served as another way to display sovereignty as part of an arsenal of symbolic communication. The institution of caliphal delegation also allowed the symbolic capital of the sultanic institution to be preserved.[42] The caliphate was part of the cultural production of the state by the sultan and his agents, and reproduced by the elites emerging around them who often used the same language of power that served their common interests.[43] As a result, the caliph could later be used for purposes of integration: just as the sultan Faraj had used the convention of Abbasid deference in his negotiations with the rebel amir Shaykh, and some years later Shaykh and Nawrūz used it again to integrate the former followers and resources left behind by Faraj.

Abbasids in a Social and Religious World

Although individual moments linked to the performance of the caliphate unfolded on a micro-stage of late medieval Syro-Egyptian-Hijazi history, the wider history, tradition and ceremonial legacy symbolised by the caliph and his office played out within the framework of a cultural matrix: a complex network of meanings and cultural modes of expression that offered political and religious elites opportunities to define and represent their respective interests.[44] While there was symbiosis and collaboration around the mutual interests of contemporaneous networks, there could still be tension in the power relationships between sultans, amirs and members of the *ʿulamāʾ*.

Observing the personal and relational ties of the caliphs adds context to their social positions and presents them as fully integrated into the late medieval social world of the Cairo Sultanate.[45] It also makes it possible to begin a discussion about their agency. The Abbasid family members were socialised in a milieu of networks composed of amirs, *mamlūk*s, scholars and everyday Cairenes. The caliphal institution itself took shape as it was being struggled over by competing networks and pursuers of power, but also internally as family members fought over the office and its associated perks. Manifest as an institution, the Abbasid Caliphate was continually changing as a virtual platform or arena where social conflict could unfold.[46] Caliphal reigns did not always follow a smooth trajectory and were often rocked by conflict or intrigue, particularly in the late fourteenth and early fifteenth centuries. Some charismatic and connected caliphs like al-Mutawakkil I, were much better (or even luckier) at playing the game of politics than his sons al-Mustaʿīn or al-Qāʾim. Upon inheriting the family office, whether through internal negotiation or appointment by the sultan and his entourage, each of the caliphs, once in office, set about forging personal ties from among the religious and military elites. Al-Mustakfī had a network of colleagues and supporters and may well have been hatching a political scheme against the sultan al-Nāṣir Muḥammad for some time. The caliphs al-Ḥākim II and al-Muʿtaḍid II made their way into the court and were able to secure positions for their family members and also begin wielding minor influence among their contacts in the scholarly world. Al-Mutawakkil had many political connections from his long period in office among Kurdish,

Bedouin and other groups, as well as local elites. Al-Qāʾim made himself available to different interest groups, but his politicking ultimately failed and he ended up exiled by the sultan Īnāl. It was not just the caliphs themselves, however, that sought to profit from clientelist or relationship ties of patronage or service.

In regard to mobility, the family members bartered influence with the sultan to compromised courtiers for access to properties and other forms of economic capital. They made use of the meagre resources they had and could often be shrewd manipulators of ceremonial and relational circumstances to negotiate their positions and social status. Evidence also suggests that the Abbasid family was largely free to make its own marriage connections independent of the outside influence of the Cairene political elite.[47] As the family grew larger in Cairo, however, competing interests came to the fore. Adult male members with fewer prospects – if they could not control the family office or household assets – sometimes tried to exert their agency outside the framework of the sultanate of Cairo by trading on the symbolic capital of the family abroad.[48] There were also far more public squabbles between rival branches of the family over resources, such as the feud between al-Wāthiq and al-Ḥākim II which preceded the final explosion of ugly confrontation between the Abbasid prince Khalīl and the caliph al-Mustamsik before all the courtiers of Qāniṣawh al-Ghawrī in the early sixteenth century, and the continuing family discord that followed their descendants in Istanbul and shocked Ottoman administrators according to Ibn Iyās.

The Caliph and the Religious Elite

In the late medieval sultanate of Cairo two foundations of religious authority remained the Abbasid caliphs and the *ʿulamāʾ*, the established spiritual elite with formal and informal relationship ties to the political elite. The caliph maintained comparably little power, while some members of the *ʿulamāʾ* wielded considerable influence in their attempts to set limits for the political elite according to *sharīʿa* and jurisprudential precedence. Even so, the *ʿulamāʾ* for their part were obliged to respect the caliphate as an important convention of Islamic tradition and a revitalising source of their own authority.[49]

As it was for the political elite, the caliphate was likewise a double-edged sword for the religious elite. On the one hand, it legitimised the position of *all* religious functionaries and helped present the established sultan's political order as an Islamic polity worthy of succeeding the well-remembered Abbasid Caliphate of Baghdad. Conversely, the prospect of a popular resident Abbasid caliph posed a latent threat to the collective strength of their own religious authority.[50]

The *ʿulamāʾ*, supplying a link between theology and social practice, therefore at least honoured the understanding that the caliphate was indispensable to the ongoing success of the state and integral to its maintenance.[51] Hassan and Broadbridge have demonstrated ways in which the jurists and chancery stylists sought to present the Abbasid Caliphate of Cairo as a portion of the imamate *du jour*, recognition of which was incumbent upon all people of Islam. The political elite thus adopted this position and consistently retained the caliph as a cornerstone of their public celebrations and succession rituals.[52]

For their part, the scholarly class seemed to be at odds over how to interpret the contemporary caliphs. One point of view exemplified by Ibn Ḥajar and al-Suyūṭī, scholars who enjoyed access to individual caliphs wanted to uphold classical caliphal rights.[53] Al-Suyūṭī even sought an increase to caliphal power that would have given them higher authority than the four chief qadis of Cairo – an idea predictably unpopular with his contemporaries.[54] On the other hand, the likes of Ibn Taymiyya, Ibn Khaldūn and al-Maqrīzī recognised the obligatory nature of the caliphate in theory, but for the time being preferred to place their faith in the office of the sultan and his delegates while hypothetically awaiting the final return of a Rāshidūn-style government. What appears to modern readers as their cynicism or detachment from the contemporary caliphate may well have been a mask for their disappointment with the Abbasid caliphs of their day and the dominance of a royal authority and theocratic sovereignty coloured as 'Islamic'.

The public support of prominent religious scholars, in addition to allegiance to the caliph, was also a source of legitimacy for the sultans of Cairo. The *ʿulamāʾ* received a degree of independence for their opinions and activities and it was in their interest to preserve the status quo. If plans to re-establish the caliphate had been a joint project undertaken by the political leaders and approved by the *ʿulamāʾ*, there was some tension over its direction and ownership.

The *ʿulamāʾ* largely prospered in medieval Cairo through their networks and ties with the political elite which provided them with *manṣab* positions and flexibility in affairs of religion.[55] Many realised that the sultans were purveyors of *mulk*, as opposed to a true or prophetic caliphate (*khilāfat al-nubuwwa*), but offered recognition on the grounds that the ruling elite were the protectors of the 'Caliphate' (such as it was). This is rather a different situation than the Ashʿarī writers of tenth- and eleventh-century Mesopotamia, who sought to protect their understanding of the idea of the historical caliphate from the encroachments of the Shiʿite Buyid amirs and the Seljuk sultans.

Apart from having the caliphs appear at investiture ceremonies, the sultans of Cairo emphasised the religious role of the caliphs by making them the centrepiece in public rituals seeking relief from drought and plague as well as denouncing the infidelity of official enemies. Beginning in the late fourteenth century, the caliphs also frequently appeared by request at a sultan's deathbed and swore to oversee the successful transition to rule by the heir apparent.[56] The symbolic presence of the caliphate was also meant to signify that *sharīʿa* was in place, the affairs of the *umma* were in good standing, and that the society was an Islamic one. The constancy of the Abbasid Caliphate in the course of changing political orders slowly reinforced its position and ability to survive political and social change.[57]

It was thus in late medieval Egypt that the caliphate recovered some of its original life-force as aspiring amirs, anxious for dominance over the political landscape, could not resist the theocratic authority linked to the Abbasid family, thereby reinvigorating some of the influence and prestige lost by the caliphate in the centuries prior to the fall of Baghdad.[58] Indeed, medieval scholars and their modern counterparts have argued that the caliphate was capable of absorbing authority by virtue of its proximity to a powerful sultan.[59]

While the caliphal idea persisted as a powerful organisational tool in the toolbox of the elites, it also remained on the minds of some *ʿulamāʾ* as an alternative mode of organisation to challenge the status quo within the sultanate of Cairo. Notions of 'Caliphate' remained at the centre of popular theological and millenarian/apocalyptic rebellions taking shape in the form of the late fourteenth-century '*Ẓāhirī fitna*' and the brief political movement formed in southern Syria around a 'Sufyānī' rebel claiming Umayyad descent in 816/1413.[60] Both movements, sometimes negatively referring to the Cairene Abbasids (and also including military elites among their supporters), wanted to see a new *dawla* within the territory of the sultanate centred around some notion of true 'Caliphate' at the expense of the 'Dawlat al-Atrāk'.[61]

The Caliph and the Masses

By promoting their ongoing loyalty and protection of the Abbasid Caliphate, the sultans and their courts hoped, in large part, to cultivate the support and sympathies of the *ʿāmma*, the (predominantly Sunni Muslim) civilian masses of Egypt and Syria (Bilād al-Shām).[62] Although contemporary Syro-Egyptian sources sometimes offer clues, the precise relationship between the caliphate and the *ʿāmma* is difficult to pinpoint.

In the absence of sources left behind by literate members of the common folk describing their own sentiments towards the caliphate, we must rely on the circumstantial remarks and hearsay of the intellectual elites who engaged in historiography and as religious scholars and chancery scribes. Although some modern historians have suggested that these historians, Sufi *shaykhs* and *ʿulamāʾ* reliably reflect public opinion, we must, in most cases (with the exception, perhaps, of Ibn Iyās), resist the temptation to suggest that their reports accurately represented the views of the *ʿāmma*.[63] It is difficult, if not impossible, to gauge the degree of interest and support which the caliphs drew from the people. Syro-Egyptian sources tend to be inconsistent in their use of the Arabic term *al-nās* as an appellation of the Citadel elite, or as a blanket designation which included the *ʿāmma*. While reflective of a popular demand for general well-being in matters of religion, reports on the public reaction towards affairs of the caliphate tend to be non-specific.

The political elite remained attuned to the mood of the masses as they sculpted caliphal policies. Baybars' investiture ceremonies were a major appeal to mid-thirteenth-century public opinion, and the sultan invited members of his subject population to witness numerous festivities featuring the caliph. In 785/1383, after rumours of a coup led by the caliph al-Mutawakkil, Barqūq had desired to publicly execute the Commander of the Faithful, but fears of a popular uprising ultimately stayed his hand. Desperate to stay in power amid a revolt led by Syrian amirs, Barqūq courted the support of the *ʿāmma* through several public appearances with the caliph at his side.[64]

The caliphs themselves were never more accessible to ordinary folk than they were during their maintenance of the Nafīsī shrine beginning in the mid-fourteenth century. Nowhere else could outsiders to the social worlds of the elites cross paths with the Abbasid caliph or his representatives. The caliph himself was said to have held court in the shrine, as he sat inside looking on as pilgrims came with donations for the chest and to pay respects to the legacy of Sayyida Nafīsa (and presumably the Abbasid family).[65] Involvement with the shrine exemplifies the ability of the caliph to straddle the political and religious worlds of the Citadel as well as the realm of a more popular piety, the lines between which were often blurred during the long history of the Cairo Sultanate.

Caliphal authority had a minor role to play in the realm of popular religious tradition. While mapping the legitimacy, charismatic blessings (*baraka*) and 'spiritual protection' (*al-ḥimāya al-rūḥiyya*) ascribed to the Abbasid caliphs in elite circles, it is difficult to ignore the parallels with the complex and influential social world of the Sufis hinted at in Chapter 4. By the late fourteenth/early fifteenth century, the influence of Sufism permeated every level of Middle Eastern Islamicate society.[66] Modern scholars often refer to the notion of a so-called 'state-sponsored Sufism' to account for extensive sultanic and amiral patronage of mosques and Sufi structures including *khānqāhs*, *ribāṭs* and *zāwiyas*.[67]

Minor similarities existed between the holy men of the Abbasid family and the Sufi *shaykhs* that enjoyed favour among the sultans. Just as Abbasid descendants were believed to be in touch with supernatural forces capable of protecting the state, Sufis were likewise regarded as bearers of a special kind of influence or a transcendental spirituality, which, in many ways, trumped the importance of the caliph. The arguably more fluid and dynamic *baraka* of the Sufi *shaykhs* was indeed different than that of the caliph, which, to some extent, the elite may have wished to keep separate from their reverence of those Sufis with a more pervasive brand of divine charisma.[68]

Although many members of the *ʿulamāʾ* were inclined towards participation in Sufi networks, some members of the Sunni religious elite frowned on the sultans' favourable tendency towards popular religion.[69] A circle of fourteenth-century traditionalist Syrian scholars, mostly the colleagues of Ibn Taymiyya, strongly disapproved of many popular spiritual practices.[70] Nevertheless, both the rulers and a sizeable portion of their subjects enjoyed a mystically-inclined religiosity and were fond of visiting the tombs of saints. As rulers, the sultans were equally proud of sheltering the caliph and ruling over the most important holy places, which, alongside their patronage of Sufi institutions, was projected as devotion and service to Islam.[71]

According to Michael Chamberlain, medieval Eurasia was characterised by an enduring legacy of universal empires (whether caliphs, popes or emperors) that allowed invading horse warriors to derive legitimacy from sacral figures who received a unique role.[72] The sultans of Cairo, like the Mongols, respected the power of shaman-like individuals, including Sufi *shaykh*s, *sayyid*s, notables possessing a sacred lineage, as well as formally appointed holy men/courtiers such as the *ʿulamāʾ*, the *shaykh al-islām* and the Abbasid caliph.[73] Given the attentiveness of sultans and amirs to popular religious practices, we may tentatively suggest that the court cultures established around the sultans, with their reverence for living holy men, may have retained at least some memory of the pre-Islamic indigenous religions of the steppe lands from which they originated.[74]

Yet another possible indicator reflecting the Turco-Mongolian past of Qipchaqī Turkish ruling elites is that there appears to be no report of a sultan ever executing or shedding the sacred blood of an Abbasid caliph in their custody, despite the numerous reports of physical mistreatment, abuse and deposition. The political culture always maintained a degree of admiration towards the caliphs' bloodline, and deemed it dangerous (and harmful to public opinion) to physically harm 'the successor of God on the Earth'. While much of the evidence remains circumstantial, some sultans strived to remain on the good side of the caliphate, perhaps for fear of the supernatural power of the prayers of a holy man against their reigns. Faced with declining political fortunes in 791/1389, Barqūq begged the Abbasid caliph al-Mutawakkil not to be upset with him for having been imprisoned for six years.[75] Al-Ẓāhir Ṭaṭar took pains to reverse the sanctions of the caliph al-Mustaʿīn by Shaykh in 824/1421.[76] Likewise, Qānişawh al-Ghawrī set right perceived wrongs against the caliph al-Mustamsik whom he had dismissed for having bad eyesight, because of worry, so we are told, that the caliph was 'upset' with him. Such gestures may have had more to do with stroking public opinion and court sensibilities or otherwise reconciling conflicted household factions; nevertheless, they also reflected a fear of offending one of Islam's holiest of holies.

Throughout the long history of the sultanate of Cairo, caliphal authority proved to be highly elastic. In addition to their performative role in the rituals of Cairene political elites, the Abbasids participated in popular religious traditions such as *mawlid* festivals celebrating the birth of the Prophet, Sufi practices at the Nafīsī shrine and funerary rites to mark the deaths of popular sultans.[77] Nevertheless, there remained some tension over what the caliphate was intended to represent: in the 825/1422 investiture deed for the sultan Barsbāy, the scribe Ibn Ḥijja boldly declares that the caliph will not be corrupted by folk understandings of the faith and will give preference only to the Qurʾān and *sunna*.[78]

Abbasid caliphs and Sufi masters alike offered themselves up as founts of charisma (*baraka*). In the context of public prayer ceremonies to combat drought, plague or to gear up for an impending battle, the caliph was one religious personality among others to offer his prayers. In times of crisis, the sultans did not discriminate between competing brands of religious legitimacy and were often anxious to hurl the power of *any* kind of holy man in an emergency, hoping that God might alleviate the latest emergency. In short, political elites courted and patronised all forms of charisma to lend spiritual power to their politics. The caliphs likely represented a more orthodox-friendly form of spiritual charisma that had important precedent and links to Islamic tradition, but that was not without significance in more popular expressions of Islam. Significantly, Abbasid authority, like *ṭarīqa* Sufism, was recognised and promoted as a symbol by religious elites. Sufis, on the other hand, were suppliers of a more ecstatic and unpredictable charisma that had more mass appeal and considerable influence with the population, but was not always as easily subject to the whims of a sultan in the way a closely-guarded and easily controllable caliph might be.

Pre-modern Islamicate Kingship

Medieval discourse on complex entities such as the caliphate and sultanate in Egypt and Syria represent one narrative strand of a broader transregional discussion and ongoing conceptual renegotiation of 'Caliphate', sovereignty, leadership and kingship in late medieval Anatolia, Mesopotamia, Iran and Central Asia from the late thirteenth to the early sixteenth centuries and beyond. Recent scholarship has highlighted some of the competing claims to sovereignty being made in the late medieval period, particularly in the Timurid, Ottoman and Mughal contexts.[79] Many of the polities in regions beyond the territories of the Cairo Sultanate were indeed moving away from traditionalist notions of 'Caliphate' and of the caliph as the supreme sovereign.[80]

The 'Abbasid Caliphate of Cairo' as it was performed through nuanced social practices and created textually through a variety of literary genres, represented merely one narrative that was revisited and repeated by traditionalist jurists and authors of Arabic historiographical writing, particularly in fifteenth-century Egypt and Syria. Other notions, arguments and ideas about sovereignty were likewise made abroad in places where Abbasid and Chinggisid ideals no longer held currency, particularly among Turko-Mongolian rulers and their subject populations.[81] Taking a step back from the sultanate of Cairo, it is possible to see a wider and highly contested discursive context alongside common vocabularies of kingship that included the competing dynastic and millenarian claims of the Ottomans, Mughals and Safavids in the sixteenth century. The regional variation of the caliphate that appeared in the territories of Egypt, Syria and parts of the Hijaz, was not separate from the highly fluid, experimental fifteenth-century 'laboratory' of claims and the ongoing state of flux throughout the Islamicate world.[82] Indeed, the idea of the 'Caliphate' itself took on a wide variety of meanings across several courtly and cultural contexts which drew from various currents such as Alid loyalty and Sufism that resulted in the more esoteric and confessionally ambiguous claims of groups like the Sarbadārs in Khurāsān, the Ḥurūfīs in Iran and Anatolia, messianic movements like the Mushaʿshaʿ in Khūzistān, the militant and millenarian Bektāshīs in Anatolia, as well as the proclaimed divinity of Shāh Ismāʿīl and the Ṣafaviyya order.[83] The fourteenth to the sixteenth centuries were thus a profoundly significant period of growth for popular religious movements which aimed to establish justice and their own forms of righteous rule.

Thus, the Arabic output of authors as diverse as Ibn Jamāʿa, al-Maqrīzī and al-Suyūṭī was part of a particular vision anchored to the role of the caliphs within the uniquely Cairene version of sovereignty tied to the juridical discourse of the 'Caliphate'.[84] It is important to stress this was but one voice in a much richer ongoing debate. As a result, notions of the 'caliphate of Cairo' remain more complex than what modern scholarship often dismisses as an anachronistic and moribund institution by the early sixteenth century.

Concluding Remarks

The Abbasid Caliphate facilitated the social behaviour of religious and political elites and furnished them with a repertoire of titles, legitimation, decrees and documents. In examining contemporary expectations and attitudes towards the Abbasid Caliphate of Cairo, it is difficult to sidestep the extreme confusion and messiness that has clouded our understanding of the sultans, their networks, political orders and policies. It is no longer easy for modern scholarship to argue that for contemporary observers, the caliphate lost *all* of its actual power throughout the span of the sultanate. Even if its profile decreased and other modes of legitimacy came to the fore, the Abbasid Caliphate was a mainstay on the political scene that became difficult to remove or replace.

Some historians point out that the Abbasid Caliphate of Cairo received only intermittent recognition from other contemporary Muslim rulers, but within Cairo we can say that it enjoyed a strong allegiance, as well as moments of socio-political leverage, because it was locally promoted as an important part of the political culture. Even when individual sultans seemed to care little about the Abbasid Caliphate, they dared not say so in public. Other scholars have advised against dismissing the personal piety of the sultans, while also remaining cautiously aware that legitimation was a real factor in the light of some sultans' pagan birth, slave origins or dubious appointment by their fathers.[85]

If the image cultivated by decades of scholarship that refers to the Cairene Abbasids as 'shadow caliphs' persists despite the palpable resonance they had among the social groupings of the late medieval sultanate of Cairo,[86] it is worth remembering that authority resides in places in which it is perceived to exist, and that the 'shadow' cast by these caliphs of late medieval Cairo was a large one indeed.

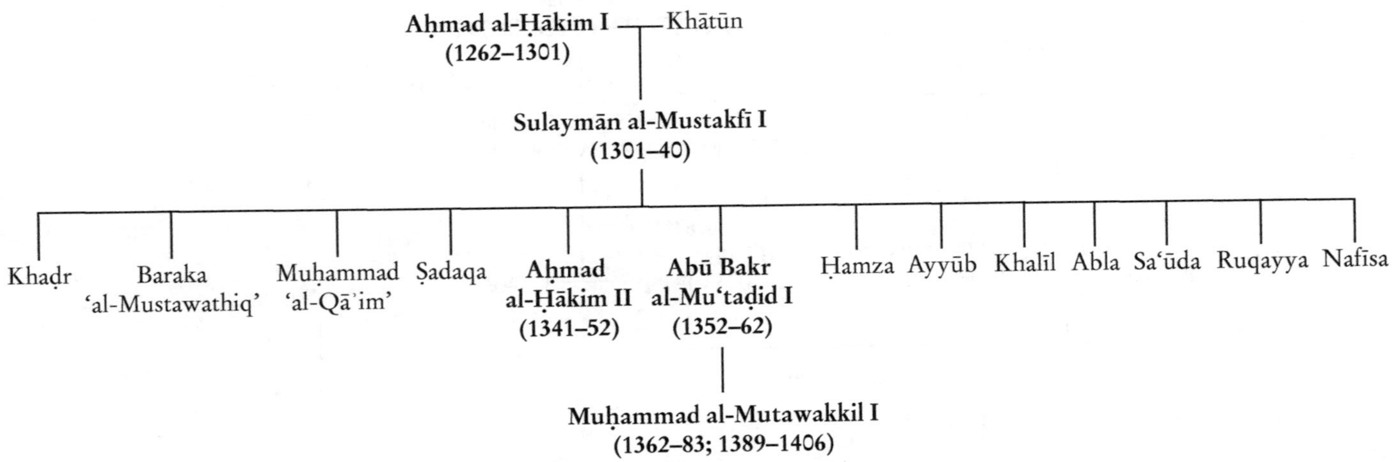

Table 10.1 Descendants of al-Mustakfī I.

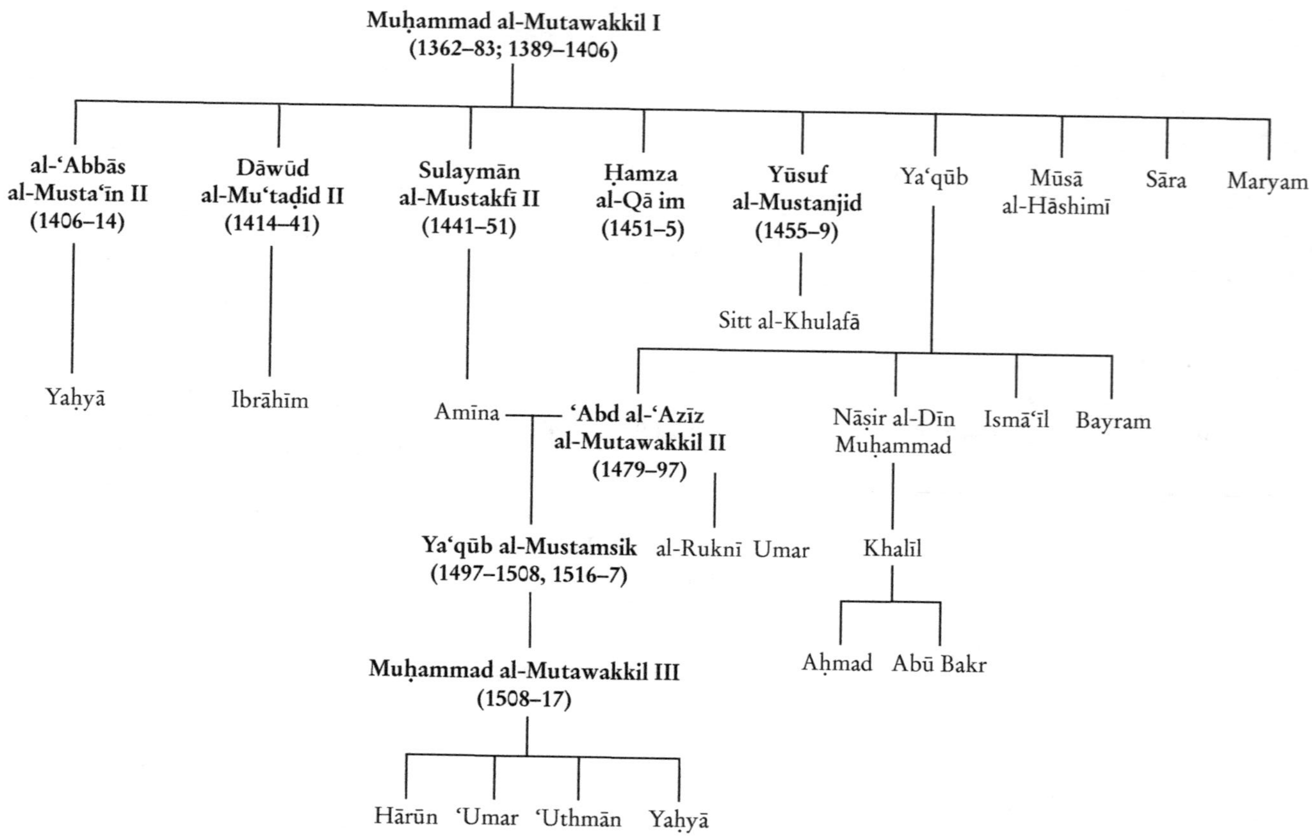

Table 10.2 Descendants of al-Mutawakkil I.

Notes

1. On this point see Al-Azmeh, *Muslim Kingship*, 187; Garcin, 'Histoire', 54.
2. Van Den Bossche, 'Past, Panegyric', 41; Van Steenbergen, ''Aṣabiyya, Messiness'.
3. Al-Azmeh, *Muslim Kingship*, 10.
4. Van Steenbergen, 'Ritual, Politics', 231.
5. Here my observations have benefited from Narotzky and Manzano, 'Ḥisba, Muḥtasib and Struggle'.
6. Hassan, *Longing for the Lost Caliphate*, 111, 115, 120.
7. Berkey, 'Mamluk Religious Policy', 12.
8. Berkey, 'Culture and Society', 386–8; Berkey, *Popular Preaching*, 21; Popper, *Systematic Notes*, 1:1–18; Lapidus, *Muslim Cities*, 79–84. The political elite were involved, symbiotically, with the men of culture. See Van Steenbergen, 'Qalāwūnid Discourse', 28.
9. For Bourdieu's discussion of social, cultural and economic capital, see Bourdieu, *Distinction*, 114.
10. Banister, ''*Ālim*-Caliph'. See also Chamberlain, *Knowledge*, 101–2.
11. Eychenne, *Liens personnels*, 24–7, 35–6, 309–11.
12. Hassan, *Longing for the Lost Caliphate*, 89, 92–3; Kennedy, *Caliphate*, xv.
13. Van Steenbergen, Wing and D'hulster, 'Mamlukization Part I', 552. See also Clifford, 'Ubi Sumus?', 46–57.
14. Hassan, *Longing for the Lost Caliphate*, 4, 67, 88, 95.
15. Kennedy, *Caliphate*, xiii–xvi, 247–50.
16. Here my thoughts have taken influence from Moin, *Millennial Sovereign*, 16–21.
17. Van Steenbergen, 'Mamlukisation', 16–17; Van Steenbergen, 'Appearances of *dawla* and Political Order', 74, 78.
18. Van Steenbergen, 'Appearances of *dawla* and Political Order', 55–63.
19. Hassan, *Longing for the Lost Caliphate*, 16–19, 26 73–5, 84; Kennedy, *Caliphate*, xv.
20. Hassan, *Longing for the Lost Caliphate*, 19.
21. Hassan, 'Poetic Memories', 9–11; Hassan, *Longing for the Lost Caliphate*, 29–31; Banister, 'Naught Remains', 245.
22. Here, I have applied the ideas of Bourdieu, 'Rethinking the State', 3–4.
23. Heidemann, *Kalifat*, 194.
24. Narotzky and Manzano, 'Ḥisba, Muḥtasib and Struggle', 35.
25. Along with the sultanate, the caliphate thus became 'part of the structural appearance of power and contributed to how power should be represented and articulated'. See Van Steenbergen, ''Aṣabiyya, Messiness'.

26. Van Steenbergen, 'Appearances of *dawla* and Political Order', 75.
27. Hassan, *Longing for the Lost Caliphate*, 88–97; Holt, 'Position and Power', 244.
28. Popper, *Systematic Notes*, 1:83.
29. Hassan, *Longing for the Lost Caliphate*, 4, 16, 67.
30. Hassan, 'Poetic Memories'; Hassan, *Longing for the Lost Caliphate*, 93–5; Wiederhold, 'Legal-Religious Elite'.
31. Moin, *Millennial Sovereign*, 6, 21.
32. Ibid., 6, 68, 93; Onimus, *Les maîtres du jeu*, 128–9; Hassan, *Longing for the Lost Caliphate*, 71–80.
33. Onimus, *Les maîtres du jeu*, 16, 128–9, 147, 153, 335, 346; Van Steenbergen, 'Appearances of *dawla* and Political Order', 62.
34. Van Steenbergen, 'Appearances of *dawla* and Political Order', 55–63; Van Steenbergen, ''Aṣabiyya, Messiness'; Hassan, *Longing for the Lost Caliphate*, 84.
35. Ibn Taghrībirdī, *Nujūm*, 11:3; Ibn Taghrībirdī, *Manhal*, 3:287; Ibn Taghrībirdī, *Mawrid*, 1:263; al-Suyūṭī, *Ḥusn*, 2:120; Surūr, *Dawlat Banī Qalāwūn*, 85.
36. Van Steenbergen, 'Ritual, Politics', 227.
37. Al-Azmeh, *Muslim Kingship*, 3–4.
38. Hassan, *Longing for the Lost Caliphate*, 13, 17, 26, 30, 45, 70–5, 83–4.
39. Al-Maqrīzī, *Sulūk*, 3:284, 290; Ibn Taghrībirdī, *Nujūm*, 11:148–9. See also Onimus, *Les maîtres du jeu*, 130–2.
40. Interactions with caliphal ceremonial could easily draw *mamlūk* recruits 'into webs of social practices and cultural meanings'. See Van Steenbergen, 'Appearances of *dawla* and Political Order', 80.
41. This question has been raised before in Wiederhold, 'Legal-Religious Elite'; Broadbridge, *Kingship and Ideology*, 150; Khūlī, *'Ulamā'*, 70–1.
42. Onimus, *Les maîtres du jeu*, 153–4, 156.
43. Flinterman and Van Steenbergen, 'Al-Nasir Muhammad', 99; Van Steenbergen, 'Is Anyone my Guardian', 58.
44. Van Steenbergen, 'Amir Yalbughā', 426; Van Steenbergen, 'Qalāwūnid Discourse', 26–7; Van Steenbergen, 'Ritual, Politics', 231; Berkey, 'Culture and Society', 386.
45. Eychenne, *Liens personnels*, 191.
46. On institutions as platforms in which struggle unfolds, see Lantschner, 'Fragmented Cities'.
47. I have explored a series of late medieval Egyptian Abbasid marriage ties demonstrating caliphal agency in my article 'Princesses born to Concubines'.

48. Ibn Khaldūn mentions one Abbasid prince who received an audience with Temür and tried to solicit his help in taking the caliphate away from al-Mutawakkil I (*Taʿrīf*, 376). Al-Biqāʿī later reports a rumour that another of the caliph's family members in Cairo sent a forged letter with a caliphal seal to the Ottoman sultan Meḥmed II requesting gifts to which he sent a reply (*Iẓhār*, 2:79).
49. Hassan, *Longing for the Lost Caliphate*, 83–8, 108–41; Holt, 'Structure of Government', 59; Petry, *Civilian Elite*, 314–15; Berkey, 'Culture and Society', 393. For an extended discussion, see Banister, '*ʿĀlim*-Caliph'.
50. The coexistence of the caliphate and the religious class in Cairo was at times uneasy. Some scholars worried that the introduction of a new caliph in Cairo might result in confusion and loss of their own influence, see Mājid, *Nuẓum*, 1:33; Jackson, 'Prophetic Action', 81–2.
51. Lev, 'Symbiotic Relations', 21.
52. Hassan, *Longing for the Lost Caliphate*, 66–97; Broadbridge, *Kingship and Ideology*, 42, 52–3.
53. Hassan, 'Poetic Memories', 14.
54. Chapoutot-Remadi, 'Une institution', 18.
55. Chamberlain, *Knowledge*, 57–66; Eychenne, *Liens personnels*, 195, 492.
56. On other ceremonial functions of the Cairo caliphs, see Banister, 'Naught Remains', 227–37.
57. Garcin, 'Histoire', 58; Becker, 'Barthold's Studien', 370; Gaudefroy-Demombynes, *La Syrie à l'époque des mamelouks*, xxix.
58. Hassan, *Longing for the Lost Caliphate*, 66–97; Ḥuṭayṭ, *Qaḍāyā*, 143.
59. Al-Ḥusaynī, *Nafāʾis*, 111; Gaudefroy-Demombynes, *La Syrie à l'époque des mamelouks*, xxii–xxiv.
60. Van Steenbergen, 'Revisiting the Mamlūk Empire', 85–6.
61. Al-Maqrīzī, *Durar*, 1:298–9.
62. The word *ʿāmma*, frequently used to refer to common people, carried a slightly negative connotation in distinction from '*khāṣṣa*', the term for the elite. On the *ʿāmma* as a broad social grouping in this period, see Berkey, 'Culture and Society', 386–7; Perho, 'The Sultan and the Common People'; Rizq, *ʿĀmmat al-Qāhira*, 33–54; Levanoni, *Turning Point*, 109–14; Shoshan, *Popular Culture*, 3, 10–11; Lapidus, *Muslim Cities*, 143–84. On the Abbasid Caliphate and its relationship with Cairene public opinion, see Ḍāḥī and Mizbān, *al-Raʾy al-ʿāmm*, 43–65.
63. Madelung, 'Treatise', 102; Ḍāḥī and Mizbān, *al-Raʾy al-ʿāmm*, 60.

64. Ibn Qāḍī Shuhba, *Taʾrīkh*, 3:110; Hassan, *Longing for the Lost Caliphate*, 91–3; Ḍāḥī, *al-Raʾy al-ʿāmm*, 46–55, 62; Wiederhold, 'Legal-Religious Elite', 213–14; Brinner, 'Struggle for Power', 234.
65. Al-Maqrīzī, *Khiṭaṭ*, 3:785; al-Maqrīzī, *Durar*, 3:293; Ibn Taghrībirdī, *Nujūm*, 11:245; Tetsuya, 'Cairene Cemeteries', 101–2; Garcin, 'Circassian Mamlūks', 303; Rāġib, 'Al-Sayyida Nafīsa', 42. It is difficult to comment on the frequency and level of interaction between the caliph and the masses, though the association was nurtured by the caliph's presence at the shrine.
66. On Sufism in late medieval Egypt and Syria and the state of scholarship, see Hofer, *Popularisation of Sufism*, 1–25; Eychenne, *Liens personnels*, 129–50; Homerin, 'Saving Muslim Souls'; Homerin, 'Sufism in Mamluk Studies'; Shoshan, *Popular Culture*, 10–22; Berkey, 'Mamluk Religious Policy', 19; Schimmel, 'Some Glimpses'. On the general importance of Sufism to the Later Middle Period, see Hodgson, *Rethinking World History*, 184–8; Hodgson, *Venture of Islam*, 2:201–54; Voll, 'Islam as a Community of Discourse', 9–11.
67. Hofer, *Popularisation of Sufism*, 35–80; Knysh, *Ibn ʿArabi*, 50–2; Little, 'Religion under the Mamluks', 172.
68. Al-Azmeh, *Muslim Kingship*, 157–8.
69. Haarmann, 'Arabic in Speech', 100; Berkey, *Formation of Islam*, 248–57; Berkey, 'Mamluk Religious Policy', 18.
70. Rāġib, 'Al-Sayyida Nafīsa', 38; Shoshan, *Popular Culture*, 67–9; Berkey, *Popular Preaching*, 91–3.
71. Broadbridge, *Kingship and Ideology*, 12–16; Schimmel, 'Some Glimpses', 384.
72. Chamberlain, *Knowledge*, 28–30.
73. In the religious experiences and expectations of Muslims of all social classes in this period, focus was often placed on highly reputed individuals, holy men, known for their learning, saintliness or pious character. These figures enjoyed the ability to negotiate social influence and were understood by common people to be able to offer 'intercession and mediation both with God and with the established authorities', even if the jurisprudential version of the faith supported by orthodox Sunni Muslim theologians discounted this as a possibility. See Sartain, *Al-Suyūṭī*, 24; Berkey, *Formation of Islam*, 250; Berkey, 'Mamluks as Muslims', 163.
74. Berkey, 'Mamluks as Muslims', 163. Devin DeWeese has attempted some explanation of the religious landscape of pre-Islamic Inner Asia. See Deweese, *Islamization and Native Religion*, 27–50; Eychenne, *Liens personnels*, 104–5.

75. Ibn Qāḍī Shuhba, *Taʾrīkh*, 1:266; Ibn Ḥajar, *Inbāʾ al-ghumr*, 2:344; al-Ṣayrafī, *Nuzhat*, 1:189; Ibn Iyās, *Badāʾiʿ*, 1:2:396–7.
76. Al-Maqrīzī, *Sulūk*, 4:2:587; Ibn Taghrībirdī, *Manhal*, 7:63; al-Malaṭī, *Nayl*, 4:99; al-Sakhāwī, *Ḍawʾ*, 4:20.
77. Schimmel, 'Kalif und Kadi', 77–8; Rāġib, 'Al-Sayyida Nafīsa', 38; Chapoutot-Remadi, 'Une institution', 17.
78. Ibn Ḥijja, *Qahwat al-inshāʾ*, 368–9.
79. Markiewicz, *Crisis of Kingship*, 3, 166; Yılmaz, *Caliphate Redefined*, 1–10, 80–96, 191–6; Binbaş, *Intellectual Networks*, 20–1; Dekkiche, 'New Source'; Moin, *Millennial Sovereign*, 1–28; Woods, *Aqquyunlu*, 1–10.
80. Arnold, *Caliphate*, 107–20; Becker, 'Barthold's Studien', 376–86.
81. Markiewicz, *Crisis of Kingship*, 6–7, 154–6, 166, 173, 176–7; Yılmaz, *Caliphate Redefined*, 1–4, 108–9.
82. Markiewicz, *Crisis of Kingship*, 3–5; Binbaş, *Intellectual Networks*, 252–3; Woods, *Aqquyunlu*, 3–4, 9.
83. Yılmaz, *Caliphate Redefined*, 89–93, 200–6; Binbaş, *Intellectual Networks*, 51–5, 150–9; Minorsky, 'Poetry of Shāh Ismāʿīl I'.
84. Markiewicz, *Crisis of Kingship*, 155–6; Hassan, *Longing for the Lost Caliphate*, 108–41.
85. Broadbridge, *Kingship and Ideology*, 12; Northrup, 'Baḥrī Mamlūk Sultanate', 255–7, 269; Schimmel, 'Some Glimpses', 356–61.
86. Hassan, *Longing for the Lost Caliphate*, 4, 19, 26, 31, 88.

Works Cited

Primary Sources

al-ʿAbbāsī, Ḥasan, *Āthār al-uwal fī tartīb al-duwal*, ed. ʿAbd al-Raḥmān ʿUmayra. Beirut: Dār al-Jīl, 1989.

Abū al-Fidāʾ, ʿImād al-Dīn Ismāʿīl, *Al-Mukhtaṣar fī akhbār al-bashar*, 4 vols, ed. Muḥammad Zaynhum ʿAzab, Cairo: Dār al-Maʿārif, 1999.

Abū Shāma, ʿAbd al-Raḥmān, *Tarājim rijāl al-qarnayn al-sādis wa-l-sābiʿ*, ed. Muḥammad al-Kawtharī, Beirut: Dār al-Jīl, 1974.

[Author Z], *Taʾrīkh salāṭīn al-mamālīk* or *Beiträge zur Geschichte der mamlukensultane*, ed. Karl Vilhelm Zetterstéen, Leiden, 1919.

al-ʿAynī, Badr al-Dīn Maḥmūd, *ʿIqd al-jumān fī taʾrīkh ahl al-zamān*, 2 vols, ed. ʿAbd al-Rāzīq al-Ṭanṭāwī al-Qarmūṭ, Cairo: al-Zahrāʾ, 1985–9.

al-ʿAynī, Badr al-Dīn Maḥmūd, *ʿIqd al-jumān fī taʾrīkh ahl al-zamān: ʿaṣr salāṭīn al-mamālīk*, 5 vols, ed. Muḥammad Muḥammad Amīn, Cairo: Dār al-Kutub wa-l-Wathāʾiq, 1987–92.

Anonymous, *Al-Kawkab al-durrī fī masāʾil al-Ghawrī*, in *Majālis al-Sulṭān al-Ghawrī: ṣafaḥāt min taʾrīkh Miṣr fī qarn al-ʿāshir hijrī*, ed. ʿAbd al-Wahhāb ʿAzzām, Cairo, 1941.

Baumgarten, Martin von, 'The Travels of Martin Baumgarten, A Nobleman of Germany through Egypt, Arabia, Palestine, and Syria', in Awnsham Churchill (ed.), *A Collection of Voyages and Travels, Some Now First Published from Original Manuscripts, others Now First Published in English*, vol. 1, London, 1732, 381–452.

Baybars al-Manṣūrī, Rukn al-Dīn, *Al-Tuḥfa al-mulkiyya fī al-dawla al-turkiyya*, ed. ʿAbd al-Ḥamīd Hamdān, Cairo: Dār al-Miṣriyya al-Lubnāniyya, 1987.

Baybars al-Manṣūrī, Rukn al-Dīn, *Zubdat al-fikra fī taʾrīkh al-hijra*, ed. D. S. Richards, Beirut: al-Sharika al-Muttaḥida li-l-Tawziʿ, 1998.

al-Biqāʿī, Burhān al-Dīn Ibrāhīm, *Iẓhār al-ʿaṣr li-asrār ahl al-ʿaṣr*, 3 vols, ed. Muḥammad al-ʿAwfī, Giza: Hajar lil-Ṭibāʿa wa-l-Nashr wa-l-Tawzīʿ, 1992–3.

al-Biqāʿī, Burhān al-Dīn Ibrāhīm, *ʿUnwān al-zamān bi-tarājim al-shuyūkh wa-l-aqrān*, 4 vols, ed. Ḥasan Ḥabashī, Cairo: Dār al-Kutub wa-l-Wathāʾiq al-Qawmiyya Markaz Taḥqīq al-Turāth, 2001–9.

al-Birzālī, al-Qāsim ibn Muḥammad, *Al-Muqtafī ʿalā kitāb al-rawḍatayn*, 4 vols, ed. ʿUmar Tadmurī, Beirut and Sidon: al-Maktaba al-ʿAṣriyya, 2006.

Çelebi, Evliyā, *Seyahatnâmesi*, ed. Yücel Dağlı et al., vol. 10,. Istanbul: Yapı Kredi Yayınları, 2007.

De Mignanelli, Bertrando, *Ascensus Barcoch (I)*, trans. Walter Fischel in *Arabica* 6 (1959): 57–74, 152–72.

al-Dhahabī, Shams al-Dīn Muḥammad, *Al-ʿIbar fī khabar man ghabar*, 5 vols, ed. Ṣalāḥ al-Dīn al-Munajjid, Kuwait, 1960–6.

al-Dhahabī, Shams al-Dīn Muḥammad, *Kitāb Duwal al-Islām*, 2 vols, Hyderabad, 1944–6.

al-Dhahabī, Shams al-Dīn Muḥammad, *Siyar aʿlām al-nubalā*, 25 vols and supplements, ed. Shuʿayb Arnaʾūṭ, Beirut: Muʾassasat al-Risāla, 1981.

al-Dhahabī, Shams al-Dīn Muḥammad, *Taʾrīkh al-Islām*, 53 vols, ed. ʿUmar Tadmurī, Beirut: Dār al-Kitāb al-ʿArabī, 1987–2000.

al-Dhahabī, Shams al-Dīn Muḥammad, *Taʾrīkh al-Islām wa-wafayāt al-mashāhīr wa-l-aʿlām. Ḥawādith wa-wafayāt, 701–746*, ed. ʿUmar Tadmurī, Beirut: Dār al-Kitāb al-ʿArabī, 2004.

al-Fākhirī, Baktāsh, *Taʾrīkh salāṭīn al-mamālīk* or *Beiträge zur Geschichte der mamlukensultane* ('Fragment einer Chronik 709–745 A. H.'), ed. Karl Zetterstéen, Leiden, 1919.

Ferīdūn Beğ, *Mecmua-i Münşeʾātü s-selāṭīn*, 2 vols, Istanbul, 1274–5/1858.

al-Ḥaṣkafī, Aḥmad ibn al-Mullā (Munlā), *Mutʿat al-adhhān min al-tamattuʿ bi-l-iqrān bayna tarājim al-shuyūkh wa-l-aqrān*, ed. Ṣalāḥ al-Dīn Khalīl al-Shaybānī al-Mawṣilī, 2 vols, Beirut, 1999.

al-Ḥusaynī, al-Ḥusayn, *Nafāʾis al-majālis al-sulṭāniyya*, in *Majālis al-Sulṭān al-Ghawrī: ṣafaḥāt min taʾrīkh Miṣr fī qarn al-ʿāshir hijrī*, ed. ʿAbd al-Wahhāb ʿAzzām, Cairo, 1941.

Ibn ʿAbd al-Ẓāhir, Muḥyī al-Dīn, *Al-Alṭāf al-khafiyya min al-sīra al-sharīfa al-sulṭāniyya al-Ashrafiyya*, ed. Axel Moberg, Lund, 1902.

Ibn ʿAbd al-Ẓāhir, Muḥyī al-Dīn, *Tashrīf al-ayyām wa-l-ʿuṣūr fī sīrat al-Malik al-Manṣūr*, ed. Murād Kāmil, Cairo: Wizārat al-Thaqāfa wa-l-Irshād al-Qawmī, 1961.

Ibn ʿAbd al-Ẓāhir, Muḥyī al-Dīn, *Al-Rawḍ al-ẓāhir fī sīrat al-Malik al-Ẓāhir*, ed. ʿAbd al-ʿAzīz Khuwayṭir, Riyadh, 1976.

Ibn ʿArabshāh, Aḥmad, *Tamerlane: the Life of the Great Amir*, trans. J. H. Sanders, London: I. B. Tauris, 2018.

Ibn al-Dawādārī, Abū Bakr ibn ʿAbdallāh, *Kanz al-durar wa-jāmiʿ al-ghurar*, 9 vols, ed. Bernd Radtke et al., Cairo: Maṭbaʿat ʿĪsā al-Bābī al-Ḥalabī, 1960.

Ibn Duqmāq, Ibrāhīm, *Al-Jawhar al-thamīn fī siyar al-khulafāʾ wa-l-mulūk wa-l-salāṭīn*, ed. Saʿīd ʿĀshūr, Mecca, 1982.

Ibn al-Furāt, Nāṣir al-Dīn Muḥammad, *Taʾrīkh Ibn al-Furāt*, ed. Qusṭanṭīn Zurayq, Beirut: American Press, 1939, vols 7–9.

Ibn al-Ḥimṣī, Aḥmad, *Ḥawādith al-zamān wa-wafayāt al-shuyūkh wa-l-aqrān*, 3 vols, ed. ʿUmar Tadmurī, Beirut: al-Maktaba al-ʿAṣriyya, 1999.

Ibn al-ʿIbrī [Bar Hebraeus], Ghirīghūryūs, *Taʾrīkh mukhtaṣar al-Duwal*, Beirut: Al-Maṭbaʿat al-Kāthūlīkiyya, 1958.

Ibn al-Shiḥna, *Al-Badr al-zāhir fī naṣrat al-Malik al-Nāṣir Muḥammad ibn Qāytbāy*, ed. ʿUmar Tadmurī, Beirut: Dār al-Kitāb al-ʿArabī, 1983.

Ibn al-Ṣuqāʿī, Faḍlallāh, *Tālī kitāb wafayāt al-aʿyān*, ed. Jacqueline Sublet, Damascus: Institut Français de Damas, 1974.

Ibn Ḥabīb, Badr al-Dīn Ḥasan, *Tadhkirat al-nabīh fī ayyām al-Manṣūr wa-banīh*, 3 vols, ed. Muḥammad Amīn and Saʿīd ʿĀshūr, Cairo: Maṭbaʿat Dār al-Kutub, 1976.

Ibn Ḥajar al-ʿAsqalānī, Aḥmad ibn ʿAlī, *Inbāʾ al-ghumr bi-anbāʾ al-ʿumr*, 3 vols, ed. Ḥasan Ḥabashī, Cairo, 1969–98.

Ibn Ḥajar al-ʿAsqalānī, Aḥmad ibn ʿAlī, *Al-Durar al-kāmina fī aʿyān al-miʾa al-thāmina*, 5 vols, Hyderabad: Maṭbaʿat Majlis Dāʾirat al-Maʿārīf al-ʿUthmāniyya, 1972.

Ibn Ḥajar al-ʿAsqalānī, Aḥmad, *Dhayl al-Durar al-kāmina*, ed. ʿAdnān Darwīsh, Cairo: al-Munaẓẓama al-ʿArabiyya lil-Tarbiyya wa-l-Thaqāfa wa-l-ʿUlūm, Maʿhad al-Makhṭūṭat al-ʿArabiyya, 1992.

Ibn Ḥijja, Abū Bakr ibn ʿAlī, *Qahwat al-inshāʾ*, ed. Rudolf Veselý, Beirut: al-Maʿhad al-Almānī lil-Abḥāth al-Sharqiyya, 2005.

Ibn Ḥijjī, Shihāb al-Dīn Aḥmad, *Taʾrīkh Ibn Ḥijjī: ḥawādīth wa-wafayāt 796–815*, 2 vols, ed. ʿAbdallāh al-Kandarī, Beirut: Dar Ibn Hazm, 2003.

Ibn Iyās, Muḥammad ibn Aḥmad, *Badāʾiʿ al-zuhūr fī waqāʾiʿ al-duhūr*, 5 vols, ed. Muḥammad Muṣṭafā, Wiesbaden: Franz Steiner, 1960–3.

Ibn Jamāʿa, Badr al-Dīn Muḥammad, *Taḥrīr al-aḥkām fī tadbīr ahl al-Islām*, ed. Hans Kofler as 'Handbuch des islamischen Staats- und Verwaltungsrechtes von Badr-ad-Dīn Ibn Ǧamaʿah', *Islamica* 6/7 (1934/1935): 349–414, 1–64.

Ibn Kathīr, Ismāʿīl, *Al-Bidāya wa-l-nihāya fī al-taʾrīkh*, 14 vols, Cairo: Maṭbaʿat al-Saʿāda, 1932–9.

Ibn Khaldūn, ʿAbd al-Raḥmān, *Al-Taʿrīf bi-Ibn Khaldūn wa-riḥlatihi gharban wa-sharqan*, Cairo, 1951.

Ibn Khaldūn, ʿAbd al-Raḥmān, *Muqaddimat Ibn Khaldūn*, Beirut: Dār al-Arqam, 2001.

Ibn Khaldūn, ʿAbd al-Raḥmān, *Taʾrīkh Ibn Khaldūn (al-musammā bi-Kitāb al-ʿIbar)*, 8 vols, ed. Muḥammad Hāshim, Beirut: Dār al-Kutub al-ʿIlmiyya, 2006.

Ibn Nāẓir al-Jaysh, ʿAbd al-Rahmān, *Kitāb Tathqīf al-taʿrīf bi-l-muṣṭalaʾ al-sharīf*, ed. Rudolf Veselý, Cairo: al-Maʿhad al-ʿIlmī al-Faransī lil-Āthār al-Shariyya bi-l-Qāhira, 1987.

Ibn Qāḍī Shuhbah, Abū Bakr, *Taʾrīkh Ibn Qāḍī Shuhbah*, 4 vols, ed. ʿAdnān Darwīsh, Damascus, 1977–94.

Ibn Ṣaṣrā, Muḥammad, *Al-Durra al-muḍīʾa fī al-dawla al-Ẓāhiriyya*, 2 vols, ed. William Brinner as *A Chronicle of Damascus, 1389–1397*, Berkeley: University of California Press, 1963.

Ibn Shaddād, ʿIzz al-Dīn Muḥammad, *Al-Aʿlāq al-khaṭīra fī dhikr umarāʾ al-Shām wa-l-Jazīra*, 3 vols, ed. Dominique Sourdel, Damascus: al-Maʿhad al-Firinsī bi-Dimashq lil-Dirāsāt al-ʿArabiyya, 1953.

Ibn Taghrībirdī, Jamāl al-Dīn Yūsuf, *Ḥawādith al-duhūr fī madā al-ayyām wa-l-shuhūr*, ed. William Popper, as 'Extracts from Abû 'l-Maḥâsin Ibn Taghrî Birdi's Chronicle Entitled Ḥawâdith ad-duhûr fî madâ 'l-ayyâm wash-shuhûr', *University of California Publications in Semitic Philology* 8, Berkeley: University of California Press, 1930–42.

Ibn Taghrībirdī, Jamāl al-Dīn Yūsuf, *Al-Nujūm al-zāhira fī mulūk Miṣr wa-l-Qāhira*, 16 vols, ed. Ibrāhīm ʿAlī Ṭarkhān, Cairo, 1963–74.

Ibn Taghrībirdī, Jamāl al-Dīn Yūsuf, *Al-Manhal al-ṣāfī wa-l-mustawfī baʿda al-wāfī*, 12 vols, ed. Muḥammad Muḥammad Amīn et al., Cairo: al-Hayʾa al-Miṣriyya al-ʿĀmma li-l-Kitāb, 1984–2006.

Ibn Taghrībirdī, Jamāl al-Dīn Yūsuf, *Mawrid al-laṭāfa fī man waliya al-salṭana wa-l-khilāfa*, 2 vols, ed. Nabīl Aḥmad, Cairo: Dār al-Kutub wa-l-Wathāʾiq al-Qawmiyya, Markaz Taḥqīq al-Turāth, 1997.

Ibn Taghrībirdī, Jamāl al-Dīn Yūsuf, *Al-Dalīl al-shāfī ʿalā al-Manhal al-ṣāfī*, 2 vols, ed. Fahīm Shaltūt, Cairo, 1998.

Ibn Ṭūlūn, Muḥammad, *Mufākahat al-khillān fī ḥawādith al-zamān*, 2 vols, Damascus: Dār al-Awā'il, 2002.

Ibn al-Wardī, ʿUmar, *Tatimmat al-Mukhtaṣar fī akhbār al-bashar*, 2 vols, ed. Muḥammad al-Khurāsānī as *Taʾrīkh Ibn al-Wardī*, Najaf, 1969.

Ibn Wāṣil, Jamāl al-Dīn Muḥammad, *Mufarrij al-kurūb fī ākhbār Banī Ayyūb*, ed. ʿUmar Tadmurī, Beirut: al-Maktaba al-ʿAṣriyya, 2004, vol. 6.

al-Jabartī, ʿAbd al-Raḥmān, *Taʾrīkh ʿajāʾib al-āthār fī al-tarājim wa-l-akhbār al-maʿrūf*, 3 vols, Beirut: Dār al-Kutub al-ʿIlmiyya, 1997.

al-Jazarī, Muḥammad, *Taʾrīkh ḥawādith al-zamān wa-anbāʾihi wa-wafayāt al-akābir wa-l-aʿyān min abnāʾihi*, 3 vols, ed. ʿUmar Tadmurī, Sidon: al-Maktaba al-ʿAṣriyya, 1998.

Khunjī-Iṣfahānī, Faḍlullāh b. Rūzbihān, *Sulūk al-mulūk*, Tehran: Intishārāt-i Khvārazmī, 1984.

Khunjī-Iṣfahānī, Faḍlullāh b. Rūzbihān, *Taʾrīkh-i ʿālam- ārā-yi amīnī*, ed. John E. Woods, London: Royal Asiatic Society, 1992.

al-Kutubī, Muḥammad, *ʿUyūn al-tawārīkh*, ed. Fayṣal al-Sāmir and Nabīla ʿAbd al-Munʿim Dāwūd, Baghdad, 1980, vol. 20

[al-Malaṭī], ʿAbd al-Bāsiṭ ibn Khalīl, *Nayl al-amal fī dhayl al-duwal*, 9 vols, ed. ʿUmar Tadmurī, Beirut: al-Maktaba al-ʿAṣriyya, 2002.

[al-Malaṭī], ʿAbd al-Bāsiṭ ibn Khalīl, *Kitāb al-Rawḍ al-bāsim fī ḥawādith al-ʿumr wa-l-tarājim*, 4 vols, ed. ʿUmar Tadmurī, Beirut: al-Maktaba al-ʿAṣriyya, 2014.

al-Maqrīzī, Aḥmad ibn ʿAlī, *Histoire d'Égypte de Makrizi*, trans. Edgar Blochet, Paris: E. Leroux, 1908.

al-Maqrīzī, Aḥmad ibn ʿAlī, *Kitāb al-Sulūk li-maʿrifat duwal al-mulūk*, 4 vols, eds Muḥammad Muṣṭafā Ziyāda and Saʿīd ʿAshūr, Cairo, 1934–73.

al-Maqrīzī, Aḥmad ibn ʿAlī, *Kitāb al-Nizāʿ wa-l-takhāṣum fī-mā bayna Banī Umayya wa-Banī Hāshim*, Cairo: Dār al-Maʿārif, 1988.

al-Maqrīzī, Aḥmad ibn ʿAlī, *Kitāb al-Mawāʿiẓ wa-l-iʿtibār fī dhikr al-khiṭaṭ wa-l-āthār*, 5 vols, ed. Ayman Fuʾād Sayyid, London: al-Furqān Islamic Heritage Foundation, 2002.

al-Maqrīzī, Aḥmad ibn ʿAlī, *Durar al-ʿuqūd al-farīda fī tarājim al-aʿyān al-mufīda*, 4 vols, ed. Maḥmūd al-Jalīlī, Beirut: Dār al-Gharb al-Islāmī, 2002.

al-Maqrīzī, Aḥmad ibn ʿAlī, *Kitāb al-Muqaffā al-kabīr*, 8 vols, ed. Muḥammad al-Yaʿlāwī, Beirut: Dār al-Gharb al-Islāmī, 2006.

Marʿī ibn Yūsuf Karmī, *Nuzhat al-nāẓirīn fī taʾrīkh man waliya Miṣr min al-khulafāʾ wa-l-salāṭīn*, ed. ʿAbd Allāh al-Kandarī, Damascus: Dār al-Nawādir, 2012.

al-Māwardī, ʿAlī, *Al-Aḥkām al-sulṭāniyya wa-l-wilāyāt al-dīniyya*, Beirut: Dār al-Kutub al-ʿIlmiyya, 2006.

Mufaḍḍal ibn Abī al-Faḍāʾil, *Kitāb al-Nahj al-sadīd wa-l-durr al-farīd fī-mā baʿda taʾrīkh Ibn al-Amīd*, ed. and trans. Edgar Blochet, *Patrologia Orientalis* 12; 14; 20, issued as one volume, Paris, 1911, 1920, 1932.

Mufaḍḍal ibn Abī al-Faḍāʾil, *Ägypten und Syrien zwischen 1317 und 1341 in der Chronik des Mufaḍḍal Ibn Abī al-Faḍāʾil*, ed. and trans. Samira Kortantamer, Freiburg im Breisgau: K. Schwarz, 1973.

al-Nahrawālī, Quṭb al-Dīn, *Die Chroniken der Stadt Mekka*, 4 vols, ed. Ferdinand Wüstenfeld, Leipzig, 1857–61.

al-Nuwayrī, Shihāb al-Dīn Aḥmad, *Nihāyat al-arab fī funūn al-adab*, 31 vols, ed. Saʿīd ʿAshūr, Cairo, 1985–92.

al-Nuwayrī, Shihāb al-Dīn Aḥmad, *Nihāyat al-arab fī funūn al-adab*, ed. Fahīm Shaltūt, Cairo, 1998, vol. 32.

Piloti, Emmanuel, *L'Égypte au commencement du quinzième siècle d'après le traité d'Emmanuel Piloti de Crète, incipit 1420*, ed. Pierre-Herman Dopp, Cairo, 1950.

al-Qalqashandī, Abū al-ʿAbbās Aḥmad, *Ṣubh al-aʿshā fī ṣināʿat al-inshāʾ*, 14 vols, Cairo: al-Muʾassasa al-Miṣriyya al-ʿĀmma lil- Taʾlīf wa-l-Tarjama wa-l-Ṭibāʿa wa-l-Nashr, 1963.

al-Qalqashandī, Abū al-ʿAbbās Aḥmad, *Maʾāthir al-ināfa fī maʿālim al-khilāfa*, 3 vols, ed. ʿAbd al-Sattār Farrāj, Kuwait, 1964.

al-Qarāfī, Shihāb al-Dīn Aḥmad, *Al-Iḥkām fī tamyīz al-fatāwā ʿan al-aḥkām wa-taṣarrufāt al-qāḍī wa-l-imām*, ed. Abū Bakr ʿAbd al-Razzāq, Cairo: al-Maktab al-Thaqāfī lil-Nashr wa-l-Tawzīʿ, 1989.

al-Qarāfī, Shihāb al-Dīn Aḥmad, *The Criterion for Distinguishing Legal Opinions from Judicial Rulings and the Administrative Acts of Judges and Rulers = Al-Iḥkām fī tamyīz al-fatāwā ʿan al-aḥkām wa-taṣarrufāt al-qāḍī waʾl-imām*, ed. and trans. Mohammad Fadel, New Haven, CT: Yale University Press, 2017.

al-Qaramānī, Aḥmad ibn Yūsuf, *Akhbār al-duwal wa-athār al-uwal fī al-taʾrīkh*, 3 vols, eds Fahmī Saʿd and Aḥmad Ḥuṭayṭ, Beirut: ʿĀlam al-Kutub, 1992.

al-Ṣafadī, Khalīl ibn Aybak, *Al-Wāfī bi-l-wafayāt*, 30 vols, ed. Hellmut Ritter et al., Wiesbaden, 1962–2004.

al-Ṣafadī, Khalīl ibn Aybak, *Aʿyān al-ʿaṣr wa-aʿwān al-naṣr*, 6 vols, ed. ʿAlī Abū Zayd et al., Beirut, 1998.

al-Saḥmāwī, Muḥammad, *Al-Thaghr al-bāsim fī ṣināʿat al-kātib wa-l-kātim*, 2 vols, ed. Ashraf Muḥammad Anas, Cairo: Maṭbaʿat Dār al-Kutub, 2013.

al-Sakhāwī, Muḥammad ibn ʿAbd al-Raḥmān, *Al-Ḍawʾ al-lāmiʿ li-ahl al-qarn al-tāsiʿ*, 12 vols, Cairo: Maktabat al-Qudsī, 1934–6.

al-Sakhāwī, Muḥammad ibn ʿAbd al-Raḥmān, *Al-Tibr al-masbūk fī dhayl al-sulūk*, ed. Aḥmad Zakī, Cairo: Maktabat al-Kulliyyāt al-Azhariyya, 1972.

al-Sakhāwī, Muḥammad ibn ʿAbd al-Raḥmān, *Al-Dhayl al-tāmm ʿalā duwal al-Islām li-l-Dhahabī*, 3 vols, ed. Ḥasan Marwa, Kuwait: Maktabat Dār al-ʿUrūba, 1992.

al-Sakhāwī, Muḥammad ibn ʿAbd al-Raḥmān, *Wajīz al-kalām fī al-dhayl ʿalā duwal al-Islām*, 3 vols, ed. Bashshār ʿAwwād Maʿrūf et al, Beirut: Muʾassasat al-Risāla, 1995.

al-Sakhāwī, Muḥammad ibn ʿAbd al-Raḥmān, *Jawāhir wa-l-durar fī tarjamat Shaykh al-Islām Ibn Ḥajar*, 3 vols, ed. Ibrāhīm ʿAbd al-Majīd, Beirut: Dār Ibn Ḥazm, 1999.

[al-Ṣayrafī] Khaṭīb al-Jawharī, ʿAlī, *Inbāʾ al-haṣr bi-abnāʾ al-ʿaṣr*, Cairo: Dār al-Fikr al-ʿArabī, 1970.

[al-Ṣayrafī] Khaṭīb al-Jawharī, ʿAlī, *Nuzhat al-nufūs wa-l-abdān fī tawārīkh al-zamān*, 4 vols, ed. Ḥasan Ḥabashī, Cairo: Wizārat al-thaqāfa, Markaz Taḥqīq al-Turāth, 1970–94.

al-Shādhilī, ʿAbd al-Qādir, *Bahjat al-ʿābidīn bi-tarjamat Ḥāfiẓ al-ʿAṣr Jalāl al-Dīn al-Suyūṭī*, ed. ʿAbdallāh Nabhān, Damascus: Majmaʿ al-Lugha al-ʿArabiyya bi-Dimashq, 1998.

Shāfiʿ ibn ʿAlī, Nāṣir al-Dīn [*Sīrat al-Malik al-Nāṣir*], Paris: Bibliothèque nationale de France, Arabe, 1705.

Shāfiʿ ibn ʿAlī, Nāṣir al-Dīn, *Kitāb Ḥusn al-manāqib al-sirriyya al-muntazaʿa min al-sīra al-Ẓāhiriyya*, ed. ʿAbd al-ʿAzīz Khuwayṭir, Riyadh, 1976.

Shāfiʿ ibn ʿAlī, Nāṣir al-Dīn, *Al-Faḍl al-maʾthūr min sīrat al-Malik al-Manṣūr*, ed. ʿAbd al-Salām Tadmurī, Beirut: al-Maktaba al-ʿAṣriyya, 1998.

al-Shujāʿī, Shams al-Dīn, *Taʾrīkh al-Malik al-Nāṣir Muḥammad b. Qalāwūn al-Ṣāliḥī wa-awlādihi*, ed. Barbara Schäfer, Wiesbaden, 1977.

al-Subkī, ʿAbd al-Wahhāb, *Muʿīd al-niʿam wa-mubīd al-niqam*, ed. Ṣalāḥ al-Dīn al-Hawwārī, Sidon: al-Maktaba al-ʿAṣriyya, 2007.

al-Suyūṭī, Jalāl al-Dīn ʿAbd al-Raḥmān, *Taʾrīkh al-khulafāʾ*, Beirut: Dār al-Kutub al-ʿIlmiyya, (n.d.).

al-Suyūṭī, Jalāl al-Dīn ʿAbd al-Raḥmān, *Ḥusn al-muḥāḍara fī akhbār Miṣr wa-l-Qāhira*, 2 vols, ed. Muḥammad Abū al-Faḍl Ibrāhīm, Cairo: ʿIsā al-Babī al-Ḥalabī, 1967–8.

al-Suyūṭī, Jalāl al-Dīn ʿAbd al-Raḥmān, *Al-Taḥadduth bi-niʿmat Allāh*, ed. Elizabeth Sartain, Cambridge: University of Cambridge, 1975.

al-Suyūṭī, Jalāl al-Dīn ʿAbd al-Raḥmān, *Rafʿ al-bās ʿan Banī al-ʿAbbās*, Tunis: Dār al-Gharb al-Islāmī, 2011.

al-Ṭūsī, Nāṣir al-Dīn, *Nasirean Ethics*, trans. George Wickens, London: Allen & Unwin, 1964.

al-ʿUmarī, Ibn Faḍlallāh, *Al-Taʿrīf bi-l-muṣṭalaḥ al-sharīf*, 2 vols, ed. Samir al-Droubi, Karak: Muʾtah University, 1992.

al-ʿUmarī, Ibn Faḍlallāh, *Masālik al-abṣār fī mamālik al-amṣār*, 15 vols, ed. Kāmil Salmān al-Jubūrī, Beirut: Dār al-Kutub al-ʿIlmiyya, 2010.

al-Yūnīnī, Mūsā ibn Muḥammad, *Dhayl mirʾāt al-zamān*, 4 vols, Hyderabad: Dar al-Maʿārif al-ʿUthmāniyya, 1955–61.

al-Yūsufī, Mūsā, *Nuzhat al-nāẓir fī sīrat al-Malik al-Nāṣir*, ed. Aḥmad Huṭayṭ, Beirut: ʿĀlam al-Kutub, 1986.

al-Ẓahirī, Khalīl ibn Shāhīn, *Kitāb Zubdat kashf al-mamālik wa-bayān al-ṭuruq wa-l-masālik*, ed. Paul Ravaisse, Cairo: Dār al-ʿArab, 1988.

Modern Research

ʿAbd ar-Rāziq, Aḥmad, *La femme au temps des Mamelouks en Égypte*, Cairo: Institut français d'archéologie orientale, 1973.

Adriaenssens, Veerle and Jo Van Steenbergen, 'Mamluk Authorities and Anatolian Realities: Jānibak al-Ṣūfī, Sultan al-Ashraf Barsbāy, and the Story of a Social Network in the Mamluk/Anatolian Frontier Zone, 1435–1438', *Journal of the Royal Asiatic Society* (2016): 1–40.

Aigle, Denise, 'Les inscriptions de Baybars dans le Bilād al-Šām. Une expression de la légitimité du pouvoir', *Studia Islamica* 97 (2003): 57–85.

Aigle, Denise, *The Mongol Empire between Myth and Reality: Studies in Anthropological History*, Leiden: Brill, 2014.

Al-Azmeh, Aziz, *Muslim Kingship: Power and the Sacred in Muslim, Christian and Pagan Polities*, London: I. B. Tauris, 1997.

Alexander, David, 'Dhu'l-Faqār and the Legacy of the Prophet, Mīrāth Rasūl Allāh', *Gladius* 19 (1999): 157–87.

Alexander, David, 'Swords from Ottoman and Mamluk Treasuries', *Artibus Asiae* 66(2) (2006): 14–29.

Allouche, Adel, 'Tegüder's Ultimatum to Qalawun', *International Journal of Middle East Studies* 22 (1990): 437–46.

Amīn, Muḥammad, *Awqāf wa-l-ḥayāt al-ijtimāʿiyya fī Miṣr, 648–923/1250–1517: dirāsa tārīkhiyya wathāʾiqiyya*, Cairo: Dār al-Nahḍa al-ʿArabiyya, 1980.

Amīn, Muḥammad, *Fihrist wathā'iq al-Qāhira ḥattā nihāyat 'aṣr salāṭīn al-Mamālīk (239–922/853–1516) ma'a nashr wa-taḥqīq tis'at namādhij*, Cairo: al-Ma'had al-'Ilmī al-Faransī lil-Āthār al-Sharqiyya, 1981.

Amitai, Reuven, 'The Conversion of Tegüder Ilkhan to Islam', *Jerusalem Studies in Arabic and Islam* 25 (2001): 15–43.

Amitai, Reuven, 'Whither the Ilkhanid Army? Ghazan's First Campaign into Syria (1299–1300)', in Nicola Di Cosmo (ed.), *Warfare in Inner Asian History (500–1800)*, Leiden: Brill, 2002, 221–64.

Amitai, Reuven, 'The Mongol Occupation of Damascus in 1300: a Study of Mamluk Loyalties', in Michael Winter and Amalia Levanoni (eds), *The Mamluks in Egyptian and Syrian Politics and Society*, Leiden: Brill, 2004, 21–41.

Amitai, Reuven, 'Some Remarks on the Inscription of Baybars at Maqam Nabi Musa', in David Wasserstein and Ami Ayalon (eds), *Mamluks and Ottomans: Studies in Honour of Michael Winter*, New York: Routledge, 2006, 45–53.

Amitai, Reuven, *Holy War and Rapprochement: Studies in the Relations between the Mamluk Sultanate and the Mongol Ilkhanate (1260–1335)*, Turnhout: Brepols, 2013.

Amitai-Preiss, Reuven, *Mongols and Mamluks: the Mamluk–Ilkhanid War, 1260–1281*, Cambridge: Cambridge University Press, 1995.

Amitai-Preiss, Reuven, 'The Fall and Rise of the 'Abbāsid Caliphate', *Journal of the American Oriental Society* 116 (1996): 487–94.

Amitai-Preiss, Reuven, 'Mongol Imperial Ideology and the Ilkhanid War against the Mamluks', in Reuven Amitai-Preiss and David O. Morgan (eds), *The Mongol Empire and its Legacy*, Leiden: Brill, 1999, 57–72.

Anjum, Ovamir, *Politics, Law and Community in Islamic Thought: the Taymiyyan Moment*, Cambridge: Cambridge University Press, 2012.

Anjum, Ovamir, 'Ibn Jamā'ah, Badr al-Dīn', in Emad El-Din Shahin (ed.), *Oxford Encyclopedia of Islam and Politics*, New York: Oxford University Press, 2014.

Arjomand, Saïd Amir, 'Legitimacy and Political Organisation: Caliphs, Kings and Regimes', in Robert Irwin (ed.), *The New Cambridge History of Islam*, Cambridge: Cambridge University Press, 2010, 225–73.

Arnold, Thomas, *The Caliphate*, London: Routledge & Kegan Paul, 1965.

Ashtor, Eliyahu, 'Baybars al-Manṣūrī', in P. J. Bearman et al. (eds), *Encyclopaedia of Islam*, 2nd edn, Leiden: Brill, 1960–2007.

Asrar, N. A., 'The Myth about the Transfer of the Caliphate to the Ottomans', *Journal of the Regional Cultural Institute* 5(2/3) (1972): 111–20.

Auer, Blain, *Symbols of Authority in Medieval Islam: History, Religion and Muslim Legitimacy in the Delhi Sultanate*, London: I. B. Tauris, 2012.

Ayalon, David, 'Studies on the Transfer of the ʿAbbasid Caliphate from Baghdad to Cairo', *Arabica* 7 (1960): 41–59.

Ayalon, David, 'Mamlūkīyyat: (A) A First Attempt to Evaluate the Mamlūk Military System; (B) Ibn Khaldūn's View of the Mamlūk Phenomenon', *Jerusalem Studies in Arabic and Islam* 2 (1980): 321–49.

Ayalon, David, 'The Mamlūks and Ibn Xaldūn', *Israel Oriental Studies* 10 (1980): 11–13.

Balog, Paul, *The Coinage of the Mamluk Sultans of Egypt and Syria*, New York: American Numismatic Society, 1964.

Balog, Paul, 'A Dirhem of Al-Kāmil Shams Al-Dīn Sunqur, Rebel Sulṭān of Syria, Hitherto Unrecorded in Numismatics (679 H. = 1280 A.D.)', *Revue numismatique* (6th series) 11 (1969): 296–9.

Banister, Mustafa, '"Naught Remains to the Caliph but his Title": Revisiting Abbasid Authority in Mamluk Cairo', *Mamlūk Studies Review* 18 (2014/15): 219–45.

Banister, Mustafa, 'A Sword in the Caliph's Service: On the Caliphal Office in Late Fourteenth-Century Mamluk Sources', Annemarie Schimmel Kolleg Working Paper 27, Bonn: Annemarie Schimmel Kolleg, January 2017.

Banister, Mustafa, 'Casting the Caliph in a Cosmic Role: Examining al-Suyūṭī's Historical Vision', in Antonella Ghersetti (ed.), *Al-Suyūṭī: a Polymath of the Mamluk Period*, Leiden: Brill, 2017, 98–117.

Banister, Mustafa, 'The *ʿĀlim*-Caliph: Reimagining the Caliph as a Man of Learning in Fourteenth- and Fifteenth-Century Egypt', in Sebastian Günther (ed.), *Knowledge and Education in Classical Islam: Religious Learning between Continuity and Change*, Leiden: Brill, 2020, 741–67.

Banister, Mustafa, 'Princesses born to Concubines: a First Visit to the Women of the Abbasid Household in Late Medieval Cairo', *Hawwa: Journal of Women of the Middle East and the Islamic World* (2020): 1–35.

Barthold, Wilhelm, 'Caliph and Sultan', trans. N. S. Doniach, *Islamic Quarterly* 7 (1963): 117–35.

Al-Bāshā, Ḥasan, *Al-Alqāb al-Islāmiyya fī al-taʾrīkh wa-l-wathāʾiq wa-l-athār*, Cairo, 1957.

Bauden, Frédéric, 'Mamluk Era Documentary Studies: the State of the Art', *Mamlūk Studies Review* 9(1) (2005): 15–60.

Bauden, Frédéric, 'The Sons of al-Nāṣir Muḥammad and the Politics of Puppets: Where Did It All Start?' *Mamlūk Studies Review* 13(1) (2009): 53–81.

Bauden, Frédéric, 'Al-Maqrīzī, Taqī l-Dīn Abū l-'Abbās Aḥmad ibn 'Alī ibn 'Abd al-Qādir', in David Thomas and Alex Mallett (eds), *Christian–Muslim Relations: a Biographical History, vol. 5: 1350–1500*, Leiden: Brill, 2013, 380–95.

Bauer, Thomas, 'Mamluk Literature: Misunderstandings and New Approaches', *Mamlūk Studies Review* 9(2) (2005): 105–32.

Bauer, Thomas, 'Mamluk Literature as a Means of Communication', in Stephan Conermann (ed.), *Ubi Sumus? Quo Vademus? Mamluk Studies – The State of the Art*, Göttingen: V&R Unipress, 2013, 23–56.

Becker, Carl, 'Barthold's Studien über Kalif und Sultan', *Der Islam* 6 (1916): 350–412.

Behrens-Abouseif, Doris, 'The Citadel of Cairo: Stage for Mamluk Ceremonial', *Annales islamologiques* 24 (1988): 25–79.

Behrens-Abouseif, Doris, *Cairo of the Mamluks: a History of the Architecture and its Culture*, London: I. B. Tauris, 2007.

Behrens-Abouseif, Doris, *Practising Diplomacy in the Mamluk Sultanate: Gifts and Material Culture in the Medieval Islamic World*, London: I. B. Tauris, 2014.

Berkey, Jonathan, *The Transmission of Knowledge in Medieval Cairo: a Social History of Islamic Education*, Princeton: Princeton University Press, 1992.

Berkey, Jonathan, 'Culture and Society during the Late Middle Ages', in Carl Petry (ed.), *The Cambridge History of Egypt*, Cambridge: Cambridge University Press, 1998, 375–411.

Berkey, Jonathan, 'The Mamluks as Muslims: the Military Elite and the Construction of Islam in Medieval Egypt', in Thomas Philipp and Ulrich Haarmann (eds), *The Mamluks in Egyptian Politics and Society*, Cambridge: Cambridge University Press, 1998, 163–73.

Berkey, Jonathan, *Popular Preaching and Religious Authority in the Medieval Islamic Near East*, Seattle, WA: University of Washington Press, 2001.

Berkey, Jonathan, *The Formation of Islam: Religion and Society in the Near East, 600–1800*, Cambridge: Cambridge University Press, 2003.

Berkey, Jonathan, 'Mamluk Religious Policy', *Mamlūk Studies Review* 13(2) (2009): 7–22.

Binbaş, İlker Evrim, *Intellectual Networks in Timurid Iran: Sharaf al-Dīn 'Alī Yazdī and the Islamicate Republic of Letters*, Cambridge: Cambridge University Press, 2016.

Björkman, Walther, 'Diplomatic', in P. J. Bearman et al. (eds), *Encyclopaedia of Islam*, 2nd edn, Leiden: Brill, 1960–2007.

Bori, Caterina, 'Il pensiero politico sunnita nel Medioevo. La questione del califfato:

al-Mawardi (m. 1058) e Ibn Taymiyya (m. 1328)', in Massimo Campanini (ed.), *Storia del pensiero politico islamico: Dal profeta Muhammad a oggi*, Firenze: Le Monnier Università, 2017, 47–67.

Bori, Caterina, 'Théologie politique et Islam à propos d'Ibn Taymiyya (m. 728/1328) et du sultanat mamelouk', *Revue de l'histoire des religions* 1 (2007): 5–46.

Bori, Caterina, 'Theology, Politics, Society: the Missing Link. Studying Religion in the Mamluk Period', in Stephan Conermann (ed.), *Ubi Sumus? Quo Vademus? Mamluk Studies – State of the Art*, Göttingen: V&R Unipress, 2013, 57–94.

Bosworth, Clifford, 'al-Ḳalḳas̲h̲andī', in P. J. Bearman et al. (eds), *Encyclopaedia of Islam*, 2nd edn, Leiden: Brill, 1960–2007.

Bosworth, Clifford, 'Al-Maqrīzī's Exposition of the Formative Period in Islamic History and its Cosmic Significance: the *Kitāb al-Nizāʿ wa-t-takhāṣum*', in Alford Welch and Pierre Cachia (eds), *Islam: Past Influence and Present Challenge: In Honour of William Montgomery Watt*, Edinburgh: Edinburgh University Press, 1979, 93–104.

Bosworth, Clifford, *Al-Maqrīzī's 'Book of Contention and Strife Concerning the Relations between the Banū Umayyah and the Banụ̄ Hāshim'*, Manchester: University of Manchester, 1980.

Bosworth, Clifford, 'Al-Maqrīzī's Epistle "Concerning What Has Come Down to Us about the Banū Umayya and the Banū l-ʿAbbās"', in Widād al-Qāḍī (ed.), *Studia Arabica et Islamica, Festschrift for Ihsan ʿAbbās on His Sixtieth Birthday*, Beirut, 1981, 39–46.

Bosworth, Clifford, *The New Islamic Dynasties: a Chronological and Genealogical Manual*, Edinburgh: Edinburgh University Press, 1996.

Bourdieu, Pierre, *Distinction: a Social Critique of the Judgment of Taste*, trans. Richard Nice, Cambridge, MA: Harvard University Press, 1984.

Bourdieu, Pierre, 'Rethinking the State: Genesis and Structure of the Bureaucratic Field', *Sociological Theory* 12(1) (1994): 1–18.

Boyle, John, 'Dynastic and Political History of the Il-K̲h̲āns', in John Boyle (ed.), *The Cambridge History of Iran*, Cambridge: Cambridge University Press, 1968, 303–421.

Brinner, William, 'The Struggle for Power in the Mamluk State: Some Reflections on the Transition from Bahri to Burji Rule', in *Proceedings of the 26th International Congress of Orientalists, New Delhi, 4–10 January 1964*, New Delhi, 1970, 231–4.

Broadbridge, Anne, 'Mamluk Legitimacy and the Mongols: the Reign of Baybars and Qalāwūn', *Mamlūk Studies Review* 5 (2001): 91–118.

Broadbridge, Anne, 'Diplomatic Conventions in the Mamluk Sultanate', *Annales islamologiques* 41 (2007): 97–118.

Broadbridge, Anne, *Kingship and Ideology in the Islamic and Mongol Worlds*, Cambridge: Cambridge University Press, 2008.

Broadbridge, Anne, 'Sending Home for Mom and Dad: the Extended Family Impulse in Mamluk Politics', *Mamlūk Studies Review* 15 (2011): 1–18.

Bulliet, Richard, 'The History of the Muslim South', *Al-ʿUsur al-Wusta: The Bulletin of Middle East Medievalists* 20(2) (2008): 59–64.

Bulliet, Richard, 'Neo-Mamluk Legitimacy and the Arab Spring', *Middle East Law and Governance* 3(1/2) (2011): 60–7.

Cahen, Claude, 'Futuwwa', in P. J. Bearman et al. (eds), *Encyclopaedia of Islam*, 2nd edn, Leiden: Brill, 1960–2007.

Casale, Giancarlo, 'Tordesillas and the Ottoman Caliphate: Early Modern Frontiers and the Renaissance of an Ancient Islamic Institution', *Journal of Early Modern History* 19 (2015): 485–511.

Chamberlain, Michael, *Knowledge and Social Practice in Medieval Damascus, 1190–1350*, Cambridge: Cambridge University Press, 1994.

Chapoutot-Remadi, Mounira, 'Une institution mal connue: le Khalifat abbaside du Caire', *Cahiers de Tunisie* 20 (1972): 11–23.

Chapoutot-Remadi, Mounira, 'Les relations entre l'Égypte et l'Ifriqya aux XIIIe et XIVe siècle d'après les autres Mamlûks', in *Actes du premier congrès d'histoire et de la civilisation du Maghreb*, vol. 1, 139–59. Tunis, December 1974; Tunis: Université de Tunis, Centre d'études et de recherches économiques et sociales, 1979.

Chapoutot-Remadi, Rachida [Mounira], 'Liens et Relations au sein de l'Élite Mamluke sous les Premiers Sultans Bahrides, 648/1250–741/1341', PhD dissertation, Université de Provence, Aix-Marseille, 1993.

Cheddadi, Abdesselam, *Ibn Khaldûn: l'homme et le théoricien de la civilization*, Paris: Gallimard, 2006.

Clifford, Winslow, '*Ubi Sumus*? Mamluk History and Social Theory', *Mamlūk Studies Review* 1 (1997): 45–62.

Clifford, Winslow, *State Formation and the Structure of Politics in Mamluk Syro-Egypt, 648–741 A.H./1250–1340 C.E.*, ed. Stephan Conermann, Göttingen: V&R Unipress, 2013.

Cobb, Paul, 'Al-Maqrīzī, Hashimism, and the Early Caliphates', *Mamlūk Studies Review* 7(2) (2003): 69–81.

Combe, Etienne et al. (eds), *Répertoire chronologique d'èpigraphie arabe*, 18 vols, Cairo: Institut Français d'Archéologie Orientale, 1931–91.

Conermann, Stephan and Anna Kollatz, 'Some Remarks on the Diplomatic Relations between Cairo, Delhi/Dawlatābād, and Aḥmadābād during the Eighth/Fourteenth and Ninth/Fifteenth Centuries', in Frédéric Bauden and Malika Dekkiche (eds), *Mamluk Cairo, a Crossroads for Embassies: Studies on Diplomacy and Diplomatics*, Leiden: Brill, 2019, 621–37.

Crone, Patricia, *God's Rule: Government and Islam: Six Centuries of Medieval Islamic Political Thought*, New York: Columbia University Press, 2004.

Crone, Patricia and Martin Hinds, *God's Caliph: Religious Authority in the First Centuries of Islam*, Cambridge: Cambridge University Press, 1986.

Ḍāḥī, Fāḍil Jābir and Asrā' Mahdī Mizbān, *Al-Ra'y al-'āmm fī 'aṣr al-Mamālīk*, Damascus, 2011.

De Fouchécour, Charles-Henri, *Moralia: les notions morales dans la litterature persane du 3e/9e au 7e/13e siècle*, Paris: Éditions recherches sur les civilisations, 1986.

De Polignac, François, 'Un "nouvel Alexandre" mamelouk, al-Malik al-Ashraf Khalîl et le regain eschatologique du XIIIe siècle', *Revue des mondes musulmans et de la Mediterranée* 89/90 (2000): 73–87.

De Rachewiltz, Igor, 'Some Remarks on the Ideological Foundations of Chingis Khan's Empire', *Papers on Far Eastern History* 7 (1973): 21–36.

Dekkiche, Malika, 'New Source, New Debate: Reevaluation of the Mamluk–Timurid Struggle for Religious Supremacy in the Hijaz (Paris, BnF ms ar. 4440)', *Mamlūk Studies Review* 18 (2014/15): 247–71.

DeWeese, Devin, *Islamization and Native Religion in the Golden Horde: Baba Tükles and Conversion to Islam in Historical and Epic Tradition*, University Park, PA: University of Pennsylvania Press, 1994.

Dewière, Rémi, 'Peace Be upon Those Who Follow the Right Way: Diplomatic Practices between Mamluk Cairo and the Borno Sultanate at the End of the Eighth/Fourteenth Century', in Frédéric Bauden and Malika Dekkiche (eds), *Mamluk Cairo, A Crossroads for Embassies: Studies on Diplomacy and Diplomatics*, Leiden: Brill, 2019, 658–82.

Eddé, Anne-Marie, 'Baybars et son double: de l'ambiguïté du souverain ideal', in Denise Aigle (ed.), *Le Bilad Al-Šam face aux mondes extérieurs. La perception de l'autre et la représentation du souverain*, Damascus/Beirut: Presses de L'Ifpo, 2012, 73–86.

Elbendary, Amina, 'The Sultan, the Tyrant, and the Hero: Changing Medieval Perceptions of al-Ẓāhir Baybars', *Mamlūk Studies Review* 5 (2001): 141–57.

Elbendary, Amina, *Crowds and Sultans: Urban Protest in Late Medieval Egypt and Syria*, Cairo: American University in Cairo Press, 2015.

Eychenne, Mathieu, *Liens personnels, clientélisme et réseaux de pouvoir dans le sultanat mamelouk (milieu XIII–fin XIV siècle)*, Damascus-Beirut: Presses de l'ifpo, 2013.

Fahd, Toufic, 'Istikhāra', in P. J. Bearman et al. (eds), *Encyclopaedia of Islam*, 2nd edn, Leiden: Brill, 1960–2007.

Fancy, Nahyan, *Science and Religion in Mamluk Egypt: Ibn al-Nafis, Pulmonary Transit and Bodily Resurrection*, London: Routledge, 2013.

Favreau, Marie, 'The Golden Horde and the Mamluks: Birth of a Diplomatic Set-Up (660–5/1261–7)', in Frédéric Bauden and Malika Dekkiche (eds), *Mamluk Cairo: a Crossroads for Embassies: Studies on Diplomacy and Diplomatics*, Leiden: Brill, 2019, 302–26.

Finkel, Caroline, *Osman's Dream: the Story of the Ottoman Empire, 1300–1923*, London: John Murray, 2005.

Fischel, Walter, *Ibn Khaldūn in Egypt*, Berkeley: University of California Press, 1967.

Flinterman, Willem and Jo Van Steenbergen, 'Al-Nasir Muhammad and the Formation of the Qalawunid State', in Amy Landau (ed.), *Pearls on a String: Art in the Age of Great Islamic Empires*, Baltimore, MD and Seattle, WA: Walters Art Museum and University of Washington Press, 2015, 101–27.

Franz, Kurt, 'The Castle and the Country: Spatial Orientations of Qipchaq Mamluk Rule', in David Durand-Guédy *(ed.), Turko-Mongol Rulers, Cities and City-Life in Iran*, Leiden: Brill, 2013, 349–84.

Franz, Kurt, 'Bedouin and States: Framing the Mongol–Mamlūk Wars in Long-term History', in Kurt Franz and Wolfgang Holzwarth *(eds), Nomad Military Power in Iran and Adjacent Areas in the Islamic Period*, Wiesbaden: Reichert, 2015, 29–105.

Frenkel, Yehoshua, 'The Mamluks among the Nations: a Medieval Sultanate in its Global Context', in Stephan Conermann (ed.), *Everything is on the Move: the 'Mamluk Empire' as a Node in (Trans-)Regional Networks*, Göttingen: V&R Unipress, 2014, 61–79.

Fuess, Albrecht, 'Sultans with Horns: the Political Significance of Headgear in the Mamluk Empire', *Mamlūk Studies Review* 12(2) (2008): 71–94.

Fuess, Albrecht, 'Mamluk Politics', in Stephan Conermann (ed.), *Ubi Sumus? Quo Vademus? Mamluk Studies – State of the Art*, Göttingen: V&R Unipress, 2013, 95–117.

Garcin, Jean-Claude, 'Histoire, opposition politique et piétisme traditionaliste dans le *Ḥusn al-muḥāḍara* de Suyūṭī', *Annales islamologiques* 7 (1967): 33–89.

Garcin, Jean-Claude, *Un centre musulman de la Haute-Égypte médiévale: Qūṣ*, Cairo: Institut français d'archéologie orientale du Caire, 1976.

Garcin, Jean-Claude, 'The Regime of the Circassian Mamlūks', in Carl Petry (ed.), *The Cambridge History of Egypt*, Cambridge: Cambridge University Press, 1998, 290–317.

Gaudefroy-Demombynes, Maurice, *La Syrie à l'époque des mamelouks d'après les auteurs arabes: description géographique, économique et administrative précédée d'une introduction sur l'organisation gouvernementale*, Paris: P. Geuthner, 1923.

Gharaibeh, Mohammad, 'Geschichtsschreibung im Dienste des ʿabbāsidischen Kalifats: Das al-Bidāya wa-n-nihāya des Ibn Kaṯīr (1301–1373) – ein geschichtstheologisches Werk', *Jahrbuch für Islamische Theologie und Religionspädagogik* 3 (2014): 95–124.

Gibb, Hamilton, 'The Islamic Background of Ibn Khaldūn's Political Theory', *Bulletin of the School of Oriental and African Studies* 7(1) (1933): 23–31.

Gibb, Hamilton, 'Constitutional Organization', in Majid Khadduri and Herbert Liebensy (eds), *Law in the Middle East*, Washington, DC: Middle East Institute, 1955, 3–27.

Gilli-Elewy, Hend, 'Baghdad between Cairo and Tabriz', in Frédéric Bauden and Malika Dekkiche (eds), *Mamluk Cairo, a Crossroads for Embassies: Studies on Diplomacy and Diplomatics*, Leiden: Brill, 2019, 340–62.

Guo, Li, 'Mamluk Historiographic Studies: the State of the Art', *Mamlūk Studies Review* 1 (1997): 15–43.

Guo, Li, *Early Mamluk Syrian Historiography: Al-Yūnīnī's Dhayl Mirʾāt al-zamān*, 2 vols, Leiden: Brill, 1998.

Guo, Li, 'History Writing', in Robert Irwin (ed.), *The New Cambridge History of Islam*, Cambridge: Cambridge University Press, 2010, 444–57.

Guo, Li, 'Songs, Poetry, and Storytelling, Ibn Taghrī Birdī on the Yalbughā Affair', in Yuval Ben-Bassat (ed.), *Developing Perspectives in Mamluk History Essays in Honor of Amalia Levanoni*, Leiden: Brill, 2017, 189–200.

Guo, Li, 'Ibn Iyās, the Poet: the Literary Profile of a Mamluk Historian', in Stephan Conermann (ed.), *Mamluk Historiography Revisited – Narratological Perspectives*, Göttingen: V&R Unipress, 2018, 77–90.

Haarmann, Ulrich, 'Khalīl, al-malik al-ashraf ṣalāḥ al-dīn', in P. J. Bearman et al. (eds), *Encyclopaedia of Islam*, 2nd edn, Leiden: Brill, 1960–2007.

Haarmann, Ulrich, 'Khundjī', in P. J. Bearman et al. (eds), *Encyclopaedia of Islam*, 2nd edn, Leiden: Brill, 1960–2007.

Haarmann, Ulrich, 'Al-Mustandjid (II) bi ʿllāh, Abu ʿl-Maḥāsin Yūsuf ibn al-Mutawakkil Muḥammad', in P. J. Bearman et al. (eds), *Encyclopaedia of Islam*, 2nd edn, Leiden: Brill, 1960–2007.

Haarmann, Ulrich, *Quellenstudien zur frühen Mamlukenzeit*, Freiburg im Breisgau: K. Schwarz, 1970.

Haarmann, Ulrich, 'Arabic in Speech, Turkish in Lineage: Mamluks and Their Sons in the Intellectual Life of Fourteenth-Century Egypt and Syria', *Journal of Semitic Studies* 33(1) (1988): 81–114.

Haarmann, Ulrich, 'Rather the Injustice of the Turks than the Righteousness of the Arabs: Changing ʿUlamāʾ Attitudes towards Mamluk Rule in the Late Fifteenth Century', *Studia Islamica* 68 (1988): 61–77.

Haarmann, Ulrich, 'Yeomanly Arrogance and Righteous Rule: Fażl Allāh ibn Rūzbihān Khunjī and the Mamluks of Egypt', in Kambiz Eslami (ed.), *Iran and Iranian Studies: Essays in Honor of Iraj Afshar*, Princeton, NJ: Zagros Press, 1998, 109–24.

al-Ḥājjī, Ḥayāt Nāṣir, *The Internal Affairs in Egypt during the Third Reign of Sultan al-Nāṣir Muḥammad b. Qalāwūn, 709–741/1309–1341*, Kuwait: Kuwait University, 1978.

al-Ḥājjī, Ḥayāt Nāṣir, *Anmāṭ min al-ḥayāt al-siyāsiyya wa-l-iqtiṣādiyya wa-l-ijtimāʿiyya fī Salṭanat al-Mamālīk fī al-qarnayn al-thāmin wa-l-tāsiʿ al-hijriyyayn/al-rābiʿ ʿashar wa-l-khāmis ʿashar al-mīlādiyyayn*, Kuwait: Kuwait University, 1995.

Hanne, Eric, *Putting the Caliph in his Place: Power, Authority, and the Late Abbasid Caliphate*, Madison: Farleigh Dickinson Press, 2007.

Har-El, Shai, *Struggle for Domination in the Middle East: the Ottoman–Mamluk War, 1485–91*, Leiden: Brill, 1995.

Hartmann, Angelika, *An-Nāṣir li-Dīn Allāh (1180–1225): Politik, Religion, Kultur in der späten ʿAbbāsidenzeit*, Berlin: Walter de Gruyter, 1975.

Hartmann, Richard, 'Zur Vorgeschichte des ʿabbāsidischen Schein-Chalifates von Cairo', *Abhandlungen der deutschen Akademie der Wissenschaften zu Berlin, Philosophisch-Historische Klasse, Jahrg. 1947* 7 (1950): 3–10.

Hassan, Mona, 'Loss of Caliphate: the Trauma and Aftermath of 1258 and 1924', PhD dissertation, Princeton University, 2009.

Hassan, Mona, 'Modern Interpretations and Misinterpretations of a Medieval Scholar: Apprehending the Political Thought of Ibn Taymiyyah', in Yossef Rappaport and Shahab Ahmed (eds), *Ibn Taymiyya and His Times*, Oxford: Oxford University Press, 2010, 338–66.

Hassan, Mona, *Longing for the Lost Caliphate: a Transregional History*, Princeton: Princeton University Press, 2016.

Hassan, Mona, 'Poetic Memories of the Prophet's Family: Ibn Ḥajar al-ʿAsqalānī's

Panegyrics for the 'Abbasid Sultan-Caliph of Cairo al-Mustaʿīn', *Journal of Islamic Studies* 29(1) (2018): 1–24.

Havemann, Axel, 'The Chronicle of Ibn Iyās as a Source for Social and Cultural History from Below', in Maḥmūd Ḥaddād et al. (eds), *Towards a Cultural History of the Mamluk Era*, Beirut: Orient-Institut, 2010, 87–98.

Heidemann, Stefan, *Das aleppiner Kalifat (A.D. 1261): vom Ende des Kalifates in Baghdad über Aleppo zu den Restaurationen in Cairo*, Leiden: Brill, 1994.

Herzog, Thomas, *Geschichte und Imaginaire: Entstehung, Überlieferung und Bedeutung der Sīrat Baibars in ihrem sozio-politischen Kontext*, Wiesbaden: Harrassowitz, 2006.

Hirschler, Konrad, *Medieval Arabic Historiography: Authors as Actors*, London: Routledge, 2006.

Hirschler, Konrad, 'The Formation of the Civilian Elite in the Syrian Province: the Case of Ayyubid and Early Mamluk Ḥamāh', *Mamlūk Studies Review* 12(2) (2008): 95–132.

Hirschler, Konrad, 'Islam: the Arabic and Persian Traditions, Eleventh–Fifteenth Centuries', in Sarah Foot and Chase Robinson (eds), *The Oxford History of Historical Writing, vol. 2: 400–1400*, Oxford: Oxford University Press, 2012, 267–86.

Hirschler, Konrad, 'Studying Mamluk Historiography: From Source-Criticism to the Cultural Turn', in Stephan Conermann (ed.), *Ubi Sumus? Quo Vademus? Mamluk Studies – The State of the Art*, Göttingen: V&R Unipress, 2013, 159–86.

Hodgson, Marshall, *The Venture of Islam: Conscience and History in a World Civilization*, 3 vols, Chicago: University of Chicago Press, 1974.

Hodgson, Marshall, *Rethinking World History: Essays on Europe, Islam, and World History*, Cambridge: Cambridge University Press, 1993.

Hofer, Nathan, *The Popularisation of Sufism in Ayyubid and Mamluk Egypt, 1173–1325*, Edinburgh: Edinburgh University Press, 2015.

Holt, P. M., 'Al-Mustaʿīn (II) biʾllāh', in P. J. Bearman et al. (eds), *Encyclopaedia of Islam*, 2nd edn, Leiden: Brill, 1960–2007.

Holt, P. M., *Egypt and the Fertile Crescent, 1516–1922: a Political History*, New York: Cornell University Press, 1966.

Holt, P. M., 'The Position and Power of the Mamluk Sultan', *Bulletin of the School of Oriental and African Studies* 38(2) (1975): 237–49.

Holt, P. M., 'The Structure of Government in the Mamluk Sultanate', in P. M. Holt (ed.), *The Eastern Mediterranean Lands in the Period of the Crusades*, Warminster: Aris & Phillips, 1977, 44–61.

Holt, P. M., 'The Virtuous Ruler in Thirteenth-Century Mamluk Royal Biographies', *Nottingham Medieval Studies* 24 (1980): 27–35.

Holt, P. M., 'Three Biographies of al-Zahir Baybars', in David Morgan (ed.), *Medieval Historical Writing in the Christian and Islamic Worlds*, London: SOAS, 1982, 19–29.

Holt, P. M., 'Some Observations on the ʿAbbāsid Caliphate of Cairo', *Bulletin of the School of Oriental and African Studies* 67 (1984): 501–7.

Holt, P. M., 'A Chancery Clerk in Medieval Egypt', *English Historical Review* 101 (1986): 671–9.

Holt, P. M., *The Age of the Crusades: the Near East from the Eleventh Century to 1517*, London: Longman, 1986.

Holt, P. M., 'The Īlkhān Aḥmad's Embassies to Qalāwūn: Two Contemporary Accounts', *Bulletin of the School of Oriental and African Studies* 49(1) (1986): 128–32.

Holt, P. M., 'Succession in the Early Mamluk Sultanate', in Einar von Schuler (ed.), *Deutscher Orientalistentag: Ausgewählte Vorträge*, Stuttgat: Franz Steiner, 1989, 144–8.

Holt, P. M., 'The Presentation of Qalāwūn by Shāfiʿ ibn ʿAlī', in Clifford Bosworth (ed.), *The Islamic World from Classical to Modern Times: Essays in Honor of Bernard Lewis*, Princeton: Darwin Press, 1989, 141–50.

Holt, P. M., 'The Sultan as Ideal Ruler: Ayyubid and Mamluk Prototypes', in Metin Kunt and Christine Woodhead (eds), *Süleyman the Magnificent and His Age: the Ottoman Empire in the Early Modern World*, New York: Longman, 1995, 122–37.

Holtzman, Livnat, *Anthropomorphism in Islam: the Challenge of Traditionalism (700–1350)*, Edinburgh: Edinburgh University Press, 2018.

Homerin, Th. Emil, 'Saving Muslim Souls: the Khānqāh and the Sufi Duty in Mamluk Lands', *Mamlūk Studies Review* 3 (1999): 65–83.

Homerin, Th. Emil, 'Sufism in Mamluk Studies: a Review of Scholarship in the Field', in Stephan Conermann (ed.), *Ubi Sumus? Quo Vademus? Mamluk Studies – The State of the Art*, Göttingen: V&R Unipress, 2013, 187–209.

Hoover, Jon, *Ibn Taymiyya*, London: Oneworld, 2019.

Humphreys, Stephen, *From Saladin to the Mongols: the Ayyubids of Damascus, 1193–1260*, Albany, NY: State University of New York Press, 1977.

Humphreys, Stephen, *Islamic History: a Framework for Inquiry*, Princeton: Princeton University Press, 1991.

Ḥuṭayṭ, Aḥmad, *Qaḍāyā min taʾrīkh al-Mamālīk al-siyāsī wa-l-ḥaḍārī, 648–923/1250–1517*, Beirut: al-Furāt, 2003.

Ilisch, Ludger, 'Inedita des ʿAbbasidenkalifen al-Mustaʿīn biʿllāh aus syrischen Münzstätten', *Münstersche Numismatische Zeitung* (1982): 39–41.

Inalcik, Halil, 'Selīm I', in P. J. Bearman et al. (eds), *Encyclopaedia of Islam*, 2nd edn, Leiden: Brill, 1960–2007.

Inalcik, Halil, 'Appendix: the Ottomans and the Caliphate', in P. M. Holt et al. (eds), *The Cambridge History of Islam*, Cambridge: Cambridge University Press, 1970, 320–3.

Inalcik, Halil, *The Ottoman Empire: the Classical Age 1300–1600*, London: Phoenix Press, 1973.

Inalcik, Halil and Donald Quataert, *An Economic and Social History of the Ottoman Empire*, 2 vols, Cambridge: Cambridge University Press, 1997.

Irwin, Robert, 'Factions in Medieval Egypt', *Journal of the Royal Asiatic Society of Great Britain and Ireland* 2 (1986): 228–46.

Irwin, Robert, *The Middle East in the Middle Ages: the Early Mamluk Sultanate, 1250–1382*, London: Croom Helm, 1986.

Irwin, Robert, 'Futuwwa: Chivalry and Gangsterism in Medieval Cairo', *Muqarnas* 21 (2004): 161–70.

Irwin, Robert, 'Gunpowder and Firearms in the Mamluk Sultanate Reconsidered', in Michael Winter and Amalia Levanoni (eds), *The Mamluks in Egyptian and Syrian Politics and Society*, Leiden: Brill, 2004, 117–39.

Irwin, Robert, 'Mamluk History and Historians', in Roger Allen and D. S. Richards (eds), *The Cambridge History of Arabic Literature: Arabic Literature in the Post-Classical Period*, Cambridge: Cambridge University Press, 2006, 159–70.

Irwin, Robert, 'The Political Thinking of the "Virtuous Ruler", Qānṣūh al-Ghawrī', *Mamlūk Studies Review* 7(1) (2008): 37–49.

Irwin, Robert, *Ibn Khaldun: An Intellectual Biography*, Princeton: Princeton University Press, 2018.

Jackson, Peter, *The Delhi Sultanate: a Political and Military History*, Cambridge: Cambridge University Press, 1999.

Jackson, Peter, *The Mongols and the Islamic World: From Conquest to Conversion*, New Haven, CT: Yale University Press, 2017.

Jackson, Sherman, 'S̲h̲ihāb al-Dīn al-Ḳarāfī', in P. J. Bearman et al. (eds), *Encyclopaedia of Islam*, 2nd edn, Leiden: Brill, 1960–2007.

Jackson, Sherman, 'From Prophetic Action to Constitutional Theory: a Novel Chapter in Medieval Jurisprudence', *International Journal of Middle East Studies* 25 (1993): 71–90.

Jackson, Sherman, 'The Primacy of Domestic Politics: Ibn Bint al-Aʿazz and the Establishment of Four Chief Judgeships in Mamluk Egypt', *Journal of the American Oriental Society* 115 (1995): 52–65.

Jaques, R. Kevin, *Authority, Conflict, and the Transmission of Diversity in Medieval Islamic Law*, Leiden: Brill, 2006.

Jaques, R. Kevin, *Ibn Hajar: Makers of Islamic Civilization*, Oxford: Oxford University Press, 2009.

Kalus, Ludvik and Frédérique Soudan (eds), *Thesaurus d'épigraphie islamique*, available at: www.epigraphie-islamique.org, last accessed 27 January 2020.

Kennedy, Hugh, *Caliphate: the History of an Idea*, New York: Basic Books, 2016.

Khalidi, Tarif, *Arabic Historical Thought in the Classical Period*, New York: Cambridge University Press, 1994.

Khan, Qamaruddin, *The Political Thought of Ibn Taymīyah*, Islamabad: Islamic Research Institute, 1973.

Khūlī, Muḥammad ʿAbd al-ʿAẓīm, *Al-ʿUlamāʾ fī Miṣr fī al-ʿaṣr al-Mamlūkī, 648–923/1250–1517*, Cairo: Dār al-Fikr al-ʿArabī, 2014.

Khuwayṭir, ʿAbd al-ʿAzīz, *Baibars the First: His Endeavours and Achievements*, London: Green Mountain Press, 1978.

Knysh, Alexander, *Ibn ʿArabi and the Later Islamic Tradition: the Making of a Polemical Image in Medieval Islam*, Albany, NY: State University of New York Press, 1999.

Lambton, Ann, *State and Government in Medieval Islam: An Introduction to the Study of Islamic Political Theory: the Jurists*, London: Oxford University Press, 1981.

Lane-Poole, Stanley, *A History of Egypt in the Middle Ages*, New York: Haskel House, 1969.

Lantschner, Patrick, 'Fragmented Cities in the Later Middle Ages: Italy and the Near East Compared', *English Historical Review* 130 (2015): 546–82.

Laoust, Henri, *Essai sur les doctrines sociales et politiques d'Ibn Taimīa*, Cairo: Imprimerie de l'Institute français d'archéologie oriental, 1939.

Lapidus, Ira, *Muslim Cities in the Later Middle Ages*, Cambridge: Cambridge University Press, 1967.

Lellouch, Benjamin, *Les Ottomans en Égypte: Historiens et conquérants au XVIe siècle*, Louvain: Peeters, 2006.

Lev, Yaacov, 'Symbiotic Relations: Ulama and the Mamluk Sultans', *Mamlūk Studies Review* 13(1) (2008): 1–26.

Levanoni, Amalia, 'The Mamluk Conception of the Sultanate', *International Journal of Middle East Studies* 26(3) (1994): 373–92.

Levanoni, Amalia, *A Turning Point in Mamluk History: the Third Reign of al-Nāṣir Muḥammad ibn Qalāwūn (1310–1341)*, Leiden: Brill, 1995.

Levanoni, Amalia, 'Al-Maqrīzī's Account of the Transition from Turkish to Circassian Mamluk Sultanate: History in the Service of Faith', in Hugh Kennedy (ed.), *The Historiography of Islamic Egypt, c. 950–1800*, Leiden: Brill, 2001, 93–106.

Levanoni, Amalia, 'The al-Nashw Episode: a Case Study of "Moral Economy"', *Mamlūk Studies Review* 9(1) (2005): 207–20.

Levanoni, Amalia, 'Who Were the "Salt of the Earth" in Fifteenth-Century Egypt?' *Mamlūk Studies Review* 14 (2010): 63–83.

Lewis, Bernard, ''Abbāsids', in P. J. Bearman et al. (eds), *Encyclopaedia of Islam*, 2nd edn, Leiden: Brill, 1960–2007.

Lewisohn, Leonard, 'Taḳwā', in P. J. Bearman et al. (eds), *Encyclopaedia of Islam*, 2nd edn, Leiden: Brill, 1960–2007.

Little, Donald, *An Introduction to Mamluk Historiography: An Analysis of Arabic Annalistic and Biographical Sources for the Reign of al-Malik al-Nāṣir Muḥammad ibn Qalā'ūn*, Montreal: McGill-Queen's University Press, 1970.

Little, Donald, 'The History of Arabia during the Baḥrī Mamlūk Period According to Three Mamlūk Historians', in Abdelgadir Abdalla et al. (eds), *Sources for the History of Arabia/Dirāsāt Ta'rīkh al-Jazīra al-'Arabiyya, vol. 1, pt. 2: Studies in the History of Arabia*, Proceedings of the First International Symposium on Studies in the History of Arabia, 23–28 April 1977, sponsored by the Department of History, Faculty of Arts, University of Riyadh, Saudi Arabia, Riyadh: Riyadh University Press, 1979, 17–23.

Little, Donald, 'Religion under the Mamluks', *Muslim World* 73 (1983): 165–81.

Little, Donald, 'The Use of Documents for the Study of Mamluk History', *Mamlūk Studies Review* 1 (1997): 1–13.

Little, Donald, 'Historiography of the Ayyūbid and Mamlūk Epochs', in Carl Petry (ed.), *The Cambridge History of Egypt*, Cambridge: Cambridge University Press, 1998, 412–44.

Loiseau, Julien, *Les Mamelouks: XIIIe–XVIe siècle; une expérience du pouvoir dans l'Islam médiéval*, Paris: Éditions du Seuil, 2014.

Madelung, Wilferd, 'A Treatise on the Imamate Dedicated to Sultan Baybars I', in Alexander Fodor (ed.), *Proceedings of the 14th Congress of the Union Européenne des Arabisants et Islamisants*, Budapest: Csoma de Kőrös Society, Section of Islamic Studies, 1995.

Mājid, 'Abd al-Mun'im, *Nuẓum dawlat salāṭīn al-mamālīk wa-rusūmuhum fī Miṣr*, 2 vols, Cairo: Maktabat al-Anjlū al-Miṣriyya, 1979.

Malkawi, Banan and Tamara Sonn, 'Ibn Taymiyya on Islamic Governance', in Asma Afsaruddin (ed.), *Islam, the State, and Political Authority: Medieval Issues and Modern Concerns*, New York: Palgrave Macmillan, 2011, 338–45.

Manz, Beatrice, 'Temür and the Problem of a Conqueror's Legacy', *Journal of the Royal Asiatic Society* (3rd Series) 8(1) (1998): 21–41.

Margoliouth, David, 'The Caliphate Historically Considered', *Moslem World* 11 (1921): 332–43.

Markiewicz, Christopher, *The Crisis of Kingship in Late Medieval Islam: Persian Emigres and the Making of Ottoman Sovereignty*, Cambridge: Cambridge University Press, 2019.

Marlow, Louise, 'Kings, Prophets and the ʿUlamāʾ in Mediaeval Islamic Advice Literature', *Studia Islamica* 81 (1995): 101–20.

Marlow, Louise, 'A Samanid Work of Counsel and Commentary: the *Naṣīḥat Al-Mulūk* of Pseudo-Māwardī', *Iran* 45 (2007): 181–92.

Marmon, Shaun, 'The Quality of Mercy: Intercession in Mamluk Society', *Studia Islamica* 87 (1998): 125–39.

Martel-Thoumian, Bernadette, *Les civils et l'administration dans l'état militaire Mamlūk: (IXe/XVe siècle)*, Damascus: Institut français de Damas, 1991.

Martinez-Gros, Gabriel, *Ibn Khaldûn et les sept vies de l'islam*, Paris: Sindbad, 2006.

al-Mashhadānī, Yāsir ʿAbd al-Jawād, *Al-ʿAlāqāt al-Miṣriyya-al-Hindiyya fī al-ʿaṣr al-mamlūkī: dirāsa fī al-jawānib al-siyāsiyya wa-l-ḥaḍāriyya*, Egypt: al-Maktab al-ʿArabī lil-Maʿārif, 2015.

Massoud, Sami G., *The Chronicles and Annalistic Sources of the Early Mamluk Circassian Period*, Leiden: Brill, 2007.

Mauder, Christian, 'In the Sultan's Salon: Learning, Religion and Rulership at the Mamluk Court of Qāniṣawh al-Ghawrī (r. 1501–1516)', PhD dissertation, University of Göttingen, 2017.

Mayer, L. A., 'A Decree of the Caliph al-Mustaʿīn Billāh', *Quarterly of the Department of Antiquities in Palestine* 11 (1945): 27–9.

Mayer, L. A., *Mamluk Costume: a Survey*, Genève: A. Kundig, 1952.

Meloy, John, '"Aggression in the Best of Lands": Mecca in Egyptian–Indian Diplomacy in the Ninth/Fifteenth Century', in Frédéric Bauden and Malika Dekkiche (eds), *Mamluk Cairo, a Crossroads for Embassies: Studies on Diplomacy and Diplomatics*, Leiden: Brill, 2019, 604–20.

Melville, Charles, 'Sometimes by the Sword, Sometimes by the Dagger: the Role of the Ismaʿilis in Mamlūk–Mongol Relations in the 8th/14th Century', in Farhad

Daftary (ed.), *Medieval Isma'ili History and Thought*, Cambridge: Cambridge University Press, 1996, 247–63.

Melville, Charles, '*Pādishāh-i Islām*: the Conversion of Sultan Maḥmūd Ghāzān Khān', in Charles Melville (ed.), *History and Literature in Iran*, London: I. B. Tauris in association with the Centre of Middle Eastern Studies, University of Cambridge, 1998, 159–77.

Minorsky, Vladimir, 'The Poetry of Shāh Ismā'īl I', *Bulletin of the School of Oriental and African Studies* 4 (1939–1942): 1007–53.

Mirza, Younus, 'Ibn Kathīr (d. 774/1373): His Intellectual Circle, Major Works and Qur'ānic Exegesis', PhD dissertation, Georgetown University, 2012.

Moin, A. Azfar, *The Millennial Sovereign: Sacred Kingship and Sainthood in Islam*, New York: Columbia University Press, 2012.

Mortel, Richard, 'The Decline of Mamlūk Civil Bureaucracy in the Fifteenth Century: the Career of Abū l-Khayr al-Naḥḥās', *Journal of Islamic Studies* 6(2) (1995): 173–88.

Mottahedeh, Roy, *Loyalty and Leadership in an Early Islamic Society*, 2nd edn, London: I. B. Tauris, 2001.

Muhanna, Elias, 'Why Was the Fourteenth Century a Century of Arabic Encyclopaedism?' in Jason König and Greg Woolf (eds), *Encyclopaedism from Antiquity to the Renaissance*, Cambridge: Cambridge University Press, 2013, 343–56.

Muhanna, Elias, *The World in a Book: Al-Nuwayri and the Islamic Encyclopedic Tradition*, Princeton: Princeton University Press, 2018.

Muir, William, *The Mameluke or Slave Dynasty of Egypt: a History of Egypt from the Fall of the Ayyubite Dynasty to the Conquest by the Osmanlis, A.D. 1260–1517*, London, 1896.

Muir, William, *The Caliphate: Its Rise, Decline and Fall*, London: Smith, Elder, 1898.

Narotzky, Susana and Eduardo Manzano, 'The Ḥisba, the Muḥtasib and the Struggle over Political Power and a Moral Economy', in John Hudson and Ana Rodríguez (eds), *Diverging Paths? The Shapes of Power and Institutions in Medieval Christendom and Islam*, Leiden: Brill, 2014, 30–54.

Nielsen, Jørgen, *Secular Justice in an Islamic State: Maẓālim under the Baḥrī Mamlūks, 662/1264–789/1387*, Leiden, 1985.

Northrup, Linda, *From Slave to Sultan: the Career of al-Manṣūr Qalāwūn and the Consolidation of Mamluk Rule in Egypt and Syria (678–689 A.H./1279–1290 AD)*, Berlin: Franz Steiner, 1998.

Northrup, Linda, 'The Baḥrī Mamlūk Sultanate, 1250–1390', in Carl Petry (ed.),

The Cambridge History of Egypt, Cambridge: Cambridge University Press, 1998, 242–89.

Onimus, Clément, *Les maîtres du jeu: Pouvoir et violence politique à l'aube du sultanat mamlouk circassien (784–815/1382–1412)*, Paris: Éditions de la Sorbonne, 2019.

Perho, Irmeli, 'Al-Maqrīzī and Ibn Taghrī Birdī as Historians of Contemporary Events', in Hugh Kennedy (ed.), *The Historiography of Islamic Egypt, c. 950–1800*, Leiden: Brill, 2001, 107–20.

Perho, Irmeli, 'The Sultan and the Common People', *Studia Orientalia Electronica* 82 (2014): 145–58.

Petry, Carl, *The Civilian Elite of Cairo in the Later Middle Ages*, Princeton: Princeton University Press, 1981.

Petry, Carl, *Twilight of Majesty: the Reigns of the Mamluk Sultans al-Ashraf Qāytbāy and Qānṣūh al-Ghawrī in Egypt*, Seattle: University of Washington Press, 1993.

Petry, Carl, 'Royal Justice in Mamluk Cairo: Contrasting Motives of Two Sultans', in Mercedes García-Arenal and Manuela Marín (eds), *Saber religioso y poder politico en el Islam: Actas des simposio inernacional Granada, 15–18 octubre 1991*, Madrid: Agencia Española de Cooperación Internacional, 1994, 197–212.

Petry, Carl, *Protectors or Praetorians? The Last Mamluk Sultans and Egypt's Waning as a Great Power*, Albany, NY: State University of New York Press, 1994.

Petry, Carl, 'Robing Ceremonials in Late Mamluk Egypt: Hallowed Traditions, Shifting Protocols', in Stewart Gordon (ed.), *Robes and Honor: the Medieval World of Investiture*, New York: Palgrave Macmillan, 2001, 353–77.

Petry, Carl, 'The Politics of Insult: the Mamluk Sultanate's Response to Criminal Affronts', *Mamlūk Studies Review* 6 (2002): 87–117.

Petry, Carl, *The Criminal Underworld in a Medieval Islamic Society: Narratives from Cairo and Damascus under the Mamluks*, Chicago: Middle East Documentation Center, 2012.

Popper, William, *Egypt and Syria under the Circassian Sultans, 1382–1468 A.D.: Systematic Notes to Ibn Taghrī Birdī's Chronicles of Egypt*, 2 vols, Berkeley: University of California Press, 1955–7.

Popper, William, 'Sakhāwī's Criticism of Ibn Taghrībirdī', in *Studi orientalistici in onore di Giorgio Levi della Vida*, vol. 2, Rome, 1956, 371–89.

Rabbat, Nasser, *The Citadel of Cairo: a New Interpretation of Royal Mamluk Architecture*, Leiden: Brill, 1995.

Rabbat, Nasser, 'Perception of Architecture in Mamluk Sources', *Mamlūk Studies Review* 6 (2002): 155–76.

Rabbat, Nasser, 'Who Was al-Maqrīzī? A Biographical Sketch, *Mamlūk Studies Review* 7(2) (2003): 1–19.

Rabbat, Nasser, *Mamluk History through Architecture: Monuments, Culture and Politics in Medieval Egypt and Syria*, London: I. B. Tauris, 2010.

Rāġib, Yusuf, 'Al-Sayyida Nafīsa: Sa Légende, son culte et son cimetière (Suite et fin)', *Studia Islamica* 45 (1977): 27–55.

Rapoport, Yossef, 'Women and Gender in Mamluk Society: An Overview', *Mamlūk Studies Review* 11(2) (2007): 1–47.

Rapoport, Yossef, 'Royal Justice and Religious Law: *Siyāsah* and Shariʿah under the Mamluks', *Mamlūk Studies Review* 16 (2012): 71–102.

Reinfandt, Lucian, 'Mamlūk Documentary Studies', in Stephan Conermann (ed.), *Ubi Sumus? Quo Vademus? Mamluk Studies – The State of the Art*, Göttingen: V&R Unipress, 2013, 285–309.

Richards, Donald, 'A Mamluk Amir's Mamluk History: Baybars al-Manṣūrī and the Zubdat al-Fikra', in Hugh Kennedy (ed.), *The Historiography of Islamic Egypt, c. 950–1800*, Leiden: Brill, 2001, 37–44.

Richards, Donald, *Mamluk Administrative Documents from St. Catherine's Monastery*, Leuven: Peeters, 2011.

Rizq, ʿAlāʾ Ṭāha, *ʿĀmmat al-Qāhira fī ʿaṣr salāṭīn al-Mamālīk*, Giza: Ein for Human and Social Studies, 2003.

Robinson, Chase, *Islamic Historiography*, Cambridge: Cambridge University Press, 2003.

Rogers, E. J., 'Notice sur le lieu de sépulture des khalifes abbassides de la deuxième dynastie', *Bulletin de l'Institut d'Égypte* (2nd Series) 4 (1884): 106–26.

Sadek, Mohamed-Moain, *Die mamlukische Architektur der Stadt Gaza*, Berlin: K. Schwarz, 1991.

Saleh, Marlis, 'Al-Suyūṭī and His Works: Their Place in Islamic Scholarship from Mamluk Times to the Present', *Mamlūk Studies Review* 5 (2001): 73–89.

Salibi, Kamal, 'The Banū Jamāʿa: a Dynasty of Shāfiʿite Jurists in the Mamluk Period', *Studia Islamica* 9 (1958): 97–109.

Salmon, W. H., *An Account of the Ottoman Conquest of Egypt in the Year A.H. 922 (A.D.1516): Translated from the Third Volume of the Arabic Chronicle of Muḥammed Ibn Aḥmed Ibn Iyās, an eye-witness of the scenes he describes*, London: Royal Asiatic Society, 1921.

Sanders, Paula, *Ritual, Politics, and the City in Fatimid Cairo*, Saratoga Springs, NY: State University of New York Press, 1994.

Sanders, Paula, 'Robes of Honor in Fatimid Egypt', in Stewart Gordon (ed.), *Robes and Honor: the Medieval World of Investiture*, New York: Palgrave Macmillan, 2001, 225–39.

Sartain, Elizabeth, *Jalāl al-Dīn al-Suyūṭī: Biography and Background*, Cambridge: Cambridge University Press, 1975.

Schacht, Joseph, 'ʿAhd', in P. J. Bearman et al. (eds), *Encyclopaedia of Islam*, 2nd edn, Leiden: Brill, 1960–2007.

Schimmel, Annemarie, 'Kalif und Kadi im spätmittelalterlichen Ägypten', *Die Welt des Islams* 24 (1942): 1–128.

Schimmel, Annemarie, 'Some Glimpses of the Religious Life in Egypt during the Later Mamluk Period', *Islamic Studies* 4(4) (1965): 353–92.

Schultz, Warren, 'The Silver Coinage of the Mamluk Caliph and Sultan al-Mustaʿin Biʾllah (815/1412)', in Bruno Callegher and Arianna D'Ottone (eds), *The 2nd Simone Assemani Symposium on Islamic Coins*, Trieste: Università di Trieste, 2010, 210–19.

Schultz, Warren, 'Mamluk Coins, Mamluk Politics and the Limits of the Numismatic Evidence', in Yuval Ben-Bassat (ed.), *Developing Perspectives in Mamluk History: Essays in Honor of Amalia Levanoni*, Leiden: Brill, 2017, 245–68.

Sharon, Moshe, *Corpus Inscriptionum Arabicarum Palaestinae, vol. 4: G–*, Leiden: Brill, 2009.

Shoshan, Boaz, *Popular Culture in Medieval Cairo*, Cambridge: Cambridge University Press, 1993.

Sievert, Henning, 'Family, Friend or Foe? Factions, Households and Interpersonal Relations in Mamluk Egypt and Syria', in Stephan Conermann (ed.), *Everything is on the Move: the Mamluk Empire as a Node in (Trans-)Regional Networks*, Göttingen: V&R Unipress, 2014, 83–125.

Sourdel, Dominique, 'Khalīfah', in P. J. Bearman et al. (eds), *Encyclopaedia of Islam*, 2nd edn, Leiden: Brill, 1960–2007.

Spies, Otto, 'Ein Investiturschreiben des abbasidischen Kalifen in Kairo an einen indischen Koenig', in S. M. Abdullah (ed.), *Professor Muḥammad Shafiʿ Volume*, Lahore, 1955, 241–53.

Subtelny, Maria, 'Tamerlane and his Descendants: From Paladins to Patrons', in David Morgan and Anthony Reid (eds), *The New Cambridge History of Islam*, Cambridge: Cambridge University Press, 2010, 169–200.

Sümer, Faruk, 'Yavuz Selim s'est-il proclamé calife?' *Turcica* 21/23 (1991): 343–54.

Surūr, Muḥammad Jamāl al-Dīn, *Dawlat Banī Qalāwūn fī Miṣr: al-ḥāla al-siyāsiyya wa-l-iqtiṣādiyya fī ʿahdihā bi-wajhin khāṣṣ*, Cairo: Dār al-Fikr al-ʿArabī, 1947.

Talib, Adam, 'Woven Together as Though Randomly Strung: Variation in Collection of Naevi Poetry Compiled by al-Nuwayrī and al-Sarī al-Raffā'', *Mamlūk Studies Review* 17 (2013): 23–42.

Talmon-Heller, Daniella, '*'Ilm, Shafā'ah*, and *Barakah*: the Resources of Ayyubid and Early Mamluk Ulama', *Mamlūk Studies Review* 13(2) (2009): 23–45.

Ṭarkhān, Ibrāhīm 'Alī, *Miṣr fī 'aṣr dawlat al-Mamālīk al-Jarākisa*, Cairo, 1960.

Taymūr, Aḥmad, *Al-Āthār al-Nabawiyya*, Cairo, 1951.

Tetsuya, Ohtoshi, 'Cairene Cemeteries as Public Loci in Mamluk Egypt', *Mamlūk Studies Review* 10(1) (2006): 83–116.

Tezcan, Baki, 'Hanafism and the Turks in al-Ṭarasūsī's Gift for the Turks (1352)', *Mamlūk Studies Review* 15 (2011): 67–86.

Thorau, Peter, *The Lion of Egypt: Sultan Baybars I and the Near East in the Thirteenth Century*, trans. P. M. Holt, London: Longman, 1992.

Tyan, Émile, 'Bay'a', in P. J. Bearman et al. (eds), *Encyclopaedia of Islam*, 2nd edn, Leiden: Brill, 1960–2007.

Tyan, Émile, *Institutions du droit public musulman*, 2 vols, Paris: Sirey, 1954–6.

Van Den Bossche, Gowaart, 'The Past, Panegyric, and the Performance of Penmanship: Sultanic Biography and Social Practice in Late Medieval Egypt and Syria', PhD dissertation, Ghent University, 2018.

Van Leeuwen, Theo, *Introducing Social Semiotics*, London: Routledge, 2005.

Van Steenbergen, Jo, 'Mamluk Elite on the Eve of al-Nāṣir Muḥammad's Death (1341): a Look behind the Scenes of Mamluk Politics', *Mamlūk Studies Review* 9(2) (2005): 173–99.

Van Steenbergen, Jo, *Order Out of Chaos: Patronage, Conflict and Mamluk Socio-political Culture, 1341–1382*, Leiden: Brill, 2006.

Van Steenbergen, Jo, '"Is Anyone My Guardian . . .?" Mamlūk Under-age Rule and the Later Qalāwūnids', *Al-Masāq* 19(1) (2007): 55–65.

Van Steenbergen, Jo, 'On the Brink of a New Era? Yalbughā al-Khāṣṣakī (d. 1366) and the Yalbughāwīyah', *Mamlūk Studies Review* 15 (2011): 117–52.

Van Steenbergen, Jo, 'The amir Yalbughā al-Khāṣṣakī, the Qalāwūnid Sultanate, and the Cultural Matrix of Mamluk Society: a Reassessment of Mamlūk Politics in the 1360s', *Journal of the American Oriental Society* 131(3) (2011): 423–43.

Van Steenbergen, Jo, 'Qalāwūnid Discourse, Elite Communication and the Mamluk Cultural Matrix: Interpreting a 14th-Century Panegyric', *Journal of Arabic Literature* 43 (2012): 1–28.

Van Steenbergen, Jo, 'Ritual, Politics, and the City in Mamluk Cairo: the Bayna l-Qaṣrayn as a Dynamic "lieu de mémoire", 1250–1382', in Alexander

Beihammer et al. (eds), *Court Ceremonies and Rituals of Power in Byzantium and the Medieval Mediterranean: Comparative Perspectives*, Leiden: Brill, 2013, 227–66.

Van Steenbergen, Jo, 'The Mamluk Sultanate as a Military Patronage State: Household Politics and the Case of the Qalāwūnid *bayt* (1279–1382)', *Journal of the Economic and Social History of the Orient* 56 (2013): 189–217.

Van Steenbergen, Jo, 'Caught between Heredity and Merit: Qawṣūn (d. 1342) and the Legacy of al-Nāṣir Muḥammad b. Qalāwūn (d. 1341)', *Bulletin of the School of Oriental Studies* 78(3) (2015): 429–50.

Van Steenbergen, Jo, '"Mamlukisation" between Social Theory and Social Practice: An Essay on Reflexivity, State Formation, and the Late Medieval Sultanate of Cairo', Annemarie Schimmel Kolleg Working Paper 22, Bonn: Annemarie Schimmel Kolleg, 2015.

Van Steenbergen, Jo, 'Appearances of *dawla* and Political Order in Late Medieval Syro-Egypt: the State, Social Theory, and the Political History of the Cairo Sultanate (thirteenth–sixteenth centuries)', in Stephan Conermann (ed.), *History and Society during the Mamluk Period (1250–1517): Studies of the Annemarie Schimmel Institute for Advanced Study II*. Göttingen: V&R Unipress, 2016, 51–85.

Van Steenbergen, Jo, *Caliphate and Kingship in a Fifteenth-Century Literary History of Muslim Leadership and Pilgrimage: al-Ḏahab al-Masbūk fī ḏikr man ḥağğa min al-ḫulafāʾ wa-l-mulūk*, Leiden: Brill, 2016.

Van Steenbergen, Jo, '*ʿAṣabiyya*, Messiness, and "Mamlukisation" in the Sultanate of Cairo (1200s–1500s)', unpublished paper, 2019.

Van Steenbergen, Jo, 'Revisiting the Mamlūk Empire: Political Action, Relationships of Power, Entangled Networks, and the Sultanate of Cairo in Late Medieval Syro-Egypt', in Reuven Amitai and Stephan Conermann (eds), *The Mamluk Sultanate from the Perspective of Regional and World History: Economic, Social and Cultural Development in an Era of Increasing International Interaction and Competition*, Göttingen: V&R Unipress, 2019, 77–108.

Van Steenbergen, Jo and Stijn Van Nieuwenhuyse, 'Truth and Politics in Late Medieval Arabic Historiography: the Formation of Sultan Barsbāy's State (1422–1438) and the Narratives of the Amir Qurqumās al-Shaʿbānī (d. 1438)', *Der Islam* 95(1) (2018): 147–87.

Van Steenbergen, Jo, Patrick Wing and Kristof D'hulster, 'The Mamlukization of the Mamluk Sultanate? State formation and the History of Fifteenth Century Egypt and Syria: Part I – Old Problems and New Trends/Part II – Comparative

Solutions and a New Research Agenda', *History Compass* (2016): 549–59 and 560–9.

Veinstein, Gilles, 'La question du califat ottoman', in Pierre-Jean Luizard (ed.), *Le choc colonial et l'islam: les politiques religieuses des puissances coloniales en terres d'islam*, Paris: Découverte, 2006, 451–68.

Veinstein, Gilles, 'Le serviteur des deux saints sanctuaires et ses *mahmal*. Des mamelouks aux ottomans', *Turcica* 41 (2009): 229–46.

Vermeulen, Urbain, 'Une lettre du Calife al-Mustakfī à Dāwud b. Yūsuf b. Rasūl (707 A.H.)', in Urbain Vermeulen and Daniel De Smet (eds), *Proceedings of the 1st, 2nd and 3rd International Colloquium organized at the Katholieke Universiteit Leuven in May 1992, 1993, and 1994*, Leuven: Peeters, 1995, 363–71.

Vermeulen, Urbain, 'La *bay'a* califale dans le *Subḥ* d'al-Qalqašandī: l'aspect théorique', in Urbain Vermeulen and Daniel De Smet (eds), *Proceedings of the 4th and 5th International Colloquium organized at the Katholieke Universiteit Leuven in 1995 and 1996*, Leuven: Peeters, 1998, 295–301.

Voll, John, 'Islam as a Community of Discourse and a World-System', in Akbar Ahmed and Tamara Sonn (eds), *The SAGE Handbook of Islamic Studies*, London: Sage, 2010, 3–17.

Watt, W. Montgomery, *Islamic Political Thought: the Basic Concepts*, Edinburgh: Edinburgh University Press, 1968.

Weil, Gustav, *Geschichte des abbasidenchalifats in egypten*, 2 vols, Stuttgart: J. B. Metzler, 1860–2.

Wiederhold, Lutz, 'Legal-Religious Elite, Temporal Authority, and the Caliphate in Mamluk Society: Conclusions Drawn from the Examination of a "Zahiri Revolt" in Damascus in 1386', *International Journal of Middle East Studies* 31 (1999): 203–35.

Wiet, Gaston, *Journal d'un bourgeois du Caire; chronique d'Ibn Iyâs*, 2 vols, Paris: A. Colin, 1955–60.

Wiet, Gaston, 'Barḳūḳ', in P. J. Bearman et al. (eds), *Encyclopaedia of Islam*, 2nd edn, Leiden: Brill, 1960–2007.

Wing, Patrick, 'Mozaffarids', in Ehsan Yarshater (ed.), *Encyclopaedia Iranica*, London: Routledge & Kegan Paul, 1983–2018.

Wing, Patrick, *The Jalayrids: Dynastic State Formation in the Mongol Middle East*, Edinburgh: Edinburgh University Press, 2017.

Wing, Patrick, 'Submission, Defiance, and the Rules of Politics on the Mamluk Sultanate's Anatolian Frontier', *Journal of the Royal Asiatic Society* (3rd Series) (2015): 1–12.

Winter, Michael, *Egyptian Society under Ottoman Rule, 1517–1798*, London: Routledge, 1992.

Winter, Michael, 'The Ottoman Occupation', in Carl Petry (ed.), *The Cambridge History of Egypt*, Cambridge: Cambridge University Press, 1998, 490–516.

Woods, John, *The Aqquyunlu: Clan, Confederation, Empire*, Salt Lake City: University of Utah Press, 1999.

Woods, John, *The Timurid Aristocratic Order* (forthcoming).

Yosef, Koby, '*Dawlat al-Atrāk* or *Dawlat al-Mamālīk*? Ethnic Origin or Slave Origin as the Defining Characteristic of the Ruling Élite in the Mamluk Sultanate', *Jerusalem Studies in Arabic and Islam* 39 (2012): 387–410.

Yılmaz, Hüseyin, *Caliphate Redefined: the Mystical Turn in Ottoman Political Thought*, Princeton: Princeton University Press, 2018.

Yüksel Muslu, Cihan, *The Ottomans and the Mamluks: Imperial Diplomacy and Warfare in the Islamic World*, London: I. B. Tauris, 2014.

Index

Page numbers in *italics* indicate illustrations

Abaqa (*ilkhan*, r. 663–81/1265–82), 39
al-ʿAbbās ibn ʿAbd al-Muṭṭalib, 322–3, 365
  legitmacy based on lineage of al-ʿAbbās, 382–4
  prophetic heritage, 405
Abbasid Caliphate
  in Baghdad, al-Maqrīzī on, 315
  extinction of, 218–19
  fall and rise of, 384–6
  resurrection of under Baybars, 28–9, 32–4
  see also Cairo Caliphate; *specific caliphs and sultans*
Abbasid family (Cairo)
  after Ottoman conquest, 212–14, 216, 218
  baraka, 91, 165, 261, 323, 353, 357, 383
  forced occupancy in Citadel, 169, 180
  genealogical claims, 292–3
  genealogical trees, *196*, *441–2*
  intrigue within house, 68–70, 196–8, 304
  living conditions, 69, 92, 153, 288, 295
  networks, 68, 77, 98, 423, 431–2, 445n48
  respect for Abbasid bloodline, 177, 423, 437–8
  squabbles within, 192, 215–16, 301, 432
  al-Suyūṭī family and, 154–5, 174, 176–7
  veneration of, 303–4, 306
  see also Abbasid family financial status; Abbasid mausoleum
Abbasid family financial status
  confiscations from, 168, 200, 213, 302
  properties and landholdings, 150–1, 153–4, 164, 168, 173–5, 180, 201, 207
  prosperity, 92, 169
  sources of, 77–8, 92, 436
  strained finances, 153–4
  see also Abbasid family; Abbasid mausoleum; Sayyida Nafīsa shrine
Abbasid mausoleum, *47*, 73, *80*, 81, 87n55, 199, 367; *see also* Abbasid family
ʿAbd al-ʿAzīz, Abū al-ʿIzz (later al-Mutawakkil II), 157–8, 170
  see also al-Mutawakkil II, ʿAbd al-ʿAzīz (caliph)
ʿAbd al-ʿAzīz ibn Barqūq, al-Manṣūr (sultan, r. 808/1405), 108, 111–12
ʿAbd al-Mālik al-Juwaynī (d. 478/1085), 239
ʿAbd al-Malik (Umayyad caliph, r. 65–86/685–705), 356
Abū Bakr ibn Khalīl (Abbasid prince), 212–13, 215–16
Abū Bakr, al-Manṣūr (sultan, r. 741/1341)
  deposes al-Wāthiq I, 74–5
  investiture ceremony, 75–6
  investiture deed, 352
  payments to Abbasid family, 78
Abū al-Faḍl al-ʿAbbās *see* al-Mustaʿīn, ʿAbbās (caliph)
Abū al-Faraj al-Iṣfahānī, 237
Abū al-Fidāʾ, Ismāʿīl (d. 732/1331), 292–3
Abū Numayy Muḥammad (d. 701/1301), *sharīf* of Mecca, 27, 44–5
Abū Saʿīd (*ilkhan*, r. 716–36/1316–35), 81
Abū Shāma, ʿAbd al-Raḥmān (d. 665/1267), 308–9
Adriaenssens, Veerle, 144
Aḥmad, al-Nāṣir (ruler of Yemen, r. 803–27/1400–24), 402, 413
Aḥmad, al-Nāṣir (sultan, r. 742–3/1342), 76–7, 78, 409
Aḥmad ibn Īnāl, al-Muʾayyad (sultan, r. 865/1461), 163–4
Aḥmad ibn Khalīl (Abbasid prince), 212–13, 215–16
Aḥmad Pasha, 216, 218
Aḥmad ibn Shaykh, al-Muẓaffar (sultan, r. 824/1421), 126, 146
Aḥmad Tegüdar (*ilkhan*, r. 681–3/1282–4), 39–40
Aḥmad ibn al-Ẓāhir *see* al-Mustanṣir, Abū al-Qāsim Aḥmad (caliph)
Āl Faḍl Bedouin, 20, 30
ʿAlāʾ al-Dawla (Ottoman leader), 171
ʿAlāʾ al-Dīn al-Bunduqdār, 25

Aleppo
Battle of Marj Dābiq, 204–6
Shaykh's base of operations, 144–5
Alexandria
as place of exile and imprisonment, 94, 104, 111, 117, 119, 126, 146, 162
water shortage, 213
ʿAlī, al-Manṣūr (sultan, r. 778–83/1377–82), 93–4, 95
ʿAlī, al-Ṣāliḥ ibn Qalāwūn, 41, 347–8
al-Alṭāf al-khafiyya (Ibn ʿAbd al-Ẓāhir), 285–6; *see also* Ibn ʿAbd al-Ẓāhir
Āmid (Turkmen capital), 149–50, 202
Amīna bint al-Mustakfī II (d. 915/1510), 177, 200
Amitai, Reuven, 33, 366
Anatolia, 144, 147, 149–50, 170–2
Anjum, Ovamir, 239, 242, 243–4
Ankara, Battle of (804/1402), 111, 144
Āqqūsh al-Barlī, 23–4, 30, 241, 284
Aqquyunlu Turkmen, 116–17, 144–5, 149–50, 259
al-Āqṣarāy, Amīn al-Dīn, 165
arbitration and intercession by Cairo caliph
for Abū al-Khayr al-Naḥḥās, 157–8
after Ottoman victory, 209–12
after Syria revolt, 80
for Baybars ibn Baqar, 152
between factions, 112–13
in fifteenth century, 180
'soft power' in politics, 426–7
see also Cairo Caliphate; ceremonial functions of Cairo Caliphate; diplomacy of Cairo Caliphate; political theory; politics and Cairo Caliphate; religious authority of Cairo Caliphate; *specific caliphs and sultans*
Armenia, attacks on, 41, 42, 364
Asanbāy al-Ashrafī, 174–5
Ashʿarī scholars, 232, 263, 434
Ashʿarī theology, 230
Ashrafī *mamlūks*, 150–1, 159, 161–2
Āthār al-uwal fī tartīb al-duwal (Ḥasan al-ʿAbbāsī), 233–6
Ayalon, David, 3
ʿAyn Jālūt, Battle of (658/1260), 20–1, 33, 364
Aynabak al-Badrī, 94–5, 430
al-ʿAynī, Badr al-Dīn Maḥmūd (d. 855/1451)
background, 312
commentary by, 128, 326, 327
as source, 44, 128, 326, 327
Ayyubids
authority over holy cities, 148, 206
Baghdad caliph and, 428
dynasty end, 20–1, 23, 24
political legitimisation model, 28
sultans of Cairo as heirs of, 259
al-Azhar mosque, 119, 120, 284–5, 366
Al-Azmeh, Aziz, 240, 428
Badāʾiʿ al-zuhūr fī waqāʾiʿ al-duhūr (Ibn Iyās), 300–6
Baghdad
attempt to reclaim, 24, 29–34
caliphs in Ayyubid period, 428
caliph–scholar relations, 232, 235
in early sixteenth century, 206
Mongol destruction of, 19
rebellion in, 92–3
Baktamur Julaq al-Ẓāhirī, 114, 118, 122
Balog, Paul, 368
Baraka al-Mustawathiq ibn al-Mustakfī, 357–8, 394–5
Bardbak (*dawādār* of al-Mutawakkil III), 209, 212, 215–16
al-Bārizī, Nāṣir al-Dīn Muḥammad (chancery chief, d. 823/1420)
chancery documents written by, 352–3
funeral, 153
made *khazīn al-kutub*, 362–3, 383, 395
Barqūq, al-Ẓāhir (sultan, r. 784–91, 792–801/1382–9, 1390–9)
death and succession, 106–7
deposition of caliph, 303
dynastic impulses, 6, 141
fitna Ẓāhiriyya, 98–9
Ibn Ḥajar on, 319
plots against, 96–7, 435–6
rebellion against in Syria, 100–1, 103–5, 249
rise to power, 95–6
sultan–caliph relationship, 303, 437
threats by Temür, 106–7
Barsbāy, al-Ashraf (sultan, r. 825–841/1422–38)
death and succession of, 150–1
foreign relations and expanding influence, 147–50
inscriptions, 367
investiture deed, 352, 354, 382–3, 398–9, 412–13, 438
al-Maqrīzī on, 313
treatment of al-Mustaʿīn in exile, 126
Barthold, Vasiliy V., 208, 219, 224n68
Bauden, Frédéric, 319
Bauer, Thomas, 340
Baumgarten, Martyn von (d. 1535), 195
al-Bāʿūnī, Aḥmad, chief qadi, 116
bayʿa
binding nature of, 413
caliphal honour, 428
and ceremonial, 407–13
ceremonial protocols, 26, 76–7
lack of removes enemies from faith, 45–6
legality of, 255
performative nature of, 425
political theory, 257
sanctity of, 319
see also Cairo Caliphate; ceremonial functions of Cairo Caliphate; legitimisation of

sultan by Cairo Caliphate; political theory; *specific caliphs and sultans*
Baybars ibn Baqar (d. 866/1461) (amir and Bedouin leader), 152, 180
Baybars al-Bunduqdārī, al-Ẓāhir (sultan, r. 657–76/1260–77)
caliphate and *futuwwa*, 179
caliphate resurrected, 28–9, 283–4, 289, 303, 308, 384–5
caliph–sultan relationship, 32–4, 284–6
foundation of 'Mamluk' Sultanate, 48
Ibn Iyās on, 303
inscriptions and coinage, 27, 366–8
investiture as sultan, 343, 344–5, 435
investiture deed, 382, 384–5
investiture of al-Ḥākim I, 34–7
investiture of al-Mustanṣir, 25–8, 343
khuṭba commissioned by, 363–4
al-Maqrīzī on, 318
military expedition to Baghdad, 29–34, 283–4, 287, 289–90
qadiships created, 325
relationship with Mongols, 34–7
rise to sultanate, 21
titles, 369, 370
Baybars al-Jāshinkīr (sultan, r. 708–9/1309–10)
Āthār of Ḥasan al-ʿAbbāsī dedicated to, 233, 234
coinage, 368
competition for power, 45
expedition against Mongols, 63
foreign relations, 361
investiture deeds, 350–2, 393, 395, 397, 399, 405, 411
usurpation of sultanate, 64, 66
Baybars al-Manṣūrī (d. 725/1325) (military historian), 289–92, 300
Baybughā Rūs, 80
Bāyezīd I (Ottoman sultan, r. 791–804/1389–1402), 106–7
Bāyezīd II (Ottoman sultan, r. 886–918/1481–1512), 170–2
Berke ibn Baybars, al-Saʿīd (sultan, r. 676–8/1277–9), 38, 345–6
Berke Khān (Golden Horde khān, r. 655–65/1257–67), 35, 40, 364
Berkey, Jonathan, 2, 7, 43, 426
Biblical and Quranic allusions, 315–16, 404–7
al-Bidāya wa-l-nihāya fī al-Taʾrīkh (Ibn Kathīr), 311
Binbaş, Evrim, 9, 178
al-Birzālī, al-Qāsim (d. 739/1339), 309, 310
Bori, Caterina, 242
Bourdieu, Pierre, 423, 425
Brinner, William, 82, 95
Broadbridge, Anne, 40, 46, 107, 433
al-Bulqīnī, ʿAlam al-Dīn (d. 868/1464) (qadi), 159–60, 162
al-Bulqīnī, Jalāl al-Dīn (d. 824/1421) (qadi), 116, 145
al-Bulqīnī, Sirāj al-Dīn (*shaykh al-islām*), 108
Burulghay al-Ashrafī, 66
Buyid amirs (Iraq and Persia), 9–10, 254–5, 369
al-Maqrīzī on, 315
understanding of Sunni caliphate, 434
use of *bayʿa*, 407

Cairo Caliphate
caliphal authority in society, 390–1
conceptions of, 82
the masses (*ʿāmma*) and, 435–8, 445n62
under Ottomans, 219
under Ottomans, administration, 209–12
under Ottomans, relations with Selīm, 212–14
under Ottomans, Selīm's perception of, 207–8
people's duties to caliph, 400–1
public profile of caliphs, 78
religious elite and, 107, 432–5
'shadow caliphate,' 1–2, 440
in social and religious world, 431–2
Sufi ties, 178–9, 436–8
see also Abbasid Caliphate; Abbasid family; arbitration and intercession by Cairo caliph; ceremonial functions of Cairo Caliphate; chancery documents; chancery documents, caliphal succession contracts; chancery documents, investiture deeds; diplomacy of Cairo Caliphate; historiographical literature; jurisprudential, advice and courtly literature; legitimacy of Cairo Caliphate; legitimisation of distant rulers by Cairo Caliphate; legitimisation of sultan by Cairo Caliphate; political theory; politics of Cairo Caliphate; religious authority of Cairo Caliphate; symbolism of Cairo Caliphate; *specific caliphs and sultans*
Cairo map, *65*
Cairo Sultanate (sultanate of Cairo)
guarantor of caliphate, 27
nondynastic legitimacy (early fifteenth c.), 141–2
Ottoman conquest of, 192–3
periodisation of, 12
political order, overview, 5–7
political realities, 426–30
respect for Abbasid bloodline, 437–8
sultans as heirs of early Abbasid caliphs, 295
see also Cairo Caliphate; political theory; *specific caliphs and sultans*
caliphal titulary protocol *see* titular nomenclature
Cem, Ottoman prince, 171–2
ceremonial functions Cairo Caliphate; *see also* Cairo Caliphate; legitimacy of Cairo Caliphate; legitimisation of sultan by Cairo Caliphate; political theory; religious authority of Cairo Caliphate; symbolism of Cairo Caliphate

ceremonial functions of Cairo Caliphate
under al-Ashraf Khalīl, 41–3
bay'a protocols, 26, 76–7, 167
bay'a ritual, 428
bestowal of authority on sultan, 326–7
demonstrations of power, 428–9
funeral prayers, 153, 166, 203
mawlid celebrations, 174, 438
pomp and protocol, 157, 158, 202, 203
Qalawunid use of symbols, 48, 82
see also religious authority of Cairo Caliphate
Chāldirān, Battle of (920/1514), 204
Chamberlain, Michael, 7, 437
chancery documents, 339–43, 371, 413–15; *see also* Cairo Caliphate; chancery documents, caliphal succession contracts; chancery documents, investiture deeds; chancery documents, various; historiographical literature; jurisprudential, advice and courtly literature; political theory; *specific caliphs and sultans*
chancery documents, caliphal succession contracts
overview, 355–7, 391–2
al-Ḥākim II, 393–4
al-Ḥākim II (701/1302) for al-Mustakfī, 357
kinship as central theme, 382
al-Musta'īn, 395, 403–4
al-Mustakfī I, 386–7
al-Mustakfī I for al-Ḥākim II, 402–3
al-Mustakfī I for Baraka al-Mustawathiq, 394–5
al-Mustakfī I for successors, 357–8
al-Mu'taḍid I for al-Mutawakkil I, 358, 387–8, 406
al-Mu'taḍid II, 382
al-Mu'taḍid II (*c.* 816/1414), 388
al-Mu'taḍid II for al-Mustakfī II, 360, 389, 407
al-Mutawakkil I, 389, 406
al-Mutawakkil I for al-Musta'īn, 358–60
see also Cairo Caliphate; chancery documents; chancery documents, investiture deeds; chancery documents, various; historiographical literature; jurisprudential, advice and courtly literature; political theory; *specific caliphs and sultans*
chancery documents, investiture deeds
overview, 343–4, 381, 391–2
al-Ashraf Barsbāy, 352, 354, 382–3, 398–9, 412–13
al-Ashraf Khalīl, 386, 410
Baybars al-Bunduqdārī, 285, 343, 344–5, 382, 384–5
Baybars al-Jāshinkīr, 350–2, 393, 395, 397, 399, 405, 411
Berke ibn Baybars, 345–6
al-Ḥākim I, 388–9
al-Ḥākim II, 387, 398, 399–401, 406, 411–12
al-Manṣūr Abū Bakr, 352
al-Manṣūr Kitbughā, 349
al-Manṣūr Lājīn, 349, 394
al-Mu'ayyad Shaykh, 352–3, 395
al-Musta'īn's testamentary document, 405–6
al-Mustakfī I inaugural prayers, 389
Muẓaffar Shāh of India, 201, 361, 383, 388, 402, 413
al-Nāṣir Muḥammad, 350, 383–4, 392–3
Qalāwūn, 346–7, 384, 385–6, 410
al-Ẓāhir Ṭaṭar, 352, 353–4, 397–8, 405, 412
see also Cairo Caliphate; chancery documents; chancery documents, caliphal succession contracts; chancery documents, various; historiographical literature; jurisprudential, advice and courtly literature; political theory; *specific caliphs and sultans*
chancery documents, various
advice to al-Nāṣir Muḥammad, 396–7
al-Bārizī's investiture deed as overseer, 362–3, 383, 395
coinage, *125*, 367–8
inscriptions, 119, *120*, 366–7
khuṭbas, 363–5
letter to Ḥizabr al-Dīn Dāwūd, 63–4, 361, 390–1
al-Musta'īn's testamentary document, 405–6
titular nomenclature, 251–2, 262–3, 367–71, 371
see also Cairo Caliphate; chancery documents; chancery documents, caliphal succession contracts; chancery documents, investiture deeds; historiographical literature; jurisprudential, advice and courtly literature; political theory; *qasīm amīr al-mu'minīn*; *specific caliphs and sultans*
Chapoutot-Remadi, Mounira, 2
Chinggisids, 9, 33–4, 99–100
Circassians, 45, 64, 95, 141–2
Citadel map, *102*
Clifford, Winslow, 7
'cultural grammar,' 4, 8
Cyprus, 147

Dahshūr, 174–5, 201, 207
Dar' ta'āruḍ al-'aql wa-l-naql (Ibn Taymiyya), 242
Dāvud Pasha, 218
'Dawlat al-Atrāk,' 6, 247, 249, 414, 426–30
al-Dhahab al-masbūk (al-Maqrīzī), 317–18
al-Dhahabī, Muḥammad (d. 748/1348)
background, 310–11
influence of Abū Shāma on, 308
as source, 67, 68
universal approach in writing, 278
Dhayl 'alā al-rawḍatayn (Abū Shāma), 308
Dhayl al-mir'āt al-zamān (al-Yūnīnī), 309–10
D'hulster, Kristof, 423–4

diplomacy Cairo Caliphate
with India, 201
diplomacy of Cairo Caliphate
with Bāyezīd II, 171
caliph's religious authority in, 153
caliph's role, 401–2
with India, 79, 82, 165, 169
with papacy, 172
with Yemen, 63–4, 361, 390–1, 401–2
Diu, Battle of (914/1509), 201
Diyar Bakr, 145, 345
d'Ohsson, Mouradgea, 214
droughts, 155, 165, 322–3
Dulqadirids, 144–5, 167–8, 171
Durar al-ʿuqūd al-farīda (al-Maqrīzī), 317

Elephant Island (*Jazīrat al-Fīl*), 69, 97, 159
Erzincan, 145
Evliyā Çelebi, 70, 216

Fabricius, Georg, 214
al-Faḍl al-maʾthūr min sīrat al-Sulṭān al-Malik al-Manṣūr (Shāfiʿ ibn ʿAlī), 287–8
al-Fallūja, 21
Faraj, al-Nāṣir (sultan, r. 801–15/1399–1412)
installation of, 108
military expedition against Temür, 109–10, 134n69, 392
rebellion against, 110, 111–13, 113–18, 127
results of reign, 141
Fatḥ Allāh (*kātib al-sirr*, d. 816/1413), 113, 114, 115, 117, 118, 124, 127, 313
Fatimids, 313, 318, 369, 370–1, 407, 428
fatwas, 97, 103, 109, 124, 204
nature of, 232–3
Ferīdūn Beğ (d. 991/1583), 211
fitna Ẓāhiriyya, 98–9, 311, 319
Flinterman, Willem, 60
foreign relations
Anatolia, 144, 147, 167–8
Aqquyunlu Turkmen, 116–17, 144–5, 149–50
Armenia, 41, 42
Baghdad, attempt to reclaim, 24, 29–34, 206
Baghdad, rebellion in, 92–3
caliph's religious authority in, 153, 261
caliph's role in, 401–2, 413
Chinggisids, 33–4, 99–100
Cyprus, 147
Europe, 172
Golden Horde, 34–7, 67
Hijaz, 123, 147, 148, 317–18
Ilkhanids, 35, 39–40, 41, 45–6, 62–3, 81
India, 79, 82, 165–6, 169, 184n51, 201
Muzaffarids (Fars), 82, 93
Ottoman sultan Bāyezīd, 106–7
Ottoman sultan Bāyezīd II, 170–2
Ottoman sultan Meḥmed II, 148–9
Ottoman sultan Murād II, 151
Ottoman sultan Selīm the Grim, 202, 204–6
Qaraquyunlu Turkmen, 145, 148–9
Temür, 106–7, 109–10, 111, 134n69
Timurids, 144–5, 148
West Africa (Mali and Borno), 82
Yemen, 63–4, 361, 390–1, 401–2
see also Cairo Sultanate; Mongols; Temür (Tamerlane); *specific caliphs and sultans*
futuwwa brotherhood, 29, 36, 55n57, 55n58, 179, 284

Garcin, Jean-Claude, 2, 73–4, 91, 163, 324–5
Gharaibeh, Mohammad, 311
al-Ghazālī, Abū Ḥāmid (d. 505/1111), 264
Ghāzān Maḥmūd (*ilkhan*, r. 694–703/1295–1304), 45–6, 62–3
Ghurid rulers, 369
Gibb, Hamilton, 246–7
Golden Horde, 35–7, 40, 67; *see also* Mongols

Haarmann, Ulrich, 260
Hafsid caliphate, 3, 27
Ḥajj (pilgrimage), 44–5, 64, 67, 78, 80, 93, 148, 221, 258–60, 259–60, 317–18, 424
Ḥājjī I, al-Muẓaffar (sultan, r. 747–8/1346–7), 79
Ḥājjī II, al-Ṣāliḥ (sultan, r. 783–4, 791/1382, 1389), 95, 103–6
al-Ḥākim I, Abū al-ʿAbbās Aḥmad (caliph, r. 661–701/1262–1302)
among Bedouin, 20–1
arrival and *bayʿa* in Cairo, 34–7
battle at Hīt, 31–2
bayʿa of Banū Taymiyya, 241
confinement, 37–8, 284, 285
death of, 47–8, 61
forced to endorse coup, 43
futuwwa initiation, 36, 55n57, 284
investiture by Baybars, 292–3
investiture deed, 388–9
investitures of sultans, 346–7, 349–50
khuṭbas, 41–2, 363–5, 392
al-Maqrīzī on, 316, 317–18
military expedition to Syria, 46, 284, 310
on pilgrimage, 44–5, 317–18
powers as caliph, 336n191
renewal of *bayʿa* pledge to, 41
search for investiture, 23–4
selection of successor, 61
submission to al-Mustanṣir, 30–1
sultan–caliph relationship, 286
support for al-Nāṣir Muḥammad, 396–7
al-Ḥākim II, Aḥmad (caliph, r. 741–53/1341–52)
bayʿa ceremony, 294
caliph 'in name only,' 296
death and succession of, 79–80
deed of appointment, 358
al-Dhahabī on, 311
duties theocratic authority and legitimacy, 403
installation of sultan al-Nāṣir Aḥmad, 76–7

al-Ḥākim II, Aḥmad (*cont.*)
investiture deed, 382, 387, 398, 399–401, 406, 411–12
investitures of sultans, 79, 352
model for 15th c. caliphs, 142
networks and influence, 77, 431
offered power, 83
petition to concerning dispute, 362
refrained from affairs of state, 81
relocated to Palestine, 77
social and political influence of, 77–8
succession contracts, 393–4
suppression of, 70, 71–2, 73
al-Ḥalabī, Shihāb al-Dīn Maḥmūd (d. 725/1325), 349, 383–4
al-Ḥalīmī, Abū ʿAbdallāh al-Jurjānī (d. 403/1012), 236–7
Har-El, Shai, 172
Hartmann, Richard, 3
Hārūn al-Rashīd (Baghdad caliph, r. 170–93/786–809), 233, 295, 355
al-Ḥasan, al-Nāṣir (sultan, r. 748–52, 755–62/1347–51, 1354–61), 79, 81
Ḥasan ibn ʿAbdallāh al-ʿAbbāsī (d. after 716/1316), 233–6
Hassan, Mona, 3–4, 8, 19, 21, 24, 26, 33, 115, 229, 239, 240–1, 242, 244–5, 245–6, 256, 278–9, 311, 312–13, 382, 404, 425, 426, 433
Ḥawādith (al-Jazarī), 309
Ḥayāt Nāṣir al-Ḥajjī, 70, 124
Ḥaydar Çelebi, 206, 211
Heidemann, Stefan, 3, 21, 24, 26, 33, 36, 43, 82, 284, 310
Hijaz
drought, 322–3
expanding influence of Caliph Sultanate in, 147, 148
prayers for caliph-sultan of Cairo, 123
al-Ḥillī, ʿAllāma (d. 726/1326), 258–9
Ḥims (Syria), 46
Hirschler, Konrad, 276, 277, 308–9, 327
historiographical literature
overview, 276–7, 325–7
awlād al-nās historians, 293–307
bureaucrat historians, 283–8
Egyptian historians, later fifteenth century, 312–25
intertextuality, 280, 309
'Mamluk' collective memory in, 278–9
military historians, 289–93
organised around caliphate, 279–80
regional and occupational considerations, 280–1, 283
Syrian historians, early fourteenth century, 307–12
ʿulamāʾ in, 277
see also Cairo Caliphate; chancery documents; chancery documents, caliphal succession contracts; chancery documents, investiture deeds; chancery documents, various; Ibn Ḥajar al-ʿAsqalānī; jurisprudential, advice and courtly literature; al-Maqrīzī, Aḥmad; political theory; *specific caliphs and sultans*
Ḥizabr al-Dīn Dāwūd, al-Muʾayyad (Rasulid ruler), 63–4, 361, 390–1, 401–2
Holt, Peter, 3, 33, 76–7, 214–15, 219, 399, 408–9
Hülegü (*ilkhan*, r. 654–63/1256–65), 34–5, 36, 37, 314
al-Ḥusaynī, Ḥusayn ibn Muḥammad, 260–3
Ḥusn al-muḥāḍara (al-Suyūṭī), 323–4

al-ʿIbar (Ibn Khaldūn), 247, 249–51
Ibn ʿAbd Rabbih, 237, 238
Ibn ʿAbd al-Salām, ʿIzz al-Dīn ʿAbd al-ʿAzīz (d. 660/1261), 26, 51n19
Ibn ʿAbd al-Ẓāhir, ʿAlāʾ al-Dīn (scribe), 351
Ibn ʿAbd al-Ẓāhir, Muḥyī al-Dīn (d. 692/1292)
al-Alṭāf al-khafiyya, 285–6
on Baybars, 37, 290
caliph–sultan relationship, 265, 286–7
chancery documents preserved by, 341, 345
chancery documents written by, 346–7, 348, 385–6, 410
Rawḍ al-zāhir, 283–5
Tashrīf al-ayyām, 285
Ibn ʿArabī, Muḥyī al-Dīn (d. 638/1240), 178
Ibn ʿArabshāh, Aḥmad (d. 854/1450), 99–100
Ibn al-Bannāʾ, Zayn al-Dīn Ṣāliḥ, 309–10
Ibn Bint al-Aʿazz, Tāj al-Dīn, 26, 325
Ibn al-Burhān (d. 808/1405), 99
Ibn Daqīq al-ʿĪd (d. 702/1302), 61
Ibn al-Furāt, 341
Ibn Ḥajar al-ʿAsqalānī (d. 852/1449)
background and works, 312, 319–23, 326
on caliphate, 433
commentary by, 120–1
funeral, 154, 323
funeral of Barsbāy, 150
al-Muʿtaḍid II and, 152
see also historiographical literature; political theory
Ibn Ḥijja, Abū Bakr al-Ḥamawī (d. 837/1434)
chancery documents preserved by, 341
chancery documents written by, 352, 354, 362–3, 382–3, 397–8, 405, 412–13, 438
see also chancery documents; chancery documents, caliphal succession contracts; chancery documents, investiture deeds; political theory
Ibn Iyās, Muḥammad (d. 930/1524)
background and works, 281, 300–7; *see also* historiographical literature; political theory
chronicle by, 216
on exiles to Istanbul, 213, 432
influence of Abū Shāma on, 308

on Khalīl ibn Nāṣir al-Dīn Muḥammad, 197, 198, 199
on al-Mustakfī II's succession, 407
on al-Mutawakkil II, 175
on al-Mutawakkil III, 210, 211, 215
popular poetry preserved, 303–4
on Qāniṣawh al-Ghawrī, 202, 203
as reporter of public opinion, 302–3, 435
as source, 432
on al-Suyūṭī, 324
Ibn Jamā'a, Badr al-Dīn Muḥammad (d. 733/1333), 238–41, 265, 308, 439–40
Ibn Jamā'a, 'Izz al-Dīn (d. 767/1366), 72–3, 75
Ibn Kathīr, Ismā'īl (d. 774/1373)
eschatological views of, 311
meets caliph al-Mu'taḍid in Damascus, 80
universal approach in writing, 278
see also historiographical literature; political theory
Ibn Khaldūn, 'Abd al-Raḥmān (d. 808/1406)
background and works, 246–51
on caliphate, 266, 276, 326, 327, 433
caliphate as organisation structure in writing, 279
influence of on al-Maqrīzī, 314
Temür meets with, 110
see also historiographical literature; political theory
Ibn Mubārakshāh al-Ṭāzī (d. 823/1420), 114–15, 117, 122, 127
Ibn al-Muqaffa', 237
Ibn Nāẓir al-Jaysh, Taqī al-Dīn (d. 786/1384), 253, 341
Ibn al-Qaysarānī, Shams al-Dīn Ibrāhīm, 350, 392–3, 396–7
Ibn Qutayba, 237
Ibn Quṭluqtamur, Ibrāhīm, 96–7
Ibn Taghrībirdī, Abū al-Maḥāsin Yūsuf (d. 874/1470)
background and works, 152–3, 295–300, 326, 331n76
on caliphate, 266, 296–300
on investiture practice, 407–8
on al-Musta'īn, 127–8
on al-Mustakfī II, 155
on al-Mu'taḍid II, 152–3
as source, 158, 162–3
see also historiographical literature; jurisprudential, advice and courtly literature; political theory
Ibn Tankiz, Muḥammad, 96
Ibn Taymiyya, Aḥmad Taqī al-Dīn (d. 728/1328)
background and works, 241–4
caliphate, 264, 265–6, 433
disapproval of popular Sufi practices, 436–7
see also historiographical literature; political theory
Ibn Ṭūlūn, Muḥammad (historian), 204, 214
Ibn Wāṣil, Jamāl al-Dīn Muḥammad, 308
Ibrāhīm ibn Muḥammad al-Mustamsi; *see also* al-Wāthiq I, Ibrāhīm (caliph)
Ibrāhīm ibn Muḥammad al-Mustamsik (later al-Wāthiq I), 61, 69
Ibrāhīm ibn al-Mu'taḍid II (d. 837/1433), 154
al-Iḥkām (al-Qarāfī), 232–3
Ilkhanids, 35, 39–40, 41, 45–6, 62–3, 81; *see also* Mongols
Īnāl, al-Ashraf (sultan, r. 857–65/1453–61)
death and succession of, 163–4
revolt against, 160–2, 163, 298
usurpation by, 158–60
Inalcik, Halil, 214
Inbāba (Imbāba), 164, 168, 173
India, 79, 82, 169, 201
embassies from, 184n51
see also Muẓaffar Shāh
Iran, 15 c. understanding of caliphate, 178
Irwin, Robert, 260
'Īsā ibn Muhannā (d. 683/1284), 20–1, 23, 24, 32
Iskandar ibn 'Umar Shaykh (d. 818/1415), 178
Ismā'īl (Safavid Shāh, r. 907–30/1501–24), 204, 258–9, 262
Ismā'īl, al-Ṣāliḥ (sultan, r. 743–6/1342–5), 77, 370
Ismā'īlī assassins (*fidā'īs*), 68
Istanbul
Abbasid caliph in, 215–16
Abbasid family members in, 218
forced exile to, 212–14
'transfer of the caliphate' legend, 214–15, 216

al-Jabartī, 'Abd al-Raḥmān, 219, 309–10
Jackson, Sherman, 29, 232
Jahānshāh (Qaraquyunlu ruler, r. 837–53/1434–49), 148–9
Jakam, 110
Jalāl al-Dīn Muḥammad Shāh (sultan of Bengal, d. 836/1433), 153, 184n51
Jān Sukkar, consort of Qāniṣawh al-Ghawrī, 203
Jānbalāṭ, al-Ashraf (sultan, r. 905–6/1500–1), 193–4
Jānībak Ḥabīb (amir), 171
Jānibak al-Ṣūfī (amir), 147
Jānim al-Ashrafī (viceroy of Damascus, d. 867/1462), 165
Jaqmaq, al-Ẓāhir (sultan, r. 842–57/1438–53)
Abū al-Khayr al-Naḥḥās affair, 157–8
consolidation of power, 150–2
death and succession of, 158
al-Mustakfī II and, 155, 156
selection of caliph, 126, 156–7
al-Jazarī, Muḥammad (d. 739/1338), 309, 310
jihād
caliph as symbol of, 63, 291, 350–1, 392–4
legality of against Mongols, 239, 291
obligation of, 364–5, 392
'protection' of caliphate, 63, 291–2
removes sin, 285

jihād (*cont.*)
sultans praised for, 384–5
see also political theory
julbān (purchased *mamlūk* recruits), 160–2
jurisprudential, advice and courtly literature
overview, 229–31, 263–6
late thirteenth century, 231–3
fourteenth century, 233–46
early fifteenth century, 246–56
late fifteenth–early sixteenth century, 256–66
advice literature, 233–4
Āthār al-uwal (Ḥasan al-ʿAbbāsī), 233–6
Ibn Taymiyya, 241–4, 264, 265–6, 433, 436–7
Kawkab al-durrī (anon.), 260
Kitāb al-iḥkām (al-Qarāfī), 232–3
Maʾāthir al-ināfa (al-Qalqashandī), 251–6
Miṣbāḥ al-hidāya (anon.), 231–2, 264
Muḥammad Ibn Jamāʿa, 238–41, 265, 308, 439–40
Muʿīd al-niʿam wa-mubīd al-niqam (al-Subkī), 244–6
Muqaddima (Ibn Khaldūn), 246–9
Nafāʾis al-majālis al-sulṭāniyya (al-Ḥusaynī), 260–3
Nihāyat al-arab (al-Nuwayrī), 236–8
Ṣubḥ (al-Qalqashandī), 251, 252, 256, 371
Sulūk al-mulūk (Khunjī-Iṣfahānī), 259–60
Taḥrīr al-aḥkām (Ibn Jamāʿa), 238–41
Taʾrīkh-i ʿālam-ārā-yi amīnī (Khunjī-Iṣfahānī), 258–9
titular nomenclature, 251–2, 262–3, 367–70, 371
Zubda (Khalīl al-Ẓāhirī), 256–8
see also al-Qalqashandī; Cairo Caliphate; chancery documents; chancery documents, caliphal succession contracts; chancery documents, investiture deeds; historiographical literature; political theory; *specific caliphs and sultans*

al-Kabsh, 44, 45, 47, 61, 62, 68, 69, 163
al-Karak, 64, 76, 77, 107, 288
as place of exile, 38, 45, 104, 348, 350, 396
Kawkab al-durrī (anon.), 260
Kennedy, Hugh, 76, 424
Khafāja Bedouin, 20, 25
Khalidi, Tarif, 277
khalīfa title, 178–9, 369–70; *see also* political theory
Khalīl, al-Ashraf (sultan, r. 689–93/1290–3)
Ibn ʿAbd al-Ẓāhir on, 285–6
inscriptions and coinage, 367–8
investiture deed, 348, 386, 410
khuṭba commissioned by, 41–2, 363–5
military campaigns, 41–2
sultan–caliph relationship, 41–3
Khalīl ibn Nāṣir al-Dīn Muḥammad (Abbasid prince), 177, 193, 196–8, 199, 221n14, 304–5
Khalīl al-Ẓāhirī (d. 872/1468), 153, 256–8, 408
Khaljī, Ghiyāth al-Dīn Shāh (sultan of Malwa, r. 873–906/1469–1501), 169
Khaljī, Maḥmūd Shāh (sultan of Malwa, r. 839–73/1436–69), 165–6
Khāyrbak (*nāʾib* of Aleppo), 205, 212, 216
Khāyrbak al-Khushqadamī, 166
Khiṭaṭ (al-Maqrīzī), 316–17
Khunjī-Iṣfahānī, Faḍlullāh ibn Rūzbihān (d. 926/1520), 168, 258–60
Khushqadam, al-Ẓāhir (sultan, r. 865–72/1461–7, 164–6, 167
Khwāja Mirjān (governor of Baghdad), 92–3
kiswa (covering for Kaʿba), 148
Kitbughā, al-Manṣūr (sultan, r. 694–6/1295–7), 43–4, 348, 368
investiture deed, 349
Knights Hospitallers of St. John, 171–2
Küçük Kaynarca, treaty of, 214
Kujuk, al-Ashraf (sultan, r. 742/1341), 76, 79

Lājīn, al-Manṣūr (sultan, r. 696–8/1296–9), 42, 43–4, 288, 348
investiture deed, 349, 394
Laoust, Henri, 241, 263
Lapidus, Ira, 423–4
legitimacy of Cairo Caliphate
Abbasid lineage, 382, 422
as arms race, 9–10
legal framework for lacking, 9
rejected by Mongols, 46
rejected by 'Ẓāhirī' scholars, 99
umma (community) as source, 243–4
see also Cairo Caliphate; chancery documents; chancery documents, investiture deeds; jurisprudential, advice and courtly literature; legitimisation of distant rulers by Cairo Caliphate; legitimisation of sultan by Cairo Caliphate; political theory; Qurayshī lineage; religious authority of Cairo Caliphate; symbolism of Cairo Caliphate; *specific caliphs and sultans*
legitimisation of distant rulers by Cairo Caliphate
from India, 79, 82–3, 153
from India (Malwa), 165–6, 169
Muẓaffar Shāh of India, 201, 361, 383, 388, 402, 413
Muzaffarids of Fars, 82–3, 93
Ottomans, 107–8, 133n55, 171
Timurids, 148
from West Africa (Mali and Borno), 82
see also Cairo Caliphate; chancery documents; chancery documents, investiture deeds; legitimacy of Cairo Caliphate; legitimisation of sultan by Cairo Caliphate; political theory; religious authority of Cairo Caliphate; symbolism of Cairo Caliphate; *specific caliphs and sultans*

legitimisation of sultan by Cairo Caliphate
Abbasid lineage seen as requirement, 94, 95
caliph's relevance questioned by historians, 301
one of several sources, 83, 440
Qalawunid dynasty, 60
see also Cairo Caliphate; ceremonial functions of Cairo Caliphate; chancery documents; chancery documents, investiture deeds; legitimisation of distant rulers by Cairo Caliphate; political theory; religious authority of Cairo Caliphate; symbolism of Cairo Caliphate; *specific caliphs and sultans*
Lellouch, Benjamin, 206
Lewis, Bernard, 214
Little, Donald, 63, 363
Loiseau, Julien, 12
Lorenzo de Medici, 172
Luʾluʾid princes, 29, 30, 32
Luqmān, Fakhr al-Dīn (*kātib al-sirr*), 344–5, 346

Maʾāthir (al-Qalqashandī), 251–6
Madelung, Wilferd, 231, 232
Majmūʿ al-fatāwa (Ibn Taymiyya), 241–2
al-Malaṭī, ʿAbd al-Bāsiṭ (d. 920/1515), 153, 169
Mamluk Sultanate *see* Cairo Sultanate
al-Maʾmūn (Baghdad caliph, r. 189–218/813–33), 235, 315
maps
Cairo, *65*
Citadel, *102*
Syro-Egypt and Mesopotamia, *22*
West Asia, *143*
al-Maqrīzī, Aḥmad (d. 845/1442)
background, 312–13, 318–19
on caliphate, 266, 326, 327, 426, 433, 439–40
on investiture practice, 407–8
on al-Mustaʿīn's deposition, 125, 127–8, 297
as source, 27, 93, 123
works addressing contemporary Abbasid Caliphate, 314–18
works on early age of Islam, 313–14
see also historiographical literature; jurisprudential, advice and courtly literature; political theory
Mārdīn, 107
Marʿī ibn Yūsuf Karmī (d. 1033/1623–4), 218
Marj Dābiq, Battle of (922/1516), 205–6
Markiewicz, Christopher, 9
Maryam bint al-Mutawakkil I, 174
al-Maṣābīḥ (al-Baghawī), *282*
Massoud, Sami, 300
Māturīdī theology, 230
al-Māwardī, ʿAlī (d. 450/1058)
on caliphate/imamate, 239, 403
influence of on al-Nuwayrī, 237
influence of on chancery secretaries, 344
influence of on Ibn Khaldūn, 247
influence of on later writers, 264
influence of on al-Qalqashandī, 252–5
sultan's authority to appoint, 346, 348
see also jurisprudential, advice and courtly literature; political theory
Meḥmed II, Ottoman sultan (855–86/1451–81), 148–9, 167, 170–1
military elite, loyalty to caliphate, 290–2, 429–30
Minhāj al-sunna (Ibn Taymiyya), 241, 242
Minṭāsh, 100–1, 103–5, 249
Mirʾāt al-zamān (Sibṭ ibn al-Jawzī), 307, 309
Miṣbāḥ al-hidāya (anon.), 231–2, 239, 264
Moin, Azfar, 231, 427
Möngke Temür (Golden Horde khān, r. 665–79/1267–80), 40
Mongols
Abbasid Caliphate as push-back to, 48
attacks in Syria (657/1259–60), 20–1
Baybars' expedition against, 287
Chinggisids, 9, 33–4, 99–100
defeat of in collective memory, 278
destruction of Baghdad caliphate, 19, 33–4
eclipse of, 81
Golden Horde, 35–7, 67
Ilkhanids, 35, 39–40, 41, 45–6, 62–3, 81
legality of *jihād* against, 239, 291, 392
rejection of caliphal authority in Cairo, 291
Shiʿism, 46
Temür, 99–100, 106–7, 109–10, 111, 134n69
see also foreign relations
Muʾayyadiyya *mamlūks*, 159
Mufarrij al-kurūb fī akhbār Banī Ayyūb (Ibn Wāṣil), 308
Mughals, 9, 177, 439
Muḥammad (817–81/1414–76) heir to caliph al-Mutawakkil II, 177
Muḥammad, al-Manṣūr (sultan, r. 762–4/1361–3), 81, 92
Muḥammad Beg, Qaramanid leader, 144
Muḥammad ibn al-Mustakfī I, 68
Muḥammad al-Mustamsik (d. 695/1296), 61, 73
Muḥammad ibn Qalāwūn, al-Nāṣir (sultan, r. 693–741/1293–1341, intermittently)
authority of, 237, 238
caliphal succession, 71–2
caliph's advice to, 396–7
caliph–sultan relations, 61–2, 68–71, 78, 239, 358
coinage, 368
creation of political elite, 66
death and succession of, 74, 351
first reign, 43, 348
foreign relations, 361
Ibn Ḥajar on, 319
investiture deeds, 350, 383–4, 392–3
al-Jazarī on, 310
military expedition against Mongols, 63
second reign, 45–6
third enthronement, 66
usurpation of by father's amirs, 61, 64, 66, 348

Muḥammad ibn Qānisawh (poet), 305–6
Muḥammad ibn Qāyitbāy, al-Nāṣir (sultan, r. 901–4/1496–8), 175–6, 193
Muḥammad Shībānī Khān, 259
Muḥammad ibn Ṭaṭar, al-Ṣāliḥ (sultan, r. 824–5/1421–2), 147
Muḥammad ibn Ya'qūb al-Mustamsik, 196–7, *196*; *see also* al-Mutawakkil III, Muḥammad (caliph)
Muhanna, Elias, 340
Mu'īd al-ni'am wa-mubīd al-niqam (al-Subkī), 244–6
al-Mukhtaṣar fī Ta'rīkh al-bashar (Abū al-Fidā'), 292–3
Muqaddima (Ibn Khaldūn), 246–9
Muqtafī (al-Birzālī), 309, 310
Murād II (Ottoman sultan, r. 824–55/1421–51), 151
Mūsā al-Hāshimī (Abbasid prince), 170
Muṣṭafā Çelebi, 212
Muṣṭafā Cenābī (d. 999/1590), 218
al-Musta'īn, al-'Abbās (caliph, r. 808–16/1406–14; sultan, r. 815/1412)
  ascension to sultanate, 114–18, 141, 255, 320
  caliph-sultan, usurpation of powers from, 121–3
  coinage, *125*, 136n93, 368
  in confinement, 142
  dates of rule, 139n131
  decrees by, 118–21, *120*
  deposed as sultan, 121–4, 297
  distinguished by name, 384
  freed from exile/confinement in Alexandria, 146–7
  Ibn Ḥajar on, 320–2
  inscriptions, 367
  investiture as caliph, 113–14
  investiture of Shaykh, 122–4, 352–3
  legitimisation of sultan of Delhi, 201, 361, 383, 388, 402
  literary commentary on, 304
  al-Maqrīzī and, 313
  politics of (overview), 127–9
  popular support for, 119–20
  powers as sultan, 116, 336n191
  sequestered and exiled, 125–6
  succession contract, 358–60, 395, 403–4
  support for as sultan, 427
  testamentary document upon succession, 405–6
al-Mustakfī I, Sulaymān (caliph, r. 701–40/1302–40)
  assumption of caliphate, 60–2
  banishment of, 68–71
  Biblical and Qur'anic allusions, 404–5
  challenge to Qalawunid legitimacy, 239
  confirmation of al-Nāṣir Muḥammad, 66
  confirmation of sultan Baybars al-Jāshinkīr, 64, 66, 350–2, 393, 395
  death and succession of, 70–4, 357–8
  exile to Qūṣ, 69–70, 294
  Ibn Ḥajar on, 319
  inaugural prayers, 389
  on military campaigns, 63, 291
  personal life, 67
  politics against al-Nāṣir Muḥammad, 64–6, 68, 431
  popular support for, 69–70
  succession contract for son Baraka al-Mustawathiq, 357–8, 394–5
  succession contract from father, 357, 386–7
  in Yemen diplomatic row, 63–4, 361, 390–1, 401–2
al-Mustakfī II, Sulaymān (caliph, r. 845–55/1441–51)
  avoidance of politics, 154–6
  drought and public prayers, 155
  at funeral of Ibn Ḥajar, 154, 323
  succession contracts, 360, 389, 407
  al-Suyūṭī family and, 154–5
al-Mustamsik, Ya'qūb (caliph, r. 903–14, 922–3/1497–1508, 1516–17)
  abdication, 195–9
  death of, 216
  later years in Cairo (914–27/1508–21), 199, 200
  literary commentary on, 304–6
  Martin von Baumgarten on, 195
  Ottoman confiscation of heirlooms and revenue, 213
  political instability in early reign, 192–5
  reinstatement as caliph, 206–7, 437–8
  succession dispute, 195–9, *196*, 301
al-Mustanjid, Yūsuf (caliph, r. 859–84/1455–79)
  death and succession of, 169–70
  Ibn Iyās on reactions to sultan's treatment, 302
  investiture of Khushqadam, 164–5
  personal life, 169
  religious ruling sought from, 167–8
  selection of, 162
  sultan–caliph relationship, 165, 301
al-Mustanṣir (Hafsid ruler), 3, 27
al-Mustanṣir, Abū al-Qāsim Aḥmad (caliph, r. 659–60/1261)
  al-Dhahabī on, 310–11
  Ibn Kathīr on, 311
  investiture, 23–4, 25–8, 283–4, 292
  investiture of Baybars, 26–7, 345
  military expedition to Baghdad, 24, 29–34, 283–4, 287, 289–90, 310
  sultan–caliph relationship, 33
al-Mustanṣir bi-llāh al-Manṣūr (Baghdad caliph, r. 623–40/1226–42), 25
al-Mustarshid al-Faḍl (Baghdad caliph, r. 512–29/1118–35), 20
al-Musta'ṣim, 'Abdallāh (Baghdad caliph, r. 640–56/1242–58), 19, 25, 123, 315

al-Musta'ṣim, Zakariyyā' (caliph, r. 788–91/1386–9), 97, 98, 100, 103, 105, 130n24
al-Mu'taḍid I, Abū Bakr (caliph, r. 753–63/1352–62), 80, 81
  succession contract for son al-Mutawakkil, 387–8
  succession documents, 358
al-Mu'taḍid II, Dāwūd (caliph, r. 816–45/1414–41)
  al-Ashraf Barsbāy and, 147–51
  dates of rule, 139n131
  diplomacy with India, 184n51
  emissaries to foreign courts, 148–9
  evocation of Prophet Dāwūd, 405
  Ibn Ḥajar on, 322–3
  investiture deed for al-Bārizī's appointment, 362–3
  investitures of sultans, 352, 353–4
  letter to al-Nāṣir Aḥmad of Yemen, 402
  networks and influence, 431
  personal life, 152–4, 295
  as rival caliph, 124–6
  scholarship, 142, 152–4
  and Shaykh's sultanate, 142, 144–5
  succession contract to brother al-Mustakfī II, 154, 389, 407
  succession contracts, 360, 382, 388
  support for sultan Yūsuf, 150–1
  in Syria with sultan, 149–50
  written commentary on, 305
  al-Ẓāhir Jaqmaq and, 151–2
  al-Ẓāhir Ṭaṭar and, 146–7
al-Mu'taṣim, Zakariyyā' (caliph, r. 779/1377), 94, 130n24
al-Mutawakkil I, Muḥammad (caliph, r. 763–808/1362–1406, intermittently)
  overview, 92
  beginning of reign, 81
  conflict with Aynabak al-Badrī, 94–5
  death of, 112
  deposition, 96–8
  disputed title, 320
  Ibn al-'Aṭṭār on, 303
  Ibn Ḥajar on, 319
  investiture of Barqūq, 95–6
  investiture of al-Manṣūr 'Alī, 93–4
  legitimacy challenged by Ẓāhirī scholars, 98–9
  al-Maqrīzī on, 317
  mission to Syrian deputies, 109
  networks and influence, 431–2
  political involvement against Barqūq, 96–8, 100–1, 103–8, 296–7, 435–6
  political involvement supporting al-Ashraf Sha'bān, 92–5
  popular support for, 98
  power offered to, 83, 93, 95
  restoration to caliphate, 100–1, 103–4, 105–6
  succession contract, 358–60, 387–8, 389, 406
  sultan–caliph relationship, 100–1, 437
al-Mutawakkil II, 'Abd al-'Azīz (caliph, r. 884–903/1479–97)
  accusations against, 173
  attempt to increase caliphal authority, 176–7, 324
  ceremonial functions, 173–4
  court rivals, 174–5
  death and succession of, 177
  delegation of powers to al-Suyūṭī, 176, 324, 354–5
  in diplomacy with Bāyezīd II, 171
  relations with al-Nāṣir Muḥammad ibn Qāyitbāy, 175–6
  relations with public, 302
  selection of, 170
  succession dispute, 301
al-Mutawakkil III, Muḥammad (caliph, r. 914–23/1508–17)
  overview, 192–3
  avoidance of meetings and politics, 200
  exile to Istanbul, 212–16, 306–7
  meets Ottoman sultan Selīm, 205–6
  military expedition against Ottomans, 202–6
  negotiator between Selīm and Ṭūmānbāy, 209
  Ottoman administrator, 209–12
  in Ottoman sources, 211
  relations with Qāniṣawh al-Ghawrī, 201, 202–3
  return from exile (927/1521), 216, 218, 225n93
  'transfer of the caliphate' legend, 214–15, 216
  written commentary on, 305–6
  see also Muḥammad ibn Ya'qūb al-Mustamsik
Muẓaffar Shāh, ruler of India (810–14/1407–11), 201, 361, 383, 388, 402, 413
Muzaffarids (Fars), 82, 93

Nafā'is al-majālis al-sulṭāniyya (al-Ḥusaynī), 260–3
al-Naḥḥās, Muḥammad Abū al-Khayr (d. 864/1459), 157–8, 180
al-Nashw, 'Abd al-Wahhāb (d. 740/1339), 68
al-Nāṣir li-Dīn Allāh (Baghdad caliph, 575–622/1180–1225), 36
al-Nāṣir Muḥammad *see* Muḥammad ibn Qalāwūn, al-Nāṣir (sultan)
Nawrūz al-Ḥāfiẓī
  caliph-sultan al-Musta'īn and, 128
  governor of Damascus, 111, 118–19
  rebellion against Faraj, 110, 113–15, 117–18
  rebellion against Shaykh, 122, 124–5, 126, 142, 144
Nihāyat al-arab fī funūn al-adab (al-Nuwayrī), 236–8
al-Nizā' (al-Maqrīzī), 314, 315
Northrup, Linda, 347

al-Nujūm al-zāhira (Ibn Taghrībirdī), 295–6; *see also* Ibn Taghrībirdī, Abū al-Maḥāsin Yūsuf
al-Nuwayrī, Shihāb al-Dīn Aḥmad (d. 733/1333), 236–8, 250, 266, 276, 278

Öljeitü (*ilkhan*, r. 703–15/1304–16), 46
Onimus, Clément, 107
Ottomans
  Abbasid caliph as Ottoman administrator, 209–12
  Abbasid caliph in exile to Istanbul, 302–3, 306–7
  Abbasid Caliphate, perception of, 207–8, 439
  Aḥmad Pasha's revolt against, 216, 218
  defeat of Cairo Sultanate, 204–9
  regional struggles, 144
  relations with Russia, 214
  succession struggle and relations with Qāyitbāy, 170–2
  Temür and, 106–7, 111
  transition period in Egypt, 300, 302–3, 306–7, 363
  see also specific sultans

papacy, Qāyitbāy and, 172
periodisation of Cairo Sultanate, 12
Petry, Carl, 167
pilgrimage (Ḥajj), 44–5, 64, 67, 78, 80, 93, 148, 221, 258–60, 259–60, 317–18, 424
Pīr Muḥammad (Timurid, d. 812/1409), 148
plague
  al-Ḥākim II's death from, 79
  al-Mustaʿīn's death from, 126
  public prayer against, 145, 152, 179, 258, 323, 434, 438
  socio-political order and, 312
political theory
  ʿaṣabiyya (group solidarity), 246, 247–8, 249–50
  authority, nature of, 242–3
  bayʿa, Khalīl al-Ẓāhirī on, 257
  Cairo as successor to Abbasid Baghdad, 252–3, 271n109
  caliphal functions, 179–80, 391–2
  caliphal functions, as symbol of *jihād*, 392–4
  caliphal functions, praying for state, 394–6
  caliphal functions, 'selecting' sultans, 396–8
  caliphate, dual nature of, 178–9
  caliphate, theological role, 311
  caliphate as idea and institution, 7, 422–5
  caliphate as moral and legal necessity, 242, 243–4
  caliphate as 'ruined institution,' 247, 315–16, 336n191
  caliphate interchangeable with sultanate, 234
  caliph's authority delegated to religious scholars, 354–5
  caliphs selected by God, 386–9
  'Dawlat al-Atrāk,' 6, 247, 249, 414, 426–30
  delegation of powers, 344, 354–5
  imām and *malik* differentiated, 237–8
  imamate, 231–3, 237–8, 250–1, 253, 254, 265–6, 408–9, 413–14
  Islamic *sharīʿa* and removal of caliph, 297
  Islamic *sharīʿa*, upholding of, 398–404
  khalīfa title, 178–9, 369–70
  legitimisation of sultan, 345–6, 440
  limitations on power, 232–3
  loyalty to caliphate, 429–30
  mulk (royal authority), 246, 247, 248, 434
  prophetic caliphate (*khilāfat al-nubuwwa*), 241, 243, 244, 266, 408, 434
  public ceremony, Khalīl al-Ẓāhirī on, 257
  seizure of power by force, 231, 239, 308–9
  sovereignty, 151, 177–8
  subjects of king, 238
  sultanate, duties of, 256–7
  sultanate government administration, 236–7
  sultanate ruling apparatus, 235–6
  sultan–caliph relationship, 234, 240–1, 248–50, 253, 255–62, 264–5, 396–8
  sultan–caliph–*imām* relationships, al-Subkī on, 245–6
  sultan–caliph–*imām* relationships, Ibn Jamāʿa on, 238–41
  sultan–caliph–*imām* relationships, Ibn Khaldūn on, 247–8
  sultan–caliph–*imām* relationships, Ibn Taymiyya on, 243–4
  sultan–*imām* relationship, 235–6, 240
  sultans as true heirs of early Abbasid caliphs, 295
  Sunni interpretation, 177–8
  theory vs. socio-political practices, 308–9, 421
  titular nomenclature, 251–2, 262–3, 367–70, 371
  transregional concepts of caliphate, 46, 178, 207–8, 434, 438–9
  ʿulamāʾ, 424, 432–5, 434–5
  umma (community) as source of legitimacy, 243–4
  wilāya, 179, 245
  see also bayʿa; Cairo Caliphate; chancery documents; chancery documents, caliphal succession contracts; chancery documents, investiture deeds; chancery documents, various; historiographical literature; jurisprudential, advice and courtly literature; Qurayshī lineage
politics and Cairo Caliphate
  late thirteenth and fourteenth centuries (overview), 91, 128
  fifteenth century (overview), 141–2
  caliph as interim candidate for sultanate, 83, 93
  caliph as political asset to sultan, 37, 40, 60, 95, 99–100, 117–18
  caliphal power and Ẓāhirī movement, 98–9

resistance to sultan over caliph selection, 72, 98, 100
see also Cairo Caliphate; *specific caliphs and sultans*
Popper, William, 426
Portugal, 200–1

qadiships, 176–7, 232, 324–5, 423; *see also* *ʿulamāʾ*
al-Qāʾim, Ḥamza (caliph, r. 855–9/1451–5)
deposition and exile, 162
Ibn Iyās on, 302
Ibn Taghrībirdī on, 297–8, 302
networks and influence, 432
opinions on, 391
politics, coup against al-Manṣūr ʿUthmān, 158–60
politics, al-Naḥḥās affair, 157–8
politics, revolt against Īnāl, 161–2, 297–8
selection of, 156–7
sources on, 162–3
Qalāwūn, al-Manṣūr (sultan, r. 678–89/1279–90)
dynastic impulses, 6, 60
inscriptions and coinage, 366–8
investiture deed, 384, 385–6, 410
rise to sultanate, 38–9
sultan–caliph relationship, 38–40, 285, 287–8
titles, 370
Qalawunid dynasty (689–784/1290–1382)
coinage, 368
dynastic impulses, 6, 60
legitimacy from Abbasid caliph, 74, 347–8
as normative in face of competing forces, 91
short-term sultans, 79, 81
sultanic line as abstraction of power, 82
see also Khalīl, al-Ashraf (sultan); Muḥammad ibn Qalāwūn, al-Nāṣir (sultan)
al-Qalqashandī, Shihāb al-Dīn Aḥmad (d. 821/1418)
chancery documents preserved by, 341, 342, 348, 361
chancery documents written by, 359–60, 405–6
on investiture of al-Mustaʿīn, 320
on investiture of al-Nāṣir Faraj, 108–9
as source, succession practices, 356–7
on titular nomenclature, 251–2
writings of, 152, 251–6, 264, 266
see also chancery documents; chancery documents, caliphal succession contracts; chancery documents, investiture deeds; jurisprudential, advice and courtly literature; political theory
Qānisawh, al-Ẓāhir (sultan, r. 904–5/1498–1500), 193
Qānisawh al-Ghawrī, al-Ashraf (sultan, r. 906–22/1501–16)
abdication of al-Mustamsik, 196–9
assumption of caliphal titles, 262–3, 370
attacks on Portuguese, 200–1
finances for war, 202–3
Ottoman threat and Battle of Marj Dābiq, 202–6
robing ceremony, 167
sultan–caliph relationships, 173, 200, 201–2, 437–8
threat of rebellion, 194–5
titles, 370
Qānisawh al-Khamsī (sultan, r. 904/1498), 193
Qarā Yülük ʿUthmān (Aqquyunlu ruler, r. 805–39/1403–35), 116–17, 145, 149–50
Qarā Yūsuf (Qaraquyunlu ruler, r. 792–823/1390–1420), 144–5
Qarābughā (Mongol commander), 21, 31
al-Qarāfī, Shihāb al-Dīn (d. 684/1285), 232–3
al-Qaramānī, Aḥmad ibn Yūsuf, 218
Qaramanids, 144–5
Qaraquyunlu Turkmen, 144–5, 149–50
qasīm amīr al-muʾminīn
al-Ashraf Khalīl's use of title, 367
Baybars' use of title, 27, 366, 367–8
on coinage, 27, 367–8
early usage, 369
on inscriptions, 366–7
Qalāwūn's use of title, 39, 368
Sunqur al-Ashqar's use of title, 39
in titular nomenclature, 251–2
see also Cairo Caliphate; political theory; titular nomenclature
Qawṣūn (d. 742/1341), 69, 74, 76
Qāyitbāy, al-Ashraf (sultan, r. 872–901/1468–96)
court culture, 172–3
death and succession of, 175–6
Ibn Iyās on, 302
military campaign in Anatolia, 167–8
opinions on, 168
relations with European rulers, 172
relations with Ottomans, 170–2
rise to sultanate, 166–7
sultan–caliph relationship, 200
ʿulamāʾ authority over, 324
al-Qazwīnī, Muḥammad, 69
Qilij al-Baghdādī, 21, 25
Qubilai (Mongol Khān), 34–5
Qurayshī lineage
for caliph, 240–1, 263, 382–3
honour for, 235
for *imām*, 231–2, 237, 254, 256, 315, 318–19
necessity for, 250–1
see also Cairo Caliphate; legitimacy of Cairo Caliphate; political theory
Qūṣ (Upper Egypt), 69–71, 78, 94, 294
Quṭb al-Dīn al-Nahrawālī (d. 990/1583), 218
Quṭuz, al-Muẓaffar (sultan, r. 657–8/1259–60), 20–1, 24

Rabbat, Nasser, 278
Ramadanids, 144–5
Rasulids of Yemen, 63–4, 361, 390–1, 401–2

Rawḍ al-zāhir fī sīrat al-Malik al-Ẓāhir (Ibn ʿAbd al-Ẓāhir), 283–5
Raydāniyya, Battle of (923/1517), 209
religious authority of Cairo Caliphate
  after Ottoman conquest, 214–15
  for excommunication of sultan's enemies, 145
  futuwwa brotherhood and, 29, 36, 55n57, 55n58, 179, 284
  inspiring loyalty to Islam, 127
  invoked with foreign rulers, 35–6, 39–40, 67–8
  invoked with *mamlūks*, 98, 194–5, 429–30
  marking transitions of power, 427–8
  mediator for human action, 19
  morale before battle, 63, 204–5, 290–1, 365, 434
  negotiation with papacy, 172
  popular religious tradition and, 436–8
  public prayers against drought, 155
  public prayers against plague, 145, 152, 179, 258, 323
  in scholarly circles, 312–13
  at sultan's deathbed, 107–8, 146, 147, 150, 158, 179–80, 434
  supernatural actor, 320–1, 323
  supporting sultan against rebels, 113, 427
  welcoming ritual for Christians, 153
  see also Cairo Caliphate; ceremonial functions of Cairo Caliphate; political theory; *specific caliphs and sultans*
Rosinus, Johannes, 214
al-Ruhā (Edessa), 149
al-Ruknī ʿUmar ibn al-Mutawakkil II (d. 913/1508), 177

al-Ṣābūnī Island, 150, 153–4, 168, 173
Ṣadaqa ibn al-Mustakfī I, 69, 70
al-Ṣafadī, Khalīl ibn Aybak (d. 763/1363) (historian), 67, 69, 294–5, 326
Safavids, 204, 218–19, 258–9, 439
al-Saḥmāwī, Muḥammad (d. 868/1464), 341
al-Sakhāwī, Muḥammad (d. 902/1497), 157, 163, 175, 258
Salāmish, al-ʿĀdil (sultan, r. 678/1279), 38
Salār, Sayf al-Dīn, 45, 47, 61, 63, 64, 361
Ṣāliḥ, al-Ṣāliḥ (sultan, r. 752–5/1351–4), 79, 81
al-Ṣāliḥ Najm al-Dīn Ayyūb (r. 637–47/1240–9), 5
Ṣāliḥiyya *mamlūks*, 20–1
Sayfiyya *mamlūks*, 159
Sayyida Nafīsa shrine
  Abbasid burial ground nearby, 48
  Abbasid family stewardship, 78, 80, 92, 98, 101, 213
  caliphal accessibility at, 78, 436, 438
  ceremony at, 101
  income from, 78, 153–4, 169, 173–4, 213
  mawlid festivals, 174, 438
  see also Abbasid family, financial status
Schimmel, Annemarie, 2, 197
Selīm I ('the Grim') (Ottoman sultan, r. 918–26/1512–20)
  Battle of Marj Dābiq, 202, 204–6
  death of, 216
  forced exile of Cairene elites, 212–14
  letter to Ṭūmānbāy, 207–8
  al-Mutawakkil III and, 215–16
Seljuks, 28, 107, 248, 264, 315, 318, 326–7, 379n147, 407, 434
Seljuks of Rūm, 369
Shaʿbān, al-Ashraf (sultan, r. 764–78/1363–77), 92–4, 367
'shadow caliphate,' 1–2, 440
Shāfiʿ ibn ʿAlī (d. 730/1330), 66, 287–8, 290, 341
Shāh Budāq (Dulqadir bey), 167
Shāh Ḥusayn (Safavid ruler, r. 1105–35/1694–1722), 218–19
Shāh Rukh (Timurid ruler, r. 807–50/1405–47), 144, 147–8, 178, 413
Shāh Shujāʿ (Muzaffarid ruler, r. 765–86/1364–85), 93
Shāh Sūwār (Dulqadir bey), 167–8
Shaykh, al-Muʾayyad (sultan, r. 815–24/1412–21)
  appointment of al-Bārizī as overseer of mosque, 362–3, 383
  death and succession of, 146
  investiture deed, 352–3, 395
  al-Maqrīzī on, 313
  military campaigns, 142, 144–5
  al-Mustaʿīn and, 118–23, 128, 297
  al-Muʿtaḍid II and al-Mustaʿīn, 139n131
  plague, 145
  social and political order, 141
  sultan–caliph relationship, 427
  usurpation of sultanate, 123–4
  see also Shaykh al-Maḥmūdī (later sultan)
Shaykh al-Maḥmūdī (later sultan), 111, 113, 114, 117–18; *see also* Shaykh, al-Muʾayyad (sultan)
Shaykh Uvays (Jalayrid ruler, r. 757–76/1356–74), 92–3
Shaykhū al-ʿUmarī al-Nāṣirī, 79–80
Shiʿism, Mongol interest in, 46
al-Shujāʿī (d. after 756/1355), 73
Sibṭ ibn al-Jawzī (d. 654/1256), 307, 309
sirr Muḥammadī, 179, 363
Sīwās, 107
Sourdel, Dominique, 356
Ṣubḥ (al-Qalqashandī)
  background, 251
  on caliphate, 256
  chancery documents preserved in, 348, 355–7, 361
  titular nomenclature, 252, 371
  see also al-Qalqashandī, Shihāb al-Dīn Aḥmad
al-Subkī, Tāj al-Dīn (d. 771/1370), 244–6, 264
Sufism
  context of *Miṣbāḥ*, 231, 232

influence and popularity of, 436–7
recognised by religous elites, 438
religious authority of Sufi *shaykhs*, 205
understanding of caliphate, 178–9
Süleymān the Magnificent (Ottoman sultan, r. 926–74/1520–66), 216, 218, 225n93
al-Sulūk (al-Maqrīzī), 314–15, 316, 317, 318
Sulūk al-mulūk (Khunjī-Iṣfahānī), 259–60
Sümer, Faruk, 206
Sunqur al-Ashqar (d. 691/1292), 39, 40
Sunqur al-Rūmī, 30, 37
al-Suyūṭī, ʿAbd al-Raḥmān Jalāl al-Dīn (d. 911/1505)
background and works, 281, 323–6
caliphal authority, attempt to increase, 176–7, 324–5, 354–5, 433
commentary on al-Mustakfī II, 73–4, 154–5
commentary on al-Mutawakkil II, 174
commentary on al-Nāṣir Muḥammad, 296
commentary on al-Qāʾim, 163
influence of Abū Shāma on, 308
as source, 121–2
sources for, 309–10
see also historiographical literature; political theory
al-Suyūṭī, Abū Bakr Kamāl al-Dīn (d. 885/1480), 154, 389
symbolism of Cairo Caliphate
jihād, 392–4
links to tradition, 305, 315–16, 404–7
religious accountability for sultan, 194–5
sacred kingship and divine election, 424
source of sovereign and theocratic authority, 425
stability, 4, 7, 179, 422
see also Cairo Caliphate; ceremonial functions of Cairo Caliphate; political theory; religious authority of Cairo Caliphate; *specific caliphs and sultans*
Syria (Bilād al-Shām)
caliph-sultan recognised in, 124–5, *125*
coinage, *125*
loss of Egyptian control, 141
Mongol attacks on, 62–3, 110, 134n69, 141
rebellion against Barqūq, 100–1, 103–4
rebellion against Faraj, 111–13, 113–14
rebellion against Khushqadam, 165
rebellion against Shaykh al-Maḥmūdī, 142, 144–5
rebellion against Ṭaṭar, 146
rival sultanate, 80
as territorial part of Cairo Sultanate, 5, 12, 277
see also specific caliphs and sultans
Syrian historians
early fourteenth century, 309–12
ʿulamāʾ historians, 307–9
Syro-Egypt and Mesopotamia map, *22*

Taḥrīr al-aḥkām (Ibn Jamāʿa), 238–41
Tarājim al-rijāl (Abū Shāma), 308
Taʾrīkh al-khulafāʾ (al-Suyūṭī), 323–4
Taʾrīkh-i ʿālam-ārā-yi amīnī (Khunjī-Iṣfahānī), 258–9
Ṭarkhān, Ibrāhīm ʿAlī, 197
Tashrīf al-ayyām (Ibn ʿAbd al-Ẓāhir), 285
Ṭaṭar, al-Ẓāhir (sultan, r. 824/1421)
investiture deed, 352, 353–4, 397–8, 405, 412
letter to al-Nāṣir Aḥmad of Yemen, 402
al-Mustaʿīn and, 126, 297, 437
rise to sultanate, 146–7
Ṭaybars al-Wazīrī, 23, 25
Ṭāz (amir), 80
Temür (Tamerlane), 92, 99–100, 106–7, 109–10, 111, 134n69, 141; *see also* Mongols
Timrāz al-Shamsī, 175
Timurbughā, al-Ẓāhir (sultan, r. 872/1467–8), 166
Timurids, 144–5, 148, 178, 439
titular nomenclature, 251–2, 262–3, 367–70, 371; *see also* Cairo Caliphate; chancery documents; chancery documents, caliphal succession contracts; chancery documents, investiture deeds; chancery documents, various; jurisprudential, advice and courtly literature; political theory; *qasīm amīr al-muʾminīn*
Töde Möngke (Golden Horde khān, r. 679–87/1280–7), 40
Toqtogha (Toqta) (Golden Horde khān, r. 690–713/1291–1313), 67
Traditionalism/Traditionalists, 230, 263, 310–11, 436–7
'transfer of the caliphate' legend, 214–15, 216
al-Tuḥfa al-mulūkiyya fī al-dawla al-Turkiyya (Baybars al-Manṣūrī), 289
Ṭūmānbāy, al-ʿĀdil (sultan, r. 906/1501), 193–4
Ṭūmānbāy, al-Ashraf (sultan, r. 922–3/1516–17)
assumes sultanate, 206–7
caretaker regent, 203
negotiations with Selīm, 208–9, 211–12
Turkmen principalities, 144–5
Turks, competition with Circassians, 95
al-Ṭūṣī, Nāṣir al-Dīn, 265

ʿulamāʾ
advisors to *imām*, 239
authority over sultan, 324
competing authorities, 232–3
excommunication of sultan's enemies, 145
as historians, 307–9
in historical narrative, 277
influence of, 432–5
al-Maqrīzī on role of, 313
as mediators, 173
opposition to al-Wāthiq, 74–5
protectors of holy law, 235
qadiships, 176–7, 232, 324–5, 423

ʿulamāʾ (*cont.*)
relations with caliphs, 67, 233, 432–5
theological rebellions, 98–9, 311, 319, 434
see also historiographical literature; jurisprudential, advice and courtly literature; political theory
ʿUmar ibn al-Mutawakkil III, 218
ʿUmar ibn al-Wardī (d. 749/1349), 73
al-ʿUmarī, Aḥmad ibn Faḍlallāh (d. 749/1349)
approach in writing, 278
on *bayʿa*, 411–12
chancery documents preserved by, 341
influence of on al-Qalqashandī, 253, 255
investiture deed of al-Ḥākim II, 75–6, 358, 382, 387, 393–4, 398, 399–401, 402–3, 406, 411–12
succession contract of al-Mustakfī I, 405
on al-Wāthiq I and al-Nāṣir Muḥammad, 72, 73, 75–6, 296
see also chancery documents; chancery documents, caliphal succession contracts; chancery documents, investiture deeds; political theory
Umayyads, 314, 315, 356
ʿUthmān Effendi ibn Saʿd al-ʿAbbāsī, 219
ʿUthmān ibn Jaqmaq, al-Manṣūr (sultan, r. 857/1453), 158–60, 298, 302
ʿUthmān ibn al-Mutawakkil III, 218

Van Steenbergen, Jo, 5, 12, 60, 66, 144, 280, 317–18, 327, 370, 423–4
Vermeulen, Urbain, 341, 390–1

waqf endowments, 100, 168, 188n105
al-Wāthiq I, Ibrāhīm (caliph, r. 740–1/1340–1)
financial support after ouster, 78
Ibn Taghrībirdī on, 296
interment in family mausoleum, 81, 87n55
ouster of, 75, 358
as rival caliph, 71–5
al-Ṣafadī on, 294
al-ʿUmarī on, 72
see also Ibrāhīm ibn Muḥammad al-Mustamsik
al-Wāthiq II, ʿUmar (caliph, r. 785–8/1383–6), 97, 98
West Africa (Mali and Borno), 82
West Asia map, *143*
Wiederhold, Lutz, 311, 312–13
Wing, Patrick, 149, 423–4
Winter, Michael, 216
Woods, John, 4

Yaḥyā ibn al-Mustaʿīn (d. 847/1443), 126, 140n138, 221n14
Yaḥyā ibn al-Mutawakkil III, 218
Yalbughā al-Nāṣirī, 100–1, 103–4, 249
Yalbughā al-ʿUmarī al-Khāṣṣakī (d. 768/1366), 81, 92–3
Yalbughāwī amirs, 93–4
Yaʿqūb ibn al-Mutawakkil II, 177
Yazdī, ʿAlī Sharaf al-Dīn (d. 858/1454), 178
Yedikule fortress (Istanbul), 216, *217*
Yemen
Abbasid descendants, 218–19
diplomatic row with Cairo, 63–4, 361, 390–1, 401–2
disputed title of Cairo caliph, 320
letter to al-Nāṣir Aḥmad of Yemen, 402
Yilbāy, al-Ẓāhir (sultan, r. 872/1467), 166
Yılmaz, Hüseyin, 9
Yüksel Muslu, Cihan, 151
al-Yūnīnī, Mūsā (d. 726/1326), 308, 309–10
Yūsuf, al-Nāṣir (Ayyubid ruler, r. 648–58/1250–60), 20
Yūsuf ibn Barsbāy, al-ʿAzīz (sultan, r. 841/1438), 150–1

al-Ẓāhir (Baghdad caliph r. 622–3/1225–6), 25
Ẓāhirī amirs, 159, 160
Ẓāhirī *mamlūks*, 113, 160–2
Ẓāhiriyya fitna, 98–9, 311, 319, 434; *see also* religious authority of Cairo Caliphate; *ʿulamāʾ*
Zangids, 28
Zubdat al-fikra fī Taʾrīkh al-hijra (Baybars al-Manṣūrī), 289–90
Zubdat kashf al-mamālik wa-bayān al-ṭuruq wa-l-masālik (Khalīl al-Ẓāhirī), 256–8

EU representative:
Easy Access System Europe
Mustamäe tee 50, 10621 Tallinn, Estonia
Gpsr.requests@easproject.com

www.ingramcontent.com/pod-product-compliance
Lightning Source LLC
Chambersburg PA
CBHW052053300426
44117CB00013B/2102

* 9 7 8 1 4 7 4 4 5 3 3 7 0 *